Contemporary Marketing and Consumer Behavior

*To our informants, those
consultants, collaborators, and friends
in the field*

Contemporary Marketing and Consumer Behavior

An Anthropological Sourcebook

John F. Sherry, Jr.
Editor

SAGE Publications
International Educational and Professional Publisher
Thousand Oaks   London   New Delhi

For information address:

SAGE Publications, Inc.
2455 Teller Road
Thousand Oaks, California 91320

SAGE Publications Ltd.
6 Bonhill Street
London EC2A 4PU
United Kingdom

SAGE Publications India Pvt. Ltd.
M-32 Market
Greater Kailash I
New Delhi 110 048 India

Printed in the United States of America

Library of Congress Cataloging-in-Publication Data

Main entry under title:

Contemporary marketing and consumer behavior: An anthropological
    sourcebook / edited by John F. Sherry, Jr.
        p. cm.
    Includes bibliographical references and index.
    ISBN 0-8039-5752-1.—ISBN 0-8039-5753-X (pbk.)
    1. Marketing—Social aspects. 2. Consumer behavior.
3. Communication in marketing. I. Sherry, John F.
HF5415.122.C66   1995
658.8'342—dc20   95-3257

This book is printed on acid-free paper.

95 96 97 98 99 10 9 8 7 6 5 4 3 2 1

Sage Production Editor: Tricia K. Bennett
Cover photo: Ravi Balasuriya

Contents

Foreword:
Does Marketing
Need Anthropology?

Does marketing need anthropology? It is a pleasure to write a Foreword to this book in answer to this question. First, the editor, John Sherry, has been a colleague of mine at Kellogg School's marketing department for several years, building my appreciation of his substantial professional and personal qualities and therefore my anticipation of this volume. Second, I found the chapters in it enjoyable to read; they are absorbing, informative, and provocative. I was also glad to see this book because it significantly furthers the role of the anthropological approach to marketing and consumer research. While such literature has been growing by way of journal articles, this volume provides the chance to contemplate that role, and its potential, in a rich and concentrated manner. Before indicating the specific content the reader will encounter, I offer a preamble to indicate the experience and outlook that I bring to bear and thereby to provide a view of the background from which this volume grew.

If it is possible to be a little bit an anthropologist, I would like to make the claim. As a student with the Committee on Human Development at the University of Chicago many years ago, I obtained an interdisciplinary education that included classes with Robert Redfield and W. Lloyd Warner, and I read fairly widely in the field. (My friends are weary of hearing this again, but I ask their indulgence in hopes of reaching a wider audience.) Since that time, I have done many research projects of an anthropological nature in both the United States and abroad. Actually, these projects fell under the heading of qualitative marketing research, as they were usually carried out with the goals of understanding particular facets of consumer behavior and furthering marketing goals. But the work also served scholarly and academic aims, finding expression in analyses and insights in my writing for the professional literature.

The context of this work was a demanding one. For a long period, from the late 1940s to the early 1960s, contributing qualitative work to the marketing field was a somewhat uphill task. In 1948, I began working with Social Research, Inc. This company (SRI) was founded in 1946 by a multidisciplinary group—Burleigh B. Gardner and W. Lloyd Warner (anthropologists), Robert Havighurst (educator), and William E. Henry (psychologist). Its work became an applied amalgam of behavioral science theory and method, using intensive interviewing, observation, and projective techniques, to illuminate social stratification, social roles, cultural change, and symbolism in the everyday life of the community. All respondents in marketing research studies were stratified according to Warner's concepts of social structure, using the Index of Status Characteristics he and his colleagues developed and reported in *Social Class in America* (Chicago: Science Research Associates, 1949).

To support this work, it was necessary to find clients who were bright, inquisitive, innovative, and sufficiently powerful in their organizations to bring in research work that differed from the conventional—and too often, simple-minded—surveys that dominated the marketing research field. But progress was made. Many business people were receptive and willing to sponsor novel and venturesome projects. One such man was John Catlin, a vice president at Kimberly-Clark. Among his responsibilities was the marketing of Delsey tissue, for which he once proposed installing cameras in toilets to gain an unobtrusive record of how the product was used. (Amusingly, I heard Margaret Mead make a similar suggestion at a program at the University of Chicago, where she talked about using photography to acquire a record of "chunks" of behavior.) Catlin also raised the cross-cultural question of why the British preferred harder tissue than Americans did.

In 1958, we also did studies of women's attitudes toward menstruation and the use of "sanitary" or "feminine" protection. The variations in response by subcultural groups to the introduction of tampons by Kotex cast light on such issues as how cultural changes occur with immigration of various ethnic groups into American society, the diffusion of customs from one group to another (e.g., from sophisticated middle-class women accustomed to using Tampax to young first- and second-generation women who thought such consumer behavior was taboo), as well as the force of new technology, products, and their promotion, in changing attitudes, self-concepts, and behavior on a large scale. Within a relatively few years, feminine protection moved from the status of a hush-hush, brown wrapper package to being casually advertised on television.

Another important client was MacFadden Publications, Inc., which sponsored a series of studies of working-class women. A full-scale report, of a markedly ethnographic character, was published as *Workingman's Wife* (New York: Oceana, 1959) in the vein of such social anthropological interpretations as *Boys in White* by Becker, Geer, Hughes, and Strauss (Chicago: University of Chicago Press, 1961).

Along with the development of this work, there was also ferment in business schools, although academia was slower, more cautious, and more resistant to change. Some of the work being done in industry was reported in the trade press and at programs of the American Marketing Association. *Tide*, a newsmagazine of advertising, marketing, and public relations, told of the work of SRI in articles in October and December 1947 and in February 1948, referring to symbolic analyses of various cultural phenomena, such as the use of greeting cards and the significance of soap operas to their audiences. Under the rubric of "motivation research," this work gained growing attention among faculty. In 1957, Joseph Newman published his doctoral dissertation *Motivation Research and Marketing Management* (Cambridge, MA: Harvard University Press), and in 1958, Robert Ferber and Hugh Wales of the University of Illinois edited the volume *Motivation and Market Behavior* (Homewood, IL: Irwin). Neither work took particular note of the anthropological nature of the research being reported; Ferber and Wales focused especially on psychology.

Although much thinking and application went on from the time I started work at SRI in 1948, the pioneering text *Consumer Behavior*, by Engel, Kollatt, and Blackwell, did not emerge until 1968. A section of that book was devoted to asserting the importance of a societal perspective and the concept of culture. Before then, in 1961, I had been hired by the marketing department of the School of Business at Northwestern University (now the J. L. Kellogg Graduate School of Management) to teach about the application of behavioral sciences to marketing. Gradually, over the past 50 years, marketing personnel on all sides have become aware that their need to understand the marketplace and the consumers in it has had to be both broader and deeper. Professionals at universities and managers in companies, with their respective skills and financial resources, addressed their common interest in solving the ever more complex problems of the marketplace that have arisen. This complexity has rapidly increased, especially in the past 25 years during which the Association for Consumer Research and the *Journal of Consumer Research* were created. This concern finds much to feed it in issues of environmentalism, consumerism, critiques of materialism, worldwide development and global competition, and the endless generation of market segments whose subjective and overt behavior invite our study and encourage the use of more varied methods.

Moving from a preoccupation with surveys and their attendant sampling and measurement problems into less charted and more ambiguous terrain, from the easy lists of actions and obvious reasons for purchase into the murkier realms of cognition, motivation, and volition, to say nothing of affect and perception, was a daunting and threatening task. Entrenched surveyers feared loss of their livelihood, new personnel had to be found and/or trained, new vocabularies had to be learned, and managers had to develop the judgment to distinguish between competence and gibberish in the face of the inexhaustible supply of con artists and sharks that quickly surfaces when fresh bread is cast upon the waters. The workers, both good and bad, came from various fields.

Most readily available and interested were psychologists. An outstanding pioneer was Ernest Dichter, who used the tools of psychoanalytic thinking toward elucidating consumer motivation. He was brilliant, provocative, and practical and found an admiring audience among corporate customers as well as a train of intellectual morticians who continue to this day to keep trying to bury Freud. There were also many other psychologists who needed the work and who could bring relevant training. Importantly, the emerging marketing concept (that marketing success depends on meeting the needs of customers) highlighted the necessity of understanding the consumer, and study of consumers intensified awareness of the idea of segmentation. George Katona pioneered with his studies in economic psychology, and Robert Ferber was an early positive gatekeeper for new ideas coming into the marketing field. Psychologists could apply personality study and had the tool of depth interviewing at hand to serve the need for fuller and richer information about consumers, and with projective methods they could lure the more daring managers.

Also up front in bringing ideas and methods to the marketing field were outstanding sociologists such as Paul Lazarsfeld, Elihu Katz, Robert Merton, and others interested in mass communications and influence. Anthropologists per se were less visible during this period in turning to the marketing field, except in the sense that they had always been there in studying the markets and consumption ways among many of the peoples on the earth. W. Lloyd Warner brought this interest forward in the United States through fostering the field of social anthropology in local American settings in the *Yankee City* series, and through his part in founding SRI as a vehicle for studying marketing research issues for varied organizations. His colleague, Burleigh B. Gardner, was also prominent for his domestic social anthropological work in *Deep South* and *Human Relations in Industry* and his subsequent leadership at SRI. My affiliation with SRI sensitized me to the importance of social structure, stratification, and change, and the symbolic character of human life. In 1974, at the August conference of the American Marketing Association, I spoke on "Myth and Meaning in Marketing," seeking to arouse more widespread awareness and involvement in exploring these typical anthropological issues in marketing. In 1978, I wrote "Hunger and Work in a Civilized Tribe, or the Anthropology of Market Transactions" (*American Behavioral Scientist*), an overview of the development of concepts in anthropological study and some parallelism in changing marketing thought, hoping again to stimulate interdisciplinary activity from this direction.

As time went by, there came to the fore most gratifyingly the work of John Sherry, Eric Arnould, and Grant McCracken and, as we see now in this volume, numerous others who pursue the study of consumer behavior while having in mind the anthropological discipline, who think about society and societies, about symbolism, lineage, and magic. I will not dwell on each of the succeeding articles; I hope the reader will find them as absorbing and instructive as I did.

The chapters in this book are examples of researchers addressing some of the issues raised by anthropology and by their own interests and diverse approaches. Following Part One, Sherry's introductory chapter, are five groupings. Part Two is about some important ways the product may be apprehended. Dan Rose provides a bold interpretation that has the character of a meditation on the complex of meanings of a shampoo and its modes of communication. Tani and Rathje show how we can learn about consumers and their use of products via the intriguing archaeological method of sorting debris. From shampoo and batteries, the text goes on in Part Three to discuss rice and pharmaceuticals, but here the products are almost incidental to the other organizational and managerial interests of the authors. Eric Arnould reminds us of the role that analysis of a traditional "anthropological" setting—African communities—can offer as such places become less traditional and move toward fuller integration in the world market where managing channel relations is a central marketing problem. Reeves-Ellington similarly provides a study of how an anthropological perspective can assist in improving sales performance in overseas markets.

Part Four focuses on the social contexts that influence consumer behavior, with Janeen Costa taking up the several elements in social organization and categorization and Barbara Olsen drawing out especially the effect of lineage on brand loyalty. In Part Five, John McCreery offers an exhilarating excursion through the craft of advertising by his linkage of Malinowski (conceivably one of the founders of marketing research via his studies of the *kula* trading system), magic, and metaphor. Rita Denny explores some of the implicit meanings that go on in the dialogue between electric utilities and customers. In Part Six, two broad investigations are reported: Duhaime, Joy, and Ross seek to capture the nature of the consumers' aesthetic experiences involved in attending museums and consuming art, and Sherry, McGrath, and Levy delineate the complex subjectivity of people when giving themselves gifts.

This summary of the book's contents suggests the importance of three large themes: how the things that people consume, whether objects, services, or ideas, have meaning in their lives; the role of relating, organizing, structuring, managing; and the rich, pervasive challenge of understanding communications. I believe this volume is an excellent beginning of such collections of literature. But it is just a start. That fact is made evident by John Sherry's Part One orientation chapter in its remarkable coverage of the possibilities as well as its apt detail. No one volume can be expected to fulfill the vision and range of potential he suggests, but he provides a great map of a wonderful and exciting terrain. In editing this collection and in contributing to it such a rich set of ideas, he answers the question I asked at the outset. Yes, marketing needs anthropology because it has so much to offer.

—Sidney J. Levy
J. L. Kellogg Graduate School of Management
Northwestern University

Preface

T he fields of marketing and consumer research are undergoing a period of almost unprecedented growth and differentiation. Much of the ferment stems from interest in the cultural and experiential dimensions of the disciplines, which is being generated by the work of researchers trained in anthropology. Simultaneously, anthropology is weathering a period of accelerated fragmentation, reflexivity, and often misplaced relevance. There is a growing demand for scholarship more tuned both to the empirical and practical realities of consumer culture. These trends conspire to produce a timely and appropriate synergy, which is resulting in the emergence of an anthropology of contemporary marketing and consumer behavior.

This is a multiple or parallel emergence of sorts. It has been a multidisciplinary rather than interdisciplinary effort and has resulted in the creation of enclaves within dominant disciplines, whose scholars often proceed in virtual ignorance of each other's contributions. It has also caused practitioners to reinvent the wheel, often using brittle spokes and warped hubs. Diffusion has been discontinuous and distorted. There is now a very timely opportunity to integrate, catalyze, and refine this emerging tradition as the interest across camps reaches a critical mass. This volume is an effort to seize that opportunity.

I have secured the cooperation of a number of colleagues to produce this sourcebook on the anthropology of contemporary marketing and consumer behavior. The book is a reader of original articles of theoretical and empirical substance, written by anthropologists who specialize in marketing and consumer research. It is intended as a sourcebook for readers interested in what anthropologists have to say about consumption and its managerial consequences.

The contributors—anthropologists and marketers—are drawn from management schools, traditional anthropology departments, and private industry. They are among the thought leaders of an anthropology of marketing and consumer research. Collectively, they have won awards for their scholarly writing, they have trained a vanguard of Ph.D., MBA, and undergraduate business students, they have advised executives of *Fortune* 500 companies as well as smaller entrepreneurial ventures, and they have plied their trade in contexts foreign and domestic. By including chapters from anthropologists working within the disciplines of marketing and consumer research as well as by those working within the discipline of anthropology proper, I have tried to achieve an "inside"/"outside" perspective of consumption phenomena. The chapters written by professional practitioners who make their living applying anthropology to the study of consumption and marketing provide additional insight and relevance to the pursuit of basic research. Finally, the remarks of eminent senior Fellows of the Association for Consumer Research, who have drawn upon anthropology to make their own seminal contributions to a number of disciplines, punctuate the volume beginning, middle, and end. A brief biosketch of contributors is provided at the end of the volume.

The topics and their treatments in this volume run a gamut of concerns from our focal disciplines. The essays are both conceptual and empirical. Elements of the marketing mix are well represented, as authors consider such matters as goods and services, brand image and equity, utility and experience, advertising and promotion, channel maintenance, relationship management, managerial intervention and stakeholder response, organization behavior, economic development, class- and gender-linked consumer behaviors, and the production of consumption. Anthropological perspectives and methods employed by the authors range from materialist to semiotic and include ethnography, archaeology, and archival analysis. Participant observation, interview, survey, projective tasking and introspection are among the techniques used to elicit information from consumers. Qualitative and quantitative methods are employed. Inquiries range across time and across cultures. Intra- and intercultural dynamics involving the United States, Canada, Japan, Africa, the Middle East, Australo-Asia, and Asia-Pacific are explored in depth by the authors, with other regions invoked through example. Contributors range across time, space, and topics in pursuit of understanding. Some have worked in the tradition of the solitary ethnographer; others have worked in teams with colleagues from other disciplines. The result is a multifaceted perspective of marketing and consumer behavior.

The book consists of 12 substantive chapters and 3 commentary pieces, organized into 7 parts. Part One is an orienting section that moves the reader into some of the issues and perspectives of an anthropology of marketing and consumer behavior. Part Two treats the objects circulating in the marketplace by examining the derivation of meaning through usage. Part Three explores the dynamics of distribution in terms of interpersonal and interorganizational relations, and considers the strategic importance of anthropology to change agency. Part Four situates consumer behavior in the material and social nexus that sustains it over time and suggests the impact that embeddedness should have on managerial action plans. Part Five is a meditation on the efficacy of one form of marketing communication in particular—advertising—as both a metaphysical system and a directed intervention. Part Six uses the vehicles of museum-going and monadic giving to broach the phenomenology of consumer behavior. Part Seven provides some closure for, and imparts some directionality to, the essays. Our respected elders bracket these contributions with their own insights.

This volume is neither a textbook nor a handbook in the encyclopedic sense of those enterprises. It is a sourcebook that reflects the polylogue that anthropologists have found marketing and consumer behavior to be. Each of the chapters, and the citation bases on which they are built, facilitate the reader's access to a larger contextual literature that, in turn, will permit future investigation of issues focused on personal interests. Encouragement of the programmatic pursuit of personalized anthropological research agendas is the ultimate objective of this sourcebook. We celebrate a diversity of topics and approaches in the service of this goal.

—John F. Sherry, Jr.
J. L. Kellogg Graduate School of Management
Northwestern University

PART ONE

Orientation

1

Marketing and Consumer Behavior

Into the Field

John F. Sherry, Jr.

Let me begin this chapter with the following enthusiastic, urgent, and unabashedly tempocentric assertion. Perhaps not since the great silver mines of Potosi (Weatherford, 1988) catalyzed the emergence of a world economic system over 400 years ago has there been an episteme whose dynamics and consequences are more in need of sensitive anthropological investigation and anthropologically sensible intervention than our contemporary culture of consumption. Consider several brief diagnostic vignettes. Each of these vignettes is a "revelatory incident" (Fernandez, 1986) of sorts, as it permits us to experience, even if vicariously, a highly charged encounter between consumption and marketing that is suffused with meaning. These examples are windows onto the phenomenology of markets and consumption:

- The spectacle attending the dismantling of the Berlin Wall became a powerful mass-mediated symbol of contending economic ideologies, concluding one decade and announcing a new one. (That the decade preceding a millennium is often a time of apocalyptic visions and millennarian activity should not be forgotten.) Whether construed as the eclipse of communism or the dawn of free-market socialism, the event itself provided a staging ground for the architects of cultural syncretism. Easterners streamed across the borders to window shop and buy and gradually to wonder how to manage emergent relationships with the Western consumption fantasy. Citizens from East and

AUTHOR'S NOTE: The author wishes to acknowledge the following colleagues for constructive comments on earlier drafts of this chapter: Eric Arnould, Meta Baba, Janeen Costa, Ken David, Rita Denny, Fred Gamst, and Sid Levy.

West swung frenzied hammers against the Wall in cathartic syncopation. The more entrepreneurial "wall peckers" among them transformed graffitoed rubble into souvenirs and rushed these relics into world markets, where consumers were soon able to own a piece of history at below-retail rates, as the artifacts were quickly remaindered to discount chains around the globe. Inevitably, an advertising firm (in this case, Saatchi and Saatchi) was able to hang its banner on the eastern side of the Wall and promote itself with a congratulatory announcement that it was "first over the Wall." Ironically now, at the time of this writing, in the formerly sleepy sector of Alexanderplatz in East Berlin, the retail shops are empty but the street has become one huge bustling open-air market, with thousands of foreign itinerant vendors working from makeshift stalls and using some of their revenues to return to the West, replenish their inventories, and resume sales in the East.

- Arnould and Wilk (1984) provide this account of transcultural consumption practices in their discussion of the appeal of Western brand-name products:

> Peruvian Indians carry around small, rectangular rocks painted to look like transistor radios. San Blas Cuna hoard boxes of dolls, safety pins, children's hats and shoes, marbles, enamel-ware kettles, and bedsheets and pillowcases in their original wrappings. Japanese newlyweds cut inedible three-tiered wedding cakes topped with plastic figures in Western dress. Kekchi Maya swidden farmers relax in the evenings to the sounds of Freddie Fender on portable cassette players. Bana tribesmen in Kako, Ethiopia pay a hefty price to look through a view-master at "Pluto Tries to Become a Circus Dog." Tibetans, bitterly opposed to Chinese rule, sport Mao caps. Young Wayana Indians in Surinam spend hours manipulating a Rubik's Cube. The most elaborate White Mountain Apache ritual, the girls' puberty ceremony, features traditional tests of endurance and massive redistribution of soda pop. When a Swazi princess weds a Zulu king, she wears red touraco wing feathers around her forehead and a cape of window-bird feathers and oxtails. He wears a leopard-skin cloak. Yet all is recorded with a Kodak movie camera, and the band plays "The Sound of Music." In Niger, pastoral Bororo nomads race to market on camelback carrying beach umbrellas. Veiled noble Tuareg men carry swords modeled after the Crusaders' weapons and sport mirrored sunglasses with tiny hearts etched into the lenses. (p. 748)

The images conjured for us by these authors suggest something of the cultural tempering processes that attend the diffusion and adoption of innovation across national boundaries.

- The brightly painted storefront murals of the El Mercado Grocery Store in urban California depict a variety of activities, among them shopping and check cashing. The paintings are quite riveting. They attract the attention of passersby, inform newcomers to the area (many of whom are not literate) of the store's multiple functions, and discourage graffiti artists from additional expression. Inside, the store is alive with Hispanic families shopping for a large variety of items, ranging from chorizo to Japanese vitamin drinks. Piñatas dangle festively from the ceiling. Contraband brand-name products are openly sold and have displaced a number of established domestic brands. Products from at least 20 Central and South American markets are in evidence. Bulk bins of generics and specials grace several aisles. Among the biggest sellers at El Mercado are the devotional candles that occupy several shelves in the store. The stock on these shelves turns over every week. Images and legends on the votive candles cover a wide spectrum of devotions and aspirations. Consumers' intentions may be offered up before a candle of the Virgen de Guadalupe or on the flame of a candle emblazoned with La Suerte de la Loteria (Lucky Lottery) and an incantation to influence Lady Luck.

- Cultural Survival is a Harvard-based nonprofit organization dedicated to the preservation of the human rights of indigenous peoples and ethnic minorities threatened by the expansion of Western ideologies of economic development and to the discovery of alternative solutions to the problems that accelerated culture contact occasions. The organization has recently launched a massive project to enable rainforest residents in Brazil to own and operate a Brazil nut processing factory and to tap into viable world markets in a way that permits 40% of the retail price of products to be returned to project financing. Sustainably harvested products are marketed in the form of Rainforest Crunch, a nut-and-candy brittle bought wholesale by Cultural Survival and retailed to consumers of the world, often through the brokerage of environmental groups. Thus not only are profits repatriated to initial producers, but the firm is able to generate revenue to fund other projects to benefit threatened indigenous peoples (D. Maybury-Lewis, personal communication, 1989). Similar community-based sustainable development efforts in the form of joint ventures between ecological activists and indigenous entrepreneurs—from Shaman Pharmaceuticals (Scott, 1994) to EcoTimber (Henderson, 1994)—are emerging around the globe.

- Just a year or so prior to the collapse of the Soviet Union, the largest to date of McDonald's 12,000 restaurants worldwide—200 outdoor seats, 700 indoor seats, and 27 cash registers—opened in Moscow. The opening was the culmination of 12 years' worth of negotiations conducted by McDonald's Restaurants of Canada with (then) Soviet officials. The deal represented a major transfer of food technology from agronomy to management, with packaging materials being the only products imported into the country. Meat and potato plants, a bakery and dairy, and quality assurance labs are part of a 10,000-square-foot distribution center built by McDonald's to process indigenous cattle and crops. Given the existing infrastructure and consumer preference patterns, the firm has been able to do little conventional marketing. Furthermore, because repatriation of profits is not yet possible, McDonald's will plough its earnings back into the venture and build an additional 19 restaurants in the city. By 1990, the firm had invested $50 million in the venture (Hume, 1990). To date, McDonald's operates three restaurants in Russia and serves over 70,000 people each day. It has also opened a 12-story office building housing numerous multinational concerns. McDonald's is a major contributor to the International Association of Children's Funds in Russia (*Backgrounder*, 1994). The Russian news source *Pravda* has dubbed George Cohon, vice chairman of the joint venture, a "Hero of Capitalist Labor," in ironic recognition of the change in the Russian ideological climate (Snegirjov, 1991).

- Economic associations in the world system reinforce the differences between cultures even as they remove impediments to intercourse. Two examples illustrate this principle. A shift from Eurosclerosis to Europhoria has attended passage of the Single Europe Act. The elimination of nontariff barriers and the harmonization of standards between the nations of Europe after 1992 was projected to create a unified European market of 320 million consumers with a projected GDP (gross domestic product) of just under $5 trillion. Almost as widely heralded, NAFTA, the North American Free Trade Agreement, linking Canada, the United States, and Mexico into a unified market of 350 million consumers with a projected GDP of $6 trillion, has also been created. As multinationals acquire local presences, labor forces become increasingly migratory, and "Eurobrands" or "Nambrands" are developed, logistics will facilitate a certain amount of homogenization within these common markets. Still, differences in local (whether national or regional) consumer preferences, patterns, language, income, exchange rates, and managerial styles will persist, making truly global strategic planning and implementation something of a semantic game. Global marketing often reinforces myths of cultural convergence, while masking the processes of cultural individuation that the world of goods abets.

- The Korean govenment has pondered a postmodern potlatch as a potential solution to the problem of beleaguered intellectual property rights in the global marketplace. In 1993, prosecutors on Seoul's Joint Investigation Team for Violators of Intellectual Property Rights seized close to 1 million counterfeit items, ranging from imitation Gucci watches to imitation Chanel bags, and have convicted nearly 400 violators peddling their counterfeit wares in tourist shopping areas. Warehousing the $12.5 million in goods has proved costly, burning or burying them would raise environmental concerns without costly processing, and removing brand labels prior to distributing the goods to the needy would cost more than the wholesale cost of the goods themselves. Leaving brand labels on the goods prior to charitable redistribution might provoke resale. Prosecutors are currently recruiting voluntary association workers (such as Red Cross volunteers) to assist in debranding and redistributing the goods (Cho, 1993).

Each of these vignettes conveys the rich texture of experience woven by the warp of marketing and the woof of consumption. Anthropological analysis is an appropriate way of appreciating this texture. I've called these vignettes "diagnostic" because they illustrate a range of critical concerns that can be fruitfully addressed from a sociocultural perspective. How might we briefly unpack these issues?

As economic systems transmute, ideologies are marketed with renewed intensity. More than merely being mass mediated, our experience is super-mediated (Real, 1989), producing a spurious, global village fellow feeling in urgent need of investigation. This experience is often tangibilized, with behavioral constellations sedimented in products (Richardson, 1987; Tambiah, 1984). We witness the entrepreneurial ebullience of informal economic systems and the ineluctable nativization of global marketing influences.

In the domestic press of multicultural diversity, yesterday's enlightened targeting strategy is today an archaic segmentation technique. The "Hispanic" consumer is virtually as massified, imprecise, and misleading a construct as any developed prior to our era of particle markets (Russell, 1990). Country of origin effects shape consumer preference formation in ways that researchers are just beginning to fathom, given accelerating patterns of migration around the globe. Acculturation-based consumer behaviors must be interpreted in view of immigrants' home country consumption complexes. Even newly arrived entrepreneurs are realizing that aesthetics must be incorporated into target hardening in the evolution of product design. Retail servicescapes impact behaviors in an increasingly segment-specific fashion. Intracorporate bootlegging reflects the conflictual nature of organizational growth, especially under conditions of accelerated globalization. Everywhere we observe the commoditization of the sacred and the sacralization of the profane. This process even includes the curious but predictable rise of what Feest (1990) has felicitously christened "cultural transvestism," whereby ethnic traditions of one group are usurped and bastardized by another.

Social marketing campaigns are being waged in the service of nonethnocentric, sustainable development. Nevertheless, the "McDonaldization" of life (Ritzer, 1993) proceeds apace. Intercultural joint ventures proliferate by expedience as well as by law. Economic strategies arising at the dawn of time—barter and patient, long-term relationship management, for example— are enjoying a renaissance among marketers.

As contemporary local consumer "realities" collide with imagined segments fantasized by managers far distant from the voices of the market, and as regional economic associations grow more powerful, dislocations in the global system will accelerate, and new organizational forms will emerge.

Ideological and legal battles over intellectual property rights (an academic mainstay to which we all resonate) are intensifying. Actuarial and humanistic models of efficient, enlightened delivery of social welfare are contending for dominance. Managers and consumers around the globe are reconfiguring the fetish of the brand. The balance of this chapter explores some anthropological approaches to consumers' marketworlds.

In contemporary hyperindustrial society, and especially in its Euro-American incarnations, work and play have become dialectically configured into a cultural focus. A focus is a part of a social system that especially concerns the members of a particular culture. Buying, selling, acquiring, and owning are at once among the most highly cathected and routinized activities in which we engage. Production and consumption are not merely mutually contingent and reinforcing; each has become an end in itself. For some, the consumption of production is paramount. For others, the production of consumption is all important. Malinowski has spoken of the "commercial libido"—a combination of commercial talent, economic avarice, and passionate interest—that fuels marketplace behavior (quoted in Drucker-Brown, 1982, p. 62). Similarly, Agnew (1986) has described the "commercial athleticism" (p. 37) that thrives in a market environment of opportunism and ambivalence when consumers contest with merchants. For better and for worse, marketing and consumption are among the most potent forces of cultural stability and cultural change at work in the world today (Sherry, 1987a). Our anthropological understanding of these forces is in its infancy. They must become a disciplinary as well as a cultural focus. In speculating that consumption may become the leitmotif of the 21st century, Nash (1990) has even envisioned the emergence of a professional Society for the Anthropology of Work and Consumption. If the globalization of markets (Levitt, 1983) or the pluralization of consumption (Levitt, 1988)—the tension between the poles of cultural homogenization and individuation—are to be harnessed in the service of empowering local peoples everywhere, anthropologists must answer a long-standing challenge.

🖂 The Challenge to Anthropology

Almost two decades ago, Cohen (1977) delivered an insightful critique of our disciplinary bias and proposed a thoughtful corrective for our strategic vision:

> Hunting, gathering, cultivation, herding, distribution, reciprocity, and so forth, are the business activities of tribal and peasant groups, though we

are careful not to use the term. If anthropologists studied industrial business organization and activities with the rigor with which they approached horticultural or pastoral business, our insights into our own societies would be greater. Unfortunately, however, it seems to be in too many people's interests to have us perpetuate the myth that kinship, religion, visiting, marriage, socialization, and the like in industrial societies are on one side of the fence, while "business" is on the other. Some of the best ethnographic data on cultures (*not* the culture) of the United States are in the daily *Wall Street Journal* and the financial pages of the *New York Times*. That is where the relationship between anthropology and business should begin. . . . Anthropology begins at home, and we have lost the art of anthropologizing. (pp. 382, 395)

As a field, we have only recently begun to respond to Cohen's challenge to redirect our ethnographic (and ethnocentric) gaze from contemporary ancestors to ancestral contemporaries, and shift our attention from the open-air dickering of the periodic marketplace to the frenetic dealing of the commodity pits (Baba, 1994). Even the most current and sweeping reassessment of cultural anthropology (Borofsky, 1994) omits consumption and marketplace behavior from its purview. Elsewhere, I have described the history of the discipline's discontinuous involvement in the study of contemporary commercial issues and its uncharacteristically reflexive critical posture toward the enterprise of business. Rather than revisit that history, in this chapter I will accept Cohen's challenge and treat two fundamentally important activities— marketing and consumption—in anthropological perspective. For initial convenience, we can view these activities in conventional terms congenial to Cohen's argument by designating consumer behavior as an adaptive strategy shaping an individual's quality of life and marketing as a directed intervention strategy of planned change. Before launching into that examination, however, it may be useful to provide a sense of the evaluative ethos that is the context from which marketing anthropology is emerging.

Shakespeare's observation that "the lunatic, the lover and the poet / Are of imagination all compact" can be turned toward my present purpose. Recognizing how thoroughly passion can animate or discourage research regimes and how contingent disciplinary advance is to the imagination of scholars (Dimen-Shein, 1977; Levitt, 1984; Mills, 1959/1975), we can envision an intersection of inquiries governed by the following metaphor. Imagine the early stages of a lunar eclipse. The bright surface of the moon represents the field of consumer behavior, broadly construed. The shadow moving across the moon's face represents the field of marketing. As the eclipse progresses, the dark shadow of marketing engulfs the disk of consumer behavior until

10 CONTEMPORARY MARKETING AND CONSUMER BEHAVIOR

the event culminates in the complete domination of the latter field by the former. From this perspective, the biobasic, culturally diverse phenomenon of consumption is inexorably marketized. Consumer behavior is so commoditized that it becomes coterminal with marketing. In this view, marketing reduces our understanding of consumption to buyer behavior, assimilates that diminished conception to a technology of influence, and applies that knowledge solely in the service of increasing sales. I think this conceit has much anthropological currency, even though the metaphor is not as well turned as it might be.

Let's invert the trope. Imagine the later stages of that same lunar eclipse. This time, marketing has a revelatory function. As the discipline of marketing advances, consumer behavior becomes more completely illuminated. Consumption is gradually revealed to be a much larger field of inquiry than marketers have heretofore imagined. Not only have certain behaviors not yet become commoditized, some actively resist commoditization in an attempt to remain unambiguously singular (Kopytoff, 1986). In this view, marketing enlightens the study of consumption beyond the narrow concerns of profit and of individual firms and orients the inquiry to more normative and macro issues. Turned this way, the metaphor is more congenial to Levy's (1976) view of marketing as a basic rather than applied discipline; marketing is more analogous to chemistry or biology than it is to either chemical engineering or medicine.

Anthropology, marketing, and consumer research are poised as linchpin disciplines in parallel intellectual domains. Each articulates broadly with contiguous disciplines within those domains and shares a type of "eminent domain" orientation that facilitates discovery, integration, and advance. By judiciously combining these various perspectives, some powerful analytic and practical synergies have been produced. And yet, one thing is clear: Convergence is occurring. Fueled by academics and practitioners in search of explanatory frameworks and managerial applications, contemporary business has been drawn into the orbit of anthropology.

Systematic anthropological investigation of such activities as marketing and consumer behavior is essential to the taming of business institutions to humane ends (Arensberg, 1978). This action orientation is the lodestar (Malinowski, see Drucker-Brown, 1982) of an anthropology of marketplace behavior. The consequences of marketing and consumption are quite varied. Traumatic dislocation and cultural transformation are possible, as among the Kalahari !Kung (Yellen, 1990). Maintenance and cultural integration are also possible, as contemporary Euro-American experience indicates (Douglas & Isherwood, 1979; McCracken, 1988). A range of hybrids between these poles is also possible, as developments throughout Asia suggest (Bohnaker, 1990; Buruma, 1984; Iyer, 1988). The processes abetting these consequences must be thoroughly studied if they are to be harnessed in the service of human development.

Toward a Common Strategic Vision

We are currently weathering the "refiguration of social thought" that Geertz (1973) has so eloquently described. The "crisis literature" in social science (Shweder & Fiske, 1986) questions fundamental assumptions about the nature of inquiry and subjects chosen for investigation. Alternative paradigms and modes of knowing have proliferated over the past decade. During this period, marketers and consumer researchers have also generated a literature of discontent that criticizes conventional wisdom and identifies frontier concerns (Sherry, 1987b). The possibility of forging a common strategic vision across these apparently disparate enterprises has never been more promising. It has been argued that marketing requires a "greater commitment to theory-driven, programmatic research, aimed at solving cognitive and socially significant problems" (Anderson, 1983, p. 28). It has also been argued that anthropology needs to "transcend the narrow, reactive, advocacy role of championing the alienated worker and to assume a more proactive, advisory role in drafting and implementing humane strategic plans at a corporate organizational level" (Sherry, 1983, p. 11). By merging these sets of needs and embarking upon a program of joint exploration, each discipline stands to benefit.

What Consumer Research and Marketing Seem to Need

Several thoughtful critics within each of these fields have provided frameworks which can be recast in a format generalizable to marketing and consumption broadly construed. Most comprehensive is Hunt's (1983) general paradigm of marketing, called the "Three Dichotomies" model. Hunt envisions the study of marketing to unfold along a set of three categories that are fundamentally dichotomous. The first dichotomy contrasts profit with nonprofit dimensions and hinges upon the presence or absence of pecuniary gain as a behavioral motivator. The second dichotomy contrasts micro- with macrodimensions and distinguishes between marketplace behavior at individual and systemic levels. The third dichotomy contrasts positive with normative dimensions and highlights the discrepancy between actual and ideal behaviors in the marketplace. Although the tradition is gradually eroding, conventional research into marketing (and managerial action plans predicated on that research) has generally concentrated on the profit-micro-positive dimensions of marketplace behavior. With a few notable exceptions (e.g., Kotler & Levy, 1969), only recently have marketers broadened their concerns to encompass nonprofit-macronormative issues in meaningful fashion. A revival of interest in social marketing and public policy is beginning, and the maturation of consumerism as an "industry" is producing an array of interesting new forms. Thus Hunt (1983) implicitly provides anthropologists with at least two distinctive avenues of contribution. They can apply their methods and perspectives to the focal concerns of marketers, adding depth and breadth to the disciplinary core. This strategy promises immediate practical benefits. Alternatively, they can push the envelope and move what have been peripheral issues to the very heart of the discipline. This strategy ensures long-term practical benefits.

Another equally congenial critical framework has been proposed by Sheth (1982), who has identified a set of shortages and surpluses in the field of consumer research. The focus of traditional research has been on the individual consumer and on rational decision making. Consequently, both group- and non-problem-solving behaviors have been neglected. The process of research and theory construction has been shaped principally by descriptive constructs imported from other disciplines. Normative constructs arising from within consumer research have been negligible. Finally, the purpose of both theory and research has been chiefly managerial rather than disciplinary. Again, anthropologists can contribute by intensifying efforts along the dominant axis or by radiating adaptively to the niches currently underexploited. A common plea of critics (e.g., Kassarjian, 1982; Zielinski & Robertson, 1982) is for integration of fields that seem fragmented and multi- rather than interdisciplinary domains. Anthropology seems especially suited to such an integrative task.

As long as marketing is viewed only as a technology of influence (Anderson, 1983) wielded by channel captains seeking to engineer consent (Tucker, 1974), anthropologists will experience ethical qualms about their involvement in the enterprise (Galt & Smith, 1976; Hakken & Lessinger, 1987; Stefflre, 1978). When painted in broader strokes, along the lines of those proposed by critics within marketing, the enterprise becomes more virtuous (Sherry, 1989). As marketing and consumer research are touched by the postmodern ethos (Sherry, 1991), the types of critical reevaluation of disciplinary ontology, epistemology, axiology, and praxis rippling through the fields virtually demand anthropological attention.

What Anthropology Has to Offer

Perspective

Without specifying exhaustively the utility of an anthropological approach to marketing and consumption (for more detailed accounts, see Sherry, 1984, 1987a, 1987b, 1991), I will use "perspective" and "method" as umbrella concepts to promote its relevance. According to Harris (1971), anthropological perspective is ecumenical, diachronic, and comparative. By aspiring to multidisciplinarity, it strives for holistic understanding of the interplay of nature and culture. By taking an evolutionary purview, it seeks to acknowledge and account for change. By interpreting local patterns of culture in light of each other, it guards against merely parochial understanding of human experience. The tension between local description and universal generalization permeates the discipline (Harris, 1968). Finally, anthropological perspective is critical (Marcus & Fisher, 1986). It can provide a cultural critique of our own lifeways and prompt an examination of our otherwise unquestioned assumptions. Such a perspective promises an amplified understanding of what is conventionally known about marketing and consumption and an improved practice of these activities in both positive and normative senses.

Whether one believes the numerous research orientations within anthropology are complementary (Johnson, 1978) or incompatible (Barrett, 1984), it is still possible to derive an orientation that provides a coherent perspective from which the investigation of cultural systems can be launched. Just such a perspective, which advances a micro-orientation based on the interrelations of the subfields of anthropology, has been used to explore the biocultural dimensions of marketplace phenomena (Sherry, 1987a). The model is reproduced in Figure 1.1.

The rationale undergirding the model has been described summarily by Sherry (1987a):

> Sociocultural anthropology is characterized by enthnographic description, which purports to represent faithfully the native's viewpoint of reality (the **emic** perspective), and ethnological analysis, which involves cross-cultural comparison resulting in generalizations derived from the experience of the native and the constructs of the analyst (the **etic** perspective). Linguistic anthropology is concerned with language generation and change in both historical and the contemporary perspective. It attempts to understand language in the varied psychosocial context in which it occurs. That broadening of "language" to include symbolic communication—such as nonverbal behavior—is an important contribution of linguistics. Biological

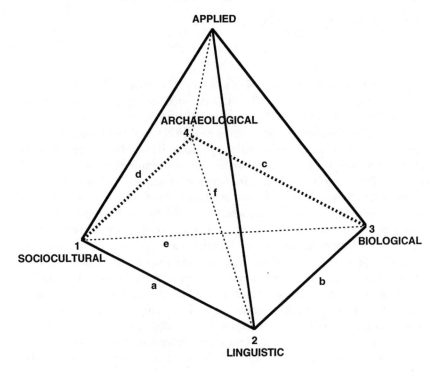

Figure 1.1   Anthropological framework for marketing behavior.
SOURCE: After Johnson (1978), adapted from Sherry (1987a).

anthropology investigates the relationship between evolution, ethology, and ecology. Biology is envisioned as a complex interplay between heredity, environment, and culture. Archaeological anthropology focuses on material culture, using the artifacts and temporal remains of past societies, along with inference and ethnographic analogy, not only to reconstruct the past, but also to discover the principles of cultural evolution which shape the present. Historic archaeology has begun to probe what we can call the contemporary past, by examining the refuse discarded by present-day consumers; techniques employed by so-called garbologists (Rathje, 1974) have already been adapted to the needs of consumer researchers (Wallendorf & Reilly, 1983). Finally, applied anthropology, which is a relative "newcomer" among the traditional subdisciplines, is oriented toward directed intervention in social behavior. It is a pragmatic enterprise which seeks to apply the basic findings of the traditional core areas to fundamental human problems. It serves an important brokerage function among the subdisciplines, and between anthropology and the other social sciences. (p. 292)

The research pathways indicated in Figure 1.1 have both disciplinary relevance and managerial implications. Adopting the vantage point of the applied perspective, a grand tour of this heuristic pyramid's bases reveals the ways in which an anthropological view of marketing and consumer behavior is illuminating. A tour is also an expedient way to situate the remaining chapters of this book within a holistic framework. The reader can refer to Sherry (1987a) for a more detailed discussion of the model.

Let's start at the Sociocultural base and move toward the Linguistic (route 1 a 2). Along this route lie some of the most fundamental issues to be addressed by managers and researchers alike. As domestic markets fragment and national economies articulate to become a global marketplace, the possibility of developing a truly comparative marketing discipline and practice seems almost palpable. How do we rehabilitate the tired aphorism "Think Global, Act Local"—the managerial imperative to "glocalize"—from simplistic platitude to a fully operational strategic plan? By developing more sophisticated and sensitive versions of cultural analysis (Barnett, 1983; Lee, 1966) that recognize the absolutely basic contribution of rigorous, descriptive local (i.e., segment-centered, whether based nationally, regionally, ethnically, etc.) accounts to theory construction, it will become possible to distinguish plausibly between the particular and the general with respect to marketplace behavior.

There is no better way to get closer to the consumer (or any other marketplace stakeholder for that matter) than by using ethnography as a bridge (Nussbaum, 1993). The challenges of cultural propriety (Sherry, 1987c) and appropriate development (Dholakia & Sherry, 1987), too often unrecognized and unanswered by conventional marketing strategists, are also best addressed in this fashion. Eric Arnould's work (this volume) on West African marketing channels makes this point apparent. Arnould describes the relative neglect of so-called informal sector marketing systems by the marketing channels literature, even though these systems distribute the bulk of necessary daily items to consumers in developing countries. In reexamining channel relationships studied by anthropologists and economists, Arnould explores the nature of environmental stresses that have given rise to particular strategies of relationship management. He draws attention as well to the forms of channel integration, the embeddedness of commercial relationships, and the segregation of these relationships from other forms of social discourse. Using data from secondary sources as well as several extended case studies, he provides insight into African channel relationships that spills over into recommendations for the academic study of marketing distribution, for the linkage of indigenous with international marketers, and for the redesign of Western channel relations at a particularly critical historical juncture.

Furthermore, if corporations are understood as vehicles for accomplishing a strategic plan, as well as culture-bearing institutions in their own right, the design and management of synergistic organizations (whether commercial or consumerist) can be enhanced through ethnographic analysis. Richard Reeves-Ellington (this volume) gives us a unique perspective of just such action research. He describes a field sales test conducted by a major international pharmaceutical firm across markets in its Africa/Asia region to demonstrate the effective merger of total quality tools and concepts, anthropological perspectives and methods, and conventional business analysis. Reeves-Ellington shows how this merger, designed to improve sales force performance, rocketed test brands to a position of market leadership within 3 years and improved the volume, sales, and profits for brands as well.

Turning the corner at the Linguistic base and moving toward the Biological (route 2 b 3), a different set of issues arises. Here we are concerned broadly with symbolic communication, verbal and nonverbal, in cross-cultural perspective. This concern can be summarized in the study of promotion as a cultural system. How do marketing and consumption as ideologies—comprising information that is both denotative and connotative—diffuse around the globe? How are these ideologies "nativized" by diffusers and adopters to articulate with local canons of evaluation and categorization? Advertising is only one of the communicative channels by which these ideologies are disseminated; arguably, it is becoming less significant in its conventionally recognized forms than it has previously been. Rita Denny's view (this volume) of communications strategy demands that we question conventional notions of advertising and virtually invites us to dimiss established literature on consumer miscomprehension as a fantasy based on a poorly turned metaphor. Denny shows how marketers miscommunicate as readily as consumers miscomprehend. Using the case example of public utility firms, she describes how customer-company relations can be improved through careful attention to the customer's voice.

Appadurai (1990) has suggested we examine global cultural flows in terms of five types of landscapes: the mobility of people (ethnoscapes), the fluid and rapid diffusion of technology (technoscapes), the disposition of global capital (finanscapes), the electronic disseminating of information (mediascapes), and the proliferation of political and ideological images (ideoscapes). Often, these flows result in what Sherry (1986) has called cultural brandscapes, that is, the creation of a material and symbolic environment built by consumers with marketplace products, images, and messages and invested with local meaning. The totemic significance of these brandscapes largely shapes the adaptation that consumers make to the modern world. John McCreery's meditation (this volume) on the ways in which advertising inspires these brandscapes is especially enlightening. In rejecting the traditional metaphors by which anthropologists have sought to apprehend advertising, he exploits the capacity of magic to account for the nuances of persuasive marketing communication. The magic worked by advertiser upon consumers, and warded off by them as well, finds parallels among Trobriand gardeners and Taoist priests. McCreery's two hats—anthropologist and creative director—grant him privileged access to this metaphysically material arena.

Rounding the turn at the Biological base and moving toward the Archaeological (route 3 c 4) in Figure 1.1, we raise what may become the most pressing issue of the decade. Here the forces of free-market entrepreneurialism collide with those of cultural ecology to affect profoundly the quality, if not the possibility, of life on the planet. Perhaps a transdisciplinary hybrid—"ecomarketing" might be an appropriate designation—can be created to foster a commercially viable sense of stewardship among consumers and marketers to halt the forces of natural and cultural degradation set in motion by the unfettered advance of capitalism. An anthropological topology of environmentalism (Milton, 1993) is one potential starting point for such an enterprise. The work of Tani and Rathje (this volume) on discarded dry-cell batteries is another. Their account of a study emanating from the University of Arizona Garbage Project's investigation of hazardous household waste disposal is laden with implications for an ecolate approach to marketing. That the common household battery is a latent threat to our welfare may surprise readers as much as the discovery that golf courses are among the most toxic threats to the global environment (Platt, 1994); yet the spread of batteries and golf courses appears integral to the present process of economic development. Tani and Rathje take the measure of an important problem and recommend ways to speed its abatement. Gauging the impact of marketing and consumption on evolutionary trends—for example, through examination of "collapse" scenarios in archaeological perspective or developmental "take-off" scenarios of historic and ethnographic record—must become a major component of cultural risk management.

If supply creates its own demand and if the diffusion of consumer products (the term "goods" is an ethically loaded conceit that should be abandoned in favor of more neutral terms such as "objects" and/or "services") is an inexorable process if not politically prohibited, then marketing anthropologists have a special responsibility with respect to the evolution of consumer culture. Bennett (1988) has remarked that the stuff, if not the consequences, of development, seems universally desired. The imminent transformation of the Second World and the continued immiseration of the Third World seem to support his view. Equitable and culturally appropriate development (as well as re- and dedevelopment) strategies empowering all of the affected stakeholders are a critical challenge to the anthropological imagination. The linking of expansion of consumer markets with the building of infrastructure may be one solution. The refinement of countertrade (Schaffer, 1989) may be another. Domestication strategies that benefit host and home countries as well as the planet itself must be discovered.

Completing the rotation from Archaeological to Sociocultural bases (route 4 d 1) in Figure 1.1, we are grounded in two constructs absolutely fundamental to marketing and consumption: "place" and "change." Anthropologists have had much to say about spatial and locational parameters of marketplaces in nonindustrial societies (e.g., Bohannan & Dalton, 1962; Cook & Diskin, 1978; Smith, 1976) but considerably less about the ethos of these places. Contemporary hyperindustrial societies have been neglected on both counts, in spite of the clear need for an interdisciplinary discipline of pathetecture or atmospherics (Sherry & McGrath, 1989). Carole Duhaime, Annamma Joy, and Chris Ross (this volume) explore some of the placeways of consumption in their investigation of consumer patronage of a contemporary art museum. They describe a phenomenology of space that mediates between consumer and art object. Theirs is a servicescape of utility and aesthetics; design is shown to be an integral component of the visitor's experience.

The relationship between market forces and cultural change awaits thorough description, in spite of the availability of historical and cross-cultural studies of trade that might be turned toward such investigation. Mintz (1985) has used sugar and Hattox (1985) coffee to show us how such an investigation might proceed. The implications of this type of investigation coupled with cultural-ecological accounts of present-day hidden costs of consumer behavior (Ayres, 1994) for the design and implementation of humane development programs are profound. Barbara Olsen's examination (this volume) of the intergenerational transmission of consumer behaviors provides insight into the micromanagement of stability and change. She integrates archival documentation on early marketing strategies for manufactured products with qualitative research on the penetration and persistence of these goods as favorite brands within three- and four-generational families. Olsen uses life history interviews to explore the transfer and rejection of brand loyalty across generations. Her observations on the centrality of kinship to object relations in hyperindustrial society provide some continuity with studies conducted in conventional anthropological field settings.

The last two routes to be considered are perhaps the most compelling for the ways in which they touch the lives of all stakeholders so directly. The Sociocultural to Biological axis (route 1 e 3) in Figure 1.1 raises some of the darker issues attendant on modern marketing and consumption. Chief among these are the biocultural determinants of risk. The resonances between the senses of consumption as acquisitive behavior and wasting disease were already apparent to contemporary observers of the transition from "traditional" to "industrial" society (Porter, 1993). Commerciogenic disease (the "terminal illness" produced by VDT/CRT monitors and the "sick building" syndrome produced by construction chemicals being two current concerns) requires anthropological investigation and intervention. So also do such aspects of consumer socialization as the relationship of marketing to biobasic behaviors, like acquisitiveness, and thence to psychosocial illnesses, such as addiction, obsessive-compulsive disorders, and the like. Social marketing campaigns around the globe would benefit from ethnographic research into such issues as infant and toddler feeding patterns, contraceptive practices, licit and illicit drug use, child labor (including prostitution), informal retail dynamics, and criminal careers.

Janeen Costa's treatment (this volume) of the social organization of consumption provides a rich conceptual context for understanding how consumers are thoroughly socialized for better and for worse. In particular, her discussions of ethnicity and of gender as these identities are mirrored in and constructed through consumption are clarion calls to comprehensive, holistic research. Adoption and ascription of identities ostensibly grounded in biology are processes fraught with difficulty, if not danger (Joy, 1988; Shipman, 1994). Gift giving is one consumption practice by which these identities are negotiated. John Sherry, Mary Ann McGrath, and Sidney Levy (this volume) use the autodon—a gift given to the self—as a vehicle for exploring some of the behaviors and fantasies of upscale women. These authors probe the ambivalence underlying monadic giving to shed light on the construction of female identity and to critique existing theories of dyadic gift exchange. They assess the role of monadic giving in the ritual reproduction of domestic economy.

The Linguistic to Archaeological axis (route 2 f 4) in Figure 1.1 serves to remind us that a discipline of object relations per se—the relationship between people and things—has yet to be fielded. That people (whether consumers or marketers) invest goods with meaning and derive meaning from goods is a semiotic enterprise that is relatively undescribed yet universally acknowledged (often as the hallmark of humanity). Miller (1987) in particular has criticized the "nihilistic" and "global" assault on consumer culture that has diverted us from intensive microlevel examination of the relationship of people to products. The production of consumption is just beginning to be probed (Appadurai, 1986; McCracken, 1988; Rutz & Orlove, 1989). The creation and detection of meaning in commodities is the essential dynamic of hyperindustrial society. It is looming ever larger in the linkage of preindustrial and transitional economies with the world system (Steiner, 1994). Dan Rose's autoethnography of consumption (this volume) becomes an opportunity for introspection, as he produces a personal meditation on the potential layers of meaning embodied in a consumer product. His analytic shift from tangible artifact to inscribed experience and back is indicative of the hermeneutic quest in which contemporary consumers are engaged. The interplay between public writing and private experience encouraged by the artifacts we call brands is at issue in his chapter.

I have used the conceit of a grand tour to take the reader quickly around the heuristic pyramid, to point out the subdisciplinary cornerstones that anchor the model, and to sketch the shape that anthropological inquiry into marketing and consumption might take. I have roughly mapped our authors' chapters along routes that blunt their contours somewhat, ignoring the many tributaries that may lead from their research streams. The discussion lacks subtlety to the degree that it ignores the gravitational pull or electron sharing that characterizes the relationship among the cornerstones of the model. Imagine the transformation of consciousness and business practice that must occur among people in transmuting command economies, where advertising was formerly banned, where persuasion was equated with propaganda, and where to get rich is now glorious. Consider the irony that the creative conversion of unaesthetic landfills to appealing golf courses, at the ultimate expense of the ecosystem, may best be appreciated by some future archaeologist, who, blessed by the bounty of these preserved middens, will misread the demise of **Homo suburbans** in the artifactual record. Ponder the challenges attending the evolution of virtual communities as culture colonizes cyberspace. The heuristic pyramid encourages such active imagination and imposes some discipline on it. The model is a holistic way of apprehending marketing and consumer behavior.

Methodology

Although it does not yet qualify as an incipient paradigm shift, a movement has arisen in marketing and consumer research over the past half decade toward methods alternative to survey and experiment (Sherry, 1991). In an extremely well-turned metaphor, Tucker (1967) lamented the fact that marketers study consumers as if they were fishermen, rather than marine biologists, studying fish. The cover story in the August 28, 1989, issue of *Business Week*, entitled "Stalking the New Consumer," suggests something of the awareness marketers have of the need to adopt novel approaches, as well as their reluctance or inability to realize the hunting metaphor as an impediment to strategic vision. Ethnography and cross-cultural comparison are promising correctives for this type of tunnel vision. Anthropologically inspired research is providing revisionist perspectives on a range of consumption issues, including retailing (Sherry, 1990a, 1990b), object relations (Appadurai, 1986; McCracken, 1988), diffusion of innovation (Arnould, 1989), brand loyalty (Belk, Wallendorf, & Sherry, 1989), biodegradation (Rathje & Murphy, 1992), advertising (Sherry, 1987d; Sherry & Camargo, 1987), and family decision making (Wilk, 1987). (A fuller account of this revisionism is provided in Sherry, 1991.)

Participant observation and a respect for folk models—that is, a willingness to engage the consumer on his or her own turf with no particular managerial worldview to defend—are the defining features of marketing ethnography. Quite often, anthropological methods are used in an exploratory fashion as a complement to conventional market research techniques. Often as well, anthropologists are consulted when conventional techniques have produced little useful knowledge or when a firm has gotten into difficulties and requires radically different data collection and interpretation strategies. Frequently, it is the ritual substratum of consumer behavior that has not been plumbed (or even considered) by the client. Sometimes, it is the literal behaviors themselves that have not been adequately described. Anthropologists may also use their skills in combination with those of other specialists in team-based approaches to consumer behavior that are more holistically conceived than conventional consumer research.

From Theory to Praxis: A Case Example

Steve Barnett is an entrepreneurial anthropologist who has left an especially effective "paper trail" of the contributions of his discipline to practitioners in marketing and consumer research. Barnett made a successful transition from academic anthropology at Princeton to an applied setting in corporate America. As the head of the Cultural Analysis Group at Planmetrics in the late 1970s and early 1980s, Barnett directed a full-time staff of six anthropologists and numerous part-time consultants (also anthropologists) on projects for such clients as Union Carbide, Royal Dutch Shell, Kimberly-Clark, Campbell Soup, Procter & Gamble, and a host of utility companies. The group has studied energy consumption, compensation schemes for the Bhopal disaster, women's roles in housework, dishwashing practices, diapering procedures, and scrip writing, among other topics (Heller, 1988; Lewin, 1986).

In the mid-1980s, Barnett moved to Research and Forecasts, a division of Ruder Finn, and Rotman, to head up anthropological studies there. Wrangler and Campbell Soup were major clients along with advertising agencies such as Saatchi and Saatchi, Hal Riney and Partners, J. Walter Thompson, and Ogilvy & Mather. Barnett's projects included studying the cultural significance of blue jeans (via observations in rodeos, bars, picnics, and stores) and the salient attributes of apples (via observations in grocery stores). The former resulted in the launch of a new product line, the latter in a new advertising campaign (Goldstein, 1988). The firm has conducted projects for 150 clients in domestic and international arenas. As a result of their work with Research and Forecasts, Colgate has now "institutionalized" the practice of ethnography, requiring its subsidiaries to conduct at least two projects each year. The firm created its Axion soap paste in Venezuela as a result of such ethnographic inquiry (Fannin, 1988).

In the late 1980s, Barnett moved to Holen North America, installing the now well-regarded ethnographic team and principles he had consolidated over the decade and bringing a number of clients with him. Holen has provided the Toyota Motor Corporation with detailed descriptions of the car shopping behavior of consumers, including aesthetic evaluations that eventually were incorporated into the advertising campaign for the luxury car Lexus. In studies conducted for the advertising agency Young and Rubicam, Holen anthropologists accompanied U.S. postal carriers on their routes to gauge consumer perceptions of the mail service. This study also had direct advertising implications. Both Procter & Gamble and Unilever have employed Barnett to conduct consumer research; the former client was concerned with clothes-washing practices, the latter with fashion consciousness. The firm has studied the consumption of cold remedies and the enjoyment value of breakfast (Foltz, 1989). Holen has studied business travelers for Hyatt hotels—revealing the highly publicized "Road Warrior" ethos of this particular segment—and microwave oven users for the Campbell Soup Company. New product development, product positioning, and packaging implications emerged from the study of microwave cooking practices (Yovovich, 1990). Barnett left Holen to become Director of Product Strategy for the

Nissan Motor Company, where he continued to introduce novel research methods into a corporate setting. Working with a consulting firm called the Global Business Network, Barnett helped Nissan revamp its planning function, using input from an interdisciplinary computerized nominal group process. Such assistance prompted a new perspective of the automobile as a cultural artifact to emerge at Nissan (Barnett, 1992). Barnett's most current transition has been from an independent consultant in the area of strategic planning and consumer behavior to a principal at Global Business Network.

This case example is not intended to be a hagiography of a particular anthropologist (in spite of the importance of origin myths or trickster tales to disciplinary advance) so much as an illustration of the practical potential of workbench anthropology in the marketplace. The sheer existence of a paper trail is of signal import. Although many consulting anthropologists—whose ranks continue to swell (Bennett, 1988; Boram, 1988; Davis, McConochie, & Stevenson, 1987; Deutsch, 1991; Giovannini & Rosansky, 1990; Jordan, 1994)—are constrained by proprietary agreements that preclude publishing results and become low-key raconteurs (or vetters) of the impressionist tale that Van Maanen (1988) has so well described, Barnett has managed to publicize the fact that an anthropologist can be a centrally interesting business person who is profoundly consequential to the success of private enterprise and yet remain an anthropologist in the bargain.

The core competencies acquired in apprenticeship confer comparative advantage on an anthropologist alive to the practical. This is recognized by such firms as Hartman International, whose JBL International group defines its future role as that of "marketing anthropologist," announces its commitment to segmentation and research procedures that are "ethnographic" in orientation and espouses "the need to embrace anthropological marketing" (Cerasuolo, 1990, p. 5). From such recognition, won in some measure by the entrepreneurial nomadism personified by Barnett, will an answer to Cohen's (1977) challenge arise.

The Market for Anthropological Consumer Research

The use of trained ethnographers to conduct observational studies is the hallmark of such anthropologically informed marketing research. Field immersion, interview skills, sensitivity to nuance and symbolism, attention to outliers and to contextual embeddedness, and a cross-cultural perspective are prerequisites to effective analysis. This background and expertise is especially critical when anthropologists function principally as analysts rather than as data collectors. For example, in the studies mentioned above, much "passive" data collection was employed by researchers. Extensive use of videotaping is a common practice, which means analysts must train informants to use equipment or, if the equipment is self-contained, "simply" analyze hundreds of hours of tape footage. Audiotaping is also widely employed, which necessitates training informants in the art of keeping an audio diary and literally talking to themselves. In effect, informants often become research instruments in their own right, and the analysts work through them (R. Denny, personal communication, 1991) to produce an interpretation. Qualitative marketing research firms such as B/R/S Group, Inc. now employ anthropologists to use these methods to track consumer behavior (Prindle, 1992).

The use of anthropology in marketing and consumer research dates back to the early days of Social Research, Inc. in the United States (Baba, 1986; Gardner, 1978; Sherry, 1987a) and to Mass Observation (Sherry, 1987a) in the United Kingdom. It is practiced by firms such as Creative Research, Inc. in Chicago (Dickie, 1982; Heller, 1988; Singer, 1986), Ross Laboratories (Heller, 1988) and Market Development, Inc. in San Diego (Fannin, 1988; Goldstein, 1988). Advertising agencies frequently hire anthropologists as consultants (Gales, 1989; Levin, 1992), while some, such as DDB Needham Worldwide, J. Walter Thompson, and Lowe Marschalk, employ anthropologists in their research departments. Anthropology has long been associated with the understanding of brand image (Gardner & Levy, 1955; Levin, 1992). Anita Roddick (1991) employs anthropologists in her Body Shop enterprise for purposes of both consumer research (tied to product development) and social outreach work of the type Kotler (1986a) has labeled megamarketing. Her sponsorship of projects advancing so-called paraprimitive solutions to contemporary social problems (Maybury-Lewis, 1992) is an intriguing application of strategic vision. Anthropologists have also been among Roddick's recent critics, as her programs have failed to meet stated ideals and marketing claims (Entine, 1994). Inevitably, professional competence and credentialing has become an issue, as critics of any privileged position for a discipline as exotic and in possession of such quintessentially low-tech methods as anthropology have begun to emerge.

Observation, interview, and focus group procedures are the chief qualitative (and for most firms arguably the only) methods employed by marketers. It is an unfortunate article of faith in the industry that anyone can perform these methods with minimal training. By combining the elements of marketing research and ethnography haphazardly, both analysis and practice can be hamstrung. The recent alarming rise in the incidence of blitzkrieg ethnography and "adnography" (Alsop, 1986; Arnould, 1992; Berstell, 1992; Foltz, 1989; Gales, 1989; Houghton, 1992; Kanner, 1989; Merritt, 1992; Miriampolski, 1988; Sherry, 1987e; Singer, 1986) is a case in point. What passes for ethnography in some firms amounts to little more than site visits, intercept interviews, eavesdropping, and voyeurism. Brief engagement with consumers can produce impressions every bit as misleading, if not more so, than those gained from focus groups. Hyped in the business press as the "Margaret Meads of Madison Avenue" (Miller, Shenitz, & Rosaldo, 1990), researchers conducting home visits a trifle more sophisticated than pantry checks, armed with conceptions of brands as myths, and appearing to have little concern with the impact of the observer on the naturalistic setting seek to get close to the consumer (Elliott, 1993). It may be that anthropology is used chiefly as a projectible field to stimulate the creativity of advertisers. Until such pop managerial notions are corrected, the impact of anthropology on marketing practice will be significantly retarded. Furthermore, as investigative journalists of the "hidden persuaders" school raise once again the alarm against increasingly intrusive forms of marketing research, even fundamentally sound ethnographic work can be made to appear ludicrous and sinister (Larson, 1992). The marketing of anthropology has critical implications for the development of an anthropology of marketing.

Growth Markets Beyond the 1990s

I have identified a number of areas where anthropology is able to make substantive contributions to marketing and consumer research. The marketing mix elements of most interest to practitioners—product, promotion, distribution, and price—are microlevel concerns that marketing anthropologists as well as traditional economic anthropologists have often addressed (Dannhaeuser, 1983, 1989; Plattner, 1989; Sherry, 1987a, 1990a, 1990b; Terpstra & David, 1991). Macrolevel issues such as politics and public relations, recently introduced by Kotler (1986a) into the marketing mix, have likewise been addressed by anthropologists, most especially those critics of contemporary business practice (Idris-Soven, Idris-Soven, & Vaughn, 1978; Nash & Fernandez-Kelly, 1983; Taussig, 1980). What remains to be developed is a programmatic identification of issues of fundamental importance to which anthropologists can make a unique contribution. Because no practical sourcebook is complete without a set of projections, I offer the following short list of growth markets for anthropological expertise. Keep in mind that the list is not exhaustive but merely illustrative. Recall as well my introductory vignettes, which focused on various levels of sociocultural integration, modalities of intercultural behavior exchange, permutations of economic philosophy, and degrees of fetish fascination resulting from the inexorable commoditization of experience. From New York to New Guinea, for better and for worse, these forces limn the lives of consumers and marketers.

Anthropology has special relevance for this particular set of managerial issues:

- Global marketing
- Domestic market fragmentation
- Strategic planning
- Organizational culture
- Economic development
- Household studies
- Consumer misbehavior
- Object relations
- Forecasting
- Basic research

The nature of the contribution anthropology can make to these issues can be briefly explored.

Global Marketing

The globalization of markets is perhaps the chief contemporary concern of business analysts and practitioners. We need to move beyond the myth of global homogenization and cultural convergence to avoid the types of premature corporate restructuring and product planning that the assumption of a worldwide leveling of tastes has produced (Wind, 1986). We must also attend carefully to the "global paradox" (Naisbitt, 1994) of the increasing power of small players in the international economy. The major red herring of the globalization debate has been the endless wrangling over the relative merits of standardization versus adaptation of the marketing mix (Kotler, 1986b; Levitt, 1983). Mercifully, Porter (1986, 1990) has attempted to shift the emphasis toward an analysis of the configuration, coordination, and linkage strategies that marketers might employ in a global marketplace. Porter's framework provides anthropologists with a timely window of opportunity for productively entering the globalization dialogue. Given the anthropological concern for context, Porter's work can be viewed as a managerial mandate both to study the world as it is and to create strategies that are cross-culturally optimal. Despite the forces of global convergence, there are clear indications of individuation emerging both from local markets and from corporate organizations. The nativization of global forces—whether brands, planning policies, interorganizational relations, or protectionistic measures—is best investigated ethnographically and this intimate local knowledge best brokered by implementation procedures monitored ethnographically (Sherry & Camargo, 1987; Tobin, 1992).

Because the emphasis of the globalization dialogue has been on consumer and industrial markets, the human dimension has been all too often neglected. Migration studies should assume increasing prominence as anthropologists enter the arena. Refugees, tourists (e.g., Belk & Costa, 1991), guest workers, and expatriate managers in particular are stakeholders whose worldviews, life chance, and brokerage functions are in urgent need of exploration. The global resurgence of ethnicity (Costa & Bamossy, 1993) also demands our attention. Articulation of local economies with the world system has produced both integration and dislocation in the lives of the world's consumers and workers. Processes such as predetermined domestication (Cateora, 1990) and nonethnocentric development (Dholakia & Sherry, 1987), which empower local actors, must be discovered, refined, and extended. The anthropological predisposition toward advocacy can catalyze these developments. Anthropologists such as Robert McConochie of Corporate Research International strive to relate their methods and perspectives to an increasingly competitive global marketplace (Laabs, 1992). McCreery's chapter in this volume illustrates one anthropologist's involvement with such marketing.

Domestic Market Fragmentation

Coinciding with the rush to globalization is the fragmenting of domestic markets. For example, in the United States, what was formerly viewed as a lucrative, homogeneous mass market is now considered, as a result of economic, lifestyle, and historical forces, a virtual confederacy of specialty markets. New buzzwords have arisen to describe this phenomenon. We speak now of "regional" markets, of "niche" markets, and lately even of "particle" markets (Russell, 1990). Marketing managers are beginning to grapple with the forces of pluralism and multiculturality. Products are now formulated in regional variants under a common brand. Bootlegging of contraband brand-name products is being combated with renewed attention to the needs of indigenous consumers. Clearly, a cross-cultural perspective is increasingly necessary to understanding consumer behavior in the United States. Costa's chapter in this volume makes this anthropological mandate apparent. Several research traditions within anthropology stand to make significant contributions to the analysis and satisfaction of consumer needs. Community studies are urgently needed to provide a descriptive database of local consumption patterns and marketing practice. Ethnic studies that incorporate consumer and marketing components into their larger agendas are absolutely indispensable, given current demographic trends (Kotkin, 1987; O'Hare, 1989; "Stalking," 1989; Waldrop, 1989; Westerman, 1989). Finally, so-called minority studies (whether of racial, income, occupation, age, or religious groups) are essential from both marketing and public policy points of view.

Strategic Planning

Strategic planning is a systematic way of relating to the future; it is the process and philosophy for which the corporation is merely a vehicle (Davidson, 1982; Davis, 1984). It needs to become the principal object of anthropological intervention (as perhaps the role played by Barnett at Nissan, described earlier in this chapter, would indicate). Recently, a group of anthropologists headed by Darcy Stapp (1992) has established a strategic think tank called Anthropological Perspectives to broker the utility of the discipline to decision makers. The group publishes a newsletter called *Anthro-Sight* to disseminate its thoughts on issues affecting marketplace and polity. Anthropologists must work diligently to transform, and ultimately eliminate, the term "externality" from the lexicon of corporate planners. Rita Denny's chapter in this volume demonstrates the feasibility of such change. With the rise of cultural risk assessment and management (David & Singh, 1991), the concept, and consequently the consequences, of "culture" will be treated less as a transaction or opportunity cost, or expendable resource where it is treated at all, and more as an end toward which marketing strategies are developed (Sherry, 1989). Arensberg's (1978) goal of humanizing the corporation, of taming it toward human ends, is an anthropological imperative. We need to reconceptualize the nature and mission of the corporation and abet the shift from maximizing shareholder value to maximizing stakeholder value. Cultural analyses and interventions are underwriting the transformation of corporations from strategy through structure as firms negotiate a global marketplace (Pucik, Tichy, & Barnett, 1992). Finally, if the buzzword "synergy" is ever to be effectively implemented, the comparative purview and attention to syncretism that characterize anthropology will be indispensable catalysts.

Organizational Culture

The anthropological study of organizational culture has grown by fits and starts; as a subdiscipline it is in its infancy despite its early origins (Jordan, 1994). A two-phase disciplinary initiative is indicated. First, extensive, comprehensive ethnographic description of corporations across industries is desperately needed. Second, a carefully considered program of directed intervention—a theoretically grounded, practically focused applied anthropology—might be undertaken. The emphasis of such study and intervention should fall on the subcultural units that are the constituting essences of organizations. Deshpande and Webster (1990) have sketched out the dimensions that a marketing-focused subcultural investigation might assume. Reeves-Ellington's chapter in this volume serves as a model for such enlightened intervention. Workman's (1992, 1993a, 1993b; Workman & Milne, 1994) ethnographic inquiry into the marketing/research and development interface in a high-tech organization has helped us appreciate more realistically the roles that marketing might be expected to play in the process of new product development. Capturing the service encounter ethnographically (Hochschild, 1983; Spradley & Mann, 1975) is of growing importance. Leidner (1993) and Reiter (1991) have each produced organizational ethnographies that balance our emergent understanding of servicescapes. Biggart (1989) and Prus (1989a, 1989b) have also examined sales organizations. In an age of mergers and acquisitions and of increasingly internationalized intra- and interorganizational relations, a well-developed understanding of substantive and processual elements of organizational culture is vital not just to market competitiveness but to corporate survival itself.

Economic Development

Development is certain to be a fundamental social, political, and ethical issue of the new millenium. Massive portions of the "First" World are in urgent need of redevelopment. At this writing, the "Second" World is transmogrifying at a rapid pace and may well assimilate to other Worlds entirely. The "Third" World, long a victim of systematic underdevelopment, is seeking to redefine its status as a source of raw materials and market for finished goods in a variety of ways, ranging from more intensive integration to active delinking with the world system. Nonethnocentric development (Dholakia & Sherry, 1987; Wiarda, 1985) is an increasingly popular option in conception as well as practice. The "Fourth" World persists as a tragically anachronistic critique of the inability or unwillingness of contemporary market economies to enhance the life chances of all its members. Empowering producers and consumers worldwide and shifting development from an economic to a cultural plane will become feasible propositions only with anthropological intervention (Bennett & Bowen, 1988; Epstein, 1991; Sherry, 1989). Eric Arnould's chapter in this volume provides a detailed account of the shift that will enable such intervention.

Household Studies

Given its status as a fundamental unit of consumer behavior, the household has been surprisingly neglected by consumer researchers. Domestic household structure and function have changed enormously since marketers first turned their attention to the family, to the point that much of our accepted wisdom is no longer accurate. Life cycles and life courses "alternative" to our mythic ideal—the employed father, homemaking mother, two children, and pet—are seen far more often in syndicated television reruns than in the culture at large; less than 6% of American families conform to this type (Schwartz, 1987). Notions of kinship and correlative behaviors have been drastically altered by demographic, historic, and social forces in ways that have outstripped consumer researchers' collective ingenuity in accounting for them. This change has also occurred, to varying degrees, on an international scale. Recently, anthropologists have stepped up their inquiry into household dynamics (Netting, Wilk, & Arnould, 1984), and consumer researchers have urged that the inquiry be accelerated (Heisley & Holmes, 1987). In particular, Wilk (1987, 1990) has examined decision-making processes and object relations within the context of households in ways that are congenial to consumer research. Wallendorf and Arnould (1991) have analyzed household consumption rituals tied to holiday celebrations. Barbara Olsen's study (this volume) of intergenerational transfer of brand loyalty is an example of the type of "getting close to the consumer" from which all sound future managerial decisions should emanate. It is through intimately knowing households in all their diversity that marketers will deliver the next-generation concept of added value.

Consumer Misbehavior

Holbrook (1985) has criticized consumer researchers for their neglect of the dark side of consumer behavior. Similarly, Miller (1987) has urged scholars to move beyond a reflexively critical, nihilistic global assault on "consumer culture" to a more intensive microlevel examination of what consumers actually do. Two and a half decades ago, Kotler and Levy (1971) proposed the concept of "demarketing" in recognition of the need to curb some of the excesses encouraged by consumer culture. The chapter by Masa Tani and William Rathje in this volume presents a cogent argument for demarketing, or social marketing, in the service of ecological restoration. There is probably no more hotly contested issue in business and the social sciences than that of ethics. Anthropologists can clearly contribute to the identification and resolution of ethical issues by directing more of their research efforts toward marketing and consumer research audiences. Anthropologists have long studied issues such as substance abuse, commerciogenic disease, and conspicuous consumption. "False consciousness" is a much used but little probed construct in need of systematic (especially emic) investigation. Studies of credit abuse, of gender stereotypes perpetuated (or changed) by advertising, and of the prioritization of demand suggest themselves. Marketing practice, personal consumption patterns, and public policy might all be significantly enlightened through the judicious communication of ethnographic findings to "nontraditional" audiences. Clearly, detailed investigations of dysfunctional consumer behaviors are warranted. A "serious examination of the social context of usage and dependency" (Mintz, 1993, p. 271), whether of drug-foods or any other product or experience (Hirschman, 1992), would seem an ethical imperative.

Object Relations

A once widely circulated quip ran something like this:
Q: What's the difference between anthropologists and sociologists?
A: We have museums, they don't.

The crux of the quip is the centrality of material culture to the anthropological enterprise. The meaning and significance of objects has always been the stock-in-trade of archaeologists, aesthetic anthropologists, and folklorists in particular, and in general of cultural anthropologists investigating ritual. Just recently have anthropologists begun to focus their interest in the world of goods on contemporary consumer culture. As noted earlier in this chapter, an object relations literature centered literally on objects is flourishing in consumer research (Belk, 1988; Belk, Wallendorf, & Sherry, 1989). This literature is beginning to plumb the experiential dimension of consumption as well as the production of consumption. For economic anthropologists willing to adopt a phenomenological perspective and explore the sedimentation of behavior, cognition, and affect in objects (e.g., exemplifed by works by Miller, 1993; Richardson, 1987; Tambiah, 1984; Thomas, 1991), the interiority of products and the nature of materiality in contemporary consumer societies await illumination. Dan Rose's chapter in this volume is an introspective account of just this type of phenomenology. That a "Distinguished Lecture" can be delivered to the American Ethnological Society in 1993 by a highly regarded senior anthropologist on the topic of the symbolic density of objects (Weiner, 1994) without a single reference to the literature of consumer research, let alone its anthropological subsets and parallels, does not bode well for the enterprise, however. Until more "mainstream" anthropologists renounce the "academic apartment syndrome" (Maruyama, 1994, pp. 182-183) and meet their neighbors on the same intellectual floor, we will continue to build knowledge silos instead of a more truly interesting interdisciplinary edifice.

Forecasting

It is often remarked that nothing is so difficult to predict as the future. With few exceptions (Barnett, 1994; Maruyama, 1982, 1985, 1991; Textor, 1980, 1990; Wallman, 1992; [I am also tempted to include the works of Ursula LeGuinn]), anthropologists have proved more reluctant than social scientists such as economists or demographers to engage in the construction of future scenarios. Even such astute observers of contemporary market societies as Mary Douglas (Douglas & Isherwood, 1979) or Marvin Harris (1981) have confined their interpretations to the ethnographic record rather than project and extrapolate their views very far forward in time. Cultural ecologists and archaeologists prefer retrodiction to prediction, even though their frameworks could be oriented to the future. What is ostensibly a scholarly virtue, however, becomes something of an impediment to managerial relevance. No matter how limited an individual manager's time horizons become as a result of routine tactical and operational considerations, the viability of a corporation depends on its ability to anticipate and influence the future. The chapter by Carole Duhaime, Annamma Joy, and Christopher Ross in this volume suggests the ways in which a sensitive evaluation study can affect an organization's future. Anthropologists have been tempocentric to the extent that they have failed to use inference and ethnographic analogy to gauge the impact of biocultural factors on emerging trends in marketing and consumer behavior. Such gauging can be couched in terms of sketching possibilities or alternatives rather than of crystal ball gazing. Given their devotion to the local, their bias toward holism, and their penchant for comparative analysis, anthropologists may be particularly suited to the type of careful scenario building required for accurate projection (Schwartz, 1991). Their advocacy orientation further disposes them to the type of informed activism that is demanded of such intervention programs as enlightened green marketing, or ecomarketing (Norberg-Hodge, 1991). New product development, corporate culture change, and category or industry transformation are just a few of the other areas to which a future-oriented anthropology might be applied. I believe the discipline will prove indispensible in helping create the visionary firm of tomorrow (Hamel & Prahalad, 1994).

Basic Research

Surveys and experiments by themselves are increasingly unsatisfactory methods of eliciting insight into fields as rich and complicated as consumer behavior. Complementary, and in some cases supplementary, analytic procedures are being adopted by researchers and managers alike (Arnould & Price, 1993; Waterston, 1994). Anthropological conventions such as naturalistic observation, contextualization, maximized comparisons, and sensitized concepts (Christians & Carey, 1981) as well as intraceptive intuition (Murray, 1943) will figure ever larger in the market researcher's toolkit (Sherry, 1991). The chapter by John Sherry, Mary Ann McGrath, and Sidney Levy in this volume represents a type of multimodal, interdisciplinary team inquiry that is diffusing into marketing and consumer research. So also will the critical perspective characteristic of the anthropologist become more necessary to managers operating in an increasingly multicultural marketplace.

Conclusion

In this chapter, I have attempted to impose a structure and a partisan point of view upon a topic that, if not entirely amorphous, is about as fluid as an emerging subdiscipline might be. Through the introductory vignettes I have sought to establish some very tentative parameters for the field of inquiry and hope to have sparked some synergistic extensions in the reader's imagination. Through discussion of an anthropological framework for marketing behavior I have suggested some particular modes of inquiry, some ways of apprehending consumption and marketing, that will help capture phenomena in something approaching their inherent complexities. Finally, through consideration of a set of projections I have explored some of the particular types of applications that anthropology may have for academics and practitioners concerned with consumer behavior, again, with the intention of stimulating the reader to imagine a more personally relevant "wish list" of agenda items. This chapter will help the motivated reader move into the field with a rough surveyor's map, if not a compass.

Throughout my discussion I have stressed the complementarity of anthropological perspectives and methods to the toolkit of conventional marketing and consumer researchers. This complementarity has both disciplinary and managerial relevance. On the one hand, anthropologists can expand the nature and scope of the basic enterprise that business academics recognize as legitimate inquiry. On the other hand, anthropologists can assist managers in matters strategic and tactical and improve both the opportunity for and quality of directed intervention in contemporary marketplaces. Anthropological practitioners have found a niche as service providers in a number of industries. Academic anthropologists must now elaborate a subdiscipline of sufficient theoretical significance and disciplinewide interest to ensure that this niche is not merely vocational nor a temporary blip in our history of ideas (Baba, 1994). This is also perhaps the most effective way to refute Kroeber's assertion—still widely credited— (quoted in Hackenberg, 1988, p. 172) that applied anthropology is merely "social work." Anthropology has traditionally been applied in the service of such marketing behaviors as health care delivery and community development (Wulff & Fiske, 1987). Over time, it has proved instrumental in areas such as new product development, especially in breaking through perceptual barriers imposed by conventional engineering- or product-driven approaches to design (Brues, 1992). Anthropologists have even studied the language of managers of U.S. pension funds (Conley & O'Barr, 1991) in an effort to understand how executives construe and implement investments. Anthropology also has the potential to contribute to meeting the needs of emerging markets (Serrie, 1991; Serrie & Burkhalter, 1994). I welcome the day when alliances and partnerships between anthropologically attuned practitioners and academics of every imaginable disciplinary stripe are as unremarkable as the problems we pursue are invigorating.

▧ References

Agnew, J.-C. (1986). *Worlds apart: The market and the theater in Anglo-American thought.* New York: Cambridge University Press.

Alsop, R. (1986, September 4). People watchers seek clues to consumers' true behavior. *Wall Street Journal*, p. 25.

Anderson, P. (1983, Fall). Marketing, scientific progress, and scientific method. *Journal of Marketing, 47,* 18-31.

Appadurai, A. (Ed.). (1986). *The social life of things.* New York: Cambridge University Press.

Appadurai, A. (1990). Disjuncture and difference in the global cultural economy. *Public Culture, 2*(2), 1-24.

Arensberg, C. (1978). Theoretical contributions of industrial and development studies. In E. Eddy & W. Partridge (Eds.), *Applied anthropology in America* (pp. 49-78). New York: Columbia University Press.

Arnould, E. (1989). Preference formation and the diffusion of innovation. *Journal of Consumer Research, 16*(2), 239-267.

Arnould, E. (1992, May 25). Research norms are not anthropology. *Marketing News,* p. 4.

Arnould, E., & Price, L. (1993). River magic: Extraordinary experience and the extended service encounter. *Journal of Consumer Research, 20*(1), 24-95.

Arnould, E., & Wilk, R. (1984). Why do the natives wear Adidas? In T. Kinnear (Ed.), *Advances in consumer research* (Vol. 2, pp. 748-752). Provo, UT: Association for Consumer Research.

Ayres, E. (1994). The history of a cup of coffee. *World Watch, 7*(5), 20-22.

Baba, M. (1986). Business and industrial anthropology: An overview. *NAPA Bulletin No. 2.* Washington, DC: National Association for the Practice of Anthropology.

Baba, M. (1994). The fifth subdiscipline: Anthropological practice and the future of anthropology. *Human Organization, 53*(2), 174-186.

Backgrounder. (1994, February). McDonald's corporate communication.

Barnett, S. (1983). Brave new wave of the '80s. *Across the Board, 20*(11), 5-12.

Barnett, S. (Ed.). (1992). *The Nissan report.* New York: Doubleday.

Barnett, S. (1994). Futures: Probable and plausible. *Anthropology Newsletter, 35*(7), 52.

Barrett, S. (1984). *The rebirth of anthropological theory.* Toronto: University of Toronto Press.

Belk, R. (1988). Possessions and the extended self. *Journal of Consumer Research, 15*(2), 139-168.

Belk, R., & Costa, J. (1991). A critical assessment of international tourism. In R. Dholakia & K. Bothra (Eds.), *Proceedings of the third international conference on marketing and development* (pp. 371-382). New Delhi: n.p.

Belk, R., Wallendorf, M., & Sherry, J. F., Jr. (1989). The sacred and profane in consumer behavior: Theodicy on the odyssey. *Journal of Consumer Research, 16*(1), 1-38.

Bennett, J., & Bowen, J. (1988). *Production and autonomy: Anthropological studies and critiques of development.* New York: University Press of America.

Bennett, L. (1988). Bridges for changing times: Local practitioner organizations in American anthropology. *NAPA Bulletin No. 6.* Washington, DC: American Anthropological Association.

Berstell, G. (1992, April 13). Slaughter the sacred cows of market research. *Marketing News*, pp. 4, 6.

Biggart, N. (1989). *Charismatic capitalism: Direct selling organizations in America.* Chicago: University of Chicago Press.

Bohannan, P., & Dalton, G. (Eds.). (1962). *Markets in Africa.* Evanston, IL: Northwestern University Press.

Bohnaker, W. (1990). *The hollow doll.* New York: Ballantine.

Boram, J. (1988, May 16). A VP of anthropology? *Industry Week*, p. 26.

Borofsky, R. (Ed.). (1994). *Assessing cultural anthropology.* New York: McGraw-Hill.

Brues, A. (1992, March). Applied physical anthropology in the Army Air Force and the development of the ball turret. *Anthropology Newsletter*, pp. 16-17.

Buruma, I. (1984). *Behind the mask.* New York: New American Library.

Cateora, P. (1990). *International marketing.* Homewood, IL: Irwin.

Cerasuolo, M. (1990). *JBL international* (Harman International annual report). Washington, DC: Harman International Industries, Inc.

Cho, N. (1993, November 19). Dump the stuff in Times Square and disposal becomes automatic. *Wall Street Journal*, p. B1.

Christians, C., & Carey, J. (1981). The logic and aims of qualitative research. In G. Stempel & B. Wesley (Eds.), *Research methods in mass communication* (pp. 342-362). Englewood Cliffs, NJ: Prentice Hall.

Cohen, Y. (1977). The anthropological enterprise. *American Anthropologist, 79*(2), 382-396.

Conley, J., & O'Barr, W. (1991, March-April). The culture of capital. *Harvard Business Review*, pp. 110-111.

Cook, S., & Diskin, M. (Eds.). (1978). *Markets in Oaxaca.* Austin: University of Texas Press.

Costa, J., & Bamossy, G. (1993). Ethnicity in developing countries: Implications for marketing and research. In L. Dominguez (Ed.), *Marketing and economic restructuring in the developing world* (pp. 407-415). Madison, WI: Omni Press.

Dannhaeuser, N. (1983). *Contemporary trade strategies in the Philippines.* New Brunswick, NJ: Rutgers University Press.

Dannhaeuser, N. (1989). Marketing in developing areas. In S. Plattner (Ed.), *Economic anthropology* (pp. 222-252). Stanford, CA: Stanford University Press.

David, K., & Singh, H. (1991). *Cultural risk in corporate acquisitions.* Working paper, Michigan State University, Department of Anthropology.

Davidson, W. (1982). *Global strategic management.* New York: John Wiley.

Davis, N., McConochie, R., & Stevenson, D. (1987). Research and consulting as a business. *NAPA Bulletin No. 4.* Washington, DC: American Anthropological Association.

Davis, S. (1984). *Managing corporate culture.* Cambridge, MA: Ballinger.

Deshpande, R., & Webster, F. (1990). *Analyzing corporate cultures approaching a global marketplace* (Marketing Science Institute Report No. 90-111). Cambridge, MA: Marketing Science Institute.

Deutsch, C. (1991, February 24). Coping with cultural polyglots. *New York Times*, p. C25.

Dholakia, N., & Sherry, J. F., Jr. (1987). Marketing and development: A resynthesis of knowledge. In J. Sheth (Ed.), *Research in marketing* (Vol. 9, pp. 119-143). Greenwich, CT: JAI.

Dickie, W. (1982). Profile of an anthropologist. *Anthropology Newsletter, 23*(9), 7.

Dimen-Shein, M. (1977). *The anthropological imagination.* New York: McGraw-Hill.

Douglas, M., & Isherwood, B. (1979). *The world of goods.* New York: Basic Books.

Drucker-Brown, S. (Ed.). (1982). *Malinowski in Mexico: The economics of a Mexican marketing system.* London: Routledge & Kegan Paul.

Elliott, S. (1993, August 23). The latest in market research: Videogenic self-analyzing shoppers. *New York Times*, p. D4.

Entine, J. (1994). Shattered image. *Business Ethics, 8*(5), 23-28.

Epstein, T. S. (1991). Client-led versus top-down development. In R. Dholakia & K. Bothra (Eds.), *Proceedings of the third international conference on marketing and development* (pp. 435-438). New Delhi: n.p.

Fannin, R. (1988). Seeing is believing. *Marketing and Media Decisions, 23*(2), 51-54.

Feest, C. (1990). Europe's Indians. In J. Clifton (Ed.), *The invented Indian: Cultural fictions and government policies* (pp. 313-332). New Brunswick, NJ: Transaction Press.

Fernandez, J. (1986). *Persuasions and performances: The play of tropes in culture.* Bloomington: Indiana University Press.

Foltz, K. (1989, December 18). New species for study: Consumers in action. *New York Times*, pp. A1, D10.

Gales, R. (1989, March 13). Consumer culture: An emerging anthropological workshop. *Adweek*, pp. 30-31.

Galt, A., & Smith, L. (1976). *Models and the study of social change.* New York: John Wiley.

Gardner, B. (1978). Doing business with management. In E. Eddy & W. Partridge (Eds.), *Applied anthropology in America* (pp. 245-260). New York: Columbia University Press.

Gardner, B., & Levy, S. (1955). The product and the brand. *Harvard Business Review, 33*(2), 33-39.

Geertz, C. (1973). *The interpretation of cultures.* New York: Basic Books.

Giovannini, M., & Rosansky, L. (1990). Anthropology and management consulting: Forging a new alliance. *NAPA Bulletin No. 9.* Washington, DC: American Anthropological Association.

Goldstein, M. (1988, October). Someone to watch over us. *Inside Print*, pp. 48-53.

Hackenberg, R. (1988). Scientists or survivors? The future of applied anthropology under maximum uncertainty. In R. Trotter (Ed.), *Anthropology for tomorrow* (pp. 170-185). Washington, DC: American Anthropological Association.

Hakken, D., & Lessinger, J. (Eds.). (1987). *Perspectives in U.S. Marxist anthropology.* Boulder, CO: Westview.

Hamel, G., & Prahalad, C. K. (1994). *Competing for the future.* Cambridge, MA: Harvard Business School Press.

Harris, M. (1968). *The rise of anthropological theory.* New York: Crowell.

Harris, M. (1971). *Culture, people, and nature.* New York: Crowell.

Harris, M. (1981). *America now: The anthropology of a changing culture.* New York: Simon & Schuster.

Hattox, R. (1985). *Coffee and coffee houses: The origins of a social beverage in the medieval Near East.* Seattle: University of Washington Press.

Heisley, D., & Holmes, P. (1987). A review of family consumption research: The need for a more anthropological perspective. In M. Wallendorf & P. Anderson (Eds.), *Advances in consumer research* (Vol. 14, pp. 453-457). Provo, UT: Association for Consumer Research.

Heller, S. (1988, June 1). From selling Rambo to supermarket studies, anthropologists are finding more non-academic jobs. *Chronicle of Higher Education,* pp. A24, A25.

Henderson, M. (1994, Spring). Rain forest crunch. *Whole Earth Review,* pp. 35-40.

Hirschman, E. (1992). The consciousness of addiction: Toward a general theory of compulsive consumption. *Journal of Consumer Research, 19*(2), 155-179.

Hochschild, A. (1983). *The managed heart: Commercialization of human feeling.* Berkeley: University of California Press.

Holbrook, M. (1985). *Consumer misbehavior: The nature of irregular, irrational, illegal and immoral consumption.* Working paper, Columbia University.

Houghton, J. (1992, May 4). Anthropologically speaking. *Advertising Age,* p. 24.

Hume, S. (1990, January 22). How Big Mac made it to Moscow. *Advertising Age,* pp. 16, 51.

Hunt, S. (1983). *Marketing theories: The philosophy of marketing science.* Homewood, IL: Irwin.

Idris-Soven, A., Idris-Soven, E., & Vaughn, M. K. (Eds.). (1978). *The world as a company town: Multinational corporations and social change.* The Hague: Mouton.

Iyer, P. (1988). *Video night in Kathmandu.* New York: Vantage.

Johnson, A. (1978). *Quantification in cultural anthropology.* Stanford, CA: Stanford University Press.

Jordan, A. (Ed.). (1994). Practicing anthropology in corporate America: Consulting on organizational culture. *NAPA Bulletin No. 14.* Washington, DC: American Anthropological Association.

Joy, A. (1988). Gender, social structure and the marketing process. In J. Littlefield & M. Csath (Eds.), *Marketing and economic development: Issues and opinions* (pp. 214-217). Blacksburg: Virginia Tech Marketing Department.

Kanner, B. (1989, May 8). Mind games. *New York,* pp. 34-40.

Kassarjian, H. (1982). The development of consumer behavior theory. In A. Mitchell & A. Arbor (Eds.), *Advances in consumer research* (Vol. 9, pp. 20-22). Ann Arbor, MI: Association for Consumer Research.

Kopytoff, I. (1986). The cultural biography of things: The commoditization of things. In A. Appadurai (Ed.), *The social life of things* (pp. 66-91). New York: Cambridge University Press.

Kotkin, J. (1987, July). Selling to the new America. *INC.*, pp. 44-52.

Kotler, P. (1986a). Megamarketing. *Harvard Business Review*, 64(2), 117-124.

Kotler, P. (1986b). Global standardization-courting danger. *Journal of Consumer Marketing*, 3(2), 13-15.

Kotler, P., & Levy, S. (1969, April). Broadening the concept of marketing. *Journal of Marketing*, 36, 46-54.

Kotler, P., & Levy, S. (1971, November/December). Demarketing, yes demarketing. *Harvard Business Review*, pp. 74-80.

Laabs, J. (1992, January). Corporate anthropologists. *Personnel Journal*, pp. 81-91.

Larson, E. (1992). *The naked consumer.* New York: Holt.

Lee, J. (1966, March/April). Cultural analysis for overseas operation. *Harvard Business Review*, pp. 106-111.

Leidner, R. (1993). *Fast food, fast talk: Service work and the routinization of everyday life.* Berkeley: University of California Press.

Levin, G. (1992, February 24). Anthropologists in adland. *Advertising Age*, pp. 3, 49.

Levitt, T. (1983). The globalization of markets. *Harvard Business Review*, 61(3), 92-102.

Levitt, T. (1984). *The marketing imagination.* New York: Free Press.

Levitt, T. (1988). The pluralization of consumption. *Harvard Business Review*, 66(3), 7-8.

Levy, S. (1976). Marcology 101, or the domain of marketing. In K. Bernhardt (Ed.), *Marketing, 1776-1976* (pp. 577-581). Chicago: American Marketing Association.

Lewin, T. (1986, May 11). Casting an anthropological eye on American consumers. *New York Times*, Section 3, p. 6.

Marcus, G., & Fisher, M. (1986). *Anthropology as cultural critique: An experimental moment in the human sciences.* Chicago: University of Chicago Press.

Maruyama, M. (1982). New mindscapes for future business policy and management. *Technological Forecasting and Social Change*, 20, 20.

Maruyama, M. (1985). Mindscapes: How to understand specific situations in multicultural management. *Asia-Pacific Journal of Management*, 2, 125-149.

Maruyama, M. (1991). International proactive marketing. *Journal of International Consumer Marketing*, 4(3), 95-107.

Maruyama, M. (1994). Epilogue. In M. Caley & D. Sawada (Eds.), *Mindscapes: The epistemology of Magoroh Maruyama* (pp. 177-188). Langhorne, PA: Gordon & Breech.

Maybury-Lewis, D. (1992). *Millenium: Tribal wisdom and the modern world.* New York: Viking.

McCracken, G. (1988). *Culture and consumption: New approaches to the symbolic character of consumer goods and activities.* Bloomington: Indiana University Press.

Merritt, S. (1992, June 15). Advertising anthropologists prowl the supermarket aisles. *Advertising Age*, p. 22.

Miller, A., Shenitz, B., & Rosaldo, L. (1990, June 4). You are what you buy. *Newsweek*, pp. 59-60.

Miller, D. (1987). *Material culture and mass consumption*. New York: Blackwell.

Miller, D. (Ed.). (1993). *Unwrapping Christmas*. Oxford, UK: Clarendon Press.

Mills, C. W. (1975). On intellectual craftsmanship. In C. W. Mills, *The sociological imagination*. New York: Oxford University Press. (Original work published 1959)

Milton, K. (1993). *Environmentalism: The view from anthropology*. New York: Routledge.

Mintz, S. (1985). *Sweetness and power: The place of sugar in modern history*. New York: Viking.

Mintz, S. (1993). The changing roles of food in the study of consumption. In J. Brewer & R. Porter (Eds.), *Consumption and the world of goods* (pp. 261-273). New York: Routledge.

Miriampolski, H. (1988, January 4). Ethnography makes comeback as research tool. *Marketing News*, pp. 32, 44.

Murray, W. (1943). *Thematic Apperception Test manual*. Cambridge, MA: Harvard University Press.

Naisbitt, J. (1994). *Global paradox*. New York: Morrow.

Nash, J. (1990). Looking back and forward: Presidential address. *Anthropology Newsletter, 31*(6), 13-14.

Nash, J., & Fernandez-Kelly, M. (Eds.). (1983). *Women, men and the international division of labor*. Albany: State University of New York Press.

Netting, R., Wilk, R., & Arnould, E. (Eds.). (1984). *Households: Comparative and historical studies of the domestic group*. Berkeley: University of California Press.

Norberg-Hodge, H. (1991). *Ancient futures: Learning from Ladakh*. San Francisco: Sierra Club Books.

Nussbaum, B. (1993, June 7). Hot products: Smart design is the common thread. *Business Week*, pp. 54-57.

O'Hare, W. (1989, November). In the black. *American Demographics*, pp. 25-29.

Platt, A. (1994, May/June). Toxic green : The trouble with golf. *World Watch*, pp. 27-32.

Plattner, S. (Ed.). (1989). *Economic anthropology*. Stanford, CA: Stanford University Press.

Porter, M. (1986). The strategic role of international marketing. *Journal of Consumer Marketing, 3*(2), 17-21.

Porter, M. (1990). *The competitive advantage of nations*. New York: Free Press.

Porter, R. (1993). Consumption: Disease of the consumer society? In J. Brewer & R. Porter (Eds.), *Consumption and the world of goods* (pp. 58-81). New York: Routledge.

Prindle, C. (1992). Anthropology's new "natives": American consumers. *CASRO Journal* [annual], pp. 149-151.

Prus, R. (1989a). *Pursuing customers: An ethnography of marketing activities.* Newbury Park, CA: Sage.

Prus, R. (1989b). *Making sales: Influence as interpersonal accomplishment.* Newbury Park, CA: Sage.

Pucik, V., Tichy, N., & Barnett, C. (Eds.). (1992). *Globalizing management: Creating and leading the competitive organization.* New York: John Wiley.

Rathje, W. (1974). The garbage project: A new way of looking at the problems of archaeology. *Archaeology, 27,* 236-241.

Rathje, W., & Murphy, C. (1992). *Rubbish: The archaeology of garbage.* New York: HarperCollins.

Real, M. (1989). *Super media: A cultural studies approach.* Newbury Park, CA: Sage.

Reiter, E. (1991). *Making fast food: From the frying pan into the fryer.* Montreal: McGill-Queen's University Press.

Richardson, M. (1987). A social (ideational-behavioral) interpretation of material culture and its application to archaeology. In D. Ingersoll & G. L. Bronitsky (Eds.), *Mirror and metaphor* (pp. 381-403). Lanham, MD: University Press of America.

Ritzer, G. (1993). *The McDonaldization of society.* Thousand Oaks, CA: Pine Forge.

Roddick, A. (1991). *Body and soul.* New York: Crown.

Russell, C. (1990). Ten particle markets. *American Demographics, 12*(8), 2.

Rutz, H., & Orlove, B. (Eds.). (1989). *The social economy of consumption.* Lanham, MD: University Press of America.

Schaffer, M. (1989). *Winning the countertrade war.* New York: John Wiley.

Schwartz, J. (1987, March). Family traditions: Although radically changed, the American family is as strong as ever. *American Demographics,* pp. 58-60.

Schwartz, P. (1991). *The art of the long view.* New York: Doubleday.

Scott, M. (1994, July/August). Responsible remedies. *Business Ethics,* pp. 15-16.

Serrie, H. (1991, April 1). The large, lucrative peasant market. *Wall Street Journal,* p. A10.

Serrie, H., & Burkhalter, B. (1994). *What can multinationals do for peasants?* (Studies in Third World Societies, No. 49). Williamsburg, VA: College of William and Mary, Department of Anthropology.

Sherry, J. F., Jr. (1983). [Review of] Staughton Lynd (1982). *The fight against shutdowns,* Singlejack Books, San Pedro, CA. *Anthropology of Work Review, 4*(4), 11.

Sherry, J. F., Jr. (1984). Some implications of consumer oral tradition for reactive marketing. In T. Kinnear (Ed.), *Advances in consumer research* (Vol. 11, pp. 741-747). Provo, UT: Association for Consumer Research.

Sherry, J. F., Jr. (1986). *Cereal monogamy: Brand loyalty as secular ritual in consumer culture.* Paper presented at the 17th Annual Conference of the Association for Consumer Research, Toronto, Canada.

Sherry, J. F., Jr. (1987a). Heresy and the useful miracle: Rethinking anthropology's contributions to marketing. In J. Sheth (Ed.), *Research in marketing* (Vol. 9, pp. 285-306). Greenwich, CT: JAI.

Sherry, J. F., Jr. (1987b). Marketing and consumer behavior: Windows of opportunity for anthropology. *Journal of the Steward Anthropological Society, 16*(1-2), 60-95.

Sherry, J. F., Jr. (1987c). *Cultural propriety in a global marketplace.* In A. F. Firat, N. Dholakia, & R. Bagozzi (Eds.), *Philosophical and radical thought in marketing* (pp. 179-191). Lexington, MA: Lexington Books.

Sherry, J. F., Jr. (1987d). Advertising as a cultural system. In J. Umiker-Sebeok (Ed.), *Marketing and semiotics: New directions in the study of signs for sale* (pp. 441-481). Berlin: Mouton de Gruyter.

Sherry, J. F., Jr. (1987e). Keeping the monkeys away from the typewriters: An anthropologist's view of the consumer behavior odyssey. In M. Wallendorf & P. Anderson (Eds.), *Advances in consumer research* (Vol. 14, pp. 370-373). Provo, UT: Association for Consumer Research.

Sherry, J. F., Jr. (1989). Observations on marketing and consumption: An anthropological note. In T. Srull (Ed.), *Advances in consumer research* (Vol. 16, pp. 555-561). Provo, UT: Association for Consumer Research.

Sherry, J. F., Jr. (1990a). A sociocultural analysis of a midwestern American flea market. *Journal of Consumer Research, 17*(1), 13-30.

Sherry, J. F., Jr. (1990b). Dealers and dealing in a periodic market: Informal retailing in ethnographic perspective. *Journal of Retailing, 66*(2), 174-200.

Sherry, J. F., Jr. (1991). Postmodern alternatives: The interpretive turn in consumer research. In T. Robertson & H. Kassarjian (Eds.), *Handbook of consumer behavior* (pp. 548-591). Englewood Cliffs, NJ: Prentice Hall.

Sherry, J. F., Jr., & Camargo, E. (1987). "May your life be marvelous": English language labelling and the semiotics of Japanese promotion. *Journal of Consumer Research, 14*(3), 174-188.

Sherry, J. F., Jr., & McGrath, M. (1989). Unpacking the holiday presence: A comparative ethnography of two midwestern American gift stores. In E. Hirschman (Ed.), *Interpretative consumer behavior* (pp. 148-167). Provo, UT: Association for Consumer Research.

Sheth, J. (1982). Consumer behavior: shortages and surpluses. In A. Mitchell (Ed.), *Advances in consumer research* (Vol. 9, pp. 13-16). Ann Arbor, MI: Association for Consumer Research.

Shipman, P. (1994). *The evolution of racism: Human differences and the use and abuse of science.* New York: Simon & Schuster.

Shweder, R., & Fiske, D. (1986). Introduction: Uneasy social science. In D. Fiske & R. Shweder (Eds.), *Metatheory in social science* (pp. 1-18). Chicago: University of Chicago Press.

Singer, K. (1986, September 29). Ethnography: Research that's up close and personal. *Adweek,* pp. 30, 32.

Smith, C. (1976). *Regional analysis* (Vols. 1-2). New York: Academic Press.

Snegirjov, V. (1991, July 31). The hero of capitalist labor: McDonald's is not a mere restaurant chain, it is an entire philosophy. *Pravda,* p. 7.

Spradley, J., & Mann, B. (1975). *The cocktail waitress: Woman's work in a man's world*. New York: John Wiley.

Stalking the new consumer. (1989, August 28). *Business Week*, pp. 54-62.

Stapp, D. (Ed.). (1992). *AnthroSight: Anthropology for decision makers*. (Available from D. Stapp, P.O. Box 1721, Richland, WA 99352)

Stefflre, V. (1978). *Jobs for anthropologists: A look at an ecological niche*. Unpublished manuscript.

Steiner, C. (1994). *African art in transit*. New York: Cambridge University Press.

Tambiah, S. (1984). *The Buddhist saints of the forest and the cult of amulets*. New York: Cambridge University Press.

Taussig, M. (1980). *The devil and commodity fetishism in South America*. Chapel Hill: University of North Carolina Press.

Terpstra, V., & David, K. (1991). *The cultural environment of international business*. Cincinnati, OH: South-Western.

Textor, R. (1980). *A handbook on ethnographic futures research*. Stanford, CA: Stanford University School of Education and Department of Anthropology.

Textor, R. (1990). Introduction. In S. Ketudat (Ed.), *The middle path for the future of Thailand: Technology in harmony with culture and environment* (pp. xxiii-xlvii). Honolulu: East-West Center.

Thomas, N. (1991). *Entangled objects*. Cambridge, MA: Harvard University Press.

Tobin, J. (Ed.). (1992). *Remade in Japan: Everyday life and consumer taste in a changing society*. New Haven, CT: Yale University Press.

Tucker, W. T. (1967). *Foundations for a theory of consumer behavior*. New York: Holt, Rinehart & Winston.

Tucker, W. T. (1974). Future directions in marketing theory. *Journal of Marketing, 38*(2), 30-35.

Van Maanen, J. (1988). *Tales of the field*. Chicago: University of Chicago Press.

Waldrop, J. (1989, March). Inside America's households. *American Demographics*, pp. 20-27.

Wallendorf, M., & Arnould, E. (1991). We gather together: Consumption rituals of Thanksgiving day. *Journal of Consumer Research, 18*(1), 13-31.

Wallendorf, M., & Reilly, M. (1983). Ethnic migration, assimilation and consumption. *Journal of Consumer Research, 10*, 292-302.

Wallman, S. (Ed.). (1992). *Contemporary futures: Perspectives from social anthropology*. New York: Routledge.

Waterston, A. (1994). Interpreting audiences: Cultural anthropology in marketing research. *Practicing Anthropology, 16*(2), 11-13.

Weatherford, J. (1988). *Indian givers*. New York: Crown.

Weiner, A. (1994). Cultural difference and the density of objects. *American Ethnologist, 21*(1), 391-403.

Westerman, M. (1989, March). The death of the frito bandito. *American Demographics*, pp. 28-32.

Wiarda, H. (1985). Toward a nonethnocentric theory of development: Alternative conceptions from the Third World. In H. Wiaranda (Ed.), *New directions in comparative politics* (pp. 127-140). Boulder, CO: Westview.

Wilk, R. (1987). House, home and consumer decision making in two cultures. In M. Wallendorf & P. Anderson (Eds.), *Advances in consumer research* (Vol. 14, pp. 303-307). Provo, UT: Association for Consumer Research.

Wilk, R. (1990). Consumer goods as a dialogue about development. *Culture and History, 7,* 79-100.

Wind, Y. (1986). The myth of globalization. *Journal of Consumer Marketing, 3*(2), 23-26.

Workman, J. (1992). From fieldnotes to ethnography: Observations on the process. In C. Allen & T. Madden (Eds.), *AMA winter educators' conference proceedings* (Vol. 3, pp. 260-269). Chicago: American Marketing Association.

Workman, J. (1993a). Marketing's limited role in new product development in one computer systems firm. *Journal of Marketing Research, 30,* 405-421.

Workman, J. (1993b). The nature of the marketing/R&D interface in a range of organizational settings. In R. Varadarajan & B. Jaworski (Eds.), *AMA winter educators' conference proceedings* (Vol. 4, pp. 353-361). Chicago: American Marketing Association.

Workman, J., & Milne, G. (1994). Breaking free of institutionalized business practices: Theory, field observations, and implications. In C. W. Park & D. Smith (Eds.), *Marketing theory and application* (Vol. 5, pp. 232-237). Chicago: American Marketing Association.

Wulff, R., & Fiske, S. (Eds.). (1987). *Anthropological praxis: Translating knowledge into action.* Boulder, CO: Westview.

Yellen, J. (1990, April). The transformation of the Kalahari !Kung. *Scientific American,* pp. 96-105.

Yovovich, B. G. (1990, April 9). Tribal rituals and how they help sell soup. *Crain's Chicago Business,* p. 18.

Zielinski, J., & Robertson, T. (1982). Consumer behavior theory: Excesses and limitations. In A. Mitchell (Ed.), *Advances in consumer research* (Vol. 9, pp. 8-12). Ann Arbor, MI: Association for Consumer Research.

PART TWO

Apprehending the Product
Artifactual Dimensions of Consumer Behavior

In this part, we explore one of the central concerns of our focal disciplines of anthropology, marketing, and consumer research. The relationship of the tangible to the intangible, the corporeal to the incorporeal, has intrigued us since the dawn of the species and surely has inspired the efflorescence of *Homo faber*. The interplay between physicality and what consumer researchers are coming to call materiality—between the thing and Kant's thing in the thing—is an issue of disciplinary and applied importance. The dialectic of having and being had impinges on private sector and public policy matters alike.

The metaphysical construction project that is the mutually constituting relationship among self, society, and stuff (Sherry, 1993a) is examined in the following chapters from perspectives of increasing interest to marketers and consumer researchers. Introspection is a current fascination (Wallendorf & Brucks, 1993) that challenges us to recall intraceptive intuition (Murray, 1943; Sherry, 1991) from its banishment to clinical psychology and to affirm the notion that the anthropologist's subjectivity is the most reliable instrument of ethnographic inquiry (Devereux, 1967). Historical archaeology, in its celebrated incarnation as garbology, has been employed to insightful effect in the study of ethnicity and consumption (Reilly & Wallendorf, 1987; Wallendorf & Reilly, 1983). Introspection and archaeology involve a delving apposite to materiality and materiel.

A venerable topic in anthropology, the meaning of objects in circulation is currently undergoing a vigorous reexamination (Schildkrout, 1992). Renewed attention to the role played by consumer products in processes of culture change—from Salisbury's (1962) steel axes in Melanesia to Manuel's (1993) cassette tapes in India—portends ever richer accounts of consumer object relations. It is methodologically suggestive as well, as one imagines merging the techniques of behavioral archaeology and introspection with the point-of-sale data collection possibilities that scanners afford to produce new insights. The priority of objects to language, the dialectic between what is utterable and what is ineffable, and inquiry into the unthought known is of increasing interest to consumer researchers. Cast in terms of a cultural poetics of consumption, we can borrow Hopkins's (Preminger & Brogan, 1993, p. 609) notions of "inscape" and "instress" to characterize this interest. Inscape is the pattern of attributes that gives an object its individuality and unity; it comprises the object's essential nature. Instress is the energy that holds inscape together and projects it into the receiver's mind. These properties of consumer object relations are revealed in analysis of consumption and disposition of the type presented in the following chapters.

Dan Rose anchors his phenomenology of products in a personal grooming ritual (Rook, 1985) and moves between an account of direct engagement with product and a poetics of fabrication. As an interpretive vehicle, his chapter is evocative of Baker's (1986) relentlessly reflexive autoethnography and Haug's (1987) impassioned critique of commodity aesthetics. Rose brackets "autonomous language" and "abstracted social theory" to create a space for apprehending the product as it is and then recontextualizes his experience to view the product as a hybrid of components not unlike Mauss's (1924) total social fact. This provocative introspection can be viewed as a detailed working out of reader response theory and a prolegomenon to programmatic ethnographic consumer research into the semiotics of promotion. Rose considers the ways that a product is animated, that consumers may inspire goods to produce consumption. His treatment leaves little doubt that a view of products as merely, or even principally, bundles of utility is myopic in the extreme.

MasaKazu Tani and William Rathje pursue a different tack entirely by shifting our gaze from the superstructural to the infrastructural level of consumer behavior. Their use of unobtrusive, nonreactive archaeological technique to explore a sorely neglected realm of consumer behavior—disposition—produces some counterintuitive findings across age and ethnic segments that lead to insightful interpretation in the present and the promise of more precise use of obtrusive, reactive measures in future studies. Their study of discarded household hazardous waste is a compelling argument for the development of an ecolate approach (Hardin, 1985) to marketing practice, consumer behavior, and public policy. Failure to anticipate the unintended consequences of decisions at managerial, consumer, and regulatory levels of the marketplace can result in ecosystem degradation of dizzying complexity and horrific result. Dry-cell batteries are a useful example of the type of transparent technology (Dubinskas, 1993) that underwrites everyday life—but with a hidden cost. As it becomes more apparent that there is no "away" to throw things to (Hardin, 1985), it is also clear that no current battery can "keep going and going, and going." Concepts like "obsolescence" and "byproduct" are now more than merely anachronistic metaphors; they are palpable threats to sustainable development. Proactive response in terms of ecolate product design and lateral cycling and reactive response in terms of precisely targeted campaigns of social marketing (Fox & Kotler, 1980) and demarketing (Kotler & Levy, 1971) are indicated by the findings of the Garbage Project. These findings contribute to the trend of rethinking materialism in the service of reducing material flows and reinforce the wisdom of practices such as efficient use, smart design, green labeling, and lateral cycling (Young, 1994).

Thus where Rose shows us that we need a cultural biography of things (Kopytoff, 1986), Tani and Rathje make it clear that we need an eschatology as well. By charting the life and afterlife of products, we should move closer to discovering the needs of consumers, both revealed and unarticulated, in a way that will produce more satisfying marketplace behaviors that are adaptive over the long term. Such charting may even result in novel presentational forms. For example, Spector (1993) has harnessed the evocative power of things in her speculative fiction, using an artifact as a projectible field in the service of feminist archaeology to produce a compelling, poetic cultural biography of a Wahpeton Dakota awl. So also has Sherry (1992, 1993b) used products in poetry exploring the nature of consumer culture. We should remain alive to the possibilities of an aesthetics *of* marketing, beyond the application of aesthetics *to* marketing or vice versa (Levy & Czepiel, 1975), which a focus on objects can stimulate.

◪ References

Baker, N. (1986). *The mezzanine*. New York: Random House.
Devereux, G. (1967). *From anxiety to method in the behavioral sciences*. The Hague: Mouton.

Dubinskas, F. (1993). Knowledge building and knowledge access: Teaching with electronic tools. In F. Dubinskas & J. McDonald (Eds.), *Electronic technologies and instruction: Tools, users, and power* (NAPA Bulletin No. 2, pp. 1-11). Washington, DC: American Anthropological Association.

Fox, K., & Kotler, P. (1980). The marketing of social causes: The first ten years. *Journal of Marketing, 44*(4), 24-33.

Hardin, G. (1985). *Filters against folly.* New York: Viking/Penguin.

Haug, W. (1987). *Critique of commodity aesthetics: Appearance, sexuality and advertising in capitalist society.* Cambridge, UK: Polity.

Kopytoff, I. (1986). The cultural biography of things: Commoditization as process. In A. Appadurai (Ed.), *The social life of things* (pp. 64-91). New York: Cambridge University Press.

Kotler, P., & Levy, S. (1971, November/December). Demarketing, yes demarketing. *Harvard Business Review,* pp. 74-80.

Levy, S., & Czepiel, J. (1975). Marketing and aesthetics. In R. Curhan (Ed.), *1974 combined proceedings: New marketing for social and economic progress and marketing's contributions to the firm and to the society* (Series No. 36, pp. 386-391). Chicago: American Marketing Association.

Manuel, P. (1993). *Cassette culture: Popular music and technology in north India.* Chicago: University of Chicago Press.

Mauss, M. (1924). *The gift.* New York: Norton.

Murray, H. (1943). *Thematic Apperception Test manual.* Cambridge, MA: Harvard University Press.

Preminger, A., & Brogan, T. (1993). *The new Princeton encyclopedia of poetry and poetics.* Princeton, NJ: Princeton University Press.

Reilly, M., & Wallendorf, M. (1987). A comparison of group differences in food consumption using household refuse. *Journal of Consumer Research, 4*(2), 289-294.

Rook, D. (1985). The ritual dimension of consumption. *Journal of Consumer Research, 12*(3), 251-264.

Salisbury, R. (1962). *From stone to steel: Economic consequences of a technological change in New Guinea.* Cambridge, UK: Cambridge University Press.

Schildkrout, E. (Ed.). (1992). Trade, ethnicity and material culture. *Museum Anthropology, 16*(3, special issue), 5-61.

Sherry, J. F., Jr. (1991). Postmodern alternatives: The interpretive turn in consumer research. In T. Robertson & H. Kassarjian (Eds.), *Handbook of consumer behavior* (pp. 548-591). Englewood Cliffs, NJ: Prentice Hall.

Sherry, J. F., Jr. (1992). Unter den Linden, Madison and mine. *Public Culture, 4*(2), 139-140.

Sherry, J. F., Jr. (1993a). Having and being had: A review essay on the cultural psychology of material possessions. *Journal of Macromarketing, 13*(2), 75-78.

Sherry, J. F., Jr. (1993b). The price of martyrdom. *International Journal of Research in Marketing, 10*(3), 225.

Spector, J. (1993). *What this awl means: Feminist archaeology at a Wahpeton Dakota village.* St. Paul: Minnesota Historical Society Press.

Wallendorf, M., & Brucks, M. (1993). Introspection and consumer research: Implementation and implications. *Journal of Consumer Research, 20*(3), 339-359.

Wallendorf, M., & Reilly, M. (1983). Ethnic migration, assimilation and consumption. *Journal of Consumer Research, 10*(3), 292-302.

Young, J. (1994). The new materialism: A matter of policy. *World Watch, 7*(8), 30-37.

2

Active Ingredients

Dan Rose

Ethnography of Objects

Early in the morning an American man stands in a hot shower, the small stall fogged by steam and streaming water. The year is 1990; the place, on the second floor of a balloon frame house in Pitman, New Jersey, on the eastern seaboard of the United States. With a bar of soap and a washcloth he soaps and washes the bridge of his nose, his neck, under his arms, his wrists, the urogenital area, and his feet. On another morning, it would be another pattern of suds and cloth. After twisting and writhing in an unpracticed Tai Chi to rinse off the soap, he reaches to the shelf for a plastic tube of shampoo. He makes sure that all the soap is rinsed from his hands, unscrews the cap from the container, and with his right hand squeezes a small—what he has determined to be an exact—portion of the viscous blue substance onto his left palm. After he replaces the tube on the shelf he leans forward, his head wet but out of the stream of water, rubs his hands together to evenly spread the shampoo concentrate, and applies it over his hair and scalp. He leaves it on for a moment and feels his scalp tingle as the pyrithione zinc affects the skin of his head. Then he ducks under the shower and starts to rinse the foam from his hair. Some miscalculation and he gets shampoo in his right eye. It stings, and the obvious thing to do is rinse it out with as much water as possible. Just to make sure, he again reaches for the tube and, with his head tilted back, opens his left eye very carefully and reads the back.

Avoid getting shampoo in eyes—if this happens, rinse eyes with water.

He follows the directions, face against the stream of water. He blinks his eye again and again and hopes he can avoid permanent eye damage. It feels as if it has been dried out and the lachrymatory lubrication stripped away.

The rinsing is complete and by blinking the eye rapidly he has reduced the discomfort.

From the location where we observe this silent activity we can see that the tube of shampoo is named Head & Shoulders.[1] It is a Procter & Gamble company personal care product sold in supermarkets and drugstores to millions of consumers around the world.

Each morning a significant portion of the female and male population of the country takes showers, soaps their bodies all over or in studied parts, and shampoos their hair. The soaping and the shampooing are accomplished with an astonishing array of products; meters of shelves in retail stores are devoted to their display. Showering and shampooing, along with brushing the teeth, have all been considered in Dewey's terms, a habit, or, drawing on anthropology, a personal body ritual. Although it is easy to appreciate the ritual features of repetition-without-critical-thinking, whether addressed to hygiene or to puberty ceremonies, there is something terribly pragmatic about showering, an efficacy for the body, a cleansing, a washing away of oils and small particles of skin, and the replacing of exhaled bodily odors with scents manufactured by large companies and associated with soaps, creams, oils, unguents, powders, aftershaves, colognes, and perfumes. I am not at all interested in the rites associated with the use of consumer products; rather, I wish to interrogate, briefly, in the space of a chapter the materiality of shampoo and tube and, starting from the informant in the shower, offer an ethnographer's prolegomenon to the ongoing studies of the material objects we consume. This is a personal essay, and the subject of materiality needs further empirical study. For example, I do not conduct an ethnography of the other consumers of a shampoo and writing on the tube but use myself as a first informant. I shall start out small and stay close to the real (Wells, 1993).

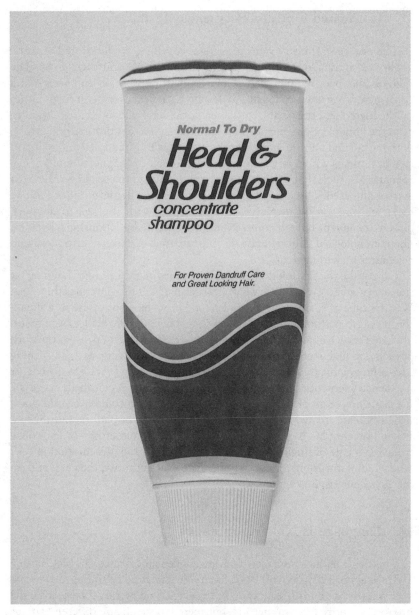

©The Procter & Gamble Company. Used with permission.

☒ Fabricated Objects, Persuasive Texts

The one central idea I want to emphasize here is the fabricated or made quality of contemporary things (Hunt, 1993, p. 294) and their prose. The tube of shampoo, its ingredients, and the writing were all engineered and constructed. My approach is not to de-engineer, deconstruct, or focus either on the ingredient, the plastic container, or the script alone. Rather, I want to treat the bundled phenomena—or phenomenon—as cultural-natural object, both nature and culture, but nature as agents, wholly modified and reorganized by humans within large corporations through the application of science to materials, such that commodities are manipulated to be sold for the mass market and used. This ethnographic inquiry requires detours, asides, oblique looks at things, a bit of play, and odd kleptics with the aim to discover, discern, or invent hidden connections and obscured relationships. I want a phenomenological ethnography of culture that discovers, critiques, and celebrates human fabrication.

Obviously, the first methodological necessity might be to go shopping on the open market of ideas to see what approach might fit such inscribed thingness. Was the tube of shampoo to be understood in its moment of use as a breakthrough into performance, as semiotic, as pragmatic knowledge, as a metaphor, as a speech event, as an utterance, as social organization, as postmodern pastiche, as high modern object of desire, as pure simulacra, as a social thing with a biography, as a necessarily fetishized commodity? Am I to decode its fragmentary sentences, deconstruct its intended meaning, classify its genre(s)? If I made any or all of those textual moves, what then could it be said that I had? If it were treated in its moment of use as ritual or performance, would I then find that life in the shower is really liminal, autoerotic, or backstage behavior, a type of singing-in-the-rain rehearsal for the presentation of self? And what of intrusion, appropriation, voice over authority, the gaze, mirroring, and mimesis, if not alterity?

☒ Language Is Not Autonomous

The idea is to draw from recent advances in empirical research (McCracken, 1989; Shelton, 1993; Sherry, 1987; Sherry & Camargo, 1987; Stern, 1989) as such inquiry has borrowed notions of language from literary theory, from the interpretive turn, or from rhetoric, but there is a significant difference in my approach from the way this research has been conducted. Rather than begin with language, whether considered to be situated in the author, the text, or the reader, whether informed by genre studies, hermeneutics, psychoanalysis, reader response, structuralism, poststructuralism, or its deconstructionist variant, I begin with a tube of shampoo and its ingredients to see what sort of object this is, set, as in the opening paragraphs, in the inauspicious context of its use, a context replicated by millions of other persons daily, a profoundly social act, despite a misleading isolation in this particular case, in the privacy of a shower stall.

Indeed, I want to distance myself from the recent plethora of interpretive efforts with product advertising and marketing by denying to language either a privileged starting point for inquiry or as an autonomous sphere artificially separated from the world as in some a priori nightmare of innate Kantian (read structural) faculties. I reject notions of language autonomy, the endless play of signifiers, contemporary culture as the consumption of pure simulacra, or the disappearance of referents, and I will not ask in any way what the scribbles on Head & Shoulders or any other consumer product *mean*. My understanding of language is not so much that it is meaning-less, though it may be, as that I consider questions about meaning as obsolete for comprehending today's commercial culture as yesterday's television news.

Along with the rejection of the autonomy of language as well as the search for meaning I will avoid starting with the queries into the sociality of the thing (Appadurai, 1986, p. 6; Wills, 1989), a topic important to social anthropologists and to students of marketing. Since Feuerbach (1841/1957, pp. 289-292) by way of Marx and Engels (1846/1957, pp. 3-78) and Durkheim (1912/1965, p. 482), the social serves as the basis for the organization of thought; the needs of society project the necessities of human social living onto the belief in or worship of gods; the ritual approach by which persons address the gods turns out to be, in this way of thinking, only the etiquette serving to facilitate interpersonal encounters (Goffman, 1953). Consumer objects do not fare well in such an uncritical social anthropology or sociology, since in the history of social theory, objects composed of matter taken from the earth have no materiality, receive no real theorizing, and can serve only as the projections of the concealed necessities of humans living in groups. Such are the assumptions underlying also the belief that the commodity, or the commodified body, serves primarily as fetishized social interest.

By bracketing (autonomous language) and (abstracted social theory) I have, for the moment, cleared a space that nevertheless remains pregnant with an absence from the received starting points from which we usually accost commodities.

Rather than beginning with language or commodities as the politics of value, I want a relatively less encumbered initial departure point that is ethnographic, phenomenological in a Peircean rather than a Cartesian sense (as I mention more fully below), and asks more primitive questions. The objective is to discuss the inquiry into a commercially produced object made up of matter and from which the ethnographer works toward language and value, and even meaning if it must be considered, but in the process opens the way for a rethinking of language, objects, and social organization taken together in the world marketplace. I draw resolve from Elaine Scarry's (1985) comment that "knowledge about the character of creating and created objects is at present in a state of conceptual infancy" (p. 280). Now, having bracketed abstract notions of language, I smuggle utterance and speech back in rather quickly, not because I am writing and you are reading words but because writing appears on the tube of shampoo and I want to know what it is doing there, those resistant and waterproof inscriptions on plastic. We could just as easily or perhaps more efficiently have been offered by retailers a plain jar of clear plastic filled with emulsion (Haug, 1986, p. 50).

Traces of Method

The philosopher Charles Sanders Peirce, in a swipe at Descartes without mentioning him explicitly, asserts that we cannot doubt everything but must begin with the state of mind we find ourselves in when we begin to philosophize (Peirce, 1905/1955, p. 256). I should like to mention the state of mind that led to an ethnographic inquiry into Head & Shoulders in part because it serves as a contribution to the knowledge of method and follows the dictum of the chemist cum anthropologist Malinowski (1923), who, pursuing standard scientific procedures, admonished ethnographers to give "a detailed account of all the arrangements of the experiments" (p. 2)—a task that I cannot accomplish in such great detail but can at least press toward.

Still enjoying the stream of hot water, finished with shampooing and soaping, gingerly blinking the right eye, the informant screws the cap back onto the top of the shampoo tube. A shower can provide a reflective moment, and he reads the entire tube and thinks to himself that the prose and poetry on it is wholly resistant to his professional understanding. It seems largely invisible to consciousness, exists outside awareness, and seems to say about itself, there is nothing here but the hard appearance of this text the moment you glance at it, nothing more. The very resistance and invisibility prove intriguing (Shelton, 1993).

🎗 A Detailed Account

In 1987, the author visited a major retrospective of the art of Marcel Duchamp at the Philadelphia Museum of Art and experienced something akin to an epiphany though actually a more sustained realization that there was a different way to conduct ethnographic inquiry, one not necessarily continuous with the pages of the *American Anthropologist* or the *American Ethnologist*. Ethnography could be altered when conducted in consumer cultures to respond to problems posed more directly to the ethnographer rather than those governed by highly monitored academic problematics and conventions set within the pages of leading journals.

Along with Picasso, Marcel Duchamp, for entirely different reasons, is proving to be one of the major influences in 20th-century art (d'Harnoncourt & Hopps, 1969, pp. 299-300). Unlike Picasso, Duchamp's work begins to dematerialize from 1912 onward with *Nude Descending a Staircase*, to reject what he called the retinal. He did not move toward abstraction only but away from what one could see, toward the conceptual. Many recent art projects derive from or pay homage to hints and suggestions he seems to have made, from Cornell's box to Cage's *Silence*, Acconci's installations, Sherman's poses, Anderson's performances, and contemporary images of identity bending (Kotz, 1992, p. 84).

I mention Duchamp, though, to extract from him this note on method. Pierre Cabanne published an interview with Duchamp a year before the artist's death at age 81. Cabanne suggested to him that he worked with technical problems before conceiving an idea. Duchamp responded, for whatever reason, "Often, yes. Fundamentally, there are very few ideas. Mostly, it's little technical problems with the elements that I use, like glass, etc. They force me to elaborate" (quoted in Cabanne, 1967/1971, p. 39).

Duchamp began his 8-year project with its little technical problems, the *Large Glass*, in 1915, a year after Roussel (1914/1983) published his novel *Locus Solus*. Ludwig Wittgenstein, serving in the Great War, was at this time keeping philosophical notebooks in brief entries that characterized his later working habits, writing down thoughts on small pieces of paper. The materials Duchamp worked with on the *Large Glass; The Bride Stripped Bare by Her Bachelors, Even* project were far from easel painting and included glass, wire, and pigment. At the same time he kept notes (like Wittgenstein's slips of paper in themselves reminiscent of Nietzsche's aphorisms) directed toward and supplementing what he was fabricating. The notes accumulated and were collected in what came to be known as the *Green Box*, a collection of scraps

Marcel Duchamp, *Large Glass; Bride Stripped Bare by Her Bachelors, Even* c. 1915. Philadelphia Museum of Art: Bequest of Katherine S. Dreier. Used with permission.

of abstract directions, notations, fictional measurements, dada poetic, allusions to private events, pseudoequations, and quasi-engineering drawings of elevation and plan for the *Large Glass*. Elements of the *Glass* were named, sketched, and some of their activities given such as "friction reintegrated," or "sounds lasting and leaving from different places," or "repeat the operation 9 times" (Sanouillet & Peterson, 1973). It is to me significant that Duchamp's fragments in the *Green Box* were modeled in a very remote and abstract sense on engineering drawings, or the type of shop renderings one learns in high school, what he called a "dry conception of art." These sorts of mechanical drawings are always meant to act upon the world; that is, they are designs for a subsequent material fabrication: an in-order-to or processual recipe. A set of orders. Duchamp played with these notions. There is no 1:1 correspondence between his notes and the physical structure of the *Large Glass*. There was nothing really scientific about the entries except what he borrowed to play with. He toyed with an extensive range of ideas about the process of rendering an ignitable bride to be stripped bare by her bachelors in a medium of glass, wire, and pigment.

I too am working with some technical problems, specifically to make sense of that tube of shampoo and its context. At the same time I need to examine the class of phenomena of which that complex agent is the merest example. The verbal context, the public writing, I think, can be thought of as a semantic landscape, a scripted geography formed in part through the marketing efforts of a great firm. Company after company makes products that they extrude through retail outlets and that form potential and often ephemeral territories of thin meaning and specific use, create zones defined by the presence of their products, presences that come into being simultaneous with our own commercially sponsored identity formation by we who have bought them. The method, then, seeks to make sense of what billions of world citizens have been doing opaquely in relation to millions of different sorts of pieces of merchandise that have formed a vast uneven landscape of commodities, a society of elements, organisms, machines, semantic strips, and humans.

Duchamp's life was characterized by his break with painting, largely through lack of interest, in the second decade of the 20th century and nonchalance toward received conventions, even to art itself. In interviews, he commented on his desire for freshness, as he did not intend to repeat himself, and his motivation for making things not from ideas but for amusement. Although he began his projects with technical problems, he was patient and worked them out over years if necessary, and I thought of ethnography this way, more embedded in living than in the year in the field, the semester off, or the summer back at the field site (Rose, 1990). His own epiphany of liberation occurred on a Monday night, June 10, 1912, when he and his friends, Apollinaire and Picabia, attended a play written and produced by the rich eccentric Raymond Roussel at the Antoine Theater in Paris. Roussel's bizarre *Impressions d'Afrique* had been greeted with extreme hostility by critics and ridiculed by the general public and was to be closed down. Artists and writers found it fecundating but curious and difficult to classify in their experience (Gough-Cooper & Caumont, 1993, p. 10; Robbe-Grillet, 1963/1987). Duchamp readily acknowledged that the strange and socially remote Roussel, who created a system of composition that generated texts by using homophones, gave him an understanding of how he, Duchamp, could move forward as an antiartist, toward the absence of repetition that he demanded and toward freshness and newness (Cabanne, 1967/1971; d'Harnoncourt & McShine, 1973).

I have derived energy from such modernist conceits and moved on two fronts, away from received conventions and toward an effort to come to terms with material objects, obdurate as they are (Ronell, 1991, p. 136). I think of the monumental triviality of studying a tube of shampoo for nearly half a decade as a turn away from the antiaestheticism and politicized polemics of the academy toward having fun, playing with materials and only the more appealing and immediately relevant ideas bequeathed by the literature.

🔰 After the Shower

After the shower, with the resistance of the text coupled with the abilities of the ingredients to remove dandruff, to be used every day, to shampoo hair, to sting the eyes, it became increasingly possible, even necessary, to talk with colleagues, family, and friends about Head & Shoulders as a field site and object of study.[2] The investigation required engagement with Procter & Gamble, and I contacted the company and was shunted to their public relations department and then to one of their outside consulting firms on Madison Avenue; I also dialed the 800 number listed on the plastic tube and talked with someone who identified himself as Mike. I discussed with Mike questions I had about the shampoo and especially the active ingredient, pyrithione zinc. He had no idea what scientific action the zinc took nor did the manual in front of him from which he looked up a stock of standard answers to standard questions.

The problem with the research, at first, was that I could easily get from corporations, which I have studied extensively, to texts because inside companies is where the texts are written; I could also easily move from corporations to commercial objects because companies manufactured them. I still could not get from texts to material objects or material objects to texts because there was no discernible intellectual bridge. At this juncture I began to examine deconstruction, linguistics, literary theory, philosophy, pragmatics, rhetoric, and sociolinguistics. It seemed necessary to review scholars who addressed language or tools: Arendt, Aristotle, Austin, Bacon, Bakhtin, Burke, Deleuze and Guattari, Derrida, Dewey, Duchamp, Foucault, Garfinkel, Goffman, Habermas, Hegel, Heidegger, Husserl, Hymes, James, Lévi-Strauss, Lyotard, Malinowski, Marx, Nietzsche, Ong, Peirce, Ricoeur, Stevens, Tedlock, and

Wittgenstein. To refute, correct, argue against, reformulate within any, several, or all of the authoritative works of these authors would prove distracting as none of them had explicitly discussed language and matter together.

Out of the review a small handful proved the most useful: Aristotle, Bacon, Bakhtin, Duchamp, and Wittgenstein. Duchamp I have mentioned; as for the others, I attempt to show briefly how they have contributed to a developing world picture. Aristotle presented the figures of speech that orators use to persuade; I assumed that words on the tube of Head & Shoulders partook of those figures to convince consumers how to proceed. From Bakhtin's notion of utterances came the idea of the speech plan in the exchange of utterances, and it seemed reasonable to expect that the writing on objects found everywhere in the commercial sphere were complex utterances that were very well planned to affect the behavior of hearers or readers. Bacon's (1627/1989) *New Atlantis* conveyed a picture of science incorporated inside a large corporation, Salomon's House or Foundation, for the purpose of effecting all things possible; from his fable I gathered that the notions of corporation, and knowledge gathered and experimented on for physical effect and human well-being, proved central. Indeed, one could write a history of the West from 1600 to the present as the course of a growing legal incorporation; one could show that the state increasingly chartered corporations that themselves incorporated nature, the fabrication of materials, and the production of knowledge into themselves.

Effective Language

In his *Philosophical Investigations*, Wittgenstein (1953) asked what would show why we think and gave the example of using calculations to build boilers rather than leaving the thickness of the walls to chance. He linked thinking to materials and to the market by suggesting that if boilers don't blow up as often as formerly, then thinking pays. With an adroit quilt work of Aristotle, Bacon, Bakhtin, and Wittgenstein, there is the possibility for breaking into the resistant object, material and writing, by considering that a pragmatic rhetoric highly planned for consumers to read and act upon is engineered in large firms coincident with the materials they manufacture to influence people, be sold on the market, and guide effective use.

This pragmatic rhetoric on and around commodities directs our lives, a significant portion of our day, it moves us, moves material, helps us assemble the next thought, a next activity, the next utterances, the next part to put in place when we construct a machine.

It is a language that offers instruction, tells us what to do, how to do it, how to accomplish something (Shelton, 1993).

The effectiveness of utterances is measured or assessed by their subsequent material, social, cognitive results.

The rhetorical and literary efforts at analysis of the language on the tube proved inadequate to comprehend its manifestation. Despite Wittgenstein's clues it was not possible to traverse the abyss from language to materials, a yawning gap that keeps us from understanding the fully material machines we have made as wholly integral to our mundane lives.

In addition to the figures mentioned above and in keeping with the autoethnography I had initiated, I then searched for an understanding of the corporeal world, for a way of addressing the blue stuff in the tube and the tube itself. As a result I began to read again in the physical sciences, mediated by a Duchampian aesthetic: computer science, cyberpunk, and nanotechnology, and scrutinized earlier readings. The influences for how to think about material objects as innocuous as shampoo containers came from reviewing not only Duchamp's "Green Box" (Duchamp, 1960) but *Science, Scientific American*, and such figures as Bohm, Dirac, Einstein, Feyerabend, Heisenberg, Prigogine, Waldrop, von Weizsacker, Wheeler, and Wigner and more recently, Drexler, Gelerntner, Lederman, Russell, and Zajonc.

The inquiry fit into an earlier quest: From 1974 to 1984 I wrote a book *Energy Transition and the Local Community* (Rose, 1981) and a series of papers, unpublished, that began to fill out for me a needed professional metaphysic of the material world, with one strut fixed by the natural sciences: "The Evolutionary Ecology of Humans and 30 Years of Unifying Theories," 1981; "The Observer Effect," 1982; "There Is No Environment, Just Strongly Coupled Systems, Observers, and Tinkerers," 1982; "The Idea of the Observer in the Evolution of Order," 1982; and "Third Order Cybernetics," 1984.

From 1983 to 1985 the ideas drawn from the readings emerged in more poetic fashion as a series of one-, two-, or three-page think pieces (Rose, 1994, 1995) that also filled out the metaphysic and which comprise a set of beliefs, in the Peircean sense of belief: that which we at least for now do not doubt but are certainly willing to question should the suspicion arise that our fixed adherence is not in accord with the way the world presents itself or the way it works.

The Universe Is Active

I reacquainted myself with the physicists, the poetic I had written, and with newer figures and came to the conclusion that the universe is active, that we can shape and deeply affect that activity with the materials of the planet, that capitalism is geared up to do this endlessly, and that we humans are active in the same sense with the same processes that the universe is, and that our language can actively engage that physical activity (Rose, 1994). Each of the sciences constructs its own working knowledge of agency, the force, for example, of physics, the living cells, of biology. Corporations have to investigate and produce innumerable lively substances. The world is composed of active ingredients, our products taken from the materials of the planet are active ingredients, and our language, in its most pragmatic forms, we use with one another to direct our activities to refashion materials so they can be manufactured, marketed, bought, sold, and used. The pyrithione zinc and the polyethylene tube are both active, just suspended in different chronological zones of relative molecular stability and both actively vended by Procter & Gamble.

Here, then, was the bridge—but not a bridge, more a way of thinking about the world, ourselves, and language at the same time: Everything is effective and in motion. Human language in its central aspect has always been pragmatic; we use words to alter one another and the world simultaneously, from "let's go fishing" or "let's go shopping" to $E = MC^2$.

My query takes flight from the confines of the shower in domestic space and drifts in imagination over all the retail outlets jammed full of products with writing on them: the Safeways, Krogers, Superfreshes, CVSs, Discount Drugs, Shop & Bags, 7-11s, K-Marts, Sam's Clubs, and Searses—then to the Japanese department stores and those in India and Europe. Writing inundates the earth, washing over products like a great flood, but it's too late to nail up an ark of some sort.

It is not just writing. Phrases are embossed *on something*. What is written on? The words materialize on materials, a physical substrate that conveys the impression of print, although often derived from added-on sprays—a painted prose. In what interior way do the materials and texts co-evolve as material artifact and sign? How, the ethnographer asks, do they act in concert, if in concert they do perform? Phenomenologically, they do not seem to be conceivable separated from one another in our visual field. I avoid materials without texts or texts so ethereal they have no material manifestation. Our informant cannot shampoo with words in part because they fail to emulsify body oils.

The ethnography I am proposing and am conversant with is grounded in *this* item here—shampoo, tube, and inscription. If we remain true to a serious study of material culture, it portends a new science of the concrete, the logic of material-cultural things, reinvented after the collapse of Marxian materialism; it begins with the empire of the empirical and goes far beyond the merely physical while never leaving it. The physical things are cultural and become, taken together, networked nature and culture into collectives of machines and humans, active agents infusing cultural life and cultural activities fecundating nature's ingredients.

There are three direct levels of the commodity phenomenon that require explication: first, the pasty ingredients inside the tube, second, the flexible polyethylene container, and third, the writing on the receptacle. These three features I treat as a single presence without wanting to privilege the writing even while examining it rather closely. These media—ingredient, tube, and text as copresented—constitute a tangible, an object, a thing, a script, a commodity, a product, a grouping of substances; it is at hand, responsive to the touch and the grasp, squeezable, an actant (Latour, 1993) capable of performing, enjoying ontic status in a commercially produced universe of stuff.

Thinking Pays

466. What does man think for? What use is it?—Why does he make boilers according to *calculations* and not leave the thickness of their walls to chance? After all it is only a fact of experience that boilers do not explode so often if made according to these calculations. But just as having once been burnt he would do anything rather than put his hand into a fire, so he would do anything rather than not calculate for a boiler.—But as we are not interested in causes,—we shall say: human beings do in fact think: this, for instance, is how they proceed when they make a boiler.—Now, can't a boiler produced in this way explode? Oh, yes.

467. Does man think, then, because he has found that thinking pays?— Because he thinks it advantageous to think?

[Does he bring his children up because he has found it pays?]

468. What would shew *why* he thinks?

469. And yet one can say that thinking has been found to pay. That there are fewer boiler explosions than formerly, now that we no longer go by feeling in deciding the thickness of the walls, but make such-and-such calculations instead. Or since each calculation done by one engineer got checked by a second one.

470. So we do *sometimes* think because it has been found to pay.

—Wittgenstein (1953, p. 134^e)

We could imagine that this language game, the one in which Wittgenstein strays from the strict philosophical question, the one that reveals a suspicion that we sometimes, if not always, think because it pays, points toward an avenue of inquiry, an avenue so very broad that we have seldom noticed that it was also a thickly congested roadway—as well as a scripted, public bazaar filled with little shops, large stores, partially concealed manufacturing firms, and the tall, bland buildings of the great corporate headquarters.

This avenue of investigation where we do "*sometimes* think because it has been found to pay" is constituted from within by discourses that have pretty much eluded a sustained literary investigation; along the concourse, these daily readings and conversations between people are demanded by their local transactions, which are, nevertheless, simultaneously exchanges on the global market.

In the corporation we think *with* boilers. We think with their thicknesses, we think about ways of devising methods of measure so they won't explode. We think into-with-about metal pressure containers; that is, we think with the physical agents of the world because it pays. Was there a boiler before there was a market for boilers? We think about boilers in ways other than measuring their walls, as in assessing how to sell them, figuring out how to build them effectively, and projecting how many consumers would buy them from us if ours do not explode as often as formerly.

To develop a phenomenology of culture we want to know how people have thought *with* objects, prose, and discussed their thoughts in carefully managed work groups as they have struggled in the firm to bring words and things to market. Ethnographic work requires that one live with substances the same way one lives with local people with the intent to document a way of life. In the phenomenology, I want to stress the phenomenon rather than the cognition of something, in other words, what ethnographers can engage directly.

It takes a number of conversations among people associated with boiler production, discussions concerning their trials and errors in making ones that won't blow up, in order to effect their calculations—their thought—such that their thought pays. Speech, as modeled here in the conversation of mechanics and technicians, or engineers, is connected by them to the imagination, thought, and language in order to achieve successes in the market.

Human beings fabricate the physical actants using speech with one another to direct their communal activities and thereby infuse the material object with ontic status, breathe some sort of life into it (the active ingredient); that is, they *animate* it (to use a word in somewhat the same way as Hobbes), however philosophically scandalous such a conception may be. Once having given the device a full sociocultural standing by inscribing prose on it, having polished its functional abilities, placing it within reach of the cultural, everyday grasp, then other humans can advertise it, pitch it, or sing about it—this *it* is a something almost complete, a homunculus, a golem, in some sense a domesticated or anthropomorphized vassal or automaton awaiting orders, an agent brought within a society of agents that can act once the switch has been thrown.

Wittgenstein, having gone beyond the invisible border of proper philosophical questions by asking *why* we think in addition to how, placed a human fabricated machine in the marketplace, the retail *agora* that Aristotle could but dimly discern as he engaged with the male citizens of Greece who conducted the political and legal discourse of the public realm.

💟 Active Ingredients

I find it necessary to pretend to begin as phenomenologist outside language and materialize it, as I mentioned, with the ingredients in the tube and the tube itself. Humans take that inorganic or organic material with its lesser or greater atomic activity and add their own scientific-technological manipulations to fashion such machines as ingredient and tube. The Head & Shoulders tube is made of polyethylene, a mass polymer, that can be thought of as a fluid solid. Of all the plastics sold for the past 30 years, the mass polymers make up 80% or more. "The systematic exploration of the relationships between property and structure in plastic materials has progressed so greatly that it is now possible *to design a material* with specific characteristics at the drawing board" (Manzini, 1989, p. 240, emphasis added).

The plastic tube is a smart actant, one that maintains shape and color for holding and dispensing ingredients, for not breaking, to have writing applied to it, and so on. The active automaton inside emulsifies the oils on the surface of the skin when applied to the scalp. The ingredients become a highly engineered soft machine for cleansing and preventing dandruff. The inscriptions that we read, then, have what I mentioned earlier as a feature of much of the writing we read in public, that is, linguistic and image-based guidance. The prose on Head & Shoulders serves to direct our interest and ability in manipulating the two interacting machines: one that holds the shampoo away from the air until ready to use and the other the shampoo itself. For example, "Lather-Rinse-Repeat," which is written on the tube (and is the epigraph for this chapter), is a pragmatic prescriptive utterance for squeezing the ingredients from the tube in order to shampoo and rinse twice in a row.

The products and commodities that humans are inventing to service themselves can be thought of as written-upon techne, contraptions, devices, gadgets, tools, instruments, utensils, appliances, automata, or robots that form networks of nature and culture combined. These commodity robots join by means of prose and conventional usage an increasingly diverse material world of other enslaved agents, such as organisms—like the genetic materials of rice or wheat or cattle—and processes whose relationships with the culture and interests of humans are not just mediated by texts, but the textual materials help us handle the physical objects. The utterances are instructive.

The phrase "Contains Pyrithione Zinc" inscribed on the container now notifies us of one of the names of the complex mix of ingredients making up the shampoo, and the written phrase mediates the physical matter with we who read it. By the prose mediator, cyborg and citizen are briefly joined. Together the zinc and the polyethylene make up a miniature social order designed by engineers to appear as a seamless production and do some things for humans.[3] Indeed, text and material demand one another; the ingredient is so strong that it requires human language in order for it to act successfully and appropriately in human society.

Pyrithione zinc, curiously, is an agent whose activities are well known but how it achieves its effects are not. It is as if the engineers have, like philosophers, effectively bracketed the "why" questions in full favor of the "how." Here, thinking pays as does not thinking. It would cost too much, in other words (to add other words), to find out why this actant is successful. The odd thing is that there is a textual gesture toward explaining how the zinc works, but even this turns out to be confused when reading various medical texts. A pharmacist's information on pyrithione zinc states that the "mechanism of action/effect" *may be* the result of antimitotic action which means that the epidermal cells cannot replicate as often, but this is clearly speculation. Although it is known that the drug sends bacteria and fungi into stasis it is not known whether or not such activity contributes to the antiseborrheic effects. The widely advertised 1993 edition of *Physicians Desk Reference for Nonprescription Drugs* (PDR) offers a slightly different take: "It is believed to control the microorganisms associated with dandruff flaking and itching" (p. 644). This is a sketchier story of ingredient action, and one might think of it as wholly unconvincing.

Humans have established innumerable relationships with physical and organismic actors, but knowledge remains partial, something like one's knowledge of one's neighbors in the same suburb. Relationships between humans and the energetic objects of their inquiry are not quite adequately addressed by theoreticians of laboratory life or science. It is not enough to think of actants as competent heroes receiving obsessive inscriptions from technicians as a result of experimentation (Latour, 1987, p. 89) or of objects scientists study; as actors we engage in a "power-charged social relation of 'conversation' " (Haraway, 1991, p. 198). Humans enslave matter to take it to market, but the bondage has momentous consequences not all capable of resolving with collegial conversation between human and organism—to pursue the metaphor of utterances as binding the human and nonhuman in direct contact. By the use of the word "enslavement," I mean to dramatize the real ways in which humans intervene with naturally occurring matter and organisms. Our relationships to the planet have been as much plunder, or even more so, as benign use. The important point here is to treat as an avenue of inquiry what sorts of complex relationships, mediated by firms and markets, we do have with planetary substances and our machines. If we do not think of humans taking matter to market, then we cannot motivate science in its multifarious practices or understand how we must engage power-charged elements we tease with other machines from their orbits and habitats. Why all the pragmatic language of the laboratory and pharmacy if not to retail active ingredients and the whole emerging world of vital machines? (Channel, 1991). It would seem that the prose is as highly engineered as the ingredients in the tube, and ideally they should work together within the mind and behavioral repertoire of the reader.

Next, I turn to the Bakhtinian speech genres of everyday life and lift out one aspect, the speech plan, to show how commercial genres are tightly bundled with the materials they must help us use. In making the return to language after rejecting so much of the received ideas about it, the objective is to show that language and materials are both active, not merely that language names, or refers to, or persuades in some sense independent of our physical lives. A theory of the commodity requires a theory of an effective, materialized language.

▨ Design of the Utterance

Like Wittgenstein, Bakhtin (1986) has a notion of speech affecting the world, but it remains undeveloped for an understanding of the commercial sphere. For Bakhtin, speech is an infinite chain without a first speaker, a closely textured and immense conversation of numerous, unclassified sub-conversations that go on forever into the human future. Each utterance is shaped by the history of previous utterances and precedes in a formative way subsequent talk or writing. Speech, whatever effect it has, then, is gathered as considered relevant into the speech that follows. In his discussion of speech genres of everyday life, Bakhtin does not distinguish between oral and written forms as the critical dimension for classification. Rather, he divides speech genres into simple and complex. The complex forms, and these are usually associated with fiction writing, take up the simple forms and incorporate them in subsequent use, as when the novelist imitates everyday speech.

He distinguishes distinctive features of speech genres, one of which is the finalization of the utterance. The hearer knows when the speaker is through, as when an army general delivers a command. "The immediate participants in communication," Bakhtin further explains, "orienting themselves with respect to the situation and the preceding utterances, easily and quickly grasp the speaker's speech plan" (p. 78). Although both Bakhtin and Wittgenstein fall short in their formulations of the operation of numerous language genres of capitalist culture that I am trying to identify, both have the idea of the effectiveness of language as human activity that accomplishes something by the utterance. Bakhtin's speech plan of the utterer, grasped by the person addressed, could be extended to mean that the speech plan, the genre spoken, contains within itself pragmatic and rhetorical features on which the hearer can or may or must act at some future time, and the machines we use in the shower are built from elaborate descriptions.

Wittgenstein's and Bakhtin's notions of language converge in that language acts upon a social world, in a sense animates or constructs that world as the word is uttered, as the story is told and the conversation unfolds. I am urging that in addition we identify a speech genre, as yet not fully understood within the universe of speech genres, whose uttering or writing makes possible some subsequent change in the material world of cyborgs, gynroids, and commodity robots. These utterances constitute the pragmatic; that is, they force or demand an accomplishment of some sort with the materials at hand, such as a shampoo tube. The word *pragmatic* is derived from the Greek word for business, and it is consummately business that trucks with material stuff—physical goods and products.

On the Head & Shoulders tube, I analyzed the speech plan by taking each phrase and interpreting it one at a time in a loose sense of the term *interpret*. Beneath each set of lines I wrote out its connections with my thinking at the moment and the literature I found relevant to explicating it. The speech plan on the receptacle looks something like this:

Side 1
   1. Type of person for whom the product is relevant
   2. Name of the product
   3. Nature of ingredient
   4. Two lines of rhyming verse
Side 2
   5. How to use the ingredients
   6. The active ingredient named
   7. Cautions
   8. If you have questions, call
   9. Where made and by whom

10. Weight of ingredients and statement of ownership
11. Two lines of rhyming verse, repeated

I shall only discuss several of these items to make the point that matter matters and text and physical object are bundled in a unified, persuasive production.

Without an authorial subjectivity richly developed as in literature, the genres of commerce appear much more stable in their meaning. The language seems depersonalized and thus conveys the impression of precision and a type of one-to-one correlation between anonymous authorial intention and the readers' understanding. Such notions have come apart as markets have very rapidly expanded over linguistic and class lines and across continents. Debates have raged, if only briefly, on whether or not an advertising campaign for world brands such as Pepsi-Cola or Coca-Cola can be universal or must be designed for specific markets and market segments. Does the same campaign play equally well in West Europe and India? How large is a semantic-pragmatic population? What constitutes understanding? Billions of dollars ride on the strategic answers to such questions.

A speech plan, as on commercial products, then, is a complex of genres that an author (speaker) constructs during an utterance and that readers (hearers) comprehend as they select from their own repertoire of genres in response. In some larger sense, all utterances are a bounded response to previous utterances. Given this kernel formulation, the writing in public appears as an endless array of flexible, partly fixed utterances—stable thematic compositions—each with its own speech plan, authored by anonymous speakers, whether coded from within the confines of a state bureaucracy, as in road signs, or within the large firm, as with the text on a Procter & Gamble home care product.

The problem with a speech plan notion is that while it does identify the generic quality of much everyday talk and semantic production it does not adequately address either the Aristotelian rhetorical figures inherent in speaking—persuasion—or the Wittgensteinian hint that we do sometimes think (converse) because it pays—a market pragmatic. "Commercial messages," as they are called by television announcers, are at once utterances composed of speech genres, persuasive figures, and made available for affecting material life through the mechanism of the market. It would be useful to think of the play of commercial conversation in companies and in the public realm as a joining together of Aristotle, Bahktin, and Wittgenstein in the close intimacy of a concrete speech production, as on the tube of Head & Shoulders, but also joined to the necessity of moving materials for the use of consumers. Although I have by no means worked out all the implications of such a junction, their labor has informed my explication. Furthermore, as will be shown, the persuasion may not persuade and the pragmatic be wildly unpragmatic, depending on who does the reading. Semantic and pragmatic indeterminacy lie at the heart of market civilization just as does the denial, particularly by some professors of marketing, of such indeterminacy, a denial that rather makes the opposing point. In large part, the uncertainty principle of language derives from its situatedness and the richness of local texture in language understandings and uses and from the associational accumulations that words and themes have picked up in their journeys through others' speeches and texts.

Side 1 of the Tube

Normal to Dry

A person walks down the aisle of the supermarket or pharmacy and pauses in front of the hair care section. Say this person is a man, one who wonders what sort of shampoo he ought to be using. He picks up a tube of Head & Shoulders shampoo and reads in English, from left to right and top to bottom the words on both sides of the package. The first three words he sees, at the very top are "Normal to Dry." Immediately he must ask himself the question, for it has been phrased that way on the packaging, "Am I 'normal to dry'?" He muses on whether he falls in the "normal to dry" category or within some other. If he is standing there with another person, perhaps he turns to that person and asks, "Do I appear to you to be a 'normal to dry' individual?" It may be at that point that some perceptive discussion ensues that clarifies the phrase "normal to dry."

What might some other category be? Abnormal to wet? If he turns his head and reads other bottles or tubes of Head & Shoulders shampoos, he will discover other classifications into which he might fall, such as "Normal to Oily."

This phrase, the very first he reads, in logical, vertical order, already identifies him in what has widely come to be called in the design professions in the most depersonalized fashion imaginable, a user. The phrase, though, forces the user to self-interrogate. The writing on the package has set up a profound, perhaps powerful connection between itself and the reader largely because it remains outside critical awareness. The reader almost instantly makes some more or less significant judgment as to whether or not he might fit into the system so described in the first words. This is a forceful move on the part of copywriters, for they have not only instantly captivated the reader but suggested that the reader engage the product in some self-selecting way, such that, perhaps, or even maybe, the person will find that he has been identified and through that identification and the active nature of the product been able to select himself as one "needing" to purchase the product in order to make a more or less significant alteration in himself with it as the tool. The instrumentality of the prose has wholly in the first words struck outward to shape not only the identity but the potential future activity of the reader.

"Normal to Dry" forces an act of identification, the vivacious quality of language that has the reader insert the prose into his own empirical experience. The rhetoricians explain that these words ask me to analyze my environment. In this statement, the reader finds his own version of reality. An invitation has been made from product to me, and these words are persuasive to the degree that they conjure. Here they conjure oneself in relation to a highly viscous substance that can be squeezed from a tube and applied to one's head.

Such is the work of the pragmatic utterance on the identity of the hearer or reader.

But with Head & Shoulders, the very first three words **normal to dry** demand that we interrogate ourselves, our corporeality, and from it take up some sort of direct and intimate relationship with or direct rejection of this tube. We are engaged by the text, the prose, the first three words. What occurs in the reader if someone of another gender buys this for the male and what does she do with the phrase "normal to dry"? Does she decide arbitrarily whether or not the male for whom she makes the purchase is dry, normal, or oily? How greased is this semantic incline? How are identities established in commercial civilization, deployed, agreed on, or disagreed with?

Separate from the author is the actant or hero who is usually a character in a narrative. In this condensed prose on a package, narrative is far more implied than made readily accessible through human characters—a vicious stepmother or a gratuitously motivated killer—who would become through description in fiction visible or explicit. In addition to anonymous author(s) in these sorts of commercial packages must be grouped anonymous readers, more than one potential consumer, and the actant, Head & Shoulders itself.

Already, in the first three words, words that precede even the name of the product, we are thrown a discursive bridge between the active homunculus in the container and the reader, who in all likelihood is shopping for a dandruff shampoo. The three words mediate the actual material and the mind of the reader which must reflect on the reader's body and on the junction constructed by the prose of the ingredient in the tube as somehow going with the scalp of the reader.

The next phrase on the tube introduces us to the name of the actant, a name that constitutes intellectual property, a subject of legal ownership, a sort of natural-substance chattel, which is a highly managed identity, a subidentity, indeed, of an ultraextensive corporate complex of identities, identities that are composed of all the products, registered under brands that it produces.

Head & Shoulders

I asked a Korean colleague what Procter & Gamble meant by giving the name Head & Shoulders to a shampoo. He answered that shoulders stood for the whole body and that this was a sort of soap or body shampoo. When I asked a Belgian observer of American life what these three words meant he answered that they were a typical American euphemism that concealed the older puritanical nature of the people. Head & Shoulders referred, he claimed, to the hairy parts of the body, and the product was to be used obviously on the hairy portions of the anatomy. When I asked an American executive from another company what the phrase Head & Shoulders referred to, he thought for a minute and then smirked, "Why it means that it stands head and shoulders above the rest of the shampoos on the market." He was referring to the common phrase "He's head and shoulders above the competition" or some such similar use of the words in American English.

Why head *and shoulders*? Why should the shoulders, of all parts of the anatomy, appear featured in the very name of the shampoo? There tends among the general populace to be little hair on shoulders that requires regular sudsing. Should one perhaps apply the shampoo to the shoulders during one's toilette? How do the human shoulders figure into a shampoo's carefully and expensively selected name? The obvious answer, obvious at least to some who use the product, is that dandruff, through the inexorable pull of gravity, falls from the head onto the shoulders, where it creates, particularly against dark fabric backgrounds, a snowy aureole of tiny flakes that cannot be readily seen by the dandruff producer but are presumably quickly, invariably, and very probably disdainfully observed by those close by. This condition of unplanned dandruff display can create phenomenally high anxiety among some members of consumer society, hence the need for a special shampoo that will control the situation.

Anxiety, along with its ameliorative second, addiction, is one of the most pervasive and insistent states of being underlying capitalist culture.

One of the most central anxieties (whose dark roots extend backward to earlier and quite diverse cultural shaping before there was mass marketing) in the culture of mass-produced societies is interactively and collusively directed toward strident, insistent, and heavy-handed control over that which the body gives off in private and public space, whether gestures of the face and hands or escaping gases, solids, and fluids, such as farts, dandruff, menstrual blood, semen, urine, and tears.

On each of the products we have pictured, there appears a pragmatic writing that, as a type of *prosopopoeia,* provides an inanimate object with the ability to enunciate or act, the package speaks to us as an implied author and demands a reaction as if it were an actor of some sort in our social world—and indeed that is what commodities become. The writing is an utterance that also offers a recipe for what actively to do with the animated contents of the tube or bottle or box. Each instruction, like a voice of quiet insistence, intends some intervention in the life of the person who makes the purchase.

The actant, which has through writing been given voice and to which the name Head & Shoulders refers in this highly compressed narrative, is the blue material stuff inside the tube that has some corporeal existence that can affect through one's course of action the surface of the skin, the scalp, and under a Proppian classificatory scheme, is properly then the *hero* but in an odd way. It is as if the hero (concealed within the tube) reaches out from the prose printed on the polyethylene tubing that wraps the blue suspension inside and seeks by means of an anonymously authored, crafted utterance to insert itself into the consciousness, daily activities, and chronological flow of life of the person reading the text, right onto the scalp itself, twice a day: "lather-rinse-repeat."

The material world, in this case a small, rather unintelligent machine, through its prose jacket, seeks to join humanity by inserting itself into the material support system that makes the culturally acceptable human presentation of self possible as a well-socialized, conforming-to-norms cultural being.

Concentrate Shampoo

Inside the container, the ingredients are compressed—concentrated—as is the prose on the tube. Not a large surface, only so much writing can be crammed onto the receptacle. But with the phrase "concentrate shampoo" arises an idea of enhanced value given the actor inside. The reasoning goes something like this: If the product is concentrated, then I can use less, it will go further or last longer; hence it has (potentially) higher value than an unconcentrated formula. "A little," the rude maxim has it, "goes a long way."

A larger issue that embraces all retail civilization is discernible in this gnomic phrase. Inherent here is the notion of portion. How much constitutes the right, correct, proper amount? What pragmatic squeeze on the tube will propel the hero from it in the proper proportion for cleaning my hair and keeping the embarrassing flakes at bay? Shuman (1981) directs our attention

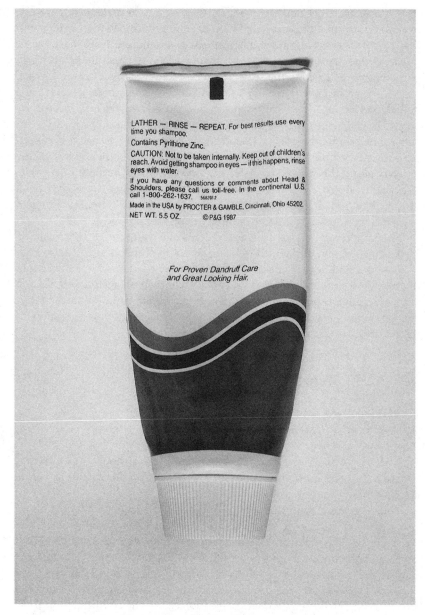

to the significance of portions particularly of repasts in middle-class society, as markers of emotional and cognitive communication among family members and with guests. Reframing her insight to extend our comprehension of public writing, we would inquire ethnographically into corporate product proportioning to understand the semantic, social, and retail significance thereof. One of the problems with the display of product quantities found in advertising and advised for use on packaging is that the producers have idealized the quantity beyond its pragmatic necessity in order to stimulate high consumption. Televised commercials for toothpaste and exemplary pictures on the packaging, for example, sometimes show a large toothbrush with a dollop of toothpaste that richly extends along the whole set of bristles and protrudes beyond either side. Whether or not this is a relevant portion to the customer is certainly open to question, and there is undoubtedly a wide range of discretion activated among laypersons in how much is thought and found to be enough.

The imagery generated by the retailer seems to preserve the romantic Hegelian cognition of the Idea—the negation of all that is particular—such as your own modified version of what constitutes a portion. Obviously, it does not always work that way but to say that mercantile package prose is in some senses Hegelian is not stretching it. By contrast, I am certain that the range of uses for a given product and the wide latitude in interpretation of instructions would astound manufacturers if compiled.

Side 2 of the Tube

LATHER-RINSE-REPEAT.
For best results use every time you shampoo.

A Möbius strip of instruction iterates indefinitely, although we know that we are to put two portions on our hair and rinse them out each time before stepping from the shower to dry our hair.

This is an addendum to the prior discussion of portions. Not only do we use it twice each time we shower but we are to use this product every time we shampoo. These phrases epitomize the entries in the codex of commercial pragmatic rhetoric, no other selection of words would more convincingly convey the results-achieving efforts of word crafting in global markets.

Part of the power of the command (or is it a suggestion) certainly derives from the impressiveness of the expertise housed in the corporation in some abstract, authoritative sense. The real strength of the command, its entitlement for being made in just this way, has everything to do with inherent, active (once again) power of the ingredient. The properties of our products can affect us appreciably, and thus the authority of the text lies in the effective agency of the manufactured cyborg that has had itself textualized, as though making utterances itself, as instructions on the tube. The logic of commands such as this one is a subset of pragmatic philosophy, although not enough attention has been placed on the users' potential and real modifications of command and ingredient through lay experimentation with the latitudes—perhaps deadly in many products—of meaning and use. Thus the logic of commands stops short and does not stray, as Wittgenstein allowed himself to do, beyond the engines of thinking, logic, and commanding—that is, into the market, human safety, and so on as bound to the command in full pragmatic effect. Instructions when executed or not executed cannot be construed as obedience or disobedience. Whereas the logicians tend almost uniformly to ignore the obedience question as intractable, any pragmatic theorizing of the use of agents manufactured from nature and turned into machines by humans requires significant elaboration of the consequences of the utterances connected to their use.

The sentence "For best results use every time you shampoo" contains the implicit contract set up by Procter & Gamble that they will through this commodity machine get your hair clean and flakefree if you use this every time you shampoo. There is also the tacit promise that this is safe to use each time you suds your hair. It is also in the finest market tradition rhetorical in that the words "every time" definitely attempt to persuade you to use this product to the exclusion of all others, a highly competitive deployment of language. These dense messages compress meaning into consummate thinness—they are, after all, only about a mercifully brief and quickly forgettable moment in the shower.

CAUTION: Not to be taken internally. Keep out of children's reach. Avoid getting shampoo in eyes—if this happens, rinse eyes with water.

In grand terms, there are two master tropes in commercial culture: The one seeks to persuade, seduce, entertain, inform, and, ultimately, sell; the other finds it necessary to warn, caution, expose, reveal, and offer counterindications. This second set of figures has had to be backed most often by state-authorized legal force. Taken together we have in the first moment, advertising with its glitzy imagery and ideal products and, in the second, an editorial press that carries the turbulent debates as to whether or not AZT should be administered early or later as the HIV-positive patient's situation deteriorates (see Angier, 1993).

The words "caution" and those that follow it on the wrappers initiate uncertainty, second thoughts, second guesses, fear, loathing, terror, and lack of balance. They are pragmatic morphemes that document what a product can do and what, in some cases, must be done if things go awry. These cautionary tales are greatly expanded in the editorial press as stories about what happened to a person or population who misused a drug or were misused by one. More critical and important for raising anxieties are those egregious failures of mass market androids and gynroids to meet expectations by damaging humans, the results often discovered years later. A recent example is that of silicon breast implants, though the list goes on and on. In a recent USA Today newspaper, an advertisement headline read

BREAST IMPLANT RECIPIENTS

and the text below noted the symptoms of the brutal side effects, such as implant rupture, immune deficiency disease, lupus, scleroderma, muscle and joint pain, extreme fatigue, and memory loss, and then made the pitch that a Milwaukee law firm could help sufferers with national product liability litigation, citing the firm's experience with the Dalkon Shield and L-Tryptophan cases, for a profit.

There is no charge for the initial consultation.
Attorney's fees are charged only if you win your case.

Crimes against women? Yes, but not only women. There are grievous delicts against consumers. I could mention asbestos and lead that affect primarily children but of both sexes.

We could all multiply horror stories and make them personal indeed, but also given time, we would tell stories of people who were saved from certain death at early ages and lived productive lives. Some of us would have to mention our own children. My point is that the texts celebrate the heroes inside the packaging and at the same time we read warnings of their powers to act beyond our own good through ignorance of scientific implications on the part of corporate authors or through misuse by consumers (Scarry, 1985, p. 295).

One of the fundamental reasons for consumer anxiousness is due to the inherently incomplete nature of the scientific enterprise itself, as I pointed out in the previous section. Scientific inquiry and its retail realization through product engineering is never finished, has no final body of knowledge, and perceives poorly (and is most often not rewarded immediately for perceiving clearly) the implications of side effects because the knowledge that today is contained in the agent may tomorrow prove to have been inadequate in the light of sustained, widespread use. It is no wonder that the use of even the seemingly innocent commodity induces mood swings particularly when unintended effects we know can become debilitating and rival the precipitating condition.

The editorial press reports a constant stream of counterrhetoric that subverts, modifies, and challenges previous findings. Reports of the responses of statistically significant numbers of Harvard mice to various injections, ingestions, and living conditions keep readers constantly off balance and on the verge of revulsion concerning the introduction of those same substances in their own bodies. Belief becomes suspended; some shoppers suffer severe apathy and resignation. Text and countertext duke it out in consumer consciousness; the entire mass market resembles an experiment station of contesting tropes where we, the subjects of the laboratory trials, have been coaxed with seductive texts and seemingly effective machines to pay for uncertain outcomes. Uncertainties fluctuate between the dueling messages, each textual type feeding off the other. Together we are offered unresolvable antinomies of persuasion-for-use and the real, but untotalizable and not wholly benign activities of the agent—activities that must be described in the discourse of counterindications.

**If you have any questions or comments
about Head & Shoulders, please call us toll-free.
In the continental U.S. call 1-800-262-1637.
Made in the USA by PROCTER & GAMBLE,
Cincinnati, Ohio 45202**

We are alerted to the made quality, where the actants were made, who made them, and where the makers are located. More interesting, we witness with this text the site of making which is one location of eruption of nature into culture, where humans draw other planetary actants into the human realm. Nature joins culture in an expanded social order.

NET WT. 5.5 OZ.©P&G 1987568207-3

These words are their intellectual property and they own them. I can use the words to read at the store before purchasing or in the shower should I need directions. Or if I were to write a scholarly paper on the text on the tube, then I would invoke the fair use rules of the U. S. copyright law. Indeed, at this moment I will claim that my use of Procter & Gamble's unidentified authors' prose falls under the law and my rights will be protected thereby and I do not need to ask their permission for my academic, educational rescripting.

Procter & Gamble has registered its trademarks and copyrighted its text as a corporate individual, but these textual wrappings enclose and socialize at once, the actant in the tube, that it has also caused to be authored in a sense, made and manufactured for consumer use. My point here is that in the West at least, natural actors are brought into the human world as *legal* entities, in an extended way, as actors belonging to actors, as subjected individuals—something like personal chattel—before the law. Unique products, combinations of actants assembled into some totality, are granted trademarks that identify the uniqueness of the goods for the commercial sphere. The corporate individual, Procter & Gamble, is a trade name; Head & Shoulders, a commodity "individual," is identified by a trademark. Nature takes on cultural identity through such legal mechanics, and it is part of the role of law to provide cultural standing for natural objects modified by humans. There is increasing interest in the academy and in international trade negotiations over the issues raised by Western legal ideas of intellectual property. These issues touch on everything from comic book figures to software programs to look-alike goods, from copyrights and trademarks through the replacement parts industries that seek to supply new parts for auto body shops, say, fenders made in Indonesia, for wrecked autos that had been manufactured and sold in Germany. Do the replacement companies infringe on the original design rights of the auto manufacturers? "Intellectual property laws are those that enable the commodification of symbols, imagery, and texts—they create limited monopolies over representational forms" (Coombe, 1993, p. 414). And, one must add, limited monopolies over matter itself: molecules, genetic codes, chemical combinations, micro-organisms, "look and feel," or the curve and shape of materials.

Conclusion

To summarize, human speech has always been pragmatic, but discourse and writing have become increasingly so; that is, people supply utterances for material effects demanded by a world market and this occurs at three levels: the language necessitated in making the active ingredients of consumer culture—the stuff in the tube; the conversations needed in constructing the container within which materials are contained and vended; and the drafting of the prose of the public commercial realm that guides human activities through the marketplace and in the privacy of their morning showers.

We have returned to language but through matter and utterances. Authors in a corporation adroitly laid down three words of text, **normal to dry,** that animate the concealed but effective shampoo machine meant to be connected to the physical condition of your scalp and hair. The language of marketing manipulates material.

In this view, language is imbricated in the production of everything and beside or on top of every human-fashioned substance, an activated verbal accompaniment guiding uses of the material stuff of the world. Contemporary discourse is intrinsic to the fabrication of the material world. In turn, the material world as we have come to know it results from science in the laboratory, whether that laboratory be in the university or in any of the millions of world companies. The thousands of products we consume in the United States have been constructed from naturally occurring materials. Over the past three centuries, matter itself has been as highly theorized as any substance, including all of the biological. Einstein's familiar equation $E = MC^2$ tells us that mass and energy are convertible into one another.

The universe is endlessly active and moving irreversibly from T_i to T_n. The point is that the stuff in the tube of shampoo is active, the tube is active, the inscription on the tube engages that activity and ours who read the inscription. A theory of contemporary discourses of the market demands a scientific notion of matter and how it and language are, in a sense, a unitary cultural phenomenon. If all the things we use in consumer society derive from laboratories, including the prepared and "natural" foods we consume, then we need to understand the discursive formation used to produce them that is embedded within and inscribed on our commodities.

Our consumer products are machines, robots, slaves, or active ingredients that owe their existence to the deployment of human language: The notion is that their active carnal being or becoming or effectiveness has been brought within culture or legally joined within the great corporations such as Procter & Gamble, given jural identity and consequently engaged in the evolution of human uses, and it is the market that rewards the manufacture and allocates such powerfully effective contrivances. We are continually modifying our materials and language within everyday conversations to make, market, and use these robots in our daily lives.

Everything, every material thing we use, is a machine contrived with pragmatic utterances in some relation to companies for a globally formed market that supplies and demands them and their sedimented linguistic labor.

With Head & Shoulders we have tapped into the code that is accumulating and that inhabits our agency, a viral complex of infinitely combinatorial linguistic-material and active possibilities.

Commodities, laboratory- and factory-fabricated substances, once they enter the marketplace and behave as they were designed to do or far beyond their intended activities, create outward from themselves lesser or greater networks that cut across human culture and nature as we know them. The introduction of plastic alters human life in ways unquantifiable. Plastic creates a hybrid that assembles chemists, companies, regulatory agencies, lobbying in Congress, fears of toxic effects among human users, a transformation of the metals industry, worldwide pollution on beaches and in landfills from plastic bags and styrofoam products, as strange an assembly as Duchamp's notes in the *Green Box*. This hybridity and organizational formation can be studied in its own right. Material things taken together form networks that cut across planetary processes; they are objects, active ingredients, are born with legal status and given a price tag, engaged by the whole market process right up to their final uses. Although these things can be thought of as machines or cyborgs, they have implications far beyond their own materiality. They mix nature and culture each step of the way.

We can study these hybrids of processes and things, for a network, as it is brought into being, exists to the extent that it affects our lives; it can be considered to come into critical view when the human observer notes it—whether politician, scientist, or essayist; it results from human-conceived projects and is made real by market possibilities (Bijker & Law, 1992; Latour, 1993). Head & Shoulders exists as a hybrid—the plastic, the prose, and the active ingredient together helping make the world of personal care products—and thus we take the brackets off and return to language and to society. The objects offer access to a partially concealed universe of corporations where the actant is the hero. We deploy our heroes with writing, and they are endlessly and in ways not well understood rich with sociality, in part because consumer objects are social creatures equipped as agents of intervention to affect our bodies, our lives.

🔯 Notes

1. Head & Shoulders is a registered trademark of Procter & Gamble.

2. Within 2 years of the showering episode I wrote a paper in 1992 on Head & Shoulders and read it at an international sociological conference where it drew laughter if not much criticism. Also, that summer I talked about it briefly at a 3-week seminar on neo-Weberian sociology at the Institute for the Study of Economic Culture at Boston University; the

participants, drawn from a number of different professions, encouraged further development. Nearly a year later, I gave a talk accompanied by 180 slides to illustrate some of the points at the Department of Anthropology, University of Virginia, and received provocative critical comment. The following spring I presented the paper to literary theorists, folklorists, and landscape architects and their graduate students at the University of Pennsylvania where incisive remarks offered rich avenues of inquiry. The last public performances were given at Drake University and the Institute for Social Anthropology at the University of Bergen in spring 1994, and criticism again provided new and tempting directions.

    3. For earlier recipes for men's hair, from falling off to turning gray, see Anonymous (1902). Chapter 13 "Business" is introduced with a photograph of Andrew Carnegie, with a caption that reads "The Prince of Business Success," and the final Chapter, "Toilette Recipes," includes the recipe to prevent the hair turning gray: "Oxide of bismuth four drachms, spermaceti four drachms, pure hog's lard four ounces. Melt the two last and add the first" (p. 422). There was nothing in the volume on dandruff control; although the recipes seemed strange and in some cases nearly unreproduceable today, the social concerns with the presentation of self in a maturing business climate seem constant, as the enlisting of nature's actants to help in that endeavor: commerce and the careful toilette, a unified production.

References

Angier, N. (1993, July 29). Australian study says AZT slows progression to full-blown AIDS. *New York Times*, p. A20.

Anonymous. (1902). *Social culture: A treatise on etiquette, self culture, dress, physical beauty, and domestic relations together with social, commercial, and legal forms.* Springfield, MA: King-Richardson.

Appadurai, A. (1986). Introduction: Commodities and the politics of value. In A. Appadurai (Ed.), *The social life of things* (pp. 3-63). New York: Cambridge University Press.

Bacon, F. (1989). *New Atlantis and the great instauration.* Arlington Heights, IL: Harlan Davidson. (Original work published 1627)

Bakhtin, M. (1986). *Speech genres and other late essays* (V. W. McGee, Trans.). Austin: University of Texas Press.

Bijker, W. E., & Law, J. (Eds.). (1992). *Shaping technology/building society.* Cambridge: MIT Press.

Cabanne, P. (1971). *Dialogues with Marcel Duchamp* (R. Padgett, Trans.). New York: Da Capo. (Original work published 1967)

Channel, D. F. (1991). *The vital machine: A study of technology and organic life.* New York: Oxford University Press.

Coombe, R. J. (1993). Tactics of appropriation and the politics of recognition in late modern democracies. *Political Theory, 21*, 411-433.

Duchamp, M. (1960). *The bride stripped bare by her bachelors, even* (G. H. Hamilton, Trans.). New York: Jaap Rietman.

Durkheim, E. (1965). *The elementary forms of the religious life* (J. W. Swain, Trans.). New York: Free Press. (Original work published 1912)

Feuerbach, L. (1957). *The essence of Christianity* (G. Eliot, Trans.). New York: Harper. (Original work published 1841)

Goffman, E. (1953). *Communication conduct in an island community.* Unpublished doctoral dissertation, University of Chicago, Department of Sociology.

Gough-Cooper, J., & Caumont, J. (1993). *Marcel Duchamp: Work and life.* Cambridge: MIT Press.

Haraway, D. (1991). *Simians, cyborgs, and women.* New York: Routledge.

d'Harnoncourt, A., & Hopps, W. (1969). *Etant donnés: 1 la chute d'eau; 2 le gaz d'éclairage: Reflections on a new work by Marcel Duchamp* [Bulletin]. Philadelphia: Philadelphia Museum of Art.

d'Harnoncourt, A., & McShine, K. (1973). *Marcel Duchamp.* New York: Museum of Modern Art and Philadelphia Museum of Art.

Haug, W. (1986). *Critique of commodity aesthetics* (R. Bock, Trans.). Minneapolis: University of Minnesota Press.

Hunt, J. D. (1993). The sign of the object. In S. Lubar & W. D. Kingery (Eds.), *History from things: Essays on material culture* (pp. 293-298). Washington, DC: Smithsonian Institution Press.

Kotz, L. (1992, November). The body you want: An interview with Judith Butler. *Artforum,* p. 84.

Latour, B. (1987). *Science in action.* Cambridge, MA: Harvard University Press.

Latour, B. (1993). *We have never been modern.* Cambridge, MA: Harvard University Press.

Malinowski, B. (1923). *Argonauts of the western Pacific.* New York: Dutton.

Manzini, E. (1989). *The material of invention.* Cambridge: MIT Press.

Marx, K., & Engels, F. (1957). *The German ideology.* New York: International Publishers. (Original work published 1846)

McCracken, G. (1989). Homeyness: A cultural account of one constellation of consumer goods and meanings. In E. C. Hirschman (Ed.), *Interpretive consumer research* (pp. 168-183). New York: Association for Consumer Research.

Peirce, C. S. (1955). *Philosophical writings of Peirce* (J. Buchler, Ed.). New York: Dover. (Original work published 1905)

Physicians desk reference for nonprescription drugs. (1993). Montvale, NJ: Medical Economics Data, Inc.

Robbe-Grillet, A. (1987). Riddles and transparencies in Raymond Roussel. *Atlas Anthology,* 4, 100-105. (Original work published 1963)

Ronell, A. (1991). Interview with Avital Ronell. *Research,* 13, 127-53.

Rose, D. (1981). *Energy transition and the local community: A theory of society applied to Hazleton, Pennsylvania.* Philadelphia: University of Pennsylvania Press.

Rose, D. (1990). *Living the ethnographic life.* Newbury Park, CA: Sage.

Rose, D. (1994). The evolution of intervention. *Anthropology and Humanism,* 19, 88-103.

Rose, D. (1995). Poems from *Architecture of the Other World,* contributed to the *Festschrift* for Kenneth Goldstein. Bloomington, IL: Trickster Press.

Roussel, R. (1983). *Locus solus* (R. P. Cunningham, Trans.). London: Calder. (Original work published 1914)

Sanouillet, M., & Peterson, E. (Eds.). (1973). *The writings of Marcel Duchamp.* New York: Da Capo.

Scarry, E. (1985). *The body in pain.* Oxford, UK: Oxford University Press.

Shelton, A. (1993). Writing McDonald's, eating the past: McDonald's as a postmodern space. *Studies in Symbolic Interaction, 15,* 103-118.

Sherry, J. F., Jr. (1987). Advertising as a cultural system. In S. J. Levy & J. Umiker-Sebeok (Eds.), *Marketing and semiotics: New directions in the study of signs for sale* (pp. 441-461). Berlin: Mouton de Gruyter.

Sherry, J. F., Jr., & Camargo, E. G. (1987). "May your life be marvelous": English language labeling and the semiotics of Japanese promotion. *Journal of Consumer Research, 14,* 174-188.

Shuman, A. (1981). The rhetoric of portions. *Western Folklore, 40,* 72-80.

Stern, B. A. (1989). Literary criticism and consumer research: Overview and illustrative analysis. *Journal of Consumer Research, 16,* 322-334.

Wells, W. (1993). Discovery-oriented consumer research. *Journal of Consumer Research, 19,* 489-504.

Wills, G. (1989). Message in the deodorant bottle: Inventing time. *Critical Inquiry, 15,* 497-509.

Wittgenstein, L. (1953). *Philosophical investigations.* New York: Macmillan.

Consumer Behavior Reflected in Discards

A Case Study of Dry-Cell Batteries

MasaKazu Tani
William L. Rathje

Most human activities involving material objects leave their traces in garbage. In industrialized societies, many material objects are short-lived. Packages, waste, and broken and used-up objects all end up in garbage. Although this fact of life often becomes the target of criticism from environmentalists who condemn wasteful "throw-away societies," garbage provides an excellent source of information for those who seek physical evidence of diverse human activities.

Love Canal. Few words are more synonymous with fear and loathing in modern America than this ironically named industrial hazardous waste dump that burst onto the public's consciousness in the late 1970s. Today, many solid waste experts are trying to expand this same awareness to include a menagerie of hazardous wastes, from used motor oil and unused nail polish

AUTHORS' NOTE: The Garbage Projects household hazardous waste research was supported by grants from the Water Quality Engineering Division of the National Science Foundation, the Office of Solid Wastes of the Environmental Protection Agency, and the Association of Bay Area Governments. Assistance and logistical support for data collection was provided by the City of Tucson Sanitation Division (currently Department of Solid Waste); the City of New Orleans Department of Sanitation; Waste Managements Recovery 1 Landfill in New Orleans; the Association of Bay Area Governments; Recycling Services in Marin County. Special thanks to Wilson Hughes, Codirector of the Garbage Project, who coordinated field operations and the logistics of sample analyses, and Garbage Project staff and students, who actually sorted and recorded garbage. The authors also thank John Sherry, Eric Arnould, and two anonymous reviewers for reading earlier versions of this chapter.

remover to leftover paints and pesticides, that frequently exit households in their garbage.

The most feared beast in the jungle of household hazardous wastes is very likely the common household battery. The rate of household discard of dry-cell batteries has nearly doubled since 1975 (Bogner, Rathje, Tani, & Minko, 1993). And no wonder. Batteries have increasingly become the power behind what most Americans view as basic necessities of living. AAAs in remote controls open garage doors and switch TV channels, AAs protect homes in smoke alarms and entertain in Walkmans and Gameboys, Cs power bike lights and small toys, Ds do the same in flashlights, bigger toys, and boom boxes, as do 9-volts in radios and remote-control toys, and a myriad of miscellaneous batteries run everything from watches and cameras to laptop computers. The disposal problem is that most of these household helpmates have both a relatively short use life and contain one or another heavy metal, such as mercury or cadmium (Tani, Rathje, & Hughes, 1994). The batteries from any one household may seem innocent enough—one is tossed out about once every 2 weeks—but aggregated at the community level, household batteries are menaces. Tucson's 260,000 households added 4 million dry-cell batteries to local landfills in 1990, and the number discarded each year has probably grown since.

Household batteries have become a primary focus of programs to collect household hazardous wastes, which now exist in more than 2,000 communities nationwide. Every one of these programs has limited resources and must allocate what it has with great care. In making decisions about ways to educate the public to properly dispose of their hazardous wastes, information about the concentrations and frequencies of household dry-cell battery discards within target communities is extremely useful (see Wilson & Rathje, 1989). The University of Arizona's Garbage Project has a database that is a start toward providing this type of information.

This chapter represents an approach to consumer behavior through discards, and it explores patterns in household battery consumption according to the socioeconomic characteristics of consumers based on the Garbage Project's hazardous waste database. The objective of this study is to identify socioeconomic groups that should be the target of environmental education for battery disposal and provide baseline information for household hazardous policy planners.

Data for analyses were generated by collecting and sorting garbage picked up at individual households. Nearly 4,000 household garbage pickups were then aggregated by census tract and collection period. Using these aggregated units as the units of analysis, data were analyzed for their associated socio-

economic variables, such as income, age, and ethnicity. Results suggest that
higher-income households tend to consume (and discard) more dry-cell
batteries. Age composition of households also appears to play an important
role in determining dry-cell battery use. However, because household median
age covaries with household income, household income needs to be controlled before the effects of age on battery consumption are characterized.
Ethnicity seems to be another factor in dry-cell battery use and discard.
Anglo, Hispanic, and African American households are represented in the
Garbage Project samples. Hispanic households consume the most batteries
and African American households the fewest, with Anglo households' battery consumption placed in the middle between the other two. Although the
difference in battery discards between Anglo and Hispanic Americans disappear when household size is controlled, African American households still
consume the fewest batteries, even on a per capita basis.

⧉ Garbage Methodology for Consumer Behavior Research

Modern material culture studies in anthropology were started as part of
archaeology. The idea was to extend the scope of archaeological inquiries to
include not only societies in the past but also contemporary societies.
Therefore, modern material cultural studies and general archaeology share
fundamentally the same research objective—to understand human behavior
through information derived from material artifacts.

The University of Arizona's Garbage Project was founded in 1973 to study
our own societies through our own garbage, just as some archaeologists learn
about ancient cultures by studying ancient garbage. Refuse analysis provides
a means for identifying and quantifying purchase, consumption, and discard
behaviors. Garbage is a material record of actual behavior rather than self-
reported behavior or self-perceptions. The Garbage Project's studies have focused on common activities, such as the procurement, consumption, and discard
of food and other household commodities, at two points along the solid waste
stream: fresh household garbage discards and garbage in landfills (Rathje &
Murphy, 1992). Domestic and international fresh household garbage studies
have been conducted in Tucson, Phoenix, New Orleans, Milwaukee, Marin
County (California), Mexico City, and Sydney. Since 1987, the Garbage
Project has excavated 15 landfills in the United States and Canada. Although garbage methodology is not designed to replace more conventional
research methods in behavioral research to study contemporary human behavior,

such as interviews and questionnaires, the information recorded from garbage certainly adds a unique dimension to characterize human behavior.

Garbage analysis possesses several advantages for behavioral research. First, the recording of refuse is a nonreactive measure of human behavior (Webb, Campbell, Schwartz, & Sechrest, 1966). Although this does not mean that garbage data are free from *any* bias, garbage data are independent of respondent biases. Second, unlike informant interviews and questionnaire surveys, refuse studies cause no respondent inconvenience. Third, the data recorded can be very specific and quantitative. Information on packages tells specific quantities, costs, and brands, which are usually well beyond a respondent's recall (Hughes, 1984; Rathje, 1979, 1984; Rathje, Hughes, & Jernigan, 1976).

Garbage methodology does, of course, have limitations, the most obvious being that refuse data cannot measure individual behaviors; instead, refuse analysis is limited to a measure of total household at-home consumption. Another limitation is that garbage analysis is only able to record the material evidence of products. Therefore, it provides data only on actual consumer purchases but not on the way consumers arrive at their purchasing decisions. Although some consumer attitudes can be deduced from discard patterns, eventually the discards from purchased products remain the only direct evidence. Refuse analysis is also prone to certain types of data absence and data loss because most of the information recorded in household garbage is derived from packages. Material data (other than the remains of the product itself) are simply absent when commodities are packaged in poorly labeled containers or are not packaged at all. Packages for many fresh fruits and vegetables are examples. Material data are lost when certain types of containers, such as aluminum cans and glass bottles, are diverted from household garbage to recycling facilities. Although this type of data loss may be partially compensated for by analyzing caps, pull-tabs, six-pack rings, and so forth, the practice of recycling still leaves some uncertainty in data related to recyclable packages. Recently, in addition to their recycling program, some communities are collecting household hazardous wastes for burial at hazardous waste disposal sites. Batteries are often one of the hazardous wastes collected. However, when the data used in this study were collected in 1985-1987, there were no systematic household hazardous collection programs in any of the study areas. Thus it is assumed that the battery discard data lost due to hazardous waste collections should be minimal.

The most important advantage of refuse analysis for this study is that refuse analysis can produce quantitative and specific data on batteries discarded in household refuse. Without hazardous waste collections, batteries in household refuse were exactly the batteries used in and discarded from sample households. As a result, detailed battery types, such as alkaline, carbon-zinc, lithium, and nickel-cadmium, and battery sizes, such as AAA, AA, C, and D, recorded in refuse sorts provide an opportunity to analyze differential use and discard of dry-cell batteries by different socioeconomic groups. These quantitative and specific aspects of refuse data analysis from a large number of sample households cannot be easily replicated by other types of survey methods.

◩ Data

Data for this study came from 3,839 household garbage pickups. A garbage pickup consists of all garbage placed out by a household for collection on a pickup day; it may be in trash cans, garbage bags, or any other type of container. These garbage pickups were collected within three communities in the United States: Marin County, California; New Orleans, Louisiana; and Tucson, Arizona. All the garbage was collected and analyzed for a study of household hazardous wastes conducted by the Garbage Project (Rathje, Wilson, Lambough, & Herndon, 1987; Wilson, Rathje, & Tani, 1994).

Data collection in Marin County was conducted in two phases, in May and in August 1986, which resulted in 1,022 garbage pickups from 12 census tracts. Another 1,109 pickups were collected from 6 census tracts in New Orleans during October 1986. Whereas these sample pickups were collected in quantity within short periods of time, the 1,708 pickups from Tucson were continuously collected a few at a time over 3 years between 1985 and 1987. Altogether, the 3,839 garbage pickups analyzed in this study weighed 82,000 pounds.

Refuse Sorting and Data Recording

Sample pickups were brought to a facility where trained sorters processed the materials. First, for each collected pickup, the census tract designation, sample number, date of collection, and the weight of the sample were recorded. Next, each individual item in the refuse pickup was systematically examined. The Garbage Project uses three distinct formats for recording information in refuse (Hughes, 1984). The first format is called a "regular sort," which is a record of all refuse items by code number, purchase weight or volume in ounces, cost, brand name, type, and waste by weight. The second format, a "weight sort," is a record of more than 40 material composition categories by weight and volume. The third format is "special pulls." A special pull is designed to record narrowly targeted information in great depth. Hazardous waste pulls are an example of special pulls. This study uses data recorded in the hazardous waste pull format.

Hazardous Waste Pulls ("Haz Pulls")

Although the Environmental Protection Agency defines household refuse as nonhazardous (Office of the Federal Register, 1987), common household products often contain hazardous substances, such as organic chemicals and heavy metals (Gurnam & Associates, 1979; Ridgley, 1982). Several studies have found that municipal solid waste—the majority of which are household refuse—landfills produce leachate as hazardous as the leachate from industrial hazardous waste landfills (Brown & Donnelly, 1988; Dunlap, Shew, Robertson, & Toussaint, 1976; Thompson, 1987). As a result, concern over the fate of household hazardous wastes has increased dramatically over the past decade (Dana Duxbury Associates, 1989). In spite of the growing concern, there is still a dearth of information on the quantities and composition of household hazardous wastes. To fill this information gap, the Garbage Project launched a comprehensive study of the characteristics of household hazardous wastes and the risks associated with their disposal in municipal solid waste landfills (Rathje et al., 1987; Wilson et al., 1994).

For the household hazardous wastes characterization study, hazardous waste pulls were designed to record detailed information on hazardous wastes in household refuse. According to a special hunting list prepared for these "Haz Pulls," listed materials in refuse were recorded. These household hazardous wastes include home pesticides and herbicides, automotive maintenance items, paints, thinners, adhesives, household cleaners, and other household products, such as batteries. Recorded information for each hazardous item included the Haz Pull code, number of items, purchase weight or volume in ounces, brand name, type of product, material composition, and commodity waste, if any. Recorded items included containers that once contained hazardous substances (e.g., paint cans), products containing hazardous substances (e.g., batteries), and products contaminated by hazardous substance-containing materials (e.g., used paint brushes).

Dry-cell batteries were recorded in Haz Pulls for their size and type, such as AA and alkaline, quantity, and brand. Because Haz Pulls recorded both containers and the products themselves, both "bubble packs" and exhausted batteries were recorded as batteries. The following analyses, however, are of actual household dry-cell battery discards only; packages for batteries were excluded.

▨ Analytical Methodology

Data Preparation for Analyses

Of the 3,839 garbage pickups examined for household hazardous wastes, 275 pickups (7.2%) contained 696 actual batteries. Battery data were compiled for analyses by battery type and by pickup (including "zero" pickups in which no batteries were found). Battery types used in this study were AAA, AA, C, D, 9-volt, and "miscellaneous," such as button, lithium, and 6-volt batteries. When no battery type was recorded, such batteries were classified as "type unknown." Although the battery count for each pickup reflected "type unknown" batteries, these were excluded from type-specific analyses.

The socioeconomic characteristics of each particular household from which garbage was collected were not known. Such information is only available at the census tract level. To analyze dry-cell battery discard data in relation to socioeconomic characteristics, battery discard data were aggregated by census tract and by sampling period. Refuse was collected once a week in Marin County and twice a week in both New Orleans and Tucson. To make battery data comparable between these areas, raw battery counts were converted to yearly (52-week projection) generation rates per household. That is, two pickups in New Orleans and in Tucson and one pickup in Marin County were treated as containing one week's refuse. The battery values of an aggregated unit represent the arithmetic means of the 52-week battery generation projection for garbage pickups in the analysis unit.

In Marin County, 1,022 garbage pickups were collected from 12 census tracts in two separate sampling periods; 8 of the 12 tracts were sampled in both periods. Altogether, 20 aggregated units were generated from the Marin County data for this study (see Table 3.1 for Marin samples and for samples from other areas). In New Orleans, 1,109 garbage pickups were collected from six census tracts in one sampling period, but because five tracts were sampled twice, 11 aggregated units are included in the analysis from New Orleans. In Tucson, 1,708 garbage pickups were collected continuously over a period of 3 years, so these pickups were aggregated by the year they were collected and by census tract. Aggregated units having less than 10 garbage pickups were excluded from the analysis. Altogether, 22 aggregated units were generated from Tucson.

Definitions of Socioeconomic Variables

Socioeconomic variables indicating income, age composition, and ethnicity were assigned to each aggregated unit. The values of socioeconomic variables were compiled from the 1990 Census (Bureau of the Census, 1993).

Income

The Census Bureau publishes several household income indicators for each census tract. They include the median and mean income of a tract, the distribution of income levels in a tract, the percentage of families below the poverty level, and more. Although each type of income indicator represents a slightly different aspect of characteristics related to household income, this study used median income per capita as its indicator of the income characteristics of census tracts. Median income per capita was derived by dividing median income per household by the number of persons per household in each census tract.

Study census tracts were further classified into three tiers—upper, middle, and lower—based on their median income per capita. These income classes are all relative to study census tracts within this study, and boundaries between income classes are somewhat arbitrary; nevertheless, census tracts in this study represent a wide range of household incomes. The study tracts range from those in Marin County, one of the highest income areas in the nation (where the median income per capita of some census tracts is more than $30,000) to those with a median income per capita of less than $3,000. Census tracts with median income per capita at $20,000 or more were designated as upper-income tracts, those with less than $20,000 but more than or equal to $10,000 were designated as middle-income tracts, and those with less than $10,000 were designated as lower-income tracts for this study.

Based on these income class assignments of census tracts, the 53 aggregated units were assigned to income classes. By this procedure, 11, 22, and 19 units were designated as upper, middle, and lower, respectively. With regard to areas, whereas New Orleans has at least one unit in every income class, Marin County lacks lower-income units, and Tucson has no upper-income unit (Table 3.1).

TABLE 3.1

Aggregated Tract Units and Associated Socioeconomic Values

Tract Unit	No. of Pickups	Income Class[a]	Median Income Per Capita	Median Age	Dominant Ethnicity (80% of tract population)
Marin County					
1	20	High	22,048	42.8	Anglo
2	23	High	20,182	43.9	Anglo
3	34	Medium	17,753	38.8	Anglo
4	65	Medium	19,019	40.0	Anglo
5	35	High	27,639	43.2	Anglo
6	86	Medium	14,993	34.4	Anglo
7	25	Medium	17,845	36.7	Anglo
8	18	Medium	10,944	27.8	N/A
9	21	High	25,979	48.8	Anglo
10	78	High	24,665	40.7	Anglo
11	47	Medium	17,753	38.8	Anglo
12	48	Medium	19,019	40.0	Anglo
13	84	High	27,639	43.2	Anglo
14	76	Medium	14,993	34.4	Anglo
15	28	Medium	17,845	36.7	Anglo
16	62	Medium	10,944	27.8	N/A
17	18	High	30,148	41.8	Anglo
18	18	High	25,482	39.4	Anglo
19	67	High	25,979	48.8	Anglo
20	149	High	24,665	40.7	Anglo
New Orleans					
1	185	High	28,727	45.6	Anglo
2	192	Low	6,915	43.5	Black
3	96	Medium	10,441	35.8	N/A
4	89	Low	4,646	32.9	Black
5	163	Medium	16,002	40.5	Anglo
6	88	Medium	15,351	34.0	N/A
7	48	Medium	15,351	34.0	N/A
8	11	Low	4,646	32.9	Black
9	29	Medium	10,441	35.8	N/A
10	107	Low	6,915	43.5	Black
11	61	High	28,727	45.6	Anglo

TABLE 3.1

continued

Tract Unit	No. of Pickups	Income Class[a]	Median Income Per Capita	Median Age	Dominant Ethnicity (80% of tract population)
Tucson					
1	23	Low	7,664	28.2	N/A
2	18	Low	5,075	29.7	Hispanic
3	159	Low	5,556	26.1	N/A
4	77	Low	9,842	31.9	N/A
5	143	Medium	15,170	37.8	Anglo
6	47	Low	5,139	25.8	N/A
7	30	Low	4,123	27.5	Hispanic
8	16	Low	4,674	26.6	Hispanic
9	33	Medium	11,160	38.2	Anglo
10	24	Low	7,664	28.2	N/A
11	82	Medium	13,111	33.2	Anglo
12	95	Low	2,264	23.1	N/A
13	25	Low	5,556	26.1	N/A
14	62	Low	9,842	31.9	N/A
15	142	Medium	15,170	37.8	Anglo
16	88	Low	4,123	27.5	Hispanic
17	59	Medium	11,160	38.2	Anglo
18	96	Medium	13,111	33.2	Anglo
19	158	Low	2,264	23.1	N/A
20	157	Low	9,842	31.9	N/A
21	123	Medium	15,170	37.8	Anglo
22	45	Low	4,123	27.5	Hispanic

a. Median income per capita: High = higher than or equal to $20,000; Medium = higher than or equal to $10,000 and less than $20,000; and Low = less than $10,000.

Age Composition

To investigate battery use by different age groups, characteristics related to the age of household members were incorporated in the analysis. First, the median age of residents in each census tract was used as an indicator of age composition of households. Based on median age, census tracts were assigned to more inclusive classes: If a median age of a tract is in the 20s, then the age class of the tract would be "20," if in the 30s, the age class would be "30," and so forth. Information on age segments is also used in analyses.

Ethnicity

There are three major ethnic groups represented in study census tracts: Anglo, Hispanic, and African American. Each census tract is assigned to the majority group if the majority group consisted of at least 80% of all population in the tract. Anglo tracts are predominant in the study units: 28 units distributed in all three areas. All four African American units are located in New Orleans, and all five Hispanic units are located in the Tucson study area. There are 16 tract-units in which no ethnic group exceeded 80% of the tracts' population; in these cases, ethnicity was not assigned.

Results

Battery Discards by Income Group

The effect of income on dry-cell battery consumption is not linear, but there seems to be a threshold. As Table 3.2 shows, although higher-income households consume more dry-cell batteries as a whole than the other two income groups, the difference between middle- and lower-income groups is not substantial. On a per capita basis, the pattern of battery discards becomes more linear along the income axis (see "Total per Capita" column, Table 3.2).

A closer look at the discards of specific battery types suggests that only certain types of battery consumption are responsible for the difference between the upper-income and the lower-income groups. The discard of AAAs and AAs among upper-income households are substantially higher than the other groups; "exotic" batteries, such as lithium, button, and 6-volt batteries, were observed almost exclusively in upper-income households' garbage. On the other hand, Cs and Ds are fairly constant across income classes. The smaller dry-cell batteries (As and exotics) usually drive more expensive devices, such as certain calculators, cameras, portable cassette and CD players, whereas the larger varieties are used in more ordinary and less expensive equipment, such as flashlights and toys. Therefore, this finding does not suggest that household income affects the ability to buy dry-cell batteries per se. Rather, it probably indicates that higher income allows

TABLE 3.2

Projected Yearly Discards of Battery Types, by Income Class

Income Class	Units	Household Size	AAA	AA	C	D	9-volt	Miscell-aneous	Unknown	Total	Total Per Capita
					Battery Type						
Upper	12	2.3	1.0	7.6	2.4	5.0	1.3	1.6	.7	19.7	8.5
Middle	22	2.1	.3	4.8	2.4	2.6	1.2	.3	1.2	12.9	6.1
Lower	19	2.9	.1	4.9	2.2	4.7	.7	.1	1.2	13.9	4.9

household members to purchase more expensive battery-operated equipment and to use such equipment more frequently.

Battery Discards by Age Group

Battery discards are also affected by the age of household members. One might expect that households with more school-aged children and teenagers would consume more batteries presumably because this segment of population is closely associated with battery-operated toys, game machines, and portable cassette and CD players.

Figure 3.1 partially confirms this expectation. It plots all battery discards projected for 52 weeks against the median age of households for the aggregated study units. As expected, units with the youngest median-age households (in the 20s) discarded dry-cell batteries at a raised level, although units whose median age is in the 40s discarded more batteries than those in the 30s (see also Table 3.3). Nevertheless, the greatest difference between age groups disappears on a per capita basis. The discard rates of the 20s and 40s groups are almost identical, and that of the 30s group is only slightly lower than the other two. Therefore, contrary to the expectation that younger generations consume more batteries, older adults appear to consume almost as many batteries as children and teenagers.

One possible reason for this is that older adults use dry-cell batteries for different purposes than children, such as button batteries for hearing aids. The patterns of discard across battery types, however, are not very different between the 20s and 40s groups. Although no age effects on battery discards are illustrated in Table 3.3, Table 3.4 indicates that age does affect battery discards. Within the same income group, the younger the median age the

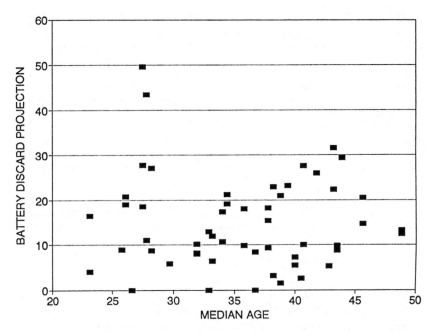

Figure 3.1   Discard projection for 52 weeks of all batteries and median age for 53 tract units.

more battery discards per capita, and within the same age group, the higher the income the more battery discards per capita, without exception. The relationship between age and income is, in general, that census tracts with older median age tend to have higher median income per capita. These two factors influence battery discards in a directly opposite way. Therefore, the effects of the age and income factors cancel each other out and generate the apparent lack of difference in total battery discards between the three age groups. In other words, once the age factor is isolated, the prior expectation about the effects of age—that households with more school-aged children will actually consume more batteries—holds true.

Battery Discard by Ethnic Group

Anglo units in all three study areas have comparable battery discard patterns (Table 3.5). Anglo tracts in Marin County discarded slightly more than those in New Orleans and Tucson, perhaps reflecting the higher income

TABLE 3.3

Projected Battery Discards, by Median Age Class

Age Class	Units	Household Size	AAA	AA	C	D	9-volt	Miscell- aneous	Unknown	Total	Total Per Capita
20s	14	3.0	.1	8.1	3.5	5.0	.6	.2	1.1	18.6	6.3
30s	23	2.1	.1	3.2	1.9	3.8	1.3	.4	1.3	12.0	5.7
40s	16	2.4	.9	6.4	2.0	3.1	1.1	1.1	.9	15.4	4.9

and larger household size within the Marin units. Although Hispanic units discarded the most batteries and African American units the fewest batteries per household, the average household size of these groups is larger than that of Anglo households (Table 3.5). After controlling for the difference in household size, battery discards per capita among Anglo Americans becomes higher than those among Hispanic Americans, and the gap in the per capita rate between Anglo and African Americans widens. Anglo and Hispanic units discarded almost three times more batteries per capita than African American units. Income does not seem to produce this difference between Hispanic and African Americans because the median income per capita of the Hispanic and African American tracts are comparable ($4,711 and $5,781, respectively). Because the African American tracts were only in New Orleans, it is possible that the difference in battery discards between this group and the other ethnic groups is caused by some geographic factor. Geographic factors can be eliminated, however, because the Anglo tracts in both Tucson and New Orleans yielded almost identical battery discards (Table 3.5). Because the median age of all Hispanic tracts is in the 20s and that of African American tracts is in the 30s and 40s, age may account for some of the difference in battery discards between the Hispanic and African American tracts. Age does not explain, however, the lack of difference between Hispanic and Anglo Americans nor the difference between Anglo and African Americans.

After eliminating the income, geographic, and age factors as a major determinant for the small quantity of battery discards by African Americans, "cultural" factors become a more likely candidate for generating this phenomenon. The reason why African Americans as a group discarded much fewer batteries at home, however, remains to be investigated. On the other hand, the main reason for the large quantity of battery discards by Hispanic

TABLE 3.4

All Battery Discards Per Capita and Median Income Per Capita, by Age and by Income Class

Income Class	Age		
	20s	30s	40s
Upper	None	9.7	8.4
		$25,482 (n = 1)	$25,736 (n = 11)
Middle	9.2	6.2	2.6
	$11,108 (n = 2)	$14,518 (n = 17)	$18,013 (n = 3)
Lower	5.8	3.4	2.5
	$5,444 (n = 12)	$7,763 (n = 5)	$6,915 (n = 2)

households seems to be their larger size. As long as Hispanic households are consistently larger than Anglos', Hispanic neighborhoods should be a target area for curbing battery discards.

✹ Discussion and Implications

This chapter examined three socioeconomic factors—income, age, and ethnicity—for their effects on consumers' battery purchase, use, and discard. All three factors differentially affect battery use. In general, income and age appear to strongly affect battery consumption and discard. Discarded batteries per capita increase as income of sample units increases and decrease as median age of the units increases. This pattern with age is not clear until battery discards are controlled for income because the effects of age and income tend to cancel each other in terms of battery consumption. These observations of battery discards in relation to age and income can, to a large extent, be explained by higher use levels of battery-operated devices among younger age groups and by the ability of higher-income households to purchase more battery-operated devices.

The next question is what makes Anglo and Hispanic Americans discard three times more batteries than African Americans? Unfortunately, no answer is provided by refuse analysis, which is not very sensitive to consumers' purchasing decisions. This is a question of the differential allocation of economic resources and behavioral habits among different ethnic groups. African Americans may use their battery-operated devices outside home more frequently than Anglo and Hispanic Americans do, and therefore the

TABLE 3.5

Battery Discard Projections for 52 Weeks, by Selected Tract-Dominant Ethnic Group

						Battery Type					Total
Income Class	*Units*	*Household Size*	*AAA*	*AA*	*C*	*D*	*9-Volt*	*Miscell- aneous*	*Unknown*	*Total*	*Per Capita*
Marin County Anglo	18	2.2	.6	5.2	2.8	4.7	1.1	1.1	.3	15.8	7.1
New Orleans Anglo	3	2.0	.8	6.5	1.4	.8	2.3	0	.9	12.5	6.3
Tucson Anglo	7	2.0	.5	4.5	1.8	2.5	.3	.9	1.9	12.5	6.2
All Anglo	28	2.2	.6	5.2	2.4	3.7	1.0	1.0	.8	14.6	6.8
New Orleans African American	4	3.3	.3	1.7	1.7	2.5	.4	0	1.3	7.8	2.4
Tucson Hispanic	5	3.4	0	6.3	5.1	7.5	.7	0	.7	20.3	6.0

batteries they use end up in public garbage. Then, too, African Americans may simply spend more time without such devices, or such devices may play a more important role in Anglo and Hispanic subcultures so that members spend more money on such devices. To investigate this question, it is necessary to conduct a more integrated study of material culture and behavioral observation, just as those done by ethnoarchaeologists, among different ethnic groups (David & Hennig, 1972; Hayden & Cannon, 1984; Kramer, 1982; Longacre & Skibo, 1994). A study that includes both comprehensive material inventories and behavioral characterization related to different types of materials would give some clue as to how each group differentially allocates economic resources. Open-ended interviews about the purchase and use of battery-operated devices, as well as about the purchase and discard of batteries themselves, would add considerable depth to material inventories. Of course, from our point of view, analysis of refuse from the same households would be essential to a comprehensive picture of battery purchase, use, and discard.

Although there is certainly valuable information for marketing batteries in the Garbage Project's initial study of battery discards, the most powerful rationale for this analysis is to protect our environment from these discards. The initial observations by this study about patterns in the household discard of dry-cell batteries clearly provide some useful information to community household hazardous waste collection programs on the most efficient ways to educate the public in proper disposal methods.

First, all households are not equal in their discard of batteries. Households with younger members, in the upper-income level, and in Hispanic neighborhoods throw out more batteries than households in other neighborhoods. This conclusion leads to another. It validates and reemphasizes the obvious need to provide multilingual educational materials, in this case in Spanish. Second, the relationship between household age-composition profiles and battery discard patterns (specifically, that more children mean a higher rate of battery discard) provides a rationale for focusing public education resources of community household hazardous waste collection programs on schools:

1. Children are the primary users of many battery-intensive devices and therefore the first to know when a battery is a candidate for discard.
2. Because schools are our most respected institutions for imparting knowledge, the need to save spent batteries for household hazardous waste collections will take on added credibility and significance.
3. The schoolchildren pathway has proved extremely effective in disseminating other types of solid waste information (specifically, on the need for and the methods of recycling) throughout the adult population. What parent can withstand the withering disdain of their offspring's disapproval, especially concerning hazardous wastes that can degrade the environment of that offspring's future?

As useful as it may be, garbage archaeology is, however, far from realizing its potential value when it is used in isolation. Despite the apparent differences in research goals and methods between cultural anthropology and garbage archaeology and between anthropology in general and marketing, these disciplines have one very important element in common. Each is viewing the same behavioral-material interactions. Like the blind men trying to describe an elephant from only the small portion that they reach (the trunk, the tusks, the legs, the tail), every individual perspective is valid. Nevertheless, when about to confront a real elephant on a jungle trail, a comprehensive view of how the trunk, tusks, legs, and tail fit together would be the most useful and could save individual investigators from making serious mistakes in interpretation.

One extremely important issue for a collaborative interview-behavioral-observation-garbage research investigation is visible in Table 3.4. The highest levels of battery use in all three income groups are within households in the youngest age bracket. The question is whether as these households move on to the next age group they will decrease their battery use or maintain, or perhaps even surpass, current levels of use and discard? Large-scale battery use is something new, so the future is unknown, but with rapidly expanding battery-powered product lines and with 3 billion household batteries discarded and consigned to landfills or incinerators last year alone, the question requires a timely and a comprehensive answer. Although each researcher would have a separate agenda—from identifying consumer demands to quantifying household discard procedures—working together would have the clear synergistic effect of generating a holistic perspective that could lead to the integration of convenient purchase with proper disposal. When the goal is to see the entire system from all angles, there can be no isolated opportunities, problems, solutions . . . or researchers.

References

Bogner, J. E., Rathje, W. L., Tani, M., & Minko, O. (1993). *Discards as measures of urban metabolism: The value of rubbish.* Paper presented at the International Symposium on Urban Metabolism.

Brown, K. W., & Donnelly, K. C. (1988). An estimation of the risk associated with the organic constituents of hazardous and municipal waste landfill leachates. *Hazardous Waste and Hazardous Materials, 5,* 1-30.

Bureau of the Census. (1993). *1990 Census of population and housing: Population and housing characteristics for census tracts and block numbering areas.* Washington, DC: Author.

Dana Duxbury Associates. (1989). *Summary of the Third National Conference on Household Waste Management.* Andover, MA: Author.

David, N., & Hennig, H. (1972). *The ethnography of pottery: A Fulani case seen in archaeological perspective.* (McCaleb Module in Anthropology No. 21). Reading, MA: Addison-Wesley.

Dunlap, W. J., Shew, D. C., Robertson, J. M., & Toussaint, C. R. (1976). Organic pollutants contributed to groundwater by a landfill. In E. J. Genetelli & J. Ciello (Eds.), *Gas and leachate from landfills* (Environmental Protection Agency Publication No. 600/9-76-004, pp. 96-110). New Brunswick, NJ: Department of Environmental Science, Rutgers University.

Gurnam and Associates. (1979) *Control of heavy metal content of municipal waste-water sludges.* Washington, DC: Author.

Hayden, B., & Cannon, A. (1984). *The structure of material systems: Ethnoarchaeology in the Mayan Highlands* (Society for American Archaeology Paper No. 3). Washington, DC: Society for American Archaeology.

Hughes, W. W. (1984). Method to our madness: The Garbage Project methodology. *American Behavioral Scientist, 28*(1), 41-50.

Kramer, C. (1982). *Village ethnoarchaeology: Rural Iran in archaeological perspective.* New York: Academic Press.

Longacre, W. A., & Skibo, J. M. (Eds.). (1994). *Kalinga ethnoarchaeology: Expanding archaeological method and theory.* Washington, DC: Smithsonian Institution Press.

Office of the Federal Register. (1987). *Code of federal regulations* (chap. 40, pt. 261). Washington, DC: Author.

Rathje, W., & Murphy, C. (1992). *Rubbish: The archaeology of garbage.* New York: HarperCollins.

Rathje, W. L. (1979). Trace measures. In L. Sechrest (Ed.), *Unobtrusive measures today: New directions for methodology of behavioral science* (pp. 75-91). San Francisco: Jossey-Bass.

Rathje, W. L. (1984). The garbage decade. *American Behavioral Scientist, 28*(1), 9-29.

Rathje, W. L., Hughes, W. W., & Jernigan, S. (1976). The science of garbage: Following the consumer through his garbage can. In *Proceedings of the American Marketing Association, 1976* (pp. 56-64). Chicago: American Marketing Association.

Rathje, W. L., Wilson, D. C., Lambough, V. W., & Herndon, R. C. (1987). *Characterization of household hazardous wastes from Marin County, California, and New Orleans, Louisiana* (Environmental Protection Agency Publication No. 600/X-87-129). Las Vegas, NV: Environmental Monitoring Systems Laboratory.

Ridgley, S. M. (1982). *Toxicants in consumer products.* Report B of the Household Hazardous Waste Disposal Project Metro Toxicant Program No. 1, Seattle.

Tani, M., Rathje, W. L., & Hughes, W. W. (1994, April). *Landfill research by the Garbage Project: A first applied archaeology.* Paper presented at the annual meeting of the Southwestern Anthropological Association, Las Vegas, NV.

Thompson, J. M. (1987). *Presence of selected organic compounds and their intermediates in municipal landfill leachates.* Unpublished master's thesis, University of Arizona.

Webb, E. J., Campbell, D. T., Schwartz, R. D., & Sechrest, L. (1966). *Unobtrusive measures: Nonreactive research in the social sciences.* Chicago: Rand McNally.

Wilson, D. C., & Rathje, W. L. (1989). Structure and dynamics of household hazardous wastes. *Journal of Resource Management and Technology, 17,* 200-206.

Wilson, D. C., Rathje, W. L., & Tani, M. (1994). *Characterization and assessment of household hazardous wastes in municipal solid wastes.* Final report to the National Science Foundation, Washington, DC.

PART THREE

Managing Channel Relations and Organizational Change
International and Interfunctional Aspects

In this part, we consider several fundamental challenges to the marketing imagination, which might be captured in the following megalomaniacal style. How can we create philosophies and organizations that tap the gifts of wildly dissimilar contributors and then harness these contributions in the service of consumer satisfaction everywhere around the globe? We can begin by returning to our earlier discussion of marketing and anthropology as linking-pin disciplines with practical linchpin applications.

These enterprises are actually "*inter*prises" in the three primary etymological senses of the prefix. First, they can be said to unfold "in the midst" of things; that is, they are supremely context sensitive and context bound. Second, they unfold "at intervals," insofar as their evolution has been discontinuous but relentless; each has advanced by annexing new intellectual territory and using that new ground as a staging area for further frontier forays. Third, they unfold with both "preventive and destructive effect," as each has enriched and immiserated, integrated, and marginalized stakeholders in its path; in theory and in practice, they have each acted as synergist and antagonist. These "interprises" speak to our need for transcultural strategies based on local input generated through and integrated by holistic interaction of all effected stakeholders. Mutuality and reciprocity are the

watchwords of such "interprises." Receptivity to cross-pollenization characterizes their progress.

Eric Arnould delivers a wake-up call to Western marketers by detailing
the realities of marketing management in what must be considered the true
global village (Iyer, 1994; Meadows, 1993). His description of channels under
duress returns the reader to the fundamentals of marketplace behavior. In
exploring and disputing the ideology of marketing and development,
Arnould reminds us that the relationship management and partnering trends
of which contemporary managers are so enamored are actually ancient
wisdom and provokes us to wonder just how many so-called paraprimitive
solutions to current business problems remain to be rediscovered (Norberg-
Hodge, 1991). Such rediscovery will be catalyzed by interdisciplinary cooperation between marketers and anthropologists, and captured in a hybrid
literature of cross cultural practicality. Once formal and informal sector
transactions are recognized and treated as part of an overarching unified
market system (Alexander, 1987; McGrath, Sherry, & Heisley, 1993; Sherry,
1990a, 1990b), and marketers forsake the notion of externality in favor of
embeddedness, the utility of anthropology to global marketing becomes
apparent. Arnould's discussion of ethnodomination of marketing channels
also portends our awakening to the multicultural diversity of domestic
marketplaces. Subcultural segmentation and entrepreneurialism are critical
forces facing marketers at home.

Shifting from the cultural ecology of marketing to action anthropology,
Richard Reeves-Ellington provides a fascinating cautionary tale for millen-
nial marketers mired in *fin de siècle* organizations. In his account, the anthro-
pologist-as-hero reengineers the firm, saves jobs, rehabilitates brands, satis-
fies consumers, and alters profoundly the philosophy of the organization.
Reeves-Ellington brings us down instructively to the workbench—or, perhaps appropriately, bush—level of operations that makes the discovery and
implementation of a transnational solution (Bartlett & Ghoshal, 1989) to
corporate business problems possible. His discussion of the details of empowering indigenous managers and bridging differences in the service of transcul-
turally efficient response (O'Hara-Devereaux & Johansen, 1994; Simons,
Vazquez, & Harris, 1993) demonstrates the wisdom of "anthropologizing" the
firm as a prelude to its "marketizing." If an organization must be predisposed
to hearing the voice of the market in order to become a long-term success,
and we realize that many, if not most, organizations are substantially hearing
impaired, then Reeves-Ellington's revitalized Pharmco serves as a compelling
example of the organization of the future. His model for engaging the cultural
context of the market, combined with such other practical directives for

organizing as the inquiry center concept of Barabba and Zaltman (1991), are prerequisites for realizing the promise of integrated marketing strategies (Schultz, Tannenbaum, & Lauterborn, 1994) of current passionate pursuit. Reeves-Ellington's attention to ethics is of special interest in our climate of renewed concern for the social impact of marketing decisions (Bol, Crespy, Stearns, & Walton, 1991).

Interest in the organizational dynamics of marketing, whether of entire economic systems such as the emerging global crime network (Sterling, 1994), culturally grounded business concerns (Janelli, 1993), or of individual corporate sales forces (Dorsey, 1994), is growing faster than traditional approaches to understanding relationship management are able to satisfy. If rumors of the death of the brand manager as a viable role are premature, the widespread move to reorganize the marketing function certainly is not. The shift to multidisciplinary teams with a category focus, the fielding of separate customer development teams, the reclamation of pricing and promotions by senior managers, and experimentation with partnering ("Death," 1994) portend a fundamental change in the way marketing is conducted. Anthropologists have already begun multidisciplinary team-based research into the ways in which work groups respond to corporate transformation initiatives and into thorny issues such as how to integrate the product development process within firms (Baba, 1994). As we enter an era of holographic marketing (Sherry, 1993), anywhere the organization chart is sectioned, from boardroom to shop floor, an emphasis on marketing will be discovered. Anthropological perspectives and methods can catalyze this reformation—from design through implementation to evaluation.

▧ References

Alexander, J. (1987). *Trade, traders and trading in rural Java*. New York: Oxford University Press.

Baba, M. (1994). Practitioner profile. *Anthropology Newsletter, 35*(6), 17-18.

Barabba, V., & Zaltman, G. (1991). *Hearing the voice of the market: Competitive advantage through creative use of market information*. Boston: Harvard Business School Press.

Bartlett, C., & Ghoshal, S. (1989). *Managing across borders: The transnational solution*. Boston: Harvard Business School Press.

Bol, J. W., Crespy, C., Stearns, J., & Walton, J. (1991). *The integration of ethics into the marketing curriculum: An educator's guide*. Chicago: American Marketing Association.

Death of the brand manager. (1994, April 9). *The Economist*, pp. 67-68.

Dorsey, D. (1994). *The force.* New York: Random House.

Iyer, P. (1994, September). Strangers in a small world. *Harper's,* pp. 13-16.

Janelli, R. (with Yim, D.). (1993). *Making capitalism: The social and cultural construction of a South Korean conglomerate.* Stanford, CA: Stanford University Press.

McGrath, M. A., Sherry, J. F., Jr., & Heisley, D. (1993). An ethnographic study of an urban periodic marketplace: Lessons from the Midville market. *Journal of Retailing,* 69(3), 280-319.

Meadows, D. (1993). Value earth. *Whole Earth Review,* pp. 79, 87.

Norberg-Hodge, H. (1991). *Ancient futures: Learning from Ladakh.* San Francisco: Sierra Club Books.

O'Hara-Devereaux, M., & Johansen, R. (1994). *Global work: Bridging distance, culture and time.* San Francisco: Jossey-Bass.

Schultz, D., Tannenbaum, S., & Lauterborn, R. (1994). *The new marketing paradigm: Integrated marketing communications.* Lincolnwood, IL: NTC Business Books.

Sherry, J. F., Jr. (1990a). A sociocultural analysis of a midwestern American flea market. *Journal of Consumer Research, 17*(1), 13-30.

Sherry, J. F., Jr. (1990b). Dealers and dealing in a periodic market: "Informal" retailing in ethnographic perspective. *Journal of Retailing,* 66(2), 174-200.

Sherry, J. F., Jr. (1993). *Cultural dimensions of international marketing.* Working paper, Department of Marketing, Kellogg School, Northwestern University.

Simons, G., Vazquez, C., & Harris, P. (1993). *Transcultural leadership: Empowering the diverse workforce.* Houston, TX: Gulf.

Sterling, C. (1994). *Thieves world: The threat of the new global network of organized crime.* New York: Simon & Schuster.

4

West African Marketing Channels

Environmental Duress,
Relationship Management,
and Implications for Western Marketing

Eric J. Arnould

Ignoring the diversity of channel contexts will impede progress in our attempts to understand how channels relationships operate in different environments.
—Frazier, Gill, and Kale (1989, p. 67)

This chapter in the applied anthropology of West African marketing channels aims at a brokerage function, urging marketers and ethnographers to explore alternative schemes to their separate, standard paradigms that dominate inquiry about marketing and development (Arnould, 1989; Bennett & Bowen, 1988). To this end, my goal is to encourage marketers and

AUTHOR'S NOTE: MM. Iddal Sidi Mohammed and Chefferou Mahatan, and U.S. Agency for International Development staff in Niger, USAID staff in other West African nations, and numerous participants in regional marketing systems contributed insight and information critical to the realization of the studies reported here. Data collection was made possible by numerous USAID projects over the years. The author wishes to thank Janeen Costa, Jan Heide, Annamma Joy, Jakki Mohr, Jack Nevin, Barbara Olsen, Linda Price, and John Sherry for helpful comments and suggestions in the conception of this chapter. Susan Cook at USF provided invaluable assistance in the preparation of the maps. I wish to credit (blame?) Jim McCullough for originally sparking my interest in linking the marketing literature to African ethnology. Errors of fact or interpretation are my own.

anthropologists to develop together a more robust comparative theory of marketing systems (cf. Frazier & Kim, 1994, p. 29), one based, above all, on the cultural relativity of marketing practices (Hampden-Turner & Trompenaars, 1993). Furthermore, the specific purpose of this chapter is to show that selected features of West African marketing channels relations are the result neither of a cultural proclivity nor an expectable outcome of the supply-side transaction costs characteristic of the marketing environment. Rather, I seek to show that the structure of marketing channels in West Africa can best be understood as a creative product of both. In other words, West African channels relations are culturally particular responses to certain types of persistent environmental duress (Ouchi, 1980; Plattner, 1989; Traeger, 1981b). Thus I want to describe African channels relationships in terms that are at once culturally relative but comprehensible to marketers, and in so doing, repudiate unexamined binary categories such as rich/poor, developed/underdeveloped, and formal/informal that inhibit the explanation of the differences between West African and other marketing systems.

Marketing systems in West Africa[1] (see Figure 4.1) provide a source of insight for a comparative, context-sensitive understanding of relationships in marketing, as well as possible defenses against the marketization of relationships (Fırat, 1991; Fırat & Venkatesh, 1993a, 1993b). Andreasen (1992) argues that research in arenas new to marketing scholars can provide a testing ground for marketing theory, a source of new insights, and at the same time provide marketers with opportunities to apply their knowledge to problems of pressing practical significance. In the context of channels research, Frazier and Kim (1994) echo this call. By adapting their descriptive and theoretical insights to the concerns of marketers, ethnographers of African marketing systems can pursue the self-critical brokerage role tempered in other development contexts (Arnould, 1989; Horowitz & Painter, 1986).

There are a number of benefits to paying attention to African marketing practices in the current climate of heightened international competition and economic stagnation in the First World. First, Africans have been successfully trading for centuries and thus provide a comparative framework for testing of marketing channels theory. Second, channels relationships in Africa have been organized and long maintained under severe environmental duress of various types. Frequently, the nature of these stresses has remained fairly constant even if their precise form has varied dramatically. As a result, channels relationships in Africa have been characterized by a high degree of embeddedness that is, I think, partly responsible for their staying power. Stated alternatively, in contrast to many sellers in the West, in Africa marketers are often deeply committed to managing their relationships with

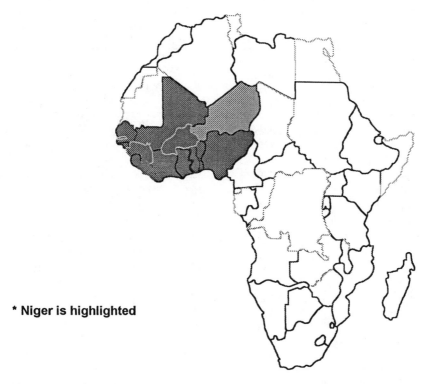

* **Niger is highlighted**

Figure 4.1 West Africa.

customers and vice versa (Dwyer, Schurr, & Oh, 1987, p. 14). Therefore, Western marketers interested in relationships might find fruitful insights from a study of relationships in African channels. Third, detailed studies of these systems should facilitate the development of a robust, comparative typology of alternative channels systems (Frazier & Kim, 1994). Finally, West Africa's so-called informal channels are responsible for delivering most items of both necessity and desire, however imperfectly, to the majority of West African consumers. U.S. marketers and marketing academics have generally ignored the African continent. When compared with Asian newly industrialized countries using the conventional categories of economic development, many nations in West Africa compare unfavorably (Table 4.1). However, given a recent 100% devaluation of the West African franc in 1994, growth in gross national product (GNP) averaging 2.2%, and a total population of 273 million in the year 2000, West Africa could be considered a long-term play

TABLE 4.1

Key Market Indicators for Selected West African Countries

Country	Population in Year 2000 (thousands)	Population Density (habitants/ sq. mi)	% Rate of Urbanization	% Literacy Rate	% GNP/ Capita	GNP Growth
Benin	6.9	111	36	23	374	1.5
Burkina Faso	11.5	88	9	18	321	5.1
Côte d'Ivoire	17.5	104	39	54	723	0.4
Ghana	20.2	170	32	60	367	2.0
Guinea	9.3	75	22	28	344	5.9
Guinea Bisseau	1.3	70	27	31	150	−0.6
Liberia	3.6	59	43	22	425	1.7
Mali	12.2	19	18	10	221	9.6
Niger	10.5	17	20	28	262	−1.3
Nigeria	159.6	323	16	42	314	−1.0
Senegal	10.5	99	36	23	627	4.2
Sierra Leone	5.3	147	28	24	233	1.8
Togo	4.9	157	22	43	362	0.5
Total	273.3					
Mean		110.7	26.7	21.2	363	2.3

SOURCE: Table compiled from P.C. Globe (1991).

in growth in consumer markets. In this context, it is well to recall that historically many multinational consumer products firms such as Unilever owe their existence to profits earned in the former colonial possessions (Suret-Canale, 1977; Williams, 1985).

▨ Background

The past decade has seen the growth of a broadened concern for interorganizational relationships in marketing and other areas of business research. A number of scholars have been propounding a new gospel of relationship marketing that foregrounds networks, relationships, alliances, and interactions (Christopher, Payne, & Ballantyne, 1992; Grönroos, 1990; Gummesson, 1993; McKenna, 1991; Sheth, 1993). The marketing channels literature has begun grappling with issues both of long-term relationship dynamics and those of cultural and institutional context (Frazier et al., 1989; Ganesan, 1994; Graham, 1985, 1993; Graham & Herberger, 1983; Johnson, Sakano, Côte, & Onzo, 1993; Spekman & Johnston, 1986). In conceptual treatments, they have emphasized the elements of duration, networks, "multiplex" obligations, trust, noneconomic sources of satisfaction and benefit sharing in relational exchanges between channel members (Dwyer et al., 1987). A similar topical thrust is observable in organizational research (Ouchi, 1980; Pfeffer & Salancik, 1978; Wilkins & Ouichi, 1983). Similarly, macromarketers have been pursuing the links between economic, institutional and cultural context and the structure of market relationships outside the first world (Dholakia & Sherry, 1987; Kumcu & Fırat, 1988; Littlefield & Csath, 1988; Olsen & Granzin, 1990; Sherry, 1989). In U.S. consumer behavior research, several authors have written about embedded markets characterized by commercial exchanges whose value transcends instrumental utility (Frenzen & Davis, 1990; Sherry, 1990). A parallel interest in the "linking value" of transactions has spawned a journal and a school of scholarship among continental business and social scientists (Berthoud, 1991; Cova, in press; Godbout & Caillé, 1992; Insel, 1991; Nicolas, 1991). Thus a paradigmatic shift is afoot to deal with marketing relationships in more holistic terms than characterized the dyadic, transactional approach of previous decades.

A number of representative propositions generated from the channels literature in marketing are recapitulated in Table 4.2. Given that useful summaries of the channels literature already exist (Frazier, 1990; Frazier & Kim, 1994; Gaski, 1984), there is no need to recapitulate them. The propositions enumerated here highlight some key channels issues raised by these summaries: channel structure, power, and conflict. They serve as a useful foil against which to organize data collected and analyzed in the West African context. In the marketing channels perspective represented in Table 4.2, structural form is said to impact the collective beliefs, sentiments, and behavior that exist in a channel. Power is the ability of a channel member to control or influence another firm's beliefs, attitudes, and behaviors. Conflict is a process reflecting divergence in expectations, perceptions, and goals between channel members.

Given these developments, it is thus strange that, with rare exceptions (Layton, 1988; Robles & El-Ansary, 1989), the relationship marketing and channels literature ignores the so-called informal sector markets in the southern hemisphere. When marketers (even macromarketers) have considered such systems they have tended to accept the crude evolutionary or economic dualism arguments put forward by neoclassical development

TABLE 4.2

Some Evidence From Empirical Studies of African Channels Relationships
for Propositions Derived From the Marketing Channels Literature

Domain	Proposition	Evidence From Informal Channels Relationships in West Africa
Structure	P1. The higher the uncertainty in the input or output sectors of the task environment of marketing channel dyads, the closer are the vertical linkages established between the dyad and other channel actors. If uncertainty arises in the input sector, backward vertical coordination is attempted. If uncertainty arises in the output sector, forward vertical coordination is attempted. (Achrol, Reve, & Stern, 1983, p. 64, P4)	High observed uncertainty in input (ecological variability) and output (thin and dispersed demand) sectors of the task environment and ubiquitous presence of ethnodominance, kin ties, and patron-client relations between channels dyads provides support. Explicit confirmation of backward (yam producers) and forward (cloth buyers) linkages in Traeger (1981a).
	P2. If uncertainty in the competitive sectors of the environment of marketing channel dyads cannot be absorbed by vertical coordination, closer linkages are established with competitors at each channel level. (Achrol et al., 1983, p. 65, P7)	Widespread informal cooperation among "competitors" in markets, by rotating credit associations, and by limiting resource pooling of smaller wholesalers to reduce marginal uncertainty, causes uncertain.
	P3. Under regulatory uncertainty, marketing channel dyads tend to enter into interest coalitions with actors in the input, output, and competitive sectors of their task environment, to counter uncertainty in the regulatory sector. (Achrol et al., 1983, p. 65, P9)	Regulatory uncertainty observed and ubiquitous presence of ethnodominance, kin ties, gender, and patron-client relations between channels dyads provides support.
	P4. If the uncertainty in the regulatory sector of the task environment cannot be absorbed by coalition behavior, marketing channel dyads tend to establish closer linkages with the regulatory agents. (Achrol et al., 1983, p. 65, P10)	Monopolization of coercive force by the state weakens effectiveness of coalitions and leads to widespread bribery and corruption involving marketers and regulators.

TABLE 4.2

continued

Domain	Proposition	Evidence From Informal Channels Relationships in West Africa
	P5. Heterogeneous channel environments will be associated with a. complex channel configurations b. decentralized decision structures c. high participation in decision making d. less formalization in procedures e. specialization of function f. more retailer control over marketing decisions (Dwyer & Welsh, 1985, p. 401, H1)	Heterogeneous channels environments observed. Proposition a. supported for high-value items like kola, livestock, salt b. supported for lower-value items but not for higher-value ones c. supported d. supported e. supported for perishables like onions and kola; not supported for grain, specialization is too risky f. not supported for crops traded across ecological and ethnic boundaries
	P6. Compared with steadfast channel environments, variable channel environments will be associated with a. less complex channel configurations b. centralized decision structures c. less participation in decision making d. formalized procedures e. less specialization in function f. less retailer control over marketing decisions (Dwyer & Welsh 1985, p. 401, H2)	Most West African channels environments are variable, yet a. not supported b. not supported c. not supported d. not supported e. supported f. supported
	P7. Under *relational channel structures* (in comparison with market channel structures), communication has a. higher frequency b. more bidirectional flows c. more informal modes d. more indirect content (Mohr & Nevin, 1990, p. 41, P1)	Enduring West African channels tend toward a relational mode, yet a. not supported because channel members rely on tacit knowledge of standard practices

continued

TABLE 4.2

continued

Domain	Proposition	Evidence From Informal Channels Relationships in West Africa
		b. more unidirectional flow because of reliance on traditional authority structures (as per Wilkins & Ouchi, 1983) c. supported given embedded nature of dyadic relationships d. supported given embedded nature of dyadic relationships
	P8. The greater volatility of the environment shrouding a transaction in a foreign market, the greater the degree of channel integration. (Klein, Frazier, & Roth, 1990, p. 200, H4)	A matter of degree: Highly volatile environments for onions are loosely integrated; moderately volatile environments for grain are more integrated; less volatile kola market is highly integrated.
	P9. The greater the diversity of the environment surrounding a transaction in a foreign market, the lesser the degree of channel integration. (Klein et al., 1990, p. 200, H5)	Not supported; products moved across ethnic and ecological boundaries tend toward greatest integration (e.g., salt, kola, livestock).
	P10. Trust in a vendor's credibility and benevolence is positively related to retailer's long-term orientation. (Ganesan, 1994, p. 4, H1)	Credibility, fostering long-term relational exchange, is nurtured through adherence to commercial (e.g., Islamic) norms, favorable manipulation of quantities, tipping, credit provision, and so on.
	P11. A retailer's perception of vendor transaction specific investments (TSIs) is positively related to the retailer's perception of the vendor's benevolence and credibility. (Ganesan, 1994, p. 4, H8)	Provision of credit is a widespread, and most common form of TSI in West African channels and influences perceptions of credibility.

TABLE 4.2

continued

Domain		Proposition	Evidence From Informal Channels Relationships in West Africa
Power	P12.	In marketing channels characterized by imbalanced power, the use of coercive power will produce a dysfunctional level of conflict. (Stern & Reve 1980, p. 58, P5)	West African channels are characterized by imbalanced power. Use of coercive power by regulatory agents increases marketers' uncertainty and risks, reduces producer prices, increases consumer prices, and reduces government tax revenues.
	P13.	Marketing channels characterized by imbalanced power and dominated by coercive influence strategies will be inherently unstable, resulting in decreased competitive viability. (Stern & Reve, 1980, p. 58, P6)	Reduced competitive viability of Nigerien onion marketing channels vis-à-vis imported onions in Côte d'Ivoire is related to imbalanced channel power and coercion in the channel. Government coercion of traders is a frequent contributing factor promoting famine.
	P14.	The greater proportion of relative power possessed by any channel member, the greater the proportion of the channel's profits that member will receive. (Stern & Reve, 1980, p. 58, P12)	Regional grain wholesalers' capital resources and assembly networks provide higher levels of profits as compared to local traders. Onion brokers' controlling relations with wholesalers and producers provide higher levels of profits compared to wholesalers and retailers.
	P15.	Under environmental uncertainty, the direction of the change in the power balance of channel dyads is determined by which member is able to cope with the sources of uncertainty. (Achrol et al., 1983, p. 64, P3)	Ethnodominance, slavery, and access to firepower were effective responses to uncertain access to product and physical threat to the channel. Patron-client relations, and boundary spanning, such as onion and livestock brokerage, are effective in coping with environmental uncertainty today.

continued

TABLE 4.2

continued

Domain	Proposition	Evidence From Informal Channels Relationships in West Africa
	P16. The higher the quality of assistances (noncoercive sources) channel member j believes he or she receives from channel member i, the more power channel member i has over channel member j. (Lusch & Brown, 1982, p. 314)	Supported here. Hausa patrons exercise considerable power over clients' through loans and "aid." Clients know, however, that patrons' power is offset by socioeconomic obligations. They too benefit. Power imbalance does not translate into exploitation.
	P17. Exercised coercive power sources will decrease satisfaction (of the target channel member) and increase intrachannel conflict. (Gaski, 1984, p. 10, P1)	Exercise of coercive power by regulators is the chief complaint in onion channel. Exercise of coercive power (i.e., monopoly pricing) by grain assemblers is chief complaint in grain channel. Conflict observed: Onion and grain producers accuse assemblers of price gouging; onion wholesalers accuse assemblers of restricting market access; grain wholesalers accuse assemblers of adulterating product; onion wholesalers accuse retailers of default on loans in kind.
	P18. Exercised noncoercive power sources will increase satisfaction and decrease intrachannel conflict. (Gaski, 1984, p. 10, P3)	Upstream channel members accept control of members who reduce uncertainty and facilitate exchange such as onion brokers despite high profits latter realize. Clients accept dependence on patrons in anticipation of future commercial and social benefits. Cooperation between channels dyads leads to increased goal attainment for all concerned.

TABLE 4.2

continued

Domain	Proposition	Evidence From Informal Channels Relationships in West Africa
	P19. Under *symmetrical power conditions* (in comparison with asymmetrical power conditions), communication has a. higher frequency b. more bidirectional flows c. more informal modes d. more indirect content (Mohr & Nevin, 1990, p. 44, P3)	Lack of communications infrastructure moderates these relationships. Dyadic partners communicate, but informality and indirectness are characteristic in West African channels regardless of power conditions. Channels members at the same level benefit from shared communication.
Conflict	P20. The higher the uncertainty in the input or output sectors of the task environment of marketing channel dyads, the higher the level of conflict within the dyad. (Achrol et al., 1983, p. 63, P1)	High uncertainty in both sectors observed. Onion and grain producers accuse assemblers of price gouging; onion wholesalers accuse assemblers of restricting market access; grain wholesalers accuse assemblers of adulterating product; onion wholesalers accuse retailers of default on loans in kind.
	P21. If uncertainty in input-output sectors of the environment cannot be absorbed by vertical integration/coordination or "coping" strategies, the level of dysfunctional conflict will escalate and the dyad is likely to move to a "looser" relationship. (Achrol et al., 1983, p. 65, P5)	Regulatory environmental and output-sector uncertainty has frustrated vertical integration in the 20th century. Hard to determine cause and effect of structural relationships longitudinally, but environmental volatility seems to have reinforced "loosening" of relationships.
	P22. In *mutually supportive and trusting climates* (in comparison with unsupportive, distrustful climates), communication has a. higher frequency b. more bidirectional flows c. more informal modes d. more indirect content (Mohr & Nevin, 1990, p. 42, P2)	Intrachannel communications relationships such as between Togolese women or within single ethnic groups relative to cross-channel communications (e.g., between Songhay and Hausa onion dealers) provide support. Infrequent external communication, and secretive information management practices are characteristic, however.

continued

TABLE 4.2

continued

Domain	Proposition	Evidence From Informal Channels Relationships in West Africa
	P23. Within channels systems characterized by high value added downstream, environmental volatility, and low replaceability of suppliers, levels of joint action in the channel relationship will be very high. (Frazier & Kim, 1994, p. 43, P16)	Cooperation between brokers, wholesalers, and retailers is high in livestock, kola, grain, and onion channels. Producers are semireplaceable, not intermediaries. Value added means certainty in clearing the market through steady customers.

economists (Galli, 1981; cf. Joy & Ross, 1989; Speece, 1990). This is unfortunate because so-called informal channels foreground relationships and operate in distinctive cultural contexts that cannot be assimilated to awkward teleologisms such as "cryptocapitalism" (Thorelli & Sentell, 1982), with their unwarranted evolutionary assumptions. In addition, alternative channels are of growing importance not only in the First World (Sherry, 1990) but more critically distribute agricultural products and other items of daily necessity to the bulk of consumers in southern hemisphere nations (MacGaffey, 1991). It is perhaps because they are indigenously organized, creative, and sometimes illegal responses to economic opportunities that the so-called informal sector marketing systems are, by and large, unstudied, unmeasured, and unrecorded by academic marketers. Perhaps as a result of disciplinary parochialism, marketers have tended to ignore the evidence for commercialization, regional and technological specialization, economic diversification, tactical sophistication, and other indicators commonly associated with economic development in West Africa (Kazgan, 1988). As a result of the neglect of West African marketing systems, marketing channels research also largely ignores important work on world systems and regional systems analysis that examines these channels relationships at a macro level, contributing to understanding the effect of macroeconomic constraints on the regional development of marketing channels (Smith, 1976).

Thus, with rare exceptions (Kumcu & Fırat, 1988), marketing in nations of the southern hemisphere has been left to anthropologists, geographers, and other nonmarketers (e.g., Bohannon & Dalton, 1962; Braadbaart, 1994; Collins, 1976; Horne, 1991; Jones, 1972; Lembezat, 1962; MacGaffey, 1991;

Meillassoux, 1971; Saul, 1987; Sherry, 1989; Smith, 1976; Traeger, 1981a, 1981b; Wilcock, 1987; Yusuf, 1975). In contrast to most of the marketing literature that assumes cultural uniformitarianism in marketing systems, the enduring central premise of anthropological studies is that marketing systems are culturally specific, locally adaptive systems in which neither constructs nor meaning are predetermined by the variant general characteristics of markets. Furthermore, the phenomena of personalism as well as those of linkage between economic, institutional, and cultural context in marketplace relationships lie at the core of the contributions of economic anthropologists (Arnould, 1984, 1985, 1986; Belshaw, 1965; Bohannon & Dalton, 1962; Davis, 1973; Geertz, 1963; Mintz, 1961; Sahlins, 1972; Saul, 1987; Traeger, 1981a, 1981b). The best work on marketing in economic anthropology brings together an analysis of external exchange processes and local interpretations of them. As discussed below, this chapter tries to meld data collected within the anthropological and world system paradigms with recent research on marketing channels.

In the next two sections, the environmental stress factors with which West African channels members contend and the forms of channels integration adopted are illustrated. Data are presented germane to the propositions summarized in Table 4.2. The aim is to depict points of similarity and contrast with expectations derived from research on channels relations in the West, primarily North America. Readers familiar with formal sector marketing in North America will also find analogies to market niching, vertical integration, relationship marketing, just-in-time inventory management, and other allegedly modern practices in the behavior of informal sector marketers in West Africa.

Data

This chapter relies extensively on numerous case studies of West African marketing systems and on data concerning the marketing system of the Niger Republic (see Figure 4.2). The latter data were collected at four points in time. The first, most exhaustive effort took place during a 13-month study of 13 regional markets (Figure 4.3) in Zinder département (or province) in 1978-1979. In this study, face-to-face interviews were conducted with nearly 1,500 traders and 800 consumers about their trading and purchasing practices (Arnould, 1985; Arnould & McCullough, 1980).

A second month-long study was conducted in 1983. The aim of this study was to determine how and why markets and traders in neighboring Nigeria were influencing markets for cereals grains and legumes in Niger. In this

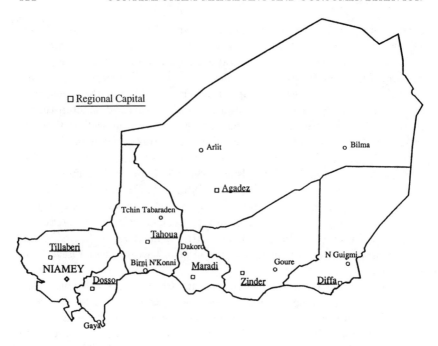

Figure 4.2   Republic of Niger: Major towns.
SOURCE: Charlick (1991).

study, merchants, marketing board officials, and researchers were interviewed in the major market towns of the border regions in north central
Nigeria and south central Niger (Arnould, 1983). In 1987, a third month-
long study sought to determine what effects liberal reform of Niger's parastatal
marketing institutions and changes in marketing policy were having on local
agriculturally based cooperative organizations, especially their financial situations. This study focused on cereals and legumes marketing. Merchants, cooperative members, and marketing board officials were interviewed in the two
south central départements of Niger, Maradi and Zinder (Arnould, 1987).

Finally, in 1992, a 2-month study of the export marketing channels for
one of Niger's emerging agricultural commodities, onions, was conducted.
This study used observation, interviews, and secondary data collection to do
a type of reverse channel mapping (Dayringer, 1983; Nayson, 1993) with
onion marketers and government officials in Niger and five onion-importing
countries in West Africa: Benin, Burkina Faso, Côte d'Ivoire, Ghana, and
Togo (Arnould with Iddal, 1992).

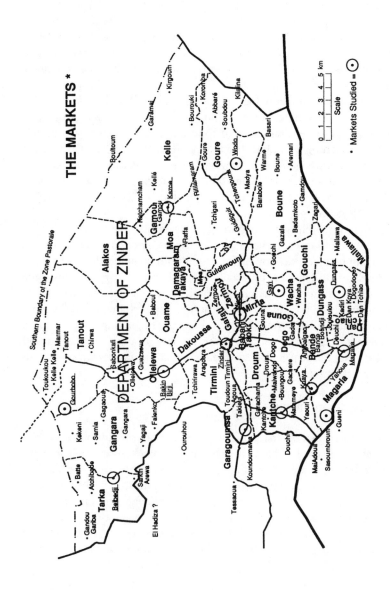

Figure 4.3   Markets of Zinder.

▨ Nature of Environmental Stresses

The marketing literature on marketing channels has recognized the importance of political and economic environments on channels relations (Stern & Reve, 1980), but empirical research is limited and centers on the management of ongoing dyadic channel relationships, and primary task environments rather than on secondary and macroenvironments, and the structure of the channel (Achrol, Reve, & Stern, 1983; Frazier & Kim, 1994; Klein, Frazier, & Roth, 1990). Furthermore, environmental factors have been weakly conceptualized, and most research assumes a Eurocentric channels environment and firm characteristics.

By contrast, recent anthropological studies of Third World market systems wed a macrolevel theoretical orientation building on economic geography and dependency theory (Smith, 1976) to in-depth case studies of channels structure and meaning (Arnould, 1985; McCorkle, 1988; Scott, 1972, 1978; Traeger, 1981b). Anthropologists, however, often neglect the dyadic dimension that is marketers' focus. A few anthropological studies employ both detailed transactional and macroenvironmental data (Cook & Diskin, 1976; Saul, 1987, 1988; Traeger, 1981a).

The present research looks at channels relations as adaptive responses to the distinctive marketing environment of West Africa. The focus of the discussion will be market channels for agricultural commodities. West African channels of distribution especially for agricultural commodities have evolved under conditions of environmental stress. The stresses are of two types recognizable to marketers: volatility (i.e., rapid change) and diversity (i.e., uncertainty; Klein et al., 1990). Preeminent among them is high environmental diversity. The next three sections discuss the nature and impact of stresses in the primary, secondary, and macrotask environments of West African channels.

Primary Task Environments

High environmental diversity refers to the presence of multiple sources of uncertainty. Diversity is evident in the primary market task environment, consisting of channel members, suppliers, and customers. At the wholesale level, this includes the existence of many small suppliers, such as small-scale farmers, and retail customers. For example, throughout West Africa, farmers often sell only enough product to finance weekly consumption needs or to fulfill social obligations (e.g., McCorkle, 1988). The average onion farmer in Niger produces no more than several hundred kilos of onions a season, although some produce much more. In Niger in the late 1970s, 50% of retail market traders in Zinder département's weekly periodic markets carried no more than 15 units in inventory! A typical grain retailer trading in four or five markets in northern Nigeria might handle less than three tons a week (Clough, 1985). Retail onion marketers may handle no more than 100 or 200 kilos of onions in a 2-week period. Small scale and poor capitalization of channels members exaggerate the diversity and complexity of the immediate task environment.

The primary task environment is also characterized by the presence of many potential or actual competitors with high dissimilarity among them. In Burkina Faso and Niger, for example, scores of poorly capitalized local wholesale and retail marketers compete for business in every marketplace (Arnould, 1986; Clough, 1985; Quinn, 1978; Saul, 1987, 1988; Traeger, 1981a). Historically and contemporaneously, the root of this diversity is the fact that channels cross distinct north-south ecological zones that also correspond to areas of distinct ethnic and political adaptations. For example, Tuareg and Fulani herders of goats, sheep, and cattle occupied the northern Sahelian zone, Wogo and Songhay fisherfolk dominated the islands of the Niger river, Diola rice farmers occupied the coastal tidal swamps of lower Senegal, and so forth. Bulk agricultural products (e.g., cowpeas, dates, dried fish, kola nuts, yams, livestock, millet, milk, onions, sorghum, sweet peppers, peanuts, etc.) have long been traded between ethnically distinct groups and across these ecological zones. For example, the Kamberin BeriBeri of Kano monopolized the kola trade in northern Nigeria (Lovejoy, 1973). Ethnic diversity and ethnic specialization increase the complexity of the primary task environment.

Another source of uncertainty is low demand density. This was a problem historically, when most Africans resided in rural areas. Today, with rates of urbanization in the region ranging from 9% to 43% and averaging only 28% (see Table 4.1), low demand density still poses a problem. In addition, the purchasing power of many channels members and both rural and urban consumers remains low (Arnould with Iddal, 1992; Saul, 1988). As Table 4.1 shows, the GNP per capita in the region is only $1 a day, or $363 per year. World Bank-sponsored structural adjustment policies imposed on the majority of West African nations during the 1980s and the 1994 100% devaluation of the West African franc used in eight former French colonies have further weakened consumer purchasing power.

To these problems may be added volatility associated with the variability and instability in the immediate input sector of most marketing channels (Achrol et al., 1983). Dramatic variations in rainfall, irrigation water resources, and pest vectors have long created periodic conditions of scarcity for most regional wholesale marketers. Alternatively, early or bumper har-vests may leave marketers holding devalued stocks, whereas spotty, regional harvests may disadvantage wholesalers without farflung assembly networks (Saul, 1987). In addition, the perishability of many traditional, high-value crops such as kola nuts and dried fish, that ill support long trips in hot, dusty conditions is high. Onions, mangos, tomatoes, and other modern cash crops remain vulnerable to spoilage due to limited economic viability and avail-ability to small-scale producers and wholesalers alike of improved packing and storing technologies. The dangers are great. In anticipation of seasonal price rises, one inexpert Nigerien wholesaler recently lost millions of francs while storing onions in inadequate facilities. Maintaining adequate storage conditions (e.g., a cold chain) across long, empty, nonelectrified distances is not simple. Variability and instability in the input sector accentuate volatility in marketing channels.

Secondary Task Environment:
Institutional Constraints on Channels Development

Channels members contend with a number of serious sources of uncer-tainty that emanate from the secondary task environment, consisting of regulatory agents and "interest aggregators" (Achrol et al., 1983, p. 57). Historical studies of African channels provide numerous examples of inten-tional disruption of preexisting channels relationships by the colonial authori-ties. For example, French colonial authorities overcame local resistance to destroy the lively trans-Saharan trade in order to export agricultural com-modities such as peanuts and cotton to France through Atlantic ports in their coastal colonies (Baier, 1974; Suret-Canale, 1977). The British effort to replace Nigerian market women with male channels intermediaries beholden to the colonial authorities resulted in major riots in the early part of the century (Leith-Ross, 1965). Other studies of channels during the early postindependence period (after 1960) show how changes in government policy, especially the panregional experiment with public marketing boards, seriously disrupted the activities and success of many independent commodi-ties producers and traders (CILSS, 1977; Collins, 1976; Grégoire, 1986; Williams, 1985). Governmental meddling in the grain trade is widely recog-nized as a contributing factor in the West African famine of the early 1970s (Franke & Chasin, 1980). Even today, despite an utter lack of expertise, the Nigerien government toys with the idea of public intervention in onion export marketing. One enduring legacy of this period is a climate of suspicion between the public and private sectors.

Today, a general climate of regulatory uncertainty constrains the extension of channels in space and the delivery of goods and services at reasonable prices to African consumers (especially rural consumers). Three common assumptions about the private sector often emerge in discussions with regulatory officials, although they are no longer part of official policy in countries of the West African Economic Community (ECOWAS). The first assumption is that the private sector, especially the informal private sector, consists of parasitic intermediaries who exploit the farmer and the consumer (Arnould, 1986; Williams, 1985). There is little popular understanding of the important functions, detailed in any undergraduate marketing text, carried out by channels intermediaries. The second assumption is that the private sector is collusive and oligopolistic (e.g., Shenton & Lennihan, 1981). Of the evidence for collusion in the trade in certain key commodities such as grain, kola, and livestock, there can be little doubt, but as suggested below, cooperation among channel members at a given level in the channel is a realistic risk reduction strategy. The evidence for oligopoly is mixed, with some support in some lines of business at some points in time (Baier, 1974, 1977; Shenton & Lennihan, 1981). However, enduring marketing dynasties are the exception in West African marketing channels. Finally, the third assumption is that private businesses obtain supernormal profits. The persistence of secretive, ethnodominated trading diaspora (Cohen, 1971; Curtin, 1971; Lovejoy, 1973; Speece, 1990) and the association between ethnicity and commercial specialization contribute to governmental suspicion of trading activities. A study of the profit margins of small-scale traders in Zinder in 1978-1979 revealed wide ranges of profitability on goods sold but average margins of less than 15% (Arnould, 1986). One small-scale grain wholesaler in northern Nigeria reportedly earned an average profit of 12% (Clough, 1985, p. 25). A recent study of profitability in the Nigerien onion trade paralleled these results (Arnould with Iddal, 1992; see Tables 4.3 and 4.4). Other studies have found that larger wholesalers may earn great short-term profits, but most traders earn modest amounts, and profitability is volatile (Grégoire, 1986; Nypan, 1960; Saul, 1987).

The three popular perceptions of conflicts of interest between the public and private sectors translate into frequent shifts in economic policy and a climate of insecurity and unreasonable scrutiny of informal sector economic operators. That is, there is manifest conflict between regulators and marketing channels members (Frazier et al., 1989). Personal, vehicle, import, export, and customs documents require numerous official stamps, signatures, and guarantees. Furthermore, without warning, the legality of exporting or importing various goods may change from year to year as may the conditions

TABLE 4.3

Variable Costs and Profitability of Niger Onion Export Marketing
(CFA Francs, $1.00 = 250 FCFA)

Destination	Niamey, Niger	Lomé, Togo	Malanville, Benin	Cotonou, Benin	Abidjan, Côte d'Ivoire	Abidjan, Côte d'Ivoire	Abidjan, Côte d'Ivoire	Ouagadougou, Burkina Faso	Cotonou, Benin	Accra, Ghana
Purchase price	9,000	8,000	7,000	6,000	2,000	2,500	8,000	8,000	3,500	8,000
Cost price c.i.f.	13,440	16,555	9,670	10,350	8,470	4,239	12,951	13,010	7,871	15,943
7% Loss	941	1,159	677	725	592.9	297	907	911	551	1,116
Cost price	14,381	17,714	10,347	11,075	9,062.9	4,536	13,858	13,921	8,422	17,060
Asking price	15,000	20,000	15,000	12,000	10,000	11,113	14,000	12,000	9,000	17,646
Margin	619	2,286	4,653	926	937.1	6,577	142	−1921	578	586
Margin % cost	4.31	12.91	44.97	8.36	10.34	145.02	1.02	−13.80	6.86	3.44

SOURCE: Table compiled from Arnould with Iddal (1992).

under which they may be marketed. Furthermore, central governments may
sometimes encourage exports, but local agents may still impose informal
charges on would-be exporters (Arnould, 1987; Arnould with Iddal, 1992;
Collins, 1976). For example, 1983 to 1984 witnessed acute disruptions in the
grain market in Burkina Faso due to political upheavals. After a series of
coups, a new revolutionary government took power and promptly issued a
string of edicts aimed at tight control of grain markets, prices, and merchants.
The government also created a nationwide youth brigade to enforce these
edicts. These measures halted or drove underground much of Burkina's
private sector grain trade for a period of months (McCorkle, 1988). Similar
measures taken in Niger on occasion throughout the 1970s and 1980s also
drove private sector trade underground. To take another example, in 1987,
agricultural cooperatives in Niger were formally authorized to export cowpeas to Nigeria, a function formerly monopolized by a public marketing
board. However, local officials disrupted cooperatives' access to funds and
export licenses (Arnould, 1987); cooperative members have been frustrated
by such intervention and in many cases abandoned joint commercial efforts
(see Table 4.2, Propositions 12, 13, & 21). Finally, in the recent past, several

TABLE 4.4

Returns to Onion Marketing, Niamey, Niger, August 1992

Katako Wholesale Market		*Petit Marche Retail Market*		
Average purchase price	7,750	Wholesale price	10,000	
Arranged tax	100	Carting		150
Intermediary	100	Market taxes		
Packing	350	@ 100 F/day	200	
Loading	100			
FOB Galmi	8,400	5% Loss		589.5
Cost price	10,939.5			
Transport	1,000			
Informal taxes	32	Revenues 120 kg		
Unloading	50	@ 100 F/kg		12,000
Miscellaneous	50			
Market taxes	10	Retail margin		1,210.5
CIF Niamey	9,542	Margin % cost		11.07
Sale price	10,000			
Wholesale margin	458			
Margin % cost	3.75			

SOURCE: Table compiled from Arnould with Iddal (1992).

countries such as Burkina Faso and Côte d'Ivoire have imposed onerous "transit fees" on imported produce (Arnould with Iddal, 1992). Such cases illustrate how government capriciously represses the private sector.

Export charges may vary significantly depending on the whims of regulatory agents. For instance, one onion trader interviewed in 1992 in Ouagadougou, the capital of Burkina Faso, claimed that duties on 15 tons of onions had varied in the recent past from $120 to $600, these amounts changing with shifts in regulatory policy and traders negotiating abilities. Furthermore, economic operators may be subject to investigation and, in theory, considerable fines may be levied for minor infractions of commercial codes.

Confusing and inconsistent regulatory requirements provide ample opportunity for blockage of private sector initiatives and illicit rent seeking. Punctilious agents can always find some irregularity in documentation if it suits their purposes and collect bribes to look the other way. Thus bribes collected on onions purchased for $4,500 in the interior of Niger and transported from the wholesale market to the Niger-Burkinabé border (600 kms) run about $200, or 4% of the value. According to one large trader, bribes on 15 tons of onions shipped between producing points in Niger and retail sales outlets in Ouagadougou amount to between $300 and $400, or 8% of the value. Bribery or rent seeking by customs agents, gendarmes, or the police tends to be rationalized in terms of the allegedly exorbitant profits earned by traders. This rationalization is reinforced by the defensive actions taken by traders to disguise and protect their earnings, such as avoiding obtaining necessary export licenses, registering exports under the names of lieutenants to avoid volume-based export fees, and so on. Marketers in Abidjan, capital of Côte d'Ivoire, and Lomé, capital of Togo, complained that bribes totaled $1,500 on 30-ton shipments of onions, or 16% of the value of the goods. Indeed, these bribes are the chief complaint of participants in the regional onion marketing channel (see Table 4.2, Proposition 17).

Refusal to pay bribes can be costly. A truck and its contents were burned at the border between Benin and Togo under mysterious circumstances when the driver working for one onion trader in Lomé refused to pay. This represented a loss of goods worth between $12,000 and $18,000 to the onion trader, an amount that would be catastrophic to all but the largest market players (Arnould with Iddal, 1992). Hence in an uncertain effort to reduce unnecessary delays and scrutiny, marketers often collude in bribery (see Table 4.2, Propositions 4, 12, & 13).

Traders and the national treasuries of the nations concerned by the interregional commerce suffer from the effects of rent-seeking by agents of the state. Rent-seeking and the transaction costs of evasion have a number of pernicious effects on West African channels costs. Because of rent-seeking, marketers seek to avoid obtaining licenses and otherwise registering their activities with public authorities. Rent-seeking and evasion raise transaction costs that motivate marketers to suppress the prices they are willing to pay to producers. High transaction costs limit Nigerien onion traders' ability to compete against European onions imported by Lebanese marketing firms in the Côte d'Ivoire (Arnould with Iddal, 1992; see Table 4.2, Proposition 13). Furthermore, consumers face higher prices than they would ordinarily. The formal economy is compelled to pay for the effects of the informal economy when, as with the cereals markets in Mali and Niger, collusive buying at bargain prices harvest results in nutritional insecurity prior to the next harvest (Arnould, 1983, 1987). Also, rent-seeking discourages marketers from undertaking investments in extending channels to consumers who are currently ill-served. It discourages them from undertaking investments in improved technologies of storage and processing that would call attention to their apparent wealth (see Table 4.2, Proposition 12).

Rent-seeking and other arrangements imposed by agents of the state on marketers, such as underweighing or undercounting of exports or outright failure to regulate cross-border flows of goods, robs national treasuries of large amounts of revenue. For example,

> in 1980 four-fifths of cocoa production was smuggled from the Volta region of Ghana to Togo . . . and in the seventies and early eighties smugglers exported 12-15% of Ghanaian gold and diamond production. . . . In 1985, the smuggling trade accounted for export of two-thirds of Senegal's peanut crop to Gambia. . . . In Sierra Leone, diamond smuggling exports an estimated two-thirds of annual production. (MacGaffey, 1991, p.16)

Peanuts were long smuggled into Niger from neighboring Nigeria because of the attractions of artificially high prices and the interest of producers in obtaining hard currency in Niger (CFA francs as opposed to Nigerian shillings and, later, naira; Collins, 1976). There is even some recent evidence for onion smuggling from Nigeria into Niger. Not only do governments fail to collect duties on all these goods, but of course, unofficial taxes (i.e., bribes) do not pay for the social services (education, health care, and retirement pensions) that West African governments struggle to provide.

Besides the above regulatory constraints, there are a number of institutional economic barriers to the evolution of West African channels. Currently, the banking system in a number of countries is in some disarray. In Niger, for example, the Nigerien National Development Bank (BDRN) defaulted in the late 1980s, the infamous BCCI came and went, and the French-owned International Bank for West Africa (BIAO), has been in a state of chronic "reorganization." With the default of the BDRN, the resources of the parastatal marketing boards disappeared along with the accounts of many of the wealthiest merchants, civil servants, and ordinary citizens. Thousands of agricultural cooperatives that were supposed to have savings accounts managed for them by the BDRN never saw any of their money either. The clouded relations between the banking sector and the commercial sector makes participants in lucrative marketing activities uncertain about placing assets with the banks. Furthermore, the lack of international transfer relationships between banks in neighboring West African countries makes it very difficult for marketers to transfer funds between nations, often forcing them to travel on an insecure highway system carrying large sums of cash. Some onion marketers complained of these dangers.

The instability of the banks together with the unwillingness or inability of most small-scale traders to register and formalize their status with the authorities means that most small-scale traders, would-be entrepreneurs, and even some of the large wholesalers avoid or have been excluded from use of commercial banks. For example, members of the loose cartel of Togolese women who control the Nigerien onion trade cannot obtain bank credits because they are not incorporated. As a result, many marketers active in the Nigerien onion trade complain that the lack of access to capital constrains the expansion of their activities.

Besides problems in the banking sector, no informal sector marketers have access to insurance that would shield them from loss of shipped product. Although total loss of shipments is unusual, it does occur. Such a loss would spell bankruptcy for most traders. The threat of unsecured loss heightens traders' perceived risk, adding to disincentives for expanded trade.

Macro Environment

In marketing parlance, "the macro environment is comprised of general social, economic, political and technological forces which impinge on the activities in the primary and secondary task environment" (Achrol et al., 1983, p. 57). Understanding these factors is critical to understanding channels relationships as much in West Africa as anywhere.

West African marketers have historically faced macroenvironmental uncertainty imposed by the long distances they must traverse to accumulate supplies of key commodities, to reach sufficient consumers to be profitable, or to tap export markets in distant North African or sub-Saharan nations. In the past, as even today, things cannot easily get from point A to point B. For example, it is 1,500 miles from Kano, an important trading city in northern Nigeria to Tripoli, an historic terminus of the trans-Sahara caravan routes on the Mediterranean coast and 1,700 miles from Kano to Dakar, Senegal on the Atlantic coast. Onion traders in central Niger must transport goods to coastal markets, the closest of which is 900 miles away, the most distant 1,200.

It is widely recognized that without transport development the rationalization of market centers is impeded (Porter, 1993). In West Africa, not only is it far between important wholesale markets, but the conditions of travel are onerous. West Africa is hot much of the time, and the climate varies from wet and very muddy to very dry and very dusty, conditions unfavorable to the transport of perishable agricultural goods. Hot, humid conditions in coastal consuming countries are one of the key risk factors faced by importers of Nigerien onions because, given their high moisture content, these onions spoil quickly under such conditions. Most national highways were not paved until the 1970s, and most secondary roads in West Africa are still unpaved. Roads within some 50 miles of national borders also often remain unpaved due to the political suspicion that characterizes many regimes. Most producers of agricultural commodities do not live near paved roads, and as distance from producing areas to paved roads increases, their degree of underpayment for food and cash crops increase (Arnould, 1987; Arnould with Iddal, 1992). Still, despite improvements in communication infrastructure in the 1970s, it is easier to telephone European capitals from the interior of West Africa than to place calls between the market towns of the interior of each West African country.

The macro environment of West African channels is also volatile. The problem of political borders and relationships was a serious one in precolonial times; over long distances, merchants always traveled in armed caravans (Baier, 1977; Hopkins, 1973; Lovejoy, 1973). The risk of robbery was great even when protection money was paid to local authorities. Such caravans persisted until World War II (Clough, 1985). In recent years, armed robbery has resurfaced in Benin, Côte d'Ivoire, and Nigeria, engendered by persistent political and ethnic unrest and negative economic growth. One response in Côte d'Ivoire, compelling traders to travel in convoys, adds significantly to their variable costs.

Like the coups and countercoups of the 1960s and 1970s, the recent democracy movement in West Africa has perturbed markets in countries such as Togo where the transition has been marked by political violence. It has also been accompanied in many countries (Benin, Mali, Niger, and Togo) by the nonpayment of civil servants' salaries. Nonpayment has tended to increase rent-seeking behavior among regulatory agents. Heightened suspicion and scrutiny of marketers, even physical violence, has often accompanied political turbulence, as occurred in northern Nigeria in the mid-1980s (Lubeck, 1987).

In precolonial times, diversity in the macro environment was exacerbated by the absence of a general purpose currency (a general purpose currency can be used for exchange, accounting, savings, payment, etc.), let alone a common currency. Today, currency differences, the weakness of some like the Nigerian naira, Ghanaian cedi, and the (artificial) strength of others such as the CFA franc, have created exchange and exchange control problems for many marketers and governmental regulators. Sometimes, Nigerien onion marketers have been unable to repatriate their profits from Ghana, compelling them to reinvest in goods obtained locally and back-haul them to Niger. Also, the overvaluation of the CFA franc used in a dozen former French colonies in West Africa against the Nigerian naira and the Ghanaian cedi (not to mention other world currencies) disadvantages franc zone exports against imports from weaker-currency nations such as Ghana and Nigeria.

Ethnic diversity linked to the exploitation of specific ecological niches is characteristic of West Africa and exacerbates macroenvironmental diversity. Boundaries between ethnic groups were and are maintained by varying religious (animist vs. Muslim), kinship (patrilineal vs. matrilineal), and political (acephalous vs. hierarchical) cleavages. Extraordinary linguistic diversity among actual and potential channels members is also a factor. Related to this, but a separate stress factor is the problem of illiteracy and innumeracy. As shown in Table 4.1, literacy in international languages currently averages only 21% in West Africa generally. This factor significantly complicates accountancy not only procedurally but in the aggregate as well. Obviously, it is hard to keep track of many deals in any one person's head. Ethnic and linguistic diversity fosters the exchange of complementary products across ethnic boundaries, but raises the risks of conflict between members of different ethnic groups. Maintaining the market peace was one traditional measure of political authority; interethnic suspicion persists, and occasional armed confrontations still occur in more remote markets.

There are also cultural particularities that constitute barriers to the evolution of African channels relationships toward those characteristic of Western-style, marketing-oriented firms. A pervasive mercantilist model of economic behavior stems from indigenous practice in the era of the trans-Sahara caravan trade. It was reinforced by the trading policies of French and English as well as Lebanese firms during the colonial period and by policies pursued by the governments in the 1960s and 1970s (Baier, 1974, 1977; Grégoire, 1986). That is to say, most successful marketers speculate in price futures and invest only in agriculture, trade, real estate, and transport but only exceptionally in industrial production.

Not surprising, analysis suggests that many West African marketers operate their businesses with different goals in mind than do Western firms. For example, among the Hausa traders of south-central Niger and northern Nigeria, profit (Hausa, *riba*) is made and spent in a particular sociocultural context which influences the meaning of the term. Typically, the purpose and use of *riba* is the maintenance and expansion of the marketers' household. Under this household mode of capital accumulation, marketers still make a profit as a balance of revenue over costs and use it to trade, buy farms, and employ wage labor. But Hausa marketers' main use of profit from commerce is in the maintenance, stabilization, and enlargement of polygynous (i.e., multiwife) households through marriage, procreation, the contracting of strategic marriages for their dependent children, and fostering close relations with their affines. They do this for reasons that are both economic and noneconomic. In fact, when questioned about their motives for becoming involved in marketing activities, almost 20% of marketplace traders in Zinder simply referred to social rather than profit motives. Household accumulation is consistent with elements of capital accumulation: profit in the accounting sense. However, the social purposes of these activities are not capitalist. This conjunction is the pervasive feature of Hausa economic life. Money profits serve kin and household values rather than social arrangements being designed to facilitate the accumulation of money values (Clough, 1985, pp. 31-32; Kirk-Greene, 1974).

Thus, although profit is surely very important to Hausa merchants in Niger, the surest form and guarantee of wealth lies in the development of extensive personalized networks of kinsfolk and clients. Indeed, when questioned about motive, only 20% of the 1,500+ Hausa-speaking traders interviewed in 1978-1979 in Zinder specifically mentioned profit as their primary motive. An enduring heritage of the emphasis on relationship equity in channels relationships, one reinforced by Islamic beliefs, is that personal worth (i.e., goodness) and wealth are measured as much in terms of political and social control over people—wives, children, and dependents (Hausa, *arzikin mutane*)—as in control over capital (Hausa, *arzikin kud'i*; Grégoire, 1986, p. 181). In Muslim Africa generally, many wives and children are a sign of a man's prosperity, not an onerous responsibility.

Wealth is realized through redistributive generosity; mere possession is de-emphasized in allocating social status (Kirk-Greene, 1974). Large-scale social gestures are common and may even take a rivalrous form between wealthy merchants. Gifts of social infrastructure such as clinics and the construction of religious monuments in the form of huge mosques costing millions of dollars rather than investment in industrial plant and equipment is an enduring legacy of many of West Africa's richest entrepreneurs (Grégoire, 1986). The benefit of such largesse is the creation of enduring reciprocal relations of dependence between wealthier marketers and far-flung networks of smaller-scale commercial operators. On the macrolevel, the cost of such values is that it is very difficult for wealthy traders to create enduring corporations, and on the microlevel to resist making even questionable loans to clamorous kinsfolk and clients, thereby dispersing capital, sometimes with negative results (Yusuf, 1975).

Islam was mentioned at several points in the foregoing paragraphs. Historical research shows that adherence to this faith provided a common cultural frame of reference for marketers in the precolonial period. Indeed, the spread of commerce and of Islam from Arab North Africa to sub-Saharan

Africa were contemporaneous (Hopkins, 1973). In West Africa today, all prominent merchants are referred to by the honorific *al hadji*, the Arabic term for those who have accomplished the pilgrimage to Mecca. The honorific is used in reference to prominent merchants regardless of the facts of their religious biographies. But the association between commerce and piety is not coincidental as merchants must rely on others' adherence to specific commercial norms encoded in the Koran, such as the prohibition on usury, as well as more general norms of interpersonal conduct for the smooth handling of affairs given the informal nature of contracts. For example, one onion merchant encountered in Kumassi, Ghana, complaining about tardy repayment on stocks advanced to retailers, said that pious persons could be expected to repay their loans speedily.

The above review of the primary, secondary, and macrotask environments is indicative of the unique context in which marketing channels develop in West Africa. The marketing environment is diverse and volatile; because there are multiple sources of diversity in the environment, commerce is fraught with risk. Marketers must contend with a volatile regulatory environment and unstable economic institutions like banks and marketing boards. Finally, there are a number of cultural particularities that impact the form of marketing channels. I now turn to a discussion of the nature of channels integration in West Africa with special reference to structure, power, and conflict. Where appropriate, reference is made to specific propositions enumerated in Table 4.2.

▧ Nature of African Channels Relationships

The first point to be made about West African channels both historically and contemporaneously is that many are lengthy, intensive, and extensive. This was true historically. For centuries, salt has been mined near Bilma in northeastern Niger and transported all over West Africa by Tuareg camel caravanners (Hopkins, 1973). Most of the ostrich feathers that decorated bourgeois ladies' hats in the Victorian era came across the desert from sub-Saharan Africa (Lovejoy & Baier, 1975). Today, Niger's onion marketers export onions grown in Tahoua département (see Figure 4.2) to consumer markets in Lomé (Togo), Cotonou (Benin), Abidjan (Côte d'Ivoire), and Accra (Ghana), each a thousand miles or more away (Arnould with Iddal, 1992; Lev & Gadbois, 1988; Mahamadou, 1987).

Not only are West African channels extended in space, they are sometimes relatively intensive as well (Saul, 1987). In some countries, where formal channels have stagnated, like Zaire, these informal sector channels are all that separate the mass of people from a state of autarky and material deprivation (Horne, 1991; MacGaffey, 1991). My studies of Zinder département (Niger) show that a relatively dense network of over 70 local market-places (Figure 4.3) has emerged since 1900 between which there are important trading links. These markets have evolved from a classic colonial dendritic spatial pattern designed merely to extract raw materials for export (Smith, 1976; Speece, 1990) into a relatively hierarchical central place arrangement, with the provincial capital at the top, numerous ephemeral periodic, retail marketplaces at the bottom, and an array of marketplaces in between. Further market channels can deliver products of primary necessity, such as cereals grains, with relative efficiency. This is suggested by a comparison of the relationships between annual price movements for millet in markets in Zinder département. Figure 4.4 shows that prices for grain are highly correlated between most pairs of markets in the département (Arnould, 1985, 1986; Arnould & McCullough, 1980).

Finally, and contrary to what has sometimes been said about channels development and economic development generally, these channels are often lengthy in the more formal terms of number of channel intermediaries (cf. Olsen & Granzin, 1990). For example, regional grain marketing often involves producer-sellers, rural assembly agents, intraregional wholesalers, private wholesale channels captains located in regional market centers such as Kano (Nigeria), Maradi (Niger), or Ouagadougou (Burkina Faso), and marketing parastatals (Arnould, 1987; Clough, 1985; Elz & Hoisington, 1986; Kohler, 1977; Saul, 1987). At the retail level, add small wholesale dealers and retailers (Arnould, 1983; Clough, 1985; Saul, 1987). Nigerien onions export channels have a length of 5 or 6, including producer-sellers, bulking agents, transporters, large wholesalers, small wholesalers, and retailers (Arnould with Iddal, 1992; Mahamadou, 1987).

Channels Integration

Given the environmental stresses enumerated above, by what mechanism are West African channels maintained and integrated? Organizational theorists have offered a useful, relatively simple theory to provide some suggestions about what to expect. This theory posits three likely forms of organizational integration arising under varying levels of transaction costs. According to these theorists, as environmental diversity and volatility increase, goal incongruence and opportunism between participants in a marketing system will likewise tend to increase, making measurement of participants' performance

	Bakin, Birji	Belbedji	Birnin, Kazoe	Dungas	Gayi	Goun-doumawa	Gourbobo	Koaya	Magaria	Matameye	Mirria	Sassoum-broum	Wodo	Zinder
Bakin, Birji														
Belbedji	.83													
Birnin, Kazoe	.72	.40												
Dungas	.95	.85	.74											
Gayi	.82	.73	.56	.75										
Goundoumawa	.83	.73	.67	.90	.76									
Gourbobo	.76	.59	.80	.81	.35	.78								
Koaya	.97	.80	.78	.97	.82	.92	.76							
Magaria	.95	.75	.77	.93	.66	.81	.92	.93						
Matameye	.91	.60	.85	.88	.82	.81	.79	.94	.92					
Mirria	.95	.77	.73	.91	.78	.79	.87	.91	.97	.91				
Sassoumbroum	.90	.76	.79	.97.	.71	.85	.86	.95	.93	.90	.88			
Wodo	.92	.88	.57	.95	.57	.78	.91	.89	.90	.74	.87	.95		
Zinder	.92	.84	.70	.95	.63	.87	.85	.92	.95	.88	.94	.92	.88	
Mean	.96	.81	.77	.98	.79	.88	.85	.98	.96	.94	.96	.97	.91	.97

Figure 4.4 Price correlations between Zinder markets for millet (Pearson's r statistic).

SOURCE: Figure compiled from Arnould and McCullough (1980).

more ambiguous. These factors increase transaction costs. The significance of this theory is that it implies that mechanisms governing exchange relationships will vary, depending on prevailing transaction costs. Obviously, other factors, such as those mentioned in the preceding sections on the marketing environment, may also increase transaction costs. Market mechanisms for controlling exchanges between channels partners can be regulated by price mechanisms efficiently only where performance ambiguity is relatively low and goal incongruence between participants is high and when cost and price related information circulates relatively freely. By contrast, where exchange relationships are subject to considerable informational ambiguity, where performance ambiguity is high as a result of environmental diversity and volatility, "clan"-based modes of interorganizational control may prevail. Where goal incongruence and performance ambiguity are relatively high, bureaucracies will prevail.

In most marketing systems, some combination of the three mechanisms for mediating interorganizational exchanges is likely to prevail. In the First World, obviously, market mechanisms prevail. But in West Africa, markets often "fail" because of exceptionally high transaction costs associated with environmental uncertainty and volatility. Hence clan mechanisms may be expected to prevail.

Of course, organizational theorists do not use the term clan the way anthropologists would use it to refer to a specific type of lineage-based kinship organization. For organizational theorists, clan-based modes of market regulation refer to systems that rely on tacit, cultural knowledge to regulate many transactions. That is, they rely on traditions rather than prices to create an implicit philosophy or point of view about how organizational relationships should work and, especially, what constitutes equity in exchange. Such systems depend on the relatively time-consuming mechanisms of socialization of participants to a general worldview and system of values and beliefs that yields a common orientation toward equity. In clan-based systems rewards are distributed according to non-performance-based criteria that rely on shared beliefs in the long-term equity of the system. Although clan-based organizations are inefficient in cost accounting terms, they are efficient under conditions of high ambiguity and are remarkably adaptive within uncertain environments because participants draw on a set of shared assumptions to derive solutions to novel problems (Ouchi, 1980; Wilkins & Ouchi, 1983).

The multiplicity of non-price-based mechanisms employed to achieve channels integration in West African channels is evident to anyone with more than a passing acquaintance with these systems. To grasp the nature of these systems, it is first important to get a sense of the context of these channels networks and commercial transactions. This context is the weekly market. Specialized traders coming from slightly overlapping areas in a given market region meet at the weekly markets to share price, demand, and supply information with each other. In every periodic, Sahelian marketplace, for example, marketers can be found sitting among groups of friends on top of or beside their livestock or their sacks of millet, yams, kola, onions, cassava, or groundnuts, adjusting and readjusting the folds in their robes. They joke, talk politics, pray, and arrange the potential sale of commodities. Much of this activity is aimed at forging links of trust through friendly discussion and communal Muslim prayer (Clough, 1985; see Table 4.2, Propositions 7 & 19).

Cultural Diaspora

African marketers mobilize several specific strategies to cope with political uncertainty and to integrate channels across political, ethnic, and linguistic boundaries. The most dramatic strategy is the ethnic trading diaspora (Cohen, 1971). In this traditional strategy, marketers establish small communities with a shared ethnic identity at important nodes in the physical channel. These ethnic communities provide their members with security. Traveling members find free lodging and warehousing with their colleagues. Product, packing, transport, and marketing knowledge is shared on a regular basis and is passed down through kin-based channels as part of the ordinary socialization process of young people (see Table 4.2, Proposition 6 & 7). Hausa traders used this technique to manage the important north-south trade in beef cattle in Nigeria (Cohen, 1971). The Diakhanke dominated trade in the headwaters region of the Niger, Gambia, and Senegal rivers (Curtin, 1971) as did the Jellaba Arabs in the southern Sudan (Manger, 1984; Speece, 1990). The Kamberin Beriberi of Kano, Nigeria employed this technique to monopolize the lucrative trade in kola nuts for 100 years. Kamberin communities were established in towns near the kola-producing areas in Kumasi (Ghana) and near Bouake (Côte d'Ivoire) as well as in the important entrepôt of Kano (Nigeria). The latter city was the gateway to the trans-Saharan caravan routes (Lovejoy, 1973).

Today, the stressful macroenvironmental uncertainty that favored the extreme form of clan organization represented by ethnic trading diaspora has eased. Nevertheless, because environmental uncertainty and volatility remain high, there is a tendency for particular channels in West Africa to assume culturally familiar ethnodominated forms. The dramatic growth in Nigerien onion marketing dates only from the mid-1970s. Nonetheless, the

Ivoirian trade is dominated by Hausa speakers, and there are parallel Hausa-and Songhay-dominated channels for onion marketing in key Ghanaian market towns. Onion production and marketing in northeastern Ghana is dominated by Hausa-speaking emigrants to the Bawku region (see Table 4.2, Propositions 1, 8, & 9).

Gender-Dominated Channels

Gender dominance is another widespread mode for organizing West African marketing channels. For example, Mfantse women dominate fish marketing around Cape Coast, Ghana (Quinn 1978). The famous "Mama Benz" dominate the private sector in the small nation of Togo, and their sisters in neighboring Benin are also aggressive marketers. In both of these nations, the trade in Nigerien onions is monopolized by small, loose cartels of women, whose business dealings may run to hundreds of thousands of dollars. Young women who are apt may expect to inherit the trade from their senior female relatives.

The mechanics of the trade are as follows: Older women station a sister or daughter at a rented home in Nigerien bulking markets like Galmi or Arewa in the onion-producing zone for periods of several weeks where they act as bulking agents. These women marketers work closely with local male market captains (*sarkin tasha*) to obtain stocks, control quality, and ensure timely shipment, reminding one of the quality teams touted by Western manufacturers. Their mothers and sisters, resident in the commercial capitals of Lomé in Togo or Cotonou in Benin, advance them money, keep them informed of market conditions in the capitals, and receive shipments of onions for bulk breaking and wholesaling (Arnould with Iddal, 1992). In Lomé, the 8 to 10 major women wholesalers operate out of two or three main wholesale points and send up to 20 women on buying trips to Niger. These relatively small numbers are indicative of their close control over the trade (see Table 4.2, Propositions 7, 10, & 11).

Up- and Downstream Partnering

Along with ethnic trading diaspora and gender-based integration strategies, marketers engage in considerable up- and downstream partnering. These channels relationships take a wide variety of forms. In the precolonial period, successful traders often held some of their representatives (Hausa, Arabic, *wakili*) in distant market towns in personal bondage (Baier, 1974; Lovejoy & Baier, 1975; Salifou, 1972). This helped ensure their fidelity. Nowadays, traders in agricultural commodities strive to maintain steady relationships with dispersed networks of suppliers even when they are not immediately profitable, as steady supplies depend on them (Saul, 1987; Traeger, 1981a). For example, in Burkina Faso,

> a grain merchant may travel widely in the post-harvest period and spend a lot of time in producing zones to coordinate buying activity. Success largely depends, however, especially for the larger merchants who operate in a wide geographic area, on a system of collecting agents. . . . There are various types of grain collecting agents employed by merchants. Some may be [village] residents who receive large funds from the merchant during the post-harvest period to acquire grain in the areas in which they live. There is a second type of agent on whom merchants rely even more importantly for the collection of grain. These are usually young people residing in the large cities, very often living with the merchant himself. They travel widely in rural areas and purchase grain for their employer in rural markets from farmers and from independent small traders, and may also coordinate the resident buyers who work for their master. They are rewarded with a commission on the volume they collect, but sometimes they are related to the merchant by a kinship or quasi-kinship tie, in which case the relationship is based less on immediate rewards and more on long-term obligations [as per Wilkins & Ouchi, 1983]. Ethnic ties are sometimes important in establishing such links, but collaboration across ethnic lines is also widespread. The association between merchant and especially agents linked by kinship often continues for several years and sometimes results in the merchant setting up his former employee as an independent trader by providing him with capital and even a wife. (Saul, 1988, pp. 90-92; Reprinted with permission)

Similar networks are found in the yam trade in southern Nigeria (Traeger, 1981a) where they take the form of "good customer" (Yoruba, *onibara*) relationships. To take another example, in onion marketing channels, five or six persons will work as collector/intermediaries under the direction of a head. These collectors are often popular and must be well-connected persons. Their functions are to find buyers, broker information, collect product from a number of regular producers often in different villages, mediate between buyers and sellers, and fix prices with buyers. Such networks help marketers cope with the quasi-absence of public channels for marketing information and the extreme volatility in produce market environments that are subject to dramatic seasonal swings in prices and supplies. On the positive side, extended networks of trade partners allow wholesale channels captains to extend their reach far into the hinterland to obtain supplies or identify markets on a low-cost basis. Togolese onion traders' close control over the channel allows them to regulate the quantities of onions imported so as to avoid glutting the market and price discounting. One Lomé-based channel captain says the wholesalers can handle 300 to 360 tons a month, but more than that causes prices to fall.

Today, market networks organized through patron-client (Hausa, *uban gida-yaro*) and patron-apprentice (Hausa, *uban gida-bara*) relationships are ubiquitous in Hausa-speaking areas (Baier, 1977; Saul, 1987). Many if not most Hausa marketers get their start as unpaid apprentices whose responsibilities and remuneration increase with demonstrated skill in business (Arnould, 1986; Grégoire, 1986; Saul, 1987). As soon as an individual is linked to another by a commercial obligation, he becomes *yaro* to the other. If the relationship becomes one of all-purpose subordination, the *yaro* becomes a *bara*. Although there is dissymmetry in the relationship insofar as the *bara* is at the *uban gida's* beck and call, there is also an exchange of protection provided by the latter to the former. The patron exploits the labor time of the client-trader, for the client spends much time buying, storing, and selling for his patron, but in return, he may receive interest-free trading loans (*jali*). Thus accumulation is based on a "multiplex" relation, in which the superior purchases the all-purpose labor time of the inferior with many types of "help"—household security for the inferior and his family, farmland, and commercial credit (Clough, 1985, p. 17). With commercial successes over a period of years, clients (*barori*) receive all sorts of regular favors (*alheri*) from their patrons, including long-term interest-free loans (*jalli*), advances of commercial goods, aid in paying the costs of marriage, and so on (Grégoire, 1986, p. 183). Loyal and successful clients may even expect their patrons to help them set up their own autonomous business; indeed, belief in this possibility is part of the glue that maintains the relationship (see Table 4.2, Propositions 10, 11, & 18).

Long-term partnering with retail clients also occurs. In onion-consuming countries such as Côte d'Ivoire and Togo, wholesale marketers rely on extensive networks of retail clients because onions must be moved quickly to avoid spoilage. Traders handling upward of 100 tons/month typically have 20 to 30 regular clients. For expensive and effectively charged manufactures, such as cloth, Yoruba traders may create a market niche through personalized ties (*onibara*) with customers; cloth traders must extend credit to most of their customers to maintain a regular clientele (Traeger, 1981a).

Partnering is important to grain wholesale and retail partners, but the reasons differ. Wholesalers need trusted downstream retail partners to avoid tying up their limited capital in stocks, that is, to facilitate stock turns (see Table 4.2, Proposition 1):

> Most rural wholesalers are relatively short of investment funds and must therefore replenish their funds. So if they have no trusted associates at the retail outlet point, their stocks may be passed over by potential buyers and their grain may be tied up at the market until the following week. [Wholesaler] M's relation with [retailer] L enables him to sell quickly and get out of the market with a profit, instead of tying down his investment funds for a week or more. (Clough, 1985, p. 29)

Grain retailers also need trusted upstream partners to buffer them from environmental volatility, especially to avoid liquidating stocks at unfavorable terms given their limited capital resources (see Table 4.2, Proposition 1):

> When [retailer] L buys and sells grain in the market, he aims at the very least to make sufficient earnings to cover a series of needs during the week. Sometimes he is left with unsold grain. If L does not know the wholesaler [who has advanced him grain for sale] well, he will give the wholesaler the agreed price for all sacks sold. This leaves L, who had expected to sell all his grain, with lower absolute earnings than he anticipated. However if L is well known and trusted by his wholesaler, then he can protect his minimum earnings by asking that payment be deferred for some of the wholesaler's sacks. (Clough, 1985, p. 28)

Even at the level of the small-scale, individual retailer, partnering occurs. Ninety percent of the 1,800 traders interviewed in a market study in Zinder département (Arnould, 1986) engage in informal cooperation with others, such as sharing transport costs, market stall maintenance, or short-term credits (Hausa, *rance*). These important reciprocal services carry very small economic costs (see Table 4.2, Proposition 3). Over time, these friendly relationships between marketers may develop into more extensive, personalized networks of clientage, partners to whom one owes favors, and from whom favors are owed (Clough, 1985). They may also provide a springboard for success. The largest onion trader in Togo began by sharing costs and product with a group of five market women. Thus long-term channels partnering in a variety of forms is a ubiquitous feature of West African channels (see Table 4.2, Propositions 8 & 9).

Competition

In West African channels, competition is based on these partnering relationships. Ethnicity or gender are easily mobilized to keep the trade in traditional hands (Cohen, 1971; Curtin, 1971; Lovejoy, 1973). The personalized networks that marketers nurture also are used to exclude potential competitors from trade. Hausa-speaking onion assemblers in central Niger, for example, exclude those not personally known to the group from participation in onion assembly. They enforce this control by refusing to buy from producers who sell to outsiders (Arnould with Iddal, 1992). Powerful local wholesaler assemblers in Niger and northern Benin's producing zones can also use their position of influence with producers to constrain exporters' direct access to producers. According to some Togolese and Beninois importers, respectively, the assemblers can influence producers to raise prices in bush markets to make buying outside established wholesale markets such as Galmi or Arewa in Niger or Malanville in Benin unattractive. Producers who bypass the established wholesale markets and attempt to undercut prices established in them may be boycotted by the assemblers (see Table 4.2, Proposition 2). Onion producers in the village of Magaria, Niger were contending with just such a boycott in July 1992. Male competitors attempting to break into the Benin women's onion trade with producers in northern Benin complained they were too "strong"; instead, men were compelled to buy Nigerian onions considered second-rate by consumers (see Table 4.2, Proposition 20).

Profitability

Effective networks that concentrate goods and customers are a source of channel power that net greater relative profits to channel members who manage them. Those who have researched grain marketing channels in West Africa find those who control the largest networks of traders also realize the greatest profits (Grégoire, 1986; Saul, 1987; Shenton & Lennihan, 1981). On account of the profit differential, the situation of clientage leads to conflicting perceptions and feelings in the client (see Table 4.2, Propositions 16):

> On the one hand, M is grateful to Z for his patronage, and very grateful for Z's willingness to allow him to convert a trading loan into a farming loan. On the other hand, M is aware that his labour-time in buying and storing grain enables the patron to make large profits on the order of 40 per cent return to his initial investment. And he is aware of the disparity between the N400 ($100) which he receives as a trading loan and the N1800 ($450) which, for example, Z made as a gross profit on the basis of M's labour in 1978. (Clough, 1985, p. 22)

Similarly in onion marketing channels, the assemblers in key bulking markets, known locally as *sarkin tasha*, reap the greatest relative profits of any channel member. By one estimate, they realize a net return of almost $350 per truckload, or 50% margin on variable costs. In a country where the average per capita income is estimated at $250, this becomes a staggering sum when multiplied over the hundreds of loads they oversee in a season (see Table 4.2, Propositions 8 & 14).

An important caveat is in order. Personal networks do not set limits on the way market forces affect price or grain movements. They facilitate the expansion of produce movements to other marketplaces over a large area. This is because traders over the expansive market areas become friends. Frequent information flows between them. The interplay between supply and demand is funneled through social interactions and therefore depends on the creation and development of personal networks (see Table 4.2, Proposition 19). As personal histories of traders as well as the margin data presented in Table 4.3 illustrate, however, personal networks do not guarantee profit margins against market forces (Grégoire, 1986; Salifou, 1972).

In the context of clan-based modes of channels integration in West Africa, uncertainty and volatility in the institutional and regulatory environment may also impede the profitability of channels. For example, cash on hand is hard to secure and is subject to many demands from dependents for consumption expenditures and for loans. Thus there is considerable incentive to invest cash in goods. Concurrently, volatility encourages frequent stock turns. Many marketers prefer brief stock turns to minimize the time their capital is tied up in goods. For a perishable crop like onions, marketers keep 50% of their working capital in cash; they put about 25% in stored onions and 25% in exported onions (Mahamadou, 1987, p. 48). In a 1960 study of Accra, Nypan (1960) found that retail marketers restocked on an average of two or more times per week. In my study in Zinder in 1978-1979, I found that half of the marketers had held goods in inventory for less than one month, and less than 10% of goods had been held for a year or more (Arnould, 1986, p. 335; Nypan, 1960, pp. 62-64). As Mintz (1961) found among Haitians, for many West African marketers "quick pennies" are better than "slow shillings." Thus money may circulate quickly, but accumulation is constrained.

Marketing Credit

Networks are a key source of marketing credits as little credit is available to informal channels members through commercial banks (Ohio State University, 1987). Smaller-scale marketers may depend on personal relationships with larger-scale marketers for access to bank credits, the latter guaranteeing the credits of the former (Grégoire, 1986, p. 181). But most traders rely on other traders for financing. Arrangements take many forms. For example, in Accra, I was told that salt belonging to Ghanaian merchants is sometimes sent to Niger for sale. A Nigerien onion merchant travels with the Ghanaian truck until it reaches Niamey, the capital of Niger. There, the Ghanaian trucker hands over the money obtained for the salt to the Nigerien merchant in the form of a loan with a one-month payback period. The Nigerien merchant buys onions that are then loaded onto the Ghanaian truck and returns to Ghana with the onions. In this way, the Nigerien merchant risks less of his own money on the trade, and the Ghanaian trucker is assured of a return load.

In the grain trade in northern Nigeria and Niger, as Clough (1985) points out,

> the importance of short-term credits (rance) received from social equals in financing the process of accumulation is as important as long-term credit (jali) received from social superiors. This is true at all levels in trading networks. For example, Alhaji Z is able to use without charge large warehouses of important trading friends in the towns for his own storage. In a sense, Hausa grain traders "accumulate together." There is a social ethic of mutual help. (p. 26)

These types of lateral arrangements may be found in many branches of trade (see Table 4.2, Proposition 2).

Wholesalers of all types often have considerable amounts of their capital tied up in credit arrangements. Fifty percent of an onion wholesaler's capital is likely to be on loan at any given time (Mahamadou, 1987), but credit runs through the whole marketing system. Most of the thousands of small-scale onion wholesalers in West Africa have access to informal sector credit. Goods are advanced to them by wholesalers, with a theoretical delay of 15 to 20 days to repay the loan amount. Of the 1,800 marketplace traders interviewed in the market study in Zinder département, 25% said they received or extended credit to other marketers (see Table 4.2, Proposition 5).

Credit can also be used as a trap to keep suppliers or retail customers loyal to wholesalers. Practices such as marketers buying standing crops from farmers at steep discounts to be repaid at harvest, making cash loans against future cash crop harvests, making volume loans in food crops against volume repayment in cash crops, and underpayment in exchange for "services" are widely reported. Some see these practices as abusive (Shenton & Lennihan, 1981), others as means of reducing risk (Arnould, 1987; Saul, 1987; see Table

4.2, Proposition 1 & 5). For example, one small-scale grain wholesaler in northern Nigeria

> distributes loans known variously as *bashi* (credit) and *kudun buhu* (the price of a sack), but chiefly as *falle*. *Falle* has the connotation of "cutting in half." In July, [wholesale] creditors advance money to half the expected value of the crop with which they are to be repaid. Thus the [producer] debtor "cuts in half" his harvest, giving one half over to the creditor. This grain is not sold immediately, but is stored to provide for future loans to the same debtors and for later sale at high pre-harvest prices. . . . The actual incidence of repayment is less than suggested by the express terms of the *falle* agreement. Some debtors pay with full sacks, some with sacks of only 30-40 measures. . . . The ability of the creditor to secure full repayment depends on their willingness to accept more general responsibilities of a patron towards a client. . . . For grain traders, *falle* is a means of purchasing crop futures. (Clough, 1985, pp. 22-23)

Still, default by retail creditors is a real possibility, and it can easily ruin a market intermediary. Such incidents are widely reported by them.

Savings

Informal networks are also the basis for most savings activities in West Africa. Many marketers eschew dealings with formal banks. Instead, they often use rotating credit associations into which each member pays on a regular schedule and from which each receives the total contributed on a similarly regular schedule. Rotating credit associations, whose membership may fluctuate after each complete turn, effectively shield capital from regulatory and taxing authorities, not to mention spouses and relatives (Touré, 1985). Rotating credit associations are often used to fund variable costs of doing business, especially by women.

Relationship-Based Marketing Tactics

Relationship-based competition also extends to market tactics. Unlike business-to-business sales in the United States and trading in North African bazaars where bargaining on price is common, West African channels members are less willing to bargain away profits through price cuts. In contrast, they are more likely to offer concessions of credit at the wholesale level and concessions of quantity at the retail level. For example, onion assemblers in the bulking markets in the producing zones are required to make up shortfalls between quantities purchased by wholesale exporters and quantities packed from their own stocks. To take another example, Nigerien onion merchants preferred to deal with Ghanaian transporters rather than Nigerien ones because the former required a 50% down payment on transport costs, with 15 days to pay after delivery of onions in Accra. Nigerien transporters, by contrast, demanded cash in advance. Some Ghanaian transporters also offered concessions on shipping rates to Nigerien wholesalers so as to obtain CFA francs, which hold their value better than Ghanaian cedis. Grain such as millet, sorghum, corn, and rice is often purchased from individual sellers by measures; it is also sold by measure. A wholesaler can grant or withhold favors from suppliers or buyers depending on the size of the "hat" piled onto the measure (Saul, 1987). A retailer can help build relationships with clientele by tossing in an extra tomato or pepper to the usual pile of five in which they are conventionally sold. Hausa marketers term this practice "healing" (*gyara*). Because price discounts have an immediate negative effect on the "bottom line," West African marketers' unwillingness to deal on price makes sound business sense.

One of the surprising features of successful, well-integrated channels is that they are often quite invisible to casual observation. For example, the wholesale entrepôt of one of the most important wholesale onion dealers in Abidjan, Côte d'Ivoire is located in a tiny, hard-to-reach cul-de-sac known mainly to the specialists involved. The wholesale entrepôt of one of the most important wholesale onion dealers in Togo is a tiny 5 m × 15 m warehouse on a quiet, residential street in Lomé. In anticipation of receipt of each 300-ton shipment from Niger, she notifies her wholesale network. As soon as the truck arrives, the dealers descend on her entrepôt, and within a matter of hours most of the sacks of onions are dispersed for resale. This sort of just-in-time, and the brevity of the stock turn that would be the envy of many First World marketers, is far from exceptional in West African channels (see Table 4.2, Propositions 3, 22, & 23).

There are several other strategies characteristic of successful relationship marketing in West African channels. One of the most common of these is within-channel niching. For example, a ubiquitous presence in many Nigerien livestock markets is the *dillali* (Hausa, pl. *dillalai*), or intermediary. A similar figure, the *sibaba*, appears in markets in southern Sudan (Håland, 1984). His role is to bring buyers and sellers together and to act as a guarantor of the transactions agreed to. *Dillalai* may also bulk livestock for wholesale exporters; many work only a few markets, in this way developing long-term relationships both with the bush-dwelling Fulani and Tuareg herdsmen who sell animals and with the cosmopolitan, urban Hausa and Yoruba wholesale buyers who are their major customers. Middlemen perform essential functions of negotiating bargains and absorbing supply from scattered producers but also, more important perhaps, of generating trust between partners to an exchange (Håland, 1984; see Table 4.2, Propositions 3, 10, & 23).

Some other examples of niching: In one study of marketers in Zinder département, Niger I found that, on average, 32% of retail traders trade only in the market in which they reside (range 12% to 59%), and many traded in only a small number of markets (see Table 4.5) regardless of the market potential theoretically available in other marketplaces (Arnould, 1986). Niching is also characteristic of financial markets in some places. Touré (1985) found that Ivoirian street bankers bundle money from investors whose individual savings are too small to interest the formal sector banks. These street bankers then place these bundled funds with the formal sector banks for their clients, depositing and withdrawing at the end of each month.

To summarize, marketers in Africa deploy gender, ethnicity, and personalized exchange networks to ensure their access to sources of supply, credit, retail customers, and consumer markets. The available investment funds, or liquid capital, of most wholesalers and retailers are limited in relation to their commitments. Long-standing personal relationships between channels dyads give partners a degree of security in an uncertain environment. Personal relations of this sort allow the social needs of both channels partners, grounded in a common religion, custom, and sense of social obligation, to be taken into account in economic transactions (Clough, 1985). Based on the classical channels literature that stresses the contingent quality of relationships between channels dyads, we might be surprised by the degree of cooperation evident among West African channels members and the degree of integration in certain channels. The facts of the case disprove the hypotheses that high levels of market diversity will reduce market integration; instead they reinforce the integrity of the dyad as a unit within the regional market system (Klein et al., 1990). Indeed, an enduring linkage of some sort *between* channel members at different levels is essential to success in the system (cf. Frazier et al., 1989). In West African channels, embedding market exchange in relationships is a technique that reduces transaction costs and spreads the risks and uncertainty characteristic of the marketing environment among channels members.

In sum, close examination of channels in West African contexts shows that the so-called informal channels deliver items of necessity and desire to millions of consumers through market price mechanisms. At the same time, these channels privilege relationships between channels entities. Indeed, consistent with Ouchi's clan-based model of organization, enduring channels relation-

TABLE 4.5
Nigerien Marketers Who Trade Only in Their Town of Residence

Market Town	Percentage of Merchants
Bakin, Birji	24.4
Belbedji	12.9
Birnin, Kazoe	29.9
Dungas	58.6
Gada	15.7
Gayi	39.3
Goundoumawa	36.7
Gourbobo	12
Koaya	27.7
Magaria	54.6
Matameye	40.4
Mirria	23.2
Sassoumbroum	42.1
Wodo	29.1
Zinder	29.3
Mean	34

SOURCE: Table compiled from Arnould (1986).

ships are characterized by a focus on relationship equity rather than brand equity or transaction-specific equity. This relationship focus has been favored by high market diversity and uncertainty and high transaction costs associated with the special characteristics of the regional marketing environment.

Weaknesses of the Market-Clan Mode of Channels Integration

Despite the strengths that enable marketers to contend with environmental stresses, the market-clan mode of channels integration in West Africa described above has a number of weaknesses. One of these is the inward-facing economic and social orientation of channels members. An inward-looking focus of channel members ill prepares them to contend for power against regulatory authorities. Thus the social networks of the two groups often do not overlap; communication between them is weak. Marketers basically adopt evasive, defensive strategies rather than offensive, environmental management strategies.

A second weakness is the inherent conservatism of the system. Although channel members respond creatively to uncertain situations, they are able to do so within a relatively narrow band of variation. A clan-based system that relies on tacit norms and values does not encourage innovation. So, for example, innovations in packing that would differentiate Niger's "Violet de Galmi" variety of onions from competitive varieties have not occurred as First World marketers would expect given new market entries and widespread consumer preference for the "Violet de Galmi." Furthermore, organized response to chaotic supply conditions that create seasonal glut or seasonal dearth in onion channels have been minimal. Thus when onion traders in Accra, Ghana find the market too glutted with onions, they find it difficult to discourage distant wholesale supply markets from continuing to ship. Traders are similarly dissuaded from making innovations in marketing tactics. For instance, questions about what onion marketers can do to attract new clients are typically greeted by references to traders' dependence on God's will for clients.

Third, the personalism that provides the glue for the system also imposes inherent limits on the size and stability of market networks. Thus although channels can be long, the distribution density of any given "firm" tends to be limited by the number of personal ties that individual traders can sustain. This leads to intraregional discrepancies in supply of particular products. Thus Nigerien onions do not reach the market hinterlands of important consumer wholesale markets because of the high opportunity cost of sustaining personal relationships in ethnically distinct, rural consumer markets where the overall density of demand is relatively low. Personalism would constrain distribution density even if environmental diversity and volatility did not contribute to such high transaction costs. Furthermore, personalism is not a perfect defense against opportunism. For instance, one onion trader stated that retailers often repay only 90% of what they owe him, claiming the stocks accounting for the remainder of the debt had spoiled. Traders can do little about this; their powers of supervision are limited. If wholesalers protest too much, clients can go to other wholesalers for supplies (cf. Clough, 1985; see Table 4.2, Proposition 23).

The personalism of the networks may also create channels inefficiencies at the system level. In most Sahelian nations, for example,

> the lack of a backflow of grain to producing areas is one of the major shortcomings of the private trading system. . . . This is so because . . . mer-

chants in regional centers . . . encounter several problems. . . . Transportation may be difficult, their restricted networks may make grain hard to find . . . and also their capital may not allow them to buy sufficiently large quantities [to provision production deficits in consuming areas]. Finally the low purchasing power of rural consumers may make it impossible for them to buy this highly priced grain. These problems create delays and dangerous breaks in the availability of grain in rural centers. [Further], the patterns in the movement of grain are more often due to the way the merchants organize their trade rather than road conditions or other physical factors. . . . [Thus grain may circulate back and forth across a country] . . . but these costs are not internalized by traders [but by consumers, because grain changes hands each time it reaches a major city], and the fact that cereals change hand several times during their journey makes it more difficult to identify the inefficiencies and estimate their magnitude. (Saul, 1988, pp. 94, 102-104; Reprinted with permission)

Finally, the existence of regulatory authorities with a near monopoly of coercive sources of power and the demonstrated ability to use it to extract resources of channels members works to inhibit channels integration. Exercised coercive power destabilizes channels through delays, draining accumulated capital into unproductive uses (e.g., regulatory agents' consumption of Pugeot 505 automobiles) through bribes and driving channel members underground. For instance, one technique used to reduce both financial and political risk to channel members is to avoid investments in infrastructure. Many merchants prefer to rent rather than own warehouse and retail space as well as rolling stock. Reducing visible signs of wealth reduces exposure to regulation, to taxation, and to rent seeking by state agents but may also reduce the viability of the channel by limiting the availability of useful processing and warehousing facilities.

Discussion

Some Implications for Western Market Practitioners

This overview of relationship marketing *à l'africain* entails certain implications for market practitioners. One of the most important things that they highlight is the benefits to be derived from relational exchanges (i.e., reduced uncertainty, managed dependence, exchange efficiencies, the social satisfactions of association, and gains in joint payoffs) as a result of effective communication and collaboration in trade (Dwyer et al., 1987, p. 14). The data also suggest, consistent with some organizational theorists, that a shared cultural orientation tends to reduce the goal divergence and opportunism that threaten relational exchanges in profit-driven economies, reaffirming the value to channels partners of taking the time necessary to nurture shared culture and norms. Such time may be time well spent even if not reflected in immediate bottom-line results. These data also suggest that when dependent members of a channel dyad perceive the exercise of power by the superordinate member as just, as in patron-client relationships, joint interests may nonetheless prevail in spite of the discrepancy in power (Dwyer et al., 1987, p. 17). Finally, the data show how relational networks can be used as a strategy of market penetration through network expansion.

The findings reported here are consistent with the recommendations of Hampden-Turner and Trompenaars (1993). In their book, *The Seven Cultures of Capitalism*, these authors argue that we must discard the notion that there is a culture of capitalism or that the world is heading in short order toward a single world culture of capitalism. Instead, capitalism, and by implication, marketing, is consistent with many cultural orientations. Indeed, these orientations exhibit distinctive comparative strategic advantages in the global marketplace. Reference has been made to numerous enduring channels of distribution for a wide range of commodities and consumer goods of value to West African consumers and suggested something of the dynamics that continue to give them their cultural specificity: personalism; embeddedness in gender, kin, and ethnic relations; long-term equity; and redistributive generosity, for example.

Marketing practitioners therefore would do well to pay attention to the structure of informal channels in West Africa. Dynamic, culturally distinctive channels relationships are likely to continue to provide the solutions to the unique environmental stresses encountered in West Africa. At the same time, West African channels do not meet the demands of consumers and small-scale producers for a wide variety of goods and services (Arnould, 1985). African channels partners often lack important resources, such as capital and the skills needed to manage corporate institutions, that would allow them to expand channels to serve broader markets. Their ability to develop novel products to meet ill-articulated, or novel consumer needs are constrained by mercantile traditions that privilege speculative profit-taking over technology acquisition, let alone research and development (Sørensen, 1988). Close study of particular informal channels can provide insight into the resources that potential African channels partners need and that expatriate marketers can provide. Thus study of onion marketing channels has shown that improved storage, packing, and presentation technologies, as well as an introduction to the world of modern import-export finance, could improve the marketability of Nigerien onions (Arnould with Iddal, 1992); yet African marketers have been slow to explore these innovations. By contrast, they have been quick to make use of improved telecommunications infrastructure, suggesting that innovation is feasible.

The cultural expectations of potential West African channels partners for First World firms will be informed by their experience of relationships within informal channels. It is likely that African channels partners will be positively influenced by successful management of long-term relationship equity rather than merely short-term profits. But the modern marketing concept is alien to the marketing practice of many channels captains in West Africa. African channels partners thus do not always appreciate the virtues of some relationship-building tools, such as augmented product features like guarantees and warranties, or marketing communications tools that can build brand and equity. For instance, onion marketers depend entirely on positive word-of-mouth to create demand for Niger's "Violet de Galmi" onion variety.

Rather than despair in the face of cultural difference, practitioners should take heart from the fact that there is a logic to informal channels in West Africa that makes sense in terms of the marketing environment. Furthermore, there are opportunities for the stout of heart. Not only are many West African economies growing at a good clip, there are numerous untapped niches. For example, there is a sellers' market for high-potency fertilizers at reasonable prices in many areas. What is needed here is probably a channel intermediary with the ability to help peasant farmers' groups establish communication links with suppliers who have the potential to transform farmers' needs into appropriate product concepts (Sørensen, 1988). To take another example, formal sector actors in at least one importing country would like to deal in Nigerien onions, if formal sector sorting, packing and financing (e.g., letters of credit) norms could be met by Nigerien producers and wholesalers. Of course, this formalization would be risky under present environmental circumstances (Arnould with Iddal, 1992).

Some Implications for Market Researchers

Fifteen years ago, Stern and Reve (1980) stated,

> Future channel research must focus on making systematic comparisons of different distribution networks within and between various environmental conditions, irrespective of whether the different networks are found in the same industry or across industries. (p. 53)

In a recent article, Frazier and Kim (1994) echoed this concern.

Conducted in this spirit, the overview of relationships in marketing channels à l'africain entails certain implications for channels researchers. These remarks are consistent with similar recommendations recently directed to consumer researchers (Andreasen, 1992). To study the role that marketing actually plays in economic development, marketers should examine systems that have been rendered invisible by the pejorative term "informal sector." Our judgments about the relationships between marketing and economic development would likely be broadened by such studies. For example, when only formal channels are studied in African nations, researchers are likely to draw the inevitable conclusion that channels development must precede economic development (Olsen & Granzin, 1990) because formal marketing channels account for so little economic activity in most African countries (MacGaffey, 1991). However, if informal channels are included in such studies, it becomes clear that a broadened perspective is required to determine how and under what conditions traditional channels do or do not contribute productively to development.

West African channels provide a fertile testing ground for various propositions that have been developed in the channels literature. Albeit anecdotal, the examples reported here provide mixed support for propositions related to channels structure, power and conflict enunciated in the recent literature and summarized in Table 4.2. For example, these data are relevant to the discussion of the relationship between the channels environments and channels structure. Environmental diversity, particularly in the input (i.e., production) and output (i.e., consumer purchasing power) sectors of the environment, leads to the development of complex and fluid onion marketing channel structure that enhances the channel's ability to cope with specialized demands and leads to considerable flexibility in channel structure, as evidenced for example with considerable movement in and out of trade. This finding is consistent with theory developed by Klein et al. (1990, p. 200) and Achrol et al. (1983, p. 63). Yet volatility in West African channels, especially those concerned with high-value products like livestock, cloth, gold, and kola, has led to interregional channels integration of the characteristically ethno-dominated form. This finding is consistent with the hypothesis (H5) propounded by Klein et al. (1990, p. 200). The West African data suggest that the risk associated with high-value products is an important moderator of the effect of volatility on integration; for low-value products, flexibility is preferred.

Data put forward concerning both grain and onions are highly supportive of Achrol et al.'s (1983) proposition (P4, see p. 64) to the effect that input sector uncertainty will lead channels dyads to seek vertical linkages between channel members at different levels in the channel. In West Africa, backward integration takes the form of enduring personal relationships between assemblers/brokers and producers.

The West African data are also relevant to the discussion of the impact of the use of power in marketing channels. The preponderance of evidence from well-developed channels such as those for grain, kola, and other basic commodities tends to support the view that channel power is related to the fact that dependent firms require resources provided by the superordinate partner to achieve their goals (Emerson, 1962). However, this is not a zero-sum game because channel leaders depend on elaborate personal networks for their power (Frazier & Kim, 1994, p. 9). What is especially noteworthy about power in this system is that between channel dyads it takes the form of legitimate power (French & Raven, 1959), that is, power legitimated by adherence to norms of reciprocity, patronage, redistributive generosity, and Islamic norms of conduct.

Channels captains such as the large-scale grain dealers of Kano (Nigeria), Ouagadougou (Burkina Faso), and Maradi (Niger) or the onion assembler-brokers of Tahoua département (Niger) accrue a greater proportion of their respective channels' profits because of their control over credit and ramified collection networks. This is consistent with Stern and Reve's (1980) Proposition 12 (p. 58). In addition, the imbalance in coercive power that is concentrated in the hands of state regulatory agents leads to instability in marketing channels, market failure, and decreased competitive viability for individual entrepreneurs, as predicted by Stern and Reve's Propositions 5 and 6 (p. 58). This is especially evident in the case of Côte d'Ivoire, where the ability of Nigerien wholesalers to compete on price with Lebanese importers of European onions is due primarily to elevated transaction costs associated with bribery and evasion in the African channels of distribution. However, uncertainty in the competitive sector seems to lead to high levels of cooperation in the form of ethnodominance only when the regulatory sector is not a significant locus of coercive power in the channel, thus providing only partial support to propositions adduced by Achrol et al. (1983, p. 64, P5 & P6). Nevertheless, collusion between marketers and regulatory agents in maintaining a pervasive system of bribes and exactions is consistent with these authors' notions that the more variable, concentrated and heterogeneous the regulatory organizations are, the more likely market channel members are to come to some accommodation with these agencies (p. 65, P10).

The data put forth here also touch on the theme of channel conflict. Certainly there is uncertainty in the input and output sectors of the task environment in which many, if not most, marketers operate. Furthermore, there is a litany of complaints that channels partners are likely to levy against one another, including price gouging, price fixing, restraining free trade, credit evasion, and so on. Coping strategies, such as clan-based organizational forms, personalized relationship management, and ethnic- and gender-based exclusion, are employed to reduce within-channel conflict. However, there is a looseness to channels structure overall, as members seek to avoid the exactions of regulatory agents. Finally, few marketers would characterize the communications climate as supportive and trusting, leading to considerable duplicity and information management both within and across channels. However, because of the embedded quality of channels relationships, the overall tenor of marketing communications inclines more toward infrequency, indirection, and informality.

The limitations of this chapter draw attention to the limitations of a number of the key concepts used in studies of marketing channels. The data reported suggest that environmental factors such as diversity, uncertainty, volatility, and relationship factors such as power and conflict do influence the structure of African marketing channels. However, it is evident that these concepts need to be unpacked and measured. As Frazier and Kim (1994) suggest, inadequate attention has been devoted to the conceptual definition and measurement of primary constructs. For example, how much and what type of uncertainty leads to ethnodominance, patron-client relations, or gender embeddedness? Certainly, there is nothing in the existing channels literature that allows us to account for the precise form that ethno- and gender-dominated channels take, nor the forms of personalism such as *uban gida-bara* or *onibara* relations take. Furthermore, when we look at West African channels, where environmental uncertainty is so pervasive, we must ask how do participants understand uncertainty? What type do they tolerate? What type do they find intolerable? Another line of inquiry that could be fruitfully pursued would be to ask what types and how much opportunism, performance ambiguity, and transaction costs lead to the existence of market- or clan-based mechanisms for channels integration. The marvelous richness of organizational forms in West African marketing systems provides an outstanding laboratory for a more rigorous investigation of these issues.

What this chapter suggests above all is the need for a sophisticated concept of culture in studies of marketing channels. The reason why this concept is needed should be obvious. Constructs such as channels length, wholesaler, retailer, broker, transaction cost, and so on are perfectly applicable in West African contexts. Given West Africa's ecological diversity, local autarky is not a real possibility. Thus, as in any marketing system, certain channels functions must be performed if goods are to be moved from producer to consumer in a timely and cost-effective manner. Furthermore, a variety of tactics should seem familiar to Western channels members: just-in-time, brief stock turns, variable credit terms, up- and downstream channel partnering, and so on. Nonetheless, nothing in the channels literature prepares the market researcher for the particular forms that channels relationships take in African contexts. The elaboration of ethnodominated channels, although illustrative of the notion of vertical channels integration, is a long way from the contractual systems familiar to students of franchises or retailer cooperatives! To understand this form of channels integration necessitates an appreciation of the dynamic cultural context that has produced this and innumerable other novel solutions to the problems of channels integration under conditions of environmental duress.

Some Implications for an Anthropology of Marketing

Anthropologists have begun to examine the contours and consequences of the contemporary world system, what might well be termed the culture of the "marketing age." In so doing, many have focused primarily, and perhaps correctly so, on its characteristic artifact, the consumer good (Appadurai, 1986; McCracken, 1988; Miller, 1987; Rutz & Orlove, 1989; Tobin, 1992). Others have looked at the culture of those institutions dedicated to the production of these goods (Baba, 1986). Although much more remains to be done in each of these areas, the cross-cultural studies of marketing channels of distribution, the mechanism that links consumers and producers in the global marketplace, is perhaps the least explored by anthropologists (cf. Dannhaeuser, 1981, 1987). The ethnocentrism and paucity of robust comparative concepts for the analysis of channels dynamics as represented in this chapter suggest that this arena is in critical need of ethnographic investigation. Not only would such investigation further the cause of a dynamic applied anthropology, it would extend theoretical understanding (Baba, 1994). Growth in theoretical understanding of channels relationships would bring channels research in marketing a cross-cultural comparative framework and extend anthropological understanding of organizational cultures.

There is one final dimension to marketing practice in West Africa that could provide a bridge between anthropologists and critical marketing scholars. This dimension concerns the segregation of markets and daily life. Some of the same mechanisms that facilitate the integration and maintenance of West African marketing channels in the face of environmental stress help to shield village communities and individuals within them from the types of alienation and fragmentation that theorists of postmodernity have noted as hallmarks of the marketing age First World (Baudrillard, 1970; Cushman, 1990; Featherstone, 1991; Fırat, 1991; Jameson, 1983). Temporal periodicity and spatial segregation of marketplaces from village communities is one aspect of marketing channels in West Africa that protects the community from the dissolving effect of the commodity. Indeed, some rural West Africans continue to treat the market as a profane place to be approached with caution (cf. Belk, Wallendorf, & Sherry, 1989). So too is the concentration of commercial transactions in the hands of trading diasporas of distinct ethnic groups, against which members of local communities may discriminate socially. Islam, which played such a great role in the marketization of West Africa (Hopkins, 1973; Salifou, 1972), also served and still serves as a point of resistance for communities practicing indigenous religions. Finally, the existence of spheres of exchange in many African societies creates barriers between the market and the community. In a number of West African societies in precolonial times, there was a sphere of goods that circulated as gifts, a sphere of products that circulated as commodities, and a sphere of exchange in which marriage partners circulated. Access to each sphere was restricted on the basis of age, gender, and status achievement. Typically, only some members of a community engaged in market exchanges (Bohannon & Dalton, 1962). Although much degraded under the influence of marketization since colonization, remnants of these systems persist (Piot, 1991). There may well be lessons here for those seeking to better understand and struggle against the alienating and fragmenting effects of postmodernity. In precolonial West Africa, the "freedom" to consume was sacrificed to the integrity of the organic community.

Ⓜ Conclusion

The current interest in cooperation, embeddedness, and relationships in marketing generally is probably a result of the current climate of intensified international competition, the decline of U.S. economic hegemony, fragmentation of the traditional corporation, a rethinking of the virtue of competition in the face of successful industrial cartels and business-government relationships in the Pacific Rim, and so forth (Hampden-Turner & Trompenaars, 1993). It is a time of crisis in Western capitalism and a fertile moment in which anthropologists and marketing practitioners could well benefit from a commingling of insights derived from close study of channels in West African and other southern hemisphere contexts. Anthropologists could use this collaboration to facilitate their linkage, brokerage, and advocacy roles vis-à-vis African marketers by anchoring their work in collaboration with market-ing experts (Arnould, 1989; Baba, 1994). Marketing researchers will benefit from the improvements in channels theory that ethnographic comparison can provide. Finally, from such a collaboration, marketing practioners can find a knowledge base with which to develop new marketing partnerships in West Africa.

☒ Note

1. For the purposes of this study, West Africa includes the nations of Benin, Burkina Faso, Côte d'Ivoire, Gambia, Ghana, Guinea, Guinea Bisseau, Liberia, Mali, Niger, Nigeria, Senegal, Sierra Leone, and Togo.

☒ References

Achrol, R. S., Reve, T., & Stern, L. W. (1983). The environment of marketing channel dyads: A framework for comparative analysis. *Journal of Marketing, 47,* 55-67.

Andreasen, A. R. (1992, September). President's column. *ACR Newsletter,* pp. 2-4.

Appadurai, A. (1986). Introduction: Commodities and the politics of value. In A. Appadurai (Ed.), *The social life of things* (pp. 3-63). Cambridge, UK: Cambridge University Press.

Arnould, E. J. (1983). *Cross-border trade between Niger and Nigeria* (Joint Program Assessment of Grain Marketing in Niger, Background Paper No. 1). Niamey, Niger: Elliot Berg Associates/ U.S. Agency for International Development.

Arnould, E. J. (1984). Process and social formation: Petty commodity producers in Zinder, Niger. *Canadian Journal of African Studies, 18*(3), 501-522.

Arnould, E. J. (1985). Evaluating regional economic development: Results of a marketing systems analysis in Zinder Province, Niger Republic. *Journal of Developing Areas, 19*(2), 209-244.

Arnould, E. J. (1986). Merchant capital, simple reproduction, and underdevelop-ment: Peasant traders in Zinder, Niger. *Canadian Journal of African Studies, 28*(3), 323-356.

Arnould, E. J. (1987). *First phase results of the cooperative cereal marketing study: Départements of Zinder and Maradi, December 3-21, 1987* (Paper prepared for Republic of Niger, Ministry of Agriculture). Niamey, Niger: U.S. Agency for International Development.

Arnould, E. J. (1989). Anthropology and West Africa development: A critique of recent debate. *Human Organization, 48*(4), 135-147.

Arnould, E. J., & McCullough, J. (1980). *Étude du système des marchés à Zinder.* Tucson: University of Arizona, Committee on Arid Lands Studies.

Arnould, E. J., with Iddal, S. M. (1992). *Export marketing of Nigerien onions* (Agricultural Marketing Improvement Strategies Project). Moscow: University of Idaho, Post-Harvest Institute for Perishables, and Abt & Associates/U.S. Agency for International Development, Niger.

Baba, M. L. (1986). *Business and industrial anthropology: An overview.* Washington, DC: American Anthropological Association.

Baba, M. L. (1994). The fifth subdiscipline: Anthropological practice and the future of anthropology. *Human Organization, 53,* 174-186.

Baier, S. (1974). *African merchants in the colonial periods: A history of commerce in Damagaram (Central Niger), 1880-1960.* Ann Arbor, MI: University Microfilms International.

Baier, S. (1977). Trans-Saharan trade and the Damergu, 1870-1930. *Journal of African History, 1*(1), 1-16.

Baudrillard, J. (1970). *La societe de consommation.* Paris: Gallimard.

Belk, R. W., Wallendorf, M., & Sherry, J. F., Jr. (1989). The sacred and the profane in consumer behavior: Theodicy on the odyssey. *Journal of Consumer Research, 16,* 1-38.

Belshaw, C. S. (1965). *Traditional exchange in modern markets.* Englewood Cliffs, NJ: Prentice Hall.

Bennett, J., & Bowen, J. (Eds.). (1988). *Production and autonomy: Anthropological studies and critiques of development.* New York: University Press of America.

Berthoud, G. (1991). Le marché comme simulacre du don? *Revue du MAUSS, 12*(1), 72-89.

Bohannon, P., & Dalton, G. (Eds.). (1962). *Markets in Africa.* Evanston, IL: Northwestern University Press.

Braadbaart, O. (1994). Business contracts in Javanese marketing. *Human Organization, 53,* 143-149.

Charlick, R. B. (1991). *Niger: Personal rule and survival in the Sahel.* Boulder, CO: Westview.

Christopher, M., Payne, A., & Ballantyne, D. (1992). *Relationship marketing.* London: Heinemann.

CILSS (Comité Interétat de Lutte contre la Sècheresse dans le Sahel). (1977). *Marketing price policy and storage of food grains in the Sahel: A survey* (2 vols.). Ann Arbor: University of Michigan, Center for Research in Economic Development.

Clough, P. (1985). The social relations of grain marketing in northern Nigeria. *Review of African Political Economy, 34,* 16-34.

Cohen, A. (1971). Cultural strategies in the organization of trading diaspora. In C. Meillassoux (Ed.), *The development of indigenous trade and markets in West Africa* (pp. 266-283). Oxford, UK: Oxford University Press.

Collins, J. D. (1976). The clandestine movement of groundnuts across the Niger-Nigeria boundary. *Canadian Journal of African Studies, 10*(2), 259-278.

Cook, S., & Diskin, M. (1976). *Markets in Oaxaca*. Austin: University of Texas Press.

Cova, B. (in press). From marketing to societing: When the link is more important than the thing. In D. Brownie (Ed.), *Rethinking marketing*. Thousand Oaks, CA: Sage.

Curtin, P. (1971). Precolonial trading networks and traders: The Diahkanke. In C. Meillassoux (Ed.), *The development of indigenous trade and markets in West Africa* (pp. 228-239). Oxford, UK: Oxford University Press.

Cushman, P. (1990). Why the self is empty: Towards a historically situated psychology. *American Psychologist, 45,* 599-611.

Dannhaeuser, N. (1981). Evolution and devolution of downward channel integration in the Philippines. *Economic Development and Cultural Change, 29,* 577-596.

Dannhaeuser, N. (1987). Marketing systems and rural development: A review of consumer goods distribution. *Human Organization, 46*(2), 177-185.

Davis, W. G. (1973). *Social relations in a Philippine market: Self interest and subjectivity.* Berkeley: University of California Press.

Dayringer, L. D. (1983). Public policy implications of reverse channel mapping for Lesotho. *Journal of Macromarketing, 2*(1), 14-19.

Dholakia, N., & Sherry, J. F., Jr. (1987). Marketing and development: A resynthesis of knowledge. In J. Sheth (Ed.), *Research in marketing* (Vol. 9, pp. 119-143). Greenwich, CT: JAI.

Dwyer, F. R., & Welsh, M. A. (1985). Environmental relationships of internal political economy of marketing channels. *Journal of Marketing Research, 22,* 397-414.

Dwyer, F. R., Schurr, P. H., & Oh, S. (1987). Developing buyer-seller relationships. *Journal of Marketing, 51,* 11-27.

Elz, D., & Hoisington, C. (1986). *Agricultural marketing policy.* Washington, DC: Economic Development Institute, the World Bank.

Emerson, R. (1962). Power dependence relations. *American Sociological Review, 27,* 31-41.

Featherstone, M. (1991). *Consumer culture and postmodernism.* Newbury Park, CA: Sage.

Firat, A. F. (1991). The consumer in postmodernity. In R. H. Holman & M. R. Solomon (Eds.), *Advances in consumer research* (Vol. 18, pp. 70-76). Provo, UT: Association for Consumer Research.

Firat, A. F., & Venkatesh, A. (1993a). Postmodernity: The age of marketing. *International Journal of Research in Marketing, 10,* 227-250.

Firat, A. F., & Venkatesh, A. (1993b). *The making of postmodern consumption.* Working paper, Arizona State University, Phoenix.

Franke, R. W., & Chasin, B. H. (1980). *Seeds of famine: Ecological destruction and the development dilemma in the West African Sahel.* Totowa, NJ: Rowman and Allanheld.

Frazier, G. L. (1990). The design and management of channels of distribution. In G. Day, B. Weitz, & R. Wensley (Eds.), *The interface of marketing and strategy* (pp. 255-304). Greenwich, CT: JAI.

Frazier, G. L., Gill, J. D., & Kale, S. H. (1989). Dealer dependence levels and reciprocal actions in a channel of distribution in a developing country. *Journal of Marketing, 53,* 50-69.

Frazier, G. L., & Kim, K. (1994). *Behavioral channels research: Present knowledge and needed research.* Working paper, University of Southern California, School of Business Administration.

French, J., & Raven, B. (1959). The bases of social power. In D. Cartwright (Ed.), *Studies in social power* (pp. 158-167). Ann Arbor: University of Michigan Press.

Frenzen, J. K., & Davis, H. L. (1990). Purchasing behavior in embedded markets. *Journal of Consumer Research, 17,* 1-12.

Galli, R. E. (1981). Rural development and the contradictions of capitalist development. In R. E. Galli (Ed.), *The political economy of rural development: Peasants, international capital, and the state* (pp. 213-226). Albany: State University of New York Press.

Ganesan, S. (1994). Determinants of long-term orientation in buyer-seller relationships. *Journal of Marketing, 58,* 1-19.

Gaski, J. F. (1984). The theory of power and conflict in channels of distribution. *Journal of Marketing, 48,* 9-29.

Geertz, C. (1963). *Peddlars and princes: Social change and economic modernization in two Indonesian towns.* Chicago: University of Chicago Press.

Godbout, J. T., & Caillé, A. (1992), *L'Esprit du Don.* Paris: Editions la Découverte.

Graham, J. L. (1985, Spring/Summer). The influence of culture on the process of business negotiations: An exploratory study. *Journal of International Business Studies,* pp. 47-62.

Graham, J. L. (1993, April). The Japanese negotiation style: Characteristics of a distinct approach. *Negotiation Journal,* pp. 123-140.

Graham, J. L., & Herberger, R. A., Jr. (1983). Negotiators abroad—Don't shoot from the hip. *Harvard Business Review, 61,* 160-169.

Grégoire, E. (1986). *Les Alhazai de Maradi (Niger): Histoire d'un groupe de riches marchands Sahéliens* (Collection Travaux et Documents No. 187). Bondy, France: Editions ORSTOM.

Grönroos, C. (1990). Relationship approach to the marketing function in service contexts: The marketing-organization interface. *Journal of Business Research, 20*(1), 3-12.

Gummesson, E. (1993). *Relationship marketing: From 4Ps to 30Rs.* Stockholm: Stockholm University Press.

Håland, G. (1984). The Jellaba trading system. In *Trade and traders in the Sudan* (Bergen Occasional Papers in Social Anthropology, African Savannah Studies, No. 32, pp. 269-284). Bergen, Norway: University of Bergen, Department of Social Anthropology.

Hampden-Turner, C., & Trompenaars, A. (1993). *The seven cultures of capitalism.* New York: Currency/Doubleday.

Hopkins, A. G. (1973). *An economic history of West Africa.* New York: Columbia University Press.

Horne, N. E. (1991). *Marketwomen's strategies buffering urban food security in Harare, Zimbabwe.* Paper presented at the annual meeting of the American Anthropological Association.

Horowitz, M. M., & Painter, T. (1986). *Anthropology and rural development in West Africa.* Boulder, CO: Westview.

Insel, A. (1991). L'enchassement problématique du don dans la théorie économique. *Revue du MAUSS, 12*(2), 110-119.

Jameson, F. (1983). Postmodernism and consumer society. In H. Foster (Ed.), *The anti-aesthetic: Essays on post modern culture* (pp. 111-125). Seattle: Bay Press.

Johnson, J. L., Sakano, T., Cote, J. A., & Onzo, N. (1993). The exercise of interfirm power and its repercussions in U.S.-Japanese channel relationships. *Journal of Marketing, 57,* 1-10.

Jones, W. O. (1972). *Marketing staple food crops in tropical Africa.* Ithaca, NY: Cornell University Press.

Joy, A., & Ross, C. A. (1989). Marketing and development in Third World contexts: An evaluation and future directions. *Journal of Macromarketing, 9,* 17-31.

Kazgan, G. (1988). Marketing in economic development. In E. Kumcu & A. F. Fırat (Eds.), *Marketing and development: Toward broader dimensions* (pp. 39-62). Greenwich, CT: JAI.

Kirk-Greene, A. H. M. (1974). *Mutumiin Kirki: The concept of the good man in Hausa.* Unpublished manuscript, University of Indiana, African Studies Program.

Klein, S., Frazier, G. L., & Roth, V. J. (1990). A transaction cost analysis model of channel integration in international markets. *Journal of Marketing Research, 27,* 196-208.

Kohler, D. (1977). Niger. In CILSS, *Marketing, price policy and storage of food grains in the Sahel: A survey. Vol. 2: Country Studies.* Ann Arbor: University of Michigan, Center for Research on Economic Development.

Kumcu, E., & Fırat, A. F. (Eds.). (1988). *Marketing and development: Toward broader dimensions.* Greenwich, CT: JAI.

Layton, R. A. (1988). Duality or diversity in the marketing systems of developing nations. In J. E. Littlefield & M. Csath (Eds.), *Marketing and economic development* (pp. 314-318). Blacksburg: Virginia Polytechnic University Press.

Leith-Ross, S. (1965). *African women: A study of the Ibo of Nigeria.* London: Routledge & Kegan Paul.

Lembezat, B. (1962). Marchés du Nord-Cameroun. *Cahiers de l'Institut de Science Economique Appliquée,* (Série 5), No. 131, 85-104.

Lev, L. S., & Gadbois, M. A. (1988). *Rapid reconnaissance of the Nigerien onion subsector: A policy-oriented analysis of market performance.* Moscow: University of Idaho, Post-Harvest Institute for Perishables, and U.S. Agency for International Development.

Littlefield, J. E., & Csath, M. (Eds.). (1988). *Marketing and economic development.* Blacksburg: Virginia Polytechnic University Press.

Lovejoy, P. E. (1973). The Kamberin Beriberi: The formation of a specialized group of Hausa kola traders in the nineteenth century. *Journal of African History,* 14(2), 633-651.

Lovejoy, P. E., & Baier, S. (1975). The desert-side economy of the central Sudan. *International Journal of African Historical Studies,* 8(4), 551-580.

Lubeck, P. M. (1987). Islamic protest under semi-industrial capitalism. In J. D. Y. Peel & C. C. Stuart (Eds.), *Popular Islam south of the Sahara* (pp. 24-49). Manchester, UK: Manchester University Press.

Lusch, R. F., & Brown, J. R. (1982). A modified model of power in the marketing channel. *Journal of Marketing Research,* 19, 312-323.

MacGaffey, J. (Ed.). (1991). *The real economy of Zaire.* Philadelphia: University of Pennsylvania Press.

Mahamadou, S. (1987). *La commercialisation des Oignons dans le Département de Tahoua, cas de la zone de Galmi.* Cotonou, Benin: Centre Panafricain de Formation Coopérative.

Manger, L. O. (Ed.). (1984). *Trade and traders in the Sudan* (Bergen Occasional Papers in Social Anthropology, African Savannah Studies, No. 32). Bergen, Norway: University of Bergen, Department of Social Anthropology.

McCorkle, C. (1988). "You can't eat cotton": Cash crops and the cereal code of honor in Burkina Faso. In J. Bennett & J. Bowen (Eds.), *Production and autonomy: Anthropological studies and critiques of development* (pp. 105-124). New York: University Press of America.

McCracken, G. (1988). *Culture and consumption.* Bloomington: Indiana University Press.

McKenna, R. (1991). *Relationship marketing.* Reading, MA: Addison-Wesley.

Meillassoux, C. (Ed.). (1971). *The development of indigenous trade and markets in West Africa.* Oxford, UK: Oxford University Press.

Miller, D. (1987). *Material culture and mass consumption.* Oxford, UK: Basil Blackwell.

Mintz, S. W. (1961). Pratik: Haitian personal economic relations. In V. E. Garfield (Ed.), *Proceedings of the Annual Spring Meeting of the American Ethnological Society* (pp. 54-63). Seattle: American Ethnological Society.

Mohr, J., & Nevin, J. R. (1990). Communication strategies in marketing: A theoretical perspective. *Journal of Marketing,* 54, 36-51.

Nayson, R. W. (1993, August). *Channel mapping: Analysis for market development in transition economies.* Paper presented at the 18th Annual Macromarketing Conference, University of Rhode Island.

Nicholas, G. (1991). Le don rituel, face voilée de la modernité. *Revue du MAUSS,* 12(2), 3-6.

Nypan, A. (1960). *Market trade: A sample survey of market traders in Ghana* (Africa Business Series, No. 2). Accra: University College of Ghana, Economic Research Division.

Ohio State University. (1987). *Rural finances in Niger: A critical appraisal and recommendations for change.* Columbus: Ohio State University Press.

Olsen, J. E., & Granzin, K. L. (1990). Economic development and channel structure: A multinational study. *Journal of Macromarketing 18*, 61-78.

Ouchi, W. G. (1980). Markets, bureaucracies and clans. *Administrative Science Quarterly, 25*, 129-141.

P. C. Globe. (1991). Tempe, AZ: Author.

Pfeffer, J., & Salancik, G. R. (1978). *The external control of organizations.* New York: Harper.

Piot, C. D. (1991). Of persons and things: Some reflections on African spheres of exchange. *Man, 26*, 405-424.

Plattner, S. (1989). Economic behavior in markets. In S. Plattner (Ed.), *Economic anthropology* (pp. 209-221). Stanford, CA: Stanford University Press.

Porter, G. (1993). Changing accessibility and the reorganization of rural marketing in Nigeria. *Journal of Macromarketing, 13*, 54-64.

Quinn, N. (1978). Do Mfantse fish sellers calculate probabilities in their heads? *American Ethnologist, 5*(1), 206-226.

Robles, F., & El-Ansary, A. I. (1989). Informal sector and economic development: A marketing perspective. In E. Kumcu & A. F. Fırat (Eds.), *Marketing and development: Toward broader dimensions* (pp. 199-228). Greenwich, CT: JAI.

Rutz, H. J., & Orlove, B. S. (1989). *The social economy of consumption.* Lanham, MD: University Press of America.

Sahlins, M. (1972). *Stone Age economics.* Chicago: Aldine.

Salifou, A. (1972). Malam Yaro, un grand négociant du Soudan Central à la fin du XIXème siecle. *Journal de la Société des Africanistes, 42*(1), 7-27.

Saul, M. (1987). The organization of a West African grain market. *American Anthropologist, 89*, 74-95.

Saul, M. (1988). The efficiency of private channels in the distribution of cereals in Burkina Faso. In J. Bennett & J. Bowen (Eds.), *Production and autonomy: Anthropological studies and critiques of development* (pp. 87-104). Lanham, MD: University Press of America.

Scott, E. P. (1972). The spatial structure of rural northern Nigeria: Farmers, periodic markets and villages. *Economic Geography, 48*, 316-322.

Scott, E. P. (1978). Subsistence markets and rural development in Hausaland. *Journal of Developing Areas, 12*, 449-469.

Shenton, R. W., & Lennihan, L. (1981). Capital and class: Peasant differentiation in northern Nigeria. *Journal of Peasant Studies, 9*, 47-70.

Sherry, J. F., Jr. (1989). Marketing and development: A review essay. *Journal of Macromarketing, 9*, 65-74.

Sherry, J. F., Jr. (1990). Dealers and dealing in a periodic market: Informal retailing in ethnographic perspective. *Journal of Retailing, 66*, 174-199.

Sheth, J. N. (1993, June). *Relationship marketing: An emerging school of marketing thought.* Paper presented at the American Marketing Association Faculty Consortium on Services Marketing, Arizona State University, Tempe.

Smith, C. A. (Ed.). (1976). *Regional analysis* (2 vols.). New York: Academic Press.

Sørensen, O. J. (1988). Development of marketing channels for agricultural supplies. In E. Kumcu & A. F. Fırat (Eds.), *Marketing and development: Toward broader dimensions* (pp. 285-316). Greenwich, CT: JAI.

Speece, M. (1990). Evolution of ethnodominated marketing channels: Evidence from Oman and Sudan. *Journal of Macromarketing, 10,* 78-92.

Spekman, R. E., & Johnston, W. J. (1986). Relationship management: Managing the selling and buying interface. *Journal of Business Research, 14,* 519-531.

Stern, L. W., & Reve, T. (1980). Distribution channels as political economies: A framework for comparative analysis. *Journal of Marketing, 44,* 52-64.

Suret-Canale, J. (1977). *L'Afrique noire; l'ère coloniale, 1900-1945.* Paris: Editions Sociale.

Thorelli, H., & Sentell, G. D. (1982). *Consumer emancipation and economic development: The case of Thailand.* Greenwich, CT: JAI.

Tobin, J. J. (Ed.). (1992). *Re-made in Japan: Everyday life and consumer taste in a changing society.* New Haven, CT: Yale University Press.

Touré, A. (1985). *Les pétits métiers à Abidjan.* Paris: Editions Karthala.

Traeger, L. (1981a). Customers and creditors: Variation in economic personalism in a Nigerian market system. *Ethnology, 20,* 133-146.

Traeger, L. (1981b). Yoruba market organization—A regional analysis. *African Urban Studies, 10,* 43-58.

Wilcock, D. (1987). *Agricultural marketing in Niger: Current situation, constraints and possible AEPRP Program components.* Washington, DC: Development Alternatives, Inc.

Wilkins, A. L., & Ouchi, W. G. (1983). Efficient cultures: Exploring the relationship between culture and organizational performance. *Administrative Science Quarterly, 28,* 468-481.

Williams, G. (1985). Marketing without and with marketing boards: The origins of state marketing boards in Nigeria. *Review of African Political Economy, 34,* 4-15.

Yusuf, A. B. (1975). Capital formation and management among the Muslim Hausa traders of Kano, Nigeria. *Africa, 45,* 167-182.

✺ 5

Anthropology and Total Quality Management

Improving Sales Force Performance in Overseas Markets

Richard H. Reeves-Ellington

The failure of major multinational corporations to meet new business challenges during the 1960s drove many large Western corporations to seek change. This chapter reports on change efforts within the Africa/Asia (A/A) region of Pharmco, Inc. (a pseudonym for a pharmaceutical company owned by a major U.S. multinational). The A/A region's product line was aging, its market position poor, and its managers were neglected and ill-trained. Customers had no image of the company. The A/A region was challenged by its management to become successful in key regional markets within 5 years. Senior company management defined success in traditional business terms: achieve breakeven in 3 years, obtain $4 million in profits within the 5-year period, and reduce its organization size to meet the fiscal challenges. They clearly stated that failure to achieve these goals would result in closure of the regional businesses.

When A/A regional personnel learned of the demands placed on them, they assumed the task was impossible. Working from a hierarchical, bureaucratic, organizational paradigm, it was. However, the new vice president of the region, a trained anthropologist, persuaded the regional managers to reconsider traditional approaches to business. He argued that if they used applied anthropological tools (e.g., participant observation), anthropological concepts (holistic sociocultural approaches), and anthropological methods (ethnographic and ethnohistorical approaches), they could meet the new goals. Indeed, they would be able to lead the company in organizational development, customer interactions, and total quality applications.

The vice president suggested a five-point program that, if addressed creatively, would bring the A/A region to a leadership position. First, the region would have to better integrate itself into the social environment of its customers and learn to work interactively with them. Second, the region would have to actually integrate its external customers into the A/A region's organization. This would require a total rethinking of what an organization is and how it works within society. (Kinship structures were of value as an alternate paradigm to the usual hierarchical Western business organization.) Third, regional personnel would have to redesign research methodologies and processes in ways that would provide new ways of looking at business. Traditional academic and business research would not provide the data needed for success. This meant that social science qualitative research would be added to the existing methods and that research responsibility would be expanded throughout the organization. Fourth, to ensure continual development and improvement, regional personnel must use the new concepts of total quality management (TQM) and strategic deployment. Fifth, all regional personnel would have to understand their existing normative and prescriptive values and build a vision and mission for the business on these values that would provide alignment of all regional personnel and their customers. The regional managers agreed that by accepting the five-point program they could achieve the organizational structure changes needed and thereby achieve not only the management goals set forth but also increase their sense of self-worth and value to their communities.

Without new products in the line, the challenge could only be met by strengthening the major brands available. Therefore, the five-point program was to focus on improved sales performance and improved regional management performance for improving the region. Regional management decided that a short-term (3-year) competitive advantage could be gained if the region's sales forces moved the two major brands from a low sixth place to first place in regional markets. Methods for achieving this growth were first tested during 1983 to 1986 in the Philippines, Australia, and the Gulf States. Given a lack of new products and limited resources, regional managers, with the agreement of the regional sales forces, agreed that they would start organizational revitalization with the sales force.

This revitalization would lead to creating a sales organization that would have a sustainable competitive advantage. The measurement of the competitive advantage would be the revival of the region's two leading brands. The

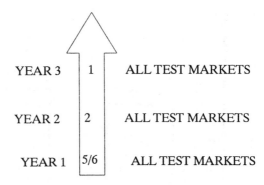

YEAR 3	1	ALL TEST MARKETS
YEAR 2	2	ALL TEST MARKETS
YEAR 1	5/6	ALL TEST MARKETS

TEST MARKETS: Australia, Gulf States, The Philippines

Figure 5.1   Brand category rank.

measurements used were brand category rank, brand volume, sales values, and profit. By these measurements, the reorganization was successful, as shown in Figures 5.1 and 5.2. Initially, in each of the test markets the organization brand placed no better than fifth in the category. Within 3 years, each brand achieved first place in its category in all test countries.

During the 3 years of improvement, the brands' promotional expenditures were steadily reduced as a percentage of sales and in absolute currency value. Much of this success was based on the implementation of the organizational changes outlined, and application of the new theoretical construct described below resulted in the A/A region's meeting and surpassing its goal of break-even in 3 years and earning a profit within 5 years. Profit was achieved by the third year. By the fifth year, the region led the division in profit as a percentage of sales. In addition, costs declined as a percentage of sales, the number of people required to produce results was 60% fewer than in other parts of the organization, and personnel from the region were heavily re-cruited by other parts of Pharmco as well as competitive companies. Finally, the company's customers in the region recognized it as an innovator and responsible citizen of the community.

During the test, field force size, its role and actions in the marketplace, and the marketing mix were constant and few personnel changes were made; thus the sales team believed that the process changes were the primary cause of improvement.

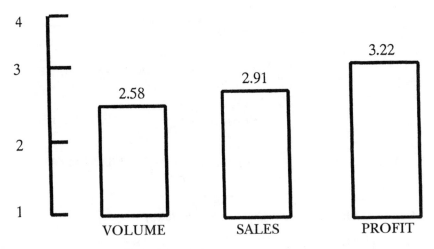

Figure 5.2   Brand indices, 1984-1985.

NOTE: Based on results in Australia, the Gulf States, and the Philippines. The first year has been indexed as 1 and the figure shows results at the end of Year 3. During the test, the field force size and marketing mix were relatively constant. However, promotional expenditures were increased in absolute terms but decreased in relation to sales.

Customer-Driven Organizations

The task required that the field force be redefined organizationally from being merely reactive to marketing needs to driving management in meeting external customer requirements.

This paradigm shift required the A/A region to use anthropological field research techniques, culture-building processes, and enculturation techniques together with total quality tools and processes of benchmarking, strategy deployment, and analytical processes. The use of these processes and tools permitted a shift in the role of the field force in the new organization and aided the new sales organization to understand where it was coming from and where it was to go. It also influenced the way the field sales organizations viewed themselves within the new organizational context. To accomplish the requisite paradigm shifts and implement them into the regional organization, the regional vice president assumed the role of corporate shaman—integrating the sacred with the profane. He performed the role of social integrator. In this role, the vice president could ensure that the underlying cultural norms and ethics were consistent with the work processes and social organization that would successfully meet the business requirements needed to

TABLE 5.1

Producer-Consumer and Customer-Supplier Paradigm Comparison

Factor	Producer-Consumer	Customer-Supplier
Focus	Reference to class or statistical group	Personal reference
Impetus	Producer driven: producer-product-user	Customer driven: user-product-supplier
Process	Impersonal, object-oriented	Interactive, inclusive participation
Quality control	Statistical acceptability	Individual satisfaction
Notion of service	An additional contract	Embedded in product
Values	Utilitarian	Communication
Organizing principle	Economic rationality; control	Relationship rationality; responsive
Strategic objective	Create demand	Respond to need

survive. He could also holistically track the progress of the project and ensure its reapplication elsewhere in the organization.

The regional sales organization had operated on a self-centered paradigm: "What is good for us is good for our customers." This was the basis of the region's poor performance. To provide a needed paradigm of understanding, a dichotomy was made between the existing "producer-consumer" paradigm and a desired interactional "supplier-customer" paradigm (Geroski, 1989; Reeves-Ellington, 1989). The difference between the two paradigms was summarized by a Japanese executive on CNN. In his words, "President Coolidge said 'The business of America is business,' but the business of Japan is relationships." The fundamental descriptors of each paradigm (Table 5.1) offer a basis for understanding whether an organization operates according to a consumer or customer paradigm.

The user of the consumer paradigm (product oriented) focuses on the habits and attitudes of the consumer of the goods and services that the producer provides, defines consumers as one of a group or class (women, Blacks, males, yuppies) and looks at consumers statistically. Underlying this model is the ethos of unilateral determinism. Users of the consumer paradigm are found almost universally in modern business and governmental organizations. For the producer, products are the central object for action and the consumer is an object to be manipulated. The producer is the prime marketplace mover of all actions throughout the distribution chain, which includes the consumer.

In contrast, the underlying principle of the customer paradigm (marketing oriented) is that the customer, through expression of needs and desires, joins with the supplier in determining what goods and services are to be developed and sold. The customer acts upon or toward the supplier and anticipates that the supplier will respond positively or negatively, which in turn influences the customer's further actions. If the customer talks, the supplier is likely to respond; thus the two will alternate in a chain of interaction until a basis of exchange or technology transfer is completed. Activation of the customer-supplier paradigm is attributed to the relationship between customer and supplier. This interchange is well exemplified by Popcorn (1991) reporting on the Japanese bicycle plant that can make a custom bike in 2 minutes but delays delivery for 2 weeks in order to make the customer feel good by anticipating the new custom-made bike. The customer process in the operating environment is defined through "interactional relativism."

Figure 5.3 shows the processes resulting from the consumer and customer paradigms. In particular, the Customer Requirements Process shows a desired method of interaction between customer and supplier that results in products that customers truly want (Reeves-Ellington & Steidlmeier, 1992). When applied appropriately, the process can lead to total customer focus and market share dominance (Reeves-Ellington, 1989). The dynamics of the customer-supplier paradigm can be summarized under the rubric of "from the customer to the customer."

Gaining consensus in the A/A region for shifting from the consumer process to that of the customer process was difficult. There was an underlying subtext of power relationships that existed in the operating consumer paradigm. For the successful application of the customer paradigm assumed in Figure 5.1, those needed to be changed. In one stormy session in which this paradigm shift was being worked through, two managers stalked out, saying "This way of working will castrate me!" It took the vice president more than a day to show these managers that if they adopted the attendant power relationships that went with the customer process they would gain a substantial competitive advantage. They would also increase their power and influence both within the legal organization and with their customers who exist outside the usual organizational definition. In short, the vice president was asking them to adopt an anthropological *Weltanshauung* by looking at the world in a holistic way. Also, the vice president assured the managers that his boss was the region's "protector" and would positively market their actions to other parts of the organization (for a fuller discussion, see Anderson & Reeves-Ellington, 1993). After A/A managers agreed to a working paradigm for the entire organization, the general managers, sales managers, and sales

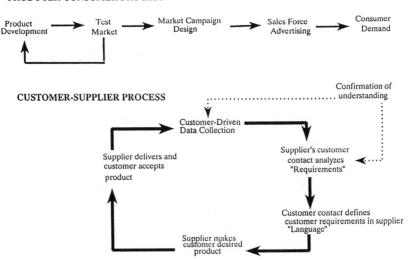

Figure 5.3 Process of operating environment definition.

people worked to develop a revised organizational construct that would improve overall organizational performance and specifically serve to improve sales and sales team performance. The meeting participants also agreed that they would have to become action researchers; that is, they would both observe and participate in the development of the new paradigms and organizational constructs.

During the initial stages of program implementation, personnel turnover exceeded 35% in all locations, 20% higher than had been previously experienced. The primary reason given for leaving was a dissatisfaction with the new work methods. Those employed at the start of the change process had been hired into the traditional, bounded organization of Pharmco. For many of these people, the shift of work expectations from one of responding to management and doing what they were told to one of thinking, creating, and recommending was a shift in social contract they did not want. As indicated earlier, this offered the major challenge within the change process undertaken. However, later into the program, a second important reason for leaving the company was cited—better opportunities elsewhere. The level of training and skill development provided left many people with a relatively high level of dissatisfaction. As one Filipino said in an exit interview, "This is a great place to be trained but a lousy place to get promoted. There aren't enough jobs." The Australians and Arabs suffered most with the level of ambiguity of the new workplace and the lack of clear direction. During the early stages, the pleas "Just tell us what to do" were constantly heard. However, the level of satisfaction with the training and skill development of those leaving was measured, in part, by the number of referrals they sent to Pharmco. Over the course of one year, the A/A region received 200 referrals (50 were hired). Within the broader community, Pharmco was seen as a caring organization, even in times of trial and change.

▨ The New Theoretical Organizational Construct

By using action research techniques, A/A region personnel agreed to shift from the traditional Pharmco paradigm to an unbounded (primarily socially defined) and "of reality" organizational paradigm. Achieving this shift of paradigm from a bounded organization or organization "for reality" (Geertz, 1973) to one of an unbounded organization "of reality" (Geertz, 1973) required that the A/A regional management develop new concepts and processes in organizational behavior. Although an overall organizational scheme was developed by the A/A region, primary focus was on the field sales organization. Specifically, focus was directed to the Philippines, Australia, and the Gulf States sales organizations.

The interpretive paradigm (Morgan, 1986) coupled with Geertz's interpretative method of understanding culture (Geertz, 1973) can be used to rethink concepts that are more appropriate for application of boundary-spanning capabilities needed to effect major organizational changes, such as downsizing and globalizing. This paradigm effects change but at a regulated pace. It assumes the world is an emergent social process created by individuals in the organization in conjunction with people identified as customers outside the traditional organization, thus creating a "social construction of reality" (Berger & Luckmann, 1967). A/A management, keeping the Greek *polis* in mind, worked on the assumption that changes in the external and internal organizational environment can force organizational members to consider change, but it is organizational members who effect the change by using shared change mechanisms and processes. Effecting such change requires adoption of the concept of the organization as social construct developed by organizational members (Aldrich, 1992; Ghoshal, 1987; Wardell, 1992; Whitley, 1992). These institutions have been called "organizations of reality" by Geertz (1973). Within this framework, the concepts of reciprocal behavior (Axelrod,

1984; Oye, 1986; Parkhe, 1993) and trust (Thorelli, 1986) must be understood and employed by all members of the socially constructed reality.

The traditional pharmaceutical sales organization operates within the producer-consumer paradigm, the marketing department being the producer of sales plans and the salespeople being the "consumer" or executor of the plans. These sales departments are "but to do or die." They are told by marketing what to say, how to say it, when to say it, and who to say it to. They keep records for others' benefit on what they do, how they do it, and what happens. They are asked to report, report, and report. They are measured by the number of calls per day they make, what is ordered by the retail pharmacist, the number of displays set up, and/or the number of conferences attended (Smith, 1983). None of these measurements reflects what salespeople consider important, nor what their customers consider important. This leads to a general customer dislike of sales people. For example, at Procter & Gamble, salespeople are so disliked that they are greeted by a sign saying "PLEASE CHECK IN WITH THE MORGUE" at one retailer's office (Swasy, 1993, p. 235). Companies actually resent the trade's place in the supply chain and do everything possible to minimize it (Smith, 1983; Swasy, 1993). As one P&G salesperson said, "Being tough with the trade was a judge of your manhood."

Within the pharmaceutical industry, salespeople are considered so unimportant that companies such as Procter & Gamble Pharmaceuticals, Abbott Laboratories, Eli Lilly, and Bristol Meyers Squibb are reducing their in-house sales forces and "renting" salespeople. These companies turn to outsiders who have a field force that can be hired for a predetermined time by the pharmaceutical company. These people are trained in understanding a specific product and product message and told who to call upon with that message. The underlying logic is that salespeople are only to deliver the messages developed by marketing and therefore are interchangeable at short notice.

However, the A/A regional sales managers wanted to redefine this selling role to one that served as a vehicle for implementing strategies that integrated the company's customer and the company by creating a shared culture (Levitt, 1983). They would do this by listening closely to what the customers had to say and by acting on this information (Barabba & Zaltman, 1991).

The Research Methodologies

To effect the organizational changes needed within Pharmco's revised working paradigms, specific research methodologies were needed. From these methodologies were to come processes that would permit the implementation of training, operating processes, and business strategies to be used by Pharmco. The desired outcome was to marketize all company employees to their external customer base by developing action research skills and the ability to integrate learning from these skills with previous academic theories.

The Action Researcher

Baskerville (1991, also personal discussions) has explored the issue of practitioner autonomy and its relationship to philosophical underpinnings of information systems research. His model, when adapted, well describes the interactions between academics and practitioners that the vice president of Pharmco used in his role of action researcher for this study. For the process to function maximally, information must flow between the theorist and practitioner, through the interaction of theorist, action researcher, and practitioner. Furthermore, the process must be continuous in ways that ensure ongoing learning. Susman and Evered (1978) and Reeves-Ellington (1993b) have described processes to achieve continuous learning for the systems, knowledge (theoretical and practitioner), and results needed. Figure 5.4 provides a schematic of the process used by Pharmco to ensure continuous double-loop learning (Argyris & Schön, 1978) between the developers of theory (academicians, action researchers, and practitioners). The process in Figure 5.2 gave users a schematic that permitted them to constantly adjust understanding of what was being done, correct actions being undertaken, and reformulate the likely outcomes of activities. In short, information gained from use of the process provided the data needed for proper implementation of policy deployment and TQM processes within the A/A region.

Action Research

The action research methods used assume that meaningful research occurs when at least one of the researchers both observes and participates in the phenomena under study. Rapoport's (1978) definition of action research offers understanding of this point of view:

> Action research aims to contribute both to the practical concerns of people in an immediate problematic situation and to the goals of social science by joint collaboration within a mutually acceptable ethical framework. (p. 588)

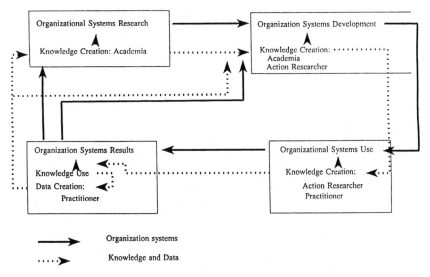

Figure 5.4 Organizational research.

The focus of action research, within Rapoport's context, is on what is to come, not, as is the case with scientific methodology applied, what has happened in the past. Hult and Lennung (1980), in their definition of action research, capture the double-loop learning as well as the continuous learning cycle. They state,

> Action research simultaneously assists in practical problem-solving and expands scientific knowledge, as well as enhances the competencies of the respective actors, being performed collaboratively in an immediate situation using data feed back in a cyclical process aiming at the increased understanding of a given social situation, primarily applicable for the understanding of change process in social systems and undertaken within a mutually acceptable ethical framework. (p. 247)

Within the A/A region, in order to adapt the general theoretical information of academe, joint efforts between academia and practitioners were led by an action researcher. He provided the business problematic (Susman, 1983) to which theory and praxis was applied. Also, the action researcher decided on what Cook (1983) calls the ontological assumptions necessary to solve a particular problem in a specific organization. This met a self-imposed requirement that organizational strategy, structure, and environment should be aligned (Miller, 1988). The resulting action research was based on qualitative data to be used in critical reflection by an analyst.

In the case of Pharmco, the vice president was the primary action researcher and leader in training others in the organization in developing action research skills. He was a trained anthropologist experienced in working with academic counterparts to translate the knowledge of academe into shared wisdom in the world of the practitioner by creating multiple practitioners in the region. To accomplish the transformation of knowledge, the A/A region's action researchers worked through native-view paradigms, used ethnoscience and ethnography, and explored multiple perspectives over time. They were able to obtain qualitative data that offer more insight than traditional survey methods usually permit (Gregory, 1983). Thus the tools for understanding were available to the firm before attempts were made to achieve intercultural and culture-specific understandings (Boyacigiller & Adler, 1991). Within this role, the action researchers functioned and acted "as fellow students, collaborators and investigators, of equal status with their managerial colleagues" (Warmington, 1980, p. 36). In addition, the action researchers had equal status with their academic consultants.

On achieving these ties, the action researchers acted as the bridges and translators between academics and practitioners. After field introduction and trial of alternate organization types and their underlying cultural assumptions, the action researchers, in conjunction with the practitioners, fed results back to academic consultants. They then critiqued the actions and, when necessary, suggested adjustments. Some examples are the use of Michigan State anthropologists and University of Utah psychologists working to provide the theory, processes, and skills of understanding and creating shared values and adjunct professors from the University of Cincinnati aiding in organization development skills and theory. After initial development, the design process was based on a self-design learning model similar to that discussed by Ledford and Mohrman (1993). These actions were undertaken jointly by the action researchers and the practitioners. All the processes created were designed to be generative in nature (Reeves-Ellington, 1993a; Reeves-Ellington & Steidlmeier, 1993; Senge, 1990). During the time of reapplication and revision, local consultants were employed within the various countries of the region. This allowed local ownership of the work being done and permitted processes to be used and reused throughout the A/A region of Pharmco on a continuous basis. In effect, a learning organization was created.

The methods for determining successful deployment of the processes were participant observation, timing of implementation of processes, and the collection of ethnographic material throughout the region. Of particular ethnographic interest was how people perceived illness and its treatment, kinship and ritual kinship roles in business, normative value orientations of those in the health delivery system, and prescriptive value orientations of health care providers. For independent evaluation, outside consultants were brought in to assess skills development, process applications, and program results. These were the people who initially helped to establish theory and processes in conjunction with the local consultants who were used. Much of this consulting work was done at little or no charge to the company. Consultants are usually permitted to use the results of their work with Pharmco in other arenas.

Although action research was valuable in planning, executing, and documenting change within the A/A regional experience, four problems manifested themselves throughout the research. First, the primary action researcher had a specific managerial position within the region (i.e., vice president). Given his perceived power position, access to detailed actions within the various business units of the region was difficult. If demands for detailed data were requested to document day-to-day changes, charges of "lack of trust" and "meddling" were forthcoming. Reliance for receiving data was based on trust between the vice president and the rest of the organization. In other words, relationship management was required—a basic tenet of anthropological fieldwork. Numerous face-to-face meetings helped to ensure good data, although there was constant worry about hearing "only the good news."

The second problem was methodological. As the action researcher was responsible for effecting the change as well as formulating and documenting it, methodology designed to create specific changes was used only as long as it was generating needed outcomes. This prevented a clean traditional experimental design and collection of statistically valid data.

The third area of concern was that the primary action researcher had a strongly intuitive and analytical personality. This resulted in some isolation from the practitioners (the field organization's managers), who felt that they and their colleagues were constantly being analyzed. As one practitioner said, "Can't you stop analyzing? You make us very uncomfortable!" This conflicted with the action researcher's role of a supportive manager. The fourth problem related to the action researcher understanding what role was appropriate at what times. For managing the region, the management role was key. For learning theory and its application to the region, the role of theoretician was prime. For transferring knowledge, the role of facilitator was indicated. For implementing new work processes, the role of practitioner came to the fore. For understanding the interaction of all aspects of regional activities, the role of action researcher was paramount. In work contexts, the roles were in conflict and led to confusion between the action researcher and his colleagues. For example, at one meeting, the vice president attended as a manager who needed to obtain results. Two outsider managers were also in attendance to learn about the business results. However, all other A/A regional managers assumed that the vice president was at the meeting to discuss and improve work processes. By failing to clarify the purpose of the meeting and the role of attendees, all parties left with a high level of dissatisfaction. The vice president was irked that no "real" results had been presented and discussed. The outsiders left believing that the region was only interested in process and not getting results. The A/A regional managers left thinking they had been set up for looking bad. These types of misunderstanding continued periodically throughout the study, even though efforts at role clarification were made before each meeting.

Ethnology and Participant Observation

As reported by Reeves-Ellington (in press), to effect major organizational change leading to the brand leadership required, sound ethnographic input is required. Eliade (1974) has reported that "concreteness (of culture) will be accentuated by the studies of the ethnologist" and that "the ethnologist will succeed in showing the circulation of the particular motif in time and space" (pp. xii-xiii). Employee collection of ethnographic data within the Pharmco context was key in providing customer and competitive environment information which was used to gain competitive advantage. The anthropological research method of participant observation (PO) provides a preferred technique for collecting ethnographic information that fits the cultural understanding of the environment of a customer-driven organization. Pharmco's preference warrants detailed discussion of good participant observer methodology.

Businesspeople need a methodological tool to help them comprehend information as others see it. PO skills, traditionally employed by the anthropologist (Finan & van Willigen, 1990; Spradley, 1980; Wheeler & Chambers, 1992), provide a tool that permits the business person to develop and use all needed channels of communication. The task of the participant observer is to find out what is important to others (Jorgensen, 1989). It involves making accessible what is normally concealed, namely, backstage and commonsense information from another person's point of view (David, 1985). Business people who employ this skill are better able to relate to those around them and to plan meaningful interactions with others.

PO is a style of behavior that creates social relationships between people (as required of a customer-driven organization) and a favorable environment for achieving mutually agreed tasks. The key point is that the participant observer spends time with others and does things with them.

Participant observation requires a combination of direct observation and questioning techniques. These techniques allow ongoing systematic acquisition of findings about what is important to people. Gaining needed information about others requires active listening. There are two main objectives of active listening. The first is to hear what is meant by listening for the vocabulary chosen and voice inflections used. The second is to "listen" with other senses for nonverbal messages (Covey, 1989; Hall & Hall, 1987). The participant observer requires specific plans for action that will move him or her from that which is easily known to that which is normally concealed. There are five action strategies that will aid in gaining concealed information: *appear to know to find out; use backstage information to get more backstage information; use others as teachers; rate others as witnesses, informants, and backstagers; and claim to really need the information.* Each of these strategies was employed in the Pharmco project.

Total Quality Management (TQM)

Strategy Deployment

The interpretive paradigm and supporting literature of organizational social constructs discussed above do not provide a sufficiently radical shift in thinking and organizational change to assist failing organizations. Effecting the change paradigm in ways that ensure thoroughness and maintain meaning requires application of total quality thinking and process application (Demming, 1982; Juran, 1989; Pernick, 1993; Rohrer, 1990). Particular emphasis on policy deployment and improved policy execution is needed (Abegglen & Stalk, 1985; Imai, 1986; Ishikawa, 1986; Reeves-Ellington & Steidlmeier, 1992). The processes used for effecting a total quality application paradigm force TQM users to constantly interact with organizational environments and provide the necessary flexibility to adapt and change (Anderson

& Reeves-Ellington, 1993). Thus processes are developed and changed as conditions demand.

Among the early exports of Deming, Juran, and other postwar quality-control advisors to Japan, however, there was a very successfully adopted decision-making and activity cycle popularly known as Plan-Do-Check-Act, or PDCA (Abegglen & Stalk, 1985; Wheeler & Chambers, 1992). In its Japanese realization, it appears that this tool fit basic cultural elements such as cognitive and value orientations about the nature of time and people (Reeves-Ellington, 1993a). The advantage of being able to observe how the Japanese operationalized PDCA adds to its advantages of Western origin and thus its potential adaptability as a reimport. As a generative process model, the purpose of PDCA, especially in the Japanese realization, is the mindful emulation of an ideal, self-correcting learning process in a constantly changing and less than fully known milieu. It has been already partially adapted as a popular rationalizing device by many U.S. businesses.

The limitation of most uses of PDCA cycles in the United States, however, has been not only that they are focused mainly on manufacturing and service outputs but that, to our knowledge, they have not been extended to tasks of organizational development. There are also the ever present culturally influenced factors: Compared with the Japanese, American firms can be generally characterized as underinvested on Plan and Check and overinvested on Do and Act. In fact, much of the time, the U.S. process of implementing anything can be characterized simply as a Plan-Act sequence, with minimal or no attempts to obtain and process feedback.

Figure 5.5 (Anderson & Reeves-Ellington, 1993) shows an adaptation of an implicit comparison made by Kinney (1988) coupled with a very similar one from Whitehall (1991), who states,

> After an idea is formulated in the Japanese company it is explained, discussed, and confirmed by all those affected. This requires considerable time (A). When the "go/no go" point is reached, however, very little time (B) is required to take action. In the U.S. case, the "go/no go" stage is reached rather quickly by top management (C). Then a massive "selling job" must be mounted taking a considerable period of time (D). In the final analysis the total time span required is not very different. (pp. 160-161)

The A/A region attempted to emulate the Japanese paradigm of PDCA rather than the American one. The time invested in planning was more than rewarded in the lack of later rework.

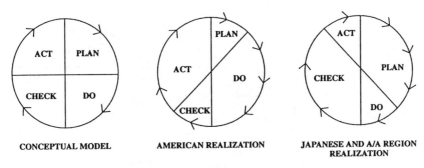

CONCEPTUAL MODEL   AMERICAN REALIZATION   JAPANESE AND A/A REGION
                                                              REALIZATION

Figure 5.5   Cultural differences in Plan-Do-Check cycle.

Analytical Tools and Processes

To effect change within the time parameters given to the sales team, every member of that team had to be able to understand the overall policy of the A/A region and that of the sales organization. They further had to be able to effect change within their specific job. For the sales team to accomplish this task and to improve key brand performance (the ultimate measure of their success) they needed several specific TQM tools and processes. (The following references for support of the analytical tools used are the most recent and more comprehensive than the ones used for the test. They are in the spirit of the work, however.)

To effect major organizational change, at either the macro- or microlevel, organizational members must use what are now well-established TQM techniques (Anderson, 1993; Bendell, Boulter, & Kelly, 1993; Demming, 1986; Mizuno, 1988; Wheeler & Chambers, 1992). Employees must benchmark themselves (Bendell et al., 1993; Spendolini, 1992), their customers, and the competition. They must identify the key factors needed for success (Mizuno, 1988; Ohmae, 1990) and develop and implement working processes that will lead to success (Beauregard, Mikulak, & Olson, 1992). This permits the organization to identify clearly what will determine possible competitive advantages within its total working environment (Porter, 1985), clearly identify its shortcomings, develop programs to overcome these shortcomings, and develop and use meaningful measurements for program success (Lock, 1994).

Pharmco, in this case, used market share standings, physician focus groups, pharmacist focus groups, internal field sales focus groups, and competitive sales

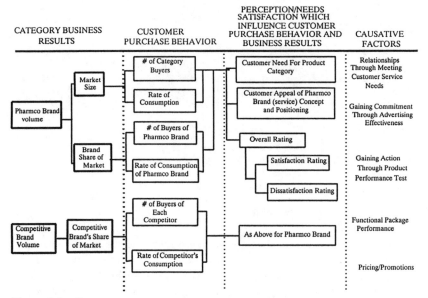

Figure 5.6   Customer measurements process.

data. Ohmae (1988) provides a clear blueprint for successful strategy development, using TQM methodologies (pp. 11-36). With the data gained from benchmarking, Pareto charting and quality evolution charting permitted clear definition of the major problems preventing the key brands from achieving leadership positions in the test markets (Crosby, 1979, 1984; Juran, 1980; Juran & Gryna, 1980). With these data, clear statements of problems and opportunities were possible. Fishboning techniques (Ishikawa, 1984; Ohmae, 1988) further identified the restraining forces in ways that permitted development of action steps to overcome such forces. Finally, work processes were needed to ensure that all necessary steps were understood and executed in the customer chain (Porter, 1980, 1985; Smith, 1983).

Measuring for Total Quality

In addition to traditional business measurements, the A/A region developed innovative customer-sales measurements that reflected the changed operating paradigm from a producer-consumer one-to-one reflecting the customer-supplier interaction. The key to measurements in a total quality

Figure 5.7   Customer satisfaction measurements.

*A +/– number represents the difference between Pharmco and the best supplier/competitor. A positive number indicates that Pharmco is stronger than others.

organization is to ensure that they reflect the desires of the customer receiving the goods and services, either inside or outside the organization. The A/A region developed a series of customer satisfaction measurements. Personnel within the region agreed that such measurements must be systematic, be defined by the customer in terms of a desired outcome, be compared to competition, relate to a predetermined time schedule, and be actionable. To ensure that all the measurement criteria were met, an overall customer measurements process was developed under the leadership of the sales groups in the test markets (Figure 5.6).

   The purpose of the process was to ensure that Pharmco's test brands were meeting the needs of the customers most likely to need and use the products. Also, the processes highlighted the need to provide services for key customers that would reflect favorably upon the brands. This is discussed in detail below. A final point was to benchmark continually the brands against those considered to be major competitors, *as defined by the customer and not by the marketing department*. The execution of the measurement program was under the control of the sales groups, who reported the results to others within Pharmco. The first user of the data was the territory salesperson, then other sales personnel in the various test markets, and finally, marketing and general

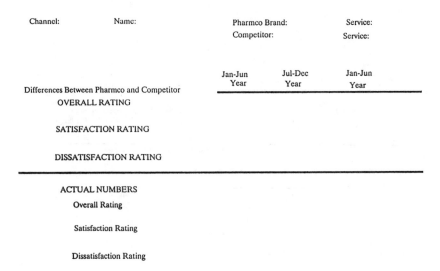

Figure 5.8   Customer satisfaction report.

management. The system was developed to measure all aspects of the field sales chain: doctors, pharmacies, hospitals, and distributors.

Two actual reporting forms were developed by the field sales teams: one for use by the customer receiving the goods and services and the other for use by the field representative as a compilation of territorial data. The measurements were taken every 6 months for every major customer in the customer chain. The one completed by the external customer, Customer Satisfaction (third-party data) (Figure 5.7), reports on the brand, related services, and competitors. The form itself was developed jointly by the field sales team and those who would complete the form. In this way the information collected would be considered important to the most important people using the data.

The second form, Customer Satisfaction Report (Figure 5.8), was developed for use within Pharmco. From the data on this sheet, appropriate policy and strategy shifts were considered and developed. These data formed much of the basis for the Check and Act phases of the PDCA cycle.

Other less formal measurements were developed by the field force members themselves. For example, in the Philippines, the sales team identified that improvements in three key uses of time would most likely improve their sales output. The improvements desired were less waiting time in the doctor's office, more time in conversation with the doctor, and an increase in the

TABLE 5.2

Time Measurements for Control Charting

Waiting time
A baseline number of 10 and 30 minutes with an average
of 20 minutes was established. A target of an average of
10 minutes was established and control charted by each representative.

Time with doctor
The baseline number was 4 minutes. A target of 15 minutes
was established and performance charted by each representative.

Frequency of visits
The average was one visit every 3 months. The target
to be charted for measurement was one visit every month.

---

annual number of visits. The team then developed baseline data for each, a control range for each activity, and a new standard desired. Table 5.2 provides the data for each. Within a 6-month period, all goals were met or exceeded.

Building Rather Than Chasing Sales

Field forces operating under the consumer paradigm are focused on and structured to "getting sales." Selling the largest amount of product to whomever will buy is the norm. Profits are not the worry of the field force. Within the Pharmco experience, the use of the consumer paradigm within the field force leads to constantly expanding sales teams, increasing direct and indirect costs, and decreasing profits. A/A sales teams within the test market altered the "get sales" paradigm to one of "building business." Figure 5.9 reflects the major steps required in executing a business building paradigm.

The first four steps of the process develop the basis of learning how to obtain organizational alignment and then actually achieving it. These skills are then useful in later customer interactions. All of the first four steps must be integrated and aligned. The next two steps—identifying customers and selecting them require a basic understanding of the customer chain—what key attributes each of the customer sets should have and the ability to select the most important individual customers from each set of customers in the customer chain. The last three steps—gaining access, delivering brand messages, and gaining action—are more traditionally accepted actions of sales forces. However, some basic rethinking was done to provide the A/A sales teams with sustainable competitive advantages over their competitors.

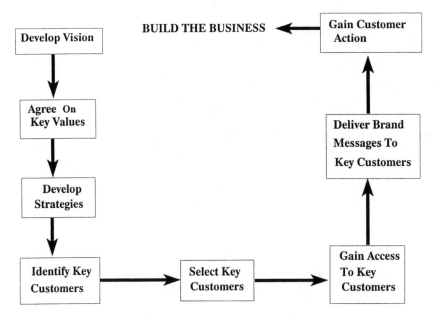

Figure 5.9   Business-building process.

Gaining Organizational Alignment

Visioning for a Paradigm Shift

To reverse the declining state of the business and to ensure the continued existence of the region, A/A regional managers needed to develop a process that would create a vision for the entire region and would provide a process that would permit all members of the organization to develop their own personal and departmental visions that would lead the region to a leadership position. Regional personnel realized that evolutionary thinking would not provide the stimulus to provoke the changes necessary to achieve a customer-driven organization. They determined that the desired organization had to be created from the imagination for the future and not from past history. Two paradigm shifts discussed above were used: an interpretive one integrating the organization into its environment and policy deployment using total quality tools. These shifts caused the region to view change as emancipating potentiality and view the organization from the standpoint that tends to be

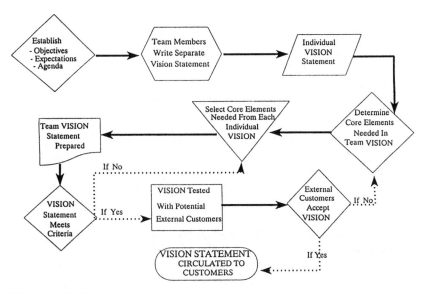

Figure 5.10 Visioning process.

realist and nomothetic. The adoption of improvement cycles and total quality techniques shifted the concept of achieving the optimum organization form (model formation) to one of constantly striving for organizational improvement (process improvements). Policy deployment permitted all employees throughout the region to understand the direction of organizational change but left them free to implement that direction in ways acceptable to them and their customers. Furthermore, it permitted everyone to participate in policy development.

The Visioning Process and Its Application

The first step in developing a radically different organization was to provide a process (Figure 5.10) by which all employees in the region could develop a vision of what they wanted and then use the process to provide a firm organizational vision (Ackerman, 1984). Through trial and error, the regional managers documented a process deemed successful to the development of their organizational vision.

The key points of the process are as follows:

TABLE 5.3

Vision Checklist

Identifies the uniqueness of the institution being developed

Provides sufficient rationale for adoption

Is compelling

Addresses mutual self-interest

Identifies external contexts

Identifies internal contexts

---

1. Each individual develops a personal vision.
2. A common vision is developed and consensus achieved—everyone has to agree to the vision.
3. The vision is "reality tested" against specific criteria (Table 5.3) to ensure that the original intent of the drafters is intact and that the vision is clear enough to provide a basis of action.
4. The vision is sufficiently clear for others to understand and support it.

The second process is one of culture building, which permits employees to capture the essence of the ethnic institution. After accepting the challenge, personnel spent 6 months developing a visioning process and testing it within the organization. During this period, several interim visions were adopted and implemented, but, until personnel probed more deeply into culture and ethics, the visions failed to provide the quantum improvements needed to meet management objectives for profit. They did energize regional personnel by providing a focus. The visioning process continued within the concept of continuous improvement throughout the entire organizational development period.

THE REGIONAL VISION

The Africa/Asia Region organization will operate as a team and have a particular identity with boundaries, culture, and community. The resulting organization will be self-defining but will assimilate itself into the national cultures of the region and the culture of the parent organization, Pharmco. The creation of value chains linking the region's organizations in a smooth continuum internally and externally will ensure assimilation in its social contexts. Within both contexts, the Africa/Asia Region will understand and emphasize its distinctive nature and identity.

The vision provides the basis of an outreaching, interpretative organization. This is in contradistinction to the traditional organization function within a producer-consumer paradigm in which the producer controls. It is rather a customer-supplier paradigm, in which both parties interact for mutual satisfaction.

With this strategic policy deployed within the region, the field forces of the Philippines, Australia, and the Gulf States developed a sales vision that was eventually to be the document used throughout the region. During a series of three meetings, each of the sales teams worked on its visions for a revitalized field force. The first meeting included learning the visioning process and practicing its application. Even before the first meeting, the regional vice president went to each of the country sites and reviewed the overall program. During these meetings, he met with every employee in the organization in order to build trust and an initial environment that would permit acceptance of the new way of doing business. These meetings were followed up by local management meetings to further encourage a trusting relationship. During the field force visioning sessions, no other management person was present. The intention was to assure each person in the selling organization that his or her work was not influenced by outside management. The resulting field force vision was the following:

FIELD FORCE VISION

1. The individual representative drives management in building the business with individual key customers.
2. The field force, as a team, will be the Region's primary sustainable advantage.

The field force vision was developed by all the test markets but first tested throughout the organization in the Philippine company. This was done to teach visioning and gain country sales vision experience. The choice of the Philippines hinged on three factors:

- The organization was the most flexible and willing to experiment with change.
- The sales force volunteered for a leadership position in this area and they were accepted by the other test markets.
- The general manager had extensive field selling and selling management experience.

As they developed, they shared both successes and failures with the other test market selling organizations. They only shared their successes with senior managers outside the Philippines. Their key learning was that successful visions had to be grounded in agreed ethical systems.

Ethics: The Drivers of the Vision

The vision requires that an organization understand and create its under-lying ethics (normative and prescriptive).

Agreeing on common ethical grounds was the most difficult step in assuring the execution of the vision. Of particular difficulty was gaining agreement on prescriptive ethics. It is these values that underpin the organization. In philosophical terms these are the metaethical foundations of behavior that are articulated in terms of values and principals and reflected in customs, traditions, and symbols (Reeves-Ellington & Steidlmeier, 1993). They are what Hofstede (1980, 1991) refers to as the "desirable" (cultural norms that people want) and what people of a culture think ought to be desired (prescriptive ethical solutions that people want).

Normative Ethics

Before processing to prescriptive ethics, acceptable normative ethics and values must be clarified and understood by organization members. The desirable or normative ethics are directional (good or bad outcomes) and ideological (absolute). These norms are applicable to all people within a culture and are used for evaluation of cultural alignment. No actions are expected from normative values. People within a given culture act and often believe that their ethical foundations are, or should be, universal rather than culturally specific. These norms set the parameters of the normative ethos of a culture. In other words, there is not a single, clearly defined, consistent normative ethical base in complex societies (Geertz, 1973), including organizational ones. In the A/A region, normative ethics were discussed and revolved around the worth of people, openness of interactions, the power of learning and the sharing of that learning, the individual's acceptance of responsibility, honesty between people, and trust between people.

Whereas the culture provides its fundamental ethos, social knowledge provides the rules of the game as expressed routinely, that is, expected behavior patterns as determined by prescriptive ethics. As Reeves-Ellington and Steidlmeier (1993) discuss, social rules, based on prescriptive ethics, reflect what people collectively find desirable. They provide specific ways of doing things within the overall structure of normative ethical parameters. The glue that holds the values of social knowledge and behavior together includes intensity (the strength of the ethic) and pragmatism (majority opinion or those with power hold sway). Those rules deemed most important by the majority of those holding power positions will receive priority. Adherence can be measured through activities and their results. Rewards for adherence include recognition of individual importance and acknowledged success (Hofstede, 1980).

Prescriptive Ethics to Advance Social Knowledge

The cultural learning process had provided the A/A region with an understanding of its social knowledge. It did not provide personnel with concepts and tools to determine prescriptive ethical behavior. Hofstede's (1980) cultural dimensions provided the needed direction. These dimensions are based on a work-related framework that Hofstede developed while he was an organizational research scientist at IBM. His study uncovered intriguing differences in terms of four value dimensions: power distance, uncertainty avoidance, individualism, and masculinity. Power distance measures the degree to which influence and control are unequally distributed among individuals within a particular group. Uncertainty avoidance measures the degree to which individuals or societies attempt to avoid the ambiguity, riskiness, and indefiniteness of the future. Individualism measures the extent to which a culture expects people to take care of themselves or the extent to which individuals believe they are masters of their own destiny. Masculinity measures the degree to which the acquisition of money and things is valued and a high quality of life for others is not valued. The A/A regional managers benchmarked themselves against the original Hofstede findings for their country and then used the measures to project how they wanted to be as a work group.

Power distance dimension. Discussions concerning power distance focused on the value of education and power distribution. The consensus was that all people within the ethnic organization had a right to extensive information and the right to receive training and educational programs that traditionally were available to managers. Organizationally, teams with leadership and power distributed throughout were to be the norm, meaning that a supportive environment was required. This focus led to a small power distance organization, leading to the selection of three power distance prescriptive ethical statements:

- Be interdependent with key customers in the entire customer chain.
- Redistribute sales and customer power from the customer to the organization through the field force.

- Use power in ways seen to be legitimate within the new paradigms and vision.

Uncertainty avoidance dimension. Discussions on uncertainty avoidance revolved around problem-solving and organizational issues. Issues addressed would be determined through interaction between suppliers and customers rather than by senior management. By involving customers, both inside and outside the legal company, regional personnel had to accept increased risk taking in that any supplier had to have power and authority to resolve customer-defined needs and problems. Therefore, all people in the organization had to have a high degree of initiative and leadership skills. Implementation of these criteria required agreement to work in a high-ambiguity environment and acceptance of uncertainty. Two prescriptive ethics emerged:

- Be tolerant and accept dissent from anyone in the organization and in the external sales chain.
- Achievement will be recognized in ways desired by customers.

Individualism dimension. Management agreed that implementation of the ethnic organization required team and group dynamics that rest on individual freedom and challenge. Furthermore, team success is based on socially encouraged individual initiative toward leadership awareness. Finally, emotional interdependence is rooted in emotional independence. However, these attributes are subjugated to a sense of "we" rather than "I." Two prescriptive ethics were highlighted:

- Team decisions will take precedence but will be congruent with individual positions.
- Values of the team will be congruent with those of individual members of the team.

Masculinity dimension. Management opted for a low-masculinity index. The organization to be developed was to be based on trust as expressed in cooperation and friendship. In addition, work and community service should be made congruent wherever possible. Finally, value differences based on sex would have no role in the organization. Two prescriptive ethical stances were adopted:

- Orient activities to people, including customers.
- Strive to combine social service with commercial activities.

The field force, again using the strategic direction of the region, developed a set of values they thought important to drive their vision.

FIELD FORCE VALUES

1. We seek, share, and use knowledge to empower ourselves, our colleagues, and our customers.
2. We are individually responsible for the attainment of professional growth of ourselves, our colleagues, and our customers.

Reaching for the field-selling vision and having some hope of gaining it required that the sales teams have clear and precise knowledge of what values they needed to support it. Only through knowledge of fundamental normative and prescriptive ethics of the vision could they design a program that aligned all of the vision's participants. All the test markets found that understanding of these values was necessary for an additional three reasons. First, they define how knowledge was to be used. Traditionally, knowledge flowed from top to bottom in the regional organization, whereas facts primarily flowed upward. The data processed "at the top" were then sent "down" as knowledge. The field-selling values redefined this pathway by implying that the knowledge originated from the person most in the know (the salesperson) and was generated throughout the organization. Second, the values adopted implied a high-context culture within the organization (e.g., knowledge shared by all its members rather than knowledge limited by the need to know). Third, the values clearly included external customers in the organization's knowledge chain. This latter point required that sales personnel share their vision, values, and knowledge with their customers.

The power of having emphasized individual responsibility for increasing knowledge and thereby furthering professional growth in others is well exemplified in an exchange between two Philippines employees—one reporting to the other. A local government authority was making several administrative rulings that were having a negative impact on the company's business. The local representative was aware of the changes but did not share the knowledge with his colleague in Manila, even though both had agreed to completely share knowledge that could have an impact on the business. The lack of sharing subsequently created an embarrassing situation for the Manila manager. During important government strategy sessions conducted industrywide, the local situation was raised, with only the Pharmco manager being unaware of the situation. The question then for the Manila manager was to address the lack of knowledge sharing between himself and the salesperson. Two courses of action were possible: order that communications improve or discuss the lack of communication in relation to the shared value of sharing information. The latter strategy was chosen and successfully employed.

▧ The Mission

The vision and values give organizational members continuity with their colleagues, both within and outside the organization. However, even an unbounded organization requires a clear mission that provides the explicit reasons for its existence. For Pharmco, the mission needed to contain both its social and commercial contexts. Clear strategies were also developed to ensure attainment of the mission and advancement toward the vision within the value contexts agreed on. The regional mission was "We will build our business through profitable sales of products for prescription by health care professionals. We will do this by staying at the forefront of institutional change." The supporting strategies were that "through the continuous application of TQM we will (a) staff our organization with individuals of strong leadership and entrepreneurial qualities, (b) empower ourselves to do business and develop partnerships with our key customers, (c) develop and utilize superior resources that have perceived value higher than actual cost, apparent cost that is an entry barrier to competition, and actual cost lower than the competition."

Following the overall strategic direction of the region, the field force mission and strategies reflect the overall regional ones but are tailored to the specific tasks of the field organization.

FIELD FORCE MISSION

Build the business by providing key customers with quality products and information important for them to improve themselves and build their business. This will be done with innovation.

The mission statement contains the premise that the field force, as a business function, will function as the primary part of the company to gain a sustainable competitive advantage with its customers in the marketplace. For such a strategy to succeed, the test market field force teams working on this problem identified two major elements for the sales structure: field sales personnel (business builders) and sales managers (people builders). Execution of this innovation is discussed below.

FIELD FORCE STRATEGY

1. Each representative will recommend, gain agreement to, and execute business-building plans for each key customer.
2. Each manager will provide the training required for the representative to be able to gain agreement to and execute business-building plans for each key customer.

The creative innovation for the business builder was to pursue activities of creating partnerships with key customers. The creation of partnerships effectively brought the key customer into the company organization. This was accomplished by sales personnel having definite strategies to create linkages between themselves and individual customers and, by creating value linkages (partnerships) with key customers, the salesperson putting organizational and cultural barriers between key customers and competitors. With strong partnership linkages to the company, the customer is, in fact, part of the organization.

The radical shift in the role of the salesperson required innovation in all field-selling management positions. They needed to understand how to cause and manage the organization change required. They also had to have the time required to create customer linkages with the field-selling personnel for whom they were responsible and to provide the requisite training to the field force. They were also faced with the challenge to keep field-selling personnel in place for longer periods of time if the key customer-salesperson link was to be fully developed. This requirement was confirmed by company research that indicated that field representatives who remain in a specific territory for 7 years or more are 25% more productive than those who have stayed in one territory for less than that period. These data had significant organizational and training implications for career development of sales personnel and for field sales managers.

Working With Customers

The remainder of the business-building processes focuses on customer identification, selection, and interactions. Prior to being able to start this phase of sales development, strong internal alignment must be in place. This alignment is required so that within the customer task environment those with the best skills for a particular task are available and willing to do it. In

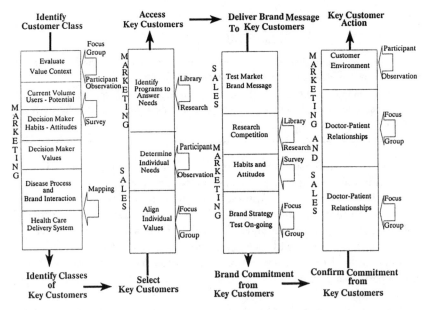

Figure 5.11 Task requirements, responsibilites, and methodologies.

addition, the best tools for accomplishing the task must be identified. Prior to starting to pursue the tasks, the organization must be certain that these tools are understood and that those who must use them are skilled in their use. Figure 5.11 is the result of A/A field force work in seeking to understand the tasks required of each step of customer interaction in the business-building process, who would best be able to accomplish the task, and what tools would best accomplish the task.

Customer Chains

Rather than the traditional organization chart (defining hierarchy and position), a customer-supplier chain chart (defining space and relationships) was used as the basis of the field-selling organization's description and actions (Figure 5.12).

Traditionally, Pharmco's selling organizations looked at its customer chain as product focused and driven by the company. It identified its customer base as wholesalers, pharmacists, hospitals, and doctors, all of which were users of products and information supplied by the marketing department. In

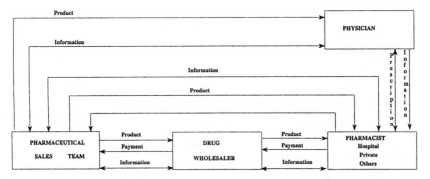

Figure 5.12 Field-selling customer chain.

discussions and information sharing with customers, the sales information flow was almost exclusively from the company to those the company wanted to inform or educate. This was particularly true of information. Originally, the information arrows in Figure 5.12 were directed to the customers rather than showing two-way communication. Application of the steps between the Key Customer Potential and Identifying Key Customers led to which class of physicians, pharmacists, and hospitals were important or probably important customers.

The A/A sales personnel then redefined the sales organization as all those in the chain (distributors, doctors, chemists, hospitals, etc.) with whom the sales-people had a primary contact. (As noted above, primary emphasis was on the physician in this stage of development.) Also, by redirecting information as a transactional activity, the field forces were able to understand more fully their various customer bases and thereby offer better responses to them. At this point, the sales teams agreed that a final identification was needed of those customers most likely to be prime users of the test market products. The total quality technique of fishboning was used to identify the major steps (Figure 5.13). Detailed steps were examined and used to fill out the original fishbone.

The sales team identified four major areas of development (the right specialty by brand, right patient population by targeted specialty, the right customer location, and the right values of the customers). The right specialty was defined, in general, as those physicians who had a large portion of their patient population with diseases for which the Pharmco test brands were appropriate therapy. Other key factors were the role of the specialists as opinion leaders in their field and their role as leaders in developing health care. A further criterion was to determine that the patients who were seen by the appropriate specialists were candidates for Pharmco products. Criteria

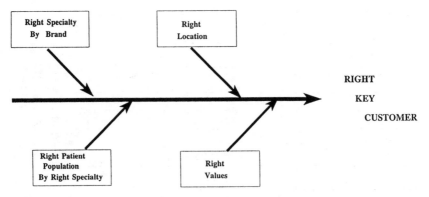

Figure 5.13   Key customer selection.

included the ability of the patient to pay for the therapy. The right-location criterion included proximity to other important customers, proximity to hospitals, and proximity to physicians who key customers might influence. To aid in determining the details of these three headings, the sales teams developed a profiling criteria outline for the key customers (Table 5.4).

Finally, the sales group determined that the greatest level of success would come from those customers who had values that were in alignment with those of Pharmco, in general, and those of the field force, in particular. A test study was done in the Philippines to determine the values and value orientations of potential physician key customers (Bantigue & Reeves-Ellington, 1986). The key findings of the study are outlined in Table 5.5. The methodology was repeated in the other test markets and confirmed the original Philippine findings.

This understanding was achieved by expanding services the company offered from strictly professional needs to include personal needs of its customers. The field force was the supplier of this information to the marketing department, which, in turn, was responsible for developing programs to support customer's stated needs. During the time covered, however, primary focus was devoted to those doctors who treated diseases for which the test brands were appropriate therapy: urologists, general practitioners, and gynecologists. For example, in Australia, urologists were having problems gaining patients for their practice. An analysis indicated this was not based on a lack of professional competence but on how other medical professionals perceived them (e.g., as arrogant know-it-alls who steal patients). With the agreement of the Australian Urology Association, the Australia company provided programs and training in personal visioning and value clarification.

TABLE 5.4

Profiling Criteria for Key Customers

Health Care Thought Leader	Therapy Thought Leader	Practice Economics
Hospital head	Professors	Size of practice
Health department	Hospital department heads	Economics of patients
Health professors	Foreign experts	Number of "right" patients
	Large general practitioner (GP) practice	
	Regulatory officials	

After several sessions, physicians started to include members of their families in the seminars. Another example comes from the Middle East. Many physicians and pharmacists in the Arab Peninsula are Egyptians temporarily located in the area. Most miss Egyptian newspapers and news of the job market in Egypt. Pharmco set up a job information and newspaper service for these people. The benefit to the transplanted medical staff is obvious. To Pharmco the benefit was in gaining access to a major sector of the medical community in the area.

Conclusions

Success in the revised field force activities was based on creating alliances rather than using the usual strong-armed tactics normally applied by field-selling

TABLE 5.5

Doctor Values

All Doctors	Urologists	Pediatricians	General Practitioners
Professional excellence	Professional excellence	Patient trust	Service
Self-actualization	Respect	Family	Socially responsible
Family	Self-actualization	Service	Patient relationships
Patient relationships	Family	Socially responsible	Professional relationships
Socially responsible			
Service			

forces. In most organizations, sales organizations are becoming counterproductive to the expectations of both their workers and their customers. They are marginalized by the company demanding that customers adapt to the needs of the company, as expressed through the field forces rather than allowing them to integrate the company and its customers into its larger environment. The success of Japanese alternatives indicates that alternative organizational models are desired. Japanese organizational successes indicate that people will respond positively to organizations that attempt to integrate into their wider societal context.

Within Pharmco, the A/A region attempted to create such an organizational alternative using the field force as its lead in organizational change. Although these changes were counterintuitive to the parent company's traditional organization, they were demonstratively more successful within the wider societies and cultures in which they operated.

Successful organizational change, especially that taking place within a short time and requiring major behavioral changes, requires that all change mechanisms and processes are transparent, generative (i.e., they are capable of being used throughout the organization to create new information that is usable within the context it is needed), and measurable by those using the processes.

This chapter has attempted to demonstrate how anthropological thought and methodologies, when used in conjunction with total quality systems and applications, are highly effective in helping organizations cope with integration into the wider community. Through this integration, as demonstrated by many Japanese and U.S. companies, superior business performance is achieved. This superior performance is coupled with personal growth of all people within the business system using anthropology and total quality. Of prime importance to the success is the holistic approach common to anthropology.

Without this approach, companies fragment their markets, leading to conflict with both external and internal customers. Although Pharmco personnel in the A/A region continued to experience personal and cultural conflict, its causes were transparent and therefore solvable. Making conflict and methods of its resolution transparent reduced pragmatic misunderstanding and misinterpretation. In addition, transparent work processes permitted greater effectiveness at cross-cultural learning and cooperation. The project results indicate that in multicultural situations the construction and display of work values and processes are important.

📓 References

Abegglen, J. C., & Stalk, G., Jr. (1985). *Kaisha: The Japanese corporation.* Tokyo: Charles E. Tuttle.

Ackerman, L. S. (1984). *Developing a vision.* McLean, VA: Linda Ackerman, Inc.

Aldrich, H. E. (1992). Incommensurable paradigms? Vital signs from three perspectives. In M. Reed & M. Hughes (Eds.), *Rethinking organization: New directions in organization theory and analysis* (pp. 17-45). London: Sage.

Anderson, A. (1993, March). *Culture, total quality, and the information age.* Paper presented at the annual meeting of the Society for Applied Anthropology, San Antonio, TX.

Anderson, A., & Reeves-Ellington, R. H. (1993, December). *Organizational change: The role of authorship, communications, and total quality.* Paper presented at the annual meeting of the American Anthropology Association, Washington, DC.

Argyris, C., & Schön, D. (1978). *Organizational learning: A theory of action perspective.* Reading, MA: Addison-Wesley.

Axelrod, R. (1984). *The evolution of cooperation.* New York: Basic Books.

Bantigue, W., & Reeves-Ellington, R. H. (1986). *Understanding physician values.* Manila: Norwich Eaton Pharmaceutical Co., Inc.

Barabba, V., & Zaltman, G. (1991). *Hearing the voice of the market.* Cambridge, UK: HBS Press.

Baskerville, R. (1991). Practitioner autonomy and the bias of methods and tools. In H. E. Nissen, H. K. Klein, & R. Hirschheim (Eds.), *The information systems research arena of the 90's* (pp. 121-144). North-Holland: Elsevier Science.

Beauregard, M. R., Mikulak, R. J., & Olson, B. A. (1992). *A practical guide to statistical quality improvement.* New York: Van Nostrand Reinhold.

Bendell, T., Boulter, L., & Kelly, K. (1993). *Benchmarking for competitive advantage.* London: Pitman.

Berger, P., & Luckmann, T. (1967). *The social construction of reality.* New York: Doubleday.

Boyacigiller, N., & Adler, N. J. (1991). The parochial dinosaur: The organizational sciences in a global context. *Academy of Management Review, 16*(2), 262-290.

Cook, T. D. (1983). Quasi-experimentation: Its ontology, epistemology, and methodology. In G. Morgan (Ed.), *Beyond method: Strategies for social research* (pp. 74-94). Beverly Hills, CA: Sage.

Covey, S. R. (1989). *The seven habits of highly effective people.* New York: Simon & Schuster.

Crosby, P. B. (1979). *Quality is free.* New York: McGraw-Hill.

Crosby, P. B. (1984). *Quality without tears.* New York: McGraw-Hill.

David, K. (1985). *Participant observation in pharmaceutical field selling.* Norwich, NY: Norwich Eaton Pharmaceutical Co., Inc.

Demming, E. W. (1982). *Quality, productivity, and competitive position.* Cambridge: MIT Press.

Demming, E. W. (1986). *Out of crises.* Boston: Institute of Technology Center for Advanced Engineering Studies.

Eliade, M. (1974). *Shamanism: Archaic techniques of ecstasy.* Princeton, NJ: Princeton University Press.

Finan, T. J., & van Willigen, J. (1990). The pursuit of social knowledge: Methodology and practice of anthropology. In J. van Willigen & T. J. Finan (Eds.), *Soundings: Rapid and reliable research methods for practicing anthropologists* (pp. 1-9). Washington, DC: American Anthropological Association.

Geertz, C. (1973). *The interpretation of cultures.* New York: Basic Books.

Geroski, P. (1989). On diversity and scale—Extant firms and extinct goods? *Sloan Management Review, 31,* 23-35.

Ghoshal, S. (1987). Global strategy: An organizing framework. *Strategic Management Journal, 8*(5), 424-440.

Gregory, K. (1983). Native-view paradigms: Multiple cultures and culture conflicts in organizations. *Administrative Science Quarterly, 28,* 359-376.

Hall, E. T., & Hall, M. R. (1987). *Hidden differences.* New York: Doubleday.

Hofstede, G. (1980). *Culture's consequences: International differences in work-related values.* Beverly Hills, CA: Sage.

Hofstede, G. (1991). *Cultures and organizations.* London: McGraw-Hill.

Hult, M., & Lennung, S. A. (1980). Towards a definition of action research: A note and bibliography. *Journal of Management Studies, 17,* 241-250.

Imai, M. (1986). *Kaizen: The key to Japan's competitive success.* New York: Random House.

Ishikawa, K. (1984). *Guide to total quality control.* Tokyo: Asian Productivity Organization.

Ishikawa, K. (1986). *Guide to quality control.* New York: Kraus International.

Jorgensen, D. L. (1989). *Participant observation: A methodology for human studies.* Newbury Park, CA: Sage.

Juran, J. (1980). *Juran's quality control handbook.* New York: McGraw-Hill.

Juran, J. (1989). *Juran on leadership for quality.* New York: Free Press.

Juran, J., & Gryna, F. M. (1980). *Quality planning and analysis.* New York: McGraw-Hill.

Kinney, J. (1988). *Policy management: A beginner's perspective.* Paper presented at the American Supplier Institute Conference on Policy Management, Cincinnati, OH.

Ledford, G. E., Jr., & Mohrman, S. A. (1993). Self-design for high involvement: A large-scale organizational change. *Human Relations, 46*(2), 143-174.

Levitt, T. (1983). *The marketing imagination.* New York: Free Press.

Lock, D. (1994). *Handbook of quality management* (2nd ed.). Brookfield, VT: Gower.

Miller, D. (1988). Organizational configurations: Cohesion, change, and prediction. *Human Relations, 43*(8), 771-789.

Mizuno, S. (Ed.). (1988). *Managing for quality improvement.* Cambridge, UK: Productivity Press.

Morgan, G. (1986). *Images of organization.* Newbury Park, CA: Sage.

Ohmae, K. (1988). *The mind of a strategist.* New York: Viking/Penguin.

Ohmae, K. (1990). *The borderless world: Power and strategy in the interlinked economy.* New York: HarperCollins.

Oye, K. E. (Ed.). (1986). *Cooperation under anarchy.* Princeton, NJ: Princeton University Press.

Parkhe, A. (1993). "Messy" research, methodological predispositions, and theory development in international joint ventures. *Academy of Management Review, 18*(2), 227-268.

Pernick, R. (1993, October). *Quality training for organizations.* Workshop presented at the annual meeting of the Society for Applied Sociology, St. Louis.

Popcorn, F. (1991). *The Popcorn report.* New York: Doubleday.

Porter, M. E. (1980). *Competitive strategy.* New York: Free Press.

Porter, M. E. (1985). *Competitive advantage.* London: Collier Macmillan.

Rapoport, R. (1978). Three dilemmas of action research. *Human Relations, 23,* 499-513.

Reeves-Ellington, R. H. (1988, December). *Relationships between multinationals and peasants.* Paper presented at the annual meeting of the American Anthropological Association, Chicago.

Reeves-Ellington, R. H. (1989, December). *Customer-supplier interaction for financial success.* Paper presented at the annual meeting of the American Anthropological Association, Phoenix, AZ.

Reeves-Ellington, R. H. (1993a). Organizational ethics and anthropologists: Moral practices of private and public organizations and people. *Anthropology of Work Review,* Summer-Fall, 1-2.

Reeves-Ellington, R. H. (1993b). Using cooperative skills for cooperative advantage in Japan organization. *Human Organization, 52*(2), 97-110.

Reeves-Ellington, R. H. (in press). Organizing for global effectiveness: Ethnicity and organizations. *Human Organization.*

Reeves-Ellington, R. H., & Steidlmeier, P. (1992, March). *Total quality programs and institutional change in business.* Paper presented at the First Biannual International Conference on Advances in Management, Orlando, FL.

Reeves-Ellington, R. H., & Steidlmeier, P. (1993). American business in China: Cultural aspects of cooperative advantage. *Anthropology of Work Review,* Summer-Fall, 6-9.

Rohrer, T. C. (Ed.). (1990). *A continuing series for implementing total quality.* Cincinnati, OH: Procter & Gamble.

Senge, P. M. (1990). The leader's new work: Building learning organizations. *Sloan Management Review, 7*(Fall), 7-21.

Smith, M. C. (1983). *Principles of pharmaceutical marketing.* Philadelphia: Lea & Febiger.

Spendolini, M. J. (1992). *The benchmarking book.* New York: American Management Association.

Spradley, J. P. (1980). *Participant observation.* New York: Holt, Rinehart & Winston.

Susman, G. I. (1983). Action research: A sociotechnical systems perspective. In G. Morgan (Ed.), *Beyond method: Strategies for social research* (pp. 95-113). Beverly Hills, CA: Sage.

Susman, G. I., & Evered, R. D. (1978). An assessment of the scientific merits of action research. *Administrative Science Quarterly, 23,* 582-603.

Swasy, A. (1993). *Soap opera.* New York: Random House.

Thorelli, H. B. (1986). Networks: Between markets and hierarchies. *Strategic Management Journal, 7,* 37-51.

Wardell, M. (1992). Changing organizational forms: From the bottom up. In M. Reed & M. Hughes (Eds.), *Rethinking organization: New directions in organization theory and analysis* (pp. 144-164). London: Sage.

Warmington, A. (1980). Action research: Its method and its implications. *Journal of Applied Systems Analysis, 7,* 23-39.

Wheeler, D. J., & Chambers, D. S. (1992). *Understanding statistical process control* (2nd ed.). Knoxville, TN: SPC Press.

Whitehall, A. M. (1991). *Japanese managemZent: Tradition in transition.* New York: Rutledge.

Whitley, R. (1992). The social construction of organizations and markets: The comparative analysis of business recipes. In M. Reed & M. Hughes (Eds.), *Rethinking organization: New directions in organization theory and analysis* (pp. 120-143). London: Sage.

PART FOUR

Hearing the Customer's Voice(s)
Contextual Grounding of Marketplace Behavior

In this part, we revisit a central premise of the volume, to reinforce and extend our belief that consumption is shaped and reflected by culture. It is only by understanding the contexts in which consumption occurs that we can hope to interpret consumer behavior in anything approaching satisfactory fashion. Marketing has been construed as a polylogue (Sherry, 1990) of stakeholder voices speaking in concert, often with little regard for conversation. Managers aspire to dialogue with consumers, although they frequently (if not invariably) conduct their business as a monologue. Increasingly, consumers are speaking in more than one voice, as lifestyle transience accelerates and the postmodern self demands ever less coherence or consistency. Grounded aesthetics and bricolage (Willis, 1990)—the local appropriation of globalized marketplace symbols and practices for purposes of personalized reconfiguration into collages of meaning—are among the primary principles of brandscape construction at work in the world today. Thus an account of consumer behavior on the ground, and on as many grounds as it occurs, is a pressing concern.

A framework for addressing the situational complexity of consumer behavior in a managerially relevant fashion was developed by Levy (1978) almost two decades ago. In laying out the sources of behavior and meaning from attribute through cosmology and tracing their interplay through individual, social and cultural circumstances in the U.S. marketplace, Levy paid particular attention to socialization processes of interest to anthropologists.

Since then, domestic ethnographies of class- and generation-based dynamics of marketplace behavior (Newman, 1988, 1993) have appeared, and international forays—into Japan especially (Creighton, 1994; White, 1993) but also France (Bourdieu, 1984)—have begun. Subcultural accounts (Hebdige, 1979) have been less common. Efforts to rehabilitate the "lifestyle" construct (Holt, 1994) are especially promising. The authors of the following two chapters seek to accelerate the anthropological exploration of socialization among consumers and marketers.

Janeen Costa delves beneath the surface of what marketing and consumer researchers commonly regard as exogenous variables to deliver a vivid impression of the richness of consumer behavior portrayed from a cultural perspective. She adroitly depicts the processes that comprise social organization and reveals the dynamics of relationship management—within and between individuals and among consumers and the stuff of the marketplace—in the bargain. She illustrates the fundamental pervasiveness of consumption in everyday life and contextualizes consumer behavior for us on a number of levels. In particular, her focus on gender, age, and ethnicity as processual constructs constituting and constituted by consumption is instructive. By demonstrating the types of meanings latent in a host of consumer behaviors and providing a set of programmatic research directives, Costa reveals our present understanding of the field to be the merest tip of a much larger iceberg than we commonly imagine.

Barbara Olsen concentrates on an especially evocative contextual arena—the household—to examine the intergenerational transfer of a particular type of consumer behavior: brand loyalty. Brand loyalty is arguably chief among the topics of most current interest and least comprehensive understanding (Aaker, 1991; Loden, 1992) in marketing. Through a variety of sins of commission and omission, managers have presided over a wholesale erosion of brand loyalty over the past decade and a half and have recently revitalized their interest in brand equity. As national brands have devolved from household gods, as loyalty has assumed the "cereal monogamy" status of secular ritual in the wake of rapidly changing family dynamics (Sherry, 1986), and as "place" has supplanted "deal" as the object of consumers' affection with the rise of private labels, it is apparent that we have not fielded a theory of brand loyalty appropriate to contemporary households. Olsen explores the heritage of brands in intergenerational perspective, with an emphasis on current purchase behavior mediated by kinship. Her investigation unfolds at the intersection of cultural biography (Kopytoff, 1986) and advertising mythology (Randazzo, 1993).

That consumerism in general, and branding in particular, antedates capitalism (Hamilton & Lai, 1989) suggests that anthropologists may have more to say about brand management than they might suspect, from both top-down and bottom-up perspectives. Pavia and Costa (1993) have begun what will hopefully become a sustained multimethod investigation that is anthropological in character into the ways in which consumers animate brands. Low and Fullerton (1994) have chronicled the evolution (and devolution) of the brand management complex in a fashion that will admit anthropological intervention into its revitalization. As ethnographies of consumption subcultures (Schouten & McAlexander, in press) proliferate and diffuse into management circles, an anthropological orientation to marketing research will gain greater currency. The heightened sensitivity to context and nuance and the bid to wed idiographic and nomothetic pursuits that are the anthropologist's peculiar preoccupations will mark this diffusion.

References

Aaker, D. (1991). *Managing brand equity: Capitalizing on the value of a brand name.* New York: Free Press.

Bourdieu, P. (1984). *Distinction: A social critique of the judgement of taste.* Cambridge, MA: Harvard University Press.

Creighton, M. (1994). "Edutaining" children: Consumer and gender socialization in Japanese marketing. *Ethnology, 33*(1), 35-52.

Hamilton, G., & Lai, C. K. (1989). Consumerism without capitalism: Consumption and brand names in late imperial China. In H. Rutz & B. Orlove (Eds.), *The social economy of consumption* (pp. 253-279). Lanham, MD: University Press of America.

Hebdige, D. (1979). *Subculture: The meaning of style.* New York: Methuen.

Holt, D. (1994). *Lifestyles as socio-cultural systems of tastes.* Working paper, Pennsylvania State University, Department of Marketing, Smeal College of Business Administration.

Kopytoff, I. (1986). The cultural biography of things: Commoditization as process. In A. Appadurai (Ed.), *The social life of things* (pp. 64-91). New York: Cambridge University Press.

Levy, S. (1978). *Marketplace behavior: Its meaning for management.* New York: AMACOM.

Loden, J. (1992). *Megabrands: How to build them, how to beat them.* Homewood, IL: Business One Irwin.

Low, G., & Fullerton, R. (1994). Brands, brand management, and the brand manager system: A critical-historical evaluation. *Journal of Marketing Research, 31*(2), 173-190.

Newman, K. (1988). *Falling from grace: The experience of downward mobility in the American middle class.* New York: Free Press.

Newman, K. (1993). *Declining fortunes: The withering of the American dream.* New York: Basic Books.

Pavia, T., & Costa, J. (1993). The winning number: Consumer perceptions of alpha-numeric brand names. *Journal of Marketing, 57*(3), 85-98.

Randazzo, S. (1993). *Myth making on Madison avenue: How advertisers apply the power of myth and symbolism to create leadership brands.* Chicago: Probus.

Schouten, J., & McAlexander, J. (in press). Subcultures of consumption: An ethnography of the new bikers. *Journal of Consumer Research.*

Sherry, J. F., Jr. (1986). *Cereal monogamy: Brand loyalty as secular ritual in consumer culture.* Paper presented at the Seventh Annual Conference of the Association for Consumer Research, Toronto, Canada.

Sherry, J. F., Jr. (1990). A sociocultural analysis of a midwestern American flea market. *Journal of Consumer Research, 17*(1), 13-30.

White, M. (1993). *The material child: Coming of age in Japan and America.* New York: Free Press.

Willis, P. (1990). *Common culture.* Boulder, CO: Westview.

6

The Social Organization of Consumer Behavior

Janeen Arnold Costa

Virginia sat at the kitchen table with her sister-in-law, Diane, to discuss the upcoming Greek Easter dinner. Although Virginia had been in the family for several years, her background was not ethnically Greek in any way. Still, she felt compelled to learn about the customs and foods required for the Greek ceremonial occasion, based on the ethnic orientation of her husband's family.

Surprisingly, Virginia's husband's ethnicity was derived from and influenced by a journey from Greece to the United States accomplished some 70 years earlier when her husband's maternal grandparents had migrated from Greece. Virginia's husband's mother grew up knowing Greek and practicing Greek customs, a second-generation Greek American herself, but had married an "American" with no other discernible ethnic background. Thus Virginia's husband had been raised in a partially Greek American home, one in which Greek was not regularly spoken and in which ethnic ties were based primarily on consumption during ceremonial occasions and on a few knickknacks placed strategically in the living room. Still, when asked, her husband would say that he was "Greek."

Virginia and Diane conferred about the upcoming dinner. Diane felt it was her role to continue the ethnic celebration, despite her parents' deaths some years earlier. Diane and her husband had bought the home in which Diane was raised, and she intended to hold all important social occasions in the

AUTHOR'S NOTE: I would like to thank Rita Denny, Dan Rose, John Sherry, and MasaKazu Tani for their comments on earlier drafts of this chapter. My research was undertaken as a David Eccles Research Associate of the David Eccles School of Business, Department of Marketing, at the University of Utah.

home, just as they had been throughout her lifetime. These social occasions included Thanksgiving dinner, Christmas celebrations, and, of course, Greek Easter. In each case, at least part of the fare and the activities would be ethnically based. Diane felt it was her role to continue these celebrations both because she herself felt Greek and because she wanted to nurture her family and provide continuity, just the way her mother had over the years.

Diane described for Virginia what would usually be included at the Greek Easter dinner in their home: lamb; feta cheese and Kalamata olives; the Greek Easter bread, *lambropsomo*; boiled eggs, dyed red as a representation of Christ's blood, for each place setting; and *koulouria*, the Greek cookies which would be twisted and shaped in the form of Christ's winding cloth. Diane recalled that they would sometimes, but not always, have *pilafi*, lemon-flavored rice; *dolmathes*, rice and meat wrapped in grape leaves; and *spanakopita* or *tiropita*, spinach or cheese pie. They decided to include *dolmathes* and *spanakopita* in their dinner plans. When the discussion turned to dessert, Diane indicated that Aunt Mary usually made enough Greek pastries for the entire extended family, and they could expect to receive a dish of these during Easter week. Nevertheless, it seemed appropriate to include *galaktobouriko*, a Greek custard pie.

Their plans for the meal completed, Diane and Virginia spent the next several days preparing the appropriate dishes. Diane occasionally thought to herself that it was nice that Virginia had chosen to express herself ethnically, to learn how to prepare the dishes, even though Virginia herself had no "Greek blood."

When the time for the dinner approached, each family member arrived and seemed gratified to find the table set just as they expected it to be, with the *lambropsomo* in the middle of the table and *koulouria* and the red eggs positioned at each plate. They began with the Lord's Prayer, spoken first in Greek by Diane, who was the only one who knew the Greek version. Then, they picked up their eggs and turned to one another, proclaiming "*Christos anesti*" (Christ is risen), followed by the response "*Alithos anesti*" (Truly, He is risen). They would crack one egg against another until the clear winner, the individual with the final uncracked egg, was declared. That person would have good luck for the entire year. Diane again thought to herself that it was interesting that they should perform this ritual because most of the family rarely attended church, only a few of them understood the meaning of the eggs and the bread, and many at the table would probably claim they were agnostic.

The feast began, with congratulations to Virginia and Diane for each dish prepared. There were comments about how Virginia had participated and about how Diane was carrying on the traditions. Each family member had married or had chosen as partners individuals who were not Greek or Greek American, yet all participated in the feast. The young children were encouraged to taste the sour feta cheese and bitter olives, and they were tutored in the appropriate egg-cracking activities, saying the Greek words without understanding them.

Despite their mixed backgrounds, the group had celebrated the ethnic holiday appropriately. They seemed to leave the table feeling they had expressed their identities, had participated in a ritual from their past that would continue in their own lives and would be passed on to their children.

🔛 Introduction

The preceding vignette is based on my own experiences. It is meant to suggest the richness and complexity of consumption behaviors as related to aspects of social organization—in this case, to individual and group ethnic identity, to gender-based social roles, and to socialization of nongroup members and of children. Of course, the behaviors and attitudes described in the vignette are not unusual in a Greek American or other ethnic context (see, e.g., Moskos, 1989; Papanikolas, 1974, 1987). In this chapter, I explore aspects of social organization and culture as they influence consumer behavior. The vignette is intended to illustrate the effects of social groups, identity, and social processes on consumer behavior, providing a basis for further discussion.

Within the social and cultural organization of a society, individuals identify themselves and others on the basis of characteristics such as age, profession, educational level, religious affiliation, sex, caste or class, income level, region or country of residence, or ethnic background. Beyond serving to identify individuals, these characteristics often serve as the foundation for the formation of social groups.

Typically treated as exogenous variables in the consumer behavior field, the full impact of these social aspects of identity and of group formation has been somewhat ignored and underresearched. It is quite clear why this is the case: The underrepresentation is related to the relatively recent use of qualitative methods and interpretive approaches in consumer research, in which the complexity of human social and cultural relations can be discovered and more thoroughly analyzed. The historic predominance of survey methods and the emphasis on cognitive psychology has contributed also to the overall dearth of consumer behavior studies focusing on aspects of social and cultural organization.

This lack has been significant and must be redressed. Social organization, as illustrated in the opening vignette and as will become clear in the following discussion, provides a framework for behavior. The attitudes, values, beliefs, expressions, and behaviors that occur on the basis of belonging to—or aspiring to belong to—a particular group, or to express a particular social identity, underlie and underline critical dimensions of consumption. It is incumbent on scholars to explore these dimensions of consumer behavior and to understand the impact and influence of social organization on consumption in general.

Thus the purpose of this chapter is to explore these social organizational constructs and to define relevant concepts; to provide examples of consumption, primarily from my own research, in which such constructs are critical components in behavior; to address the relative lack of attention paid to these social dimensions in the literature currently; and to suggest fruitful domains for further inquiry. I have provided a proposed research agenda, the intention of which is to urge scholars to focus more on social organization, specifically social status and role, and group and individual identity formation, expression and influence. To delineate the effects of these aspects of social organization on consumption, it is suggested tht scholars use more extensively the anthropological research techniques of fieldwork and participant observation, in addition to the well-established methods of formal and informal, unstructured or semistructured interviews and group interviews or focus groups.

Culture, Social Organization, and Consumption

Culture, a concept which at its most general refers to all learned behavior, contributes to and accounts for variation in customs, attitudes, values, beliefs, behaviors, and so on. Culture can be said to serve as a framework for thoughts, actions and behaviors, imparting meaning to the vast majority of all that we, as humans, do. In anthropology, culture as a concept is regularly and fruitfully used to describe and analyze both the varieties and generalities of human behaviors, values, choices, preferences, practices, beliefs, attitudes, and so forth throughout the world. In marketing and consumer behavior research, however, use of the concept has been minimal; it has been common for marketers and consumer researchers to ignore the great depth of the concept and its implications for the analysis of human behavior. Instead, culture is often treated superficially, as an independent variable and in the context of "cross-cultural" studies (Costa, 1993b).

Culture has deeper, broader, and more significant implications for marketing and consumer behavior, however, than has been evident in most published studies. Specifically, it is suggested here that the processes of culture, the pervasiveness of culture as an influence in human life, and the embeddedness of behavior in cultural constructions of the past and present should be addressed more fully in marketing and in consumer behavior studies and should become an inherent part of the way in which marketing researchers and theorists approach their studies. This implies that cultural approaches illuminate behavior in ways that other approaches cannot. The fruitfulness of such approaches is apparent in the few works that have analyzed consumer behavior from an anthropological perspective; these include, among others, analyses by Arnould (1989, also Chapter 4, this volume), Costa (1989, 1992), Joy, Hui, Kim, and Laroche (1995), McCracken (1988, 1989), Sherry (1990), and Sherry and McGrath (1989) (this list is suggestive rather than exhaustive). Overall, the number of studies and theorists using an anthropological perspective is small, however. Therefore, despite these exceptions, the concept of culture is, in general, underused and misused in consumer behavior and marketing studies. This chapter provides examples of the ways in which culture and social organization can be used more fruitfully.

Within the domain of cultural anthropology are disciplinary emphases on social organization, on political organization, on religious systems, and so on. Hence it is further suggested that the specific subarea of cultural anthropology that focuses on social organization has also been underused. Although it is relatively easy to *identify* social organizational variables, mere identification leads to only a cursory understanding. For example, age, gender, ethnic background, and other aspects of social organization are variables that can be ascertained through survey data and can be used to describe consumers. However, such usage seldom moves beyond this superficial level. For example, a survey sent to Diane and Virginia, discussed in the opening vignette, would reveal that both are women, in the age range of 30 to 40, have children, and are white, urban middle-class American citizens. If the survey were designed to inquire about ethnic background, Diane may have identified herself as Greek American. A particularly well designed and lengthy survey might even find that Diane, and perhaps Virginia, occasionally consume ethnic foods in certain contexts. Beyond that, it is unlikely that any of the complex behaviors discussed in the opening vignette would be exposed and thereby available for analysis. Thus we could say that although social organizational variables are sometimes considered in consumer research they are often underexplored, misunderstood, or misinterpreted.

Social Organization:
Individuals, Statuses, and Roles

This chapter, then, focuses on a specific aspect of culture: social organization. Anthropological treatments of social organization have often focused on the statuses and roles of individuals. Unlike the lay concept of status as prestige, the social scientific concept of *status* refers to simple social position, without hierarchical implications. Linton (1936) observed that all individuals have a number of statuses or social positions (see also Turner, 1988; Webster & Foschi, 1988). For example, a single individual may have the multiple statuses of father, brother, son, husband, employee, salesperson, friend, fishing partner, president of a charitable association, and neighbor, all at the same time. In the context of consumption, an individual may be a consumer of gourmet foods, of reggae music, of tennis and golf sporting goods and activities, of late-night television programs, of New Age spiritual paraphernalia, of clothing based on a cowboy or American West motif, of mystery or romance novels, and so forth. These statuses may be referred to as *consumer statuses.*

Associated with each status are the expected behaviors, rights, and obligations, or *role*, of that social position. In reference to the first example above, for instance, a fishing partner may have the role of occasionally driving to a fishing destination, purchasing and sharing fishing bait with his companions, offering advice on where to fish, how to tie a specific knot, what to do when a fish is on the line, what fishing equipment is most desirable, how to handle purchases in a given angling store, and so on. All of these behaviors are part of the role of a fishing partner, and some of these behaviors focus on consumption activities.

The consumer statuses mentioned above are inherently based on consumption of certain products, but the analysis must move into an exploration of the *consumer roles* associated with these statuses. How does the reader of romance novels or the viewer of late-night television perceive him- or herself? How does he or she interact with others who consume in the same way—are there group activities involving these consumption behaviors, for example? What is expected of the individual who engages in tennis or golf as leisure activities? How does she or he act in the process of consuming? Do others think the activities themselves say something about prestige or skill? How does consumption of tennis and golf products relate to self-definition of the individuals? In other words, it is not enough, from an anthropological perspective (or, I would suggest, from a consumer research perspective in general), to say that someone does this or that, consumes this or that. Rather, the entire, complex, full social role involved in being a consumer of a particular product must be explored.

The same individual also holds statuses other than that of fishing partner or of late-night television consumer, and each status carries with it a role. Thus, because individuals have numerous statuses, they have numerous roles (first described by Linton, 1936). So, an individual may hold the numerous consumer statuses related to consumption of golf, New Age paraphernalia, gourmet foods, and Western clothing all at the same time. Each of these consumer statuses would carry with it a fully elaborated consumer role as well.

Of interest, however, is that, based on an individual's self- or group identity, she or he may be more likely to consume products that societally represent a cohesive identity. Thus, in a stereotypical example, the consumer of gourmet foods may also consume French wines, vacation abroad at luxury resorts, wear designer clothing, listen to classical music, drive a European-made luxury car, and furnish his or her home with antiques, Euro-design furniture, Persian rugs, and Lalique glass. Also stereotypically, the reader of Louis L'Amour novels may drive a 4 × 4 truck, wear cowboy boots and occasionally other clothing with a cowboy motif, always wear Levi button-down jeans, be an above-average consumer of American beers and of American fast food, enjoy country-western music, and be an avid fisherman. In each of these cases, the consumption represents a cohesive *consumption identity* of numerous products related to one another through the overall identity they represent.

In addition to the phenomenon of multiple statuses and multiple associated roles, a *single* status may carry with it an array of roles, based on the interaction of the individual with others in the context of enacting his or her status. Merton (1957) coined the term *role-set* to refer to this multiplicity of roles associated with a single status:

> By role-set I mean that complement of role-relationships in which persons are involved by virtue of occupying a particular social status. Thus, in our current studies of medical schools, we have begun with the view that the status of medical student entails not only the role of a student vis-à-vis his teachers, but also an array of other roles relating him diversely to other students, physicians, nurses, social workers, medical technicians, and the like. (p. 111; see also Parsons, 1949; for analysis and critique of Parsons and Merton, see Habermas, 1987; Munch, 1988)

Examination of this multiplicity of roles associated with a status is of use in consumer behavior studies. Clearly, a medical student, for example, has particular consumption needs, desires, and behaviors in these various roles, purchasing and using textbooks, clinical garb, and equipment in certain ways, depending on the social context and the individuals with whom he or she is interacting. We can well imagine that a medical student, for example, might wear his or her stethoscope around the neck, only using it, with hesitation, when a teaching physician asks him or her to do so. Similarly, we can imagine this same individual proudly displaying the stethoscope to family and friends when it is first purchased, shown to be indicative of his or her position and standing as a medical student, allowing children to listen to their pulse through the earpieces. In this situation, the medical student is using the same consumer product to express a multiplicity of roles associated with the status of medical student. The consumer object itself takes on different meanings—expresses the student's status and role differently—in the disparate social contexts.

Further sociological and anthropological elaboration of role has led to examinations of *role expectation, role performance,* and *role perception.* In each of these cases, behaviors are manipulated and interpreted on the basis of expected enactment of a given role. The parameters of expected and accepted behaviors are socially defined, individually performed, and perceived and responded to by others. A husband may be societally expected to perform his role in a particular way, for example. Thus the role expectation for an American husband includes the duties, responsibilities, rights, and obligations the society deems fit for this role and may include activities of production, of sexual access, of emotional caring, and so forth. From a consumption perspective, the husband may be expected to choose and purchase a home, be responsible for purchase and maintenance of cars and certain other products, and express the emotional caring for his wife through the purchase of gifts, of romantic dinners, of weekend vacations, of flowers. Again, the description is stereotypical, but as such it draws upon American societal expectations involving the ideal role of the husband as related to consumption.

An individual's performance in the given role is then examined by others and by oneself on the basis of the expectations. Individuals may adjust their role performance to conform to role expectations. Furthermore, individuals perceive their own roles and the roles of others in particular ways. This role perception similarly leads to adjustments in role performance. It is interesting to note that perception of adequate role performance may be based on consumption activities. Does the husband perform his role by remembering his wife's birthday, their anniversary, and other special occasions and by purchasing products appropriate to the occasion? Does the student perform his or her role by purchasing textbooks, as well as books related to relevant topics in class, by taking extensive notes in purchased notebooks, using yellow and neon green highlighters to emphasize important areas in the text, by devoting available time to study and, therefore, dressing in inexpensive clothing indicative of someone who studies rather than is gainfully employed, and so on?

Each of these elaborations of role is tied to the dramaturgical interpretation of social interaction, whereby individuals are constantly engaged in presentation of self to others in a social context. According to Graburn (1971), the concept of role and its extensions are derived from observation of the ways in which individuals act on an everyday basis: "The concept of role has long been present in lay ideas on the nature of society. Implicit in this concept is the notion that life is drama and that individuals, throughout their lives, play parts in this drama" (p. 289).

Goffman (1959) and Berreman (1962) are the social theorists most well known for the focus on drama in social interaction; recent significant treatments include Becker and McCall (1990), Deegan and Hill (1987), Lamont and Fournier (1992), and Lyman (1990). The resulting branch of anthropology/sociology known as interaction theory/symbolic interactionism

> concentrates upon the examination of social life in terms of "encounters" between social persons in particular situations. Abandoning the more static anthropological concepts of people playing normative, culturally defined roles, interaction theorists have shown how individuals modify their behavior in terms of their perceptions of situations, their self-perceptions, and their perceptions of how the other social person expects them to act. Thus, interaction theory resembles, in many ways, a detailed study of "face," the mechanisms by which a social person chooses what role to play in each situation. (Graburn, 1971, p. 290)

In consumer research, Belk's (1988) "Possessions and the Extended Self" provides an exploration of the underlying premises of interaction theory as they apply to consumer behavior. Focusing on the way in which individuals use and feel about their possessions, Belk's analysis has important implications for the presentation of self to others. As individuals derive meaning from, and define themselves through, their possessions, they also communicate their identity to others through their possessions. For example, in the United States, individuals are thought to communicate their identities through their style of clothing, the cars they drive, the restaurants they frequent, and so on. In this sense, we are what we consume, and others identify us through those consumption behaviors. Furthermore, we manipulate our identities and our associated consumer behaviors on the basis of those with whom we interact.

Consumption situations in which interaction theory, the presentation and perception of self and identity, is important to the consumer behavior are numerous. At ceremonial occasions like those discussed in the opening vignette, individuals present their social statuses and roles, their expressions of identity to themselves and to others, through the foods they eat, the shopping behaviors in which they engage, and the ritual activities in which they participate. For example, in early childhood, American boys and girls begin to express their gender identity through preference for certain toys, of certain colors, presented in certain ways. Their friends look at their toys and tell them "that's for girls!" or "that's for boys!," using consumption to identify gender as well as to express it. Clearly, the dramaturgical approach to social interaction, focused on the consumption of products, provides much insight into this behavior.

Groups and Identity

Social structure includes both individuals and groups in a given society. All societies are composed of social groups, or collections of people who share common characteristics (see Fox, 1967; Murdock, 1949; Service, 1971). Social groups comprise individuals who see themselves, or are seen by others, as belonging to a particular community of individuals or as being similar to that community in such a way that they are then included by others in the category of people who belong to that community. Membership in social groups, then, is both a matter of choosing to belong and of being designated as belonging by others. The perspective is both from that of the individual in self-identification and from that of others in the society in terms of categorization.

Anthropologists have focused primarily on groups that are formed on the basis of kin ties, that is, formed through ties of marriage or of blood relationship. Group identity and membership can be based on non-kin principles, however; and, in modern industrial societies, most groups are non-kin based. Anthropologists have studied numerous societies in which groups based on age are very important, resulting in the formation of age grades or age sets. An example of such a group in American society, based at least partially on age, would be neighborhood gangs, whose behavior is ritualized, often violent, and is consumption oriented—membership in the gang is shown through the wearing of specific colors of clothing and through emblems on clothing, cars, bags, and even on the skin itself in the form of tattoos. Gang members "hang" together, consume together. Another example of an age-based group in

American society is the small, fluid groups of teenagers who interact socially for periods of time and who affect one another in terms of consumption styles. These are sometimes referred to as cliques or groupies (currently), and the individuals who form these groups emulate one another in terms of clothing styles, music, and activities. For example, in the early 1990s, young American teenagers wore Girbaud jeans and T-shirts, Nike sports shoes, listened to rap music, and played laser tag and Super Nintendo. In these social situations, continued membership and acceptance in the group is often based on the ability to consume appropriately.

Non-kin groups also can be formed on the basis of gender. In this context, the reference is not to all men or women who behave in a particular way because of their overall gender roles in society. Rather, behavior is generated and modified on the basis of belonging to a particular group that is gender based. Feminist book groups or male sports associations are examples of such groups in the United States. Fischer and Gainer (1994) indicate, for example, that "organized sports is an institution in which a sharp divide between men and women is defined and reinforced" (p. 86). Through formation of and association with such non-kin groups, members may come to see others in the group as reference points in their consumption behaviors. Again, Fischer and Gainer suggest that

> consumption of organized sports helps men to develop and reinforce their masculine self-identities . . . [and] reinforces a hierarchical form of social bonding among men . . . through their choices or constraints in the consumption of sports, men will display a varied range of masculinities. . . . Women experience feelings of marginalization in their consumption of organized sports. (pp. 92, 94, 97, 99, respectively)

In this example, the consumption behavior becomes the means by which individual identity is expressed, manifest, and manipulated and how group membership is defined, complete with designations *within* the group, as well as delineating inclusivity and exclusivity.

A final example of a non-kin-based group of interest here is the voluntary association, referring to a group organized on the basis of common interests. Clearly, this is an important organizing principle for group membership in complex industrialized societies. Similar to the groups mentioned above, which are organized on the basis of age or of gender, voluntary associations are groups that may also influence the consumption behavior of individual members of the group by providing social pressure to emulate or by providing role models for consumption. These voluntary associations may even require specific consumption behavior in order to join or maintain membership in the group. This would be the case for certain types of leisure/recreation-based groups, for example. Men, women, and their families who belong to the National Muzzle Loading Rifle Association, for instance, or to local black-powder rifle or muzzle-loading rifle organizations, participate regularly in reenactments of the mountain man rendezvous, which occurred in the western United States between 1825 and 1840. Participation in the national rendezvous requires elaborate and expensive consumption activities. Local rendezvous reenactments may last only a few days, whereas national rendezvous will last 8 to 10 days. During that time, participants must wear only clothing that would have been worn during the 1825 to 1840 time period, sleep in white canvas tents or tepees reminiscent of that period, cook on open fires with cast iron utensils, pots, and pans, eat from dishes and with utensils that would have been available in the early 1800s, sit on furniture from the period, and so on. Anyone who does not conform will be informed of their inappropriate behavior by neighbors or by the "dog soldiers" who are assigned to peruse the camp for consumption conformity. Consistent nonconformity results in expulsion from the camp. At a national rendezvous, casual spectators or tourists are not allowed, because they disrupt the "authentic" atmosphere created by appropriate consumption behaviors.

The daily rendezvous activities include "shoots" with special rifles from the period, typically costing anywhere from a few hundred to several thousand dollars, shopping on "traders' row" for more objects to make the camp and the individuals who inhabit it appear "authentic," costume contests and exhibitions in which the authenticity and elaborateness of individuals' apparel are judged, and classes for participants to learn how to bead, quill, carve arrows, tan hides, or engage in other activities that will help individuals consume appropriately at the rendezvous.

With all of the special consumption required to acquire and maintain membership in this group, annual purchases can amount to thousands of dollars. Some members find the overall investment too high, but, compelled by the desire to remain part of the activity and the group, they engage in "trading," selling special items they have purchased or, more often, made during the year or trading them with others in order to outfit themselves appropriately (Costa, 1993a; Costa & Belk, 1995).

In general, the social and behavioral ramifications of group membership and group identity have been well explored in anthropology. A useful illustrative example is the anthropological treatment of ethnic groups. Although it was certainly not the first work on the subject, Barth's book, *Ethnic Groups and Boundaries: The Social Organization of Culture Difference*, published in 1969, focused attention on the formation and maintenance of group boundaries. Barth suggested that ethnicity is a social *process*, formed through the interactions of members of the group among themselves and with those who do not belong to the group. Through this emphasis, Barth revolutionized the field of ethnic studies by suggesting that social processes rather than lists of cultural traits define groups. Glazer and Moynihan (1963) were also concerned with ethnicity as process; they suggested that the maintenance of ethnic identity and the formation of ethnic groups may be an inherent part of all complex human societies. In a theoretical approach that helps clarify the interaction of individual and group identity, Epstein (1978) suggested that the powerful process of ethnic self-identification involves emotion and affect, which eventually serve to reinforce and maintain the boundaries of the group (see also Isaacs, 1975). In certain cases, the powerful identification of the individual with the group has led to ethnic conflict and violence (Bell, 1975; Glazer & Moynihan, 1975; Horowitz, 1975; Yinger, 1994).

Each of these aspects of group identity has potential interest for consumer behavior research, where they remain relatively unexamined in the scholarly literature (see, however, Costa & Bamossy, 1993, 1995a, 1995b—all chapters). In the trade literature, though, certain elements of ethnic consumer behavior *have been* explored, although again typically on a superficial level. For instance, *American Demographics* consistently publishes information on ethnic segments and associated behaviors. It reports, for example, that "blacks value status more than Hispanics or Asians . . . do not buy unknown brands just to save money . . . [and] are willing to pay more for quality products" (Crispell, 1993, p. 15). Similarly, "Hispanics surpass the U.S. average in participation in aerobics, basketball, bicycling, hiking, racquetball, running, soccer, softball, swimming, tennis and weight training" (Kate, 1993, p. 22). It is typical for the analysis to stop there, however, with the superficial report of differences in characteristics or behaviors.

It would be appropriate for scholars to take such information as a *starting point* and to push the analysis further through an in-depth exploration of the *meaning* of such behaviors, the way in which they are expressed in group activities and in self- and group identity. For example, how do those Blacks who "value status" express that status to one another through consumption behaviors? In which social situations would a dramaturgical approach to presentation of self be fruitful in illuminating the behavior? Does this emphasis on prestige help define the ethnicity of some segment of the Black American population? In the Hispanic example, is participation in sports an ethnic expression of group membership? Do processes of in-groupness and out-groupness take place in the sports context? Can interethnic conflict be generated or be alleviated through sports play? A trained cultural anthropologist would be most likely to assume *any/all* of these situations as possible and would begin to explore their manifestations in actual behaviors. Consumer researchers, on the other hand, often conclude their analyses early with the statement that differences exist, but they fail to pursue further exploration, fleshing out meaning and the social organizational implications of the behaviors.

Occasionally, *American Demographics* reports push the analysis to a higher level. For instance, in a discussion of the home-buying interests of Asians, underlying Chinese cultural values were explored:

> Imagine a curving path leading to a house nestled in the hills. In the backyard glistens an ornamental pool. . . . Those qualities, along with many others, translate into *feng shui*—literally, "the wind and the water." Rooted in China's centuries-old agrarian culture, *feng shui* . . . often guides many Asians' beliefs about good and bad luck in a home. . . . Many Asians believe that a home loaded with right angles will bring them bad luck. . . . *Chi* represents an important part of *feng shui* beliefs. "Vicious, harmful *chi* travels on a straight line." . . . "Beneficial, gentle *chi* travels on a curved, irregular path." (Fost, 1993, pp. 23-24)

Scholarly efforts could further explore the ways in which particular beliefs about *feng shui* and *chi* influence the formation of ethnic-based communities and senses of belonging and of exclusion.

Other dimensions of group formation and identity have been examined by anthropologists and have potential applications in the consumer behavior field (see, e.g., Hansen, 1988; Little, 1988; Rosaldo, 1989). Although the main anthropological emphasis on group has been with respect to corporateness (property holding) and to rules of inclusion (Mair, 1972), it is recognized that membership in groups can be fluid and that groups can be somewhat undefined and invisible in certain social circumstances. Ethnic groups are again an example; in many instances, ethnicity and ethnic groups are invisible or unemphasized. A person may feel that he or she belongs to an ethnic group, for example, without ever actually participating socially with other members of that group, beyond the members of his or her own nuclear family from which the ethnic identification is derived. Similarly, if pushed to respond, an individual may indicate that he or she is a member of the "middle class" in American society. Yet social enactment of class membership may be visible primarily to the outside analyst, assessing the consumer behavior of the individual in question, for example. So, a marketing researcher may decide to categorize a person as a member of a particular class on the basis of the type of home owned, the car driven, the clothes worn, and the leisure activities undertaken, whereas the individual largely fails to self-identify specifically as belonging to a particular class unless pushed by a researcher or other questioner to do so. Again, all of these aspects of group social organization have ramifications for consumption behavior.

It is important to note that further explorations of demographic variables, with sufficient elaboration to be characterized as studies fully emphasizing social organization, have taken place. Among the most prominent are Weiss's (1988) *Clustering of America,* Mitchell's (1983) *The Nine American Lifestyles,* and Fussell's (1992) *Class: A Guide Through the American Status System.* In each of these examples, the author has taken demographic or social variables—geographic neighborhood (based on zip code), values and lifestyles (VALS), and class, respectively—and has written about the marketing and consumer behavior implications of these variables. In the case of Weiss's (1988) clustering, for example, 40 neighborhood types are identified, "each with distinct boundaries, values, consuming habits and political beliefs" (p. xii). Weiss's geodemographic perspective, based on Claritas's PRIZM (Potential Rating Index by Zip Markets), measures consumption patterns of literally thousands of different products and shows clusters of consumers who live near one another and consume in similar ways. Mitchell's (1983) work on lifestyles is derived from the Social Research, Inc. (SRI) developed VALS program, in which values and lifestyles for nine categories of American consumers are documented. Values refers to "the entire constellation of a person's attitudes, beliefs, opinions, hopes, fears, prejudices, needs, desires, and aspirations that, taken together, govern how one behaves. One's interior set of values . . . finds holistic expression in a lifestyle" (Mitchell, 1983, p. vii). Values are an inherent part of culture, and their expression in a lifestyle can be said to be an aspect of social organization which affects consumer behavior. In a similar fashion, Fussell's (1992) analysis is based on class and status in American society.

Each of these studies, and others like them, contributes to the understanding of social organization and consumer behavior in important ways. However, I would suggest two possible research directions based on these books: First, scholarly researchers must use these approaches to consumer behavior more consistently and thoroughly in their own studies; second, studies using geodemographics, VALS, class, or other sociodemographic variables must be pushed further in the direction of full exploration, looking at the ways in which these variables are manifest in actual consumer behavior and assessing the impact and influence of individuals and social groups in the context of these variables.

Extant approaches to consumer behavior focus to a large extent on the individual, with particular emphases on cognition, information processing, and decision making. In anthropological approaches, the behavior and attitudes of the individual are incorporated into social and cultural domains. Whereas anthropologists may "study" an individual, even using a *single person* as a focus of study (see, e.g., Black Elk, 1961, and Mountain Wolf Woman, 1961, where anthropologists collected and translated single-life histories, published as autobiographies), such an approach is most often intended as a "case study" of sorts, whereby the actions, behaviors, attitudes, and so forth are thought to be illustrative of, to exemplify, the social and cultural dimensions of the larger group to which the individual belongs. The exploration of the individual in the fields of ethnopsychology and cognitive anthropology, among others, further demonstrates ways in which anthropologists have concentrated on the individual (see Casson, 1981; Dougherty, 1985; Hamill, 1990; Kearney, 1984). Within the context of anthropological approaches to consumer behavior, focus on the individual would have similar dimensions; that is, it would largely be intended to illustrate *not* individual behavior but the larger social and cultural domains of which the individual is a part.

It may be useful also at this point to distinguish more clearly between social and cultural approaches, particularly in the context of consumer behavior. Culture, as detailed earlier, refers to *shared* ideas, attitudes, behaviors, and so forth; cultural approaches to consumer behavior can emphasize any/all of these. This is the case even when, as just indicated, the actual "subject" of the study seems to be "individual," as in the opening vignette, the point of which was to refer to Greek American shared attitudes and beliefs about appropriate ways in which to consume at Easter. It is not Diane or Virginia per se who is of particular interest; rather, it is the social and cultural group of which both are a part, in which they express membership via consumer behavior.

Whereas culture refers to shared, learned behaviors and so forth, society refers to the social group that shares the culture. When the scholarly focus is on groups and the ways in which they are *organized*, on the rules and processes for learning the rules of behavior, or on a specific society, the approach can be said to be "social." To return to the opening vignette, Diane's tutelage of Virginia is an example of socialization, learning the appropriate rules for behavior; the group formed by the ethnic-identified individuals is a social group; and the gender and ethnic roles are enactments of social organizational expectations and socially defined prescriptions for behavior, organized into guidelines that transcend the individual but also organize the individual. However, social approaches are, like approaches focusing on the individual, *also* cultural approaches, albeit with an emphasis specifically on groups, rules, roles, statuses, socialization processes, and so on. These are cultural as well, in the sense that they vary cross-culturally and that they are shared, learned behaviors, expressing cultural values, beliefs, attitudes, and so forth. Diane's role was an expression of the Greek American value emphasizing the desirability of maternal care and of group religious celebrations with a focus on the family, for example. Thus individual/social/cultural approaches both diverge from one another in their specific foci *and* are integrated with one another in a larger, holistic fashion under the rubric of "culture" in general.

Consumer Behavior Examples and Social Organization

This section provides further examples of consumer behavior and social organization, drawing on the intersection of individual and group identities in consumption activities.

Gender Roles

Increased use and elaboration of the concepts of status and role in consumer behavior studies would lead to greater insights. Status is not just an attribute but a combination of attributes, which then carries with it a framework for action, a role. One of the areas of consumer behavior inquiry in which the analysis of role is beginning to emerge is that of gender. Gender roles, because they have received recognition as a named, legitimate (at least in the opinion of some scholars) research domain, are perhaps a good illustrative example of the fruitfulness of role analysis in consumer behavior studies. Studies in this area are beginning to flesh out the full dimensions of gendered consumer behavior (see Costa, 1994a), with a recognition that gender-role performance, expectation, perception, and enactment of role-sets are all rich areas for fruitful inquiry.

Some consumer behavior studies have found that American women are often primarily responsible for certain consumption activities—gift buying and gift giving, specific types of shopping, preparation of items for consumption, disposition, and so on (i.e., Cheal, 1987, 1988; Davis & Rigaux, 1974; Fischer & Arnold, 1990; Fischer & Gainer, 1991, 1994; Herrmann, 1991, 1993; Lavin, 1991; Qualls, 1987; Sherry & McGrath, 1989). However, in some instances, American men, in enacting their gender roles, choose gifts and are responsible for consumption activities related to certain types of goods (i.e., Belk & Coon, 1993; Milner, Fodness, & Morrison, 1991; Rudell, 1991, 1993).

The analyses of these scholars point to the usefulness of greater attention paid to role enactment and to various other aspects of role-based behaviors. The complexity of role enactment is explored, so that we begin to understand how American masculinity and femininity are *enacted* and *expressed*. Again, it is not enough to simply suggest that gender differences in consumption exist; the tapestry, the underlying fabric of the differences, must be explored:

> Merely suggesting that men and women, boys and girls, do things differently, behave differently in terms of consumption, is not enough. It is time to stop accepting such a finding as important—the field of gender and consumer behavior has progressed to the point that the response to such a simplistic finding should be, "of course." The questions, the issues for analysis, then become—why, how, and in what way? (Costa, 1994b, p. 373)

The scholars cited above move in this direction: Rather than merely stating that gender is a variable, they explore *why* and *how* gender is manifest in consumer behavior.

Perhaps a comprehensive example would be useful at this point. Research on gender and consumer behavior in Greece reveals an elaborate gendered dichotomy of possessions and of behaviors related to those possessions. In some sense and at a very general level, Greek men and women "possess" separate spaces. The public domain of the fields, streets, communal buildings, town square, the right-hand side of the church, and most retail and service outlets are essentially male dominated, male controlled, male owned. The domain of the home, including its walled surroundings, is associated with females (Campbell, 1964; Costa, 1989; Dimen, 1977; Dubisch, 1986; du Boulay, 1978; Friedl, 1962; Herzfeld, 1985; Hirschon, 1978; Hoffman, 1974).

The gendering of domains is based on enactment of gendered roles and on the cultural dimensions of the gender stereotypes in Greek society. Through gendered space, women enact gender roles based on the expectations that women care for the home and for children and refrain from public associations with others and from public appearances in general (Campbell, 1964; Dubisch, 1986; Friedl, 1962). Dubisch (1986) notes, for example,

> The house is the focus of Greek family life. . . . Within the walls of the house are carried out the daily activities that sustain family life in all its physical, social, and psychological aspects; the preparation and consumption of food, the socialization of children, adult sexual activity, the discus-

> sion of private family matters. . . . The house is the special responsibility of the woman, and she is both functionally and symbolically associated with it. (p. 197)

Dubisch goes on to discuss the way in which the objects in the home are part of a woman's domain. In this respect, the kitchen and its associated objects are most important. A woman fulfills her social role of mother, nurturer, and caretaker all through specific consumption activities in this room and elsewhere in the house. In the kitchen, the woman cleans vegetables and prepares other foods for cooking, mends and knits, throws bedding over the door to air out, cleans laundry, entertains and socializes, and counsels her family on important household decisions (see also Hirschon, 1978).

Within the Greek home, then, certain rooms are more "male" and certain rooms are more "female," based on the occasions for use of the room, the types of objects in the rooms, and the activities that take place there. In each situation, gender role is again enacted:

> The tools required for work outside the home, for farming, for the care of work animals, for fishing and—in those regions affected by modernization— the car, are all men's possessions. The women own the tools and appliances associated with the kitchen and their tasks in the home. . . . Animals may be owned separately also, with the work animals belonging to the men, and the milk goats, chickens, and housecats owned by women. It appears then, that men usually own those things which "establish a family outside the home" (Hoffman, 1974, film narration). Some theorists have gone so far as to claim that "all valuable items belong to men." (Costa, 1989, p. 563)

In urban areas of Greece, a gender-based pattern of ownership is also found: Men are often associated with technical products, and women continue to be associated with nontechnical and home-related items. This pattern of gendered possessions is similar to that found in other European societies and in American societies, where the association of women with the nontechnical and with the home and of men with work and with technical products has been documented. Rudell (1991) indicates, for example, that "there is much historical and social evidence of differences in males' and females' relationship to technology" (p. 189); this gender difference is then manifest in consumption of technical products:

> The picture that emerges is one of children being socialized to regard technology as more appropriate for males. As a result, males are more

involved with technology, feel more confident and comfortable with it, and derive greater pleasure from its toy-like qualities. Females are less involved or comfortable with technology, viewing high-tech products as tools to help them accomplish tasks efficiently. Adoption of a high-tech product by a female consumer may depend more on its ability to "get the job done" with least disruption to current habits and minimum risk of failure, while male consumers may be drawn to the power and pleasure afforded by its use. (pp. 193-194)

In their study of gender differences in the use of similar products in the Netherlands, Bamossy and Jansen (1994) indicate that "within Western industrialized cultures there is the generally held belief that, compared with females, males are more involved with technology, feel more confident and comfortable with it, and derive greater satisfaction from using it" (p. 144). Bamossy and Jansen go on to document this "influence of gender socialization with respect to attitudes toward computers in young Dutch students" (p. 155; see also Costa & Pavia, 1993; Pavia & Costa, 1993; Rudell, 1993).

Role enactment or performance does not merely involve the use of objects associated with specified gender-dichotomized work tasks and work space, however. In Greece, women are said to be in closer contact with the supernatural and are placed in charge of caring for the dead, of curing the ill (with folk rather than Western medical practices), and of the spiritual well-being of family members, for example. As part of that role, Greek women purchase or make items for use in folk or Greek Orthodox religious rituals, prepare the grave goods and bring objects to the graves of loved ones on a daily or weekly basis after burial, purchase amulets for protection of their children and grandchildren, and so on. In these consumption activities, they are enacting their roles as spiritual caretakers of the family.

In Mediterranean societies in general, males are expected to behave stereotypically as producers in agriculture and in business, as being in charge of relations between the nuclear family and the rest of society, and as more respectable (than are women) in God's eyes through basic masculinity and associated cleanliness. As with women, the gender role for Greek men goes beyond their duties in production. Greek men are responsible for presentation of the family to the outside world, for instance. For this reason, the one room in the home specifically designed and decorated for presentation of the familial "self" to the community is analyzed by some as a male domain and by others as both a female and a male domain (Costa, 1989). This is in contrast to the overall "ownership" of domestic space by women. In addition, the male, as representative of the family and its wealth and abilities, generally engages in more conspicuous consumption than do females of the family for presentation of the family to the larger community. The male owns and takes care of any vehicles, often dresses quite fashionably and meticulously, and consumes publicly in a way that reflects positively on his family—for example, being generous when socially necessary. According to Herzfeld (1985), "there is less focus on 'being a good man' than on 'being *good at* being a man'—a stance that stresses *performative excellence*" (p. 16; emphasis in the original). In general, Greek men see themselves as constantly "on display" and consume and present themselves accordingly.

Greek masculinity is most clearly expressed in certain consumption rituals; specifically in drinking alcohol and in eating meat. Herzfeld explains that, in toasting rituals associated with drinking, "drinking involves the substances of masculinity, sexuality and death. . . . The act of drinking is . . . an affirmation of manliness" (p. 126). This association with "manliness" is accomplished through the challenges to one another that occur in the toasts themselves, through the symbolism of the wine as blood, and through competitive performances that are part of the Greek male expression of identity. Herzfeld (1985) further suggests that both "meat and wine . . . are quintessentially male substances" (p. 130). Presentation of meat to guests represents the honor of the male and of his family—the more meat he is able to present at a given time, the more manly he is considered to be. And, in line with the emphasis on performance, the best meat is that which has been stolen. The consumption of such meat symbolizes daring and hardship, which both build and represent male strength: "Meat thus becomes a medium for encoding the relative values of . . . [Greek] manhood" (p. 131).

These examples from Greek social organization and anthropological treatments thereof suggest the richness that can be derived from extensive investigations of consumption behaviors as they are related to social organization through the individual and the group.

Individuals and Groups

Marketers and consumer researchers *have* analyzed social groups through the strategic process of market segmentation. Baby boomers, perhaps the most famous of all market segments in the U.S. market, for instance, are characterized by their age, materialistic aspirations, educational profile, attitudes toward health and fitness, dual-career orientation, delay in childbearing, focus on family life, and so forth. Baby boomers constitute 30% of the American population and head 44% of U.S. households. Their purchasing power and sheer numbers make them an often cited segment in marketing studies and education.

Specific aspects of consumer behavior among baby boomers can be ascertained and understood on the basis of this segmentation. An important characteristic is that they are "absorbed in family life" (Russell, 1991, p. 26) and consume accordingly—44% of boomers own their own home, have spent money on their own education and plan to do the same for their children, and stress quality and value in their products. A "Demogram" provided by *American Demographics* focused on the familial emphasis of baby boomers:

> George Mitchell is staring at a pool table covered with shoes: ski boots, ice skates, baseball spikes, ballet slippers, flip flops, high heels, and roller blades. It is his family's net worth in footwear. . . . Everyone seemed to enjoy the idea that their family might be a textbook example of kid-centered spending. In fact, other than some furniture and maybe the Mr. Coffee, I hadn't seen anything that wasn't for kids. . . . As everyone scrambled upstairs, Mary Ann turned around. "I want to show you what six gallons of milk look like." (Parker, 1991, p. 31)

In the process of market segmentation, marketers adjust aspects of their product offering and marketing mix to appeal to a targeted market segment. For example, marketers must offer baby boomers products for their family and products that ease the lifestyle of dual-income families. Similarly, marketers must recognize that they need to adjust the advertising/promotion aspects of their marketing mix because "baby boomers are insulated from advertising messages. . . . They are too busy juggling jobs and parenthood to pay attention to marketing efforts . . . [and] a proliferation of advertising is competing for their attention" (Russell, 1991, p. 27). The strategic analysis of specific groups of consumers within the larger population and the resulting designed procedures to reach them through marketing efforts are common among marketing practitioners.

It is important for an expanded usage of the segmentation construct to occur in consumer research. Moving beyond the list of traits associated with given market segments, we must understand social groups in the context of social interaction within and outside the group. Ethnicity again provides a useful example here. It has been suggested that "it is often precisely at the point of interaction that ethnicity is expressed through marketing practices and in consumer behavior" (Costa & Bamossy, 1995a, p. 9), for example. Ethnicity becomes visible, and is often emphasized, in the context of the market. Employment is certain industries can be related to ethnicity (Boissevain et al., 1990), distribution channels can be ethnically controlled (Arnould, 1993, also Chapter 4, this volume), and ethnic groups can be identified with and specialize in specific retail sectors (Waldinger, Aldrich, & Ward, 1990).

Ethnicity is particularly visible in consumer behavior. Following Belk's (1988) analysis of possessions as extensions of self, ethnicity can be expressed visibly through objects of consumption. In describing and interpreting the meaning of objects owned by a particular family, for example, Costa and Belk (1990) indicated,

> Their emphasis on the combination of past and present is most apparent in the items which they choose to illustrate their ethnic identity or heritage, particularly when such objects were used by parents or grandparents. Hanging on the wall in their recreation room, for example, Phil and Catherine have the shoemaking tools which Phil's father used in his trade in Italy, as well as an implement his mother used to wring out her mop. On the same wall, Catherine has placed instruments from her own mother's kitchen. . . . Irene has purchased, either on trips or for anniversary presents, vases and other items which invoke her Italian heritage. While he denies specific influences, Rob is adding columns and peristyles to the interior of his home as decorations which invoke a classical heritage, albeit in a post-modern form. (p. 112)

Similarly, Joy et al. (1995) found that, for Italian immigrants in Montreal,

> home . . . serves as a looking glass, reminding Italians of who they are in a Canadian context. Italians demarcate and sacralize space in the home as a tribute to their "heritage." . . . Each object reveals a part of the identity of those who own it and is thus a window to the world(s) they live in. (p. 175)

In the opening vignette, we saw that Virginia and Diane expressed ethnicity through choice and preparation of foods and through consumption rituals surrounding an ethnic ceremony. Virginia's desire to belong to the group, to move from out-group to in-group, and Diane's intent to preserve the ethnic identity of the family after the death of her parents and as part of her gender role were expressed through ethnic-based consumption.

Levy (1978) points out that market segmentation thinking has moved through phases of usage and importance. He concluded that the fourth, and most recent, phase involves a questioning of segmentation's efficacy in marketing and social policy. I would suggest that, in fact, the use of segmentation in marketing and consumer research should move into a fifth phase, whereby the full *meaning* of belonging to a segment, manifest on both an individual and a group level, must be explored. Such exploration of meaning would include, for example, inquiry into how individuals and groups indicate membership through consumption, what social messages are inherent in their consumer behaviors, and whether or not group or individual ends and goals are somehow displayed or achieved through the consumption process.

◊ Conclusion

Consumer researchers often appear to be satisfied with a superficial analysis. A consumer may be said to have certain attributes of age, gender, family position, and so on. The consumer is merely described as possessing these attributes, rather than fully analyzed on the basis of what the possession of those specific attributes implies in terms of actual behavior and what underlying meaning can be attributed to consumption of given products. When analysis does take place, it is again on a superficial rather than substantial level, and this is the crux of the problem. It is not enough to state that differences in behavior exist on the basis of possession of specific attributes.

When consumer researchers *have* studied social organization, they have typically treated attributes as static structures, variables in a descriptive equation. So, for example, some researchers have reported the results of their studies and conclude that, in fact, men and women do seem to behave differently. Surprisingly, the analysis stops there. Typically, there is no further investigation, no placing of the fact of differential behavior on the basis of sex in any type of cultural context. Similarly, researchers may report that Hispanics shop differently than do non-Hispanic Americans. The implication is that marketers should direct their marketing efforts to Hispanics in a distinct fashion. Again, no cultural context, with a full exploration of social organizational dimensions, is provided. What does it mean that Hispanics shop differently? Where does this behavior come from? How does it fit into the full context of the ethnic behavior of the group and of the individuals in that group? These questions deserve further exploration.

The Hispanic example is also useful in illustrating other problems in analysis related to this superficial use of social organizational concepts. For example, Hispanics, categorized as such on the basis of language, constitute a large, varied group that does, indeed, behave differently in certain ways from other ethnic groups and from the typical "white" American. But Hispanics *do not* form a single, homogeneous ethnic group. Researchers who suggest that Hispanics behave differently often commit the basic error of assuming that all Spanish speakers share the same culture rather than differentiating between Mexican Hispanics, Spanish Hispanics, Colombian

Hispanics, and so forth. In fact, "it is well known that Hispanics of different national origins have different attitudes and values" (Frey & O'Hare, 1993, p. 32). Of course, it would be a mistake to suggest even *within* nation-based Hispanic ethnic groups that all individuals behave in precisely the same manner. In either case, by overgeneralizing we run the risk of misunderstanding culture's influence on consumption as manifest in aspects of social organization.

It is suggested that consumer researchers focus to a greater extent on providing context and meaning for behavior. Through a more comprehensive exploration of social organization, researchers can examine the dynamism of social interaction and enactment of attributes in the process of social and individual identity. This suggested emphasis would lead to greater overall understanding of both specific consumption activities and consumer behavior in general. A consumer, aged 36, female, with an income of $30,000 per year, would be analyzed not just in terms of these attributes but in terms of how these relate to actual behavior. Her purchases, the use of the items she purchases, what these items seem to say about her, her choice of certain products over others, her presentation of her "self" to others through the use of certain products—all need to be analyzed and understood. The meaning of the attributes and the ways in which these attributes define, influence, or give meaning to her actual behavior are the dynamic social interactional aspect of social organization.

Research Agenda

This discussion of social organization and consumer behavior provides a context for the following suggestions concerning future directions for research:

- We must *move beyond* the mere statement that differences in behavior exist on the basis of social organizational variables.
- We must *move beyond* the superficial description of market segments.
- We must *move beyond* the simple assertion that individuals are what they consume.
- In all of these cases, the "move beyond" must involve a greater exploration of *how* and *in what way* the behaviors differ, *why* the differences exist and are manifest by some individuals and groups and not by others in some situations and not in others, *when* and *under what circumstances* we can expect the behaviors to vary or to remain the same, and *what the underlying meaning is* of the different behaviors.

Analysis and understanding of this final point is most critical and facilitates further assessment of how, why, and when behaviors differ.

The research agenda must focus on social organization, specifically on the formation, expression, and influence of groups, and on various aspects of individual identity. In the case of groups, issues involving manifestation of membership, of order and interaction within the group and between the group and those who are nonmembers, of ways in which one becomes involved or excluded from the group, all through various aspects of consumption, must be explored. With respect to individuals, it is suggested that a focus on status and role is most fruitful at this point in time; that is, researchers may find that the most expeditious and fruitful way to proceed is through the initial determination of the social status that an individual is enacting or attempting to enact through the consumption behavior. Further exploration of the role associated with that status, through analyses of role perception, performance, and so forth, would enrich our understanding of the consumption and its meaning. In particular, exploration of specific *consumer statuses,* *consumer roles,* and holistic *consumer identities* would be valuable.

It is further suggested that the exploration of social organization and consumption would be facilitated through increased emphasis on research techniques already in use and fully developed within the anthropological discipline. The research methods of fieldwork and participant observation are misunderstood and underused in consumer research, where they often have been lumped under the term "ethnography" and have referred to research periods of as short as a few hours. The complexity of culture and of social organization in the context of consumption demands that prolonged periods of research be undertaken. This is admittedly difficult for researchers who are used to short periods of contact—or to a total lack of personal contact when survey data collection is undertaken. Nevertheless, more time and care *must* be taken in the collection and interpretation of qualitative data. "Blitzkrieg ethnography" suffers from a far greater likelihood of misinterpretation of the data, and those who read such research are suspicious (correctly, I might add) about the quality of the research and of its results. The prolonged engagement suggested requires extensive training and commitment, but the benefits of this process will be enormous.

In conclusion, social anthropology provides us with full and useful analyses of various aspects of social organization. We must draw upon and expand anthropological perspectives in consumer behavior studies. Of particular interest are the concepts of status and role and their various manifestations and extensions; much room remains for research in these particular areas. Also of interest are the social processes of individual and group identity as they relate to consumption behaviors in modern society. The phenomenon of the group remains relatively underresearched in our field, and again there is ample room for expansion of our research endeavors. The concepts exist, are fully defined, elaborated upon, and used fruitfully. Although it is an effort that requires much time and energy, the avenues of further inquiry are open and inviting, and it is incumbent upon consumer behavior scholars to expand our analyses of consumer behavior and social organization.

◪ References

Arnould, E. (1989). Toward a broadened theory of preference formation and the diffusion of innovations: Cases from Zinder Province, Niger Republic. *Journal of Consumer Research, 16,* 239-267.

Arnould, E. (1993, January). *Barriers to entrepreneurship in Niger.* Paper presented at the Fourth International Conference on Marketing and Development, San Jose, Costa Rica.

Bamossy, G. J., & Jansen, P. G. W. (1994). Children's apprehension and comprehension: Gender influences on computer literacy and attitude structures toward personal computers. In J. A. Costa (Ed.), *Gender issues and consumer behavior* (pp. 142-163). Thousand Oaks, CA: Sage.

Barth, F. (Ed.). (1969). *Ethnic groups and boundaries: The social organization of culture difference.* Boston: Little, Brown.

Becker, H. S., & McCall, M. M. (Eds.). (1990). *Symbolic interaction and cultural studies.* Chicago: University of Chicago Press.

Belk, R. W. (1988). Possessions and the extended self. *Journal of Consumer Research, 15,* 139-168.

Belk, R. W., & Coon, G. S. (1993). Gift giving as agapic love: An alternative to the exchange paradigm based on dating experiences. *Journal of Consumer Research, 20,* 393-417.

Bell, D. (1975). Ethnicity and social change. In N. Glazer & D. P. Moynihan (Eds.), *Ethnicity: Theory and experience* (pp. 141-174). Cambridge, MA: Harvard University Press.

Berreman, G. D. (1962). *Behind many masks: Ethnography and impression management in a Himalayan village* (Monograph No. 4). Ithaca, NY: Society for Applied Anthropology.

Black Elk. (1961). *Black Elk speaks, being the life story of an Oglala Sioux.* Lincoln: University of Nebraska Press.

Boissevain, J., Blaschke, J., Grotenbreg, H., Joseph, I., Light, I., Sway, M., Waldinger, R., & Werbner, P. (1990). Ethnic entrepreneurs and ethnic strategies. In R. Waldinger, H. Aldrich, & R. Ward (Eds.), *Ethnic entrepreneurs* (pp. 131-156). Newbury Park, CA: Sage.

Campbell, J. R. (1964). *Honour, family and patronage: A study of institutions and moral values in a Greek mountain community.* Oxford, UK: Clarendon.

Casson, R. W. (Ed.). (1981). *Language, culture, and cognition: Anthropological perspectives.* New York: Macmillan.

Cheal, D. (1987). "Showing them you love them": Gift giving and the dialectic of intimacy. *Sociological Review, 35,* 151-169.

Cheal, D. (1988). *The gift economy.* London: Routledge.

Costa, J. A. (1989). On display: Social and cultural dimensions of consumer behavior in the Greek saloni. In T. Srull (Ed.), *Advances in consumer research* (Vol. 16, pp. 562-566). Provo, UT: Association for Consumer Research.

Costa, J. A. (1992). The periphery of pleasure or pain: Consumer culture in the EC Mediterranean of 1992. In T. M. Wilson & M. E. Smith (Eds.), *Cultural change and the new Europe: Perspectives on the European Community* (pp. 81-98). New York: Westview.

Costa, J. A. (1993a, June). *Mountain women in a mountain man's world.* Special session presentation at the Second Conference on Gender and Consumer Behavior, Salt Lake City, UT.

Costa, J. A. (1993b, August). *Using the culture concept: A comparison of marketing and anthropology.* Paper presented at the 18th Annual Macromarketing Conference, Kingston, RI.

Costa, J. A. (Ed.). (1994a). *Gender issues and consumer behavior.* Thousand Oaks, CA: Sage.

Costa, J. A. (1994b). Gender issues: Gender as a cultural construct. In C. T. Allen & D. R. John (Eds.), *Advances in consumer research* (Vol. 21, pp. 372-373). Provo, UT: Association for Consumer Research.

Costa, J. A., & Bamossy, G. J. (1993). Ethnicity in developing countries: Implications for marketing and research. In L. V. Dominguez & C. G. Sequeira (Eds.), *Proceedings of the Fourth International Conference on Marketing and Development* (pp. 408-415). Madison, WI: Omnipress.

Costa, J. A., & Bamossy, G. J. (1995a). Perspectives on ethnicity, nationalism, and cultural identity. In J. A. Costa & G. J. Bamossy (Eds.), *Marketing in a multicultural world: Ethnicity, nationalism, and cultural identity* (pp. 3-25). Thousand Oaks, CA: Sage.

Costa, J. A., & Bamossy, G. J. (Eds.). (1995b). *Marketing in a multicultural world: Ethnicity, nationalism, and cultural identity.* Thousand Oaks, CA: Sage.

Costa, J. A., & Belk, R. W. (1990). Nouveaux riches as quintessential Americans. In R. W. Belk (Ed.), *Advances in nonprofit marketing* (Vol. 3, pp. 83-140). Greenwich, CT: JAI.

Costa, J. A., & Belk, R. W. (1995). *The mountain man rendezvous: A consumption reenactment.* Working paper, University of Utah, Department of Marketing, Salt Lake City.

Costa, J. A., & Pavia, T. M. (1993). Alpha-numeric brand names and gender stereotypes. In J. A. Costa & R. W. Belk (Eds.), *Research in consumer behavior* (Vol. 6, pp. 85-112). Greenwich, CT: JAI.

Crispell, D. (1993, August). Materialism among minorities. *American Demographics*, pp. 14-16.

Davis, H., & Rigaux, B. (1974). Dimensions of marital roles in consumer decision-making. *Journal of Marketing Research, 7*, 305-312.

Deegan, M. J., & Hill, M. R. (Eds.). (1987). *Women and symbolic interaction.* Boston: Allen & Unwin.

Dimen, M. (1977). Review of Kypseli: Women and men apart—A divided reality. *American Anthropologist, 79*, 194-195.

Dougherty, J. W. D. (Ed.). (1985). *Directions in cognitive anthropology.* Urbana: University of Illinois Press.

Dubisch, J. (Ed.). (1986). *Gender and power in rural Greece.* Princeton, NJ: Princeton University Press.

du Boulay, J. (1978). *Portrait of a Greek mountain village.* Oxford, UK: Clarendon.

Epstein, A. L. (1978). *Ethos and identity.* Chicago: Aldine.

Fischer, E., & Arnold, S. (1990). More than a labor of love: Gender roles and Christmas gift giving. *Journal of Consumer Research, 17*, 333-345.

Fischer, E., & Gainer, B. (1991). I shop therefore I am: The role of shopping in the social construction of women's identities. In J. A. Costa (Ed.), *Gender and consumer behavior: Proceedings of the Conference on Gender and Consumer Behavior* (pp. 350-357). Salt Lake City: University of Utah Printing Service.

Fischer, E., & Gainer, B. (1994). Masculinity and the consumption of organized sports. In J. A. Costa (Ed.), *Gender issues and consumer behavior* (pp. 84-103). Thousand Oaks, CA: Sage.

Fost, D. (1993, June). Asian homebuyers seek wind and water. *American Demographics*, pp. 23-25.

Fox, R. (1967). *Kinship and marriage.* London: Penguin.

Frey, W. H., & O'Hare, W. P. (1993, April). Vivan los suburbios! *American Demographics*, pp. 30-37.

Friedl, E. (1962). *Vasilika: A village in modern Greece.* New York: Holt, Rinehart & Winston.

Fussell, P. (1992). *Class: A guide through the American status system.* New York: Simon & Schuster.

Glazer, N., & Moynihan, D. P. (1963). *Beyond the melting pot.* Cambridge: MIT Press and Harvard University Press.

Glazer, N., & Moynihan, D. P. (Eds.). (1975). *Ethnicity: Theory and experience.* Cambridge, MA: Harvard University Press.

Goffman, E. (1959). *The presentation of self in everyday life.* New York: Doubleday.

Graburn, N. (1971). *Readings in kinship and social structure.* New York: Harper & Row.

Habermas, J. (1987). *The theory of communicative action.* Cambridge, MA: Polity.

Hamill, J. F. (1990). *Ethno-logic: The anthropology of human reasoning.* Urbana: University of Illinois Press.

Hansen, E. C. (1988). Drinking to prosperity: Hedonism and modernization in Villafranca. In J. B. Cole (Ed.), *Anthropology for the nineties* (pp. 231-242). New York: Free Press.

Herrmann, G. (1991). Women's exchange in the American garage sale: Giving gifts and creating community. In J. A. Costa (Ed.), *Gender and consumer behavior: Proceedings of the Conference on Gender and Consumer Behavior* (pp. 234-243). Salt Lake City: University of Utah Printing Service.

Herrmann, G. (1993). His and hers: Gender and garage sales. In J. A. Costa (Ed.), *Gender and consumer behavior: Proceedings of the Second Conference on Gender and Consumer Behavior* (pp. 88-98). Salt Lake City: University of Utah Printing Service.

Herzfeld, M. (1985). *The poetics of manhood: Contest and identity in a Cretan mountain village.* Princeton, NJ: Princeton University Press.

Hirschon, R. (1978). Open body/closed space: The transformation of female sexuality. In S. Ardener (Ed.), *Defining females* (pp. 66-88). New York: John Wiley.

Hoffman, S. (1974). *Kypseli: Women and men apart—A divided reality* [Film, with R. Cowan and P. Aratow]. Produced by University of California EMC.

Horowitz, D. L. (1975). Ethnic identity. In N. Glazer & D. P. Moynihan (Eds.), *Ethnicity: Theory and experience* (pp. 109-140). Cambridge, MA: Harvard University Press.

Isaacs, H. R. (1975). Basic group identity: The idols of the tribe. In N. Glazer & D. P. Moynihan (Eds.), *Ethnicity: Theory and experience* (pp. 29-52). Cambridge, MA: Harvard University Press. (Material expanded to book length in *Idols of the tribe, group identity and political change,* by H. R. Isaacs, 1975, New York: Harper & Row)

Joy, A., Hui, M., Kim, C., & Laroche, M. (1995). The cultural past in the present: The meaning of home and objects in the home of working-class Italian immigrants in Montreal. In J. A. Costa & G. J. Bamossy (Eds.), *Marketing in a multicultural world: Ethnicity, nationalism, and cultural identity* (pp. 145-179). Thousand Oaks, CA: Sage.

Kate, N. T. (1993, June). Hispanics hit the hoops. *American Demographics,* p. 22.

Kearney, M. (1984). *World view.* Novato, CA: Chandler & Sharp.

Lamont, M., & Fournier, M. (Eds.). (1992). *Cultivating differences: Symbolic boundaries and the making of inequality.* Chicago: University of Chicago Press.

Lavin, M. (1991). Husband dominant, wife dominant, joint: A shopping typology for the 1990s? In J. A. Costa (Ed.), *Gender and consumer behavior: Proceedings of the Conference on Gender and Consumer Behavior* (pp. 358-366). Salt Lake City: University of Utah Printing Service.

Levy, S. J. (1978). *Marketplace behavior: Its meaning for management.* New York: AMACOM.

Linton, R. (1936). *The study of man.* New York: Appleton-Century-Crofts.

Little, K. (1988). The role of voluntary associations in West African urbanization. In J. B. Cole (Ed.), *Anthropology for the nineties* (pp. 211-230). New York: Free Press.

Lyman, S. M. (1990). *Civilization: Contents, discontents, malcontents, and other essays in social theory.* Fayetteville: University of Arkansas Press.

Mair, L. (1972). *An introduction to social anthropology.* New York: Oxford University Press.

McCracken, G. (1988). *Culture and consumption: New approaches to the symbolic character of consumer goods and activities.* Bloomington: Indiana University Press.

McCracken, G. (1989). Who is the celebrity endorser? Cultural foundations of the endorsement process. *Journal of Consumer Research, 16,* 310-322.

Merton, R. K. (1957). The role-set: Problems in sociological theory. *British Journal of Sociology, 8,* 110-118.

Milner, L., Fodness, D., & Morrison, J. (1991). Women's images of guns: An exploratory study. In J. A. Costa (Ed.), *Gender and consumer behavior: Proceedings of the Conference on Gender and Consumer Behavior* (pp. 199-208). Salt Lake City: University of Utah Printing Service.

Mitchell, A. (1983). *The nine American lifestyles.* New York: Macmillan.

Moskos, C. C. (1989). *Greek Americans: Struggle and success.* New Brunswick, NJ: Transaction.

Mountain Wolf Woman. (1961). *Mountain Wolf Woman, sister of Crashing Thunder: The autobiography of a Winnebago Indian.* Ann Arbor: University of Michigan Press.

Munch, R. (1988). *Theory of action.* London: Routledge & Kegan Paul.

Murdock, G. P. (1949). *Social structure.* New York: Free Press.

Papanikolas, H. Z. (1974). *Toil and rage in a new land.* Salt Lake City: Utah State Historical Society.

Papanikolas, H. Z. (1987). *Aimilia-Giorges* [Emily-George]. Salt Lake City: University of Utah Press.

Parker, T. (1991, May). Demogram: Tuxedo, New York. *American Demographics,* p. 31.

Parsons, T. (1949). *Essays in sociological theory.* New York: Free Press.

Pavia, T. M., & Costa, J. A. (1993). The winning number: Consumer perceptions of alpha-numeric brand names. *Journal of Marketing, 57,* 85-98.

Qualls, W. (1987). Household decision behavior: The impact of husbands' and wives' sex role orientation. *Journal of Consumer Research, 14,* 264-279.

Rosaldo, R. (1989). *Culture and truth: The remaking of social analysis.* Boston: Beacon.

Rudell, F. (1991). Boys' toys and girls' tools? An exploration of gender differences in consumer decision-making for high tech products. In J. A. Costa (Ed.), *Gender and consumer behavior: Proceedings of the Conference on Gender and Consumer Behavior* (pp. 187-198). Salt Lake City: University of Utah Printing Service.

Rudell, F. (1993). Gender differences in consumer decision making for personal computers: A test of hypotheses. In J. A. Costa (Ed.), *Gender and consumer behavior: Proceedings of the Second Conference on Gender and Consumer Behavior* (pp. 1-16). Salt Lake City: University of Utah Printing Service.

Russell, C. (1991, May). On the baby-boom bandwagon. *American Demographics*, pp. 25-31.

Service, E. R. (1971). *Primitive social organization: An evolutionary perspective.* New York: Random House.

Sherry, J. F., Jr. (1990). A sociocultural analysis of a midwestern American flea market. *Journal of Consumer Research, 17,* 13-30.

Sherry, J. F., Jr., & McGrath, M. A. (1989). Unpacking the holiday presence: A comparative ethnography of two gift stores. In E. Hirschmann (Ed.), *Interpretive consumer research* (pp. 148-167). Provo, UT: Association for Consumer Research.

Turner, B. S. (1988). *Status.* Minneapolis: University of Minnesota Press.

Waldinger, R., Aldrich, H., & Ward, R. (Eds.). (1990). *Ethnic entrepreneurs.* Newbury Park, CA: Sage.

Webster, M., & Foschi, M. (Eds.). (1988). *Status generalization: New theory and research.* Stanford, CA: Stanford University Press.

Weiss, M. J. (1988). *The clustering of America.* New York: Harper & Row.

Yinger, M. J. (1994). *Ethnicity: Source of strength? Source of conflict?* Albany: State University of New York Press.

7

Brand Loyalty and Consumption Patterns

The Lineage Factor

Barbara Olsen

This chapter is concerned with nostalgic consumers, their socialization and patterns of behavior that have evolved over the last century to perpetuate a consumer culture. It integrates archival documentation on early marketing strategy for convenience goods from the 1880s to the 1930s with qualitative research on the persistence of favorite brands through several generations of the same families.

In the spirit of paradigmatic pluralism, I incorporate several theoretical approaches to interpret the past, and the past in the present, as it relates to a cultural biography of brands and brand loyalty. Cultural materialism facilitates an understanding of the causes and anomalies emerging from historical analysis. In using the historical method to trace patterns and other behavioral trends, the diachronic functionalist approach offers insight into why objects are adopted for convenience and for their various social and environmental utilities (Harris, 1979; Kroeber, 1963; Smith & Lux, 1993).

Communications theory also contributes to understanding changes in behavior and brand adoption that is integral to exploring the cultural biography of brands. By using an interpretivist, semiotic analysis of family history narratives, we may infer the significance of brand heritage in real-life

AUTHOR'S NOTE: The author would like to thank the many students who informed this research, as well as Barry Armandi, Janeen Arnold Costa, Hyginus L. Leon, Dan Rose, and John F. Sherry, Jr. for their thoughtful and constructive comments on initial drafts of this chapter, and gratefully acknowledges the support of the NYS/UUP and the Research Foundation of SUNY-Old Westbury for funding research in the J. Walter Thompson Company Archives held by Duke University Library.

experiences (Douglas & Isherwood, 1979; Geertz, 1983; Kopytoff, 1986/ 1988; Sahlins, 1976). Hebdige (1988) interprets marketing and promotion efforts as a distinct "moment of mediation" between production and consumption which contribute to the " 'cultural significance' " inherent in product consumption (pp. 80-81). Brands have symbolic utility and are adopted for what they communicate for the user. An interpretive analysis of American material culture is necessary to understand its reciprocal relationship with the social so we can trace where we, as a society, are headed in the coming millennium.

This chapter is concerned specifically with an analysis of various aspects of brand loyalty for the nostalgic consumer. The heritage factor in consumption and brand preference is traced through cultural biography for consumers who exhibit high involvement with regard to either intergenerational transmission or its blockage. The methodology integrates historical analysis from archival data with ethnographic research, participant observation, and life history documentation.

Anthropology, and especially its ethnographic methods—participant observation, depth interviews, and emic interpretations—are becoming increasingly popular sources from which to borrow tools to investigate marketing and consumer behavior in the late 20th century (Belk, Wallendorf, & Sherry, 1989; Fairhurst & Good, 1993; McCracken, 1990, 1993; Schouten, 1991; Schudson, 1984; Sherry, 1991; Solomon & Assael, 1987). This chapter, however, applies an anthropological perspective to an analysis of early marketing, advertising, and promotion for particular insight into the continuing lineage effect on our consumption experience. Data on early advertising and marketing strategies were gathered for this section from the J. Walter Thompson Company Archives, which are held by Duke University Library, during summer 1991.

I use qualitative research to trace the history of product use, brand loyalty, and intergenerational transfer in several families. During a period of 4 years, from 1989 to 1993, family histories were gathered from students using "self-as-instrument" (McCracken, 1988, p. 32) who participated as "junior collaborators" (Wallendorf & Arnould, 1991) in a marketing class project that traced product use within several generations of their own families. Anonymity was ensured, and permission to use their findings did not impact on their grade. The goal of the research was "discovery oriented." The method, however, is opportunistic as it relies on a convenience sample narrowly restricted to college students (Wells, 1993) who conducted their own interviews. This methodology is also considered controversial because it relies on the trustworthiness of data collected by junior fieldworkers for course credit (Wallendorf & Belk, 1989). Although the students are taught the tools of ethnographic data collection, the senior researcher can only interpret that which has been collected secondhand. In this naturalistic inquiry, however, the methodology did provide a wider sample than a single researcher could obtain.

The project was conceptual and exploratory in nature. It was launched to determine if any patterns existed. I used an ethnographic approach, combining participant observations with depth interviews. Life histories collected from family members produced a broad range of shopping patterns and brand experiences for analysis. The results demonstrate that within the process of consumer socialization we adopt and reject consumer behaviors and product preferences. We use brands as bonding agents that "bridge" us with previous generations and also use them as "fences" to symbolically negate an influence (Douglas & Isherwood, 1979). Brands can be useful tools for everyday life. They are also our weapons in an increasingly complex social world.

Fred Posner, an executive with the advertising agency N. W. Ayer, claims that certain brands become our "friends" (Aaker, 1991, p. 34). We build relationships with things that help us interpret meaning in the context of statuses and transitions during our lives (Csikszentmihalyi & Rochberg-Halton, 1981). Over the life cycle we often reflect on favorite brands that held particular meaning in a sentiment of nostalgia (Davis, 1979; Holbrook, 1993; Holbrook & Schindler, 1991). Sometimes, brand preference passes from one generation to the next, often without awareness. Considering the intergenerational component of nostalgia, each generation's members incorporate elements of their parents' lives, who incorporated elements of their parents' lives, including a collection of behaviors and goods that flavor the texture of the present (Havlena & Holak, 1991). Many of us take for granted that we have always used Scott toilet tissue and shopped at Sears.

To prosper, marketers must continuously expand their market share. Traditional marketing theory demands the solicitation of new users. Marketers get existing users to consume more, find new uses for the product, or alter its design or composition in some way to extend life through line extensions. This chapter explores both historical and current campaigns that reflect these approaches in advertising appeals. Internationally marketed brands, such as Gerber, are now confronting East European markets in stages of development reminiscent of America in the 1920s. They are replicating historical strategies stressing benefits of nutrition and sanitary packaging that educated resistant consumers to a new world of manufactured goods. When a Polish mother was recently asked why she refused to use Gerber's products, she replied, " 'I've never tried Gerber. My grandmother prepared my mother's baby food, who in turn prepared mine. I don't see why I should change a trusted recipe that's been used for generations' " (Perlez, 1993, p. D1).[1]

Baudrillard (1988) says that Americans have domesticated "modernity" (p. 79). However, in the process he senses an absence of "culture," claiming that "one should speak rather of an 'anthropological' culture, which consists in the invention of mores and a way of life" (p. 100). Toward the creation of the American "way of life" that is our culture, there is a reflexive quality between our social relationships and the goods and artifacts we produce (Childe, 1951). This occurs not just from the social relations manifest in production but also from the symbolic qualities we invest in goods, especially as we increasingly communicate through things to articulate definitions of ourselves (Douglas & Isherwood, 1979; McCracken, 1990, 1993). Kopytoff (1986/1988) describes how these things become culturally loaded:

> In the homogenized world of commodities, an eventful biography of a thing becomes the story of the various singularizations of it, of classifications and reclassifications in an uncertain world of categories whose importance shifts with every minor change in context. As with persons, the drama here lies in the uncertainties of valuation and identity. . . . A society orders the world of things on the pattern of the structure that prevails in the social world of its people. (pp. 89-90)

In this chapter, I trace the cultural biographies of a number of brands. I first provide the historical background of the transformation from a producer to a consumer culture and then explore the legacy of equity in nostalgia. Younger generations communicate in a "dialogue with history" through the memories of the sensual experience provided by heritage brands. Next, I present the transformation from home production to consumer brands for the grandparent generation and then trace how marketers, as secondary socializers, promoted new packaging, food forms, soap, toothpaste, and toilet paper to the marketplace through aggressive advertising. I then analyze aspects of consumer socialization for a base on which to interpret the biography of brands through heritage tracing in contemporary second and third generations. The narratives reflect brand associations for nostalgic consumers that are interconnected with symbolic meaning from their family histories. Marketers, not oblivious to the power of nostalgia, continue to reinforce family themes that connect us to the products we buy. I conclude by contextualizing contemporary branding and describing the current state of equity and loyalty. I speculate on how loyalty shapes and reflects social relations and offer some suggestions for future research and brand practice.

🔱 Historical Transformation to a Consumer Culture

To situate the presence of brands in contemporary American life, we must look backward, briefly, at the historical transition from a "producer" to a "consumer" culture, and from a "commodity" culture to a "brand" culture. American industry until the Civil War had been concerned with building the transportation and communication infrastructure, the railroad, steamship, and telegraph systems. The Civil War generated demand specifically for ready-made, mass-produced clothing of wool and cotton for uniforms and portable food provisions, particularly in tin cans. Industry responded with an effort that would later feed, clothe, shelter, and convenience a growing national population expanding into new habitats.

By the 1880s, continuous-process machinery was mass-producing goods for mass consumption. Agriculture, among other things, provided fruit, vegetables, grain, and oil that were transformed into new convenience goods: biscuits, cereal, preserved produce and processed meat, paper products, and improved soap. The new infrastructure facilitated their sale on a national scale.

The "long depression," however, from 1873 to 1894, introduced price competition. Because the evolutionary nature of capitalism is predicated on changes in production, distribution, and consumption, when profits fell the manufacturers found they could compete on a nonprice level by introducing new commodities to capture market share. Product differentiation was the logical alternative, and this period, from the 1870s to the 1890s, was significant for the first registration of trademarks and the establishment of many heritage brands.

As products were originally produced and distributed in bulk, branded goods that could be packaged and labeled symbolized proof of quality for fearful new consumers. Brand names were recognizable and predictable. They were especially helpful for immigrants and rural migrants who found themselves far from home and family. Brand reference also became a means by which relocated and dislocated individuals established collective identification through what Boorstin (1974), broadly speaking, calls "consumption communities." Disparate populations with nothing else in common could identify through the consumption of popular brands. Popular literature stressed progress and modernization. This trend was reinforced by the close contact of urban life and social pressure in the new work environments. Department stores and new retail establishments appeared. People socialized each other to their new shopping reality. Marketers, as secondary socializers, heavily advertised in newspapers and popular magazines how their brands would ensure social acceptance and advancement. Ad themes impressed the populace with the need to use the best so not to be left behind. Marketers promoted trademarked brands with inventive distribution tactics, offering free samples and other incentives to transform old patterns of subsistence into reliance on consumer goods.

This heritage in marketing history is woven in the cultural biography of brands and reported in the narratives. Advertising influenced the transition from homemade to brand adoption for the grandparent generation as first-time users. For instance, women learned to replace rosewater as a moisturizer with Pond's Cold Cream. Wives learned how to prepare better dinners by using Libby's canned vegetables and Hellmann's mayonnaise. Mothers replaced camphor with Vicks VapoRub to treat colds. They adopted Scott tissue to prevent family members needing rectal surgery. Mothers helped their children advance in school by teaching them to brush their teeth with Colgate toothpaste. This marketing history is embedded in the cultural biography of these brands.

For second- and third-generation nostalgic consumers, their narratives reveal a sentiment buried in the symbolic attachment to certain brands because they are reminders of favorite relatives. This link of branding development and intergenerational transfer with nostalgia is revealed through cultural biography. Informants discuss their preferred brands and connect them explicitly to parents and grandparents. In some narratives, it is a shopping habit that was learned and maintained. In other instances, new behaviors were specifically adopted because of a rupture in a social relationship.

Brand Loyalty and Nostalgia

Brand loyalty implies a relationship incorporating a "psychological commitment (i.e., the beliefs, feelings, and intentions) that results in the consistent repurchase of the same brand over time" (Jacoby & Chestnut, 1978, p. 9). However, there is a broad range of brand based behaviors. A high level of brand loyalty signifies consistently purchasing the same brand "over a period of years in the life of an individual" (Guest, 1944, p. 17). Expanding on Guest's initial analysis, Jacoby and Chestnut (1978) cite G. H. Brown's 1953 loyalty types that monitored sequential purchasing. Besides noting " 'single brand' " loyalty, Brown characterized " 'unstable loyalty' as the brand sequence AAABBB, or the consistent buying of first one and then another brand," and " 'divided loyalty' " alternated between two choices ABABAB (quoting Brown, p. 12). Within their range of loyalty behaviors, Jacoby and Chestnut also incorporate Cunningham's 1956 analysis of "proportional purchasing" in which a family is considered brand loyal if they made more than half of their product purchases with one brand.

Today, there is strong evidence that brand loyalty is on the wane as shoppers place saving money above brand loyalty. This has as much to do with the recession continuing from the 1980s as it does with competition on a nonprice basis, similar in response to the "long depression" a century ago. Today, there are just more alternatives to choose from, including less expensive store and "generic" brands.

Recent research among baby boomers (born between 1946 and 1964) shows that, considering both sexes, their degree of loyalty spans from 30.1% who are "very loyal" to 57.5% who are "somewhat loyal" to 12.0% who exhibit no loyalty at all to specific brands (Schlossberg, 1994, p. 2). Most consumers vacillate among several loyalty behaviors—"unstable," "divided," "proportional purchasing" to totally loyal for specific brands. The narratives reflect staunch loyalty for Quaker State and Castrol motor oil, Ford and Dodge automobiles, Craftsman tools, Ivory and Palmolive soap, Nescafe coffee, Mazola oil, AT&T, Domino sugar, Morton salt, Gold Medal flour, Arm & Hammer baking soda, Breakstone butter, Hellmann's mayonnaise, Bumble Bee tuna, Johnson & Johnson baby shampoo, Vicks VapoRub, and Colgate and Crest toothpaste. Another narrative considers the alteration in loyalty caused by divorce. Her husband, as buyer, reflected the "unstable" type during the marriage, but as a nostalgic consumer, she reverted to "single brand loyalty" for childhood brands after the divorce.

Considering nostalgia, Miller (1990) notes the difference between emotional nostalgia and retrofad appeal. Baby boomers today exist in a precarious midlife quandary where they nurture comforting memories from a more secure past while peering into a fear-filled future. Baby busters and teenagers (born after 1965), who use symbolic elements of the past, are "more likely making a fashion statement than a social one" (p. 1).

It was during the early 20th century that many of the brands reported in the narratives became established fixtures in the lives of most Americans. Brands that used the most persuasive appeals with enticing promotions entered into lasting relationships with us and our families. If brand equity is the accumulated history and sentiment attached to a particular brand, it is nurtured by corporations and supported by the loyal following who continue to purchase it on a regular basis (Aaker, 1991). If we consider the cultural value for consumers, when we participate with a brand we extract values that have been previously incorporated through advertising as well as the investment of our own meaning during use (Davis, 1979; McCracken, 1990, 1993).

Certain moments in our lives become powerful memories interconnecting brands, people, and places. Holbrook and Schindler (1991) suggest a peak period that freezes cultural phenomena and social events during critical years in our life cycle. For some, this may be the end of the teenage years; for others, it is early adulthood. Also, in their calculation of a "nostalgia index," they recognize that individuals may be differentially prone to nostalgia in varying intensities experienced at different periods and for different preferences (p. 332; see also Davis, 1979; Havlena & Holak, 1991; Holbrook, 1993). A cultural biography of brands must take into account the peak period during which consumer taste was imprinted at a particular moment in time. Thus crystallized, certain goods, whether they be food, toiletries, appliances, music, or geographic locations, become part of our continuing dialogue with the past.

When we consider the relevance of things situated in time, Davis (1979) notes that

> nostalgic sentiment dwells at the very heart of a generation's identity. . . . And, in large part it is because human consciousness can forge "generations" from the raw materials of history that the generations come to speak to each other, as it were, each reminding the other of "precious things" about to be lost or forgotten. Thus the dialogue of history is itself enriched and given dramatic form far beyond that which could be evoked from a mere chronology of places, persons, and events. (p. 115)

Memories from the family interviews illuminate how this "dialogue of history" is woven from our past. A 62-year-old Mexican grandmother reminisces to her granddaughter why she will always use Palmolive soap:

> She says that she won't change it for any other brand because the smell of it reminds her of her mother when in the evenings she used to take a shower and sit down under a cotton tree in the back yard to weave and that she (my grandmother) will contemplate her sitting right in front of her and, with the breeze, the smell of the soap will get to her. The smell brings her back memories of her mother—"besides the fact that it is a great soap" she said.

The "raw materials of history" that nostalgic consumers can psychologically manipulate are the brands we grew up with. They give sensual essence to our experience. This grandmother hangs onto the memory of her mother weaving in the yard through the precious whiff of Palmolive soap. She contextualizes a relationship as well as the "dearly departed past." As the Indian philosopher Krishnamurti said, death ends a life but not a relationship. We can reinvent this past through our own correspondence with history.

We invest things with memories of loved ones and through nostalgic reminiscing find help negotiating our way through transitions related to life stage passages or geographical dislocations (Davis, 1979). A young adult, aged 22, of Filipino descent reported that he followed a family tradition of purchasing certain goods because

> I believe that seeing the Whirlpool brand in my own kitchen makes me feel that my family is still around near me and not across the continent in California. I always remember my grandma's RCA television, my parents never bought any other brand than RCA, and when my turn came to go to Sears to buy my first television and VCR, with no further looking around, I automatically purchased an RCA TV and VCR.
>
> My parents were always loyal to Colgate, Listerine and Ivory products. I find myself automatically picking these items when I am at the supermarket; it makes me feel sort of at home in my own bathroom in sunny California. I remember my mom bathing my sister and me and we used to play with the bubbles of the Johnson & Johnson baby shampoo; well, I still use the same product. When I feel down with the cold and alone in my apartment with no mother to care for me—a whiff of Vicks VapoRub always reminds me of my grandmother by my side and my mom's never-ending pampering.

This man finds himself "automatically" purchasing the same products from his youth. He has incorporated warm memories in brands that make him feel "at home" in California with his family. The colder climate and physical dislocation from his loving, nurturing family stimulate deep sentimental attachments to textures, tastes, and smells of his childhood. Even shopping in the same store and taking his "turn" buying the family's familiar heritage brands brings peace and security to life away from home for this homesick consumer.

Brands also offer comfort when we feel insecure. A young woman discussing the history of brands used by her family found that "my mother mentioned that she hasn't used Blue Grass in a long time because it reminds her of my father but that she went out and bought a bottle during the Gulf War." In this narrative, where the smell of Blue Grass had previously resurrected memories of loss and remorse, during the war, the same essence symbolized strength and protection functioning as a buffer in a time of political unrest.

Memories also connect us to important places in our personal histories. A male in his 20s from Hong Kong stated,

> My father told me that he is loyal to AT&T long distance service because when we were in Hong Kong AT&T was the only company which had long distance service there. So he is loyal to AT&T. Several times, some mail or salesmen from other companies [contact him] like MCI, which give a cheaper price, but he just says "no" to them.

In our highly mobile society today, we often have longer relationships with our brands than with the places and people we have known. For this father, AT&T captured a share of mind by being the only supplier in his homeland. In his new residence, far from home, the brand represents a personalized connection with his homeland as well as predictable reliability. This prior relationship takes the risk out of having to make another choice.

The Mexican grandmother still used many brands she bought in the "old country" as a young girl. When asked why she was still loyal to Nescafé, Mazola oil and Palmolive soap she answered: "Because they are not only goods, I grew up with them in my house with my father and mother and I feel like they are part of my life now. For example, my day wouldn't be the same without a hot cup of Nescafé." These brands are a connection to the traditional culture of her Mexican heritage and her deceased parents. They are more than "goods"; they have been woven (like the smell of Palmolive soap) into the tapestry of her everyday life and are reflective moments from history.

These nostalgic sentiments represent powerful memories and are indicative of successful socialization experiences. As the family is the primary force in consumer socialization, it is among the most important means by which we are introduced to and learn consumer skills.

In an industrial economy defined by a capitalist mode of production, survival depends less on household production and more on procurement from the commercial landscape. Historically, peoples' lives were shaped by the relationships that were formed between people. The traditional social bonds ensured that adequate production levels were met from subsistence farming activities and domestic chores to guarantee families' needs for the year. In time, manufactured goods replaced hand-crafted home production. For many families, this transition is still within living memory.

Transition From Homemade

Research from the family interviews revealed that many grandparents made their own products, especially remedies. In some families, these remedies are still used. For others, home preparations were replaced by brand-name goods.

From an African American female in her mid-20s:

> My great-grandmother is an Alabama native and set up her home in Indiana. She made the decision to live off the land. My great-grandmother was never satisfied with the quality of soap on the market. Once a year she makes an oil-based lye soap. It's all-purpose—she uses it for her body, hair, and also for washing her clothes, preferring the older type of washer with ringer and scrub board.

This great-grandmother's decision to be self-sufficient gives her a great sense of independence. She also prides herself on growing and canning her own produce. What she could not raise herself (certain fruit, freshly made juices and meat) she had delivered to her home. The granddaughter recognized a strength in character that she used as a role model. She also adopted her skepticism of manufactured brands.

From a Chinese American male in his early 20s:

> In my grandparent's generation, in China, people didn't use toothpaste, shampoo, or toilet paper. Instead, they used the paper which had been used for something else for toilet paper. They used salt as the toothpaste and used their fingers or a little stick as a toothbrush.

Both toothpaste and toilet paper are products that took decades to build a consumer franchise. At the turn of the century, oral hygiene was not yet part of the daily American ritual. When there was a need to clean one's teeth, households had functional alternatives that had been used for generations. "Chew sticks" or a wash cloth and soap was adequate. Baking soda, found in most kitchen cupboards, was also used as a dentifrice. Toilet paper was obtained from newspaper and catalogues, and in rural areas, they used corn cobs. Eventually, brands from the store were perceived to be more effective and convenient alternatives.

From a German American female in her early 20s:

> One of my grandmother's beliefs was that if you had a headache, potatoes could cure it. She sliced them up and put them inside a cold rag, then applied to the head. When the potatoes turned black, your headache should be gone! If you had trouble falling asleep, warm milk and honey or butter was the cure. For a cold, she used to tie camphor around her neck to make breathing easier. Now, she just rubs some "Vicks" on her chest.

Another women, an Italian American in her late 20s, discovered similar homemade preparations from her grandmother and replacement by store brands:

> My grandmother would mix honey and figs and make her own cough syrup. Camomile tea acted as a remedy for stomach ailments. Rosewater was used to moisturize skin. When she had a headache, she would put a slice of potato on her forehead. When the potato turned black, the headache would be gone. Kirkman's soap was used as a laundry detergent, shampoo, dish detergent and body soap.
>
> Kirkman's soap was eventually replaced by Lux soap, Breck shampoo, Ivory liquid and Dash. The camomile tea was replaced by Mylanta and rosewater by Pond's Cold Cream. As for headaches, although she swears the potato worked, my grandmother bought Bayer aspirin and now uses Tylenol.

In both narratives, Old World traditional cures for medical problems were made from available products found in the home and handed down from mother to daughter. Marketers of new brands had to confront the belief that traditional remedies worked best. Advertising and pressure from "more modern" peers sent the message that those not using store-bought brands were old-fashioned. Lever Brothers began heavy advertising for Lux flakes in 1917 with a strategy that "exploited it as something magical, mysterious and in the same way synonymous with fashion." Headlines ran, asking "Which are the hands of the rich man's wife?" and "Do women with maids have lovelier hands?" (Account Histories, Representatives' Meeting, December 3, 1929, J. Walter Thompson Company Archives, Duke University Library).[2] The middle class was striving to move up, and the perception of a shortcut could be found in store brands. An increasing number of products became available for both real and contrived concerns.

Looking at Pond's Cold Cream, which replaced rosewater, early ads from 1882 represent Pond's Extract as an all-purpose cure, "The Ladies' Friend," and "The vegetable pain destroyer." A 1911 ad says Pond's Extract Company's Vanishing Cream "effectively promotes that fineness of skin texture so requisite to a clear and beautiful complexion." By 1917, Pond's was advertising "Every Normal Skin Needs Two Creams—Learn how to use them intelligently!" Pond's Cold Cream was used to massage and cleanse and Pond's Vanishing Cream would protect and soften. A coupon was attached for a free sample (Chesebrough-Pond's, Account File, J. Walter Thompson Company Archives, Duke University Library).

▨ Marketers as Socializers

It has been argued that advertising reflects the cultural codes of our social world (Ewen, 1976; Fox, 1984; Leiss, Kline, & Jhally, 1990; Schudson, 1984). It functions as a medium through which consumers not only hunt and gather for the availability of goods but also ascertain current notions of style. For the corporation, advertising represents an investment in brand equity that accumulates over time in profitability and expanded market share involving various intensities of brand loyalty (Aaker, 1991; Aaker & Biel, 1993). One study analyzing the strongest brands in 1985 among 22 product categories found that of the leading brands in 1925 the strongest in 19 of the categories remained the same: Swift bacon, Everready batteries, Nabisco biscuits, Kellogg cereal, Kodak cameras, Del Monte canned fruit, Wrigley chewing gum, Life Savers mint candies, Sherwin-Williams paint, Prince Albert pipe tobacco, Gillette razors, Singer sewing machines, Crisco shortening, Ivory soap, Coca-Cola beverage, Campbell soup, Lipton tea, Goodyear tires, and Colgate toothpaste (second to Crest) (Thomas S. Wurster, "The Leading Brands: 1925-1985," *Perspectives*, Boston Consulting Group, 1987, in Aaker, 1991, p. 71). Many brands with a loyal following and accumulated equity are now "heritage brands," leaders in their category, that continue to build on their rich history through nostalgic revivals or line extensions (Marney, 1990; Schoenfeld, 1990).

> *Pears'*
> *My grandmother used Pears' Soap;*
> *perhaps yours did, too. We owe them*
> *gratitude for that.*
> *Use Pears' for the children; they soon*
> *acquire the habit.*
> *Established 1789*
>
> —In Calkins and Holden (1905/1985, p. 307)

This turn-of-the-century advertisement addresses the value of consumer socialization. In the process of incorporating certain goods as artifacts of convenience for everyday life, our grandparent generation socialized their children, thus contributing to a process of intergenerational transfer for brands used by several generations.

In defense of both Ewen (1976, 1988) and Boorstin (1974), industrialism contributed to antagonizing class differences as well as democratizing a population of disparate backgrounds. The difference lies in how the goods were promoted and consumed. For the rural-to-urban migrant and the new immigrants, both caught between two cultures, goods could be purchased by all social and ethnic groups that not only performed better than homemade preparations but helped perfect the image they were American and middle class (Ewen, 1988, p. 73). Advertising communicated how this "good life," that was stylish, clean, and efficient, could be obtained. Marketing analysts carved the American populace into segments based on aspirations, needs, and lifestyles appropriate for targeting their brands.

How did certain brands come to capture the consciousness of America, establishing a niche in our minds that would last in some families for several generations? New food preparations, notions of hygiene, toiletries, and paper products represented labor-saving, healthful alternatives as well as risks to new users. Early advertising had to build a need for a product, demonstrate how to use it, and offer incentives, usually coupons or free samples, to get people to try these new goods and adopt them into their lives.

The Convenience of Packaged Food

Initially, there was consumer resistance to new food forms because preparation at the time was deeply linked to cultural tradition. In their ethnography of American culture, Lynd and Lynd (1929) discovered,

> Under the old rule-of-thumb, mother-to-daughter method of passing down the traditional domestic economy, when the same family recipe and doctor book—with "Gravy" in its index followed by "Gray hair, how to treat"—was commonly cherished by both mother and daughter, the home tended to resist the intrusion of new habits. (p. 157)

The diffusion of most manufactured goods in America is facilitated by circumstances necessitating convenience, and this is also true for food. Soda biscuits were one of the earliest commercially available snack foods. Their acceptance paralleled innovations in packaging and distribution.

Early initiation to the availability of commercially produced biscuits evolved from a distribution process described by Calkins and Holden (1905/1985), where the product was

> supplied loose, in bulk from a barrel, from which the grocer weighed out the necessary quantity. [However,] the method was unclean and unsanitary, and crispness was lost. It required an unnecessary number of handlings which took time and were distasteful. The name, soda-biscuit, meant

> several kinds of biscuit in bulk; the customer seldom knew them apart; the
> most intelligent thing she could do was to point them out. (p. 8)

The manufacturing of safe and convenient packaging was not perfected
until the late 1800s. In fact, "until 1841 such collapsible packaging as there
was had been made from animal bladders" (Boorstin, 1974, p. 439). In an
economy that was increasingly based on mass production for national consumption, the time and transportation factors involved in bulk distribution
became inefficient and wasteful. A spate of inventions ensued for machines
that made paper bags (1867), folding paper boxes (1879), and metal tubes
(1870). Packaging products in individually available portions also presented an
opportunity for advertising on the container. By 1898, the National Biscuit
Company (currently RJR Nabisco) began marketing prepackaged Uneeda biscuits in tins. Demand from advertising produced by N. W. Ayer was greater than
the tin supply, and the manufacturer resorted to cardboard boxes on which they
displayed their trademark and slogan: " 'Lest you forget, we say it yet, Uneeda
Biscuit' " (Fox, 1984, p. 39). Packaging conveyed brand identity, easy recognition, and a belief that the product was safer to consume because of less
handling and greater protective wrapping. Consumers thus became

> familiar with the name of a biscuit in a package, wrapped first in a sanitary,
> waxed, air—and moisture—proof wrapper, then in a compact, handy car-
> ton, and finally in a decorative wrapper. This package would now be
> recognized by a large percentage of the population in the United States at
> a glance. (Calkins & Holden, 1905/1985, p. 9)

The Lynds' (1929) ethnography of Middletown reveals a culture typical
for most of North America in the 1890s and 1920s. Comparing the two eras
illuminates the diffusion of innovations from one generation to the next. The
most profound changes involved new methods of production, consumption,
and changing attitudes toward food and hygiene. In the northern climes,
canning and refrigeration introduced seasonal variety into an otherwise
inadequate diet. In 1890, the two diets were described as " 'winter diet' and
'summer diet.' " The winter diet consisted of various combinations of " 'steak,
roasts, macaroni, Irish potatoes, sweet potatoes, turnips, cole slaw, fried
apples, and stewed tomatoes, with Indian pudding, rice, cake, or pie for
dessert.' " Another informant said they typically ate meat for all three meals:
" 'Breakfast, pork chops or steak with fried potatoes, buckwheat cakes and
hot bread; lunch a hot roast and potatoes; supper, same roast cold.' " Consequently, the summer diet of vegetables, fruit, and herbs, available from May

to October, cured the body of the "spring sickness" brought on by the winter diet (Lynd & Lynd, 1929, pp. 156-157).

Canning or preserving perishable fruit and vegetables became commercially available for home consumption in America after 1875. By 1883, the continuous flow system was capable of making 3,000 cans an hour (Strasser, 1989, p. 32). During the same period, the availability of central heating made homes too warm in winter to keep produce stored without spoiling, and the proliferation of city apartment houses did not accommodate root cellar storage for tenants (Boorstin, 1974, p. 325). For many city dwellers, and especially for the lower-income groups, canned goods meant a better diet when fresh produce was out of season and too expensive to buy. A stigma, however, attached to women who fed their families from cans (Lynd & Lynd, 1929, p. 156).

Helen Lansdown, an executive at J. Walter Thompson in 1916, successfully directed the marketing of many products targeted toward women. During a sales convention for Libby, McNeil, and Libby, packers of canned vegetables, she reiterated the importance of consumer education in each Libby ad. For instance, in such monthly magazines as *Woman's Home Companion* and the *Ladies' Home Journal*, ads would be run with

> photographs of various dishes in tempting style, with recipes covering the material and methods for producing the dishes. . . . It will carry the message one step further, in that it will advise the consumer not only what article to use, but whose product to buy in order to produce the recipe. It will also have the advantage of color, so that the appetite-value of the foods can be represented to the consumer in the most attractive form. (*JWT News Bulletin*, Number 23, November 26, 1916, p. 5, J. Walter Thompson Company Archives, Duke University Library)

A review of several women's magazines from the teens through the 1920s found that Crisco shortening, Carnation milk, Del Monte canned fruit, Royal baking powder and Pillsbury flour were consistent advertisers using this educational copy formula for extending product application.

Hellmann's Mayonnaise

(Although the current brand name reads Hellmann's, the spelling of the inventor's name in the archives is spelled Hellman, therefore, I have chosen to use the spelling found in the agency's records when referring to him.)

In the 1910s, Mr. Hellman was a new immigrant who had become a successful grocer on the upper west side of New York City and while on holiday in Paris observed the preparation of mayonnaise. Returning to New York he began production with distribution from his store and other grocers willing to carry his product. By 1914, Hellman's sole business became the making of mayonnaise. He packed it in "wooden boats" before perfecting what he believed to be "the first jar with a screwed top." Hellman brought his account to JWT in 1926 and was convinced that the success that led to additional manufacturing facilities in San Francisco, Dallas, and Tampa, Florida, was due to his unique jar with the label on top. Meanwhile, he had competition, but research conducted in 1927 with consumers and dealers revealed that the competition came primarily from the ease with which anyone with a $20 mayonnaise-making machine could produce the mixture. Local brands abounded, and the jar with similarly labeled tops was replicated as well. Almost everyone, and especially the urban middle class, bought the commercial version because of its convenience. Strategy for the initial Blue Ribbon mayonnaise campaign began with advertising in women's magazines having the greatest urban circulation. The ads suggested its use in salads, emphasizing "This is the best flavor you can buy—it comes from recipes which you can't duplicate. Only 25c for one-half pint." The ingredients in Hellman's product cost more than the competition because it was said "Mr. Hellman buys Colman's Mustard and claims he can't get the same consistency with any other Mustard. . . . This is the secret plus the knowledge of mixing that makes the product so good. No one is allowed in Hellman's spice room but himself" (Staff Meeting Minutes, May 31, 1927, pp. 2-4, J. Walter Thompson Company Archives, Duke University Library). The distinctive flavor still accounts for its being the number one brand of mayonnaise today. Kraft mayonnaise is number two.

Soap

After the Civil War, soap producers began perfecting the quality of their ingredients and methods of distribution. However, manufacturers also had to communicate the hygenic benefits of cleanliness and the many applications of their product:

> All the first makers operated on a purely local basis. Practically all soap was made from garbage and the maker went on weekly rounds of the homes in his town. He exchanged soap for garbage, leaving two or three bars. . . . Ultimately he established retailer connections and used advertising to secure a brand identity for his product, which was easily trade-marked. (*Printers Ink*, 1938/1986, p. 23)

Soap was molded in a form that made it easy to transport and to use. The greatest challenge was creating a soap that smelled fresh and clean. Soap made from "garbage" contained animal lard, which spoiled and "as the animal oils become rancid the odor reached to the heavens." However, by combining the animal fat with vegetable oils soap makers overcame the problem of perishability and went into serious production with wider distribution (*Printers Ink*, 1938/1986, p. 23). There were many soaps available by the 1890s; Sapolio, Pearline, Pear's, Kirks, Packer's Tar, Fairy, Cuticura, Woodbury's, and Wool soap. Ivory gained the early lead and, as a heritage brand, maintains the highest brand share among "exclusive users," with a percentage of 22.6 against Basis with 19.1 and Dial with 17.1 (*BrandAdvantage*, 1992). It has, however, fallen in market share (as measured in supermarket sales) from 1985 to third in 1991, behind Dove and Dial ("America's Top 2,000," 1992).

Procter & Gamble, as soap and candle makers, produced a floating soap by error and called it White soap. In 1879, the name was changed to Ivory by Harley Procter after he heard a psalm in church that mentioned "ivory palaces." Ivory was successfully marketed with the slogan "99 44/100 percent pure" and "It floats" in advertisements that began in 1881 (Aaker, 1991, p. 1; *Printers Ink*, 1938/1986, p. 24; Strasser, 1989, p. 8; Vinikas, 1992, pp. 80-81). Soap has a very large profit margin and manufacturers wanted to sell as much as possible. Besides patent medicines, the soap companies were among the earliest manufacturers to advertise. The many soap campaigns found a ready market in the multiple uses for the product. An early Ivory soap ad promoting its success in the laundry was written in the form of a poem:

> *John Anderson, my jo, John,*
> *When first I was your wife,*
> *On every washing day, John,*
> *I wearied of my life.*
> *It made you cross to see, John,*
> *Your shirts not white as snow;*
> *I washed them with our home-made Soap,*
> *John Anderson, my jo.*
> *Ah, many a quarrel then, John,*
> *Had you and I thegither (sic);*
> *But now all that is changed, John,*
> *We'll never have anither (sic).*
> *For washed with Ivory Soap, John,*

> *Your shirts are white as snow;*
> *And now I smile on washing day,*
> *John Anderson, my jo.*
>
> —*The Century Illustrated Monthly Magazine,*
> September 1885, p. 40

This ad concluded with the plea "If your grocer does not keep the Ivory Soap, send six two-cent stamps, to pay the postage, to Procter & Gamble, Cincinnati, and they will send you *free* a large cake of Ivory Soap." Two other Ivory ads from 1893 promoted it as both horse soap and women's shampoo:

> Keep a cake of Ivory Soap at the stable, it is most excellent for washing galled spots and scratches on horses, for it will cleanse without irritating, and the vegetable oils of which it is made are cooling and healing in effect. (Calkins & Holden, 1905/1985, p. 321)

The other ad reflects 19th-century shampooing habits:

> Women with long, thick hair find it difficult to keep in proper order without too frequent washing, which renders it dry and harsh. The following method is effectual and need only be repeated once in two months, if the hair is well brushed each night.
>
> Beat the white of an egg sufficiently to break it, rub this well into the scalp. Wash it off thoroughly with Ivory Soap and warm water, rinse off the soap and when the hair is dry it will be found soft and glossy. Ordinary soaps are too strong, use only the Ivory Soap. (Calkins & Holden, 1905/1985, p. 318)

With a change in hair styling from long to short by 1925, Procter & Gamble were encouraging women to shampoo more frequently. One ad suggested, "You can keep your hair beautiful and fluffy and glossy by cheerfully shampooing it two or three times a month with pure soap and soft water. . . . The elves just naturally *assume* that you will use Ivory" (appearing in *The Delineator,* September 1925, p. 4). Ivory's success was a deliberate effort by Procter and Collier, the in-house agency, to conduct consistent marketing and advertising. Through prominent package labeling, educational advertising, and promotion, the power of the Ivory brand became permanently scrubbed into the skin of America. Booklets entitled "What a Cake of Soap Will Do" featured elves mixing coconut and cotton oil in heated vats that produced rectangular cakes with "Ivory" embossed on top (p. 116). The brand became so prominent among its competition that "by 1909, some ad men argued that a million dollars' worth of advertising could not destroy

Ivory soap—in essence, that Procter and Gamble had made itself invulnerable to competition" (Strasser, 1989, p. 57).

Toothpaste

The transition of tooth powder to paste was made possible by the invention of metal tubes originally designed for encasing "artists' colors." "By 1892 a Connecticut dentist was putting up toothpaste in tubes, and soon afterward, Colgate's pioneered in the large-scale marketing of toothpaste in this form" (Boorstin, 1974, p. 439). A competitive battle was waged among competing brands in the war for clean teeth and healthy gums. Most dental formulas at this time were made from harsh chemicals with corrosive effects. However, around 1890, a German physician, Dr. Unna, discovered the healing properties of potassium chlorate for mouth sores. He produced a tooth powder that was later perfected by P.B.& Co. as a paste combining its chemical compound crystals with chalk, glycerine, and a powerful flavoring. This neutral base did not harm mucous membranes in the mouth nor destroy enamel, which occurred with the stronger products. The toothpaste's brand name, Pebeco, was adopted from the corporate initials and was manufactured in the United States by Lehn & Fink, Inc. using German ingredients. Aggressively advertised beginning in 1907, it rapidly became the best-selling toothpaste until World War I. Quality control faltered during the war when supplies became irregular. The paste increasingly solidified in the tube and when "tons" were returned to the manufacturer, consumers defected to the two other leading brands, Kolynos and Forhan's (Lehn & Fink Pebeco Case History, January 28, 1926, p. 1, Account Histories, J. Walter Thompson Company Archives, Duke University Library).

Colgate began marketing its Ribbon Dental Cream in 1905 with early success due, in part, to a slogan promoting its unique tube "that molded toothpaste so it 'Comes Out a Ribbon, Lies Flat on the Brush' " (Strasser, 1989, p. 97). A 1912 *Ladies' Home Journal* ad for Colgate's dental cream claimed it "Cleanses safely because it is wholly free from grit—antiseptically—destroying decay-germs making the mouth wholesome and non-acid—and pleasantly with a delicious flavor; so different from the usual 'druggy' taste" (from an ad reproduced in Strasser, 1989, p. 96). This copy challenged consumers' problems with Pebeco: too strong, gritty, and leaving a bad taste in the mouth.

Ultimately, it was Colgate's toothpaste that became the most widely used. Promotions to parents and teachers in public schools helped teach the importance of dental hygiene. This 1912 Colgate ad to parents stressed their socializing theme:

It has been proved beyond question that children having seriously defective teeth, take at least six months longer to complete the school course than those possessing good teeth.

It is for you as a parent to urge the teaching of dental hygiene in the schools and to practice it in your home.

The twice-a-day use of the tooth-brush is a pleasure as well as a duty if you choose such a delicious dentifrice as—Colgate's Ribbon Dental Cream. (reproduced in Strasser, 1989, p. 96)

Marketers, as secondary socializers, use their advertisements to acculturate potential consumers to new lifestyles that necessitate using their products. Ads were initially instructional, simply telling us how to use products because they performed better than alternatives. The selling point in an ad could also be highly persuasive, using intimidation, social pressure, and parody in which consumers saw themselves as a consequence of the product's use.

Roland Marchand (1985) claims that "as an economic force, advertisements functioned as efficient mass communications that rationalized and lubricated an impersonal marketplace of vast scale" (p. 9). His extensive analysis of advertising from the 1920s through the 1930s expresses how advertisements helped cultivate a receptive audience for the "modernization" that was being manufactured and sold in the marketplace. Advertising visuals portrayed " 'participatory' anecdotes" in which people as consumers "dominated illustrations as advertisers sought to induce the potential customer to play a vicarious, scripted role as protagonist in the ad" (p. 12; see also Hebdige, 1988; Pollay, 1985). Increasingly, ads showed people using the products and receiving the benefits derived from use. Copywriting became a more refined art as it evolved from the John Powers' "reason why" style, offering straight, factual, functional copy appeal to situational contexts that emphasized social stigma for impression management.

Toilet Paper

We have seen that many manufactured goods initially were homemade or had convenient alternatives. Toilet paper is no exception. Conversations with the elder generation reveal the application of existing paper products for toilet needs. Parents and grandparents recall using paper from telephone books, the Sears and Montgomery Ward catalogs, and tissue wrapping, which was packaged around fruit from grocers, for toilet paper.

In the studies conducted with the junior collaborators and their families, the favored toilet paper is Scott tissue. Today, although Charmin has the lead in market share, Scott maintains the leading brand share of 42.1 among "exclusive users" to Charmin's 26.5 (*BrandAdvantage*, 1992). Interestingly, Scott was not the first toilet paper, but it was one of the first to use aggressive advertising. The Scott family manufactured paper products under many labels until 1909 when it developed brands under its own name. In 1899, the company made a revolutionary innovation in the packaging of toilet paper from bulky sets of sheets to presenting their tissue on hand-sized rolls with convenient perforations that made it easy to tear for each use (Schlereth, 1991, p. 129; Strasser, 1989, p. 58). In any product category, the brand that is able to capture early market share attains the strongest presence in the marketplace. The equity invested in the brand from promotional advertising ensures a loyal following.

By using an emotional plea with a negative appeal, certain copy styles became a calculated effort to convince the public, especially women, of the necessity for using particular brands. Scott toilet paper in the 1920s was the leading brand, with a 15% share of the market. According to JWT, 85% of toilet paper users selected from papers of varying quality, the worst being "glazed-surfaced and brittle, . . . quite rough and full of ground wood splinters." Therefore, the copy approach used "a medical appeal which is amply substantiated by good authorities on rectal disease. This appeal emphasizes to women the fact that bathroom paper is not just a modern convenience but that it has also definite medical significance" (Minutes of the Staff Meeting, Importance of Strategy in Copy, by William Day, p. 12, June 4, 1930, J. Walter Thompson Company Archives, Duke University Library). At a staff meeting in 1931, Mr. Legler, an executive with the company, explained Scott's negative copy appeal this way:

> Back of our advertising campaign on Scott Tissue and Waldorf is the sharp pointed appeal of fear. It is not enough to say that these brands are soft and absorbent—that they are the choice of discriminating housewives. Our copy says: 'if you continue to use the inferior brands of toilet tissue you are now using, you stand a very excellent chance of getting rectal trouble, which more than likely will result in a painful operation.' And we present sufficient medical evidence to convince the reader that perhaps he *had* better buy Scott Tissues from now on. (Minutes of the Staff Meeting, p. 2, September 1, 1931, J. Walter Thompson Company Archives, Duke University Library)

One ad in this campaign integrated the agency's "Mother-Daughter" theme with a fear appeal:

> 'Tell Mother What's the Matter'

> When children complain of irritation it may be toilet tissue illness.
>
> Is it serious for a child to have an inflamed rectal condition? This question has caused many mothers considerable anxieties, for very little information has been printed on the subject.
>
> The answer is—yes, it may be quite serious! Especially if the trouble was caused by harsh or chemically impure toilet tissue. . . .
>
> Doctors, Hospitals, Health Authorities approve Scott Tissues for Safety. (Minutes of the Staff Meeting, Exhibit B, September 1, 1931, J. Walter Thompson Company Archives, Duke University Library)

One line of thought in the advertising debates maintains that agencies became the "captains of consciousness." Ewen (1976) claims, "The functional goal of national advertising was the creation of desires and habits. In tune with the need for mass distribution that accompanied the development of mass production capabilities, advertising was trying to produce in readers personal needs which would dependently fluctuate with the expanding marketplace" (p. 37). Although much of the earlier ad copy represents factual instruction for useful products that made our lives better, later copywriters positioned similar products with emotional appeals that emphasized one's sense of inadequacy and self-worth (see Leiss et al., 1990, pp. 327-348). They related products for hygiene to one's character, social class, and responsibility for self and others and used a persuasion that sullied and shamed a generation of Americans into needing many products that have since become personal necessities.

Of particular significance for this chapter is the intergenerational appeal found in earlier ads linking mothers with daughters. Contemporary advertisers continue this theme but have extended it to both genders and, as we will see, to several generations. Their advertising merely reminds us how certain brands have become family "friends."

⬚ Consumer Socialization

Consumer socialization is defined as the ways in which people at all ages learn the values and appropriate roles for success in the marketplace. Although much of the research focuses on how children learn to be consumers (Bahn, 1986; Carlson, Grossbart, & Walsh, 1990; Foxman, Tansuhaj, & Ekstrom, 1989; Moschis & Churchill, 1978; Moschis & Moore, 1979, 1983; Moschis, Moore, & Smith, 1984), the process is now understood to extend throughout the entire life cycle (Moschis, 1987). Consumer socialization analysis has evolved since the 1970s (Ward, 1974) into a critique of various learning perspectives. These range from the social learning approach (Moore & Stephens, 1975; Moschis & Churchill, 1978; Ward, Wackman, & Wartella, 1977) and cognitive development approach (Alba & Hutchinson, 1987; Bahn, 1986; Bettman, 1979; Foxman et al., 1989; Hoch & Deighton, 1989; McNeal, 1987) to research involving the emotional quality of the family setting (Alderson, 1957/1978; Csikszentmihalyi & Rochberg-Halton, 1981).

Some of the more fruitful data on consumer socialization will continue to come from research investigating the family's emotional context. Toward this direction, researchers have compared communication strategies between parents and children. Descriptions of two family types have emerged from this research. The socio-oriented family represents a rigid, dogmatic environment in which children defer to parental authority, and the concept-oriented family is one in which children's opinions and initiatives are encouraged for them to be more active in the marketplace (Moore & Moschis, 1981; Moschis, 1985, 1987; Moschis & Moore, 1979). Carlson et al. (1990) have concentrated particularly on these orientations, focusing on the relationships between mothers and their children.

Intergenerational influence on brand loyalty and consumption patterns is a consequence of our socialization experiences. Much more work, however, needs to be done to understand fully the process by which it occurs. Glass, Bengtson, and Dunham (1986) studied three generational families for attitude similarity covering politics, status, and gender roles and concluded that there is significant persistence for religious and political attitudes. This may help account for religion and other ancestral influences contributing to children's product preferences in adulthood (Bahn, 1986; Hirschman, 1985).

Research on the parent generation's influence for adult children's product choices began with Guest's (1955, 1964) longitudinal investigation that traced the same individuals from youth into adulthood. He found that brand loyalty nurtured in childhood extends over the lifetime. Critical intergenerational research focuses on how and why this transference occurs, considering culturally constituted family forms—that is, nuclear versus extended (Childers & Rao, 1992) and strength of familial ties (Heckler, Childers, & Arunachalam, 1989). Other analyses have been more strategy and product specific (Allen, 1993; Hill, 1970; Miller, 1975; Woodson, Childers, & Winn, 1976) and gender relational, seeking analogies between mothers and daughters (Moore-Shay & Lutz, 1988).

The family histories that inform this chapter reflect both concept and socio-oriented socialization experiences as well as varying emotional contexts and strength of kinship ties. Douglas and Isherwood (1979) contend that "goods are neutral, their uses are social; they can be used as fences or bridges" (p. 12). It was found in the present analysis that conscious rejection of a parent's shopping habits or brands used during childhood conveyed a form of rebellion in which rejected goods/habits represented "fences" symbolically communicating a fracture in the relationship. On the other hand, replication of parental buying behavior symbolically "bridged" the emotional bond with another.

For instance, an Italian American male reported that his mother continued to purchase "almost every brand" bought by her mother because "she is scared to try anything else . . . and would feel bad not buying something that has been with her for so long." His aunts also used the same brands. Another informant's grandmother and mother shopped together every week, buying identical products. Parental socialization to the marketplace is a strong factor in shaping lifelong shopping patterns. As we age, many consumers form shopping cohorts with others. The people in these relationships continue to reinforce or influence our buyer behavior.

Not surprising, every semester the project was conducted, congruence emerged as a trend among many families. Consider this comment by an Italian American female in her early 20s:

> My mother's mother always used Gold Medal flour, Morton salt, Arm & Hammer baking soda and powder, and Domino sugar. My mother said she buys these products because her mother used to. I asked my sister M_____. She listed all the same products. When I asked her why, she said, "Because that's what Mom uses." Ditto for my sister S_____, my sister B_____, and myself. I don't even think we know what any other product is like.

This informant had never considered the significance of the products she bought. It was only after interviewing her sisters that the pattern became apparent. They all adopted the brands they grew up with as an automatic shopping response. There is a strong inclination for maternal influence, especially in food brands. In the replication of culture, these expedients represent both practicality and utility (Sahlins, 1976).

A male in his late 20s of Russian ancestry, in a follow-up interview, mentioned that his family was "faithful" to the Jewish religion and compared it to their brand loyalty. Belk et al. (1989) have noted that we often distinguish between "sacred and profane" consumption experiences in which the most mundane can become transcendental in particular contexts. This man related his family's habits in similar terms:

> All of us have used Crest toothpaste, Breakstone butter, Hellmann's mayonnaise, and Bumble Bee tuna. All these products have been passed on and

we all have remained incredibly loyal. Brand loyalty is almost mystical. It transcends time. We all use these products today.

When considering the cultural biography of brands, Kopytoff (1986/1988) reminds us that in "complex societies" people strive to decommodify or to sacralize certain goods, such as hierlooms and prized possessions. In follow-up conversations with this man, the significance of keeping a Kosher home was very important for his family. Consequently, when discussing the history of product use, his mother and grandmother sentimentalized certain consumer goods into a realm above and distinct from ordinary varieties. These had become family fixtures in a way that "the longevity of the relation assimilates them in some sense to the person and makes parting from them unthinkable" (Kopytoff, 1986/1988, p. 80). When this man changed his diet to healthier alternatives he maintained the same brands but bought versions that had reduced salt, oil, fat, and cholesterol. Thus the "singularization" process effectively kept these brands part of the family heritage.

Besides loyalties attached to certain brands, informants reported adopting parental shopping habits: frequenting the same stores, using "price clubs," and relying on coupons. These behaviors were both time—and money—savers for them. One male in his mid-20s said that, even after living for several years on his own, he found that he was "conditioned to use coupons" by his mother. He currently saves "hundreds of dollars" each year through promotional sales incentives:

> I used to take frequent grocery shopping trips with her when I was a child and could remember holding the coupons that she passed to me after picking up the item off the shelf and placing it into the shopping cart. I had the responsibility of guarding these valuable pieces of paper until we reached the cash register.

His use of coupons today and the utility it inspires brings him closer to his mother. This is a classic example of successful socialization in the market-place. Heckler et al. (1989) found that parents continued to influence adult children in the area of convenience goods: "The best explanation for this effect seems to be that knowledge of parental choices is used as a time-saving heuristic when the products are not complex or involving" (p. 283). As a child, he was given an important responsibility to guard and protect what were then only "valuable pieces of paper." The consequence of this experience has a functional application in the economy of his current shopping habits. He projects his pride in saving money to his respect for his mother. However, on another level, when he shops with his coupons today, they also represent a precious connection to her and she remains with him in spirit.

A consistent transfer of automotive brand loyalties was found between fathers, sons, and other male relatives.

From an Italian American male in his early 20s:

> Father was exposed to cars by his uncles. His uncle preferred to buy cars from Ford, so my father still today prefers to buy Ford cars. . . . I traced it all the way back to his uncle's first car, a Model T Ford.

Male children are taught to play with cars and trucks and often relate to older males in their families through playing with mechanical toys. As we grow, the toys get more expensive and the relationships more utilitarian in terms of the experience we can gain to avoid risk.

Another son, a German American in his early 20s, found an introspective moment with his father while they both were working on the family car:

> I happened to notice that we were working on a Dodge and that all our cars were Dodges. I also noticed that he was using Craftsman tools, drinking Schaeffer beer, and smoking Camel cigarettes. I asked him about these products and he said he got them from his father, all except the Camels which he started with his friends. I find that I am very influenced by my father in terms of cars, auto parts, the tools that I use, and my newspaper.

Although the transfer of car brands between male kin was widely reported, other brands that fathers influenced were tools, newspapers, liquor, beer, cigarettes, cologne, and motor oil. In this narrative, the significance of the father adopting Camel cigarettes from his friends suggests a "contaminating" factor. The transfer of automobile, beer, and tool brands was connected to his father. These brands have been "singularized." They have become extraordinary, made special by their heritage. The Camels were not as legitimately acquired and thus operate under a different object code (Kopytoff, 1986/ 1988, p. 78).

A similar heritage factor was reflected in the cultural biography of motor oil, as expressed by an Italian American male in his mid-20s;

> In the area of motor oil it's very simple, the brand is Quaker State. My grandfather, my father, and myself have always used it and will continue to use it in all our cars. As the saying goes, "The Q stands for Quality, it always has and it always will." My father loves that saying.

An Italian American male in his early 20s comments,

> When I do my oil changes on my car I will only put Castrol oil into my car. If a store doesn't have it I will travel until I find a store that has it. My father does the same thing.

The motor oil in these narratives has been "personally singularized." As a biographical reference, they have been family members for several genera-tions, and each brand is perceived to be the best in its category. Quaker State and Castrol, for each family, is the only choice. Advertising also reinforces a unique status with the slogan that one father has internalized in his belief system. Contamination with another brand would be tantamount to a trans-fusion with a different blood type.

Although there is a symbolic dimension to sharing the same brands and habits across the generations that expresses often latent emotions of rever-ence, respect, affection, and love, the opposite of the "bridge" is the "fence" constructed of independent behaviors and product preferences. These choices often reflect dysfunctional socialization experiences and other stressful fam-ily relationships. One mother "felt forced as a child to use her parents' products." Her family always used Ivory soap and it was among the goods she abandoned in order "to break free and have her own identity." Interpreted in the cultural materialist paradigm, "dysfunctional ingredients . . . are func-tional in a diachronic sense, since they are responsible for the emergence of a new adaptive system out of the old" (Harris, 1968, p. 235). As a response to our earthly problems, we change our strategies for survival. This is equally true in our social relations. Brands become weapons when they symbolize aspects of intimidation and independence. They reflect the perception of who we want to be.

Another woman, an Anglo American in her mid-20s, discovered that her father had been raised in a poor family where all products were purchased on sale. He had no brand loyalty. During the marriage, he feared that his wife would overspend so he controlled household purchasing:

> My mother was comfortable with many particular brands that she grew up with (Del Monte sauce, Betty Crocker baking goods, Campbell's soup, Lipton iced tea, Pledge, Windex, Boar's Head cold cuts, Woolite), and I found it very interesting that even for over 15 years she probably hardly ever used these brands because brand loyalty did not exist at this time, since my father did all of the shopping and only bought what was the cheapest brand that week. When she did begin to shop she chose to buy the particular brands that she was loyal to from her past.

This woman was freed by divorce. She could redefine her "self" in the marketplace and did so by returning to the "comfort" of her youth. Creative identity reconstruction is often subsumed in symbolic consumption and alternative consumer behaviors after divorce (McAlexander, Schouten, & Roberts, 1992). When the transition is more difficult, we selectively appropriate powerful symbols from our past (see also Fellerman & Debevec, 1992; McAlexander, 1991). Marriage and divorce represent critical psychic adjustments. Humans are territorial, and shelf space often constitutes valuable real estate in the home. Sharing space and a grocery budget often becomes a battle ground of egos and economics. In this narrative, the mother relinquished one facet of her "self" during marriage. She regained it back through her economic autonomy after divorce. The integrity of her ego and symbolic identity was restored when she could again define herself in terms of the brands of her youth.

Much less is understood about the consumption patterns of survivors of other dysfunctional socialization experiences. Further research will benefit from contributions with adult children of chemically dependent parents and survivors of physical and emotional abuse. Alderson (1957/1978) observes that "for some children the problem of growing up is partly that of achieving normal development in spite of their parents" (p. 186).

The experiences of another junior collaborator are poignant. Now in her late 20s and an incest survivor, after several follow-up interviews, the observation was made that she and her sister (early 40s) were raised in a family with three brothers who were "treated like royalty." Both daughters experienced emotional neglect. The elder sister moved out at the age of 19 when the informant was 5. She has never been able to ask her sister if she was also abused by their father as their own relationship is less than cordial. She was able to discuss their product histories and found some interesting analogies:

> I have come to the conclusion that my sister and I rebelled against the products my mother used. My mother completely mandated all product usage in our household. If any of us brought home a product other than the usual ones, she would pass derogatory remarks about the product. Reading between the lines, she was telling us that if she did not approve the product, it was not good.
>
> As a result of this rebellion my sister (age 42) and I turned to different types of products altogether. My mother uses frozen vegetables, we used canned. My mother drinks cola, we drink the "uncola." My mom buys Campbell's (canned) soup, we use Lipton (packaged). And the list goes on (tea, toothpaste, cough syrup, mustard, detergent, cars).

What is significant about this narrative is the fact that the sisters did not abandon the product categories used during childhood. Instead, their symbolic liberation was realized by changing brand and product form. By altering the constitution of the products and changing brands, both were able to divest themselves of their mother's heritage. The mother had, in fact, already rejected the daughters during the socialization experience when they went shopping for her. The sisters were given negative reinforcement in the form of "derogatory remarks" which they interpreted as the product "was not good." On a deeper level, the communication that was internalized was that each daughter "was not good." When we cannot please our generalized others, we often stop trying and protect ourselves. In this case, ego preservation was maintained by changing product form and brand loyalty.

In the reconstruction of our selves through creative consumption, many of us are able to articulate symbolic messages originating in our histories. In an attempt to deal with our pain, we try to establish new levels of emotional comfort through the goods we buy.

Conclusion

In this chapter, I have been concerned with the biography of brands and heritage tracing with nostalgic consumers over several generations. Marketers, as indirect socializers, used persuasive advertising to first-generation consumers who adopted these brands because they represented efficiency and convenience while conveying an image of modernity. Product history from family narratives shows how some brands facilitate a symbolic communication of nostalgia in generational heritage. Family brands become part of the tool chest in strategies for survival during critical life passages. Certain brands are good to "think" in the same way that certain animals in traditional societies are relegated to a totem status within clan social structure (Douglas & Isherwood, 1979; Lévi-Strauss, 1963; Tambiah, 1969).

Considering the state of brands today, customers of the 1990s are looking for price benefit, value and convenience in their products. This theme is a continuation of consumption patterns discussed in previous sections. However, there is a smaller percentage of single-brand loyalists. Consumers alternate between name brands and private labels, and a majority use sales, coupons, or special deals to determine choice. Families appreciate savings by joining price clubs, buying in bulk and in larger quantities. With more two-income families, children become the shoppers for the household and increasingly determine what brands are brought into the home.

Marketers, as socializers, are targeting this youthful market to generate lifelong customers. Reminiscent of Colgate's early promotion campaign in public schools are recent incursions by companies, such as Nike, Reebok, AT&T, IBM, Pepsi-Cola, and Coca-Cola, to supplement school supplies in return for strategically placed logos and trademarks. Direct mail campaigns and kids' clubs are creating little loyalists for entertainment media, holiday destinations, and fast-food chains. Christopher Whittle's "Channel One" offers televisions, video players, and news programming with product commercials to schools. These forays are justifiably criticized for compromising education with advertising messages to children in what should remain a commercial-free environment. However, marketers now understand the value of capturing brand loyalty at an early age.

Successful managers of heritage brands recognize the power in established brand equity. Many years of consistent advertising, nurturing trademark, product quality, and customers alike, ensure stature in building a brand's longevity. Some, like Procter & Gamble are turning to everyday low pricing to maintain loyalty and avoid habit-forming promotion deals. With the number of new offerings introduced each year failing at a rate of nearly 90%, heritage brands with strong equity fare better as their loyal following extends to new brand and line extensions.

Loyalty is the strongest factor that builds heritage brands. What Boorstin (1974) called the "consumption communities" of the 1800s have been reconstituted in the 20th century as image tribes ("Image Gains," 1989). Shared cultural meaning is manifest in brands that have charisma for communal identity. Image tribes can range from the oppositional loyalties, characteristic of Durkheim's (1915) "mechanical solidarity," to Turner's (1974) "communitas," a generalized sentiment of informal social bonding through shared brand recognition. Brand relationships link contemporary peers with each other, as the sneaker wars amply demonstrate. They also connect us to a history of brand identification—from Werther's Original (candy) to Ford families.

The lineage factor in marketing persuasion has not been forgotten by contemporary marketers. Generational themes continue to remind us of loved ones who used the products in the past and introduced us to our favorite brands. They also imply that we are responsible for continuing the tradition. One of the most sentimental from this genre is Werther's Original candy, with its slice-of-life television commercials portraying an elderly gentleman buying Werther's from an old-fashioned candy counter. He reminisces that when he was 4 years old, his grandfather bought the same candy for him. Now, he buys this treat for his young grandson. These commercials also communicate the symbolic quality of gender bonding through brand loyalty transfer.

The advertising message that best reflects the narratives' portrayal of brand transfer in lineage consumption patterns is a 1988 print ad by Richardson-Vicks for VapoRub. The headline, simply positioned above a picture of the familiar blue jar as "hero" of the ad, states, "Recent clinical studies prove your Grandmother was right." It continues, "Today it's known for a fact that Vicks VapoRub not only relieves congestion like a pill, it also relieves coughs like a cough syrup. And nothing can match that warm, soothing VapoRub feeling. All of which goes to show that your grandmother did know what was best for you." Marketers are tapping into these memory banks with nostalgia marketing that recollect our "personally experienced past."

Where do we go from here? The intergenerational legacy has potential for future research. What is particularly characteristic about American culture is that our competitive marketplace offers an infinite variety of goods to an increasingly acquisitive populace that, although at times wistful for the past, celebrates innovation. As consumer cohorts age at the same time, brand development could benefit from research into peak periods and residual nostalgic content for each age group. Life's passages can trigger significant experiences from a cohort's collective past that could predict trends for product themes.

Brand loyalty is waning; yet established brand names are a company's greatest asset. As it costs more to generate new customers than to keep the existing franchise, future research will continue to explore ways to bond the brand with the customer. Considering the mobile, transient nature of American society, many individuals form longer "friendships" with brands than with people and places. These brands represent trusted reliability in functional and symbolic performance. This emotional context should be explored more fully. What is the extent of consumer feelings for brands we consider friends? How do we compensate for disappointment when brands disappear?

Marketing will also greatly benefit from continuing research on the ethnic dimension. The family narratives showed that different cultures demonstrate high involvement with specific product categories. This should be researched in greater depth.

In terms of the intergenerational study of product use that launched the research for this chapter, a valuable contribution can be made by successive follow-up reports. Building on Guest's (1944) original longitudinal work conducted over 50 years ago, I intend to track these students in 5-, 10-, and 20-year increments to trace brand loyalty, continuity, and change as they distance themselves from families of influence.

Continuing research on the evolution of marketing will reveal how generational and gender, ethnic, racial, and other power relationships are established and reinforced. We must learn how we reconstitute the past in the present so we can alter the course for the future.

⚏ Notes

1. Copyright © 1993 by The New York Times Company. Reprinted by permission.

2. All excerpts from the J. Walter Thompson Company Archives reprinted by permission of the John W. Hartman Center for Sales, Advertising, and Marketing History at Duke University Library.

⚏ References

Aaker, D. A. (1991). *Managing brand equity.* New York: Free Press.

Aaker, D. A., & Biel, A. L. (1993). Brand equity and advertising: An overview. In D. A. Aaker & A. L. Biel (Eds.), *Brand equity and advertising: Advertising's role in building strong brands* (pp. 1-8). Hillsdale, NJ: Lawrence Erlbaum.

Alba, J. W., & Hutchinson, J. W. (1987). Dimensions of consumer expertise. *Journal of Consumer Research, 13,* 411-454.

Alderson, W. (1978). *Marketing behavior and executive action.* New York: Arno. (Original work published 1957)

Allen, A. (1993). Brand loyalty. *Confectioner, 78*(1-2), 21-26.

America's top 2,000 brands. (1992). SuperBrands section of *AdWeek's Marketing Week.*

Bahn, K. (1986). How and when do brand perceptions and preferences first form? A cognitive developmental investigation. *Journal of Consumer Research, 12,* 382-393.

Baudrillard, J. (1988). *America.* New York: Verso.

Belk, R. W., Wallendorf, M., & Sherry, J. F., Jr. (1989). The sacred and the profane in consumer behavior: Theodicy on the odyssey. *Journal of Consumer Research, 16,* 1-38.

Bettman, J. R. (1979). *An information processing theory of consumer choice.* Reading, MA: Addison-Wesley.

Boorstin, D. J. (1974). *The Americans: The democratic experience.* New York: Vintage.

BrandAdvantage. (1992). Wilmette, IL: Standard Rate and Data Service.

Calkins, E. E., & Holden, R. (1985). *Modern advertising.* New York: Garland. (Original work published 1905)

Carlson, L., Grossbart, S., & Walsh, A. (1990). Mothers' communication orientation and consumer-socialization tendencies. *Journal of Advertising, 19,* 27-38.

Childe, V. G. (1951). *Man makes himself.* New York: New American Library.

Childers, T. L., & Rao, A. R. (1992). The influence of familial and peer-based reference groups on consumer decisions. *Journal of Consumer Research, 19,* 198-211.

Csikszentmihalyi, M., & Rochberg-Halton, E. (1981). *The meaning of things: Domestic symbols and the self.* Cambridge, UK: Cambridge University Press.

Davis, F. (1979). *Yearning for yesterday: A sociology of nostalgia.* New York: Free Press.

Douglas, M., & Isherwood, B. (1979). *The world of goods.* New York: Basic Books.

Durkheim, E. (1915). *The elementary forms of religious life.* New York: Free Press.

Ewen, S. (1976). *Captains of consciousness: Advertising and the social roots of the consumer culture.* New York: McGraw-Hill.

Ewen, S. (1988). *All consuming images: The politics of style in contemporary culture.* New York: Basic Books.

Fairhurst, A. E., & Good, L. K. (1993). Teaching marketing concepts: An ethnographic approach. *Marketing Education Review, 3*(3), 47-51.

Fellerman, R., & Debevec, K. (1992). Till death do we part: Family dissolution, transition, and consumer behavior. In J. F. Sherry, Jr. & B. Sternthal (Eds.), *Advances in consumer research* (Vol. 19, pp. 514-521). Provo, UT: Association for Consumer Research.

Fox, S. (1984). *The mirror makers.* New York: Vintage.

Foxman, E. R., Tansuhaj, P. S., & Ekstrom, K. M. (1989). Adolescents' influence in family decisions: A socialization perspective. *Journal of Business Research, 81*(2), 159-172.

Geertz, C. (1983). *Local knowledge.* New York: Basic Books.

Glass, J., Bengtson, V. L., & Dunham, C. C. (1986). Attitude similarity in three-generation families: Socialization, status inheritance, or reciprocal influence? *American Sociological Review, 51,* 685-698.

Guest, L. (1944). A study of brand loyalty. *Journal of Applied Psychology, 28,* 16-27.

Guest, L. (1955). Brand loyalty—Twelve years later. *Journal of Applied Psychology, 39*(6), 405-408.

Guest, L. (1964). Brand loyalty revisited: A twenty-year report. *Journal of Applied Psychology, 48*(2), 93-97.

Harris, M. (1968). *The rise of anthropological theory.* New York: Crowell.

Harris, M. (1979). *Cultural materialism: The struggle for a science of culture.* New York: Random House.

Havlena, W. J., & Holak, S. L. (1991). "The good old days": Observations on nostalgia and its role in consumer behavior. In R. H. Holman & M. R. Solomon (Eds.), *Advances in consumer research* (Vol. 18, pp. 323-329). Provo, UT: Association for Consumer Research.

Hebdige, D. (1988). *Hiding in the light.* New York: Comedia.

Heckler, S. E., Childers, T. L., & Arunachalam, R. (1989). Intergenerational influences in adult buying behaviors: An examination of marketing factors. In T. Srull (Ed.), *Advances in consumer research* (Vol. 16, pp. 276-284). Provo, UT: Association for Consumer Research.

Hill, R. (1970). *Family development in three generations.* Cambridge, MA: Schenkman.

Hirschman, E. (1985). Primitive aspects of consumption in modern American society. *Journal of Consumer Research, 12,* 142-153.

Hoch, S. J., & Deighton, J. (1989). Managing what consumers learn from experience. *Journal of Marketing, 53,* 1-20.

Holbrook, M. B. (1993). Nostalgia and consumption preferences: Some emerging patterns of consumer tastes. *Journal of Consumer Research, 20*(2), 245-256.

Holbrook, M. B., & Schindler, R. M. (1991). Echoes of the dear departed past: Some work in progress on nostalgia. In R. H. Holman & M. R. Solomon (Eds.), *Advances in consumer research* (Vol. 18, pp. 330-333). Provo, UT: Association for Consumer Research.

Image gains importance as consumers form tribes (1989, November 11). *Marketing News,* p. 8.

J. W. Thompson, Company Archives, Duke University Library.

Jacoby, J., & Chestnut, R. W. (1978). *Brand loyalty measurement and management.* New York: John Wiley.

Kopytoff, I. (1988). The cultural biography of things: commoditization as process. In A. Appadurai (Ed.), *The social life of things: Commodities in cultural perspective* (pp. 64-91). Cambridge, UK: Cambridge University Press. (Original work published 1986)

Kroeber, A. L. (1963). *An anthropologist looks at history.* Berkeley and Los Angeles: University of California Press.

Leiss, W., Kline, S., & Jhally, S. (1990). *Social communication in advertising.* Scarborough, Ontario: Nelson Canada.

Lévi-Strauss, C. (1963). *Totemism.* Boston: Beacon.

Lynd, R. S., & Lynd, H. M. (1929). *Middletown: A study in American culture.* New York: Harcourt, Brace.

Marchand, R. (1985). *Advertising the American dream: Making way for modernity 1920-1940.* Berkeley: University of California Press.

Marney, J. (1990, December). Now's the time for brand loyalty: Market dominance helps stop consumer switching. *Marketing* (MacLean-Hunter, Toronto), pp. 10, 24-31.

McAlexander, J. H. (1991). Divorce, the disposition of the relationship, and everything. In R. H. Holman & M. R. Solomon (Eds.), *Advances in consumer research* (Vol. 18, pp. 43-48). Provo, UT: Association for Consumer Research.

McAlexander, J. H., Schouten, J. W., & Roberts, S. D. (1992). Consumer behavior in coping strategies for divorce. In J. F. Sherry, Jr. & B. Sternthal (Eds.), *Advances in consumer research* (Vol. 19, pp. 555-556). Provo, UT: Association for Consumer Research.

McCracken, G. (1988). *The long interview.* Newbury Park, CA: Sage.

McCracken, G. (1990). *Culture and consumption.* Bloomington: Indiana University Press.

McCracken, G. (1993). The value of the brand: An anthropological perspective. In D. A. Aaker & A. L. Biel (Eds.), *Brand equity and advertising: Advertising's role in building strong brands* (pp. 125-139). Hillsdale, NJ: Lawrence Erlbaum.

McNeal, J. V. (1987). *Children as consumers.* Lexington, MA: D. C. Heath.

Miller, B. C. (1975). Intergenerational patterns of consumer behavior. In M. J. Schlinger (Ed.), *Advances in consumer research* (Vol. 2, pp. 93-101). Ann Arbor, MI: Association for Consumer Research.

Miller, C. (1990, November 26). Nostalgia makes boomers buy. *Marketing News,* pp. 1-2.

Moore, R. L., & Moschis, G. P. (1981). The effects of family communication and mass media use on adolescent consumer learning. *Journal of Communication, 31,* 42-51.

Moore, R. L., & Stephens, L. F. (1975, September). Some communication and demographic determinants of adolescent consumer learning. *Journal of Consumer Research, 2,* 80-92.

Moore-Shay, E. S., & Lutz, R. L. (1988). Intergenerational influences in the formation of consumer attitudes and beliefs about the marketplace: Mothers and daughters. In M. J. Houston (Ed.), *Advances in consumer research* (Vol. 15, pp. 461-467). Provo, UT: Association for Consumer Research.

Moschis, G. P. (1985). The role of family communication in consumer socialization of children and adolescents. *Journal of Consumer Research, 11,* 898-913.

Moschis, G. P. (1987). *Consumer socialization: A life-cycle perspective.* Lexington, MA: Lexington Books.

Moschis, G. P., & Churchill, G. A. (1978). Consumer socialization: A theoretical and empirical analysis. *Journal of Marketing Research, 15,* 599-609.

Moschis, G. P., & Moore, R. L. (1979). Family communication and consumer socialization. In W. L. Wilkie (Ed.), *Advances in consumer research* (Vol. 6, pp. 359-363). Ann Arbor, MI: Association for Consumer Research.

Moschis, G. P., & Moore, R. L. (1983). A longitudinal study of the development of purchasing patterns. In P. E. Murphy et al. (Eds.), *Proceedings of the educators' conference* (pp. 114-117). Chicago: American Marketing Association.

Moschis, G. P., Moore, R. L., & Smith, R. B. (1984). The impact of family communication on adolescent consumer socialization. In T. C. Kinnear (Ed.), *Advances in consumer research* (Vol. 11, pp. 314-319). Chicago: Association for Consumer Research.

Perlez, J. (1993, November 8). In Poland, Gerber learns lessons of tradition. *New York Times,* pp. D1, D3.

Pollay, R. W. (1985). The subsiding sizzle: A descriptive history of print advertising, 1900-1980. *Journal of Marketing, 49,* 24-37.

Printers ink: Fifty years, 1888-1938. (1986). New York: Garland. (Original work published 1938)

Sahlins, M. (1976). *Culture and practical reason.* Chicago: University of Chicago Press.

Schlereth, T. J. (1991). *Victorian America: Transformations in everyday life, 1876-1915*. New York: HarperPerennial.

Schlossberg, H. (1994, January 31). Survey sheds light on "typical" boomer. *Marketing News*, p. 2.

Schoenfeld, G. (1990). Capitalize on your brand's heritage. *Marketing News*, 24(21), 10-11.

Schouten, J. W. (1991). Personal rites of passage and the reconstruction of self. In R. H. Holman & M. R. Solomon (Eds.), *Advances in consumer research* (Vol. 18, pp. 49-51). Provo, UT: Association for Consumer Research.

Schudson, M. (1984). *Advertising, the uneasy persuasion: Its dubious impact on American society*. New York: Basic Books.

Sherry, J. F., Jr. (1991). Postmodern alternatives: The interpretive turn in consumer research. In T. S. Robertson & H. H. Kassarjian (Eds.), *Handbook of consumer behavior* (pp. 548-591). Englewood Cliffs, NJ: Prentice Hall.

Smith, R. A., & Lux, D. (1993). Historical method in consumer research: Developing causal explanations of change. *Journal of Consumer Research*, 19(4), 595-610.

Solomon, M. R., & Assael, H. (1987). The forest or the trees? A gestalt approach to symbolic consumption. In J. Umiker-Sebeok (Ed.), *Marketing and semiotics: New directions in the study of signs for sale* (pp. 189-217). Berlin: Mouton de Gruyter.

Strasser, S. (1989). *Satisfaction guaranteed: The making of the American mass market*. New York: Pantheon.

Tambiah, S. J. (1969). Animals are good to think and good to prohibit. *Ethnology*, 8, 424-459.

Turner, V. (1974). *Dramas, fields, and metaphors: Symbolic action in human society*. Ithaca, NY: Cornell University Press.

Vinikas, V. (1992). *Soft soap, hard sell: American hygiene in an age of advertisement*. Ames: Iowa State University Press.

Wallendorf, M., & Arnould, E. J. (1991). "We gather together": Consumption rituals of Thanksgiving day. *Journal of Consumer Research*, 18(1), 13-31.

Wallendorf, M., & Belk, R. W. (1989). Assessing trustworthiness in naturalistic consumer research. In E. C. Hirschman (Ed.), *Interpretive consumer research* (pp. 69-84). Provo, UT: Association for Consumer Research.

Ward, S. (1974). Consumer socialization. *Journal of Consumer Research*, 1, 1-16.

Ward, S., Wackman, D. B., & Wartella, E. (1977). *How children learn to buy*. Beverly Hills, CA: Sage.

Wells, W. D. (1993). Discovery-oriented consumer research. *Journal of Consumer Research*, 19, 489-504.

Woodson, L. G., Childers, T., & Winn, P. R. (1976). Intergenerational influences in the purchase of auto insurance. In W. Locander (Ed.), *Marketing looking outward* (Business Proceedings, Series No. 38, pp. 43-49). Chicago: American Marketing Association.

Amidword

Anthropology, Metaphors, and Cognitive Peripheral Vision

Gerald Zaltman

This chapter calls for a more eclectic approach to the study of customer behavior (which includes both ultimate consumers and organizations). This requires the development of wide cognitive peripheral vision in the pursuit of disciplinary-based research. While preserving the value of one's own disciplinary orientation, it is necessary to systematically seek perspectives that may at first seem irrelevant to an issue but which may be the springboard for making recent research accomplishments seem old-fashioned quickly.

The discussion begins with a commentary on how the administrative structure of two institutions, academia and business, are organized for efficiency rather than effectiveness and may not fit with the external environments they seek to understand. Mention is made of strategies that might enhance effectiveness. Next, the subject of human or cultural universals is introduced. It is noted that various disciplines in the humanities and social and biological sciences offer insights about many of the same patterns of universal thought and behavior.

The major and concluding section suggests that the study and use of metaphors may be an effective way to understand these universals. Metaphors are of interest to most disciplines and are themselves based on the idea that seemingly irrelevant comparisons can provide relevant insight. Thus metaphors are useful in their own right for understanding the content of customer behavior from multiple disciplinary perspectives. At another level, they are also a guiding concept as a research strategy for perceiving the relevance of falsely defined irrelevancies. The latter is mentioned in this chapter as a major source of ignorance.

✍ Disciplinary Bias and Polite Lies

Administrative arrangements within higher education fosters the idea that the world at large—its individuals, organizations, and institutions—is organized as universities are, namely, along specific disciplinary lines. In fact, the very term "discipline" is a revealing metaphor suggesting enforced patterned behavior, control, order, rules, and even punishment that is uncharacteristic of a more dynamic, fluid, and sometimes unruly social world. "Inter-" and "multi-" disciplinary efforts to overcome artificial boundaries still preserve "discipline" as their root and are often troubled orphans as academic enterprises.

Mismatches between internal organizational arrangements and the nature of their external environments are found outside academia as well. For example, in commercial organizations, different functional areas, such as manufacturing, marketing, and finance, often see the world differently, fail to communicate with one another, and thereby forego opportunities to make creative and constructive use of these differences in forging more useful insights. This is known as the silo effect or chimney effect. A firm's customers, however, seldom distinguish one function from another when developing their understanding of and responses to the firm's offerings. Some companies have discovered that (a) how they are perceived by customers and how customers think they are perceived by the company does not correspond to (b) how managers in any function actually view their customers nor to their impressions of what customers think of them. The silo effect, or lack of integrated thinking, within these firms appears to be one factor contributing to this mismatch in customer and firm constructions of reality. This mismatch is interesting given the importance that companies place on understanding the world as perceived by their customers.

The Basic Unit of Analysis

To understand the academic version of this problem more fully, it will be helpful to offer a definition of customer behavior. Customer behavior consists of the acts, processes, and social relationships displayed by individuals or groups before, during, and subsequent to an exchange process. Three *commingling* phenomena characterize customer behavior: *people*, including individuals and informal and formal groups of varying sizes, engaging in *activities*, including actions, processes, and interpersonal relationships, that create *experiences*, including those associated with obtaining, using, and dealing with the consequences of goods and services.

Although it is easy to focus on the traditional buyer role in this definition, the people, activities, and experiences referred to also include sellers. The seller cannot avoid a presence in the customer's mind and vice versa. When testing alternative advertising cues, we are asking customers to convey their comprehension of stimuli in which are embedded the beliefs that marketing specialists have about these customers and about the product or service. This also provides the opportunity (usually foregone) to learn about vendors or ourselves as researchers. Thus, at a minimum, the fundamental unit of analysis in customer behavior is a dyad in which each party to the exchange both gives and gets something of perceived value. In the process of enhancing this value, each party has thoughts and actions that shape and are shaped by the other.

Researcher Habits of Mind

For better or for worse, neither people nor their consumption-oriented activities and experiences, reflect the discipline-based administrative arrangements of university life. No one discipline can lay unique claim to any facet of this complex, dynamic process of commingling, co-occuring phenomena. We understand a given activity or experience from an anthropological, sociological, psychological, economic, physiological, linguistic, or cognitive neuroscientific perspective, for instance, because those are the perspectives available to us. They are researchers' habits of mind. This does not mean customers have corresponding systems of thought and behavior. There is no cartridge, cassette, or software package for anthropology or psychology that customers pop in and out of their minds depending on what they are thinking or doing. Because researchers can make productive use of such cassettes or frameworks it is easy to think customers possess them, too. But customers know better, even if researchers do not.

The fact that very different specialists can feel confident explaining, say, the meaning of a specific product (without necessarily having similar or even compatible explanations) suggests that customer behavior is far richer than any one framework can capture. This argues for multi- or interdisciplinary approaches to a given issue. It also suggests that no single academic discipline, be it in the humanities, social sciences, or biological sciences, has exclusive ownership of the best analytic tools.

The point of these observations is not to suggest doing away with or reorganizing existing disciplines. To the contrary, these enterprises have great independent value and must be pursued in order to reveal as much as we can. But we also need the wisdom to know that in doing so we are missing much as well. We must take our usual perspectives with a major grain of salt and recognize that each tells a polite lie when it offers an explanation. Each discipline is a metaphor and thus both reveals and hides certain insights (Soyland, 1994).

Eclecticism

If each discipline both reveals and hides matters of interest, and as researchers we are "It" and committed to playing hide and seek, a strategy is required. We need to be more eclectic as individual scholars in recognizing the relevance of a diverse array of research traditions and freely choose theories, concepts, research methods, and findings from among them, subject only to our ability to use them appropriately.

Eclecticism requires a frontal attack on one of the two major components of ignorance. The first component (not addressed here) is believing something is so when it is not. The second is judging something to be irrelevant to a topic when it is relevant. Coping with this component of ignorance requires us to think in more generic terms, reaching out more broadly to literatures that are often uninviting to the uninitiated, and thinking more imaginatively, with its attendant greater risks and costs as well as rewards. Basically, we need wider cognitive peripheral vision: We need to do a better job at imagining the potential relevance of ideas outside our normal viewpoint and actively explore this potential. Having a particular viewpoint is important, not to mention unavoidable, and so I am not suggesting an eclecticism that tries to be free of a disciplinary bias. (Personally, I really enjoy my home discipline of sociology!)

Fewer polite lies and certainly fewer bold ones will be told if, for a given issue, we ask, "What appropriate concepts and methods beyond our home discipline would help us understand it?" This process might be started by asking why someone in another field would be interested reading about the issue in a customer behavior context. What do they and we have in common despite different contexts of application? This helps focus attention on the generic or fundamental issue being studied, which, in turn, helps identify other potentially relevant areas of inquiry. Consider, for example, the concept of loyalty, which is of interest to brand managers. It has also been studied by people concerned with political parties, voting behavior, volunteerism, cohesion among military units, nationalism, fund-raising, family dynamics, and so on. What is known about loyalty in these contexts, especially where findings converge, has relevance to brand managers. This approach contrasts with one that stays within a preferred discipline and asks how the issue can be structured so that it is amenable to the tools of that discipline. The chapter by Barbara Olsen (Chapter 7) provides a nice example of the richness of looking at brand loyalty through the broad metaphor of lineage.

Another question is very helpful in broadening cognitive peripheral vision once a certain comfort level is reached with a set of research results: "How can I make these results seem outdated as quickly as possible?" Typically, this requires searching for new ideas and integrating them with current ideas. Having the question in mind seems to serve as a quasi-conscious filter or perhaps magnet for catching relevant ideas that might otherwise be missed during normal recreational professional reading.

There is one discipline that seems to me to have wider cognitive peripheral vision than others. This is anthropology (although I dearly wish I could say sociology). Let me add to the offense that nonanthropologists will take by saying it is not something inherent about anthropology or other disciplines that warrants this statement. Indeed, no one field has an inherent intellectual, substantive, or methodological advantage over another, despite claims to the contrary. Rather, it is the practice of anthropology that seems to invite more eclecticism with respect to customer behavior. The chapters by Eric Arnould (Chapter 4) and Richard Reeves-Ellington (Chapter 5) are exemplars of this point.

Having expressed—though not justified—my thoughts about anthropologists as inviting more eclecticism and broadening our habits of mind, I would like to address two issues more directly related to the substance of customer behavior. The first deals with the idea of cultural universals; the second addresses the topic of metaphors.

◪ Cultural Universals

Cultural studies tend to highlight differences among cultures or subcultures, and for good reasons. According to one source, "It is reasonable to estimate that between 25% and 50% of behavior is culturally determined" (Gannon & Associates, 1994, p. 348). Consequently, it is important to look at cultural variation to understand variation in behavior.

Recent thinking among anthropologists, however, is also giving more attention to what are called human universals or near universals. These are traits and behaviors that are found in all or virtually all societies. This focus has been stimulated partly by findings that have overturned widely held previous beliefs about the distinctiveness of different cultures. For example, Margaret Mead argued that adolescence in Samoa did not involve the same trauma as found in Western societies; Malinowski argued that the Oedipus complex was peculiar only to certain types of societies; Edward Sapir and Benjamin Whorf hypothesized that categories of language shape perceptions of the world; and others have argued that the meaning of facial expression varies by culture. These important and influential beliefs have all been found to be in error. For example, the evidence is much more supportive of the idea that thought shapes language rather than the reverse. Where differences in thinking exist among people who speak different languages they are not found to be the result of qualities inherent in their spoken or written language, although such differences are important in other ways.

A sample of universal or near universal qualities is presented in Box 8.1. Fortunately, the list of universals that are relevant for a product or service category or for a specific brand concept and positioning is relatively brief. Some managers and researchers recommend identifying the relevant universals prior to introducing a product into a new cultural market. The universals represent either a specific need or the source of a specific need to which a product should be linked. Then they ask whether, in each market, these universals manifest themselves in different ways that might require changes in the marketing mix.

Monitoring changes in the way universals are enacted by people in a target market provides a basis for determining whether changes in the marketing mix are necessary. It also provides a basis for identifying opportunities for new goods and services. For instance, if people in two different market segments are becoming more (less) similar in how they conceive of success and failure, then some standardization in communications might be (in)appropriate for products related to the achievement of success and avoidance of failure. If issues of success and failure are becoming more salient in a particular culture, then this might represent an opportunity for a new product or a new concept for an existing product. Knowing, for example, that fashion and food products (i.e., what we place on and in our bodies) relate to a widely held need of self-expression may help in developing a common promotional theme to be used for these products in several countries (Domzel & Kernan, 1993). Moreover, there may be certain visual cues that have the same or similar meaning in those several countries and that will activate ideas about self-expression that are relevant to the food or fashion product being advertised. This can result in a more efficient use of promotional and packaging resources.

The presence of commonalities does not mean that the exact same advertisement, package design, and so forth is warranted in each country, nor does it mean that just any execution of an ad will work well for all

BOX 8.1. Universals

• Change through time • Use metaphors • Regulate sex • Have a system of status and roles • Share cognitive organization • Regulate the expression of affect • Control disruptive behaviors • Dream • Mark time • Use space • Record numbers • Conceive of success and failure • Have standards by which beauty and ugliness are measured • Are ethnocentric • Choose pragmatically • Have followers of leaders who are apathetic, regimented, "mature," and autarkic • Believe in the supernatural • Have a range of temperaments • Categorize color • Empathize • Dominate • Foster inequality • Hold similar attitudes toward: supernatural occurrences, fear, hope, love, hate, good, bad, beautiful, ugly, murder, theft, lying, and rape • Experience ambivalence (due to competing tendencies in human nature) • Use symmetry • Use polite expressions • Dance • Sing • Tell tales • Create literary art • Create verse that uses beats and lines • Symbolize • Recognize signs • Marry • Create and use tools • Groom each other • Solve problems using trial and error, insight, and reasoning • Establish rules and leadership to govern the allocation of important resources • Lose their tempers • Trade and transport goods • Conduct activities by dyads and groups • Supervise • Lead • Adjust joint activities to personalities • Regulate individual action by the group • Kill for retribution • Establish morals • Set expectations of responsibility • Create a sense of duty and indebtedness • Experience male sexual jealousy • Develop similar cognitive functions • Consider some aspects of sexuality private • Convey erotic, reproductive, and gender meanings using objects, actions, symbols, signals, and sayings • Hold a conception of reproduction • Practice abortion • Think about social relations between other individuals: triangular awareness • Establish etiquette • Need novelty • Experience approach-avoid ambivalence • Express surprise • Name objects • Are curious • Raise their tonal frequency when talking to children (especially mothers) • Express emotion with their faces • Smile • Communicate contempt with the same facial expression • Interpret rather than merely observe human behavior • Transform and elaborate the human body • Impose order on the universe • Reciprocate (in both positive and negative [tit-for-tat] ways) • Give gifts • Establish identity • Understand concepts of the same and opposite • Establish cause • Categorize shapes • Relate cues to consequences in avoidance learning • Create a religion that holds serious moral "oughts" grounded in conceptions of the way the world is • Associate music with ritual • Perceive pitch and musical contour • Are consciously aware of memory, emotions, experience of acting on the world, and making decisions • Experience being in control as opposed to under control • Consult in collective decision making • Follow rules about inheritance •

Equate social and physiological maternity • Display personality apart from social role • Recognize ascribed versus achieved status • Get bored • Feel hostility, altruism, pride, shame, sorrow, and need • Prohibit murder and untruth (under certain circumstances) • Offer restitution • Suffer from greater male violence and homicide than female • Believe in spiritual entities such as the soul • Experience dissatisfaction with individual culture • Deny unwelcome facts • Prefer faces that are average in their dimensions • Give hair symbolic value • Use language with a universal underlying structure • Overestimate the objectivity of our thought • Provide for the poor and unfortunate • Demand truth in certain conditions • Are unable to transcend guilt • Need to explain the world • Sacrifice one's self for one's group • Consume substances to partake of their properties • Expect women to care for children more than men do • Recognize a male need for achievement • Think men and women are different in more than only procreative ways • Intend • Promise • Experience inner states • Anthropomorphize • Employ capital punishment • Rape (and disapprove of it) • Wish to allure • Feel pride, shame, amusement, and shock • Forego present pleasure for a deferred good • Evidence negative effects on the personalities of children who have been rejected by their parents • Use same basic color categories • Identify the same geometric forms • Confront the issue of the haves versus the have-nots • Consider the relationship of nature to culture • Acquire as children linguistic features in similar order • Think rationally • Consider morally right and wrong methods of satisfying needs • Form a personality structure that integrates needs (id), values (superego), and executive- response processes (ego) • Establish psychological self-defense mechanisms • Attach meaning to what is essentially meaningless • Play games of skill and chance • Include homosexuals • Have juvenile delinquents • Hold male activities that exclude females • Express loyalty • Include people who attempt to cure the ill • Deceive themselves • Associate poetry with ritual • Predict • Use red, white, and black to symbolize the same things • Use words whose meanings are transparent and opaque • Employ 13 semantic primes in language: I, you, someone, something, world, this, want, not want, think of, way, imagine, be a part of, become • Form personalities based on solidarity versus conflict and dominance versus submission •

SOURCE: Adapted from *Human Universals* (pp. 157-201), by Donald E. Brown (1991). New York: McGraw-Hill, Inc. Reprinted with permission of McGraw-Hill, Inc.

segments within countries. In fact, the "country" may not be the appropriate unit of analysis. For a certain target market, such as young adults, in several countries, fashion ads that use lifestyle formats, fantasy, visuals, emotions, and self-identity may have more universal appeal than ads for the same product whose execution gives more attention to culture, art, history, and more abstract concepts (Domzal & Kernan, 1993). The latter themes will appeal more to older adults in these countries. In this case, differences exist not so much across or between countries as between segments or subcultures related to chronological age.

The extensive list of universals represents at some very fundamental or generic level categories of thought that are the same among different populations. Common *categories* of thought and behavior, however, may or may not give rise to common content for those thoughts and behaviors. Moreover, common content may or may not be expressed in similar ways. In fact, a central activity in marketing is to determine across different market segments whether or not there are similarities in categories of thought, the content of those thoughts, and in the ways they are represented. This has major implications for decisions about whether, how much, and with regard to what it makes sense to standardize the marketing mix for different populations or subpopulations. This means that although a product or service may address a need or cluster of needs shared by many different markets it may have to be designed, delivered, and communicated in very different ways corresponding to how different customers think and behave with respect to that need.

A fruitful way of understanding the representation of the thoughts and behaviors shown in Box 8.1 is to study metaphors, the subject of the next section. All societies have metaphors expressing these universals. Accordingly, the particular experience and hence meaning of these universals for any culture or subculture can be found by analyzing the dominant metaphors used to express them. For instance, Martin J. Gannon and Associates (1994) suggest that each nation has a dominant metaphor that captures many of its significant themes. For Germany it is the symphony, for India the dance of Shiva, for Italy the opera, for Turkey the coffee house, and so on. Moreover, these metaphors provide a basis for assessing certain universal dimensions such as the individualistic-collectivistic dimension. The German symphony reflects subordinated individualism, the Italian opera expresses exteriorized individualism, American football captures competitive individualism, and Irish conversation reflects religion-focused individualism.

Metaphors

In response to the question "How do people represent their thoughts?" it is suggested that thoughts are represented primarily by metaphors. (I am sidestepping the questions "What is a thought?" and "What is *it* that has or holds a thought?") Metaphors are fundamental to sense making; they shape attentional and perceptual processes and comprehension. They are also a primary means by which new ideas are developed. Metaphors are central to understanding the human mind (Leary, 1990) and thus of interest to scholars in many fields beyond linguistics, especially in cognitive psychology (for reviews of the historical treatment of metaphors, see Billow, 1977; Black, 1993; Haskell, 1987a, 1987b; Hoffman, 1983; Johnson, 1987; Leary, 1990; Ortony, 1993; Parmegiani, 1987/1988; Rumelhart, 1993).

Metaphors are so prevalent in everyday representation of thought that we are often unaware of their use. Ordinary metaphors are reflective of deep thought structures, which are organized as stories and symbols, stored in long-term memory and shared in social groups. Properly elicited and used, metaphors can be effective in uncovering diverse types of "hidden" as well as more surface knowledge. As representations of varying types and levels of thought, metaphors can be effective in identifying the conceptual ecology shared by a market segment for a given topic. Depending on whether one takes a manager's or a consumer's perspective, a firm's offerings and the consumer's needs can be viewed as metaphors for one another.

Representing Thought Through Metaphor

A metaphor involves the understanding and experiencing of one thing in terms of another (Lakoff & Johnson, 1980, p. 5). Alternatively, it is the perception of one thing as if it were a different type of thing (Dent-Read & Szokolszky, 1993, pp. 227, 230).[1] For example, in a study of the value of marketing (Coulter & Zaltman, 1994), one person described marketing as being "like the color orange, which is a hungry color and the color worn by hunters" (p. 7). In a corporate image study, a customer used a news photo of a gorilla as a pictorial metaphor of how that company perceived its customers. This particular metaphor represented the belief that the company in question thinks its customers have a low level of intelligence. Another customer used a photograph of a flock of sheep to express her view that the company thinks people can be easily led. Interestingly, managers in this company used metaphors describing their customers as having a high level of product knowledge and sophisticated decision-making skills.

The position that thinking is represented primarily through metaphors is consistent with the interactionist view that the creation of new thoughts is shaped by metaphors. In fact, "the vast majority of linguistic metaphors reflect underlying conceptualizations of experience in *long-term memory* that are *already structured by metaphorical schemes*" (Gibbs, 1992, p. 572, emphases added; see also Johnson & Henley, 1992). Metaphorical schemes would include physical dimension (up/down, over/under, central/peripheral, far/near, in/out, etc.), containers, personification, construction, and so on. We find metaphorical schemes reflecting basic dimensions of culture such as time, information flows, primary modes of activity, assumptions about relationships between people, individualism, and so on.

Conceptual metaphorical schemes, stored in long-term memory, help us make sense of literal metaphors (see Katz, 1992, and esp. Glucksberg, 1991, for a psychological treatment of the interplay between figurative and literal phrases). Metaphors not only make sense of what we perceive, they direct our attentional and perceptual processes. "Metaphorical projection is one fundamental means by which we project structure, make new connections, and remold our experience" (Johnson, 1987, p. 169).

I. A. Richards (1936) argued that thought is ultimately and irreducibly metaphorical and that linguistic metaphors are the outcroppings of metaphoric thought:

> The processes of metaphor in language, the exchanges between the meanings of words which we study in explicit verbal metaphors, are superimposed upon a perceived world which is *itself a product of earlier or unwitting metaphor.* (Richards cited in Johnson, 1987, p. 69, emphasis added)[2]

The "earlier or unwitting" metaphor refers to the projection and elaboration of image schemata that are central not only to existing thought but to the creation of new thought (see, e.g., Johnson, 1987, chap. 4). This widely accepted perspective (called the interactionist perspective) holds that metaphors create emergent meanings. The use of a metaphor involves an "active partial transformation of the topic under the guidance of the vehicle" (Dent-Read & Szokolszky, 1993, p. 230; see also Black, 1993). For example, the meaning of "time is money" (e.g., we invest, budget, borrow, spend, save, and make profitable use of time) goes well beyond the simple mapping of the properties of one object or event onto the other (Lakoff & Johnson, 1980). When using variants of this core metaphor, the entire system of implications from the money domain interact with those of the time domain in a way that produces a new, irreducible system of implications. Simply comparing the initial money and time domains is insufficient to understand the cognition involved in the "time is money" utterance (Black, 1993).

Emergent meanings may or may not have intended or helpful consequences. For instance, over time the use of biological life cycle concepts to understand the management of products has shaped thinking about product management. The life cycle metaphor highlights certain ideas and hides others; in the process it causes us to reconceptualize product management in terms of the metaphoric vehicle (e.g., the biological concept of unvarying, unidirectional life cycle stages). Although this has been helpful, it has also led to some difficulties (for a discussion of the dysfunctional use of the product life cycle metaphor because of "imported" assumptions from biology, see Dhalla & Yuseph, 1976; Tellis & Crawford, 1981).

The interactionist perspective surfaces in Schön's (1993) concept of generative metaphors. He notes that "metaphor [is] central to the task of accounting for our perspectives on the world: how we think about things, make sense of reality, and set the problems we later try to solve" (p. 137). Although Schön develops this concept within the context of social policy problem-setting, it applies equally well to business contexts. Nonaka (1991) presents a similar position:

> Through metaphors, people put together what they know in new ways and begin to express what they know but cannot yet say. As such, metaphor is highly effective in fostering direct commitment to the creative process in the early stages of knowledge creation. (p. 100)

The generative capacity of metaphors has received attention in educational psychology (e.g., Wong, 1993). It is relevant to marketing professionals when consumers must develop understandings in a context of incomplete knowledge. Such instances would include understanding relatively discontinuous innovations and first-time purchases in a product category. People are adept and active in generating new metaphors for dealing with unstructured problems, especially those not necessarily having a single correct solution (Perkins, 1981; Wong, 1993). A metaphor becomes self-generated through continual refinement and synthesis of fragmented knowledge and is a tool for achieving understanding rather than an end in itself.

The use of metaphors as basic units of thought is of great importance to marketing. From a communications standpoint, for example, Paivio and Clark (1986; also Paivio & Walsh, 1993) have explored metaphor comprehension using dual coding theory and the conceptual peg hypothesis; "High imagery words are especially effective as 'conceptual pegs' for storage and retrieval of associated information" (p. 369). As part of their research they evaluated the relative importance of high and low imagery vehicles (the metaphoric reference) versus high and low imagery topics (e.g., a product or brand) in the comprehension of metaphors. One finding was that people spend significantly more time thinking about the metaphor vehicle than the topic and that the imagery value of the metaphor vehicle has a major impact on information processing.[3] Stated differently, "while the topic is the focus of attention, the vehicle does the bulk of the work" (Winner, 1988, p. 258). This suggests that advertisers and others must pay substantial attention to their use of metaphors to convey information.

Although the suggestion above may seem obvious, metaphors are so basic to the representation of thought that communicators and audiences alike are often unaware of their use, and hence the significance of metaphors in the creation and expression of thought may escape attention. "Conscious scrutiny of an explanatory metaphor is an important aspect of [its] productive usage" (Gentner & Grudin, 1985, p. 190, brackets added). This is true whether it be in scientific discourse (Kuhn, 1993; Leary, 1990; Roediger, 1980), product and service design (Caroll & Mack, 1985; Dent-Read, Kelin, & Eggleston, 1994; Dumas, 1994), or the creation of marketing communications. In fact, the interpretation of metaphorical meaning is difficult, if not impossible, to inhibit even when it is irrelevant to and distracts from task performance (Glucksburg, Gildea, & Bookin, 1982). Experiments show that subjects, using only a few basic relational concepts, will make sense of randomly generated metaphors (Johnson & Henley, 1992). Thus sensitivity to metaphors is especially important because consumers are likely to process information metaphorically even when that is not the communicator's intent.[4] Conscious scrutiny not only avoids the danger of false credibility (Gentner & Grudin, 1985) but permits the use of certain guidelines or rules of thumb that can lead to more effective metaphors (cf. Gibbs & Kearney, 1994; Marschark, Katz, & Paivio, 1983; Paivio & Walsh, 1993).

Metaphors and Hidden Knowledge

Metaphors can be especially effective in surfacing hidden knowledge. Several investigators in the field of psychotherapy (Pollio, 1977; Shell, Pollio, & Smith, 1987; Weiser, 1993) have found that explicit use of metaphors is effective in helping patients make unconscious experiences progressively more conscious and communicable. Because metaphors can elicit cognitive processes beyond those displayed by literal language, they can also surface important mental states or content that literal language may underrepresent or miss altogether (Entin, 1981; Krauss & Fryrear, 1983; Weiser, 1988). This implies that different cognitive processes tend to be associated with different constructs. If so, metaphorical and literal language may have varying probabilities of uncovering particular ideas. Ellen Winner (1988) notes,

A novel metaphor surprises the listener and challenges him to solve a puzzle by mapping attributes and relations between the stated or implied elements being linked. Literal descriptions do no such thing but simply describe the world in established ways. In the sense that metaphors force us to understand one thing in terms of another, metaphors must elicit cognitive processes not ordinarily called upon by literal language. (p. 17; see also Gentner, 1983; MacCormac, 1985, cited in Winner, 1988)

Thus, by using both metaphors and literal language, the likelihood of uncovering important consumer and manager mental constructs is increased. In fact, metaphors are not stored verbatim in memory but abstractly in modality-free language. They are stored in terms of the so-called ground, that is, in terms of the understood shared properties between vehicle and topic. This abstract understanding becomes part of our image schema (Chandler, 1991). Abstract understandings, of course, are the primary components of mental models.

The Role of the Senses:
Image Schemata, Physicality, and Metaphors

The hidden knowledge that metaphors elicit are rooted in image schema (Weiser, 1993). Image schemata appear to be physiologically based (Johnson, 1987; see also Johnson & Henley, 1992, p. 71) although distinguishing physical from cultural bases of metaphors can be difficult (Classen, 1993; Howes, 1991; Lakoff & Johnson, 1980, p. 19). Johnson (1987), for instance, argues that image schemata are recurring patterns arising from bodily movements and our manipulation or perceptual interaction with objects. More specifically, "image schemata *are* those *recurring structures of, or in, our perceptual interactions, bodily experiences, and cognitive operations*" (p. 79, emphases in original). Stated differently, they are recurring patterns of our perceptual interactions and motor programs that provide structure and coherence to our experience (see Lakoff, 1987; Lakoff & Johnson, 1980, chap. 4). The thesis that abstract thought is rooted in sensory visual systems receives compelling support from many different areas (Arnheim, 1969; Barlow, 1990; Danesi, 1990; Humphrey, 1992; Leyton, 1992). The chapter by Carole Duhaime, Annamma Joy, and Christopher Ross (Chapter 10) is a wonderful use of vision as a metaphor for grasping or comprehending.

Other researchers provide further elaboration, suggesting that metaphoric processes originate in neurological substrates tied to sensory-motor-affective systems (see Beck, 1987; Marks, 1978; Marks & Bornstein, 1987). Again, the use of metaphors involves projecting patterns from one area of experience on to another to help structure or repattern the second area of experience.

By projecting patterns in our sensory experience onto our abstract under-standing we organize that understanding (McAdams & Bigard, 1993). For example, abstract understanding of quantity (e.g., a price change) is achieved in terms of the physical experience of verticality (e.g., up, down), which, in turn, may carry judgmental associations ("up" has many more positive associations than "down"). Similarly, the abstract understanding of good and bad is often achieved in terms of smell (it stinks) or touch (he's abrasive) (see Danesi, 1990, for an excellent discussion of the thinking is sensing, especially seeing, hypothesis).

One of the more interesting approaches to the physiological aspect of metaphors involves synesthesia or cross-modality perception in which one mode of sensory perception transfers to another (see Marks, 1978; Marks & Bornstein, 1987). An example is colored speech perception, such as the association of soft- and low-pitched sounds with dark colors (for more on colored speech perception, see Baron-Cohen, Harrison, Goldstein, & Wyke, 1993). When asked, most people will say a sneeze is brighter than a cough. There is strong evidence that associations between sensory metaphors are patterned; that is, different individuals (within the same culture) display the same systematic connections between dimensions of specific modalities.[5]

Synesthetic capacity is more widespread than previously acknowledged (Marks, 1978, p. 8). (Interestingly, it is much more evident among children than adults.) Marks, Hammeal, and Bornstein (1987) suggest that "rather than being 'abnormal,' synesthetic perception may rest on a universal under-current of cross-modal equivalence" (p. 3). They note,

> Cross-sensory "translations" underlie the way people appreciate many cross-modal metaphors in poetry; such appreciation may rest therefore on relatively simple and possibly innate, perceptually based connections among the senses. (p. 5)

Different cultures approach the sensorium differently (Classen, 1993; Stoller, 1989; Trehub & Trainor, 1993), and the interactions among senses will differ accordingly (Howes & Classen, 1991). One culture might favor sound/vision combinations, whereas another might favor sound/taste com-binations. Moreover, the practical value of a particular sense may correspond to its cultural or symbolic importance (Classen, 1993, chaps. 4, 6; Stoller, 1989, esp. chap. 4). Understanding metaphors, including those whose origins are rooted in sensory perceptions and motor experiences, is central for the understanding of current schemata and the emergence of new ones, includ-ing those facilitated by innovative marketing mix decisions. Thus an interesting avenue for exploration is whether there are cross-modal or synesthetic patterns for particular goods and services and for particular customer segments that can be identified in metaphoric expression. If so, this would offer an intriguing basis for market segmentation with major implications for advertising, point-of-purchase displays, and purchase environment design.

Metaphors, Imagination, and the Linking of Needs and Products

The significance of metaphors for marketing managers is partly based on their centrality to imagination. The process of imagining (i.e., creating or arriving at what it is we know) shapes the content of knowledge. "Without imagination, nothing in the world could be meaningful. Without imagination, we could never make sense of our experience. Without imagination, we could never reason toward knowledge of reality" (Johnson, 1987, p. ix).

The concept of originality closely resembles imagination and is essential in the discovery aspect of science. Indeed, to ignore this aspect "is to ignore most of the scientific enterprise" (Royce, 1988, quoted in Shames, 1991, p. 344; see also Goldman, 1986, pp. 247-249, for a discussion of the importance of originality as a topic for epistemology). "Figuration" is the cognitive undergriding of insight and discovery and hence basic to studying the nature, origins, and criteria of knowledge. Metaphoric aptitude, as Shames (1991) notes in his treatment of metaphor in creativity and epistemology, is a highly evolved cognitive process of insight inherent in language and is probably grounded in the central nervous system (given the perspective that symbolization is an inherent function of the nervous system). Metaphor should displace "scientific method" at the center stage of epistemology (Shames, 1991). Imagination, then, is very important. However, *without metaphors, we cannot imagine: Metaphors are the engine of imagination.*

In general, marketing has not given much attention to the significance of imagination in reasoning and comprehension among consumers. Nonetheless, metaphor is the primary means by which firms and customers interact. The notion of becoming market based by hearing the voice of the market (Barabba & Zaltman, 1991) requires that managers understand customer needs and then structure the goods and services they offer accordingly. Customer needs, in effect, serve as metaphors for managerial thinking about product offerings and other marketing mix decisions (see Dumas, 1994, for a discussion of the explicit use of metaphor by a product design team).

Similarly, a firm's offering is seen by consumers as a metaphor for their needs. Consumers imagine (the term is used here as a perceptual process) the relevance of goods and services in terms of their needs. To establish the relevance of an innovation to a need is a challenging task for managers. It is still more challenging when the need is latent, emerging, or not yet understood by the consumer. The interaction of the product and need domains produces a new understanding that becomes part of the consumer's image schema. The more managers know about preexisting metaphors the more creative they can be in establishing a novel connection between a specific brand and a need.

Ⓜ️ Some Concluding Thoughts

Anthropology is a lens that broadens our cognitive peripheral vision. It might be thought of as a fisheye lens with telescopic capacity. Anthropology, as evidenced by the chapters in this sourcebook, is capable of construing a major enterprise such as advertising in terms of such broad and different metaphors as magic and religion while at the same time providing specific communication guidance for a utility company whose customers see its transmission lines as containers whose overflow has potentially unhealthy consequences.

The concept of a lens is itself a metaphor as are the concepts of broaden, cognitive, peripheral, and vision. We often think of a lens as a corrective device, a way of restoring 20/20 vision, a convention that is somehow supposed to be normal, true vision. However, even if such immaculate perception, the intellectual equivalent of 20/20 sight, were possible, it would not be very helpful. Normal vision isn't useful for obtaining abnormal (i.e., innovative) insight. Thus the utility of the anthropological lens, this fisheye with telescopic capacity, lies in its ability to distort ordinary, vanilla vision.

Each chapter in this book uses metaphors that offer the broad perspective of a fisheye lens or the highly focused insight of a telescopic lens. For instance, there is a very interesting chapter by John McCreery (Chapter 8) comparing magic and religion as broad metaphors for viewing advertising in which the unique (and common) distortions of each of these lens are identified and evaluated. These distortions are helpful in understanding in the enterprise of advertising more fully than we would in the absence of either lens. The chapter by Rita Denny (Chapter 9) is more telescopic in nature, focusing in on specific customer perceptions of a regional utility company's power lines in terms of the containment of electromagnetic fields and unhealthy spillover. Denny describes the frames of reference that customers use when thinking about health and electromagnetic fields. By coincidence, I have recently conducted research for a utility company in a different region of the country than the two reported in Denny's work and encountered some of the same issues. (My approach required customers to generate visual and other sensory metaphors to express their overall thoughts and feelings about the company; for more about this method, see Zaltman & Higie, 1993.) Containers constituted one of several deep metaphors that customers use in thinking about this company. And speaking of containers, Dan Rose's chapter on active ingredients (Chapter 2) is exceptionally rich with metaphors, and we find interesting perspectives on the meaning of, for instance, head and shoulders as elements of a brand name for a shampoo.

John Sherry, in his introductory chapter, makes use of a pyramid as a geometric metaphor to help create coherence among diverse research orientations. His use of a pyramid caught my eye because of a recent interview I conducted with a vice president of a *Fortune* 100 company. The interview concerned this person's approach to ill-structured or messy problems. One phase of the interview required him to visualize and verbally describe a movie or vignette expressing this approach. (This "movie" was later created on a computer.) A component of the movie involved a pyramid emerging from a roiling sea of moving, psychedelic colors and contrasting textures. This person attached several meanings to the pyramid. One was that its sharp lines and smooth surfaces represented the type of order that needs to emerge in defining a messy problem; another meaning was that the pyramid represents structural strength. The same can be said for Sherry's conceptualization.

A concluding caution is in order. Metaphors may be appealing and effective as a mechanism for eliciting socially shared cognitions because they happen to map onto existing cultural understandings or models that are structured in terms other than metaphors or image schemas. It is not clear what these other bases are for the structuring of cultural understandings. Whatever they might be, they may not involve metaphors in a prominent way. Thus we should enjoy the excitement that metaphors offer but not ignore the possibility that something more basic might be going on that shapes shared understanding. This gives anthropology a special opportunity. Because anthropology has broad cognitive peripheral vision while retaining the ability to focus on detail, and because of the richness of marketing as a context of (a) applied social science and therefore (b) a playground for developing social science theory, the practice of anthropology in marketing contexts may provide exciting insights about largely unanswered questions about the structure and functioning of the human mind. The fisheye with telescopic capacity might encounter something far more profound than metaphors.

⚘ Notes

1. An analogy is a metaphor when the two sets of objects are not of the same type. An iconic sign is a metaphor when the vehicle [metaphoric reference] is a sign of one thing independently of its role in the metaphor *and* is also a sign of a second thing in its role as a vehicle (Dent-Read, Kelin, & Eggleston, 1993, p. 9, brackets added).

2. For a good discussion of the interplay between spoken language and thought and particularly the evidence concerning the primary impact of human cognition in shaping language (rather than the reverse), see Sweetser (1990), Glucksberg (1988), and Pinker (1994). Glucksberg also makes a compelling argument for thinking of language in a multimodal way rather than simply as speech.

3. There is debate about whether imagery plays a central or a peripheral role in metaphor processing and comprehension and also about how imagery functions in metaphors.

4. It appears, too, that there is no difference in the speed of processing, in the interpreting and arriving at meaning, between metaphorical and literal language (Ortony, Shallert, Reynolds, & Antos, 1978).

5. We are speaking here only of systemic connections between modalities. Other data suggest that important individual differences may be common. Some individuals may comprehend a given literary or nonliterary metaphor easily while others may not. Differences also may exist as to whether the metaphor is judged good or bad (Katz, Paivio, & Marschark, 1988).

⚘ References

Arnheim, R. (1969). *Visual thinking.* Berkeley: University of California Press.

Barabba, V. P., & Zaltman, G. (1991). *Hearing the voice of the market: Competitive advantage through creative use of market information.* Cambridge, MA: Harvard University Press.

Barlow, H. (1990). What does the brain see? How does it understand? In H. Barlow, C. Blakemore, & M. Weston-Smith (Eds.), *Images and understanding* (pp. 5-25). New York: Cambridge University Press.

Baron-Cohen, S., Harrison, J., Goldstein, L. H., & Wyke, M. (1993). Coloured speech perception: Is synaesthesia what happens when modularity breaks down? *Perception, 22,* 419-426.

Beck, B. E. F. (1987). Metaphors, cognition, and artificial intelligence. In R. E. Haskell (Ed.), *Cognition and symbolic structures: The psychology of metaphoric transformation* (pp. 21-27). Norwood, NJ: Ablex.

Billow, R. M. (1977). Metaphor: A review of the psychological literature. *Psychological Bulletin, 84*(1), 81-92.

Black, M. (1993). More about metaphor. In A. Ortony, *Metaphor and thought* (2nd ed., pp. 19-41). New York: Cambridge University Press.

Brown, D. E. (1991). *Human universals.* New York: McGraw-Hill.

Caroll, J. M., & Mack, R. (1985). Metaphor, computing system, and active learning. *International Journal of Man-Machine Studies, 22,* 39-57.

Chandler, S. R. (1991). Metaphor comprehension: A correctionist approach to implications for the mental lexicon. *Metaphor and Symbolic Activity,* 6(4), 227-258.

Classen, C. (1993). *Worlds of sense: Exploring the senses in history and across cultures.* New York: Routledge.

Coulter, R. H., & Zaltman, G. (1994, August). *Seeing the value of marketing: An application of the Zaltman metaphor elicitation technique.* Paper presented at the Value of Marketing Conference, Stanford University, Stanford, CA.

Danesi, M. (1990). Thinking is seeing: Visual metaphors and the nature of abstract thought. *Semiotica,* 80(3-4), 221-237.

Dent-Read, C. H., & Szokolszky, A. (1993). Where do metaphors come from? *Metaphor and Symbolic Activity,* 8(2), 227-242.

Dent-Read, C. H., Kelin, G., & Eggleston, R. (1993). *Metaphor in visual displays designed to guide action.* Unpublished manuscript, University of Connecticut, Center for the Ecological Study of Perception and Action, Department of Psychology.

Dhalla, N. K., & Yuseph, S. (1976, January/February). Forget the product life cycle concept. *Harvard Business Review,* 54, 102-112.

Domzal, T. J., & Kernan, J. B. (1993). Mirror, mirror: Some postmodern reflections on global advertising. *Journal of Advertising,* 22(4), 1-20.

Dumas, A. (1994, Winter). Building totems: Metaphor-making in product development. *Design Management Journal,* pp. 71-82.

Entin, A. D. (1981). The use of photographs and family albums in family therapy. In A. Gurman (Ed.), *Questions and answers in the practice of family therapy* (pp. 78-93). New York: Brunner/Mazel.

Gannon, M. J., and Associates. (1994). *Understanding global cultures: Metaphorical journeys through 17 countries.* Thousand Oaks, CA: Sage.

Gentner, D. (1983). Structure mapping: A theoretical framework for analogy. *Cognitive Science,* 7, 155-170.

Gentner, D., & Grudin, J. (1985, February). The evolution of mental metaphors in psychology: A 90-year retrospective. *American Psychologist,* pp. 181-192.

Gibbs, R. W., Jr. (1992). Categorization and metaphor understanding. *Psychological Review,* 99(3), 572-577.

Gibbs, R. W., Jr., & Kearney, L. R. (1994). When parting is such sweet sorrow: The comprehension and appreciation of oxymora. *Journal of Psycholinguistic Research,* 23(1), 75-89.

Glucksberg, S. (1988). Language and thought. In R. J. Sternberg & E. E. Smith (Eds.), *The psychology of human thought* (pp. 214-241). Cambridge, UK: Cambridge University Press.

Glucksberg, S. (1991). Literal meanings: The psychology of allusion. *Psychological Science,* 2(3), 146-152.

Glucksberg, S., Gildea, P., & Bookin, H. (1982). On understanding nonliteral speech: Can people ignore metaphors? *Journal of Verbal Learning and Verbal Behavior,* 21, 85-98.

Goldman, A. I. (1986). *Epistemology and cognition.* Cambridge, MA: Harvard University Press.

Haskell, R. E. (1987a). Cognitive psychology and the problem of symbolic cognition. In R. E. Haskell (Ed.), *Cognition and symbolic structures: The psychology of metaphoric transformation* (pp. 85-102). Norwood, NJ: Ablex.

Haskell, R. E. (1987b). Giambattista Vico and the discovery of metaphoric cognition. In R. E. Haskell (Ed.), *Cognition and symbolic structures: The psychology of metaphoric transformation* (pp. 241-256). Norwood, NJ: Ablex.

Hoffman, R. R. (1983). Recent research on metaphor. *Semiotic Inquiry, 3*, 335-361.

Howes, D. (Ed.). (1991). *The varieties of sensory experience: A sourcebook in the anthropology of the senses.* Toronto: University of Toronto Press.

Howes, D., & Classen, C. (1991). Sounding sensory profiles. In D. Howes (Ed.), *The varieties of sensory experience: A sourcebook in the anthropology of the senses* (pp. 257-288). Toronto: University of Toronto Press.

Humphrey, N. (1992). *A history of the mind.* New York: HarperCollins.

Johnson, M. (1987). *The body in the mind: The bodily basis of meaning, imagination, and reason.* Chicago: University of Chicago Press.

Johnson, M., & Henley, T. B. (1992). Finding meaning in random analogies. *Metaphor and Symbolic Activity, 7*(2), 55-75.

Katz, A. N. (1992). Psychological studies in metaphor processing: Extension to the placement of terms in semantic space. *Poetics Today, 13*(4), 607-632.

Katz, A. N., Paivio, A., & Marschark, M. (1988). Norms for 204 literary and 260 nonliterary metaphors on 10 psychological dimensions. *Metaphor and Symbolic Activity, 3*(4), 191-214.

Krauss, D. A., & Fryrear, J. L. (Eds.). (1983). *Phototherapy in mental health.* Springfield, IL: Charles C Thomas.

Kuhn, T. S. (1993). Metaphors in science. In A. Ortony (Ed.), *Metaphor and thought* (2nd ed., pp. 533-542). Cambridge, UK: Cambridge University Press.

Lakoff, G. (1987). *Women, fire and dangerous things.* Chicago: University of Chicago Press.

Lakoff, G., & Johnson, M. (1980). *Metaphors we live by.* Chicago: University of Chicago Press.

Leary, D. E. (Ed.). (1990). *Metaphors in the history of psychology.* Cambridge, UK: Cambridge University Press.

Leyton, M. (1992). *Symmetry, causality and mind.* Cambridge: MIT Press.

MacCormac, E. (1985). *A cognitive theory of metaphor.* Cambridge, MA: Bradford.

Marks, L. E. (1978). *The unity of the senses: Interrelations among the modalities.* New York: Academic Press.

Marks, L. E., & Bornstein, M. H. (1987). Sensory similarities: Classes, characteristics, and cognitive consequences. In R. E. Haskell (Ed.), *Cognition and symbolic structures: The psychology of metaphoric transformation* (pp. 49-65). Norwood, NJ: Ablex.

Marks, L. E., Hammeal, R. J., & Bornstein, M. H. (1987). *Perceiving similarity and comprehending metaphor* (Society for Research in Child Development, Serial No. 215, 52, 1). Chicago: University of Chicago Press.

Marschark, M., Katz, A. N., & Paivio, A. (1983). Dimensions of metaphor. *Journal of Psycholinguistic Research, 12*(1), 17-40.

McAdams, S., & Bigard, E. (1993). Introduction to auditory cognition. In S. McAdams & E. Bigard (Eds.), *Thinking in sound: The cognitive psychology of human audition* (pp. 1-9). Oxford, UK: Clarendon.

Nonaka, I. (1991, November/December). Knowledge creating company. *Harvard Business Review*, 96-104.

Ortony, A. (1993). *Metaphor and thought* (2nd ed.). New York: Cambridge University Press.

Ortony, A., Shallert, D. L., Reynolds, R. E., & Antos, S. J. (1978). Interpreting metaphors and idioms: Some effects of context on comprehension. *Journal of Verbal Learning and Verbal Behavior, 17,* 415-477.

Paivio, A., & Clark, J. M. (1986). The role of topic and vehicle imagery in metaphor comprehension. *Communication and Cognition, 19*(2-4), 367-368.

Paivio, A., & Walsh, M. (1993). Psychological processes in metaphor comprehension and memory. In A. Ortony (Ed.), *Metaphor and thought* (2nd ed., pp. 307-328). Cambridge, UK: Cambridge University Press.

Parmegiani, M. (1987-1988). A critical review of traditional theories of metaphor and related linguistic issues. In M. Danesi (Ed.), *Metaphor, communication and cognition* (Monograph Series of the Toronto Semiotic Circle, No. 2, pp. 1-7). Toronto: Victoria College, University of Toronto.

Perkins, D. N. (1981). *The mind's best work.* Cambridge, MA: Harvard University Press.

Pinker, S. (1994). *The language instinct: How the mind creates language.* Cambridge: MIT Press.

Pollio, H. R. (1977). *Psychology and the poetics of growth: Figurative language in psychology, psychotherapy, and education.* Hillsdale, NJ: Lawrence Erlbaum.

Richards, I. A. (1936). *The philosophy of rhetoric.* Oxford, UK: Oxford University Press.

Roediger, H. L. (1980). Memory metaphors in cognitive psychology. *Memory and Cognition, 8*(2), 231-246.

Rumelhart, D. E. (1993). Some problems with the notion of literal meanings. In A. Ortony (Ed.), *Metaphor and thought* (2nd ed., pp. 71-82). New York: Cambridge University Press.

Schön, D. A. (1993). Generative metaphor: A perspective on problem setting in social policy. In A. Ortony (Ed.), *Metaphor and thought* (2nd ed., pp. 137-163). New York: Cambridge University Press.

Shames, M. L. (1991). On the transdisciplinary nature of the epistemology of discovery. *Zygon, 26*(3), 343-357.

Shell, J. E., Pollio, H. R., & Smith, M. K. (1987). Metaphor as "mitsein": Therapeutic possibilities in figurative speaking. In R. E. Haskell (Ed.), *Cognition and symbolic structures: The psychology of metaphoric transformation* (pp. 205-223). Norwood, NJ: Ablex.

Soyland, A. J. (1994). *Psychology as metaphor.* Thousand Oaks, CA: Sage.

Stoller, P. (1989). *The taste of ethnographic things: The senses in anthropology.* Philadelphia: University of Pennsylvania Press.

Sweetser, E. (1990). *From etymology to pragmatics: Metaphorical and cultural aspects of semantic structure.* Cambridge, UK: Cambridge University Press.

Tellis, G. J., & Crawford, C. M. (1981). An evolutionary approach theory. *Journal of Marketing, 45,* 125-132.

Trehub, S. E., & Trainor, L. J. (1993). Listening strategies in infancy: The roots of music and language development. In S. McAdams & E. Begand (Eds.), *Thinking in sound: The cognitive psychology of human audition* (pp. 231-277). Oxford, UK: Clarendon.

Weiser, J. (1988). See what I mean? Photography as nonverbal communication in cross-cultural psychology. In F. Poyatos (Ed.), *Cross-cultural perspectives in nonverbal communication* (pp. 245-290). San Francisco: Hogrefe.

Weiser, J. (1993). *Phototherapy techniques: Exploring the secrets of personal snapshots and family albums.* San Francisco: Jossey-Bass.

Winner, E. (1988). *The point of words: Children's understanding of metaphor and irony.* Cambridge, MA: Harvard University Press.

Wong, E. D. (1993). Understanding the generative capacity of analogies as a tool for explanation. *Journal of Research in Science Teaching, 30*(10), 1259-1272.

Zaltman, G., & Higie, R. H. (1993). *Seeing the voice of the customer: The Zaltman metaphor elicitation technique* (Working Paper No. 93-114). Cambridge, MA: Marketing Science Institute.

PART FIVE

Communicating
Through Advertisements
Consideration of the Craft

In this part, we travel to the world of advertising, a pilgrimmage as obligatory as the visit to a Oaxacan *zocalo*. Advertising has long been an anthropological fetish focus (Sherry, 1987a), a metatextual voodoo doll of sorts to be pierced with the ideological pins and needles of cultural critique. Reflexive criticism of advertising is an anthropological *rite de passage,* an often smug attempt to parse through customs in our own society en route to more exotic sites not yet enthralled by the false consciousness engendered by the aesthetics of mercantile realism. Despite being viewed most often as the cause of contemporary malaise and the driving force of an irrational economic system, advertising is regarded as an accurate reflection of our devaluation of marginalized others and "outsiders" (O'Barr, 1994). Even critics within the industry believe that anthropologists can use advertising as a Rosetta Stone for interpreting evolving lifeways (Garfield, 1994).

Thoughtful readings proceed apace (Danna, 1992; Goldman, 1992; Rutherford, 1994), providing sturdy etic frameworks that should now be made to bear the weight of emic empirics. If a precise definition of advertising has eluded anthropologists, the evocative power of the phenomenon has prompted them to probe a host of metaphors. Is advertising philosophy? Art? Religion? Ritual? Myth? Sport? Folk narrative? Delusional system? Culture-bound syndrome? All of these genres? Perhaps. Ironically, these rhetorical questions have yet to be translated into empirical ones beyond the merely textual. While we await a rigorous ethnographic investigation of advertising as experienced and employed by consumers, a writerly or producerly oriented discussion of advertising is begun in the following chapters by anthropologists inside the industry.

John McCreery uses personal reminiscence to marry classical anthropological theory to contemporary advertising practice, giving us a glimpse of a creative director's implicit theory of communication that Kover (in press) has explored among copywriters. Although McCreery's observations emanate from a Japanese context of the type described by Moeran (1995; Moeran & Skov, 1993), they resonate with accounts produced by Randazzo (1993) and Leiss, Kline, and Jhally (1986) of Western advertising practice. He plumbs the ritual substratum of one of our premier contemporary technologies of influence to uncover a preexisting ancient one. Like a palimpsest, magic underlies advertising. Magic is manipulative rather than supplicative and harnesses impersonal powers formulaically in the service of the practitioner's desires (Lessa & Vogt, 1972); action through a distance occurs via a secret sympathy among things (Frazer, 1963). The advertising magician conjures sympathetically, tuning our system of objects with a semiotic precision governed by belief more than empirical calibration. McCreery helps us become a sorcerer's apprentice for a brief moment by revealing the creative director's kinship with the more familiar ritual specialists of ethnographic record.

Rita Denny, in her cautionary tale of the semiotics of proactive marketing, demonstrates the perils that attend relationship management when stakeholders speak past each other. Using a discourse analytic perspective that is diffusing into consumer research (Parker, 1988; Scott, 1993; Sherry, 1987b; Stern, 1993), Denny shows how a particular polylogue is rife with slippage, as each stakeholder to the transaction is able to frame information in a way that mitigates personal responsibility and fosters blaming. This demonstration should cause us to rethink our notion of consumer miscomprehension and to search for a more appropriate trope to capture what actually happens during marketplace communications. In her quest to reveal and interpret the symbolic vocabularies used by consumers, Denny opens an intriguing window onto the areas of crisis management and contingency planning. She makes it apparent that marketers must also become astute political analysts and reaffirms the need for an ecolate view of marketing. Anthropologists are aware of Hardin's (1985) dictum that marketers cannot do merely one thing, that decisions have consequences which are both unpredictable and unintended. Unanticipated consequences can be detected prior to implementation through sensitive anthropological analysis.

Fine and Leopold (1993) correctly observe that an entire system of provision, consisting of a "comprehensive chain of activities between the two extremes of production and consumption" (p. 33)—that is, distribution finance, marketing, and functions other than mere advertising—guides the sociocultural construction of products and services. Thus magic may well be pervasive in marketing (Dégh, 1994). Recognizing the primary communicative function of marketing in all of its manifestations, we have need of an an-trope-ology (Fernandez, 1974) of transactions among stakeholders. This an-trope-ology might productively explore *all* marketing communication as a "political economy of sign value," an especially urgent undertaking in an era of "declining half-life" of sign value (Goldman & Papson, 1994, pp. 50, 51). The reciprocal impact of marketing and marketized communication on contemporary poetic discourse (Perloff, 1991) would also be a fit study for such an an-trope-ology.

 ## References

Danna, S. R. (Ed.). (1992). *Advertising and popular culture: Studies in variety and versatility.* Bowling Green, OH: Bowling Green University Press.

Dégh, L. (1994). *American folklore and the mass media.* Bloomington: Indiana University Press.

Fernandez, J. (1974). The mission of metaphor in expressive culture. *Current Anthropology, 15*(2), 119-145.

Fine, B., & Leopold, E. (1993). *The world of consumption.* New York: Routledge.

Frazer, J. (1963). *The golden bough.* New York: Macmillan.

Garfield, B. (1994, August 15). Please, please mind manners. *Advertising Age*, pp. 5, 22.

Goldman, R. (1992). *Reading ads socially.* New York: Routledge.

Goldman, R., & Papson, S. (1994). Advertising in the age of hypersignification. *Theory, Culture & Society, 11*(3), 23-53.

Hardin, G. (1985). *Filters against folly.* New York: Viking/Penguin.

Kover, A. (in press). Copywriters' implicit theories of communication: An exploration. *Journal of Consumer Research.*

Leiss, W., Kline, S., & Jhally, S. (1986). *Social communication and advertising: Persons, products, and images of well being.* New York: Methuen.

Lessa, W., & Vogt, E. (1972). Magic, witchcraft, and divination: Introduction. In W. Lessa & E. Vogt (Eds.), *Reader in comparative religion: An anthropological approach* (pp. 413-415). New York: Harper & Row.

Moeran, B. (1995). *A Japanese advertising agency.* Richmond, UK: Curzon Press.

Moeran, B., & Skov, L. (1993). Cinderella Christmas: Kitsch, consumerism and youth in Japan. In D. Miller (Ed.), *Unwrapping Christmas* (pp. 105-133). Oxford, UK: Clarendon.

O'Barr, W. (1994). *Culture and the ad: Exploring otherness in the world of advertising.* Boulder, CO: Westview.

Parker, R. (1988). Conversational interaction: Directions for qualitative marketing and consumer research. *Research in Consumer Behavior, 3,* 211-245.

Perloff, M. (1991). *Radical artifice: Writing poetry in the age of media.* Chicago: University of Chicago Press.

Randazzo, S. (1993). *Myth making on Madison avenue: How advertisers apply the power of myth and symbolism to create leadership brands.* Chicago: Probus.

Rutherford, P. (1994). *The new icons? The art of television advertising.* Toronto: University of Toronto Press.

Scott, L. (1993). Spectacular vernacular: Literacy and commercial culture in the postmodern age. *International Journal of Research in Marketing, 10*(3), 251-276.

Sherry, J. F., Jr. (1987a). Advertising as a cultural system. In J. Umiker-Sebeok (Ed.), *Marketing and semiotics: New directions in the study of signs for sale* (pp. 441-461). Berlin: Mouton de Gruyter.

Sherry, J. F., Jr. (1987b). Market pitching and the ethnography of speaking. In M. Houston (Ed.), *Advances in consumer research* (pp. 543-547). Provo, UT: Association for Consumer Research.

Stern, B. (1993). Feminist literary criticism and the deconstruction of ads: A postmodern view of advertising and consumer response. *Journal of Consumer Research, 19*(1), 556-566.

8

Malinowski, Magic, and Advertising

On Choosing Metaphors

John McCreery

To Malinowski (1935/1965a), advertising was "the richest field of modern verbal magic" (p. 237). He may have meant this statement literally; today we read it as metaphor. We are, as James Fernandez (1991) puts it, at a "metaphorical moment" (p. 1) in the history of anthropology and the other human sciences, having learned that what we had taken to be straightforward descriptions of ethnographic realities are, in fact, metaphoric interpretations that often conceal as much as they reveal (Clifford & Marcus, 1986; Geertz, 1988; Sperber, 1989). Deconstructionist trends in recent critical theorizing have made us deeply aware of how metaphor (and other tropes) permeate even the strictest scientific discourse, which raises the problem behind the problem I wish to discuss here. If our theories are metaphors and are thus not literally true or false, how can we choose between them?

Malinowski equates advertising with magic. Reading metaphorically, we recognize that his statement may not be literally true. If literal truth is not the issue, why choose to link advertising with magic? Why not with art? or politics? or, especially, with religion? Are there reasons for choosing one over another? Or is choosing a trope just a matter of whim? Can we make an informed decision? Or do we pick at random, like a shopper confronted with a shelf of similar products and no good reason to prefer any one of them? (The image is John O'Shaugnessy's, 1987, in *Why People Buy*.)

To an anthropologist who has worked in advertising in Japan for more than 10 years, these questions are poignant. As a copywriter and creative director at Hakuhodo Incorporated,[1] I am constantly looking for verbal and visual metaphors that will add meaning to the messages my clients wish to communicate. I have heard it said that in other parts of the world an agency may offer its client a single proposal. In Japan, the rule is three or four. (Two may be sufficient if the job is small and the agency-client relationship a long and happy one. If the job is big or a pitch for new business, or the agency-client relationship has soured, five or six or more are not unusual.) The inevitable question is which is better? Which will the agency recommend? Shrewd presenters offer good strategic reasons for each proposal and then ask their clients which reasons seem most important to them. Clumsy presenters offer no reasons, leave the choice to clients' impressions, and—all too frequently—wind up with all their proposals rejected. To someone who has been involved in both types of presentations with major pieces of business at stake, it is all too clearly a matter of some urgency what will count as a good strategic reason. Truth alone is never enough.

Thus it is that when I consider Malinowski's equation of advertising and magic, I find myself raising the same issues I would in assessing an ad proposal: What is he saying? Why do I find it attractive? What else could we say? How else could we say it? Truth remains a factor; we can't say anything blatantly false. But what I really want to know is, given some alternatives, which is the "bigger" idea? Which is "closer to the heart of the matter"? Which is "more campaignable"? The bigger idea will be the one that encompasses more of what we know about the business. The idea that is closer to the heart of the matter will capture more of how the business feels. The more campaignable idea will suggest more lines of development; that means more interesting problems to research and, for the anthropologist, perhaps more salable products in the intellectual marketplace.[2] What, then, of the metaphorical claim that advertising is magic?

In this chapter, I first examine Malinowski's theory of magic and why, as an advertising man, I find it attractive. I then describe an important alternative: the proposal revived by John Sherry that advertising resembles religion. Next, I introduce the key terms in which I compare two metaphors: ritual (where advertising, religion, and magic may seem to converge) and knowledge and property (where their differences are, I will argue, quite marked). I follow this with three brief case studies. Two are examples of magic: magic as practiced in the Trobriand islands, as described by Malinowski and reanalyzed by Annette Weiner (1984), and magic as practiced by the Taoist healers with whom I have worked in Taiwan. The third case is a work of fiction: *Murder Must Advertise* by Dorothy Sayers (1967). Malinowski recommends it as an accurate picture of advertising, as practiced, that is, in Britain in the early part of this century. In all three cases, I use my own agency experience working in Japan in the 1980s as a counterpoint to the voices we hear. My own voice is best considered that of a thoughtful informant who speaks from the catch-as-catch-can experience provided by his job. Reader be warned: It does not reflect systematic research. In my concluding remarks, I explain why, given a choice of metaphors, advertising as magic or religion, it looks like magic to me and why the common core of both metaphors, the equation of ads with rituals, needs reexamination.

Malinowski on Magic

In *Coral Gardens and Their Magic*, Malinowski (1935/1965a) develops a theory of magic, which is part of a larger theory of language. As humans we are born helpless. Our cries bring us the food and nurture without which we could not survive. Growing up, we learn to shape our cries, to speak in ways appropriate to the situations in which we find ourselves and the others to whom we speak. We learn to communicate information and we also learn to communicate feelings. We communicate information pragmatically, speaking clearly and to the point about things over which we have control. We communicate feelings magically, by speaking in ways that may make no pragmatic sense but do express emotions.

The pragmatic and the magical permeate human speech, but their ratio varies. Malinowski states,

> Having started by using language in a manner which is both magical and pragmatic, and passed gradually through stages in which the magical and pragmatic aspects intermingle and oscillate, the individual will find within his culture certain crystallised, traditionally standardised types of speech, with the language of technology and science at one end, and the language of sacrament, prayer, magical formula, advertisement and political oratory at the other. (p. 236)

Advertisements are ranked with sacrament, prayer, political oratory, and magic proper as types of speech in which the magical element predominates. Like religion, politics, and magic, advertisements speak to a world in which human hopes outrun the limits of human control.

To many anthropologists, Malinowski's theory may seem too simple, too crude to be taken seriously. To someone who makes advertising, it speaks to an everyday problem. We sell ideas to clients whose decisions we cannot control. They in turn must sell their products to consumers who spend their money as they please. All the efforts of marketing science do not determine the outcome. In an effort to shape purchase decisions, we generate images, chant incantations, and tell each other stories that we hope will appeal to clients' and ultimately consumers' emotions. In talking about their brands, at least one major international corporation makes it a matter of dogma: A brand is conceived as a triangle, an image uniting functional benefits, on the one hand, with emotional benefits, on the other. If I read Malinowski and think of my three criteria, only one thing is sure. His metaphor goes to the heart of the matter. It feels right. Is it big enough? Or campaignable enough? That remains to be seen. We must first consider an important alternative.

Is Advertising Religion?

In "Advertising as a Cultural System," John Sherry (1987) revives the proposition that, conceived as a cultural system, advertising resembles religion.[3] He notes that others may not agree (see, e.g., Schudson, 1993, pp. 10-11), but he still regards the metaphor as a useful and productive one. His argument can be summarized as follows:

- Advertising is one of the key components in marketing, and marketing itself is among the most potent agents of cultural change and cultural stability at work in the contemporary world (Sherry, 1987, p. 442).
- Like religion as conceived by Clifford Geertz (1973), advertising is a system of symbols whose meanings include both models of and models for human behavior. Its practitioners hope to induce long-lasting moods and dispositions in consumers who read ads.
- Ads themselves are analogous to rituals. Like rituals, ads appeal to fundamental motives and values and use dramatic and aesthetic devices to heighten the meanings their symbols convey.
- So far as these two analogies hold, the products of anthropological research on religion and ritual symbolism have a special value in the intellectual marketplace, with direct economic consequences as well as theoretical interest.

This metaphor is a big idea. It claims for advertising a major and paradoxical role like that which is frequently assigned to religion in anthropological studies: Like religion, advertising is seen as both a central support for social order and an engine of social change. Given the assumption (which may be false; see Douglas, 1973, pp. 19-39) that religion is highly visible and pervasive in the tribal and traditional cultures that anthropologists usually study, the high visibility and saturation of advertising in contemporary culture lend credence to the claim.

As Sherry's own work demonstrates, this metaphor is clearly campaignable. Religion is a subject much studied by anthropologists, and given the basic analogical assumption that

advertising: contemporary culture = religion: tribe and tradition

the researcher in search of ideas has a vast literature to mine. What, then, could be better? To this advertising practitioner, this metaphor's logic seems clear. Still, somehow, it misses the heart of the matter.

Once again, I recall a familiar situation in agency life. On the table are several proposals for ads. Some are clearly on strategy; they also say precisely what the client wants to hear. They're not bad, but . . . Look at this one! It feels so right. What's frustrating is that we can't yet say exactly why. We need a fresh perspective.

Ritual, Knowledge, and Property

Advertising is magic. Advertising is religion. The common ground for both these metaphors is the analogical proposition that ads resemble rituals. Like rituals, ads are intended to interrupt the ongoing flow of everyday life and practical, technology-governed activity. Both use dramatic and aesthetic effects to underline their messages and associate them with strong emotion. Both appeal to received ideas and established social categories and principles. All these similarities apply as much to magic as religion. Why, then, do these metaphors feel so different?

Describing what first comes to mind when advertising is likened to magic, Tokyo copywriter Stephen Benfey puts it this way (personal communication): It is, he says, "easy to think of a slogan as a charm, a trademark as an amulet, a jingle as a spell." Try substituting "prayer" for "charm," the "sign of the Cross" for "amulet," and "hymn" for "spell." The analogies falter. Why should this be?

Reading Malinowski suggests several answers. In all cultures, he says, we find the distinction between the profane (the realm of rational, empirical knowledge) and the sacred (the realm in which action is governed by emotion shaped by tradition). In the latter, we find two kinds of ritual. One, religion, is seen as obligatory and performed as an end in itself; the other, magic, is a practical art directed to ends outside itself. To these basic distinctions, he adds another derived from Durkheim's claim that magic involves the private use of public symbols, where the latter are collective representations (Malinowski, 1954, pp. 88-89). He also observes that magic is typically the prerogative of specialists. In contrast, religion is something in which, at least in principle, all of a community's members are involved. On these grounds alone, advertising, which is practical, private, and practiced by specialists, already seems more like magic as Malinowski conceives it. Still, even though the feeling is right, other issues remain. Is magic big enough, or campaignable enough, to be a metaphor worth pursuing?

Consider, again, Benfey's remark that he finds it easy to think of "a slogan as a charm, a trademark as an amulet, a jingle as a spell." To look in this direction is to focus our attention on what, adapting a term from S. J. Tambiah (1968), we might call the "inner frame" of symbolic action: the ways in which word, image, and object work together to generate rhetorical force.[4] In these respects, advertising, religion, and magic all look very similar. Their differences emerge when we look instead at the "outer frame," that is, the sociocultural contexts within which advertisments are made and religious and magical rites performed. Here, again, we have Malinowski to thank for pointing us toward the key issues: their claims to represent knowledge and, as Simon Harrison (1992) also suggests, their status as intellectual property.

⫶ Classic Magic, The Trobriand Case

In describing Trobriand garden magic, Malinowski presents a world of stunning simplicity. Spells belong to those whose ancestors owned them. So firmly is ownership of garden magic respected that its status as the garden magician's property is never contested. To those of us whose sense of magic is shaped by Tolkien, The Arabian Nights, the Salem witchcraft trials, and Nintendo fantasy games, the implication is stunning. Magic is not a secret. It is something everyone knows; "there is no secrecy about it" (Malinowski, 1935/1965b, p. 12).

We must remember, however, that Malinowski's key informants were, like Bagido'u, "the proudest garden magician of the island," the self-proclaimed and widely acknowledged ruling elite of the Trobriands. The simplicity of the statements that Malinowski (1935/1965b) recorded is ideology's mark. In other fields of magic and other moments of Trobriand history, things were not so simple.

Consider, for example, love magic, a "complex and somewhat chaotic subject," where a simple description "suggests more precision and system than actually exists" (p. 314). Here, Malinowski reports, several competing systems were jumbled together and only a few Trobrianders had full sets of spells belonging to the same system. Then he makes a truly startling claim.

He remarks that for every spell he wrote down in his fieldnotes he had to reject several others as "spurious, fragmentary or not understood by the natives" (p. 314). "No native in the Trobriands," he writes,

> would be able to judge magical texts as well as myself. For no human memory is a match for a written comparative collection. Towards the end of my field-work, I found little difficulty in deciding whether a spell recited to me was genuine or corrupt; and, in the latter case, whether it was deliberate deception, self-deception, or deception on the part of my inform-ant's predecessor, or just lack of memory. (p. 314)

What, then, was a Trobriander to do, if all that he or she knew was "spurious, fragmentary, or not understood"? The answer that Malinowski provides is faith supported by experience (love magic, it seems, will frequently seem successful) and, we should note, by experiment. He describes a youth, who knowing only a spell or two, and sometimes only a fragment of each, will still believe in their virtue. And, says Malinowski, "very often experience strengthens his belief" (p. 314). If he tries them with one type of leaves and fails, he will try them again with other herbs until he achieves success.

In Malinowski's Trobriands, then, there were, at least, these two poles: *garden magic*, public knowledge, the undisputed property of those who claimed to be masters of the land, and *love magic*, private and only partially known, fragments jumbled together from several competing systems and empirically tested for effectiveness.

Malinowski's reports are based on fieldwork conducted from 1915 to 1918. It was 1971 and 1972, over 50 years later, when Annette Weiner did her research. Despite a half-century of time and the impact of World War II, Weiner (1976) found the Trobriands to be much the same place that Malinowski had studied. "Many superficial elements have changed," she writes, "but the dynamics of social interaction and the ways people relate to, attract, and use each other still seem fundamentally grounded in the traditional cultural system" (p. 25). There were, however, differences, both in the way research was conducted and in Trobriand society itself.

Unlike Malinowski, Weiner lived in a village with no high-ranked man in residence: a village composed of six hamlets, each with its own "manager." None of the managers was of high rank, and none had been able to establish himself as leader of the whole village (p. xvii). During the second phase of her fieldwork, in 1972, she had access to men of high rank, Vanoi and his heir-apparent Waibadi, "the most powerful and influential men in Kiriwina" (p. xvii). But during her stay, their power was, she says, "seriously contested."

It was, perhaps, a visible sign of this changed political situation that, while gardens continued to look much as they had in Malinowski's photographs and individual garden magic was still highly valued, the long cycle of public magic that Malinowski studied had not been performed for over a decade (p. 30). In the Trobriands that Weiner studied, magic is deeply involved in exchange and thus, of course, politics.

According to Malinowski, garden magic belongs to the *dala*, the matrilineal subclan whose ancestors already owned it when they took possession of the subclan's land. In contrast, Weiner (1976) notes an important distinction. *Dala* "blood" is eternally pure and determined absolutely at birth. The property associated with *dala*, which includes magic together with land, body decorations, and taboos, cannot remain pure. "Property circulates, it is loaned to others, it is stolen, it becomes lost forever. In other circumstances, property can also increase" (p. 39).

No automatic rule of inheritance fixes the teaching of magic. Like other valuables, a man's magic is doled out to other men who make the gardens that provide the yams that fuel the exchanges on which political power depends. (Aristocratic rank is a necessary but not sufficient condition for holding real power.) The relation of magic to politics is vividly dramatized when a man dies. His death becomes the occasion for a game in which other men display their knowledge of magic spells, and he who knows the most wins (p. 70). This political "game" demonstrates clearly that detailed knowledge of magic is not uniformly distributed. With ownership the point of the contest, secrecy comes into play. To demonstrate the range of the magic a man controls, he will always include the name of the previous owner when chanting a spell. To protect his knowledge, he will, however, chant only a portion of the spell (p. 71).

We should note, too, a historical difference between Malinowski's and Weiner's accounts. Malinowski's notebook made him, the anthropologist, the authority on which Trobriand spells were accurate. In 1972, Trobrianders had notebooks, too. On the night of the game Weiner (1976) describes, the winner was Bunemiga whose "magic was written in a thick notebook that his son read to him for part of the time he chanted" (p. 72). For Bunemiga, however, his notebook was, it seems, simply an aid to memory. It enabled him to shout more spells than anyone else and thus emerge the winner of the game. There may be Trobriand scholars who examine such texts with a critical hermeneutical eye. If so, they have gone unrecorded.[5]

In summarizing her own views of Trobriand magic, Weiner attributes to Malinowski the proposition that magic substitutes for technology and that primitive man turns to magic to deal with a hostile physical environment.

She rejects this view, arguing that to a Trobriander the problem is how to control other people. The physical environment is only dangerous when someone else's magic has made it so. Where, for example, Malinowski argues that sea fishing requires magic but lagoon fishing does not, Weiner replies that magic is also used when fishing in the lagoon: when, that is, the catch is to be used in exchange (p. 217). Her principle applies to gardens, too. Not all gardens are treated with magic. Only when the harvest is used in exchange is magic performed (p. 217).

As Weiner sees it, both magic and exchange are primarily means of controlling those others on whom social success depends. Magic, however, is seen as inherently powerful in a way which exchange is not. Trobrianders conceive each individual as autonomous, with a self that constitutes a private, personal space. Unlike the objects used in exchange that must stop at self's borders and wait to be accepted, magic is seen as penetrating that space directly:

> The words of magic spells are the fantasies of private thought and, when spoken, these words are the projection of power. The practice of magic extends the strength of one's creative and manipulative intent to control and publicly displays one's autonomy. (p. 214)

Substituting "ads" for "words" and "products" for "objects," it is hard to imagine a finer description of advertising's intent. In a world where advertisers cannot be content to mutely offer their products, ads strive to seize consumers' attention, break through their resistance, and make the product irresistible. Magic, indeed.

In fairness to Malinowski, we should note that what Weiner attacks is a view of magic formulated in Malinowski's (1931) article "Culture," which appeared in the *Encyclopedia of Social Science,* in which we find a picture of primitive desperation in the face of an uncontrollable natural world. In *Coral Gardens and Their Magic,* we find instead a world in which economic surplus is expended on nonutilitarian goals. Here we find that Trobrianders work hard to make their gardens beautiful. They put in far more effort than is necessary for the growth of what they plant. Their conscientiousness, says Malinowski, is especially evident in magic, where every detail is treated carefully.

To someone who works in advertising, where the way an ad is finished may be more than half the battle in winning client and consumer approval, this all sounds very familiar. To achieve aesthetic effects, those who create advertising often work far harder than would seem necessary if the goal were simply to communicate a proposition. Camera angles and lighting in photos, touch and tone in illustrations, the size and placement of type in layouts, the choice of words in copy, and music in the case of television—all are checked and checked again. Why do people in advertising put in all that extra effort?

First, of course, the bottom line: Like Trobriand gardeners, they are putting food on their tables, and clients who spend great sums of money don't like slipshod work. Besides cash in hand, there are other rewards: dancing and feasting, pleasant overseas expeditions, renown, and the satisfaction of vanity—all are listed by Malinowski as goals the Trobriander seeks and all are among the perks of successful agency careers. There is also the intrinsic craftsmanlike pleasure of doing a good job (that feeling of accomplishment my Japanese colleagues call *shokuninkatagi*). And we mustn't forget sheer love of the game.

There is, writes Malinowski (1932/1968), "a desire in every one of us to escape from routine and certainty" (p. 290). We may (as so much of anthropological theory suggests) value order in our lives, but even the most skeptical may rebel against blind causality and prefer the gifts of chance good fortune. If, as Malinowski notes, "love, gambling and magic have a good deal in common" (p. 290), so does business in a market economy and, most especially, advertising.

Would-Be Professionals: Taoist Magicians

When reading about Trobriander magicians, this advertising practitioner feels at home. The costumes that Trobrianders wear and the objects they exchange may not be what I'm used to, but in their zest for competition and the tensions, fears, and ambitions that drive them, they are clearly my kind of people. If all I knew were Taoist philosophy, Taoists might seem a world apart.

John Lagerwey (1987) describes the ideal Taoist as follows:

> The Real Man (*chen-jen*) is the man of pure potency; he "accomplishes without having to act" (*Lao-tzu* 47).
>
> . . . He has *realized* man's *potential* to be, of all beings, the most potent and so naturally all the less potent beings of the body of the universe—the Count of the Wind, the Master of the Rain—are at his beck and call. Whenever he solicits, Nature responds. This Real Man, described already in the third century b.c. text of the *Chuang-tzu*, is the prototype of the modern Taoist priest. (pp. 6-7)

Like Bagidou's account of Trobriand garden magic, this, too, is ideology. To which we must add that, given the scope of China's history, the reality is far more complex.

Malinowski was the first anthropologist to record Trobriand magic in writing. The *Tao-te ching*, the earliest text in the Taoist Canon, may date to as early as the 7th century B.C. Of the Trobriand magician Bunemiga, Weiner (1976) could still write that "all his magic was written in a thick notebook" (p. 72). The Taoist Canon, the *Tao-tsang*, is not a book but a library of several thousand pages in its latest edition. The Harvard-Yenching catalog lists 1,466 separate titles (Strickmann, 1981, p. 6). As Strickmann notes, the name "Canon" may be misleading. The *Tao-tsang* contains a vast and motley collection of texts whose value to the historian lies precisely in the fact that, far from defining an orthodox system, they represent the accretion of numerous sources over time. Their heterogeneity is far from surprising, given their authors' uncertain status.

In *Le corps taoïste*, Schipper (1982) notes that Taoism is notoriously hard to define. Taoists are not a congregation. With no fixed dogma or liturgy and no interest in proselytizing, they are neither church nor sect. They are, instead, a group of "local sages," who, initiated into mysteries, put themselves at the service of communities for whom they perform ritual services. Substituting "creative wizards" for "sages," "clients" for "communities," and "the making of ads" for "ritual services," it sounds like advertising to me. At least one thing is very sure. Like people involved in advertising, Taoists present themselves as professionals. Others scoff at their claims.

In 1970, while doing my first fieldwork in Taiwan,[6] I was introduced to Tio Sin-se[*], a man then in his 50s who identified himself as a "red-head Taoist master" (*hung-t'ou tao-shih*; in Taiwanese, *ang-thau to'-su*). On the walls of his storefront temple, he proudly displayed a portrait of the 63rd Heavenly Master (*T'ian-shih*; Taiwanese *Thian-su*), the lineal descendant of Chang Tao-ling, the founder of the Taoist religion, and a meter-tall paper charm (*fu*; Taiwanese *hu-a*) in the Heavenly Master's hand. Photographs showed Tio Sin-se[*] dressed in Taoist priestly robes, and a framed diploma showed that he was certified by the National Taoist Association (*Chung-hua min-quo tao-chiao hui*) as a Great Magician (*ta fa-shih*; Taiwanese *tai hoat-su*).

Tio Sin-se[*] was a man of extraordinary empathy, with a truly exceptional willingness to let other people tell their stories, not leaping in with "helpful" or critical remarks. He was also a craftsman who paid close attention to fine detail in making his rituals beautiful. As someone involved in advertising, I now admire these traits more than ever. I thought of him then as a healer.

He was also a truly great salesman and producer. These, however, were personal traits. They were by no means characteristic of other Taoists I later encountered. They did not change the social fact. Like other Taoists, Tio Sin-se* claimed professional status. His claim was clear. His status was not.

Tio Sin-se* was one of several brothers who were active in wholesale vegetable marketing in Taichung, the nearest large city. He had come to the town where I met him to help set up the local wholesale vegetable market and had founded his temple only after losing a battle for control of the market. Detractors claimed that he'd bought the credentials he so proudly displayed. This, I learned, was not unusual.

At the 1971 conference whose papers were published as *Religion and Ritual in Chinese Society* (Wolf, 1974), participants included both Kristopher Schipper, who worked in southern Taiwan, and Michael Saso, who worked in northern Taiwan. Both asserted the orthodoxy of the masters with whom they studied and were eager to differentiate the "orthodox" Taoist priest (*tao-shih*; Taiwanese *to'-su*) from the "heterodox" magicians (*fa-shih*; Taiwanese *hoat-su*) with whom they overlap. To Wolf (1974), it came as a revelation that one school's magic was seen as "mortally opposed" to that of another, leading not only to name-calling but to great physical battles for control of temples and cities and to "magical jousts fought with conjurations, mudras and spirits" (p. 17).

In working with Taoists and other ritual specialists in Taiwan, I noticed how rarely they had a good word to say about each other. In public encounters, they would treat each other with respect. In private, however, they freely accused each other of ignorance ("doesn't know much"), moral turpitude (sexual scandals and "only in it for the money"), and outright evil (heterodox practice and sorcery). With these accusations they contributed to a climate of opinion in which all claims to ritual knowledge and magical powers are treated with skepticism and yet, paradoxically, cults of every shape and kind flourish. It is, after all, quite possible to believe that most who make such claims are charlatans and still believe that you know someone who really knows magical secrets and really possesses magical powers. The problem, of course, is to find them. Or seen from the marketing side of the issue, how to support a magician's claim to be the real thing.

In his conference paper, Schipper (1982) argued that whereas priestly rituals include the use of written prayers, the magician depends on oral spells alone. Only the priest (*to'-su*) is entitled to perform the great communal rites of renewal called *chiao* (Taiwanese *chio*), and only the head priest (*tao-chang*; Taiwanese *to'-tiu**) is formally ordained in the "Orthodox Church of the Heavenly Master" and receives the registers (*lu*; Taiwanese *liok*) that list the spirits required to obey his commands (p. 311). In everyday life, however, priest and magician are hard to distinguish. Like the magician, the priest also acts as an exorcist and healer. Both perform the same rituals, "composed of the same, vernacular, incantations." The priest then wears the red turban or headscarf, which identifies the "red head" magician (p. 310).

When I posed this question to Tio Sin-se*, his reply was a model of candor. A Taoist, he said, can support his claims in one of two ways. He can point to a lineage that goes back to the master who first received the special knowledge he claims to possess. Alternatively, he can say that he himself has received a new revelation from a god. The latter claim will be accepted only if he is, in fact, *ling* (Taiwanese *leng*): able to demonstrate magical powers.[7] In my notes to myself, I find the words "Nothing succeeds like apparent success." In retrospect, the adman says, "I must agree."

In 1976-1977, I worked with one of Tio Sin-se*'s disciples, a man to whom I have given the pseudonym Ong. Ong grew up in the town where Tio Sin-se*'s storefront temple was located. As a young man he earned a reputation as a rascal and wastrel. He had been possessed by a god but declined to become a spirit medium, preferring the role of magician. He had met Tio Sin-se* and become his disciple. When I met him, he had his own storefront temple in a suburb of Taipei. He, too, had a certificate from the National Taoist Association in which he was labeled a Great Magician. He, too, had his detractors.

While watching Ong perform rituals that I, too, had learned from Tio Sin-se*, I made what seemed at the time a shocking discovery. By definition, I believed, rituals repeat set forms. While similar in name and overall pattern, Ong's rites were visibly different in many details from those which I had been taught. How could this be?

When I challenged Ong and later pursued the same issue with other ritual specialists, the explanation was clear. All told me that they had worked with several masters and taken from them what seemed to have spiritual power. To see the force of this explanation, it helps to know that masters and disciples are competitors in a market for ritual services. Thus, although having disciples is a mark of success and to keep disciples a master must gradually reveal his secrets, no master will ever reveal all that he knows. Intelligent disciples supplement what they learn from one master by learning what others do. Then, like the young Trobriander who knows only a fragment of love magic, they try things out and see what seems to work for them. The result is an ongoing re-creation of tradition in which basic patterns persist and individual elements are constantly being recombined in what may be novel ways (McCreery, 1976).

From Magic to Advertising

When I look at Taoist magic from an adman's point of view, I note many similarities with the world in which I work. Like Taoist magicians, advertising and marketing people also want to be seen as professionals. We too have our certificates and associations but lack the legal authority granted, for example, to priests, lawyers, and doctors. We too occupy an ill-defined liminal state between laypersons and professionals whose status is legally defined. And, of course, we have our detractors. Competition and the tensions it generates are facts of life in what we call the "advertising game." Surrounded by skeptics and critics, we support their skepticism through factionalism and backbiting. Like Taoists and Trobrianders both, we too assemble our skills by observation, trial and error, recreating traditions as we go along. How, then, are we different?

To those who would understand the world of advertising, Malinowski recommends a classic English mystery, *Murder Must Advertise* by Dorothy Sayers (1967). Consider, for example, the following discussion of what makes a good ad:

> "It will come," said Mr. Hankin. . . . "Let me see what you are doing. You are starting with the headlines? Quite right. The headline is more than half the battle. IF YOU WERE A COW—no,no, I'm afraid we mustn't call the customer a cow. Besides we had practically the same headline in—let me see—about 1923, I think. Mr. Wardle put it out, you'll find it in the last guard-book but three. It went 'IF YOU KEPT A COW IN THE KITCHEN you could get no better bread-spread than G.F. Margarine'—and so on. That was a good one. Caught the eye, made a good picture, and told the whole story in a sentence." (Sayers, 1967, p. 18)

Note, in particular, the objection raised "because we had practically the same headline in—let me see—about 1923." For the Trobriander, magic is rooted in the ground from which the ancestors emerged; innovation is unperceived or ignored. For the Taoist magician, too, magic is rooted in the nature of things; revelation may legitimate innovation, but it does so without disturbing this basic assumption. In both cases, what is inconceivable is magic being rejected because it resembles an earlier model.

In advertising, what we sell is "creativity." Our work may, in fact, be derivative. It is always presented as something new. In brainstorming sessions in Japan, the only comment more damning than *mo furui* ("already old") is pointing out that certain words or images have already been used either for the product in question or for one of its competitors. Once having appeared in print or on TV, both words and images must wait for several years before being seen as fresh again. Even then, some twist is needed to avoid the appearance of imitation.

Both Trobriander and Taoist magicians are forced by the nature of their training to reconstruct fragmented traditions. Admen, too, are bricoleurs. Magicians, however, work in worlds where precedent rules. New magic cannot be very different from what has come before. In the advertising business, creativity warrants destruction. In the adman's constant search for new material, the past is looted but always transformed. One result is the shape of what we think we've learned. Our knowledge is more a heap of common sense than a carefully constructed theory (Schudson, 1993). Consider, for example, the following passage:

> Mr. Bredon had been a week with Pym's Publicity, and had learnt a number of things. He learned the average number of words that can be crammed into four inches of copy; that Mr. Armstrong's fancy could be caught by an elaborately drawn lay-out, whereas Mr. Hankin looked on art-work as waste of a copy-writer's time; that the word "pure" was dangerous, because if lightly used, it laid the client open to prosecution by the Government inspectors, whereas the words "highest quality," "finest ingredients," "packed under the best conditions" had no legal meaning, and were therefore safe; that the expression "giving work to umpteen thousand British employees in our model works at so-and-so" was not by any means the same thing as "British made through-out"; that the north of England liked its butter and margarine salted, whereas the south preferred it fresh; that the Morning Star would not accept any advertisements containing the word "cure," though there was no objection to such expressions as "relieve" or "ameliorate," and that, further, any commodity that professed to "cure" anything might find itself compelled to register as a patent medicine and use an expensive stamp; that the most convincing copy was always written with the tongue in the cheek, a genuine conviction of the commodity's worth producing—for some reason—poverty and flatness of style; that if, by the most far-fetched stretch of ingenuity, an indecent meaning could be read into a headline, that was the meaning that the great British Public would infallibly read into it; . . . that the great aim and object of the studio artist was to crowd the copy out of the advertisement and that, conversely, the copy-writer was a designing villain whose ambition was to cram the space with verbiage and leave no room for the sketch; that the lay-out man, a meek ass between two burdens, spent a miserable life trying to reconcile these opposing parties; and farther, that all departments alike united in hatred of the client, who persisted in spoiling good lay-outs by cluttering them up with coupons, free-gift offers, lists of local agents and realistic portraits of hideous and uninteresting cartons, to the detriment of his own

interests and the annoyance of everybody concerned. (Schudson, 1993, pp. 33-34)

What I emphasize here is the form of this list and the items that compose it: a motley collection of rules of thumb without the coherence of science or dogma. There may be an underlying system. If so, it is buried in something with a family resemblance to Borges' Chinese encyclopedia, where animals are classified as belonging to the Emperor, embalmed, tame, sucking pigs, stray dogs, and so on (Foucault, 1970, p. xv). Far from being a theory, it is, at best, the form of knowledge that Pierre Bourdieu (1990) calls a *habitus*.

What, then, of property? and secrecy? Creators retain a proprietary interest in what they have made, and making an ad gives its creators an unimpeachable claim. In agency life, no sin is more grievous than stealing ideas or neglecting to acknowledge the source of a borrowed idea. Here again, I quote a passage that beautifully illustrates a typical situation:

> "Tell me, timeless houri," demanded Mr. Bredon, "what was wrong with my lamented predecessor? Why did Miss Meteyard hate him and why does Ingleby praise him with faint damns?"
> This was no problem to Miss Parton.
> "Why, because he didn't play fair. He was always snooping round other people's rooms, picking up their ideas and showing them up as his own. And if anybody gave him a headline and Mr. Armstrong or Mr. Hankin liked it, he never said whose it was." (Schudson, 1993, p. 39)

In my office at Hakuhodo, I too have seen a writer make himself despised by appearing to be a snoop. I observe every day that because our office follows the typical Japanese pattern, with coworkers sitting side by side, only those on official business will approach desks that are not their own. Being asked over the phone to check for messages is one excuse. Another is looking for a document involved in a shared project. To look for anything else or to spend more time than necessary arouses suspicion.

From a broader perspective, who owns an ad is a complex issue. In submissions to shows and contests, copywriters and art directors own the right to have their names associated with the ads they create. The agencies that produce ads include them in their own promotional material. Clients pay for creation, production, and publication of ads, but photographers, illustrators, and models restrict the use of their work to specified media, times, and places. If an image appears elsewhere, they may claim additional compensation. There are more than enough tangles to keep agency legal departments busy.

As regards secrecy, ads follow a curious cycle. While being planned they are kept secret, lest ideas be stolen and used before they are scheduled to appear. Once published or shown on TV, they enter the public domain, subject, of course, to the ownership claims sketched above. Then, however, they become, as it were, negative models that reduce the value of similar ads that appear later. There is no room in advertising for ancient wisdom's loss or recovery, no place for the hermeneutic motives that drove both Malinowski and the Taoist Canon's compilers as they gathered and arranged their texts. There is, at most, nostalgia. Coming full circle again, history is merely historical, something to be either exploited or simply avoided in the endless search for something new.

Where Do We Go From Here?

James Carrier, who was kind enough to read an earlier version of this chapter, asked if it really amounted to more than an exercise in typology (an old-fashioned sort of thing to do). The answer is "No."

Typologies fix positions in an intellectual space that is organized hierarchically. They are, I suggest, most useful when our thought is precise enough for hypothesis testing and we need clear categories to organize our statistics. Both as an anthropologist and as someone working in advertising, I rarely find myself in this particular situation. I am, instead, involved in discussions where, far from fixing positions in a hierarchically organized space, metaphors are being used to push them around (Fernandez, 1986). The issue that constantly comes up is "Where should we go from here?"

Here, we began with two metaphors: One says that advertising is magic; the other says that advertising is religion. Neither is literally true. Both, however, are true enough to be interesting. Then we raise the adman's questions: Which is the bigger idea? Which is closer to the heart of the matter? Which is more campaignable? The case for religion is strong. It's a big idea and campaignable. Still, however, magic feels closer to the heart of the matter. Now we can say more clearly why.

In the cases examined here, magic shares with advertising the tensions of a highly competitive business, the rewards of success, the fear of defeat, the quiet pleasures of craftsmanship, and the sheer love of the game. Ads do, indeed, articulate cultural categories and principles (McCracken, 1990). They rarely, if ever, form the basis for solidarity groups; they are public but not collective acts (Schudson, 1993, pp. 159-160). Ads speak for products, companies, or candidates, more rarely on behalf of the public good. They are not produced as ends in themselves. Where religion suggests self-sacrifice and the muting of private wants and desires in favor of ultimate values, magic is selfish, competitive, contested. So is advertising. If we had to choose religion or magic, it feels like magic to me.

Still, one nagging issue remains. Comparing these two metaphors, we find in them a common core. Like religion, magic is rooted in ritual, and in their use of symbols, ads and rituals seem alike. But here, especially, caution is needed. For where rituals are said to repeat traditional patterns and are validated by faithfulness to their prototypes, ads are supposed to be new creations. In the realm of ritual, innovations are either ignored or, if recognized, justified as rediscoveries or revelations. Ritual repeats received ideas. Ideally, at least, ads do not.

In advertising, innovation is openly celebrated. As in scholarly research, plagiarism is evil, flagrant imitation a sin. Ads belong to a world in flux, where "meaning is constantly flowing" (McCracken, 1990, p. 71) and, thanks to new technology, the ownership of meaning is more than ever up for grabs (Barlow, 1994). Ritual assumes a settled world in which cultural categories are fixed, where cultural principles never change. Advertising assumes a world in which traditions are being replaced, where media-based messages propose transformations in relationships between persons and goods (Leiss, Klein, & Jhally, 1990, p. 62).

If our categories and principles now seem as uncertain as the truth in our metaphors, that is the world in which we live. In our rampant jungle of symbols (no orderly forest this; see Turner, 1967), we need strategic reasons to guide us. Our metaphors point in many directions. As makers, researchers, and managers, we need, I propose, more thought devoted to how we choose among them.

▧ Notes

1. Founded in 1895, Hakuhodo Incorporated is Japan's second largest advertising agency, with annual billings that in fiscal 1993 made it the sixth largest in the world.

2. Like Victor Turner (1974), the teacher to whom I owe much of my inspiration: "I am not opposed to metaphor here. Rather I am saying that one must pick one's root metaphors carefully, for appropriateness and potential fruitfulness" (p. 25).

3. In American history, this metaphor goes back at least to the 1920s. Sinclair Lewis (1922/1980) describes George Babbitt as a man for whom "these standard advertised wares—toothpastes, socks, tires, cameras, instantaneous hot-water heaters—were his symbols and proofs of excellence; at first the signs, then the substitutes, for joy and passion and wisdom" (p. 81). In a 1926 speech, Calvin Coolidge is reported to have said that "advertising ministers to

the spiritual side of trade," and Bruce Barton, perhaps the greatest advertising man of the age, vigorously promoted the equation of advertising and Christianity (Fox, 1984).

4. Pursuing this line leads to many interesting questions. It is, for example, the core of both liberal and Marxist criticism, which sees in advertising a type of black magic that stimulates and manipulates irrational wants in consumers. For a summary of these arguments, see Leiss, Klein, and Jhally (1990, pp. 15-33). Taussig (1993) and Jameson (1992) develop similar themes in important works of postmodern cultural criticism. Cook (1992) examines advertising rhetoric in terms of applied linguistics and literary theory; I have never seen it done better. "Magic" is also sometimes used simply as a synonym for "extraordinary experience" (see, e.g., Arnould & Price, 1993).

5. We know, however, that disputes over land can be won by telling a myth "correctly" and lost by telling one "incorrectly" (Weiner, 1984). Here, however, the judgment appears to be based on the unaided memories of those who were hearing the case. Written texts were not involved.

6. In 1969-1971, my research in Taiwan was supported by grants from the National Science Foundation and the Cornell China Program. In 1976-1977, I returned to Taiwan with a grant for advanced Chinese language study provided by the American Council of Learned Societies. On both occasions, my work would not have been possible without the generous support of Professor Li Yih-yuan and other members of the Institute of Ethnology, Academia Sinica, Republic of China.

7. This may not be as difficult as it sounds. Medical research suggests that many complaints are self-limiting and spontaneously cured with or without treatment. In a modernizing country with a rising standard of living, many people may, in fact, find their prayers answered. For many problems, a sympathetic ear and a plausible explanation are sufficient to make someone feel better. Whatever the cause, news of apparent success spreads quickly to those who are searching for magical cures. Those who feel that they have been helped will cling to the power they believe they have found, supporting a snowball effect. Those who are disappointed disappear in the crowd, their complaints lost in the routine din of skepticism that surrounds all claims to magical power. We must remember, too, that we never hear of those whose claims to magical power go unaccepted. The successful may not write history, but only they are recorded there.

References

Arnould, E. J., & Price, L. L. (1993). River magic: Extraordinary experience and the extended service encounter. *Journal of Consumer Research, 20,* 24-45.

Barlow, J. P. (1994). The economy of ideas. *WIRED* 2.03, 84-90, 126-129.

Bourdieu, P. (1990). *The logic of practice* (R. Nice, Trans.). Stanford, CA: Stanford University Press.

Clifford, J., & Marcus, G. E. (1986). *Writing culture: The poetics and politics of ethnography.* Berkeley: University of California Press.

Cook, G. (1992). *The discourse of advertising.* London: Routledge.

Douglas, M. (1973). *Natural symbols.* New York: Random House.

Fernandez, J. W. (1986). The mission of metaphor. In J. W. Fernandez, *Persuasions and performances: The play of tropes in culture* (pp. 3-27). Bloomington: Indiana University Press.

Fernandez, J. W. (1991). *Beyond metaphor: The theory of tropes in anthropology.* Stanford, CA: Stanford University Press.

Foucault, M. (1970). *The order of things: An archaeology of the human sciences.* New York: Random House.

Fox, S. (1984). *The mirror makers: A history of American advertising and its creators.* New York: William Morrow.

Geertz, C. (1973). Religion as a cultural system. In C. Geertz, *The interpretation of cultures* (pp. 87-125). New York: Basic Books.

Geertz, C. (1988). *Works and lives: The anthropologist as author.* Stanford, CA: Stanford University Press.

Harrison, S. (1992). Ritual as intellectual property. *Man, 27,* 225-244.

Jameson, F. (1992). *Postmodernism or, the cultural logic of late capitalism.* Durham, NC: Duke University Press.

Lagerwey, J. (1987). *Taoist ritual in Chinese society and history.* New York: Macmillan.

Leiss, W., Kline, S., & Jhally, S. (1990). *Social communication in advertising: Persons, products and images of well-being* (2nd ed.). Scarborough, Ontario: Nelson Canada.

Lewis, S. (1980). *Babbitt.* New York: New American Library. (Original work published 1922)

Malinowski, B. (1931). Culture. In *Encyclopedia of the social sciences* (Vol. 4, pp. 621-646). New York: Macmillan.

Malinowski, B. (1954). *Magic, science and religion and other essays.* New York: Doubleday/Anchor.

Malinowski, B. (1965a). The language of magic and gardening. In B. Malinowski, *Coral gardens and their magic* (Vol. 2). Bloomington: Indiana University Press. (Original work published 1935)

Malinowski, B. (1965b). Soil-tilling and agricultural rites in the Trobriand Islands. In B. Malinowski, *Coral gardens and their magic* (Vol. 1). Bloomington: Indiana University Press. (Original work published 1935)

Malinowski, B. (1968). *The sexual life of savages* (3rd ed.). London: Routledge & Kegan Paul. (Original work published 1932)

McCracken, G. (1990). *Culture and consumption.* Bloomington: Indiana University Press.

McCreery, J. (1976). The parting of the ways: A study of innovation in ritual. *Bulletin of the Institute of Ethnology Academia Sinica, 46,* 121-136.

O'Shaughnessy, J. (1987). *Why people buy.* New York: Oxford University Press.

Sayers, D. L. (1967). *Murder must advertise.* New York: Avon.

Schipper, K. M. (1982). *Le corps taoïste—corps physique—corps social.* Paris: Fayard.

Schudson, M. (1993). *Advertising, the uneasy persuasion: Its dubious impact on American society.* London: Routledge.

Sherry, J. F., Jr. (1897). Advertising as a cultural system. In J. Umiker-Sebeok (Ed.), *Marketing and semiotics: New directions in the study of signs for sale* (pp. 285-306). Berlin: Mouton de Gruyter.

Sperber, D. (1989). *On anthropological knowledge.* New York: Cambridge University Press.

Strickmann, M. (1981). *Le taoïsme du Mao Chan—chronique d'une révélation: Mémoires de l'IHEC XVII.* Paris: Presses Universitaires de France.

Tambiah, S. (1968). The magical power of words. *Man, 3,* 175-208.

Taussig, M. (1993). *Mimesis and alterity: A particular history of the senses.* New York: Routledge.

Turner, V. (1967). *The forest of symbols: Aspects of Ndembu ritual.* Ithaca, NY: Cornell University Press.

Turner, V. (1974). Social dramas and ritual metaphors. In V. Turner, *Dramas, fields and metaphors: Symbolic action in human society* (pp. 1-57). Ithaca, NY: Cornell University Press.

Weiner, A. B. (1976). *Women of value, men of renown: New perspectives in Trobriand exchange.* Austin: University of Texas Press.

Weiner, A. B. (1984). From words to objects to magic. In D. Brenneis & F. R. Myers (Eds.), *Dangerous words: Language and politics in the Pacific* (pp. 161-191). Prospect Heights, IL: Waveland.

Wolf, A. (Ed.). (1974). *Religion and ritual in Chinese society.* Stanford, CA: Stanford University Press.

9

Speaking to Customers

The Anthropology of Communications

Rita Denny

But what are they doing with my money?

This chapter, at its most specific, is about making sense of questions like this one, which was posed by an electric utility customer to fellow customers. More generally, it is about interpreting the meanings of what people ask or say in order to make relevant responses. Taken at face value, the question posed above is simply a query for information. Judged by the supporting chorus of "yeahs" voiced by fellow customers when it was raised and the frequency with which the question is posed (by virtually any group of customers across the country), it is a question that is in sore need of an answer. Efforts by companies to respond by merely providing the apparently sought-for information often fail to silence the crowd—the information is not believed or not "heard." For example, when residential customers are shown direct mail pieces outlining company costs in the form of pie charts, graphs and the like, they respond with skepticism: "How do we know these numbers are accurate?" "How can this [fuel, labor, operations, etc.] cost so much?" Surrounded by customer voices such as these, I get the distinct impression that no matter how many times these customers are spoken to, their questions will keep coming. Lots of answers, no satisfaction.

AUTHOR'S NOTE: I would like to thank my corporate clients without whom research like this would never be done. This chapter has also greatly benefited by the comments of its reviewers. To each of you, thanks much.

The view taken here is that words speak of larger truths about the subject, whether the subject is a product, issue, service, or company. These truths are culturally based beliefs constructed through daily experience, historical understanding, advertising, or some other form of communication. In this case, beliefs about utility companies are implicit in the question: These companies are accountable to customers in ways that other companies are not.

Customers' beliefs about utilities are framed by assumptions they make about big business, monopolies, and the government (Denny & Russell, 1994)—and more specifically, about how they think companies think about them. "But what are you doing with my money?" is a question not asked of the local supermarket, department store, or car dealer. We do ask it of the government, in reference to our tax dollars, and of free-market companies only if we are stockholders. The point is that the ways individuals choose to talk tells us something about the implicit relationships between speaker and subject, and these relationships need to be understood by corporations whenever the subject "speaks" to customers—in the form of services and products, advertising, or policy development.

I use the recent concern about electromagnetic fields, or EMF, as a way to demonstrate the richness of speech and the benefits of analysis when designing communication strategies. Public concern about EMF has risen dramatically in the past few years. Paul Brodeur (1990a) made headlines with his book "Currents of Death" and made EMF a household term through subsequent articles and talk show appearances. Articles about EMF appeared in *Family Circle* (Brodeur, 1990b) and *The New Yorker* in the early 1990s. The topic has been addressed by Ted Koppel on *Nightline* (March 9, 1990) and by Larry King on CNN (January 28, 1990). The concern is with the link between childhood leukemia and exposure to electromagnetic fields. Although the scientific evidence isn't clear, some of the epidemiological data support the claim that exposure to EMF increases the probability of childhood leukemia.

Electric utilities have felt the impact of customer concern because "power lines" are often targeted as the source of EMF by media. As a consequence, the issue is a focus of communication for electric utilities. Impetus for resolving the issue has only grown as lawsuits are filed and receive attention (Richards, 1993). A suit against San Diego Gas & Electric (Lane, 1993) for knowing that high voltage lines can cause cancer, heard in the spring of 1993, was lost by the plaintiffs. While other suits have met with similar results, the unspoken fear is that one day a suit will be won, leaving utilities extremely vulnerable. As task forces are convened within companies to grapple with the limits of their responsibility and the practical implications of policy decisions, consumer concern grows in fits and starts, locally and nationally.

Customers' views of company actions and companies' views of customer needs often elicit looks of shocked surprise from company executives and customers, respectively. Resolving the discrepant perspectives is a necessary prerequisite for developing a successful EMF policy.

The data cited here were collected in two separate studies. In the first (from 1991), my client was a southern electric utility concerned about potential fallout from customers in response to EMF publicity. At this point, there was no company policy directing communications about EMF, the history of nuclear plant communications disasters were still capable of making company executives squirm uncomfortably, and the company had plans to extend high-voltage wires in urban and rural areas. Their goal was to gauge customer concerns about EMF and to construct a communications policy that directly responded to these concerns. In the second study (from 1993), my client was also an electric utility, this time in the northeastern United States. Their EMF policy was quite developed, involving interfaces with state agencies, individualized response to customer queries, and funding of EMF research, among other things. They were also facing an EMF-related lawsuit. The director of corporate communications, in this case, still felt that company communications were lacking. Something.

So, in both cases, my role as a research supplier was to give these companies a way to think about their communications needs (in common parlance, a strategy): What were the problems? What were the constraints? What were the corporate options within these constraints (e.g., make EMF go away? make it manageable? make the utility a good guy? nonobstructive? customer partner?)? As an anthropologist, my goal was to understand EMF in cultural context: native definitions and symbolic weight. From an analytic standpoint, I was interested in customers' definitions of EMF—the meanings implicitly and explicitly attached to the term, the frames of reference invoked by customers to interpret information on EMF. The logic was that by understanding this cultural etymology, so to speak, we would have a better chance to respond to significant customer needs. As a linguistic sort of anthropologist, I looked to the ways customers spoke about the issue as the primary means for understanding its meaning.

Point of Departure

In focusing on how people use words to voice larger truths about themselves and others, this work is a practical application and contemporary illustration of ethnography of speaking, a movement that in the past 30 years has studied the ways in which speech is organized in social life. Often pushed forward by Hymes (1962, 1972), this coalition of linguists, sociologists, and anthropologists argues against the notion of a linguistic system that is independent of the culture within which it lives or the social process within which it is cast about and toward which it contributes.

Much ethnography of speech has focused on documenting the scope and nature of linguistic regularities in social context. This might mean the differential distribution of sounds—for example, use of postvocalic |r| across social classes (Labov, 1966)—speech styles (Hymes, 1977; Joos, 1967), terms of address, pronominal usage—for example, use of formal and familiar |you| forms in Russian (Friedrich, 1966)—taking turns in conversation (Denny, 1985), or the performative social roles that speech enables (Bauman & Scherzer, 1977). The terms of address used, the form of pronoun chosen, or the way speaking turns are transacted say something about (or point to) the relationships among the speakers. Qualities such as deference, solidarity, or distance are communicated. What anchors this work is a premise about the way language works—a dynamic system that reflects, perpetuates, and creates social, not merely cognitive, action.

In a similar vein, Lakoff and Johnson (1980) focus on how a culture's metaphors structure experience. Metaphor is not simply a poetic, literary device (e.g., LOVE IS A ROSE). Rather, metaphors are chosen, displayed, and negotiated in everyday speech. They show systematic and pervasive patterns that reflect a society's particular assumptions about the world we live in and the way it works—its worldview and its ethos (Sherry, 1984). In the United States, for example, TIME IS MONEY:

> Corresponding to the fact that we act as if time is a valuable commodity . . . we conceive of time that way. Thus we understand and experience time as the kind of thing that can be spent, wasted, budgeted, invested wisely or poorly, saved or squandered. (Lakoff & Johnson, 1980, p. 8)

Use of these (or related) analytic frames in consumer research are few and far between, and when they are found they typically reference advertising texts (Mick, 1986; Sherry, 1987; Sherry & Camargo, 1987; Stern, 1988) or other forms of sales pitches (Pinch & Clark, 1986; Sherry, 1988). Somewhat ironic is that the methods applied to the analysis of advertising are typically not applied to everyday speech—as though the former constitutes a performance and the latter does not.

If ethnography of speaking was identified as such in the past 30 years, the effort received a significant push from an earlier group of linguistic scholars, the Prague structuralists of the 1940s and 1950s. This group includes Mukarovsky, Havranek, Trubetzkoy, and, in the United States, Jakobson. These scholars viewed language as having distinct functional styles that through careful observation of speakers could be identified and meaning derived. Styles are bound to contexts of occurrence—what might be appropriate in one context would not be for another. Contexts themselves are defined linguistically and, more applicable for our interests here, by individuals—their social roles, their reason for speaking, and so on. These styles can be thought of as conventions—culturally based ways for communicating.

In anchoring their focus to context of use, these theorists articulated indexical properties of language, in contrast to symbolic. Following the distinction of Peirce, articulated at length by Silverstein (1976), indexical signs are those "where the occurrence of the sign vehicle token bears a connection of understood spatio-temporal contiguity to the occurrence of the entity signaled" (p. 27). Conversationally based indexicals include sound patterns ("wash" vs. "warsh," e.g., points to region and social class), pronouns, terms of address, or use of silence. Consumer examples are red suspenders, popular necktie patterns, or the white band of skin on a "wedding finger." In each case, significance stems from an original spatial and temporal relationship between object and context of its occurrence: the wearing of red suspenders and ties of certain patterns by Wall Street's power brokers in the 1980s or the state of being married. Indexicals are opposed to icons, which bear a physical relationship to the entity signaled (e.g., pictures), and to symbols, which bear an arbitrary relationship (currency is a good example in the consumer world). By their use, social roles and relations may be reflected and perpetuated.

In the example used above—"But what are they doing with my money?"—the nature of the question says something about the customer-utility relationship. It is clear from the question that the customer assumes that money paid to the company is still the customer's (indicated by use of "my") and that the company is accountable to customers for their spending decisions. Chrysler customers don't feel the company should consult them on capital investment decisions, yet utility customers are often angry that the company didn't consult them before investing in nuclear plants (or other types of generating plants). These assumptions point to a long-lasting, mutually dependent relationship rather than short-lived contractual arrangements characteristic of American purchasing in general.

Considered within the world of market research, I reference the Prague model in a few ways. First, I think of the relationship between consumer and producer as a dialogue, if not always a direct one. Producers "speak" in the form of advertising, services or products. Consumers "speak" in the form of protests or purchases or in the ways they talk about the producer/product. Clearly, my notion of exchange is broadly construed and includes the social and symbolic dimensions, not merely the economic (Levy, 1978).

Second, by studying the speech conventions used by consumers, we can better understand the subject (be it product, service, company, or issue). Whether we analyze them or not, individuals draw on these conventions to express themselves. And these conventions are culturally based. They might be linguistic markers such as pronouns, but they might be in the form of metaphors, use of speech events like questions, or the display of apparently contradictory opinions. Think of someone's talk as a poem rather than an immutable display of descriptive fact. The "poetic structure" provides a window for gleaning a richer understanding of what is being expressed by speakers. In our case, the interest is in the beliefs individuals have about utility companies, energy production or consumption, or environmental threats.

Third, the Prague structuralists identified a mechanism for articulating the meaning of linguistic signs. Today, we refer to markedness of a sign (speech or otherwise), but this characterization stems from Havranek's (1955) distinction between automatized or foregrounded uses of a particular convention within contexts of speech. Following Havranek, when an occurrence of a sign (an indexical in Peircean terms) is an expected or usual event it is automatized. Its use would function as a simple affirmation of shared knowledge. For example, the use of a term of address such as "Doctor" by a patient would be considered usual or expected and points to the authority and expertise accorded the physician's status. When appearing in an unexpected time or place, then the use is marked or foregrounded (e.g., the use of "Doctor" by a spouse, probably in a sarcastic tone). Drawing on its unmarked context for significance, a foregrounded use may be a comment on behavior (that the individual is acting like a physician and not a spouse) and perhaps a directive to the hearer to behave differently. Tannen (1993), in an article appearing in the *New York Times'* Sunday magazine used markedness to talk about men and women's dress codes. Men, she argued, constitute the unmarked case (vis women)—their ubiquitous jacket and tie says they are males in the workplace. Women's dress is marked—*whatever* they choose to wear is saying something or, at least, will be interpreted as a comment by her on her role and attitude toward the workplace.

In the present case, the great significance of "what are they doing with my money?" is the fact that it is an unusual query with reference to American commerce (it is a marked or foregrounded use). And the interpreted meaning is located in its automatized or unmarked use—when referencing government or, even more literally, when stated by stockholders. Marking has the effect of transferring indexical meanings to new referents; in this case, utility customers are referencing themselves, unconsciously but clearly, I think, as shareholders.

Analytically, we observe conversations (audiotapes or transcripts) and ask the following: What must be true about the world for this utterance (or set of utterances) to make sense for speaker and fellow discussants? What is implicit in the speech about the subject at hand? What tones of voice are used? What metaphors surface? How are questions phrased? What descriptors are used by respondents? Importantly, where else have we heard these ways of expression? Comparison allows us to discern some of the marked and unmarked uses of conventions. In all, analysis unearths some of the cultural baggage that, in this instance, infuses consumer understanding of a particular environmental threat.

To view a given speech event systematically, Jakobson's (1980) "Metalanguage as a Linguistic Problem" is helpful, as he lays out the various functions of language as they are brought to bear in communicating. For example, he discusses the emotive function, which refers to the attitude of the speaker towards his subject, the conative function, which refers to the orientation of speaker to hearer, and so on. Another, but more limiting, way of interpreting speech is by looking at the illocutionary force of utterances as described by Austen (1963). The approach of the firm I am associated with (B/R/S Group, Inc.) reflects the interests and proclivities of its researchers. So we tend to focus on the questions people ask (what is assumed by the query vis the speaker's worldview and/or ethos?) or other formal (typically indexical) characteristics of the speech events. For example, in a recent study on Microsoft's brand image we noticed that the words typically used in describing the company were |-ing| words: leading, driving, exciting, and so on. The particular theory and method is less important than applying one in the first place.

 ## "Currents of Death": Talking About Electromagnetic Fields

The Data

The data consist of 10 group discussions, each group having 10 to 12 participants. Four of the groups took place in Louisiana (1991), the remainder in the northeastern United States (1992-1993). In each case, the participants reflected a local demographic profile. In each group, half the respondents were male and half were female. They ranged in age from 25 to 60 and tended to have children at home. In the South, income ranged from $20,000 to $50,000, and education ranged from high school to college graduates. In the Northeast, household incomes were higher ($30,000-$70,000) as was educational level (reflecting the client's sense of the key target audience for EMF communications). Participants were only recruited if they felt they were at least "somewhat familiar" with EMF. Concern with the issue varied from none at all to extreme. Each was audiotaped, and the Louisiana groups were transcribed.

The most similar format to our approach to group discussions is the focus group. Like focus groups, our respondents are recruited by local market research facilities, screened for designated criteria, asked to participate, and paid for their time ($30-$45). Each discussion is about 2 hours long, and each is audiotaped.

Unlike focus groups, these conversations are organized with a series of "tasks" that respondents complete as a group, with minimal intervention by us. These tasks are designed to get at potentially deep issues and allow respondents to use their own language to voice their opinions. For example, groups in the Northeast were asked to "write" an editorial for the *New York Times* on EMF. Groups were asked to debate positions or outline magazine articles on new technology. Participants completed these tasks out loud through discussion that was managed more or (often) less by an appointed chair. The editorial, for example, would have a designated editor-in-chief who would direct the groups' discussion of what points to include in the editorial, the stand the group wanted to take, and so on. Although the scope of topics is determined by us in the "task" format, the ways in which opinions, concerns, or "facts" are articulated are relatively unconstrained. Finally, the goal is not the completion of each task but the examination of the process by which respondents give voice to their thoughts. Our aim is to discern the meaning embedded in their talk—in this case, about EMF and about electric utilities.

The Folk Definition of EMF

If a single sentence were to summarize customer concern about EMF emerging from our groups it would have to be "Does it cause cancer?" The question is a loaded one, and attempts to answer it are all too often met with a disappointed (sometimes disgusted) shake of the consumer's head. In particular, the question is loaded with expectations of corporate response, which, in turn, stem from particular beliefs about business and technology. These beliefs tend to frame customer interpretation of EMF information, reactions to EMF stories, or opinions about the EMF issue.

American Industry

In the absence of evidence to the contrary, customers generally assume that the utility industry will follow the historical precedent of industry in general, or at least their idea of industry and its history. So, for example, respondents believed their electric company might sacrifice safety for profit or withhold key information on EMF:

> They're avoiding prevention to save on costs.

> Hey, we'd save a lot of government money if we stopped doing this dance . . . and make them come clean . . . and say "Hey, we know you know" and "You know we know you know" . . . and get on to the solutions and stop the dance.

> Are they sharing all that matters?

These statements assume an adversarial relationship in which EMF is viewed as a consumer problem, not one shared by the company. Moreover, the industry most called upon by analogy is the tobacco industry: powerful, greedy, and self-interested. The unusual relationship between company and customer (based on long-lasting interdependence) does not provide a counterpoint to the negative view of "industry" in general. Instead, it appears to compound it and catalyze greater emotional feeling behind the question "Does EMF cause cancer?" Resolution of the issue, or an adequate response, is all the more important because of the interdependence characteristic of the company-customer relationship.

Even without the imputation of malfeasance, our respondents tended to be blind toward company actions:

> I haven't heard them address the problem.

> We're not condemning the fact that [the company is] standing still but . . .

And, taken to an extreme, consumers' lack of knowledge itself is seen as an intentional act by the company:

Why *weren't* we told?

Why are most people ignorant about EMF? Is it a cover-up?

Taken together these statements imply that the company ought to be doing something. Indeed, the lack of visible action spurs ever greater skepticism about motives.

Electric Technology

Customers exhibit a lack of surprise when faced with EMF headlines. Nods and an air of resignation are more typical responses. This reaction stems in part from ambivalent feelings about technology in general. Although technology can represent excitement, innovation, and power over surroundings, it is also thought to threaten social relations and be harmful through unintended effects. Technology is definitely a mixed blessing (Sherry, 1984).

At its most positive, technology confers power and excitement. Microwaves and cellular phones, two examples cited by respondents, allow individuals greater control over time, computer networks easily override traditional limits of geography, and medical applications have extended or improved quality of life. Consumers expect technology to be a source for future stimulation and fun—"the best is yet to come" attitude. But with the positive is an expected downside. Technology carries an implication of social harm ("We let technology control us"): "Too much" TV, computer games, and so on are thought to affect the quality of social relationships. Technology can be harnessed for destruction (e.g., smart missiles). Breakthroughs at one time yield disaster at a later time. The initial headlines about EMF are understood within this frame—another technological feat gone awry.

However, electric companies in particular are singled out by customers. High-voltage wires offer a powerful construct of danger for customers, offering them a means for visualizing EMF, or making it concrete. Customers further elaborate through their own experience with electricity:

It's like static electricity when you walk across the carpet.

You can feel your hair stand up near an electric pole.

It's what happens when you put a fluorescent bulb in a microwave or near a power line and it lights up.

Hear 'em singing.

The new information for customers is that proximity, not just touch, is enough to be dangerous.

Some of our respondents also assumed that EMF is a by-product of electricity. As such, it is an avoidable phenomenon:

> Residual electricity.

> It's too much current on the line.

> Overload.

> Why does it have to be leaking out?

Underlying these beliefs are metaphors of both quantity and containment. More is worse/less is okay ("What is the level that can be tolerated?"), and solutions are technical ones that have to do with containment ("shielding," "wrapping," or, for some, "burying").

A key aspect of technology, then, is control: the ability to manage it. Otherwise, chaos threatens. EMF becomes an example of "unmanaged" technology, raising the question "Why wasn't it managed better? And how can it best be managed now?" As the company is culturally implicated, if you will, in the EMF issue, it is looked upon to respond to these implicit questions.

Implications for Communications

Beliefs about American industry and electric technology together with the customer-company relationship put electric companies in a paradoxical space. Customers will continue to ask their local company "Does EMF cause cancer?" and not hear, accept, or otherwise favorably respond to the company's answer.

In my experience, electric utilities have tended to respond by taking the question "Does EMF cause cancer?" at face value. They adhere to the myth of objectivism (Lakoff & Johnson, 1980) in their belief that the world is composed of objects whose properties are independent of the individuals who experience them, that we can make statements of unequivocal truth or falsity about this world, that words have fixed meanings and individuals just need to be skilled enough to use words precisely and appropriately (Lakoff & Johnson, 1980, p. 187). Implicit in this view is that linguistic expressions are objects and communication is likened to a conduit metaphor (fixed message from sender to receiver). If only customers, employees, communicators, and so on were more competent in using words appropriately! (This view surfaces in a variety of corporate contexts when designers, marketers, CEOs, or whomever disparage customers for just not getting it or believe their communication problems would be solved if customers were just educated on the topic.) Utility companies may or may not make scientific reports available to customers, but in any case they summarize such studies by stating that "research is inconclusive," that "more studies are being done," and that the company is making every effort by "continuing to fund research." Yet the answers seem, at best, unsatisfying and, at worst, intentional obfuscation.

Company attempts to explain or define EMF can also have the same effect. Diagrams sometimes look as though they are cut from engineering books, and language can unwittingly play on the concerns that customers have without addressing them. For example, EMF is described as "an invisible force" that "surrounds" any flow of current in which "the magnitude of the force" depends on current and proximity to the source. This is education? From a customer's standpoint, this sounds like radiation. Common measures of EMF (in milligaus) around the home are sometimes given, yet customers have no way to evaluate the significance of these numbers. Indeed, the company may say there *is* no way to evaluate significance.

"Does EMF cause cancer?" The question presupposes an expertise on the company's part. In asking it of the company, customers are granting the company authority on the subject in some way. Given the belief that customers have about technology (namely, that it has unintended consequences), the content of the question might be rephrased as "What are the unintended side effects of electricity production?" or "What's the downside?" Implied also in the question, I believe, are the other questions deriving from the technology mindset: "Why do we have this problem?" and "What are you doing about it?" Beliefs about the way big business functions and the unusual nature of the company-customer relationship are additional factors through which corporate responses are filtered and interpreted by customers. There are a number of implications:

- Silence can be damning. Apparent silence, in the face of public concern, takes on a specter of active avoidance. Furthermore, the burden appears to be on the utility to grab the attention of its customers. It isn't enough to be able to point to communications efforts; the company must be able to point to efforts that succeeded. This is done most convincingly if customers feel they themselves have been reached. Acting out of the ordinary, as an indication that EMF is not "business as usual," would have this effect. Candor about the way customers view the company's actions around environmental threats would be a first step. Resonating with customers' ideas indicates that the company has spent time trying to understand them. (Picture an ostrich on a full page in the

Wall Street Journal with a headline something like "This is us when it comes to EMF," followed with an explanation of why the metaphor would no longer be appropriate. Guaranteed to be seen by customers, but oh so unlikely to get past company legal departments.)

- If central to the (perceived) problem, companies should be central to the solution. This means demonstrating leadership and leveraging their expertise. "Funding research" or responding to customer questions, two frequent corporate responses, lack a proactive stance that typifies leadership. Instead, inertia is signaled, so the clout that customers associate with big business is not being used to customer advantage. Thus a neutral or "supporting" position is interpreted as an act of noncompliance.

- The utility is, at best, an active guide of consumer understanding. Data dumps of "the facts" to customers won't help mediate the perceived opposition of company and customer ("They're passing the buck"). Facts about the issue are important to give, but so is a way to interpret the facts. Customers have to come to their own conclusions, the company cannot do this for them—for example, in the form of "we don't have a problem." But it is critical that the company provide a means for allowing customers to think through the issue; if they don't, another frame of reference will be invoked, one less complimentary of the corporate position.

Conclusions

The need to understand company-customer relationships is particularly acute when the marketplace is changing, bringing corporate entities into focus when they might otherwise be invisible. And change is here today. New technology is catalyzing a repositioning of communications and entertainment companies. Deregulation and environmental threats are making gas and electric utilities more conscious of themselves and their image. The mainstreaming of environmental concern places chemical companies and the issue of federal regulations in consumer focus. Rapid technological advances keep the computer industry in a state of flux. Globalization raises the question of whether to leverage the corporate brand as a means for introducing particular products.

In all these cases, the role of the corporate brand is at issue (in marketing terms, its equity). Following Blackston (1992), I differentiate a brand's fundamental equities deriving from its products, pricing, and so on from its "added value" equities. In the terms of this chapter, a brand's added value equity is the cultural baggage that hangs onto the brand—the set of assumptions that consumers will make about the company's products or services before they even experience them. In times of change, companies may well rely on these meanings when they "speak" to customers via advertising, new policies, or products. Equally likely, they will be hampered by these meanings. In leveraging the corporate brand, the logic behind communications runs something like "If they know us and like (or trust) us, they'll choose (support, believe) us." Yet knowing what is meant by liking or trust depends on understanding the sources of distrust and being able to mediate them effectively.

I've argued here that literal expressions of like/dislike cannot be taken at face value, that understanding rests on interpreting the ways opinions or statements are made. Communication is not a closed system. It is not an objective enterprise between sender and receiver. It's messy. It's variable. Most important, it's interactional. It's also systematic. Ethnographers of speech recognize this and use speech as a means for understanding broader social codes and the dynamics of change and meaning (re)formation. I apply these principles to corporate and consumer environments, working with marketers, communications executives, advertising research directors, and so on to understand a customer point of view. What I do, of course, is help them understand their own point of view and, through the process, (re)solve specific communications problems: developing an EMF policy, repositioning the Jeep brand, figuring out a worldwide creative strategy for Microsoft.

A critical piece of any communications strategy is defining a realistic goal. In the EMF case, persuading customers that EMF is not a problem is unrealistic (and absolutely a waste of time). Persuading customers that EMF is not a utility's problem is similarly unrealistic. Nor should the strategy attempt to make consumers into engineers. Resorting to the "education" of consumers as the means for implementing change in all likelihood won't work. One isn't so much imparting knowledge as arguing for a particular experiential worldview and, moreover, arguing its superiority. It might be more useful to construct the goal in terms of a desired (and achievable) company-customer relationship—allies, perhaps, in determining the nature of this particular risk. Given that the starting point is an adversarial we-they relationship, the strategy has to outline a progression of steps, not least of which is being heard in the first place.

I have used electric utilities to illustrate the need of ethnographic readings of speech because they make a lot of mistakes, errors that stem from misreadings of customer talk. But U.S. utility executives are not alone—their actions are simply more visible (by dint of culture). Consumer expectations of corporate identity and behavior and the beliefs spurring them will, of course, vary, depending on native views of industry distinctions (Merrill Lynch vs. Commonwealth Edison vs. Chrysler) and on change over time (IBM in 1980 vs. IBM in 1990). Defining the constraints against which any communication strategy must work is necessary if it is to be successful, or heard as intended. IBM, for example, faces a radically different world in 1994. Hardware is increasingly a commodity; competitors are outstripping its market share and its ability to define technological change. Like an electric utility, IBM cannot change who it is overnight. Just as utilities cannot be understood easily by consumers as "free market" companies, IBM cannot be Microsoft. Yet change it must. How ads (corporate or product) speak to customers will be based on past "conversations" and our ability to interpret their import. Understanding talk—theirs and ours—is key.

References

Austen, J. (1963). *How to do things with words*. New York: Oxford University Press.

Bauman, R., & Sherzer, J. (Eds.). (1977). *Explorations in the ethnography of speaking*. Cambridge, UK: Cambridge University Press.

Blackston, M. (1992, February). *Beyond brand personality: Building brand relationships*. Paper presented to the Advertising Research Foundation, New York.

Brodeur, P. (1990a). *Currents of death*. New York: Simon & Schuster.

Brodeur, P. (1990b, September 25). Danger in the schoolyard. *Family Circle*, pp. 61-66.

Denny, R. (1985). Marking the interaction order: The social constitution of turn exchange and speaking turns. *Language in Society, 14*, 41-62.

Denny, R., & Russell, V. (1994, August 1). Fighting bias through public relations. *Fortnightly*, pp. 14-17.

Friedrich, P. (1966). Structural implications of Russian pronominal usage. In W. Bright (Ed.), *Sociolinguistics* (pp. 214-259). The Hague: Mouton.

Havranek, B. (1955). The functional differentiation of the standard language. In P. Garvin (Ed.), *A Prague school reader on aesthetics, literary structure and style* (pp. 3-16). Washington, DC: Washington Linguistics Club.

Hymes, D. (1962). The ethnography of speaking. In T. Gladwin & W. C. Sturtevant (Eds.), *Anthropology and human behavior* (pp. 15-53). Washington, DC: Anthropology Society of Washington.

Hymes, D. (1972). Models of interaction of language and social life. In L. J. Gumperz & D. Hymes (Eds.), *Directions in sociolinguistics* (pp. 38-71). New York: Holt, Rinehart & Winston.

Hymes, D. (1977). Ways of speaking. In K. Basso & J. Sherzer (Eds.), *Explorations in the ethnography of speaking* (pp. 433-452). Cambridge, UK: Cambridge University Press.

Jakobson, R. (1980). *The framework of language*. Ann Arbor: Michigan Studies in the Humanities.

Joos, M. (1967). *The five clocks.* New York: Harcourt, Brace & World.

Labov, W. (1966). *Sociolinguistic patterns.* Philadelphia: University of Pennsylvania Press.

Lakoff, G., & Johnson, M. (1980). *Metaphors we live by.* Chicago: University of Chicago Press.

Lane, E. (1993, February 22). SDG&E prepares for March court date in key EMF case. *Energy Daily,* p. 4.

Levy, S. J. (1978). Hunger and work in a civilized tribe. *American Behavioral Scientist, 21,* 557-570.

Mick, D. (1986). Consumer research and semiotics: Exploring the morphology of signs, symbols and significance. *Journal of Consumer Research, 13,* 196-213.

Pinch, T., & Clark, C. (1986). The hard sell: "Patter merchandising" and the strategic (re)production and local management of economic reasoning in the sales routines of market pitchers. *Sociology, 20,* 169-191.

Richards, B. (1993, February 5). Electric utilities brace for cancer lawsuits though risk is unclear. *Wall Street Journal,* p. A1.

Sherry, J. F., Jr. (1984). Some implications of consumer oral tradition for reactive marketing. *Advances in Consumer Research, 2,* 741-747.

Sherry, J. F., Jr. (1987). Advertising as a cultural system. In J. Umiker-Sebeok (Ed.), *Marketing and semiotics* (pp. 441-461). Berlin: Mouton de Gruyter.

Sherry, J. F., Jr. (1988). Market pitching and the ethnography of speaking. *Advances in Consumer Research, 15,* 543-547.

Sherry, J. F., Jr., & Camargo, E. G. (1987). "May your life be marvelous": English language labeling and the semiotics of Japanese promotion. *Journal of Consumer Research, 14,* 174-188.

Silverstein, M. (1976). Shifters, linguistic categories and cultural description. In K. Basso & H. Selby (Eds.), *Meaning in anthropology* (pp. 11-55). Albuquerque: University of New Mexico Press.

Stern, B. B. (1988). How does an ad mean? Language in services advertising. *Journal of Advertising, 17,* 3-14.

Tannen, D. (1993, June 30). Wears jump suit. Sensible shoes. Uses husband's last name. *New York Times Magazine,* pp. 18-19.

PART SIX

Being in the Marketplace
Experiential Consumption

In this part, we describe some of the mechanisms of consumer apperception by tracing the interplay of cultural ideology and individual experience. We introduce the reader to consumers embedded in both a literal and figurative marketplace—the aesthetic agora of a museum and the moral economy of gift giving—to demonstrate how, in the piquant language of Shweder's (1990) cultural psychology, "You can't take stuff out of the psyche *and* you can't take the psyche out of the stuff" (p. 2). Relationship management within and between individuals as well as between individuals and objects (Armstrong, 1971; McKenna, 1991) produces the affecting presence that is the heart of the consumer's experience. Marketing acts to condition that experience, whether positive or negative, neutral or ambivalent.

In the case of the museum, objects are retired from private circulation, socialized via enshrinement in consecrated space, and revered for their ability to facilitate an exalted experience (Becker, 1982; Bourdieu, 1984) of production, consumption, and disposition. The packaging of these objects—the servicescape (Bitner, 1992) that is museum exhibition—may help or hinder this facilitation (Karp & Lavine, 1991). In the case of gift giving, objects are transformed from impersonal commodities to vessels bearing elements of the donor's essence (Carrier, 1993), appropriated by the recipient into a sacral possession via consumption and disposition (Carrier, 1990a), and animated by an ideology that imperfectly reconciles altruism with obligation (Carrier, 1990b). In each of these cases, the consumer's experience consists of a

347

complex interplay between cultural processes, his or her own creative production of symbolic value, and marketing design as reflected in architectural
and artifactual dimensions of the built environment.

Carole Duhaime, Annamma Joy, and Christopher Ross tread boldly into
one of the most ideologically volatile arenas of our contemporary "cultural
wars" (Hunter, 1991)—the normative function of brokerage in the commoditization of aesthetic experience—as consumer advocates in search of an
effective servicescape (Bitner, 1992). Implicitly and explicitly, they raise
provocative questions in their evaluation study. What is the anthropological
propriety of museum practice (Clifford, 1988; Jones, 1993)? Are there aspects
of consumer behavior that should remain outside the orbit of the marketplace
(Belk, Wallendorf, & Sherry, 1989; Codrescu, 1986; Levy & Czepiel, 1975;
Norman, 1994a, 1994b)? Should nonprofit enterprises be conducted like
for-profit ones (Kotler, 1982)? What is the proper relationship between public
policy (including such issues as the impact of multicultural initiatives on
national identity) and consumer preference? Duhaime and her colleagues
couch these questions in terms of the effect of the built environment on
patrons' perceptions of art objects and the differential awareness of that
effect on the part of museum officials. The museum is seen as a medium
through which transient meanings must flow en route to being sedimented
in and liberated from particular objects.

John Sherry, Mary Ann McGrath, and Sidney Levy present the findings
of a long-term collaborative investigation into gift-giving practices among
upscale urban U.S. women. They describe a cycle of research that began with
ethnography, progressed to projective tasking, and culminated in interpretations that promise to lead the team back inexorably to the study's ethnographic origins. Sherry and his colleagues focus on the behavior of monadic
giving (Mick, in press), and, eschewing conventionally exclusionary "either/or"
distinctions, position it in postmodern perspective as an "and/both" phenomenon that contradicts the ideology of the dyadic gift even as it perfects that
ideology. Their fascination with the ineffable dimension of consumer experience and with the unthought known is indicative of the type of existential-
phenomenological issues challenging consumer researchers to expand the
scope of their inquiries and the variety of their methods. Sherry et al. employ
monadic giving as a vehicle for exploring female consumption roles, the
evolution of interaction ritual, and the production of consumption.

Whether we consider the ceremonial site of a consumption experience or
the ceremonial object itself, anthropological analysis takes us directly to the
ritual substratum of consumer behavior. Increasingly, the ritual is secular and
the space liminoid, but the cumulative impact of the built environment and

the sacralization of commodities is profound nonetheless. As Mintz (1993) observes, the "desire to consume, powerful as it is, does not rest easy on the American psyche. The feeling that one must pay for one's excesses is at least as American [dare we say Canadian, as well?] as the consumption itself. The feeling that in self-denial lies virtue, and in consumption sin, is still powerfully present" (p. 269). Giving a gift to the self, in either the indulgent form of a personal present or the civic form of museum patronage (via taxes or tariffs), seems always an occasion tinged with ambivalence and an opportunity for reflecting on the tension between individual desires and cultural mandates. Wrapping the gift, whether in a package or a museum, ennobles the object and harnesses its power.

References

Armstrong, R. (1971). *The affecting presence: An essay in humanistic anthropology.* Urbana: University of Illinois Press.

Becker, H. (1982). *Art worlds.* Berkeley: University of California Press.

Belk, R., Wallendorf, M., & Sherry, J. F., Jr. (1989). The sacred and profane in consumer behavior: Theodicy on the odyssey. *Journal of Consumer Research, 16*(1), 1-38.

Bitner, M. J. (1992). Servicescapes: The impact of physical surroundings on customers and employees. *Journal of Marketing, 56*(2), 57-71.

Bourdieu, P. (1984). *Distinction: A social critique of the judgement of taste.* Cambridge, MA: Harvard University Press.

Carrier, J. (1990a). Reconciling commodities and personal relations in industrial society. *Theory and Society, 19*(5), 579-598.

Carrier, J. (1990b). Gifts in a world of commodities: The ideology of the perfect gift in American society. *Social Analysis, 29,* 19-37.

Carrier, J. (1993). The rituals of Christmas giving. In D. Miller (Ed.), *Unwrapping Christmas* (pp. 55-74). Oxford, UK: Clarendon.

Clifford, J. (1988). *The predicament of culture: Twentieth century ethnography, literature, and art.* Cambridge, MA: Harvard University Press.

Codrescu, A. (1986). Obsolescence. In A. Codrescu (Ed.), *A craving for swan* (pp. 288-289). Columbus: Ohio State University Press.

Hunter, J. (1991). *Culture wars: The struggle to define America.* New York: Basic Books.

Jones, A. (1993), Exploding canons: The anthropology of museums. *Annual Review of Anthropology, 22,* 201-220.

Karp, I., & Lavine, S. (1991). *Exhibiting cultures: The poetics and politics of museum display.* Washington, DC: Smithsonian Institution Press.

Kotler, P. (1982). *Marketing for nonprofit organizations.* Englewood Cliffs, NJ: Prentice Hall.

Levy, S., & Czepiel, J. (1975). Marketing and aesthetics. In R. Curhan (Ed.), *1976 combined proceedings: New marketing for social and economic progress, and marketing's contributions to the firms and to society* (pp. 386-391). Chicago: American Marketing Association.

McKenna, R. (1991). *Relationship marketing.* Reading, MA: Addison-Wesley.

Mick, D. (in press). Self-gifts. In C. Otnes & R. Beltramini (Eds.), *Gift giving: An interdisciplinary anthology.* Bowling Green, KY: Bowling Green University Popular Press.

Mintz, S. (1993). The changing roles of food in the study of consumption. In J. Brewer & R. R. Porter (Eds.), *Consumption and the world of goods* (pp. 261-273). New York: Routledge.

Norman, M. (1994a, January 30). A book in search of a buzz: The marketing of a first novel. *New York Times Book Review,* pp. 22-23, 25.

Norman, M. (1994b, February 6). Reader by reader and town by town, a new novelist builds a following. *New York Times Book Review,* pp. 28-30.

Shweder, R. (1990). Cultural psychology: What is it? In J. Stigler, R. Shweder, & G. Herdt (Eds.), *Cultural psychology* (pp. 1-43). New York: Cambridge University Press.

10

Learning to "See"

A Folk Phenomenology of the Consumption of Contemporary Canadian Art

Carole Duhaime
Annamma Joy
Christopher Ross

Cultural objects make visible the cultural principles and categories that form the basis of any society. Art objects are no exception. However, unlike other aspects of material culture, they not only reflect, persuade, and convince the community of the importance of these rules (McCracken, 1986) but also critique and challenge the very fabric of society. To substantiate this view, we would like to draw the reader's attention to the controversy that arose over the presentation of an exhibit entitled "Into the Heart of Africa" at the Royal Ontario Museum in Canada in 1989. Because the intention of the curator was to show how the exhibited objects were acquired, the spatial layout of the exhibit featured a military gallery, a missionary gallery, and a gallery showing contemporary cultural and other events. The African Canadian community and some art critics felt that the exhibit, organized around the theme of precolonial and colonial contact, perpetuated racist stereotypes and demonstrated a lack of respect for the community. The passionate reactions of community members are not an isolated event but, rather, quite commonplace in both Canada and the United States. They also raise important ethical issues relating to the politics of representation and sponsorship

_____
AUTHORS' NOTE: The authors wish to gratefully acknowledge financial support from the Social Sciences and Humanities Research Council in Canada.

(Jones, 1993). This chapter considers the number of ways in which art is perceived and experienced in the context of a museum. We begin with the following vignettes (all names pseudonyms):

> Caroline is Belgian born. She has lived in Canada for 18 years. She speaks four languages but has no formal degree. She does not like to go to museums, partly because she was taken there very often as a child and partly because of the formal tradition of viewing art that was imposed on viewers during visits. A recurrent theme of concern for her was the "burden of the past." She grew up in a 14th-century house in Brussels, an oppressive environment that reflected the society that she lived in. Caroline is 42.

> Barbara is a sporadic museum visitor. She does not like museums in Montreal because she feels they lack the sense of excitement of the Guggenheim, the Metropolitan, or the Prado. Barbara has a degree in fine arts and has worked in film. She is also a writer, having completed a screen play for a feature film. She is 25 and has not taken any courses in art history or art criticism.

> Jocelyn is married and has two children. She is 27 and possesses a bachelor's degree in music. She associates museum viewing with travel. As a teenager, she visited the Prado and the Louvre. A visit to a museum gives her background information on history and culture. At the same time, it provides her with the possibility of new discovery.

> Beatrice is in her late 20s. She is a student of fine arts at Concordia University. She is from South America, although she is very reticent about her ethnicity. She is an artist herself, having started with oils and then moved on to pastels. She associates art with her youth, with a time when she started visiting museums by herself. Although she likes all forms of art, she prefers sculpture, murals, and works by artists of a Spanish/Latin American descent. She likes to go to operas, despite their prohibitive costs, but she does not attend plays because she finds it difficult to identify with them.

> Matthew is an artist in his early 40s. He is married with two children. He has a graduate degree in fine arts and teaches courses in that field. Although his parents did not visit museums very often, they were involved in amateur operatics and theatre. Although he did not visit museums very often as a child, he was later encouraged by his family to do so.

These brief vignettes give glimpses into the lives of some people interviewed. They illustrate the view that "learning to see" depends, in part, on the preparation people have to see and on their early induction to the process of seeing. A sense of the past and their experiences with the past provide museum visitors with a framework for positive and negative responses to contemporary art. Although the thematic focus of this chapter draws extensively on the interviews with these five core visitors, the voices of others who were part of this study can also be heard.

A critical concern that informs much of this chapter is whether cultural objects have a stable set of meanings or whether their meanings derive from the interaction between the viewer and the object. A number of studies in consumer behavior have dealt with the issue of the meaning of objects to consumers (Bal, 1992; Belk, Sherry, & Wallendorf, 1988; Belk, Wallendorf, & Sherry, 1989; Belk, Wallendorf, Sherry, & Holbrook, 1991; Hirschman, 1986, 1988; Hirschman & Holbrook, 1982; McCracken, 1986; Mick, 1986; Rook, 1985). McCracken (1988, 1990), for instance, refers to objects as conduits of meaning from the culturally constructed world to the individual consumer. According to him, meaning is always in transit, and objects can be used in the creation and manipulation of meaning. Our research suggests that the cultural meaning of art objects is created in the process of interaction between the artists, the museum, and the individual viewer. Artists find expression in their art and invest meaning in the objects they create. The museum authenticates this meaning through research, acquisitions, documentation, accreditation, and, finally, interpretation. The museum's endorsement and the meaning that it invests in objects mark their status as works of renown. The very fact that art objects are located in discursive space within a museum gives them an aura of value. This sets the stage for the final transfer of meaning (McCracken, 1990) from the institution to the individual. The interaction between individual and product is the final step in the evolution of meaning.

Teaching to "see" creates a dilemma for the museum because its wish to educate the public is contradicted by curatorial attempts to interpret objects in a manner that makes them totally inaccessible to the public. Indeed, the use of the term "public" reveals the conflicting principles embodied in the museum. An element of distancing is involved in the use of the term. As Duncan (1991) notes,

> The public museum produces the public as a visible entity by literally providing it a defining frame and giving it something to do. Inversely, the political passivity of citizenship is idealized as active art appreciation and spiritual enrichment. Thus the art museum gives citizenship and civic virtue a content without having to redistribute real power. (pp. 93-94)

Although the individual fluctuates between the museum's attempt to teach him or her how to "see" and to the process of learning to "see," this chapter focuses on the latter.

Cultural objects vary in their coherence and in the meanings vested in them (DiMaggio, 1987). This is particularly evident in contemporary art, which is defined as a "process in the making." We were able to explore in a free-flowing manner the themes and topics that were of interest to our informants. The reviews provided by individual viewers contrast with those of the curators, the artists, and the publications that accompany an exhibit. Three themes emerged from this ethnographic study: Artists "see and use," museums "teach to see," and individuals "learn to see." In what follows, we present a description of the ways in which individuals experience art in the context of a museum. Our goal is to understand and abstract activities within this setting.

▨ The Literature

A growing body of work in anthropology, sociology, and art education relates to museum viewer behavior. These works can be organized into two sections: visitor sociodemographic and psychological profiles and person-object relations in the museum.

Visitor Profile

Research suggests that the clientele of art museums tends to be young, to enjoy a high income, and to possess a higher level of education than the general public. Bourdieu (1993), in particular, refers to the process of acquiring culture capital by this privileged few. In his words, "culture is not what one is, but what one has, or rather what one has become" (p. 234). Bourdieu goes on to describe the individual appropriation process that involves deciphering the work of art at various levels. Substantiated by a number of other studies, his research also shows that the level of education seems to be the most important variable in predicting the frequency with which people visit the museum (DiMaggio, Useem, & Brown, 1978; Kelly, 1987a; Lynes, 1980). Cross-cultural research in Canada, Sweden, England, the United States, and France confirms the importance of two variables in predicting visitor behavior in museums: education and wealth. Of these two, education seems to be more significant.

Studies suggesting ways of increasing the number of visitors to the museum have also been conducted (Hoope-Greenhill, 1988). McCall and Ellenport (1990) argue that the public has to be seen as the target for activity rather than as an irrelevant complication to museum activity. According to them, although the figures of museum visitors have not declined and show no signs of declining, the visitors they interviewed noted being bored with what was shown and suggested ways that exhibits might be improved. Roederer (1990) likewise argues that the public desires a different experience than what it gets in a museum. Roederer refers to the new hedonism that is multisensual rather than merely visual and that affects the public's experience of museums. These recommendations contrast sharply with what many museums actually do: sanctify art and set it apart from everyday life. This sacralization is visible in the architecture, the mandate, and the representation of art and artifacts in the museum.

Another study of the Canadian public and its attitudes toward the museum notes that although a positive image of the museum exists in people's minds this does not guarantee that these people will visit a museum. In a study of the museum of art in Toledo on the consumer allocation of leisure time, Hood (1983) found that adults identified six major positive attributes of museum attendance: being with people, doing something worthwhile, feeling comfortable and at ease in one's surroundings, having the challenge of new experiences, having an opportunity to learn, and participating actively. Hood also identified three different audience segments of museum visitors: frequent participants, occasional participants, and nonparticipants. It is not surprising that frequent visitors associated the museum with the attributes described above, whereas nonparticipants described the museum as difficult and requiring special skills to understand the museum code.

Apart from providing the sociodemographic profile of museum goers, Dixon, Courtney, and Bailey (1987) identified other reasons for frequenting the museum. The most common were "I wanted to learn something," "I wanted to enjoy myself," and "I wanted to see a special exhibit that I had heard about" (p. 190).

Other research on the museum experience deals with stages of aesthetic understanding that viewers undergo. According to Housen (1983, 1987), there are at least five such stages: accounting, constructive, classifying, interpretative, and re-creative. Furthermore, he suggests that certain stages are necessary in order to experience more complex ones. From an ethnographic point of view, the studies summarized above provide only "thin descriptions." Our study attempts a more holistic and humanistic description of art appreciation in a museum.

Person-Object Relations

Goffman (1983) argues that individuals bring certain "presuppositions" to any encounter that is important to them. In this context, we are referring to the knowledge, the expectations, the mental schema, and the values that individuals bring to their experience of art. According to Goffman, a presupposition can be defined very broadly as "a state of affairs we take for granted in pursuing a course of action" (p. 1). When a cultural object brings to the fore some of these assumptions held by individuals, a cultural interaction or positive encounter is said to have occurred. Such a view suggests that meaning does not reside in the object alone but, rather, is fashioned and created when individuals or groups interact with the object(s). The recognition of the artist and the interpretation of his or her artwork through the exhibits is only one level of this meaning-creation process. The second level involves an examination of the percipience of the viewer to the object (Griswold, 1986). Although this experience is highly individualized and heavily influenced by one's background, social class, gender, and personal biography, some themes distinguish themselves from this seemingly disparate set of ethnographic details. In this particular case, knowledge or the lack of knowledge of contemporary art seems to create the great divide.

McCracken's (1990) study of person-object relations in the context of a museum provides insight into how objects are vested with meaning in the North American context. According to McCracken, in North America, more than in any other part of the world, consumer goods are vehicles of cultural meaning that are constantly in transit from the world to the good and, ultimately, to the consumer. Museum objects, albeit noncommercial artifacts or goods, are also expected to be repositories of cultural meanings. McCracken argues that when these objects are from one's own culture, the decoding of meaning is easier than if these objects were from a culture very different from one's own. Consequently, matching cultural categories and principles across cultures through appropriate selection and pairing of objects is offered as one solution to the problem of interpreting cultural meaning.

Kelly (1987a, 1987b, 1993) raises an important issue: whether person-object relations end with the gallery visit. Through his research, he shows that this relationship can be extended by the acquisition of souvenirs or mementos relating to the exhibit or to the museum. In a study of visitors to an ethnographic museum in British Columbia, Kelly (1987a) argues that a number of people do not actually view the exhibits. Instead, they go to the gift store and buy souvenirs to remind themselves of it as well as to tell others that they had been there. This suggests that experiencing art has less value to some people than having been to the museum (and having socially visible evidence thereof).

Baxandall (1991) also considers the interactions between the artist, the exhibitor, and the viewer. He identifies the space between the object and the explanatory label as the point of intersection of the three. This is the space where a dialogue between the art object and the viewer can take place and where viewers demand a certain type of art criticism they will use to sharpen their own perceptions of the object. Consequently, Baxandall argues that, instead of seeking to control or direct the viewers' perception, the museum must try to enlarge this space by offering more stimulating interpretation. Ultimately, it is the viewer who has to make the connections between his or her life and the cultural object. Alpers (1991) and Gurian (1991) also offer insights into the manipulation of this viewer space. Gurian suggests that the interaction between object and person can be stimulated by a new style of writing labels. She recommends allowing the audience to participate in writing the labels and proposes that texts of different reading levels be included on the same label (i.e., separate texts for children and adults). Our investigation is an extension of the study of person-object relations employing both marketing and consumer research perspectives (Heinich, 1988). The implications of our research for the marketing of the arts in general and the marketing of museums in particular are many (Berry & Parasuraman, 1991; Bitner, 1992; Congram & Friedman, 1991; Kotler, 1982).

Method

This is primarily an ethnographic study of one museum employing an interpretive paradigm and multiple data collection processes. We focus on one particular site, Montreal's Museum of Contemporary Art, for the following reason. Although there are a number of other museums and galleries in the city, there is no other major outlet for exhibiting contemporary art. Indeed, this museum was built in response to specific needs expressed by local artists. However, over time this vision was lost, and disgruntled artists have created a new forum for exhibiting their work. This avenue, entitled the "100 Days of Art," an alternate to the museum exhibit, is an annual event located in an alternate space—a local factory warehouse.

Participant observation and in-depth interviews were the methods used (McGrath, Sherry, & Heisley, 1993). Data collection took place over a period of 2 years and involved visits to the museum and other city venues where contemporary art was displayed. Interviews conducted with about 45 visitors allowed us to explore the expectations and experiences they brought to the exhibits as well as to the museum.

Six researchers conducted this study, three of whom were codirectors and received funding for such purposes. Of the three directors, one is a consumer researcher with a quantitative background, the second is interested in strategic implications and has a marketing background, and the third is an anthropologist experienced in conducting and using qualitative techniques. The three graduate research assistants had background knowledge in literature and fine arts and prior experience with issues of representation and interpretation. The bulk of the interviews were conducted by the assistants, although the anthropologist not only made periodic visits to the site and helped in data collection but also directed and debriefed the others on a regular basis. Although the assistants participated in the iterative process, most of the analysis, interpretation, and writing was primarily done by the anthropologist. However as we see it, the outcome of the research is a jointly negotiated interpretation of how visitors perceive contemporary art in a museum setting (Joy, 1991).

The study of viewing behavior, collected primarily through participant observation, was conducted in a variety of ways. In some cases, we observed individuals as they moved through the exhibits. At other times, we observed several visitors or groups of visitors vis-à-vis specific exhibits. All researchers attended *vernissages* (opening ceremonies), tours, children's workshops, and a number of art-related events to get a sense of the various faces of the museum.

The interviews brought home the fact that articulating experiences such as a visit to a museum is a very difficult task. Language seems to constrain the expression of such an experience because there are dimensions that language cannot capture. Sherry, McGrath, and Levy (1993), for instance, note the difficulty in eliciting information regarding certain aspects of gift giving. To overcome this difficulty, they used projective techniques to uncover, for example, instances of negativity and ambivalence regarding gift exchange. Regrettably, we did not use any such projective techniques in our research. We also realized the importance of the unwritten norms of behavior in a museum. As noted earlier, the museum experiences a conflict in terms of its mandate to bring art to the people and its curatorial practices that sanctify it. This sacrality is communicated through the use of space and the artistic interpretation provided by the museum (Becker, 1982; Clifford, 1985; Lynes, 1980). Viewers, on the other hand, express discontent at the fairly formal contexts in which they are encouraged to see the exhibit. If they could have their way, the idea of the museum as a citadel of learning would be replaced by a more democratic approach to art. Ironically, such informality is evident along the museum margins, in its few "commercial spaces" such as the gift store and the café. In contrast to the formal and controlled exhibit activities, these commercial spaces are both vibrant and more accessible. The cultural model (the idea of the "sacred self") projected by the museum is challenged by the more pervasive cultural models (the "profane other") from the periphery (i.e., consumer culture).

Unlike conventional consumer research techniques that require a priori reasoning and the development of a plan of action, naturalistic inquiry is dependent on emergent design (Lincoln & Guba, 1985). Participant observation on site and in-depth interviews provide the basis for the various themes that have been and are to be explored. The theme, "learning to see," around which this chapter is structured, was developed after our being in the field for a few months and after several interviews with visitors, curators, and other museum personnel. Because the study lasted 2 years, we were able to participate and observe all the year-around variants of museum life. For instance, in the summer when the tourist season is at its peak, we were able to interview people from outside the country as well as those from around the city. Likewise, in the fall and winter, there were more regular types of visitors and more visits from schoolchildren. Thus we were able to achieve maximum variation in the sample chosen. Continuous debriefing sessions held after each interview allowed us to identify the gaps and questions to be pursued. As we moved from the museum to warehouses where contemporary art was also displayed (this shift in traditional exhibit location occurred in response to artists', art lovers', and art critics' perceptions of the inadequacy of the museum to display the art that was actively being produced and viewed), we reaffirmed our themes as they emerged.

Field notes were maintained by all researchers. In addition, we each maintained a field journal of our own experiences, noting emerging themes, changes in these themes, and other relevant observations of how we saw and interpreted data. This journal is critical in tracing the researcher's own growth in the process of data collection and in evaluating the implications of the "self" in such a process. Whether one likes it or not, ethnographers are always implicated at the hyphen between the "self" and "others." By exploring how we relate to those we study and the contexts in which this occurs, we gain a much better understanding of the multiplicity of our relations and a realization that the story that is narrated is only one of several negotiated outcomes between the researchers and the people studied (Fine, 1994; Marcus & Fischer, 1986). The journal also provides a metaframework for interpreting the interviews with individual visitors and museum personnel (Belk et al., 1988; Geertz, 1973; Hirschman, 1986). In some instances, in-depth interviews were tape recorded. However, because it was inconvenient to tape every interview, the research assistants made brief notes during the interviews and then expanded on them as soon as the interview was over.

Thus, overall, we tried to obtain as much verbatim information as possible from the informants and the personnel.

Over the course of this study, we were able to provide some feedback to the museum personnel regarding our observations, which were of interest to them. Although this was not a formal condition of our access to the museum, it was clear to us that they would appreciate such an effort. That ethnographers have to show more immediate forms of accountability is not new (Sherry & McGrath, 1989). Such action also allowed us to establish the necessary rapport with the museum personnel in order to pursue our study. The most difficult part of this study was to conduct in-depth interviews with viewers both because of the nature of the subject and because many of them were not regular museum visitors. For art students, critics, and regular museum goers, the vocabulary of the art world was very familiar, and hence questions relating to their experience of art did not pose much difficulty. However, those who were less knowledgeable about art felt a little threatened at first and seemed somewhat reticent to share their experiences with us.

Finally, we did not use outside auditors to examine the various pieces of data. From time to time, we provided drafts to some of the regular visitors, curators, and other museum personnel as member checks. Our goal was to develop a thick description of viewer behavior in the context of a museum and to assess the managerial relevance of our findings.

The Ethnography: The Museum of Contemporary Art

The following is a brief account of how people view art in a museum. Pseudonyms are used throughout the account, and, as is customary in ethnographic writing, the account is reported in the present tense.

The Setting

The Museum of Contemporary Art is a study in modern/postmodern neutrality. The old building, which was the site for the present ethnographic study, is an austere gray building with a restrained, muted reference to material and construction. All references in this chapter are made to this building.[1] Even the logo posted on a gray pillar outside the building is not readily visible unless one is looking for it. Consequently, the museum is what one can describe as perfectly indistinct space. Furthermore, it is located in an inaccessible part of town, away from the city center. The museum even has its own bus service to encourage more visitors.

Background and History of the Museum

The Museum of Contemporary Art was created in 1964 by the Ministère des Affaires Culturelles at the request of contemporary artists. The museum holds a permanent collection of 4,800 works, of which 60% are by Quebec artists and the rest by other Canadian and international artists. Its most recent acquisition has been the Lavalin collection, a corporate collection in Montreal. Half of the museum's collection is made up of engravings and etchings, and the other half is composed of paintings, sculptures, drawings, photographs, stained glass, and tapestry. The mandate of the art museum is to acquire, conserve, and diffuse contemporary Quebec art dating from 1939 onward. The museum is also mandated to ensure the presence of Canadian and international contemporary art so as to provide a point of reference for Quebec works. The museum sees itself as maintaining the artistic heritage of Quebec as well as promoting the production of visual art. It also has a major educative role to play and thus desires to serve all types of publics, whether they be amateurs or specialists. It wishes to open its doors as wide as possible and to expose all types of art while respecting the vocation of other art museums in the city.

The museum's current policy on acquisitions is to achieve a balance in its collection. Hitherto, its collection had been primarily Quebecois, but now it hopes to achieve a distribution of 25% Canadian art, 25% works of art by internationally renowned artists, and the remaining 50% comprising Quebec art. Lack of funding appears to have been a serious problem in making acquisitions, although political considerations seem to have had an effect as well. Until recently, even American art was deemed unimportant. As one of the museum's curators observed, "Quebec art cannot continue in the ghetto." The current strategy is to purchase the works of an artist early on in her or his career, despite the risk that this artist may not later be recognized. As one of the curators explained, "It gives us the flexibility of developing a major collection without the prohibitive expenses."

Physical Layout of the Museum

The administrative offices are located to the left of the entrance, with the reception area and gift store on the right. The lack of visual cues is a trifle disorienting, particularly because there are glass cases with art objects for sale at the reception area. Beyond these glass cases, the viewer can find posters, books, magazines, and slides for sale. On the left, past the offices, are the cloak room and washrooms. Beyond those, one finds vending machines, behind which are the café and service center. Between the café and the gift store, located in the rear, are the stairs to the galleries and to the library. What is most obvious to the visitor is the lack of signs identifying the various spaces in the museum. For example, there seems to be a great deal of ambiguity regarding the use of the reception area. It appears to be a "no man's land" because of the different uses of this space: greeting visitors, giving information, selling objects from the boutique, and so forth. One of our field note entries reads as follows:

> It is astonishing that on many occasions there is no attendant at the reception desk to welcome visitors or to provide them with information. Consequently, visitors are often at a loss about what to do and where to go when they enter the museum. While there are salespeople at the counter, on one occasion, the customer was made to wait a long time without being attended to. When customers ask for information, sometimes imprecise information (i.e., regarding the objects for sale) is given. The salespeople answer questions, but show little enthusiasm toward customers.

The café is not operated by the museum itself but by a concession owned by independent operators and subsidized by the museum. Although the museum deems this space as essential, the café is located in a small area, virtually tucked away from sight. What is interesting, however, is its popularity among museum visitors. On occasion, especially on weekends, the number of tables and the supplies of cups and saucers are inadequate to respond to the clientele, and the attendant is unable to service all the customers.

The library is also tucked away and fairly inaccessible. Located behind the stairwell on the second floor, it is a space untraversed by the regular viewer but only by those who deliberately seek it out. This documentation center features rows of filing cabinets containing slides, photographs, and current as well as older catalogues of the museum's permanent collection. Two walls are devoted entirely to books on art and art criticism, with another wall reserved for current periodicals. There are also audio-visual materials that may be consulted on the premises. This center does not lend out its resources: it functions primarily as a reference library.

Finally, workshop sites are virtually hidden from view, and there are no directions to indicate where the workshops are held.

TABLE 11.1

Artists/Exhibits at the Museum of Contemporary Art[a]

Name	Age	Birthplace	Type of Artist	Materials Used	Artistic Vision/ Focus
Miquel Barcelo	37	Majorca	Painter	Canvas, oils	Biographical/ allegorical in nature
Joseph Beuys	74	Germany	Sculptor	Felt, fat, everyday matter	Reinvent art and society
Charles Gagnon	60	Quebec	Photographer/ painter/ filmmaker	Film	Combines rational with emotional
Jacques Hurtubise	55	Quebec	Painter	Canvas, oils	Visual experience
Jannis Kounellis	58	Greece	Painter/ sculptor	Canvas, oils, wood, metal	Poetic and political considerations
Suzelle Levasseur	40	Quebec	Painter	Canvas, paints	Human figure in iconic fashion
Ken Lum	37	British Columbia	Conceptual art	Any material	Critique of commercial art and media
John Lyman	—	Canada	Painter	Canvas, oils	Representational work
Liz Magor	40	British Columbia	Sculptor	Wood, metals	Critique of being excessively literal
Gordon Matta Clark	50	United States	Sculptor/ architect	Buildings/ warehouse/ photography	Social responsibility
Mario Merz	70	Italy	Sculptor	Natural materials: wood, metals, and so on	Separation of nature versus culture

a. Compiled from descriptions given in brochures and pamphlets about the artists.

Exhibits: Structure and Interpretation

During the course of this research, the following exhibits were staged by the museum: Barcelo, Beuys, Gagnon, Hurtubise, Kounellis, Levassuer, Lyman, Lum, Magor, Matta Clark, and Merz. Table 11.1 provides a summary of these artists and their work.

In general, the exhibits are located in the galleries. On occasion, they start on the ground floor and extend to the first level. Special exhibits receive particular care. For example, in the case of one such exhibit, the entire entrance and gift store areas were reorganized to allow space for the objects displayed.

Besides allocating more space, the museum communicates to the public the importance of an artist by providing guided tours, by organizing family workshops around the exhibits, by scheduling conferences on or by the artist, and by posting a sign in the lobby with the artist's name on it.

In general, exhibits are arranged either in a chronological and linear order or thematically. Generally, there is a title card beside each work. However, in some instances, the title cards are grouped together at the entrance so that the works can be viewed as a whole. With creativity and imagination, exhibits can be structured visually and spatially so as to give due consideration to the viewer. Indeed, on occasions, exhibits are not arranged in the usual fashion, and reflect a preoccupation for creating an element of surprise and adding to the viewers' enjoyment. However, these are special occasions and not the usual pattern of exhibits.

English and French audiotapes are available to guide the viewer through exhibits. In addition, group tours are offered in both languages, and special tours are organized for children. Generally, guided tours are very animated, informative, and encourage visitors to "see" in directions that they may wish to explore. Generally speaking, the museum's attendants are formal with visitors and seem unsure of how much they should interact with the public. Their interactions seem limited to instances when visitors have tried to touch an object or peek beneath the surface of a painting to see what materials were used. Very few visitors approach these attendants to ask art-related questions, and when they do, they are answered brusquely. On occasion, the attendants themselves seemed unsure of how best to help the visitors in the museum.

Important Museum Events

In this section, we briefly describe selected artistic events to provide an overall impression of the many activities that both visitors and museum personnel are involved in. The opening ceremony, or vernissage, of a special exhibit is a common activity at the museum. It signals the commencement of an exhibit. Talks by artists/art critics, film shows, workshops, school/guided tours, and experimental theatre and dance presentations are also scheduled and held within the museum premises. The following vignettes provide a sense of the researchers' observations on these occasions.

Vernissage of Donors
For this museum, this is an odd exhibit—a mixture of works ranging from Lyman, Pellan, Hurtubise, Goodwin, Warhol, and Moore. The exhibit

occupies all galleries. There is a thin thread of historical development, but the exhibit stands without any accompanying literature from museum personnel. Consequently, it does not offer much to the viewer. I think the problem might be that the museum attempted to plant the exhibit squarely and evenly in the center of a complex of intersecting activities: the individual collector and donor; the museum as recipient, collector, and exhibitor; the artist as generator; and the public who is invited to see. A change from other vernissages observed was in the amount of socializing the museum management engaged in. People were very well-dressed. The importance of the donors could be assessed by the fact that the personnel spoke to every one of them. This is clearly a public relations activity.

Observation of a School Tour

The group of mostly fifth and sixth graders arrived at 10 a.m. The children were led to the stairs, where they paused before the Kounellis work placed there. The guide asked them what they saw in it and whether they could identify the materials used. The children recognized the fragments of statues and the artist's use of steel. They noted that the steel looked warm, rather than cold. She handed them samples of materials used by the artist. They could touch, smell, and look at the samples. She then asked them which scent pleased them the most and which the least. She also asked them to describe the feel of some of the materials like jute, unspun wool, charcoal, etc. For the children, the smells they judged as pleasant had some association with places and events in their memories. It is by using such associations that the guide brings them toward a better understanding of the art they are looking at. After taking them through the exhibits, she had them make music on the wooden seats lining the stairwell and make the bannister "sing." She also had them feel the rough concrete wall with their backs near the Kounellis exhibit. For the pictures, however, there was always the admonishment to "touch only with your eyes, three feet away."

25th Anniversary Celebrations

When I [Joy] arrived, the parking lot was full. Inside, the museum was crowded. At the entrance, a jazz band was playing. Decorations consisted of purple and white helium balloons. The café walls had an exhibit of AIDS art. Coffee and croissants were available. This seemed to be a pretty successful event, and people seemed to be enjoying themselves. But the art was also viewed. Clothing was casual, but generally stylish. Museum attendants appeared less conspicuous although an 11-year-old was chastised for having dirt on his shoes. The boy tried to escape, but the attendant held onto him and told him to clean his shoes. No doubt the attendants will be held responsible if any damage is done.

Special Workshop on Glass

This workshop was to demonstrate the contradictory characteristics of glass. It was meant to be an adjunct to the Merz exhibit that featured an enormous igloo and spiral table. The workshop consisted of four display tables, the first of which was a sealed case with samples of glass in various stages of the refining process. The second case consisted of glass pieces of various shapes and weights. The third consisted of pieces of glass rods, squares of glass, and a crystal ball. The final exhibit was a table of different sized glass jars filled with water. When tapped, they made different sounds. There was no formal demonstration and, except for the fact that the objects could be handled, the activity was essentially passive. It appears to me [Duhaime] that the activity department has difficulty organizing these events and that it also suffers from a lack of imagination.

Special Presentation of Dance/Photographs

The people waiting for the show to begin wandered through the galleries before settling down on the seats near the stairwell. This group was predominantly young, in its mid-20s, and dressed in black or generally darker colors. I counted 45 who attended the show. Entrance to the auditorium was through black curtains leading to a black room lit by spot lights. There were no seats: the performance was to be experienced standing up. The disorientation caused by going from a bright hallway to a dark room caused some confusion. This was a planned effect since the performance continued undercutting habitual orientations. As soon as everyone had entered, the performance began. There was a large screen behind the performance platform on which black and white pictures were projected. These were pictures of the hands and feet of one of the dancers who stood beside it, dressed in black. Five minutes into the performance, a second dancer appeared in the audience, her body moving through a series of silent crouches. Her presence was momentarily terrifying, and people moved away from her. This remarkable performance was a juxtaposition of dance, photographic images, and music.

Film Shows

The event for the day was three short films by Charles Gagnon. At least 60 people came to see the films, although some did wander in later. Gagnon makes films for filmmakers. One such film was very accessible because I [Duahime] had seen it before on Radio Canada and at the repertory. It is very emotional in its representation of Gagnon's understanding of war. The other two films were more abstract, more involved with the techniques of creating the image on the screen and so on. People left during the showing of these two films. The films are difficult to understand.

Visitors' Profiles

The observations reveal the presence of several profiles (or segments) of visitors differing in several ways from one another. The types of visitors varied according to the day of the week, the season, the type of exhibit, and the event. Although there is a great deal of variation among people who visit contemporary museums, (i.e., in their age, gender, ethnicity, level of education, occupation, and income), some commonalities do exist. The following segments are one way of classifying people from an etic point of view. Clearly, we are describing ideal types in this categorizing framework. The different segments were obtained strictly through observation of visitors' behavior and by interviewing people as much as possible.

Artists. This segment constitutes the core group (also the largest) of museum visitors. Their dress and behavior suggests that members of this group are either artists or art students. They tend to be young (in their 20s and early 30s) and dress in individualized clothes (black or dark colors and natural fibers—mostly cotton and leather). Some have limited income. Several of them come to the museum on a regular basis. They often know one another and like to socialize with their friends. They frequently visit the exhibits or look at certain works on exhibit more than once before leaving the galleries. Their viewing behavior suggests an overriding interest in art techniques. They look at the objects, the materials, the colors, and the forms from very close range, and sometimes even touch the works if no one is around to watch. A brief on the spot interview with one of them revealed that his interest was not recreational: "I want to see what other artists are doing. It gives me energy, ideas, even if I don't like what they have done very much." This particular visitor used the documentation center facilities on a regular basis, almost every week, mainly to look at art catalogues, slides, and art magazines. He mentioned visiting all new exhibits, some of them several times. In talking about the perception process, another artist noted,

> I look for connections between the paintings I like and those I do not like.
> I always look through the corner of my eyes to see three or four paintings
> and look at them as a whole. I know these paintings are not hung by chance
> because I have exhibited as well. . . . Probably in the artist's mind there is
> [a connection] but in your mind you are questioning.

Sociable visitors. This relatively small group is composed of people who, by dress and attitude, appear to be in the artistic community but for whom museum going does not seem to have anything to do with art. They trickle in, maybe one couple or group per day, racing through the galleries and only stopping to discuss mutual acquaintances or the last film they saw. They are most noticeable for saying virtually nothing about the art they are standing in front of. For these people, museum going is a purely social event. In one instance, four young women who came together spent more time looking for things at the gift store than at the art. They scanned the art very quickly, making comments to each other such as "gorgeous," "nice," "pretty," and so on. The interviews reveal that they do not know much about art and see the visit much like a shopping trip. Their lack of interest is due to an unfamiliarity with contemporary art, but they like to be around it.

Patrons. People in this group tend to be older (mid-40s to mid-60s), expensively dressed, and mostly professionals or people with family money. They often know one another and show up mainly during vernissages, dressed in expensive suits and semiformal dinner dresses. They form a small group only. On one occasion, a well-dressed couple wanted to know why a particular picture was chosen for a fund drive. A friend of theirs, a young man in an elegant gray suit, explained that it was one of a series of five by the same artist, that the museum already had the others, and that it was important to acquire this one to complete the series. Patrons are also fairly knowledgeable about the art exhibited.

Tourists. Individuals in this category form a rather disparate group in terms of age, income, and apparent knowledge of contemporary art. They visit the museum both during the week and on the weekend, especially during the summer months and holidays. They often come as couples or in a group, and they are dressed very comfortably: Hush Puppies or sneakers, sunglasses, and casual clothes. Brief conversations with some of them revealed that museum going is part of their irregular activities during vacations. Some of them have been to several museums in Europe and the United States. As Marge observed, "Wherever I happen to be, I hit all the museums, all the churches, and all the shopping centers." A visit to this museum is often part of an itinerary suggested to them by the Tourist Board. One of the tourists observed, "We saw this thing in the paper, and we came. We had been here and at the McCord Museum a few years ago, but this museum is isolated. It really requires a lot of effort to get here."

Families. This segment is mostly composed of families with preschoolers and school-aged children. Less often, they include children in their late teens. The parents are generally between 25 and 40 years of age. Some of them dress in casual but not inexpensive clothes. Families tend to visit the museum mostly during the weekend, usually on Sundays. The average family run through the exhibits is faster than others, partly because of the impatience of children. However, on occasion, children show a great deal of interest, as in the case of the Joneses, a family consisting of parents and two children who crouched for about 10 minutes in front of an igloo by an artist named Merz. They looked very carefully at the construction, exchanging ideas, and the parents answered their children's questions. Families tended to use the café more often than other groups.

Groups. Regularly during the week, visitors arrive at the museum as members of groups. The various groups include school groups (the largest segment being children from either day care centers or primary or secondary school), tourist groups, and groups of adult students enrolled in art history or fine art classes. The school groups benefited from the help of a tour guide hired by the museum.

Academics. Members of this group are college and university professors. They tend to be middle-aged and often wear corduroy pants and tweed jackets. They often attend public lectures, and they spend long hours visiting the exhibits, sometimes going over them twice. Many academics were pleased with the academic content and form of the lecture given by a curator on the artist Kounellis. Of particular interest to them was the artist's European background and his reception in North America. Finally, this group uses the documentation center facilities and often buys art catalogues. Academics visit the museum during the week and on weekends.

Film, dance, and theatre people. Although members of this segment resemble the artists in dress, age, and income, they differ from them in that they come to the museum strictly for art-related performances. They socialize among themselves and seem to know a lot of people. Cindy was one of them. She was dressed somewhat gypsy-like. Her shoes were plain, yet very light, and she seemed to dance or float. She was very interested in contemporary dance, given that she is an amateur dancer herself and practices dance therapy. She was happy to participate in the event, noting that "it is important to take time to listen to ourselves and those around us." She did not, however, view the exhibit.

Senior citizens. During the weekdays, older people tend to tour the exhibits. They often come in groups and are dressed comfortably. They are not necessarily knowledgeable about contemporary art. Overall, this group seems to be small relative to other groups.

Besides the above, there were other types of visitors who could not be easily classified. Also, the composition of museum visitors at any given time differed according to the day of the week, the season, the type of exhibit, and the type of event. On weekends, observations indicated the regular presence of artists, sociable visitors, tourists, families, groups, and academics. During the week, there were fewer visitors, mainly artists, some tour groups, academics, and senior citizens. Families primarily came on weekends.

Likewise, the summer crowd also differed from those who came the rest of the year in that it included larger groups of both tourists and families. Similar observations were made during the holidays and on long weekends. Different types of exhibits attracted different segments of visitors. For example, the exhibit of Ken Lum, an artist of Chinese descent, attracted larger than usual groups of visitors of Asian descent, whereas Barcelo seemed to be popular with Spanish-speaking people. Lyman seemed to have an appeal for the older (over 50) group, whereas Kounellis attracted a lot of younger viewers, mostly art students and younger artists. He also seemed to be popular with children.

Finally, the types of visitors differed, sometimes drastically, according to the type of event scheduled that day. Vernissages, for example, tended to attract art patrons, artists, academics, and young professionals, whereas special workshops involved young couples and groups with older children. The audience for talks or lectures varied depending on who gave the talk. Finally, art-related shows attracted people who, from our observations and interviews, specialize in a corresponding discipline: Dance performances, by and large, attracted dance people; film showings attracted film students or theatre people. This variation of visitor types in relation to the type of event may well reflect the success of the museum's promotional strategy, which is based on a segmentation approach.

Learning to "See"

Although individuals bring knowledge and their past experiences to an exhibit, their viewing experience is also influenced by the preparatory work done by the museum's curators, although sometimes the meanings vested in art objects, either by the artist or by the curator, may not always be apparent to visitors. Thus the artist creates meaning through his or her works of art, and the museum interprets this work for the public. The museum "teaches

to see," the artist "transforms and creates," and the individual "learns to see."
Our research suggests how this three-way interaction occurs.

Preparation for Seeing

The five vignettes at the beginning of this chapter provide a basis for
considering the background and preparation for "seeing" of those individuals.
In Caroline's case, forced visits to museums and an early exposure to formal
ways of viewing created a negative response to museum visits. Even though
she had taken art lessons during her youth, she very often repeated that she
was not very good at "seeing art." For Caroline, art and its personal importance cannot be forced or hastened. It takes time for her to "see," a process
that she vividly describes in her attempt to come to terms with Rembrandt
as the master of light. She observed,

> But Rembrandt is always so dark. . . . I couldn't figure out why he was the
> master of light. Years later, when I went back to the Rembrandt museum, I
> finally understood. It took me a long time. I studied those paintings, and,
> suddenly, I was able to see it.

This was a moment of self-discovery. Caroline wished to minimize the
influence of art critics and others on her experience of art. She truly wanted
to shake away the burden of the past.

On the other hand, Barbara had little to say about her childhood memories of museums and art. Jocelyn made a brief reference to having visited the
Prado and the Louvre as a teenager. She spent 3 days in the Prado, partly
because she wanted to get away from heat and pollution but also because it
featured a large collection of Bosch paintings. What fascinated her about
these paintings was their seeming modernity, despite their actual date of
creation. It was for Jocelyn "a first and fresh encounter." Years later, she wrote
a paper on Bosch and his work. The background knowledge she gained
through her research helped her "understand the paintings better."

Beatrice brings her personal life, her identity, and her biography to viewing
art. As a child, she felt alone in her interest in art. Although her parents
recognized her aptitude for painting, they did not actively encourage it. They
never took her to museums, and, to a large extent, they dissuaded her from
considering art as a career. At 13, she started painting. Initially, she was
fascinated with oils, but she quickly learned that she could not handle them.
As a result, she moved on to pastels, which offered her more control. She
thinks of art as "nostalgia," associating it with her youth.

Finally, Matthew recognizes the debt he owes his parents for encouraging his interest and aptitude in art. His father's interest in theatre and amateur operatics gave him ample confidence in presenting and doing things. Matthew visited museums from an early age, and he was allowed to dabble in paints. Although the family did not own works of art, he remembers a landscape painting owned by his mother:

> An incredible painting . . . very classical, very mundane. I guess that was an important icon in some ways. It was of two figures by a brook looking into a small woodland or copse. The act of "seeing" by these figures created a greater awareness of the importance of it and entering into the painting's reality.

Scholastic enrichment programs were also excellent ways of developing Matthew's interest and aptitude in art. He attended workshops that allowed him to dabble in art materials and pursue his knowledge and interest in a relatively uninhibited fashion. Attending art shows in the neighborhood was an important practice that he began early in his life. Whenever his father went to London, he went with him and spent the day at the Tate Gallery. As soon as he could travel by himself, he made trips to London and spent time at the Tate.

As Matthew spoke, one of the researchers recalled the importance of "seeing" and "learning to see" in her own past. She remembered the fascination she had with a painting reproduced in a book on the Louvre. It was a painting of Saint Joseph, a Dutch painting that showed an old man at work being both watched and illuminated by a small child holding a candle:

> For me, the magic of the work lay in the light shed by the candle. I was engrossed by the quality of that light, by the way it shone through the skin of the child's fingers. I used to experiment by holding my own hands near a candle to see if the artist had really seen it. Thematically, the act of perceiving light ran through the rest of my life also. I would watch the late afternoon sun on the trees as long as it lasted, or I'd watch that same light streaming through a window. I think that is what the painting really brought to me—the recognition of another's vision . . . that another had seen this light and showed what he had seen.

There were several others who spoke about their early socialization in the arts. In some instances, the families collected art, and in other instances, they were regular museum goers. For Josh, a 40-year-old clothing designer, museum going is a part of a variety of cultural events, including ballet and jazz concerts, that he attends regularly. For Martha, a fairly frequent museum visitor, coming to view art seems like second nature because she herself "dabbles in art." This interest in art began as a child and seemed to be nourished by her husband who does silverwork. Like Martha, there are several others who are involved with the arts at various levels. For them, their background and socialization in arts were critical for their current occupation.

Developing Intimacy With Art Objects

Whereas preparation for "seeing" was essential to the positive or negative responses that individuals felt when they saw specific art objects, the process of developing an intimacy with art and cultural objects over their lifetime seemed to have a tremendous influence on their appreciation of art.

Caroline's description of her realization that Rembrandt was the master of light suggests her intimacy with paintings and cultural objects. It was important for her to come to terms with these works of art, with little influence from knowledgeable people or critics. Her private and personal experience of art from an early age colors her contemporary vision of it.

Barbara briefly refers to developing an intimacy with art objects related to her childhood, a period during which she was oversocialized in regard to proper museum behavior. One of the important lessons that she learned was not to touch a picture or a sculpture even though her hands longed to reach out. After touching a piece of the exhibit, she noted, "In the back of my mind is the certainty that even if nobody is around, they are going to know if I put even a fingernail on something."

While Jocelyn had little to say about developing a certain sense of intimacy with art objects, Beatrice seemed hesitant to talk about it. From the time she was 17, she had visited museums in South America. She was interested in contemporary art because, as she noted, "it belongs to my time." Even as a teenager, she went several times to see a show or an exhibit "just to see . . . to look at it." Her sense of loneliness and longing helped her find solace in the art that she saw and loved. For Beatrice, this intimacy with art appeared to fill the gap she seems to have experienced in her life.

Matthew talked a lot about developing an intimacy with art. From the start, what seemed to have fascinated him are pictures of the "process of creation." He has memories of being "infatuated" with one particular picture in the Tate Gallery that he returned to see several times. Each time, he wished to know whether it had changed since he had last seen it. This thrill of bringing his previous experience to a picture and discovering that he could never go back to the first time rendered him unspeakable delight. This sort of personal growth and biography seem to have influenced his current experiences of museums and art.

Another visitor who was interviewed spoke about being emotionally involved with the objects she viewed. Looking at an Asian carpet that was part of an installation, she was reminded of the carpet in her own living room and was thus able to enter into a more intimate space than the object invoked. Likewise, another viewer who was very taken with the works of Joseph Beuys described them as having an "incredible amount of movement and swirling." Being very knowledgeable about Beuys, he noted, "The hat of course is Beuys's trademark . . . a beaten-up felt hat." Most of all, he seemed to enjoy the underlying religious connotation of one of the pieces. Commenting on its mock sacredness, he said, "It is like a religious icon . . . similar to religious paintings of the Renaissance. . . . Every bird, every flower, and every color can mean something."

Loren, who was interviewed at the "100 Days of Art" exhibit, had this to say:

> Sometimes I respond very strongly to a piece of art. Sometimes I connect with them. There is a similarity. I am on the same wavelength. I need the contact . . . the idea, and feeling. That is why conceptual art leaves me cold after the first 10 minutes. There's no humanity in it . . . which I think is important. I cannot develop an intimacy with art of that style.

Expectations and Experience Brought to Exhibits

The dominant theme that seemed to emerge from the interviews was the sense that, in contrast to daily events and occurrences, viewing art was sacred or unique. There are a number of ways in which individuals experienced a sense of sacrality in seeing and/or doing art. Some of the emerging themes are the return to the familiar, the wish to be surprised, humor, play, the irresistibility of the piece, an emotionally charged experience, intimacy, discovery, self-knowledge and growth, and feeling "right there." We deal with these in turn.

Return to the Familiar

There were not many references to this theme. Contemporary art is so abstract that it precludes any sense of recognition or return to what is familiar. In many instances, unless the title indicated the representation, individuals could not identify it. In Caroline's case, she was visibly disturbed by Lyman's landscapes. These landscapes, supposedly of familiar places, did not elicit any sense of recognition. She made quick scanning motions as if to confirm her

displeasure with the artist's presentation. In particular, she was very dis-
pleased with a landscape entitled *Tunis*, saying that she could have accepted
the painting without a title but that it bore no resemblance to Tunis at all.
Furthermore, when viewing a landscape of Cowansville, she remarked that,
although it looked like a scene she knew, the colors were strange. In her own
words,

> I couldn't see the landscapes. I could only see the portraits. The colours were
> weird. There was that one that I thought was a place I knew. That was a weird
> place. I thought it was a weird place. The painting looked like that.

The characterization of the familiar in this particular form of art seemed
to disturb Caroline. Similarly, Barbara also seemed disturbed by her identification of the familiar in the paintings of Levasseur. She shook her head from
side to side and described them as too "nihilistic." What she seemed to
recognize in them were memories of the Holocaust. To her, these paintings
had little humor or optimism, although the colors suggested energy that she
equated with optimism.

Jocelyn perceived elements of the Kounellis exhibit as interesting because
they reminded her of fragments of Greek and Roman statues. Part of this
pleasure came from her identification with something that she had already
experienced in museums elsewhere. Beatrice's fondness for the works of
Spanish or Latin American artists was in many ways also a response to what
was familiar. These works aroused in her a sense of nostalgia, a sense of
coming to terms with herself and her emotions evoked by symbols from her
past. In her words, what interests her in art is the reflection of some of her
own experiences:

> Eighty percent of the time, I already know something about the artist. If I
> do not know but like the work of an artist, I try to learn more. I really try
> to get myself in touch with the works before I go.
>
> Re Barcelo: I find this artist great. . . . He always uses enclosed rooms
> with just a splinter of light. There is a certain symbolism that is related with
> our times, with the obscurity of our times, with a sense of hopelessness that
> invites you to enclose yourself. I cannot differentiate all of this out of
> art . . . and I relate very well to it.

For Matthew, the work of Quebec artists such as Hurtubise and Gagnon
is very interesting because it is familiar. He feels that it is important to see
the concerns exhibited by these artists because they are currently influential
in the Quebec context. The works of art are also fascinating to him because

they reflect a process of evolution and development in Quebec art—very much akin to his fascination with art that reflects the process of creation.

Bianca was likewise drawn to the German exhibit because she was familiar with the style emanating from that part of the world. She said, "You know that in Germany, the level, the intensity of cultural manifestation is of great magnitude." Another woman who was interviewed remarked that she loved the works of Betty Goodwin. She does not necessarily prefer female artists, but she is interested in knowing how feminist ideas get translated into female motifs, symbols, and styles. She noted, "It's a language that I can comprehend . . . and want to understand more. I see in these works a valuing of women, an empowering of women, and, in that sense, it interests me."

The Wish to Be Surprised

When Caroline saw certain objects made by Kounellis, her eyes lit up and she became very excited. She moved very quickly toward the objects, read the titles, and then moved away from them in the most animated fashion to get a better view. She spoke more quickly and asked a number of questions with a great deal of pleasure. Clearly, she likes contemporary art because of the element of surprise. It makes her see things in a totally different perspective. She said, "The world is so drab; reality is drab . . . and then you see this work which suddenly makes you see things. It's like being in another reality." This sense of surprise and excitement at seeing something unexpected explains her preference for art galleries that she enjoys visiting on her way home from work—suddenly dropping in on a place she has just discovered and seeing the art there. For her, art is a very personal and intimate experience she wishes to discover accidentally, on her own, and in an intimate surrounding. This sense of surprise is evident whenever she speaks of being happy to find Kounellis in the Metro. This unusual juxtaposition of art and life fascinates her: "I would like to pass that every day on the way to work. It would be nice." This passion for surprise has been a part of Caroline's fantasy for a long time. In her words, it is like "following a narrow winding sidewalk and spontaneously discovering and entering a new doorway to find a magical reality."

Kounellis produced excitement and a sense of surprise because of the unusual juxtaposition of the materials that he worked with. It elicited metaphors of delight in her:

> The steel was warm, gasjets sound like water, and washbasin with charcoal. I saw an old washing basin. There should be water in there, but there's coal. I suppose it really should have been a flame.

Although the element of surprise in works of art was not as important to Barbara, the Kounellis exhibits did, however, create a great deal of excite- ment in her. She asked a number of questions about the gasjets and the fabrication of a particular piece in the gallery. She definitely found this work "different and interesting." What was important was that the process of questioning generated by the Kounellis exhibit seemed to inspire her to do more active viewing of the rest of the objects and the museum in general. Several other visitors also mentioned the desire to be surprised by an exhibit. They also remarked using this sense of the unexpected as inspiration for their work activities. A Montreal designer who now works in Toronto drops in to the museum every time he visits the city for that very reason. Although all exhibits do not inspire him in the same fashion, he likes to sharpen his own knowledge of what pleases him and what does not.

Matthew referred to the pleasure of being surprised by the Irene Whittome show at the Montreal Museum of Fine Arts. Although this has little bearing on the Museum of Contemporary Art, he suggests that museums can convey a sense of the unexpected by bringing together a set of works that challenge the museum, that "raise questions about the legitimacy and the validity of the museum itself."

Another visitor observed, "If the artist is too clear, if the artist tells us too much . . . that's too much and renders the work uninteresting. A certain sense of ambiguity enhances the value of the art." Commenting on a structure that included computers and terminals, another viewer also alluded to the desire to be surprised. He said,

> The screen blinded us. Nevertheless, my impression was that we were invited to touch the keyboard . . . to send ourselves messages. I was also hoping to see other illusions inside the structure when I looked through the broken metal parts.

Humor/Play

Although the element of surprise made people aware of the comical or absurd conveyed through art, viewers did not make any references to humor. During our observations, we noted how much time people spent in front of exhibits and their physical reactions to the art. We noted that many viewers burst into laughter or had a beaming smile when they saw some of the exhibits. Caroline's experience of the Kounellis exhibit was, at best, cautious and tentative. Although the open flame seemed to make her a little less spontaneous, she asked, "Is this the force of life?" and then laughed.

Barbara was distressed at the Levasseur exhibit because of its lack of humor and optimism. She observed that even though its use of color reflected energy and optimism, the forms in the pictures were anguished and in pain. In contrast to this, she found the black-and-white paintings very pleasing. Their shape suggested some humor to her, although this was later dissolved by the use of color. This dissolution of whatever form was initially apparent disturbed her, but then she found that the juxtaposition of text with sculpture was interesting and conveyed humor. She found the next exhibit, *Four Remarkable Bears*, both satisfying and very funny. Although Jocelyn, Beatrice, and Matthew responded to various unusual and unexpected elements of contemporary art, they never used the word "humor" to describe them.

Many visitors expressed enjoyment over various forms of puzzle-solving as they viewed the art works. One individual who liked the Matta Clark exhibit (architectural in orientation) elaborated on the analogy between Clark's process of investigation and discovery of architecturally defined space and the relation between the body and the self. Remarking on the object (*Splitting II*) he said,

> I found it intriguing because, well, it reminded me of a kind of dissection on a living body, and I thought that when you carry the analogy further it is a bit perverse in the sense because it had neither the authority of a grotesque presentation of the decimated body, so it wasn't like shock and horror, and, at the same time, it didn't really seem to have a kind of valid reason, such as biological research. It seemed a bit creepy, a bit disturbing . . . and yet it seemed like the artist was playing with the boundaries . . . breaking the boundaries. He was really playing with form and light.

At the "100 Days of Art" exhibit, viewers were also vocal about the absurd that was presented in art. Christine noted that she loved the humor in Pat Steir's work. For her, the humor resided in the fact that it was created out of blackboard and chalk, materials that she never thought would be used in art. She also remarked that the drawings of infants on the inside of the cube made her think of a womb. There were also others who noted the importance of the absurd in art.

Discovery of "Self"

Under this rubric, a number of themes could be subsumed: art as an emotionally charged experience, the irresistibility of the piece, its sense of play or lack thereof, a sense of intimacy, personal growth, and a concomitant sense of well-being. Not all informants used the same words to refer to their experiences, but it is clear that their links to art were similar to their discovery and definition of "self."

Caroline is very clear about what pleases and displeases her. She does not like to be influenced in her viewing by expert opinions. She is resolute in her view that art must contain an element of surprise to compensate for the drabness of reality. She dislikes the mix of art in the Museum of Fine Arts' permanent collection so much so that she only goes there to see special exhibits. She remarks,

> I hate that stuff. . . . It makes me sick. I really don't like it. Such exhibits are displays of ornaments and have a heavy bourgeois significance of things, and the burden of things from the past.

Art is a part of her life, and she would like it to remain that way in order to break the monotony of the real world. Art forces her to think about life, and it appears that the negative aspects of her life are compensated by the revitalizing effect of her discovery of self through art. "It is important to sit and muse about one's experiences," she observed, "and to digest it within the context of one's life."

Her final comments about an outdoor exhibit she viewed as she left the museum reveals her understanding of "self" and the role art plays in her own self-development. The exhibit featured a miniature landscape made of moss and lichen and resembling the human brain. She quickly bent over the piece and spontaneously identified and described the various forms of lichen used. She was not self-conscious about the classification process that she engaged in, almost as if it were important to her sense of well-being and identity.

For Barbara, art is an emotionally charged experience. Art as an intellectual exercise does not fascinate her. In fact, if an object does not arouse her emotions and her senses, she loses interest in discovering more about it. To her, trying to deconstruct a piece of art in order to understand it is truly laborious and unexciting. Although the conceptual basis of a work of art is important, she feels that art that requires such mental maneuvers is "cold and emotionally repressed." She does not derive a sense of play from the combination of logic and art.

Jocelyn's view of art and its impact on her life is equally emotionally charged. She dislikes the use of innocuous objects, such as the bedspring that formed part of one of Kounellis's exhibits. It bothered her, and she referred to it as "trashy." Although she disliked the exhibit, it incited her curiosity to find out more about the artist and the work. Because art is "opaque" to Jocelyn, she needs background information and knowledge. Her recollection of the works of Bosch in the Prado suggests that although she was intensely moved by the pictures her later attempt to write an essay on the artist opened up many doors for her own discovery, pleasure, and personal growth. Her visit to the Cairo museum and her memories of the visit confirm the importance of background information and knowledge for her appreciation of art. She is like a designer who frames her sense of "self" through her understanding of the objects on display. As she puts it,

> There were blocks of buildings and stuff from the tombs, and when you finally found out where they were from, they were 4,000 years old. You could rummage and discover the identity of these things in all that chaos. That was truly exciting.

Beatrice appreciates art through her heart, her soul, and her mind. Being a fine arts student, she has the necessary knowledge to bring to her experiences. However, despite the importance of understanding art from a historical, political, and sociocultural perspective, she feels a need for personal growth and involvement in what she sees. Thus it is important that art reflect her life, her experiences, and her total "self." The works of Spanish and Latin American artists please her because she can identify with them. Because of her Spanish background, the symbols and colors and textures used are familiar to her.

Given her views on art and her sense of isolation, art provides her with much solace. To get more out of any show, she likes to familiarize herself with the works of the artist before going to see the exhibit. Most of the time, she already knows about these artists, especially if they are Spanish or Latin American. Her emotional involvement with Barcelo is evident in her discussion of the work of this artist and her contrast of his work to that of Ken Lum. In her words,

> I like his ability to work with textures. I like colors, and although there is not much colour in his paintings, he was able to acquire light and shadows out of the textures of his art, and I think that is quite a feat. That's what I like most about this artist. In a way, any artist is limited by technique, but he freed himself from technique by using another material, a scrap of paper, for instance, just to give the idea. He shows that he is not limited by technique really. . . . Lum, on the other hand, is very precise—the colors, the shapes, the letters—it's mostly graphic art, and I miss something from it. I feel that something's missing. I find him more of a sign painter than an artist.

Her use of metaphor to express the rather indescribable feeling that Barcelo evokes in her is very revealing. She refers to this feeling as "inside reciprocity." The oneness that she feels with the works of this artist reflects her mind, her body, and her soul. Considered separately, each of these dimensions, while analytically useful, cannot fully capture that sense of the "whole" she senses. She continues,

> Nothing has delineance really. It's really, in a way, disorganized. I feel a constant "inside anxiety." . . . It's like being disturbed. That's what I appreciate. Ken Lum, on the other hand, is very precise, very clear, very clean, very well delineated, colourful but limited too. It shows me less "inside."

This feeling is so sacred and so important to her that she feels great joy on going to see an exhibit. She enjoys art so much because she looks at it from the point of view of history, politics, and culture. Although all these elements are in a sense distinct, they all affect the artist and his or her works. They are not visible all the time, "but they are there—hidden in some ways." For Beatrice, art is life and vice versa. The two cannot be separated because art encodes the complexities of life. In her view, the individual is part of this reality and grows with it.

Perhaps for Matthew, art has always been a part of his life and central to his personal growth and maturity. To him, it is a personal experience and will always remain so. That intimate link with cultural objects is witnessed in his preference for solitude—to commune with objects without distractions. The thrill of looking at something and realizing how important it was to see it and gain some form of intimacy with it is a significant goal of his life. He describes this as a "dialogue with cultural objects." To convey this pause that occurs when viewing an object of personal significance is, he observes, a very important aspect of life. Recalling a feeling that he had on viewing a painting by Vermeer, he said,

> You looked at a time which somehow expanded. You were looking at the moment in which it was painted, a particular period, and you know that the anxiety of the moment did not abide in that work; somehow it had expanded. And you gained an incredible insight as to the attitude, feelings going on between the painter and subject, and for one crazy moment, you really felt as though you had been invited in and you could create all kinds of personal projections which were encouraged by that experience.

This sense of well-being that he feels when he is around art is projected in his fantasies of having a Vermeer in his home. He said he would "like to see the picture when having breakfast, when drunk, in candlelight, or while having an intimate conversation with someone." Vermeer, above all, is a painter of interiors, of intimate private moments—very much like the land-scape painting Matthew recalls. Time, according to Matthew, expands and draws an individual into the picture, as it were, if only briefly. That brief encounter provides much revitalization of the mind, the body, and the spirit.

Not all museums nor all types of art evoke the same intimacy that Matthew experiences when he sees Vermeer paintings. It depends on the mood he is in, the space in the museum, and the way the exhibits are set up. A conglomeration of objects or exhibits that are loosely coupled makes it difficult for him to get into such an intimate mood. He feels pulled in many directions and unable to experience these works as a whole. He finds this stressful, as if it were an act of compartmentalization of the "self":

> The juxtaposition of the three shows (Barcelo with other Quebec artists) is intellectually interesting. You can make all sorts of jumps and associa-tions. You can think about culture, assimilation, and so forth. But it seems contrived. It's too much for me to be there. It's like going to three different places in one place. It might be a good experience in itself, but for me it's too much. What I might have to do is to go to one, then see the other exhibits at another time.

The experience is total and charged with emotions.

For Marjorie, the works of Betty Goodwin were very important. She observes,

> I would go back because I felt something. . . . Her paintings are very intense, and I think it is hard to absorb all of it in one session. In fact, I seem to have only one of her images in my mind right now. But there were enough there that were intriguing and touched me both here (touching head and heart), and you know you want to go back. You know you want to look at them again . . . which is really a positive statement about her art.

Literal Representation

It seemed ironic that this issue would come up in a contemporary art museum since, by definition, contemporary art challenges and critiques traditional representational modes. However, Caroline made some observa-tions regarding Lyman's portraits of a woman. They were both of the same woman: In one, she was clothed and had a stern, but serene expression; in the other, she was nude and had a very antagonistic expression. Caroline was fascinated by these portraits and spent a great deal of time looking for similarities and differences. Finally, she concluded that it was the same woman in both portraits that seemed to pique her curiosity further. "He got her to pose nude," she observed, "and she is skeptical. . . . She does not like doing this at all!" In trying to understand these paintings, Caroline was involved in a dialogue with herself. She tried to identify the model's feelings that would lead to these representations. To her, viewing Lyman's portraits as literal representations heightened the pleasure of the moment. However, none of the other informants seemed to be concerned with this particular aspect of art.

Visitors to the "100 Days of Art" exhibit showed appreciation in a similar literal sense, with reference to Pat Steir's chalk drawings of human figures. A mother with three children discussed the dimensions marked on the figures as these dimensions related to the age of the figures. She pointed out the difference in the circumference of the sweep of the arms between the younger figures and the adult ones. Another group of women, likewise, noted the differences between the male and female figures. Both these groups examined and understood the work in its most literal sense, seeing it as a comparative study of various body types.

The "How" of Works of Art

Although in the appreciation of a piece of art the emotional and the intellectual ways of seeing art gained prominence, occasional references were also made to how these objects were constructed. Caroline seemed to be concerned with the construction of the Kounellis exhibit. The surprise she felt on finding a bedspring as an integral part of the object prompted her to consider its other aspects. When a work of art pleased her, she wanted to know more about its composition.

Barbara seemed to be particularly interested in both the materials and the construction of the piece. In particular, sculptures seemed to arouse her desire to know more about how the piece was fabricated. This interest in the construction of the object led to disappointments as well as surprises. She found the use of lead a bit incompatible with her expectation of works of art. However, it caused her some surprise, and she derived pleasure from such knowledge.

Jocelyn also seemed to be interested in the "how" of art, especially when she viewed Kounellis's exhibit. Her curiosity was unexpectedly aroused by the recognition of day-to-day items such as a bedspring. Although she considered the use of the bedspring "trashy," she wanted to know the purpose of the piece within the overall framework and was quite willing to reconsider her original opinion of it. With respect to the gasjet installation, she was fascinated by the many parts that constituted the piece. She wanted to know about each of these parts and the materials that were used, the source for the jet, the effect of the heat created by the gas, and so forth. Because art is opaque to her, it is important for her to understand what the piece is made up of or to have background knowledge in order to appreciate it.

Beatrice's infatuation with art does not motivate her to appreciate objects from this particular perspective, yet she does observe the use of technique in Barcelo's work. Furthermore, although she identifies technique as paramount, she prefers artists who are not constrained by it—hence the pleasure she derived from observing Barcelo's work in contrast to Lum's.

Matthew finds pleasure not only in viewing art but also in learning from it. He recalled that he and his friends had once distracted museum guards in order to lift the paintings and test their tautness by tapping on their back. He observed that although these are the types of activities that museums frown on they are critical for an artist. Another time, he and his wife had a rather embarrassing situation when she ran her hands over a painting. He mused that although this was a natural reaction, it was not right considering the value of the painting.

Likewise, Josephine showed great interest in the works of Joseph Beuys, particularly in his blackboard art works. She noted,

> It interests me because you can feel that he is involved in the making of the work. You can feel the sensitivity radiating from the blackboard. Even in the writing, you can sense the efforts, the emotions that comprise the atmosphere during the creationing . . . he's writing, he's erasing . . . we can feel that he is absorbed by the piece.

For Paul, the "how" of works of art could only be comprehended through the piece's appropriate location within the museum. Commenting on Becher's piece *Blast Furnace Heads*, Paul explains, "Since the composition is very large, we need more distance to appreciate the work better. The materials can be viewed from nearby, but it does not make sense as a work of art unless we gain perspective."

Experiences and Expectations of Museums

Having considered the various dimensions of experiencing art, we now consider the views that these informants had of the museum that housed these exhibits.

Museums as Sacred Spaces

In this section, we argue that museums are sacred spaces, set apart from other types of institutional spaces. In the minds of visitors, museums facilitate intense emotional and intimate involvement with cultural objects. This involvement is also evident in the behavior associated with these spaces. Museums generally enforce a code of conduct that respects individual appreciation of art with minimal distractions. This includes the control of sounds like talking, laughing, shuffling of feet, and, particularly, children's behaviors. The sacredness of museum space is also evident in the ways curators use space. They prefer to use all of it for the exhibit rather than for cafés or boutiques. It is in this sense that we use the term "sacred" to suggest that space is a metaphor for the multifaceted and deep involvement that individuals have with cultural objects.

For Caroline, museums, in general, are formal spaces that inhibit the individual from achieving a sense of well-being and intimacy with art. Insofar as museums are set apart from everyday spaces, they serve to distance art from life. Particularly in the case of contemporary art, works could be well incorporated in public spaces such as the Metro so that an individual could see and enjoy them on a daily basis, without the element of personal intimacy and spontaneity being removed from the viewing experience. To Caroline, museums such as the Museum of Fine Arts, with its eclectic collection, are too ornamental and bourgeois. For her, museums kill any sense of surprise that art can evoke and, generally, stifle the viewer's personal growth and intimacy with works of art. Her major complaint about the Museum of Contemporary Art was that it lacks spaces for sitting and contemplating works on exhibit. She feels that museums should provide the individual with the opportunity to recuperate from this encounter. In her words, "I like to sit far away and look at them from a distance and decide which ones I want to see more closely. Then I get up and go and look at them from near."

She also felt that the Lyman exhibit was too crowded. The walls of the museum inhibited viewing Lyman exhibits from a distance. She said that a place to have coffee and recall what was seen is essential for the resolution of a sacred and emotionally charged experience. Once this experience has been digested, it is then possible to go back into the real world and deal with its problems and issues. Because life to her is extremely drab, seeing art and being around it offers that bit of hope for lifting her spirits. This contrast of drab life with exciting and fulfilling art experiences summarizes, for Caroline, the importance of art and the housing and location of such art in museums.

Barbara was more vociferous in her dislike of the Museum of Contemporary Art. She is unhappy with its location, its building, and the size of its galleries. She noted that the colors inside were all gray and cold and that the galleries were all of the same shape and size. To her, architecture is an integral part of understanding and loving art. Her memories of the Prado and the

Smithsonian suggest that she likes to have small rooms off galleries, where more private viewing is possible. She noted that such rooms also allow for viewing an object or a small number of objects apart from the exhibit and without surrounding people. It allows for at least some moments of intimacy with the art object. The neutrality created by this undifferentiated use of space makes it difficult for her to appreciate contemporary art, although she believes that this is a deliberate choice by the museum to match the architecture with the art exhibited.

For her, a museum visit is a sensual and emotionally charged experience that includes not just the art on display but also the use of space. "The architecture and decor should be special, varied, and unique," she observed. "It should convey the importance of the aesthetic experience which it encompasses." She also views museum visits as "events or occasions" with some amount of ceremony and ritual. She argues that, in general, Montreal museums are very conservative and safe and house art "that is watered down."

What she finds disturbing in the Museum of Contemporary Art is that although the building reflects the challenge posed by avant-garde art, this effect is diluted by the presence of very conservative-looking guards hired by the museum. Similarly, the lobby suggests a conventional and restrained approach to avant-garde art. It is ironic that contemporary art, defined by its lack of constraint and control, should be housed in a space that evokes these very qualities. Barbara noted that the contemporary sense of experimentation and discovery is stifled by the museum.

For Jocelyn, visiting museums is like visiting a new country: The sense of discovery, pleasure, culture, and history is replicated in such visits and is the central focus of such activities.

Beatrice attends museums at least two or three times a month. She is a part-time volunteer for certain exhibits at the Museum of Fine Arts. Her comments about the Museum of Contemporary Art reveal the importance she attaches to museums and their use of space to enrich her experience of art:

> I find it small . . . very, very small. It has some big spaces that is very nice, such as the entrance . . . and that's very interesting . . . gray carpet, white walls, nothing out of the ordinary. But I expect to find more glass, more play with materials that they have used in the construction, more art display. I expect to find high ceilings and open glass ceilings that let in the light. I like this feeling. It's like going to a temple. It's like going to church.

She elaborates on this feeling of transcendence that occurs. She feels a "presence there . . . to raise myself, my spirit, to the level of the presence." Her imagery is of soaring vertical spaces, of churches, and of places where the individual expects and sometimes experiences a sense of spiritual well-being. That experience is sacred to her and important for her own growth and personal sense of happiness. The architecture raises her to great levels of ecstasy that few places can. Beatrice contends that the Museum of Contemporary Art fails to do so because it is too square a building and appears as if it is made up of "blocks." Architecture is an important element of the aesthetic expression, and unless this expression is incorporated in the design, "it is merely shelter."

This intent is visible in the Museum of Fine Arts, which is both classical and modern. This integration provides that extra source for the release of emotions. She likens this to a religious experience intended through ecclesiastical architecture.

Her opinions as to how to improve the Museum of Contemporary Art are also clear and unequivocal. She suggests that museums must provide a frame of reference because people don't know what to expect. Viewers wonder and ask themselves whether the paintings or objects are what art is purported to be. Beatrice asserts that if the museum raises this critical awareness in individuals it has served its purpose. She concludes,

> For those reasons, it is important that museums invite people to explore today's art, today's way of expression—not to make it harder to understand but to make it accessible, make it easy, something they can personally relate to.

Perhaps of all people interviewed, Matthew was most vociferous in his criticism of the use of space at the Museum of Contemporary Art and the importance of space in relation to the art displayed therein. As noted earlier, museums have been an important part of his life. He has visited several of them, some more often than others. In his mind, there is no such thing as an ideal museum—that would suggest some form of standardization. He believes that museums should reflect the places where they are located. As an example, he made these observations about the national museum in Washington, D.C.:

> The conveyor belt in the museum is much like its use in a factory. People are shuttled across to the various parts of the museum. This, with the mock proportions of the building, the allusion to French architecture really made sense in the capital city.

Likewise, museums that convey a sense of proportion and time in relation to the objects they house are exceptional, he observed. Although he is not consciously aware of his expectations regarding a museum visit, he is aware that space and art cannot be viewed neutrally. "It would be great to view a museum and only afterwards realize what it was," he observed wistfully. The impossibility of this ideal, however, is very clear to him. He notes that a museum can provide "a very anonymous setting for a terrifically intimate experiencing . . . that frees an individual to experience the art in a manner that is meaningful to him." By taking an active role as interpreter and authenticator of cultural products, the museum limits the individual's freedom to develop an understanding and personal link with art.

About the Museum of Contemporary Art, Matthew is unsure of the image it conveys—didactic or glossy. Although he finds the Museum of Fine Arts appalling, he feels that it conveys a sense of critique and challenge in the way exhibits are organized. Rather than take it for granted that the museum authenticates art, it is important to raise the issue. Matthew is of the opinion that when objects are made primarily for viewing in a museum the museum has not served its purpose and the works of art have lost their critical edge.

Loren, who had visited the museum as well as the alternate annual exhibit in the city, observed that the museum was remiss in its duty as educator. She was referring to the representation of Joseph Beuys's work. She had overheard a group of people referring to one of the pieces, *Rock on Floor*, as a phallic symbol. At this point, she had interrupted the conversation to inform them that the artist's overriding concern was with the environment. Loren felt that this type of misunderstanding happened because the museum had failed to explain Beuy's philosophy to the public. She also thought there was too little of his work shown for an individual viewer to grasp the magnitude of the artist's work and philosophy.

At the Museum of Contemporary Art, there seems to be a split between the curatorial and administrative approach to the use of space. The commercial tilt in design supported by the administrators should not come as a surprise because, as the American Association of Museums suggests, museums are big business. The art museum as a social meeting place and a cultural department store is an American idea that has taken root. Libraries, lecture halls, coffee shops, and sales counters are very common in these buildings. The flip side of being very appealing to the visitor is that this takes away from the contemplation of art. A long trek past gift stores and varieties of coffee may be wearing on an individual who is interested in the art and who may find that in the end the art is dull and boring compared to what else was already seen (Posner, 1988).

Other Museums, Other Times

All the informants contrasted pleasurable experiences at other museums with their experiences at the Museum of Contemporary Art. Many of them had visited museums around the world and had special recollections of the space, the intimacy, the variety, and the uniqueness of experience these museums offered. To many, the contrast between the Museum of Fine Arts and the Museum of Contemporary Art was very sharp, with most preferring the former.

The Politics of Art/
The Self-Consciousness of Quebec Art

The final element of the museum experience, articulated by both Beatrice and Matthew, is central to the organization of the museum and the structuring of exhibits within its space. According to a study conducted by the University of Montreal in 1982, the Museum of Contemporary Art was created by the Ministère des Affaires Culturelles at the request of contemporary artists. Initially, 100% of the funding came from the government— hence no search for alternate commercial sources of funding was undertaken. Although this freed the museum from compromising its artistic priorities, it has also made the museum more insular than others of its kind.

The importance of how politics impinges on art and artists was articulated by Beatrice and Matthew, partly because of their knowledge of art and museums and also because of their experience with the Museum of Contemporary Art. To Beatrice, social, cultural, and political influences affect the artist and are displayed in his work, although these influences cannot be separately identified or delineated. Art is to be experienced in its totality and as a reflection of society. Politics is much more central to Matthew's view of art and museums. In his comments on the Museum of Contemporary Art, he remarked that it has an "anesthetized political feel to it"—in other words, the works selected by the museum can easily be contained within it and do not challenge it. In this context, it is interesting to note that Barbara, Beatrice, and Jocelyn all commented on the "safe art" that the museum purchases and displays. This art does not question the museum's "trusteeship" nor reflect the democratic ideals that the museum may wish to convey.

The politics of art is also conveyed through the relationship of the artist to the museum. Matthew feels that the Museum of Contemporary Art has treated artists very badly because of an imbalance of power between the museum and the artists. He notes that the museum does not give the artist much say in the organization of space and the exhibit of his or her work within that space. He suggests that if the museum does not invite the artist to set up his or her own exhibit, then that artist has to be wary of how the curator interprets his or her work because the use of space may radically change the meaning of the work.

With regard to specific shows by Quebec artists, Matthew is very puzzled by the self-consciousness of culture presented in the art. He views art as a by-product of culture and notes that Canadians seem to be very self-conscious about culture:

> There is always an attempt to make it pronounced, as viable and objectified as it possibly can be. Culture is something which occurs and not something you make. . . . It's a by-product and not the central issue.

Matthew further notes that the Museum of Contemporary Art is very self-conscious in its approach to Quebec art. He feels, however, that it is important to see these exhibits because they take the familiar and throw it into relief. In that manner, the museum has defamiliarized the process of viewing art. From an intellectual perspective, art can be viewed as historical artifact: It can symbolize the evolution of the society from which it evolves.

The sense of disappointment with the museum experienced by contemporary artists is displayed most vividly in the actions they have undertaken. Every year, artists hold an art show in a local warehouse where they display current works—mostly by artists who have never shown at the museum. Our observations on viewer behavior showed that, on average, people who came to this alternate exhibit stayed longer to view the art and actively read the accompanying catalogue.

Barbara, a very vocal visitor to the museum, noted that she was a little disturbed about the museum's lack of English in its signs and pamphlets. (As a point of reference to the reader, the museum does produce pamphlets in both languages, but English versions are only available upon request.) Although she understands that the museum is intended to reflect Quebec society, she feels it ridiculous not to use English. She argued that "if they [the museum] wanted to promote Quebec art, then they have to reach out, past the confines of the province. This means accommodating visitors who are not French."

Conclusions and Research Implications

This chapter explored the ways in which visitors perceive art in the context of the museum. We have documented the process by which data were gathered. We also identified the behaviors associated with exhibits, vernissages, the library, the gift store, guided tours, and so on both from the point of view of the individual viewers and that of the museum personnel. Finally, we elaborated on some of the important themes that emerged from our observations and interviews.

Three significant themes are "learning to see," "teaching to see," and "creating and transforming." Whereas the artist and the museum teach to see, the individual learns to see. The meaning of cultural objects, we argue, lies not merely in the works created by the artist but in the process by which the museum interprets and authenticates them and in the ways in which individual viewers experience them. Thus it is a three-way process, with meaning arising out of this interaction between the works of art, the interpretation of the museum that houses this art, and the individual viewer's perspective of it.

For many viewers, art as "discovery of self" is a cherished outcome of person-object relations. Although contemporary art is less understood by the general public, most viewers consider it an emotionally charged experience, where a sense of play, intimacy, well-being, and personal growth are all involved. Art forces individuals to think about life and provides a sense of connection with the rest of humanity. In a manner of speaking, art is life and encodes the complexities of life. To contemplate life with art objects is the wish expressed by many. Contemporary art, in particular, is contrasted with art from the past and is defined in terms of whether it is challenging and provocative. For many, the disappointment comes only when the works are not on the "cutting edge" and when the museum does not dare to take risks. By looking at the "how" of works, by "developing an intimacy with objects," by "seeing the humor in art," or even by viewing "art as literal representation," viewers recognize the clever internal balance of the elements (and sometimes the lack thereof) that may initially appear grammatical. But as the gaze extends and viewers recognize the familiar or are surprised by the unexpected, the different elements and the tensions they create begin to reveal a spellbinding poetry that leads the individual down the road to self-discovery.

However, the dialogue between person and object does not occur in a vacuum. In this context, it is enhanced by the space and the interpretation of the object by the museum. Two issues are significant: first, the notion of the museum as a citadel of sacred lore, and second, the notion of the museum as a department store. According to Belk (1994), the underlying principles of the first type are order, taxonomy, and decontextualization and recontextualization of the object as art. Objects are viewed as sacra and sanctified through scientific and historic lore. As sacra, they are also set apart and, within such a ritual context, removed from contamination by touch. Many curators subscribe to this view, although more recently, the move has been toward the notion of the museum as a bazaar. Although objects cannot really be touched, the museum has metamorphosed into a center for social gathering, fitted with coffee houses, lecture halls, gift stores, and libraries.

The museum's mission of bringing art to the people, while desired by many of those interviewed and adopted with great zeal by the museum administrators, may actually have the effect of trivializing the art it houses. The hype of the market, the glitz of commercial products, and the traversing through commercial space before the art is viewed may, indeed, jade the viewing process. The desire of visitors to sit in the museum café and muse upon the works of art or to buy postcards, souvenirs, or books on art should not be read as giving priority to commerce. The uneasy balance between art museums and business, with the tilt toward commerce, however, represents the direction that many museums are now seeking. As Kelly (1987a) notes, person-object relations can be extended beyond the gallery, but selling scarves and renting halls for corporate gatherings may signal the danger of commoditizing art.

The extensive observations of visitors to the museum as well as the in-depth interviews conducted and reported in this chapter suggest some actions that the museum personnel can take to improve the performance of its role and public attendance. Bitner's (1992) study of "servicescapes" provides many valuable insights as to how visitors or viewers can be positively influenced within the context of the museum.

As noted earlier, the mandate of the Museum of Contemporary Art is to acquire, conserve, and diffuse contemporary Quebec art. This art is defined as dating from 1939 onward. The politics of Quebec art cannot be ignored given the province's position in Canada. The museum is also mandated to ensure the presence of Canadian and international contemporary art so as to ensure a point of reference for Quebec works. The museum sees itself as both maintaining the artistic heritage of Quebec and promoting the production of visual art. The museum also has a major educative role to play and thus desires to serve all types of publics whether they be specialists or amateurs. It wishes to open its doors as wide as possible and to expose all types of art while respecting the vocation of other museums of art in the city. The mandate and role of the museum thus forms the framework within which we outline our implications.

As suggested in the earlier discussion, visitors to this museum comprise different segments. These segments are sufficiently distinct regarding what they visit and when they visit that it would seem that radically different strategies are required to entice these segments. For example, the required promotional strategy may be quite different depending on whether the segment of concern is the artists' group or the tourists'. Even though the artists' group is larger, the museum's mandate suggests that it is constrained by policy to consider all segments equally and attempt to satisfy their needs. This is a common dilemma facing organizations operating in the not-for-profit sector (Kotler, 1982). In spite of this constraint, the idea that the museum should vary its promotion and marketing to respond to the needs of the largest segment or segments still holds. The only condition that should constrain such action is the museum's possible loss of vision.

Besides the segments suggested by the observations, the in-depth interviews also suggest some additional segmentation characteristics that may be potentially useful for marketing decision making by the museum. These characteristics are variations in the level of sophistication and knowledge in the manner of viewing the exhibits. For example, some segments, such as the artists and the film, dance, and theatre group, seek out different types of benefits from the exhibits than, say, the tourists or senior citizens. The difference in level of sophistication and in viewing behavior is clearly shown by the need of artists, relative to that of the tourists, to closely examine the materials, substances, colors, and forms used. These variations mean that the museum cannot assume that all its visitors are equally sophisticated. Depending on the groups expected, written explanations could be tailored to meet their needs. In this context, it is critical to recall Baxandall's (1991) suggestion of viewing the space between the object and the label as the viewer's space. This shuttling process is active rather than passive, and the onus lies on the museum to provide nonmisleading and stimulating conditions within which learning can occur.

A further implication of the findings is that for some groups, especially children and artists, merely using the sense of sight is insufficient. Children love to touch, and the artists, because of their need to know, also love to examine closely and touch art objects. It may be worthwhile for the museum to develop some mechanism within its exhibition space that would allow these groups to satisfy their need to touch. A multisensual approach to art has been experimented with in other museum contexts. The only caution that might be necessary is to guard against the "Disneyfication" of the museum (Belk, 1994).

The childhood experiences that were outlined during the interviews suggest that these play a critical role in determining museum behavior in adulthood. It would seem, therefore, that if the intent of the museum is to foster museum going and make it more commonplace among the population, then it would be useful to begin exposing children to more and more interesting museum experiences. Certainly, any attempt to involve children in regular museum going and to stimulate both their sense of sight and touch would pay off in the long run. Actively reaching out to children is an investment in the future (Perrachio, 1993).

The need for consistency among the various elements of the museum's offering was also clearly brought out in the interviews. The visitors seemed uncomfortable with the apparent inconsistency among the stern-looking guards, the lack of directions, the blandness of the buildings that housed the exhibits, and the exhibits of the art objects themselves. Thus, within the constraints of location and the physical structure of the building, museum person-nel should strive for consistency in their offerings (Berry & Parasuraman, 1991; Bitner, 1992; Congram & Friedman, 1991).

The museum experience should be viewed in a holistic sense. Bitner (1992) recommends such conceptualization for all servicescapes. The mu-seum experience encompasses not only the exhibits but also the personnel who are visible to visitors, the boutique, the café, and the styling of brochures and other literature available to visitors. The museum provides a total experience, and although the exhibits are a major contributor to this expe-rience they are only one factor. The other factors mentioned here should also be taken into consideration. Again, the growing alliance between art and commerce is a paradoxical development. The vision of the museum cannot be subjected to its commercial calling. Given the large crowds that attended the talks and dance performances, it would seem unwise for the museum not to put greater emphasis on the promotion of these events. The observations suggest that promotion was primarily word-of-mouth, with the audience members knowing each other fairly well. It may therefore be useful to target special promotional literature to the segments that attend these events, such as, for example, the artists or the academics.

Visitors to the museum arrive with a set of expectations and unique experiences. The emergent themes suggest new and useful ways of structur-ing museum exhibits. Typically, the museum structures exhibits around particular artists or around specific time periods. The use of emergent themes as a way of structuring showings offers the possibility of integrating the exhibits with different segmentation levels of sophistication and knowledge. For instance, the idea of art as humor can be used effectively in staging such an attempt. However, more research on the museum clientele may be needed in order to sucessfully carry out this restructuring. In this context, McCracken's (1990) warning to think of the marketing concept as metaphor is also useful. According to him, the marketing concept suppresses our vision of the interaction between individual and object as a complex social and cultural event (pp. 41-42).

Finally, although one can argue that the museum is viewed as sacred by both the visitors and the museum personnel, there is some room for the use of commercial sponsors in promoting and funding exhibits. If the role of the museum is to diffuse contemporary art among the population, then the recent cutbacks on subsidies on the part of the provincial government means that the museum must find alternate sources of funding. Although the use of commercial sponsors might be seen as somewhat profane, this is not necessarily so (Joy, 1993). More and more, businesses are associating themselves with art and the art world, and they have become important sources of support for the society's cultural heritage. Rather than introducing an element of profanity in the museum, it is likely that the support of a museum by business makes business appear to be less profane. Marketing and corporate sponsorship and the role of the museum are not always mutually exclusive, although the uneasy balance may tilt in the direction of commerce. Although the objectives of business in the arts may be self-serving and may not provide a critique of society, what business does with art may have the unintended consequence of transforming the many publics who come into contact with it.

 ## Note

1. The museum moved to a downtown location in 1991. According to some of the curators, the decline in the number of museum visitors to the old site was primarily an outcome of poor location. When the architectural planning for the new building took place, these same curators were very vocal about the merits of a downtown location and its proximity to other art buildings. Such inputs did pay off, and more visitors do enter its portals today, although curators lament the lack of knowledge of some of these viewers who come to browse just because of its central location.

References

Alpers, S. (1991). The museum as a way of seeing. In I. Karp & S. D. Levine (Eds.), *Exhibiting cultures* (pp. 25-32). Washington, DC: Smithsonian Institution Press.

Bal, M. (1992). Telling, showing and showing off. *Critical Inquiry, 18,* 556-594.

Baxandall, M. (1991). Exhibiting intention: Some preconditions of visual display of culturally purposeful objects. In I. Karp & S. D. Levine (Eds.), *Exhibiting cultures* (pp. 33-42). Washington, DC: Smithsonian Institution Press.

Becker, H. (1982). *Art worlds.* Berkeley: University of California Press.

Belk, R. (1994). *Collecting in a consumer society.* Unpublished manuscript.

Belk, R., Sherry, J. F., Jr., & Wallendorf, M. (1988). A naturalistic inquiry into buyer and seller behavior at a swap meet. *Journal of Consumer Research, 14,* 449-470.

Belk, R., Wallendorf, M., & Sherry, J. F., Jr. (1989). The sacred and the profane in consumer behavior: Theodicy on the odyssey. *Journal of Consumer Research*, 16, 1-38.

Belk, R., Wallendorf, M., Sherry, J. F., Jr., & Holbrook, M. (1991). Collecting in a consumer culture. In R. Belk (Ed.), *Highways and buyways: Naturalistic research from the consumer behavior odyssey* (pp. 178-215). Provo, UT: Association of Consumer Research.

Berry, L., & Parasuraman, A. (1991). *Marketing services: Competing through quality*. New York: Free Press.

Bitner, M. J. (1992). Servicescapes: The impact of physical surroundings on customers and employees. *Journal of Marketing*, 56(2), 57-71.

Bourdieu, P. (1993). *The field of cultural production*. New York: Columbia University Press.

Clifford, J. (1985). Objects and selves—An afterword. In G. W. Stocking, Jr. (Ed.), *Objects and others: Essays on museums and material culture* (History of Anthropology, Vol. 3, pp. 236-245). Madison: University of Wisconsin Press.

Congram, C. A., & Friedman, M. L. (Eds.). (1991). *The AMA handbook of marketing for the services industry*. New York: AMACOM.

DiMaggio, P. (1987). Classification in art. *American Sociological Review*, 52, 440-455.

DiMaggio P., Useem, M., & Brown, P. (1978). *Audience studies of the performing arts and museums: A critical review*. Washington, DC: National Endowment for the Arts.

Dixon, B., Courtney, A. E., & Bailey, R. H. (1987). *The museum and the Canadian public* (Report for Arts and Culture Branch, Department of the Secretary of State, Government of Canada). Ottawa: Culturcan.

Duncan, C. (1991). Art museums and the ritual of citizenship. In I. Karp & S. D. Levine (Eds.), *Exhibiting cultures* (pp. 88-103). Washington, DC: Smithsonian Institution Press.

Fine, M. (1994). Working the hyphens: Reinventing self and other in qualitative research. In N. K. Denzin & Y. S. Lincoln, (Eds.), *Handbook of qualitative research* (pp. 70-82). Thousand Oaks, CA: Sage.

Geertz, C. (1973). *The interpretation of cultures*. New York: Basic Books.

Goffman, E. (1983). Felicity's condition, *American Journal of Sociology*, 89, 1-53.

Griswold, W. (1986). *Renaissance revivals: City comedy and revenge tragedy in the London theatre from 1576 to 1980*. Chicago: University of Chicago Press.

Gurian, E. H. (1991). Noodling around with exhibition opportunities, in I. Karp & S. D. Levine (Eds.), *Exhibiting cultures* (pp. 176-190). Washington, DC: Smithsonian Institution Press.

Heinich, N. (1988). The Pompidou centre and its public: The limits of a utopian site. In R. Lumley (Ed.), *The museum time-machine* (pp. 199-211). London: Routledge.

Hirschman, E. (1986). Humanistic inquiry in marketing research: Philosophy, method and criteria. *Journal of Marketing Research*, 23, 237-249.

Hirschman, E. (1988). A sociology of consumption: A structural-syntactical analysis of "Dallas" and "Dynasty." *Journal of Consumer Research, 15,* 344-359.

Hirschman, E., & Holbrook, M. (1982). Hedonic consumption: Emerging concepts, methods and propositions. *Journal of Marketing, 46,* 92-101.

Hood, M. G. (1983). Staying away—Why people choose not to visit museums. *Museum News, 61*(4), 50-57.

Hoope-Greenhill, E. (1988). Counting visitors or visitors who count. In R. Lumley (Ed.), *The museum time-machine* (pp. 214-238). London: Routledge.

Housen, A. (1983). *The eye of the beholder: Measuring aesthetic development.* Unpublished doctoral dissertation, Harvard Graduate School of Education.

Housen, A. (1987). Of pluralism. In *Art education here* (pp. 29-39). Boston: Massachusetts College of Art.

Jones, A.-L. (1993). Exploding canons: The anthropology of museums. In B. J. Siegel (Ed.), *Annual review of anthropology* (Vol. 22, pp. 201-220). Palo Alto, CA: Annual Reviews, Inc.

Joy, A. (1991). Beyond the odyssey: Interpretations of ethnographic research in consumer behavior. In R. Belk (Ed.), *Highways and buyways: Naturalistic research from the consumer behavior odyssey* (pp. 216-233). Provo, UT: Association of Consumer Research.

Joy, A. (1993). The corporate Medicis: Corporations as consumers of art. In R. Belk & J. Costa (Eds.), *Research in consumer behavior* (pp. 29-54). Greenwich, CT: JAI.

Kelly, R. (1987a). Culture as commodity: The marketing of cultural objects and cultural experiences. In M. Wallendorf & P. Anderson (Eds.), *Advances in consumer research* (Vol. 14, pp. 347-351). Provo, UT: Association of Consumer Research.

Kelly, R. (1987b). Museums as status symbols II: Attaining a state of having been. In R. Belk (Ed.), *Advances in nonprofit marketing* (Vol. 2, pp. 1-38). Greenwich, CT: JAI.

Kelly, R. (1993). Vesting objects and experiences with symbolic meaning. In L. McAlister & M. Rothschild (Eds.), *Advances in consumer research* (Vol. 20, pp. 232-234). Provo, Utah: Association of Consumer Research.

Kotler, P. (1982). *Marketing for nonprofit organizations* (2nd ed.). Englewood Cliffs, NJ: Prentice Hall.

Lincoln, Y., & Guba, E. (1985). *Naturalistic inquiry.* Beverly Hills, CA: Sage.

Lynes, R. (1980). *The tastemakers: The shaping of American popular taste.* New York: Dover.

Marcus, G., & Fischer, M. (1986). *Anthropology as cultural critique: An experimental moment in the human sciences.* Chicago: University of Chicago Press.

McCall, S., & Ellenport, M. (1990). The production of a "consumer based strategy" plan for the museum of Victoria. In *Symposium proceedings on research and marketing for the arts* (pp. 37-55). Amsterdam: ESOMAR.

McCracken, G. (1986). Culture and consumption: A theoretical account of the structure and meaning of consumer goods. *Journal of Consumer Research, 13,* 71-84.

McCracken, G. (1988). *Culture and consumption: New approaches to the symbolic character of consumer goods and activities.* Bloomington: University of Indiana Press.

McCracken, G. (1990). Matching material cultures: Person-object relations inside and outside the ethnographic museum. In R. Belk (Ed.), *Advances in nonprofit marketing* (Vol. 3., pp. 27-49). Greenwich, CT: JAI.

McGrath, M. A., Sherry, J. F., Jr., & Heisley, D. (1993). An ethnographic study of an urban periodic marketplace: Lessons from the Midville Farmers' Market. *Journal of Retailing, 69,* 280-318.

Mick, D. (1986). Consumer research and services: Exploring the morphology of signs, symbols and significance. *Journal of Consumer Research, 13,* 196-200.

Peracchio, L. (1993). Young children's processing of a televised narrative: Is a picture really worth a hundred words? *Journal of Consumer Research, 28,* 281-293.

Posner, E. (1988). The museum as bazaar. *Architecture, 3,* pp. 67-70.

Roederer, B. (1990). Sociocultural trends and how they affect the public's reactions to art museums. In *Symposium proceedings on research and marketing for the arts* (pp. 71-78). Amsterdam: ESOMAR.

Rook, D. (1985). The ritual dimension of consumer behavior. *Journal of Consumer Research, 12,* 251-261.

Sherry, J. F., Jr., & McGrath, M. A. (1989). Unpacking the holiday presence: A comparative ethnography of two gift stores. In E. Hirschman (Ed.), *Interpretive consumer research* (pp. 148-197). Provo, UT: Association of Consumer Research.

Sherry, J. F., Jr., McGrath, M. A., & Levy, S. (1993). The dark side of the gift. *Journal of Business Research, 27,* 225-244.

Monadic Giving

Anatomy of Gifts Given to the Self

John F. Sherry, Jr.
Mary Ann McGrath
Sidney J. Levy

> *Maybe all presents are presumptions.*
> *Giving, we test our affinity*
> *with hidden wishes. Yet asking changes both desire and deliverance,*
> *as when lovers must say touch me*
> *there. . . .*
>
> —Alice Fulton, "Self-Storage" (1990, p. 11)

A confluence of traditions is prompting consumer researchers to reassess their discipline's understanding of the dynamics of gift giving. Among the most intriguing of the discoveries driving this reappraisal is the phenomenon of gifts given to the self (Mick, 1991; Mick & DeMoss, 1990a, 1990b, 1992; Sherry & McGrath, 1989). Monadic giving[1] challenges our fundamental notions of gift giving as a dyadic enterprise, notwithstanding conceptions of a "postmodern" (Cushman, 1990; Ogilvy, 1990) or "dividual" (DeVos, 1985)

AUTHORS' NOTE: The authors wish to acknowledge the following colleagues for their constructive comments on earlier drafts of this chapter: Kalman Applbaum, Annamma Joy, David Mick, Peter Shabad, and Melanie Wallendorf.

self. In this chapter, we seek to deepen our understanding of gifts given to the self by exploring the ambivalence by which the activity is tinged. This exploration compels us to examine the cultural ideology of the gift. What follows is a sociocultural account of monadic giving.

In the poem from which our epigraph is borrowed, Alice Fulton (1990) captures much of what we have learned about gift giving at the level of cultural ethos. Donors often seek to produce an artificial or mechanical transformation of recipients. Acquiescence or compliance is bought at a high price: a recipient will commonly shelve the authentic self and endure a kind of remaking at the hands of a donor. Although this endurance may be tested to the breaking point (i.e., the dissolution of the dyad; Sherry, 1983), it is more often merely strained, provoking dissonance between the ideology and the ritual itself (Sherry, McGrath, & Levy, 1992, 1993). The "otherness" of the recipient is more often suppressed than celebrated. When celebrated, it is frequently muted via the donor's use of hints, wish lists, and other order-taking devices that become gift giving by proxy at best and inefficient personal provisioning at worst. Even though recipients always get it (i.e., the literal present), donors rarely "get it" (i.e., the right present and the affect it encodes). One consequence of such an unsatisfying personal experience of an ostensibly ennobling cultural convention is the co-optation of that convention by the self. Levy (1982) suggested as much in his assessment of the gift-giving literature over a decade ago when he advocated considering personal use as a form of gift giving to the self. Both the complexities and meanings of gifts and giving are illuminated when we explore how "I as subject" transacts with "me as object" (Levy, 1982, p. 542). Monadic giving short-circuits some of the disappointment and futility that recipients often feel in their transactions with donors. As our epigraph makes clear, the abiding rightness of the "touch," the unassisted, unerring discovery of the "*there*" are palpably at stake.

The findings we report in this study represent renewed interest in the semiotic significance of the gift. Bird-David (1990) maintains that gift giving has not yet been conceptually or analytically distinguished from reciprocity. Implicit in her argument is the conviction that reciprocity itself has already been adequately understood. More recently, Weiner (1992) has asserted that even reciprocity, especially in its pristine form as practiced in so-called "primitive" societies, has not yet been adequately understood by social scientists. She believes that gift giving affords us a particular opportunity to analyze reciprocity properly. We will seize this opportunity momentarily. Finally, Shabad (1993a) has called attention to the "rigid split between giving and receiving in our narcissistic culture" (p. 490) in such a way as to make it apparent that we have little understanding of the dynamics of gift *receiving*. The interplay between gender and receivership requires our consideration.

Parry's (1988) discussion of the ideologies of gift giving—the intermingled coexistence of interest and disinterest long ignored by analysts—offers still another challenge to consumer researchers. Even inadequately plumbed, the emics of gift exchange are far richer than our etic analyses have allowed. If gift giving in contemporary consumer culture, let alone the variegated local cultures that comprise this global phenomenon, has not yet been satisfactorily interpreted (Cheal, 1988), it is largely because we have failed to explore either the indigenous categories of meaning or the ideological core (Raheja, 1988) of the phenomenon itself. We attempt each of these two kinds of exploration in this chapter.

Our present account is one of a series of attempts by consumer researchers to redress these shortcomings and fundamentally redirect the nature of inquiry into giving. Sherry and McGrath (1989) reintroduced the topic of gifts given to the self in an ethnographic field study of gift shopping. Although concerned primarily with the semiosis of gift giving, the field study had strong feminist roots (Joy, 1989) and highlighted the gendered nature of gift-giving phenomena in the United States. This ethnography gave rise in turn to a series of articles (Sherry et al., 1992, 1993) exploring the contrast between cultural ideology and personal experience of women engaged in gift rituals. This research stream coincides with an increasing interest in the role of women in a host of consumption activities (Costa, 1991; Bristor & Fischer, 1993; Hirschman, 1993; Sherry, 1990; Stern, 1993; Wallendorf & Arnould, 1991). In another series of articles, Mick and DeMoss (1990a, 1990b, 1992) began an investigation of some of the surface features of gifts given to the self. They define such gifts as "personally symbolic self-communication through special indulgences that tend to be premeditated and highly context-bound" (Mick & DeMoss, 1990a, p. 328). The predominant contexts of self-gifting are those of reward and therapy; life transitions and periods of discretionary plenty also occasion these gifts (Mick & DeMoss, 1990b). The study we describe below is an attempt to braid these varied strands of semiosis, monadic giving, and feminism into a common cord.

In a sweeping reassessment of the literatures of reciprocity and gift giving, Weiner (1992) has usefully contrasted the categories of alienable and inalienable possessions. The latter objects are of particular interest to postmodern researchers concerned with such issues as sacralization (Belk, Wallendorf, & Sherry, 1989), interiority of the artifact (Sherry et al., 1992, 1993) and the extended self (Belk, 1988). Inalienable possessions are invested with the essence of their owner. Although psychologists and anthropologists have long been involved in the study of the interplay between materiality and fantasy (see Thomas, 1991, for a current example), consumer researchers have come somewhat lately to the game. Weiner (1992) identifies a phenomenon she calls "keeping while giving" that animates inalienable possessions. "Keeping while giving" further sacralizes the essence of what Mauss (1924) initially identified as the "spirit" of the gift. Weiner (1992) eloquently interprets the spirit of the gift as the power of females—the domestic equivalent of masculine power exercised in the political economy—sedimented in the object and motivating its circulation. This power emanates from rituals surrounding the exclusive roles of women in spheres of production and reproduction, which gives them a domain of authority in their own right. It is a tangible recognition of the efficacy of women that is otherwise muted in mundane discourse.

Briefly rehearsed, Weiner's (1992) argument takes the following form. In a heroic effort to secure their role in social life over time, individuals invest objects with a life force, which is the stored accumulation of meanings attached to objects by emergent tradition. Because these objects are authenticated by forces outside the present, they are semiotically charged with great power and value. Individuals resist placing such inalienable possessions into circulation until they are virtually compelled to do so, preferring instead to exchange less psychosocially significant possessions. Should an inalienable object be introduced into circulation, it is expected eventually to be returned to its original owner. Both this reluctance and return comprise "keeping while giving." In Weiner's (1992) view, women have a political presence insofar as they produce cosmological authentication in people and objects; that is, women create both inalienable possessions and the kin relations in which these possessions are embedded.

We argue in this chapter that "keeping while giving" is most emphatically enacted in the phenomenon of gifts given to the self. Recognizing the existence of multiple ideologies of giving, we posit an ambivalent tension between the cultural prescription of disinterested giving and the personal stake in interested giving. This tension will be especially palpable for women, who are the principal conductors of gift rituals in contemporary consumer culture. They negotiate the meanings of both the gift and the giving. This negotiation is rarely glimpsed in the literature of consumer research. If the mirroring process by which we individuate is reclaimed from the realm of developmental psychologists and recast in terms of a gift relationship between self and essential other (Shabad, 1993b), and if the capacity to receive is imagined to be impaired or impoverished during this essential period of gender socialization and reinforced over the life course, reverberations in gifting dynamics might be expected to result. In this chapter, we examine some of the ambivalence experienced by women who give gifts to themselves.

Let us emphasize that we are addressing the far end of a continuum in gifting. This continuum ranges from extreme selflessness, in which one gives a gift that is perhaps totally self-abnegating (maybe even pretending to no desire for thanks or reciprocity of indebtedness), to the utmost in egocentricity and selfishness. Because our society makes demands for and exalts sociality and self-denial, gifts to the self are looked down on; they make us anxious, ashamed, and guilty. Also, ours is an individualistic society and time, as these things go (in comparison to Asian cultures where gifting is highly prescribed and dominated by fears relating to loss of face), and giving one's self gifts is acceptable as part of our praise of individuality, self-development, and the narcissism and pride that go with achievement.

Monadic giving resonates as well with the self-orientation that goes with being self-conscious about having neuroses and requiring therapy. Given the therapeutic roots of consumer culture (Lears, 1983) and the current commoditization of therapy (Cushman, 1990; Gergen, 1991), such resonance may be inescapable. From this orientation results the psychic rewards and compensations to which we are entitled when successful (e.g., a new car, an ice cream treat) or unsuccessful (e.g., masturbation, a new coat, an ice cream cone). Also devolving from this orientation is the anxious ambivalence we feel about asserting our hedonism in the face of being part of the socius. These basic ideas underlie the materials relating to women's conflicts with regard to agentic and communal expression that we present in this chapter.

⚅ Methodology

> Man is least himself when he talks in his own person. Give him a mask and he will tell the truth. (Wilde, 1969, p. 389)

Having observed consumers in retail settings engaged in the search for and selection of gifts to be given to themselves and having interviewed these consumers at length about the practice of giving to the self (Sherry & McGrath, 1989), researchers eventually discovered a limit to their ability to elicit articulate insights from informants about their own motives. To extend the inquiry beyond participant observation and depth interviews, we created a projective instrument to be administered to consumers drawn from the client base of the stores that had been studied ethnographically. We thus hoped to tap issues that individuals might be enjoined to suppress as a matter of cultural ideology. Indirect elicitation is an especially appropriate way of assessing the semiotic intensity of such a fundamental convention as gift giving.

Other work (Sherry et al., 1992, 1993) has outlined the historical, theoretical, and methodological development of projective techniques and has demonstrated their utility in tapping information not readily accessible via traditional research procedures. Most notable is the ability of projective methods to investigate unconscious material, socially unacceptable motivations, and consumer fantasy. Researchers have also illustrated that, within the projective toolbox, each of a variety of these techniques yields responses different in focus and length and that a number of projective methodologies used collectively can provide both a broad and deep spectrum of responses to a topic that a respondent may find either too trivial or too sensitive to respond to directly (McGrath, Sherry, & Levy, 1993).

With respect to gift giving and receiving, researchers have found that direct questioning (in one case about the difference between a gift and any other purchased commodity) yielded terse, abbreviated, sometimes tongue-tied responses, in essence due to the respondent perception that the answer to the question asked of her was at the same time so obvious and yet so inexplicable, being part of the fabric of a shared cultural experience, that she could not or would not fashion a detailed response. Projective responses on the same topic appeared to be more complex, diverse, abstract, imaginative, and creative. Also, various projective formats revealed socially unacceptable and unconventional responses that appear to be difficult to articulate through other methods.

The Respondents

The voices in this chapter belong to members of a group of 83 women who comprise a judgmental sample drawn randomly from the mailing lists of two upscale urban gift shops that were the focus of an earlier ethnographic study (Sherry & McGrath, 1989). We chose a nonprobability sampling strategy because of the ethnographic grounding and exploratory nature of our investigation; prior to hypothesis generation and selection of follow-up cases for intensive study, such a strategy is favored by ethnographers (Bernard, 1988). Because sampling errors and biases are not computable for this type of sample, the data cannot be employed in statistical testing procedures but, rather, used to suggest or indicate conclusions (Miller, 1991). By using our collective research skill and prior knowledge to select respondents (Bailey, 1978), we depart from more conventionally positivist consumer research regimes and emphasize again the discovery-oriented nature of our interpretive efforts. We do not quantify responses and expect our contribution to emerge from the qualitative richness of the data rather than from statistical power.

Using the framework of the 40 PRIZM clusters (Weiss, 1989) to analyze the zip codes occurring on the stores' mailing lists indicates that the customers are a homogeneous group, hailing predominantly from older, upper-middle-class suburban communities (pools and patios) and wealthy bedroom suburbs (furs and station wagons). Their specific demographic profile and suburban locale as well as their choice of gift-shopping domains characterize our respondents as upscale individuals. The demographic specifics have been exhaustively detailed in other work (McGrath et al., 1993; Sherry et al., 1992, 1993). The majority were married (58%) and college graduates (72%), with median annual family incomes between $50,000 and $75,000. We selected this upscale educated sample for two reasons. First, the respondents were shoppers at the stores in the field study that had originally revealed the unexplained phenomenon of monadic giving. Second, their upscale situation eliminated economic barriers to monadic giving and, we surmised, probably increased its propensity. Our goal was to explore the phenomenon among women who were arguably most familiar with it.[2]

The participants in this study were women who were willing to share their views on various aspects of gift exchange in a written format. Our research goal was to elicit a range of responses for analysis rather than to measure any construct or occurrence. The sheer existence of the phenomenon of monadic giving, not its distribution through a population nor its frequency of occurrence, is our preoccupation. We make no claim that our sample is representative of the population of all women gift shoppers, although we believe that the sample reflects a conservative bias in that these women have little economic reason to recoil from self-indulgence. The women were offered a small indirect incentive for participation in the form of a contribution to the local United Way. Judging from their thoughtful and elaborated responses, the women who agreed to participate in this study appeared to have adequate discretionary time as well as income.

The study allowed the respondents the flexibility to complete the self-paced but lengthy questionnaire at their leisure. As evidenced by their agreement to participate and their prolific written remarks, we surmise that these female respondents possess a higher-than-average proficiency and comfort with written communication. They wrote lengthy and detailed responses that may not be readily obtainable from less educated respondents (whose own eloquence might conceivably be captured best by audiotape). Furthermore, by using projective tasks we sought to address some of the gender-linked difficulties associated with the formal interview that have been identified by feminist analysts. For example, Devault (1990) believes the "halting, hesitant, tentative talk" of her female respondents "signals the realm of not-quite articulated experience, where standard vocabulary is inadequate and where a respondent tries to speak from experience and finds language wanting" (p. 103).

Our sample may also have had an above-average interest and involvement in gift exchange. The respondents appear to comprise a group that marketers label "heavy users" and often seek as expert narrators in focus groups and depth interviews. Completed questionnaires were returned to us by mail in stamped, self-addressed envelopes. Many contained notes to the researchers; some were explanations and apologies for incompletions, and others were expressions of interest in learning our findings.

Let us emphasize once more the special nature of our sample. Because previous work has indicated the female-dominant nature of gift giving in U.S. society, we are concerned to extend our understanding of women's experience of gift giving. We have grounded our effort in ethnography among female informants. We have used ethnographic material as a staging ground for deeper analysis of women's gift worlds. We are not concerned with men's experience of gift giving in this study in any but the most oblique of fashions. We agree with Abu-Lughod (1991) that "from Simone de Beauvoir on, it has been accepted . . . in the modern West [that] women have been other to men's self," and that the "process of creating a self through opposition to an other always entails the violence of repressing or ignoring other forms of difference" (pp. 39-40). In keeping with postfeminist inquiry that resists treating "self" and "other" as given, we have focused our attention on female voices only. Masculine perspectives of gift giving await their own detailed investigation. The mediation of gift giving by gender roles is of increasing interest to consumer researchers (Belk & Coon, 1993; Gould & Weil, 1991).

The Instrument

Respondents in the study filled out a self-paced written instrument that consisted of unambiguously direct questions about gift giving, three types of projective devices, and demographic information. The projective portion of the questionnaire was designed to "evoke from the subject what is in various ways expressive of [her] private world" (Frank, 1948, p. 47). We capitalized on the flexibility and latitude of the techniques, inherent in Lindzey's (1961) definition: "A projective technique is an instrument that is considered especially sensitive to covert or unconscious aspects of behavior . . . permits or encourages a wide variety of subject responses, is highly multidimensional, and . . . evokes unusually rich and profuse response data" (p. 45). He adds further that "the stimulus material presented by the projective test is ambiguous, interpreters of the test depend upon holistic analysis, the test evokes fantasy responses, and there are no correct or incorrect responses" (p. 45). Projective techniques can assume a variety of formats. Rabin (1968) suggests a classification consisting of five categories: association techniques (word associations, the Rorschach), construction techniques (the TAT [Thematic Apperception Test], storytelling), completion techniques (sentence completion), choice or ordering techniques (Picture Arrangement Test), and expressive techniques (psychodrama, painting). The projectives used in this study were completion and construction techniques in the form of sentence completion tasks, the elicitation of a dream fantasy, and storytelling in the presence of ambiguous pictorial stimuli.[3]

Analysis

In the analysis of our data, responses were grouped by each projective stimulus. Each of the projective techniques yielded a particular type of data, which we report and interpret separately in the Results section. The analysis of the sentence completion tasks generally involved ordering or classifying them along emergent continua and dichotomies. For example, many of the stem responses could be sorted along a positive-neutral-negative continuum. As we sought to explore and categorize the range of responses, other classifications were added, including tangible-intangible, emotional-intellectual, goods-services, and lavish-limited. Dream fantasies were examined individually, sifted for emergent themes, and grouped by similar themes.

Several approaches were used to ensure the integrity of our analysis. Among them was triangulation. The use of varied projective stimuli allowed us to triangulate via technique. As a team of bi-gender, multidisciplinary analysts with a range of clinical and field experience, we posed, explicated, justified, and negotiated interpretations. This nuanced process of triangulating among analysts has been described by semiotically- and phenomenologically-inclined consumer researchers variously and exhaustively as "close reading" (Stern, 1989), "hermeneutics" (Thompson, Locander, & Pollio, 1989), "interpretive tacking" (Hirschman & Holbrook, 1992) and "devil's advocacy" (McAlexander, Schouten, & Roberts, in press). Contextual concerns were addressed by embedding the projective investigation within the setting of a larger ethnographic study. By drawing the sample from a previously studied population we were able to frame our interpretations with the benefit of preexisting familiarity with emic viewpoints. Although we designed our projective instrument to elicit insight into several dimensions of gift exchange behavior revealed in the earlier ethnographic study, we address only the topic of gifts given to the self in this chapter.

Results

In this section, we detail the reactions of our respondents to the projective stimuli provided to them related to monadic giving. To provide structure to the presentation, we discuss each of the projective devices separately. We begin with the completion task presented by the sentence stems and conclude with the construction of dream fantasies.

Sentence Completion: Filling a Void

Sentence completions allow a wide range of variability in their degree of structure and use of explicit personal reference (Kline, 1973). Results have correlated with those of other less structured presentations, such as the Rorschach and TAT (Murstein, 1965). Some of the stems in our study employed first-person referents, which have been found to elicit more effectively references to self than do third-person stems (Sacks, 1965). Stems were written to be less rather than more directive by omitting verbs or prepositions that might suggest categories of appropriate response. Written instructions reassured respondents that the exercise had neither correct nor incorrect answers.

The distinct themes that emerged from the sentence completion tasks are summarized in the following paragraphs. The actual sentence stems used are in boldface type, and all verbatim responses have punctuation and grammar of respondents kept intact. Although our interpretations are based on the entire corpus of data collected in this study, we include a selection of all the verbatims to give the reader the flavor of the qualitative responses.

Bittersweet Affect

The act of monadic giving carries with it both joy accompanying perfection and the dark underside of guilt, loneliness, and real or perceived isolation. Self-givers are characterized by themselves and others as prudent and practical as well as immature and shamefully self-indulgent. The "lift" that characterizes the therapeutic function of the self-gift is only temporary;

the transitory high of a quick fix may soon dissipate, leaving the participant steeped in remorse and occasionally in financial liability.

The feelings of social aberrance and personal failure connected with "solo" consumption that Rook (1986) predicted would moderate over the life course have in fact abated, if our sample is any indication, but our respondents have still not shaken their ambivalence toward the practice. Nor, it is clear, have marketers made great strides in reducing the institutional reinforcers of this ambivalence (Goodwin & Lockshin, 1992). It is clear that we still need to nudge Rook's (1987) vision of a phenomenology of impulsive consumption a bit higher up on the agenda of consumer research. Our respondents suggest that monadic giving is neither mere impulsive purchasing nor enlightened personal provisioning, although it may resemble either. It is also not simply a hybrid of these options. Rather, it represents the dialectical tension between desiring and deserving, between entitlement and perquisite. Monadic giving is volitional ceremonial self-care. It is a metaphysic.

Responses to two sentence stems, *If I give a gift to myself* and *If I give myself a gift*, are varied and reveal both positive and negative affect. The therapeutic motive mentioned by Mick and DeMoss (1990b) emerges as several responses indicate that the autodon produces "a lift" and is also reflected in verbatim completions such as "I get a kick out of it," "I love it!," "it makes me feel good," and "it's always fun!" Gifts to self are employed to "cheer me up," "when my spirits are low," or "when I'm down and out." But positive responses hint at guilt associations in the form of the unsolicited denial of such notions: "I feel fine about it (rather than guilty)" and "I feel smug—but not guilty." There is a bittersweet dimension to giving a gift to the self: "It makes me happy—but not nearly as much as if someone else had given it."

On the negative side, the gift to the self is sedimented with a number of odious feelings. Monadic giving may lead to direct admission of guilt: "I feel guilty about who I could have spent the money on otherwise" or "I sometimes feel guilty." The response that *If I give a gift to myself* "it's after everyone else's needs have been met" exhibits anger and self-pity. The monadic gift is bemoaned as "often perfect" but leaves out the relational possibilities with "someone outside myself which makes me feel known" or "it doesn't give me as much pleasure as one from someone else." The autodon may be given in desperation; it may become a last resort—"it's because I don't expect to get it from anyone else." In addition, it may make its self-recipient feel "lonely" or "silly."

Some respondents react to the concept of monadic giving with outright denial or with an affirmation of its sporadic nature: "I don't," "it's rare," or "I seldom do." Overall, the admission of the frequency of gifts given to the self ranged from "daily" to "never." Responses hinted that such gifts might signal victory in an intrapsychic battle—"when I can rationalize why I should have it. (Sometimes I win)." Similarly, "when I need it for some useful purpose to indulge my ego," necessity contends with luxury, instrumentality with expressiveness.

Consequential Contents

The content of gifts to self is instructive. *If I give a gift to myself* "it must be something I really want," "it is something I either need or have wanted for a long time," "it is something lovely or distracting." Intensity and duration of longing coupled with seductive evocation are cited in defense of giving gifts to the self. The gift must cast a spell (in contradistinction to the pitchman's—i.e., clerk's or ardent recipient's—*spiel*) that the respondent can use to induce enchantment. Elements of premeditation and positive affect suggested by Mick and DeMoss (1992) emerge here: "It's usually something expensive and something I've always wanted," "I think about it very carefully," and "I always get just the right thing." But the content of what respondents perceive as a gift to self also includes small and sometimes serendipitous indulgences: "it is of time," such as "time to lie down and read a book" or "an hour off—a special sweet—a long hot bath." The longing for thinly veiled downtime is both a recognition and denial of being overworked. A common response included rationalization and apologetic embarrassment, indicating "it's usually something small." It is almost as if the object were stolen or siphoned from some imagined household inventory of limited goods, thereby enriching the recipient at the expense of (presumably more deserving) others. A critique of entitlement and the moral economy of domesticity is immanent in these responses.

In response to the sentence stem *I give myself a gift*, the content of such gifts focused more on inexpensive and abstract indulgences than on substantial extravagances. Frequent responses involved gifts of time (to read, relax, bathe, "a walk"), "of comfort in clothes or surroundings," and of intangible indulgences such as in "mysticism" or "encouragement." Tangible responses included "a special sweet," "fresh flowers," "clothes," "earrings," and "trips."

In response to the stem *I hesitate to give myself*, respondents say they shrink from autodons as extravagances, luxuries, and frivolities of which they characterize themselves as undeserving. Examples of such unmerited largesse are "anything too large and expensive," "an expensive gift that I consider unnecessary," "extravagant things," "anything too large, expensive," "power and money," and "frivolous gifts that I don't really need." By virtue of their mention, however, they appear to be items that these women want. Alluding to the power that objects have to alter relationships, one respondent hesitated to give herself "anything that would break up the household." Specific mentions were made of "nonessentials," "expensive clothes," "expensive jewelry," "a fur coat," "sexy lingerie," and "something impractical." Although some respondents emphatically claim that "I never hesitate!," others poignantly observe that I *hesitate to give myself* "free time," "a compliment," and mundane or "practical gifts" such as "socks, bras, underwear." The hesitation and hope associated with deferred monadic giving is that it is "something I think someone else will get me for a special occasion." The autodon may come too easily, as reflected in one woman's hesitation to give herself "things that I could make if I took the time." Another woman balks at the monadic gift "because I receive so much." Others assert that they hesitate to give themselves "nothing I really want" or an associated "guilty feeling." One woman posed and emphatically answered her own rhetorical question: "At this stage in my life, if I want it and can afford it, what's wrong with getting it? Nothing."

Between the horns of self-indulgence and self-denial lies the central dilemma of our respondents. The dilemma is a material analog of the dynamics of bulimia and anorexia (Brumberg, 1989), which themselves are gender-skewed, culture-bound syndromes. The behavior is not as remarkable in either its presence or its absence so much as in its qualified, conditional, equivocally calibrated reception. Few women give unstintingly to themselves; few are complete abnegates. Those more aggressive in their gift care eschew the merely practical, as if the relative infrequency of the occurrence demanded departure from the mundane. Those more passive in their gift care hedge their guilty pleasure with practicality. Here the motivation is reactive: The violation of the cultural injunction (i.e., dyadic giving) demands an affirmation of almost pure utility. Something of the murkiness of the boundary between luxury and necessity is implicit in these responses as well.

Self-Diagnosis and Self-Medication

In completion of the stem I *give myself a gift*, the gift to self emerged as a self-penned prescription, frequently overlaid with embarrassment and rationalization: "I used to, when I was 'down.' Like when my mother-in-law visited too long and I'd have to put up with a bunch of junk. Of course, I was a lot younger then." Although the palliative is linked to immaturity, the agonistic role of giving in kin relations is clearly identified (Sherry et al., 1992). I *give myself a gift* "to raise my spirits," "when I feel low," "when I'm depressed," "when I'm down and out," "when I need my self-esteem to be raised," or "when I'm stressed out" are a sample of the diagnostic responses. The gift-as-antidepressant motif that recurs throughout our corpus is more than simple acknowledgment of the phenomenon of retail therapy (Cushman, 1990). It is also more than a reflection of gender-skewed susceptibility to culture-bound syndromes and propensities to seek therapeutic intervention. Our upscale female respondents, for whom money would seem to be no object, especially in gift transactions with significant others, self-medicate in the closet for complex reasons. Gift care is at once an affirmation of the object's healing potential and a lonely lamentation of the limits of dyadic giving. Gift care addresses disorders at the levels of personal aspiration and social relations.[4]

Compensatory eating and drinking are popular antidotes. *I give myself a gift* "by eating something fattening," "by buying chocolate," "by buying myself a cookie," "with food," "with a good lunch"/"by going to lunch." This need be "no big deal. McDonald's or Burger King is fine." Respondents report that *I reward myself while gift shopping* by "stopping for some coffee" or "a tea break" or "with a cappuccino coffee reward!" or with "a glass of wine." A shopping trip may also precipitate "going out to the nearest liquor store." That the reward is drawn from the universe of food, and more specifically, food popularly regarded as indulgent, dangerous, or sinful, is perhaps entirely predictable and, given the dynamics of eating disorders in contemporary society, could be considered appropriate in a tragically ironic key (Brumberg, 1989). A universal gift emblematic in our culture of domesticity and inclusion, food bonds communicants. Special foods mark ceremonial or ritual occasions; they represent departure from mundane convention. Furthermore, nourishing others is a cultural injunction that is heavily gender marked, as is the relative stigma attached to (over-)feeding oneself nonnutritive foods.

Other compensations take the form of intangible yet sensory indulgences such as "looking at whatever interests me for awhile," "looking at all the merchandise," "taking my time to look," and "looking at all the things I like." There was innate pleasure and perceived personal reward in "exploring everything in the store" and "letting it be fun." The psychosocial significance of the window shopping or "just looking" phenomenon in contemporary consumer culture has been explored by Sherry (1990).

Autodon as Benchmark for Perfection

In other work (Sherry et al., 1992) we have characterized the "perfect" gift as that which is successfully incorporated into the recipient's life. Information instrumental to the choice of a gift to the self may be of an intimate nature and inaccessible to others. Our respondents hope that all their gift choices fit recipients as unerringly as autodons suit the self. Furthermore, since they sense that their own choices are consistently appropriate for themselves, they frequently project the same tastes and lifestyles onto their recipients. Donors may duplicate their personal choices for others, hoping to enjoy with their recipients not only the material objects that give them pleasure but also the recipients' pleasure in sharing the form and function of these objects as they assume comfortable and orderly patterns in daily lives.

Responses to the sentence stem *the gift I hated to give away* revealed elements of the perfect gift, frequently referenced to the self. Women regretted giving away an object that "I thought would not be appreciated as much as I did," "one I'm obligated to give," or "something I wouldn't buy for myself (too bad)." Undervaluation, ingratitude, and wistful grieving are each occasions for questioning the cultural ideology of the gift. Several women recalled specific items they reluctantly gave but whose loss they harbor and grieve. Givers lamented parting with presents they themselves "wanted" or "loved." These were frequently gifts that embodied a heavy personal investment, such as "a handmade sweater," "the hand-embroidered caftan I made for my daughter-in-law," "my own cashmere coat," "a very old but wonderful mink coat that was not appreciated by the recipient," or "when I spent $50 on a needlepoint Christmas stocking I made for a baby nephew and I knew the parents wouldn't appreciate the effort or cost of it." There is resentment in giving an expensive gift that attempts to compensate for lack of sentiment between the giver and receiver—"when I've spent too much so I wouldn't be perceived as unloving by my family members." Rather than reinforcing strained kin relations, as ideology would have us believe, gift giving can poignantly highlight the frustrating futility involved in forging family ties.

Some respondents admit that they hate to give "any" or "all gifts," whereas others have "almost asked to have back" gifts once given. In several cases, the gift that the informant hated to give away was "duplicated" or "kept for my own enjoyment," becoming a post hoc gift to self. One woman indicated that "if I loved it, I would buy two and keep one for myself. If there was only one to buy, I would keep it and buy something else to give." Gifts may be withheld, recalled, or appropriated. Cultural convention may be derogated or arrogated.

Some respondents recalled incidents from their childhoods related to *the gift I hated to give away*. Nostalgic recollections such as "red shoes when I was 10," "a toy truck when I was 4" or "a Barbie doll" illustrate a powerful salience and the early understanding of a perceived tension between giver and recipient within the gift exchange dyad. This also relegates hesitation to give and the preference to keep to the realm of selfishness associated with childish immaturity. Self-denial is thought to be a hallmark of maturity. These traits are also gender marked.

Not wanting to part with a gift was not always positioned negatively but, instead, was used by some women as the ultimate litmus test of appropriateness in gift choice. Several respondents indicated that they chose gifts based on their personal tastes and preferences. *The gift I hated to give away* "was a music box—in fact—three or four of them. I give them because *I* love them so much" and "an Apple computer to my college-bound daughter. I wanted one!" In the best case, it is the gift that "the receiver loved" and it "gave me pleasure to think about later (and I didn't have to dust them)." One generous donor described this gift as "something I admired and/or treasured but wanted to share with a loved one." As a strategy for gift choice, one respondent claims that she hates to give away "lots of them. I tend to buy what I like unless it's a special request." One respondent explained that *the gift I hated to give away* was "all of them and none of them. If they weren't special, I wouldn't get them in the first place." The donor's projected pleasure, mirrored in the actual or imaged response of the recipient, becomes a gift given to the self. The donor receives vicariously by proxy.

In all cases, *the gift I hated to give away* represents the perfect gift as it "was singular in some way, with a character of its own," carried the potential to be "very pleasurable to me," "is one which tells something about my personality" or, on the negative side, "is one that I thought would not be appreciated." Such a gift seems literally a gift of the self; the gift embodies the donor's authentic self and is a proper object of (re)incorporation. Its rejection is a threat to the integrity of the self.

Our respondents' candid remarks offer a number of insights and clarifications to the multifaceted nature of monadic giving. The autodon may preempt a potentially unbalanced gift exchange or may offer the monadic giver a moment of reprieve from a harried lifestyle and sometimes from the pressure to find and choose the perfect gift for another. Monadic giving is the potential energy to the kinetic energy of dyadic giving. Each motivates and informs search but in different orbits. Monadic giving is a source of solace to which the self suspects but cannot confirm entitlement.

The autodon appears to vary in reality and fantasy. When comparing the findings of the two types of projective methodologies employed in this study, it is clear that respondents *in reality* delight in small indulgences, but *dream* of luxurious consumer excesses. Indulgent fantasies, however, are often tempered by reality, as we illustrate below.

Monadic Fantasies:
Some Themes From the Dreams

Respondents were asked to imagine a dream in which they could envision buying a present for themselves. We have reduced their responses to a set of four interpretive themes whose significance we will explore in some detail. These themes are the intrusion of ideology into fantasy, the labor value theory of worthiness, the minimal material nucleus, and the ritual substratum of gift giving.

Intrusion of Ideology Into Fantasy

Personal narratives are often as instructive in the omission of material as they are in its inclusion (McAdams, 1993). Our respondents' dream scenarios are noteworthy for the rarity of their expression of unalloyed joy. Here is one such exceptional account:

> I am in an antique store browsing. It is dusty and dingy. All of a sudden, a bright meticulously carved carousel horse sort of stands out in the gloom. I say Wow, this is it. [I] [b]uy the horse and go home feeling terrific.

The hierophany (Belk et al., 1989) depicted in this story is transformative both of the dramatic tone and of the narrator herself. Joyful accounts encoding greater pathos are somewhat bittersweet but still insist on fundamental transformation of the self. Here is a story of psychological transference and individuation, tinged with a moralizing practicality:

> I had this dream that I was going to this fur store to get the furs my mother had given me out of storage. The furs did not fit on anyone. As I got to the store and saw all the beautiful fur coats inside I even decided to put some coats on. They felt so good and I felt so special in the few coats especially the white ones. I decided then and there that it was time to buy myself a present. When the girl brought out my mother's fur coats they looked so shabby and not any good looking. However, when I tried on the new fur coats they looked beautiful on me. So I ask the lady how much the coats cost and she even said today we are having a special on the fur coat you are looking at so I took out my check book and gave her a check for the coat plus the old fur coats. I felt so beautiful when I put it on and special.

Finally, an account grounded in deprivation redressed describes the transformation of the narrator:

> I've dreamed this fantasy dream over and over. After all these years as a widow. I will be a bride again. Not a bride in a court house. But a real wedding. I'll buy myself a dress that is cream or ice blue. Mid-calf length—with high victorian collar. A little lace on the cuffs of the "leg-o-mutton" sleeves, and lots of covered buttons. My three granddaughters will be there—two 15 years old, [o]ne 5 and I will buy them old fashion matching dresses. We will carry baskets of daisies. It will be a morning wedding—in June with lots of sunshine and much hugging and happiness for all.
>
> All the children will be there. His and mine. I'm going to give myself a beautiful wedding—and take a new life for both of us.
>
> Now my imaginary dream—is going to be a reality. I'm buying myself a present tomorrow—a wedding dress that is cream or ice blue.

Without interpreting the other motifs of these stories (which will echo in our later discussion) it is clear that where joyful experience of an unmitigated giving to the self occurs, the self has been appropriately transfigured. An authentic self has been realized. In these few instances only, the self is presented as a vehicle of personal transformation (i.e., agentic) in a way that the narrator does not find problematic. Self-transformation is quickly problematized, however, even in those rare instances in which the narrator struggles to be her own deliverance. For example,

> I am in a forest—dark, wet, lonely. But I am lost. As I wander through the trees, I suddenly observe a depth of shining color gleaming among the rocks in the stream that flows nearby. I am drawn to this rainbow image, and as I move towards it I realize it is a beautiful opal set in a simple gold ring. I reach in to take it, but my hand freezes just above the water. To whom does this lovely ring belong? I love to watch it; first the green, then the blue, the fire. Suddenly I know it was meant for me; it will help me find my way out of the forest. Once again I reach in to dislodge it from among the rocks. It is even more beautiful out of the water. I slip it on my finger and it fits perfectly. This is my gift—to myself, but I am never really sure from whom. I only know that wearing it makes me feel proud and humble, awed by its changing lights, gifted and stronger and clear sighted. As I wake from this dream I know that even the dream itself is a gift.

Not knowing for sure, but suspecting that perhaps transcendence can be self-induced, is the state that best characterizes the plight of our most celebratory dreamers. This conflict is literally engendered in the Arthurian romance of the narrative just cited. In this thinly veiled masturbatory fantasy, the ideal of courtly love is transmuted into an autoerotic experience that is not merely sexual. The heroine achieves a transcendental awakening.

Healthy narcissism or benevolent egoism is rare in our respondents' fantasies. We hear repeatedly of the reluctant indulgence. Even when given "permission" to fantasize, respondents make conditional stories. Sometimes the mere frequency of dreaming is restrained:

> Once in a great while I dream and this dream continues to be about clothes, clothes and more clothes!
>
> My dream always starts with a long aisle of clothes, separated by styles according to dates. We start out with the 40s and jump to the 80s and back to the 20s. A style show takes place and each piece of clothing is modeled by a well-known person such as Jacqueline Onassis and many other celebrities.
>
> The final phase of my dream is the best. Each beautiful piece shown in the show end up in my closet and accessories are furnished also.

Sometimes the dream is converted to a nightmare:

> I screamed with delight. The person on the other end of the telephone just told me I had won a 12-hour shopping spree at Marshall Fields. It was the State Street store on a Sunday when the store was closed. I could take whatever I wanted as long as it was all put in carton boxes that were available to me in every department and stacked by the Lake & Wabash entrance at the end of the 12-hour period. Was I dreaming—I couldn't believe my eyes. A limo would pick me up at 8:30 a.m. & I would have the whole store to myself from 9 a.m.-9 p.m. What a day. I started on the 1st floor in the Chanel Boutique. I was less discriminating in my selections, but was still cautious. I only took what I really wanted and by the end of that day had amassed 82 cartons at the entrance. It lined up 3 boxes high all over the candy dept. and we had to move the luggage displays into a tight mound to fit the cartons near the door. It was so wonderful. Was I dreaming? Suddenly, I noticed on my return home a letter in my mailbox. I opened it up and read 30 pages of charges amounting to $856,422.51 from Marshall Fields. A bad dream. . . .

In a variation of this department store fantasy, the dream is aborted by the pettiness of a spouse:

> One day I'm casually walking through Old Orchard. I walk into Copper and Copper looking for a warm cut stylish coat. I come upon a beautiful

> brown full length Shearling coat. Its leather exterior has the feel of butter. The salesman tells me "it looks great on you" (as they all say about anything and everything). I ask "How Much?" He says, "a mere $1,300"; I say "charge it!" Then I walk out into the below zero weather feeling all warm inside. Then I wake up freezing because my husband has all the covers.

Rational calculation in the service of self-indulgence is punished. Impulsive behavior or spontaneity in the service of self-indulgence is similarly punished. Neither practicality nor frugality introduced (as a defense mechanism) into fantasy in service of cultural ideology is sufficient to protect the consumer from disappointment:

> I have been looking at the fur coat ads since early Fall, checking prices and styles. Now that Christmas is over, the real sales will start. I am looking for a 3/4 length shadow fox coat. The first place I go is Dion Furs. These coats are skimpy and look cheap. Next I try Evans. Their coats are full and the prices are really good, but I want to be sure and get the best price. Next I try Field's and there is a fabulous full length coat at a very good price, but it's $700 more than I want to spend. But, I really want it, so I look at other coats, but I don't like them, so I don't buy anything.

The hard work of producing consumption yields bitter fruit in this account. Echoes of Tantalus's predicament or that of Aesop's fox are audible in this fantasy.

Desire contends with decorum in most of our stories. "Reality" in the form of the cultural ideology of disinterested giving intrudes on the fantasies of our respondents. This reality is punitive. Practicality recurs as a theme because self-indulgence must be rationalized. Guilt must be mitigated. Conditions must be placed on purchases. If others can be implicated in the web of consequences (as auxiliary beneficiaries of a gift to self or as critics of the self-gifting enterprise), so much the better.

Labor Value Theory of Worthiness

Earlier work on gift shopping (Cheal, 1988; Sherry et al., 1992) has described the labor value theory that consumers employ to infer the merit of and invest meaning into gifts. Simply put, the symbolic value of a gift is often linked (by donor and recipient) to the amount of mental, emotional, or physical effort believed to have been expended in the process of search. This theory shows up in our database as well: "I dreamt I was going to buy myself a full length mink coat! Expensive, beautiful, luxurious—why not? I deserve it." Our respondents' fantasies also suggest an analogous theory applied to the perceived worthiness of the self. Their accounts indicate a belief that a gift must be earned or deserved; effort must be invested in meriting. For example, one respondent muses,

> I was walking up and down the aisles of our antique show. I was particularly interested in the jewelry. I'd lost a lovely watch a few years ago and I kept hoping I'd find it at a show. The watch originally belonged to my mother-in-law. It was made of white gold or platinum. It had a rectangular face that was surrounded by diamonds. After a long time, perhaps an hour or more, I saw the watch in a display case. I was delighted. I asked to see the watch and asked the price of it. The woman told me the watch had been sold. I offered more money than the price. I told her I had a police report of the loss. I asked her to describe the purchaser and what she was wearing. I started to run up and down the aisles as I looked for the purchaser. After what seemed like an eternity, I wake up.

Despite the frustration ultimately involved, she has labored mightily to reacquire the gift. Another respondent confounds reality and fantasy in her account of the heroic earning of the gift:

> I don't have to imagine. I'll tell you a true story. A few years ago, two to be exact, I went to Water Tower and got a job at Lord and Taylor department store. I was assigned to the fine jewelry section. I worked three evenings a week and all day Saturday and Sunday. On the weekends, I was assigned to the special watch display section. It featured Seiko, Jaz, etc. . . . And, they had a sales promotion, whereas every time we sold a Jaz watch we would write the style # and amount on a card, given by them, and after the promotion ended December 31, we would send the card in and for every $100 total, we would be entitled to $10 toward a Jaz watch. . . . One day while tagging, a beautiful Jaz watch came to my attention. It was gold and silver. The design was elegant. It could be worn during the day or night. Its price $150.00. To have the watch I had to sell $1500.00 in value of Jaz watches. I had to push all the watches and pray many of the people wanted a Jaz. Two weeks before the promotion ended I dreamed I came into the store, went to the display case as a customer and someone brought me my watch. I couldn't see who made the gift purchase, nor who sold it, but it was mine. The weekend came and my first Jaz sell was to a woman . . . and she purchased my watch for herself. My heart stopped. It was our last. We had other styles, but not this one. My thoughts raced . . . how could someone get it for me when she just got the last one? Never mind, I thought, just keep selling Jaz. I sold $1000.00 in value (selling price) of Jaz. I looked at the styles costing $100.00, none were for me. The only one costing

exactly $100.00 was ugly to me. It had a gold trim face, small numbers and black straps. Nothing like mine. Mine, it had a silver and gold face, the numbers were small gold dots for each hour. The band was a bracelet of silver rope with gold notches. The band it was trim and elegant. And, there were no more and even if there were I didn't have enough sales. I turned in my card. And, even though there were no more, I wrote my watch down as my first choice. I didn't give a second or third choice. A month passed, then a call from Jaz headquarters came. My watch, I could have [it] . . . there was one left located in New York. A week later it was mine. A dream comes true.

Despite apparent setbacks as fate takes its course, the narrator recounts a happy ending. Worthiness triumphs, aided enormously by heroic diligence. These gifts are clearly expensive, both monetarily and emotionally. In the stories presented above or considered below, the gift must allow the narrator to be more or do more than she could unaided. The gift becomes a vehicle of mastery as much as anything else. It may also be emblematic of the gendered nature of entitlement. The gift is earned, paid for in fact, with a bonus, making it a literal gift exchange with sacrificial overtones. Self-indulgence is funded with explicitly discretionary income.

Minimal Material Nucleus

Given the unlimited possibilities for inflaming and satisfying desire that fantasy would promise to enfranchise, the tightly circumscribed range of gifts our respondents imagine giving themselves is quite remarkable. As narratives already reported suggest, clothing is the most frequently fantasized gift to the self. Furthermore, clothing often resolves to a single (albeit luxurious) garment: a coat. That consumers most desire this particular item is curious. Perhaps the coat best represents the new or discardable persona. It attracts, disguises, and enhances. It may be regarded as parasomatic packaging, a literal second skin. It can be shed or changed, offering the wearer a set of chameleonic options (Bouchet, 1991) in an overdetermined social routine. She may flout political correctness or flaunt naturalness.

The vacation is the next most commonly envisioned gift to the self. The vacation is awarded as a blessed relief to unbearable sameness and repetitive routine. It may be guiltily enjoyed or shared with others:

> If I could buy myself a dream gift—I'd have a hard time but I guess make arrangement to go on a trip to Gunda—it's a beautiful island in the Caribbean and would like to get and stay for a week with my husband and our two grown children with their husbands.

> Would be costly but really would like to go there someday down the road
> when we can see our way clear.

It may be doubly institutionalized, affording the narrator both time and place
away from care:

> I would buy a cleaning lady and never think about cleaning again. I would
> need her 2 or 3 times a week. What a relief. Then I would travel around
> the world.

A trifecta of sorts is described by one respondent. Escape is not embodied
merely in relief from mundane drudgery and nonreciprocal caretaking as
much as it is in the abiding rightness of the selection:

> My dream would be of a truly wonderful gift—a super vacation trip, a
> dramatic new dress, perhaps a vacation house. I would select and inspect
> the gift—it would be perfect in every detail. The stumbling block would be
> its price, but I would buy it anyway.

That propriety is absolutely critical resounds through the narratives. One
account reinforces the effort generally needed to achieve perfection:

> I would have a dream house to furnish. I would decorate each room. Money
> is not a problem. Finding the right piece is.

Many of the narratives recounted above describe the search for the unique
or the antique. The quintessential gift (Belk et al., 1989) embodies the "right
stuff"; its rightness is often revealed in hierophany.

Ritual Substratum

Thomas (1991) has spoken of the "optical illusion" that we are offered by
material culture:

> We take the "concrete and palpable" presence of a thing to attest to the
> reality of that which we have made it signify; our fantasies find confirmation
> in the materiality of things that are composed more of objectified fantasy
> than physical stuff. Not that this mystification is a veneer of falsehood; the
> dialectic of reification and consumption is as necessary and fundamental
> as anything else constitutive of human sociality, but the truths are truths
> of seduction rather than presence. (p. 176)

If we demystify the dreamworks and sound the seductiveness our respondents have portrayed for us, we gain some insight into the ways in which guilt and obligation can stifle authentic desire. Our female respondents have apparently muted their agentic impulse and amplified their communal voice. Many of our respondents' fantasies emphasize domesticity, communality, and family over and above self. Given permission and encouragement to dwell on and indulge the self, our respondents have learned to prefer to defer. And demur. Their capitulation to the ideologies of both disinterested giving and hegemonic political economy verges on complete; the resulting repression of even the range of choice that might contribute to self-indulgence as a viable option is quite thoroughgoing. These women are the producers and makers of gift ritual primarily. They are relegated to the secondary role of consumer and beneficiary of gift ritual. In the social reproduction of culture in this particular sphere, the ritual subject has great difficulty becoming—or even approximating—the ritual object.

Believing that political power lies at the heart of the sacred, Weiner (1992) reads through Bataille to revise Mauss in her assertion that reciprocity is motivated by a "desire to keep something back from the pressures of give and take" (p. 43). She identifies this something as a "possession that speaks to and for an individual's or group's social identity" (p. 43); the difference between persons or groups is thereby affirmed. Weiner assesses the absolute value of an inalienable possession as the authenticity of its symbolic representation of an individual's or group's "distinctiveness" (p. 51). For the reproducer of domestic culture to present herself with the embodiment of cultural generativity, to arrogate to herself the reproductive principle is an apparently threatening prospect. It may even be construed as dangerous. It clearly jeopardizes the existing division of power and disrupts the role repertoires in contemporary social relations. Such a presentation to self is perhaps so evocative of the female donor's distinctiveness that its foregrounding challenges the androcentric myth privileging political economy over domestic. It invites us to consider whether it truly is a man's world or whether such a world is worth having; it offers principles of resistance, if not integration. Yet the degree to which monadic giving is a ritual in transition from a hyperextension to a reversal of commodity feminism (Goldman, Heath, & Smith, 1991)—the depoliticization of social critique that occurs when marketers fetishize feminism—is a fundamental question that future research must address. Surely, our women respondents do not give themselves the same gift care they give kith and kin. Perhaps they cannot, or will not, accord themselves equivalent gift care. They may actually become so entrapped in the "circular compulsivity of mandated giving and entitled needfulness" that, feeling bereft of "spontaneous desire or sense of genuine caring" (Shabad, 1993a, p. 488), the autodon becomes a palliative. The degree to which they are unaware of their penchant to slight self-care remains a provocative empirical question.

Conclusion

> Oh bright box ripping in its own good time. (Fulton, 1990, p. 11)

Is it conceivable that the only "pure" gift, if such a thing can be said to exist at all in contemporary consumer culture, is a gift to one's self from one's self? This may in fact be the only situation wherein the ideologies of interest and disinterest coincide perfectly. Nor does this coincidence imply balance, harmony, or cancellation. Rather, it appears to generate a tension that results in a reassessment of the nature of gift giving itself. If, as Alice Fulton (1990) implies, the self is an emergent gift, it may explain why those "inflammatory abstracts," such as "love, forgiveness, [and] faith," are among the most preferred gifts that our ritual makers would give to themselves.

Beidelman (1989), in particular, has taken great pains to reintroduce students of the gift to the original writings of Mauss (1924) and Simmel (1971, 1978) and to stress the polysemic nature of the gift. He notes that Mauss, having outlined the process of agonistic exchange (involving formal pretense and social duplicity), neglected the concept in favor of a theory that featured exchange as a conflict reduction mechanism. Simmel, on the other hand, envisioned exchange as a process of tension and struggle, sacrifice and resistance, that served to heighten divisiveness. Whereas Mauss believed that gifts and the self encoded therein eventually returned to the donor and that this knowledge of eventual return created value, Simmel maintained that both gift and encoded self were often lost and that this risk of loss created value (Beidelman, 1989). Although the role of ambiguity and ambivalence is weighted differently by each of these theorists, the centrality of agonistic exchange to the creation of a social self seems apparent. The discrepancies between the private self and its persona(e) are negotiated, if not always resolved, through agonistic exchange. Gifts enable the individual to gauge the commensurability of her appraisal of self with that of others (Beidelman, 1989). Among our respondents, the recognition of a need to augment or offset deficient appraisals that is implicit in monadic giving represents both a critique and a supersession of kith and kin relations. Monadic giving is at once a source of personal autonomy and existential doubt.

Let us begin to integrate some of the larger themes emerging from our study. Recent consumer research (e.g., McCracken, 1988) in contemporary Western society has confirmed what anthropologists working in indigenous non-Western societies have long asserted: Objects are animated by invested meaning. Whether charisma (Tambiah, 1984), pathos (Beidelman, 1989), or other behavioral components (Richardson, 1987) are sedimented in the object, the object can become singularized (Kopytoff, 1986) until it acquires the status of an inalienable possession (Weiner, 1992). The "radiating power" of withholding such possessions from circulation generates the "thrust" of exchange and endows their owners with "hegemonic dominance" over others (Weiner, 1992, p. 180). Thomas (1991) clarifies the distinction between alienable and inalienable objects in a useful way. Noting that the issue is "the way in which an object is socially consequential" (which in turn determines whether it "can, must, or cannot be circulated"), he designates the singularity of the object as a matter of "context and narrative" (p. 100). When the ideologies of interested and disinterested giving collide, as they do in our consumer narratives, the ambivalence created by "keeping while giving" is palpable.

The result of this disharmony of ideologies is the creation of a metanarrative or metasocial commentary on the nature of gendered exchange. This commentary is both ironic and oblique. It is ultimately critical as well. It reveals that the burden of ritual responsibility is borne with reverence and resentment. It suggests that our ritual makers must be incentivized beyond obligation and altruism if the ritual is to have a binding force that will resist alienation. It prompts us to wonder if broadened or more diversified participation in social worlds can be achieved without a corresponding compromise or diminution of personal integrity based on authority. Finally it may signal the demise of gift giving itself as a mechanism of sociocultural integration in the late 20th century and herald a more atomistic era. The metanarrative repackages the adage "What goes around comes around." For our female respondents, monadic giving represents the short-term possibility of shifting from entrapment to empowerment. In the long run, a generalized mastery of the autodon could produce a reenchantment of dyadic giving. One could imagine redrafting the metanarrative as a postmodern cautionary tale that combined the moral economies of Lysistrata and The Little Red Hen.

The women in our study are rewiring the totemic circuitry of gift exchange (Plath, 1987; Sherry & McGrath, 1989). In nonmarket society, where a prosumption ethic (Toffler, 1980) obtains, the gift circulates through networks to return to the donor. Others mediate the gift given to the self. In market society where a production ethic obtains, the gift literally becomes a commodity exchanged with others. Whether it is sacralized or not, the gift is usually retired from circulation; its disposition affects the nature of dyadic ties. In hypermarket or postmodern society, the ethic of "prosumption" is revived on an ad hoc basis. The actively producing consumer (whose production is now largely symbolic and focused on the creation of experience) may circulate or retire gifts; she may pursue both of these routes. A third option is now apparent. Consumers may appropriate gifts directly to themselves. Respondents in our study are the obverse of Toffler's (1980) "prosumer." Collectively, they might be termed the "conducer," insofar as their goal is to reconcile interest and disinterest, to balance or integrate agenetic and communal orientations. Conducers literally "lead" by "bringing together"; community is both a cause and a consequence of their agency. Whereas gift giving in market society has always served as a cultural vehicle of conduction, it becomes a personal vehicle in postmodern society. The autodon is given to a protean self engaged in multiple life projects. It is an autoerotic activity entirely appropriate to the era (Brooks, 1993). It is a manifestation of the cultural poetics of desire (Halperin, Winkler, & Zeitlen, 1990; Sherry et al., 1993) and a reminder that erotica is a larger realm than mere sexuality.

The split between domestic and political economies in postmodern consumer culture is in many ways less pronounced than in the past. Women may exercise or reject the option of participating in the political economy. This "mere" option can be quite stressful. If the option is exercised, women often face the prospect of limited advance and retain responsibility (de facto) for material and ritual reproduction of domestic economy. If the option is rejected, women often come to feel "less than" more multiply engaged counterparts and suffer qualms over being responsible for only the material and ritual reproduction of domestic economy. Living in an era when the inherent dignity of all work goes largely unrecognized or unacknowledged is a source of much contemporary malaise. This malaise returns us to the inexplicably neglected theme of sacrifice (Cheal, 1988; Mauss, 1924; Sherry et al., 1993; Tambiah, 1984; Weiner, 1992) as a blueprint for gift giving.

Market culture has enforced a norm of self-sacrifice among women. This norm has had dysfunctional as well as functional consequences. It has resulted in deprivation as well as liberation. Women are expected to sacrifice self in the service of domestic and political economy. This expectation is often simultaneously joyfully embraced and bitterly resented; it is rarely the object of conscious reflection in consumer research investigations. Where embraced, the expectation produces a view of gift as an investment of life that animates objects and others. Where resented, the expectation produces a view of gift as a loss of life, either to no avail or to the parasitic benefit of a vilified other. Either way, the gift is a sacrifice on the cosmological level on the order of the theft of fire or on the mundane level on the order of provision of starter dough. Some *élan vital* is rekindled or extinguished through the gift. Whether we invoke the labor theory of value, the theory of extended self, the theory of sacralization, or any other folk model of understanding, the female self is incorporated into rituals reproducing domestic culture.

The limitations of the present study must be reemphasized and the opportunities for future inquiry briefly sketched. Our interpretation is based on an intimate familiarity with a particular population, and although it is certainly suggestive, it is not generalizable to other populations at this time. We are aware of the pitfalls inherent in theorizing female subjectivities—totalizing, privileging gender as a unit of analysis, applying preconceived theories of female experience to women's texts, privileging select texts, and considering women's tests apart from those of men, to name a few (Costello, 1991, p. 125)—and stress both the exploratory nature of this investigation and the holistic character of our larger enterprise. A pluralistic research regime is essential to the unpacking of gift-giving dynamics in contemporary U.S. society.

Detailed investigation of monadic giving across a range of female populations of varied socioeconomic status, age, household composition, and ethnicity is clearly indicated. Exploration of male gift worlds in comparable depth is also warranted. These worlds are incompletely described in the consumer research literature. Cross-cultural investigation of monadic giving, especially in regions affected differently by the diffusion of late capitalism, would be a productive undertaking. India, for example, where gender roles and relationships between the individual and the collective differ from those in the United States, might prove to be a productive comparative field site. A cultural account of the ongoing transformation of gift economies might be one result of such a study. Finally, a return to the ethnographic roots of our study is appropriate. Our present projective analysis can now be introduced into our original field sites, where informants can be engaged in refining the understanding of the phenomena we have probed in this chapter. The sociocultural account we have provided here incorporates elements of a critique of everyday life. It may serve as a foundation for the truly critical postfeminist account of consumption practices that we have not attempted to develop here.

Changes over time in mating rituals and patterns, family and household structures, and conceptions of the self conspire to produce the phenomenon of gifts given to the self. Gift care can be understood in part as an adaptive response to a repressive patriarchal social structure that proves stressful to the individual female respondent in the short run. Monadic giving is then a market correction that helps the domestic economy to persist over time as well as an individual strategy of personal regeneration. It is one way of observing the metaphysical injunction (stemming from indifference and true ignorance) our culture places on its ritual makers: heal thyself. It is also a material manifestation of the painstaking selectivity of women coping with an "empty" self. Restricting the domain of those from whom she will receive gifts may reveal the unconscious directedness of her experience of need (Shabad, 1993a, p. 486).

A gift to self produces both satisfaction and guilt. Given an uncertain, unknowable, undervalued, multiple self,[5] I get what no one else can or will give me with no apparent strings attached (i.e., a pure or altruistic gift) but at a cost to "them" and at a cost to my traditional sense of self. By relaxing my other-serving vigilance and recentering that vigilance on my self, through ritual self-care I (re)make myself. Both the gift and its giving are presents. By relinquishing the vigilance required by cultural convention, by diverting time, effort, and money from others to the self and by suspending the essence of self as extrinsically determined, the collective "I" of our female respondents sacrifices the collective "you" of the generalized other that comprises a conventional recipient pool. Although neither a scapegrace nor a scapegoat, the woman engaged in monadic giving dreads such designation and its imagined consequences. The autodon is at once a guilty secret, a sheepish self-indulgence, a hegemonic artifact, and an emancipatory opportunity. It should serve as well as a warning to the passive recipients of received wisdom, whether they are social scientists or jaded donors.

 Notes

1. We are the heirs of an unfortunately turned label. The term "self-gift" has been employed in the consumer research literature. Most gifts are self-gifts in that donors project, invest, and otherwise impute personal meaning into their offerings. Donors give of self and shape self. If a neologism must be used to denote the object given and received, we favor the term "autodon," which connotes both anachronism and tenacious cultural survival (continuity from pre- to postconsumer society). Self-gift is too ambiguous in its apparent simplicity. We prefer to use "monadic giving" as the cover term for the ritual process itself. The term self-gift is used in this chapter as a bridge to existing literature only.

2. In fact, a reviewer of this chapter suggested that we point out that the upscale bias of our sample is an advantage for examining this phenomenon rather than a limitation. The upscale sample provides a conservative bias, as upscale women should be better able to justify giving to themselves, thus pointing out that our findings of hesitation cannot be accounted for

with economic explanations. The reviewer further added, "Just imagine what the results would be if a middle class or downscale sample had been used."

3. In our larger study, respondents performed a thematic apperception task, writing stories to 3 of 15 different pictures. One of these pictures was designed specifically to elicit the concept of monadic giving and had, in fact, been used by one of our focal gift stores in an advertisement that suggested that the gift buyer will want to keep gift purchases made at this store for herself. Unfortunately, in none of the stories did respondents specifically connect this picture to a gift to the self. Respondents interpreted the visual cues with stories of a sexy, sophisticated woman (often themselves) who may be giving or receiving a gift. One respondent identified the figure as "me kidding my husband that he actually went shopping." Thus our attempt to capture visually the stimuli related to monadic giving was not successful, although Mick, DeMoss, and Faber (1992) accomplished this by combining a picture with a verbal prompt. Rather, we approximated an interesting advertising concept test, one that might inform retailers trying to convey this idea. We determined that although the visual portion of a store's advertisement did not communicate the retailer's intended message to its clientele the advertisement served to communicate by virtue of showing a wrapped present a number of other notions associated with gift exchanges.

4. The ritual of gift search may provide a synergistic boost to gift care, as this response suggests: "Sometimes I buy things for myself when I am actually looking for gifts for another." Search may prompt the seeker to apply her diagnostic acumen to her own unrequited situation. It invites serendipity and fosters the illusion of dyadic exchange, mitigating guilt in the bargain. That this ritual and synergy need not be seasonal is revealed in our discovery of the phenomenon of "gift closets" maintained by some of our respondents. For example, one woman observes, "I'm a very organized person—make a lot of lists—most of the time I know what I'm looking for and if I see a gift for even 6 months away I purchase it and put it in my 'gift' closet. Find that this closet has been a life saver many times." As symbolic medicine chests, these closets store gifts for specific and generalized others and occasions. They also function as projectible, dispensable hope chests, permitting owners to engage in provisioning fantasies prior to literal disposition.

5.

> *Do I contradict myself?*
>
> *Very well then, I contradict myself,*
>
> *(I am large, I contain multitudes.)*
>
> —Walt Whitman, "Song of Myself"
>
> (1959/1977, p. 27)

References

Abu-Lughod, L. (1991). Writing against culture. In R. Fox (Ed.), *Recapturing anthropology: Working in the present* (pp. 137-162). Santa Fe, NM: School of American Research Press.

Bailey, K. (1978). *Methods of social research.* New York: Free Press.

Beidelman, T. O. (1989). Agonistic exchange: Homeric reciprocity and the heritage of Simmel and Mauss. *Cultural Anthropology, 4*(2), 227-259.

Belk, R. (1988). Possessions and the extended self. *Journal of Consumer Research, 15*(2), 139-168.

Belk, R., & Coon, G. (1993). Gift giving as agapic love: An alternative to the exchange paradigm based on dating experiences. *Journal of Consumer Research, 20*(2), 393-417.

Belk, R., Wallendorf, M., & Sherry, J. F., Jr. (1989). The sacred and profane in consumer behavior: Theodicy on the odyssey. *Journal of Consumer Research, 16*(1), 1-38.

Bernard, H. R. (1988). *Research methods in cultural anthropology.* Newbury Park, CA: Sage.

Bird-David, N. (1990). The giving environment: Another perspective on the economic system of gatherer-hunters. *Current Anthropology, 31*(2), 189-196.

Bouchet, D. (1991). Marketing as a specific form of communication. In H. Larsen, D. Mick, & C. Alsted (Eds.), *Marketing and semiotics* (pp. 31-51). Copenhagen: Handelshøjskolens Forlag.

Bristor, J., & Fischer, E. (1993). Feminist thought: Implications for consumer research. *Journal of Consumer Research, 19*(4), 518-536.

Brooks, C. (1993). Hand jive. *Utne Reader,* No. 56, 132-134. (Reprinted from *Isthmus,* September 4, 1992)

Brumberg, J. (1989). *Fasting girls: The history of anorexia nervosa.* New York: New American Library.

Costa, J. (Ed.). (1991). *Gender and consumer behavior.* Salt Lake City: University of Utah Printing Service.

Cheal, D. (1988). *The gift economy.* New York: Routledge.

Costello, J. (1991). Taking the "woman" out of women's autobiography: The perils and potentials of theorizing female subjectivities. *Diacritics, 21*(2-3), 123-134.

Cushman, P. (1990, May). Why the self is empty: Toward a historically situated psychology. *American Psychologist,* pp. 599-611.

Devault, M. (1990). Feminist interviewing and analysis. *Social Problems, 37*(1), 96-116.

DeVos, G. (1985). Dimensions of the self in Japanese culture. In A. Marsella, G. DeVos, & F. L. K. Hsu (Eds.), *Culture and self: Asian and Western perspectives* (pp. 141-184). London: Tavistock.

Frank, L. K. (1948). *Projective methods.* Springfield, IL: Charles C Thomas.

Fulton, A. (1990). *Powers of congress.* Boston: David Godine.

Gergen, K. (1991). *The saturated self.* New York: Basic Books.

Goldman, R., Heath, D., & Smith, S. (1991). Commodity feminism. *Critical Studies in Mass Communication, 8*(3), 333-351.

Goodwin, C., & Lockshin, L. (1992). The solo consumer: Unique opportunity for the service marketer. *Journal of Services Marketing, 6*(3), 27-36.

Gould, S., & Weil, C. (1991). Gift-giving roles and gender self-concepts. *Sex Roles, 24*(9-10), 617-637.

Halperin, D., Winkler, J., & Zeitlen, F. (Eds.). (1990). *Before sexuality: The construction of erotic experience in the ancient Greek world.* Princeton, NJ: Princeton University Press.

Hirschman, E. (1993). Ideology and consumer research, 1980 and 1990: A Marxist and feminist critique. *Journal of Consumer Research, 19*(4), 537-555.

Hirschman, E., & Holbrook, M. (1992). *Postmodern consumer research.* Newbury Park, CA: Sage.

Joy, A. (1989). Beyond the odyssey: Interpretations of ethnographic writing in consumer behavior. In R. Belk (Ed.), *Highways and buyways: Naturalistic inquiry from the consumer behavior odyssey* (pp. 216-233). Provo, UT: Association for Consumer Research.

Kline, P. (1973). *New approaches in psychological measurement.* London: Wiley.

Kopytoff, I. (1986). The cultural biography of things: Commoditization as process. In A. Appadurai (Ed.), *The social life of things* (pp. 64-91). Cambridge, UK: Cambridge University Press.

Lears, T. J. J. (1983). From salvation to self-realization: Advertising and the therapeutic roots of the consumer culture, 1880-1930. In R. W. Fox & T. J. J. Lears (Eds.), *The culture of consumption* (pp. 3-38). New York: Pantheon.

Levy, S. (1982). Symbols, selves, and others. In A. Mitchell (Ed.), *Advances in consumer research* (Vol. 9, pp. 542-543). Ann Arbor, MI: Association for Consumer Research.

Lindzey, G. (1961). *Projective techniques and cross-cultural research.* New York: Appleton-Century-Crofts.

Mauss, M. (1924). *The gift.* New York: Norton.

McAdams, D. (1993). *The stories we live by.* New York: Morrow.

McAlexander, J., Schouten, J., & Roberts, S. (in press). Consumer behavior and divorce. *Research in Consumer Behavior.*

McCracken, G. (1988). *Culture and consumption.* Bloomington: University of Indiana Press.

McGrath, M. A., Sherry, J. F., Jr., & Levy, S. J. (1993). Giving voice to the gift: The use of projective techniques to recover lost meanings. *Journal of Consumer Psychology, 2*(2), 171-191.

Mick, D. G. (1991). Giving gifts to ourselves: A Greimassian analysis leading to testable propositions. In H. H. Larsen, D. G. Mick, & C. Alsted (Eds.), *Marketing and semiotics: The Copenhagen symposium* (pp. 142-159). Copenhagen: Handelshøjskolens Forlag.

Mick, D. G., & DeMoss, M. (1990a). To me from me: A descriptive phenomenology of self-gifts. In M. E. Goldberg, G. Gorn, & R. W. Pollay (Eds.), *Advances in consumer research* (Vol. 17, pp. 677-682). Provo, UT: Association for Consumer Research.

Mick, D. G., & DeMoss, M. (1990b). Self-gifts: Phenomenological insights from four contexts. *Journal of Consumer Research, 17*, 322-332.

Mick, D. G., & DeMoss, M. (1992). Further findings on self-gifts: Products, qualities, and socioeconomic correlates. In J. F. Sherry, Jr. & B. Sternthal

(Eds.), *Advances in consumer research* (Vol. 19, pp. 140-146). Provo, UT: Association for Consumer Research.

Mick, D. G., DeMoss, M., & Faber, R. J. (1992). A projective study of motivations and meaning of self-gifts: Implications for retail management. *Journal of Retailing, 68*(2), 122-144.

Miller, D. (1991). *Handbook of research design and social measurement.* Newbury Park, CA: Sage.

Murstein, B. I. (1965). Assumptions, adaptation level, and projective techniques. In B. Murstein (Ed.), *Handbook of projective techniques* (pp. 49-68). New York: Basic Books.

Ogilvy, J. (1990, February). This postmodern business. *Marketing Research Today,* pp. 4-20.

Parry, J. (1988). The gift, the Indian gift and the "Indian gift." *Man, 21,* 453-473.

Plath, D. (1987). Gifts of discovery. *Liberal Education, 73*(4), 12-16.

Rabin, A. I. (1968). *Projective techniques in personality assessment.* New York: Springer.

Raheja, G. (1988). *The poison in the gift: Ritual presentation and the dominant caste in a north Indian village.* Chicago: University of Chicago Press.

Richardson, M. (1987). A social (ideational-behavioral) interpretation of material culture and its application to archaeology. In D. Ingersoll & G. Bronitsky (Eds.), *Mirror and metaphor* (pp. 381-403). Lanham, MD: University Press of America.

Rook, D. (1986). Targeting the "solo" consumer. In J. L. Chandon & V. Venkatesan (Eds.), *Quality and innovation policies, market segmentation and positioning* (pp. 142-155). Aix-en-Provence, France: Institut l'Administration des Enterprises.

Rook, D. (1987). The buying impulse. *Journal of Consumer Research, 14*(2), 189-199.

Sacks, J. M. (1965). The relative effect on projective responses of stimuli referring to other persons. In B. Murstein (Ed.), *Handbook of projective techniques* (pp. 823-834). New York: Basic Books.

Shabad, P. (1993a). Resentment, indignation, entitlement: The transformation of unconscious wish into need. *Psychoanalytic Dialogues, 3*(4), 481-494.

Shabad, P. (1993b). Repetition and incomplete mourning: The intergenerational transmission of traumatic themes. *Psychoanalytic Psychology, 10*(1), 61-75.

Sherry, J. F., Jr. (1983). Gift giving in anthropological perspective. *Journal of Consumer Research, 10*(2), 157-168.

Sherry, J. F., Jr. (1990). A sociocultural analysis of a midwestern American flea market. *Journal of Consumer Research, 17*(1), 13-30.

Sherry, J. F., Jr., & McGrath, M. A. (1989). Unpacking the holiday presence: A comparative ethnography of two gift stores. In E. Hirschman (Ed.), *Interpretive consumer research* (pp. 148-167). Provo, UT: Association for Consumer Research.

Sherry, J. F., Jr., McGrath, M. A., & Levy, S. J. (1992). The disposition of the gift and many unhappy returns. *Journal of Retailing, 68*(1), 40-65.

Sherry, J. F., Jr., McGrath, M. A., & Levy, S. J. (1993). The dark side of the gift. *Journal of Business Research, 28*(3), 225-244.

Simmel, G. (1971). *On individuality and social forms* (D. Levine, Trans.). Chicago: University of Chicago Press.

Simmel, G. (1978). *The philosophy of money* (T. Bottomore & D. Frisby, Trans.). London: Routledge & Kegan Paul.

Stern, B. (1989). Literary explication: A methodology for consumer research. In E. Hirschman (Ed.), *Interpretive consumer research* (pp. 48-59). Provo, UT: Association for Consumer Research.

Stern, B. (1993). Feminist literary criticism and the deconstructing of ads: A postmodern view of advertising and consumer responses. *Journal of Consumer Research, 19*(4), 556-566.

Tambiah, S. (1984). *The Buddhist saints of the forest and the cult of amulets.* New York: Cambridge University Press.

Thomas, N. (1991). *Entangled objects.* Cambridge, MA: Harvard University Press.

Thompson, C., Locander, W., & Pollio, H. (1989). Putting consumer experience back into consumer research: The philosophy and method of existential phenomenology. *Journal of Consumer Research, 16*(2), 133-161.

Toffler, A. (1980), *The third wave.* New York: William Morrow.

Wallendorf, M., & Arnould, E. (1991). "We gather together": Consumption of rituals of Thanksgiving Day. *Journal of Consumer Research, 18*(1), 13-31.

Weiner, A. (1992). *Inalienable possessions.* Berkeley, CA: University of California Press.

Weiss, M. (1989). *The clustering of America.* New York: Harper & Row.

Whitman, W. (1977). Song of myself. In F. Murphy (Ed.), *Whitman: The complete poems* (pp. 63-124). New York: Viking. (Original work published 1959)

Wilde, O. (1969). The critic as artist: A dialogue, part II. In R. Ellman (Ed.), *The artist as critic: Critical writings of Oscar Wilde* (pp. 371-408). New York: Random House.

PART SEVEN

Conclusion

◿ 12

Anthropology of Marketing and Consumption
Retrospect and Prospect

John F. Sherry, Jr.

W e have asked the reader to wander the outback of interdisciplinary inquiry from behavioral archaeology to projective fantasy as a way of discovering some of the issues of contemporary relevance to theorists and practitioners interested in biobasic and marketized aspects of consumer behavior. In the course of this walkabout we have exposed the reader to artifacts and organizations, physical and social architecture, sacred and profane economies, superstructural and infrastructural public writing, cultural ideology and intrapsychic dynamics, fantasies and realities, prescriptions and proscriptions, and managers and consumers both foreign and domestic. I return the reader to our point of embarkation in the following pages by way of an interpretive summary of our enterprise.

◿ Issues and Directions

Although anthropological attention to contemporary marketing and consumer behavior has been discontinuous and selective, we have shown that it is currently being trained on these areas with greater precision and fervor. In this sourcebook we have explored four broad topics in particular: the world of goods and services, the role of motivation in marketing and consumer behavior, the experience of emplacement in institutional perspective, and the managerial relevance of anthropology to marketing. This exploration opens further the door to those experiential consumption worlds (Holt, in press) or market worlds (Sherry, 1993) of interest to researchers probing the phenomenology and cultural psychology of marketing and consumption. A synopsis of these four topics and a concluding assessment of the trajectory their anthropological investigation might assume are in order.

Let me begin by espousing the antireductionist, nonexclusivist position adopted by Orlove and Rutz (1989) without championing any of the traditions of economic anthropology—individual, political, social or cultural—that they view as stakeholders in the anthropology of consumption and without adopting their classificatory system of authors in those traditions. This position is the principle upon which our sourcebook is founded. Believing, like Fine and Leopold (1993), that one general theory of consumption would require "too much *ceteris paribus* to swallow" (p. 4), even if fielded by a holistic discipline such as anthropology, and, having celebrated diversity of perspective, I will impose an expedient framework upon the sociocultural inquiry of marketing and consumption to bring our discussion to fruition.

The World of Goods and Services

Perhaps this section should be retitled "Worlds of Materiality and Materiel" in recognition of the projectible, shape-shifting nature of the objects, experiences, and behavior exchanges that we have shown comprise marketing and consumption. "Goods" and "services" represent at worst a metaphoric denial of the dysfunctional or dark side of transactions and at best a masking of their neutrality as vessels of human agency. We might speak as productively of "bads" and "disservices"—as well as of "longages of demand" in lieu of "shortages of supply" (Hardin, 1985)—in our analysis of the role played by marketing and consumption in everyday life. At any rate, we have worked toward a cultural understanding of the corporeal and noncorporeal components of consumer and marketplace behaviors that can be recounted here.

It has become an anthropological commonplace since the Douglas and Isherwood (1979) assessment that products and services are a nonverbal medium of communication that make our cultural categories stable and visible. Products and services and our cognitive faculties are mutually constituting. We have illustrated some of the many ways that consumption pervades experience and is used strategically to recruit individuals to an array of projects. For Douglas and Isherwood (1979), consumption is ultimately about sociality and power. As we have emphasized, consumption serves societal and individual interests.

The sociality of consumption has been most vigorously pursued by anthropologists, yet its psychological significance has been relatively neglected by them. We have indicated how this emphasis is beginning to shift. That products and services are not exclusive to so-called modern industrial societies, that the creation of value is a politically governed procedure, that consumption is subject to social control and political redefinition, and that the politics of value is often a politics of knowledge are each amply depicted in Appadurai (1986a) and amplified by his colleagues (Appadurai, 1986b). We have elaborated on these themes throughout this volume. The role of products and services in the cultivation of a self, perhaps most compellingly explored in detail originally by Csikszentmihalyi and Rochberg-Halton (1981), has led to the postulation of two types of materialism: terminal and instrumental. The moral, pragmatic valuation of materialism in terms of purpose rather than simple existence has generated an object-relations subdiscipline among consumer researchers of anthropological bent. Differentiating between materiality as a relational condition and materialism as philosophy or strategy (perhaps even a syndrome) of acquisitiveness is the current project of this subdiscipline.

Motivation in Marketing and Consumer Behavior

If we accept the existence of a world of goods, how can we account for its animation? What type of cultural interpretation can we make of the motives of marketers and consumers? Although each of the contributors to this volume has offered some insight on this score, an effort at closure is warranted.

McCracken (1988) opened the anthropological window onto motivations by faulting conventional semiotic accounts of products and services for failing to deal with the transience of meaning in cultural systems. He tracked this mobility of meaning from its origins in the culturally constituted world, then through its investment in products and services, and on to its ultimate unpacking by individual consumers. Given that meanings are constantly in transit, McCracken became concerned to examine the occasions and investments of meaning transfer as a way of understanding the trajectory of those meanings. He has explored institutions such as advertising, fashion, design, and product development as well as personal rituals such as possession, exchange, grooming, and divestment in pursuit of the processual, constituting essences of consumption phenomena. This exploration has spawned something of a hermeneutic quest for vessels of consumption, especially among ethnographers eager to interpret the multileveled complexity of marketplace behavior depicted in this volume.

By demonstrating that the cultural logic of modernity is characterized by a tension between rationality and passion and that the "dynamism" of

Western culture stems from the "strain between dream and reality, pleasure and ability," Campbell (1987, p. 227) has moved our discussion of consumer behavior from an ideological platform of mere risk aversion and utility calculation to a more progressive emphasis on risk seeking and hedonism. This dialectic between asceticism and sentimentality, discipline and desire (Agnew, 1993, p. 26), has driven the emergence and efflorescence of a consumer culture whose complications and sequelae we have examined in this book. Modern autonomous imaginative hedonism has given rise to and has been substantiated by contemporary consumption.

In Campbell's (1987) view, the "essential activity" of consumer behavior is "not the actual selection, purchase or use of products, but the imaginative pleasure-seeking to which the product image lends itself" (p. 89). We have seen that the function of advertising in particular (Leiss, Kline, & Jhally, 1986) and marketing in general (Gardner & Levy, 1955) is to create this image. Our current ethnographic fascination with the production of consumption stems in no small measure from the interaction of this romantic impulse with the commercial libido we invoked throughout this volume. The practical resuscitation of branding will depend for its success on a deeper understanding of this impulse.

Most recently, Falk (1994) has sought to revise the work of McCracken and Campbell in his interpretation of the ways in which desire interacts with object-relations. Falk perceives both an introjective and a distinctive logic to be guiding contemporary consumption. Exercise of the former logic results in an inclusive, individually constructed self. Exercise of the latter logic results in an exclusive, socially constructed self. The interplay between the incorporating activity of the individual self and the distinguishing activity of the social self animates the pursuit of completion, around which the system of consumption revolves. The individual's life project is driven by a desire that, paradoxically, is at once objectless and constituted through objects, referring back to an undifferentiated state of being preceding ontogenic separation. Thus, ineluctably, elaboration of a cultural poetics of desire returns us to biology.

Tracking transient meaning across domains of consumer experience beyond the merely economic—marketing semiosis broadly construed (Larsen, Mick, & Alsted, 1991; Umiker-Sebeok, 1987)—has become a preoccupation among some consumer researchers during the past decade. This preoccupation is in large part a response to the postmodern climate in which our research regimes are unfolding (Firat, Sherry, & Venkatesh, 1993; Hirschman & Holbrook, 1992; Sherry, 1991). We have shown how ethnographers have concentrated on contextuality to make sense of things. Parallel investigation by researchers employing an existential-phenomenological approach emerging from psychology (Mick & Buhl, 1992; Thompson, Locander, & Pollio, 1989, 1990) has focused on the lived experience of consumers. We have seen something of a merging of anthropologists' semiological inquiry into cultural process with psychologists' semiotic inquiry into individual process in recent naturalistic (Belk, 1991) and humanistic (Hirschman, 1989) treatments of marketplace behavior; experiments with hybrid forms such as telethnography (Sherry, 1994a) reflect this trend as well. I expect this merger to intensify as research teams become more facile in combining ethnographic techniques, depth interviewing, and projective tasking.

In their exploration of consumers' and marketers' motivations, postmodern researchers have adopted a critical posture (Sherry, 1991). Their criticism has been both disciplinary and cultural. By broadening their inquiry beyond information processing, they are exposing dimensions of actors' experience in a manner that dampens the reflexively judgmental enthusiasm of an earlier generation of macro thinkers and promotes an enlightened, thoughtful criticism of the cultural conditions of slippage in marketing, consumer, and public policy sectors.

The Experience of Emplacement

We are witnessing the emergence of a marketing and consumption-based research tradition that can be characterized as the phenomenology of emplacement (Sack, 1992; Sherry, 1994b). On one level, this tradition is concerned with behavior on the ground and specifically addresses issues arising directly from institutions both formal and informal. On another more abstract level, this tradition is concerned with the kaleidoscopic individual "worlds" inhabited by stakeholders in the marketing transaction. The former aspect deals with the impact of the built environment on marketplace behavior; the latter deals with the individual elaboration of that environment as a projectible field for personal fantasy. Each aspect contributes to the experiential state we identify as "being-in-the-marketplace." Together they take us into the heart of the "embeddedness" issue we have broached in this book.

The sites of emplacement studies have begun to proliferate. Formal organizations such as marketing firms and advertising agencies are being investigated. Marketplaces themselves, from swap meets to upscale specialty boutiques, are becoming increasingly prominent field sites. The marketing of places (Kotler, Haider, & Rein, 1993) promises to become a growth industry of the future and will require a phenomenology of place to sustain it. Informal organizations, such as individual households and families (Heisley & Levy, 1991; Willis, 1991), are being studied for the light they can shed on the production of consumption. Experiential "worlds," both tacit and manifest, created by consumers in interaction with marketers (Holt, in press; Sherry, 1993) are proving to be more interestingly configured than our conventional dispassionate conceit of "the Market" (Carrier, 1994; Dilley, 1992) would suggest. As the ethos of retail theatre diffuses across all elements of the marketing mix, we will require more sensitive methods to apprehend our engagement with it.

"Place" may eventually become the predominant element of the marketing mix. It profoundly shapes the nature and reception of the other variables. Indeed, in a post-instant-gratification era where the interlude between a wish and its fulfillment becomes vanishingly small, one of marketers' most pressing concerns is to reach "the person who doesn't know that he or she wants to shop at that moment in time" ("Shopping," 1994, p. 27). Our understanding of place as a phenomenological address—whether utopia or dystopia—is in its infancy. We have attempted to speed up its maturation a bit in this book.

Relevance of Anthropology to Marketing Management

Anthropology provides a powerful challenge to the ontological, epistemological, and axiological assumptions of conventional marketing and consumer research (Hudson & Ozanne, 1988; Sherry, 1987). It provides a worldview, methodology, and values system that not only complement traditional approaches but also threaten to supplant aspects of positivist paradigms currently incapable of apprehending the empirical and theoretical richness of marketplace behavior. In terms of praxis, the discipline is well suited for managers' nascently anthropological theories-in-use and is supremely compatible with either the management-by-wandering-around or management-by-interfunctional-team philosophies currently esteemed. As a management tool or research orientation, it gets us about as close to customers as is presently possible. We have taken the reader "up close and personal" throughout the volume.

For over a decade, as an educator, consultant, and trainer, I have demonstrated to managers the utility of an anthropological approach to the marketplace. It has been my experience that practicing managers have often been more receptive to a marketplace anthropology than have many of my academic research colleagues. Other contributors to this volume have had similar experiences. As practitioners cater to emerging and evolving segments everywhere around the globe, an anthropological lens will become indispensable to their strategic and tactical vision. Anthropology is a practical discipline, anchoring the blue-sky thinking it encourages firmly to the local ground that it inhabits.

Conclusion

Recall our positioning of this volume as a sourcebook. The limitations of our treatment are apparent. The volume is not a textbook on marketplace behavior. The vigilant reader will observe that pricing alone among the marketing mix variables has been treated obliquely in this volume. Although such short shrift is unintentional, anthropological attention to pricing (e.g., Alexander, 1992; Lave, 1988) has been fleeting in comparison to other marketing elements, although the use of quasi-ethnographic techniques to understand pricing dynamics in retail settings (Dickson & Sawyer, 1990) may portend change. Nor is this volume a consumer behavior textbook. It is encouraging to note the increasing frequency with which anthropological perspectives are appearing in traditional consumer research vehicles (Sherry & Sternthal, 1991; Solomon, 1994; Wallendorf & Anderson, 1987; Wilkie, 1990), and we await the appearance of a textbook on the anthropology of consumption.

Neither is this volume a textbook on economic anthropology. Horticulturalists (Johnson, 1989) and peasants (Cancian, 1989; Hodges, 1988; Roseberry, 1989), central places and itinerary (Plattner, 1989), and formalist-substantivist-Marxist-local metaphorist debates (Sherry, 1989) have been elided in our discussion, although the exploration by marketers of preference formation in non-Western settings (Arnould, 1989) and of the overall relationship of marketing to development (Dholakia & Sherry, 1987) suggests that these issues may grow more relevant to managerial practice. As subsistence sectors of advanced and peripheral economies are integrated into the global system, the very existence of capitalism is threatened (Nash, 1994) in a way that may dwarf the collapse of command economies of the former Soviet bloc; this imminent threat lends greater urgency to the rigorous empirical search for marketing universals (Dawar & Parker, 1994). Contrary to gung ho conventional wisdom (Levitt, 1984), it may not ultimately be in anyone's best interest for marketers to push local preference patterns to their absolute limits. We must heed Dilley's (1992) admonition that "the market" cannot be disembedded from the culturally specific bodies of knowledge that generate, model, and deploy it in discourse (p. 14).

Studies emerging from the fields of anthropology, economics, history, literary criticism, and sociology (Sherry, 1991) make it increasingly apparent that, in Agnew's (1993) delightful phrase, "the productionist, supply-side and hegemonic interpretation of consumer culture has been shaken, if not overthrown, leaving one dimensional man marooned on a small and ever shrinking island of history" (p. 23). Perhaps, as the historiography of consumption matures and as the ethnography of marketing accelerates, we will understand how consumer behavior precludes and preempts possible futures, how it becomes a comprehensive *mentalité*, how it encourages us to oscillate between the existential conditions of *Homo edens* and *Homo gulosus* (Brewer & Porter, 1993), and how, if apprehended in situ though extended experiential participation of researchers (Arnould & Wallendorf, 1994), its credible interpretation can reform managerial practice. Only rigorous empirical research will help us decide whether a unified field theory (as opposed to less ambitious middle-range theories) of marketing and consumption, of the universal generalizability currently prized as the grail of academic pursuit, or the profoundly relativistic, situational systems of provisioning view of marketplace behavior (Fine & Leopold, 1993) best suits our interpretive needs.

References

Agnew, J. C. (1993). Coming up for air: Consumer culture in historical perspective. In J. Brewer & R. Porter (Eds.), *Consumption and the world of goods* (pp. 19-39). New York: Routledge.

Alexander, P. (1992). What's in a price? In R. Dilley (Ed.), *Contesting markets: Analyses of ideology, discourse and practice* (pp. 79-96). Edinburgh, UK: Edinburgh University Press.

Appadurai, A. (1986a). Introduction: Commodities and the politics of value. In A. Appadurai (Ed.), *The social life of things: Commodities in cultural perspective* (pp. 3-63). New York: Cambridge University Press.

Appadurai, A. (Ed.). (1986b). *The social life of things: Commodities in cultural perspective.* New York: Cambridge University Press.

Arnould, E. (1989). Preference formation and the diffusion of innovations: The case of Hausa-speaking Niger. *Journal of Consumer Research, 16*(2), 239-267.

Arnould, E., & Wallendorf, M. (1994). Market-oriented ethnography: Interpretation building and market strategy formulation. *Journal of Marketing Research, 31*(4), 484-504.

Belk, R. (Ed.). (1991). *Highways and buyways: Naturalistic research from the consumer behavior odyssey.* Provo, UT: Association for Consumer Research.

Brewer, J., & Porter, R. (1993). Introduction. In J. Brewer & R. Porter (Eds.), *Consumption and the world of goods* (pp. 1-15). New York: Routledge.

Campbell, C. (1987). *The romantic ethic and the spirit of modern consumerism.* New York: Blackwell.

Cancian, F. (1989). Economic behavior in peasant communities. In S. Plattner (Ed.), *Economic anthropology* (pp. 127-170). Stanford, CA: Stanford University Press.

Carrier, J. (1994). *Introduction.* Working paper, University of Virginia, Department of Anthropology.

Csikszentmihalyi, M., & Rochberg-Halton, E. (1981). *The meaning of things: Domestic symbols and the self.* New York: Cambridge University Press.

Dawar, N., & Parker, P. (1994). Marketing universals: Consumers' use of brand name, price, physical appearance and retailer reputation as signals of product quality. *Journal of Marketing, 58*(2), 81-95.

Dholakia, N., & Sherry, J. F., Jr. (1987). Marketing and development: A resynthesis of knowledge. In J. Sheth (Ed.), *Research in marketing* (Vol. 9, pp. 119-143). Greenwich, CT: JAI.

Dickson, P., & Sawyer, A. (1990). The price knowledge and search of supermarket shoppers. *Journal of Marketing, 54*(3), 42-53.

Dilley, R. (1992). Contesting markets: A general introduction to market ideology, imagery and discourse. In R. Dilley (Ed.), *Contesting markets: Analyses of ideology, discourse and practice* (pp. 1-34). Edinburgh, UK: Edinburgh University Press.

Douglas, M., & Isherwood, B. (1979). *The world of goods.* New York: Norton.

Falk, P. (1994). *The consuming body.* Thousand Oaks, CA: Sage.

Fine, B., & Leopold, E. (1993). *The world of consumption.* New York: Routledge.

Firat, A. F., Sherry, J. F., Jr., & Venkatesh, A. (1993). Postmodernism and the marketing imaginary. *International Journal of Research in Marketing, 10*(7), 215-223.

Gardner, B., & Levy, S. (1955). The product and the brand. *Harvard Business Review, 33*(2), 33-39.

Hardin, G. (1985). *Filters against folly.* New York: Viking/Penguin.

Heisley, D., & Levy, S. (1991). Autodriving: A photoelicitation technique. *Journal of Consumer Research, 18*(3), 257-272.

Hirschman, E. (Ed.). (1989). *Interpretive consumer research.* Provo, UT: Association for Consumer Research.

Hirschman, E., & Holbrook, M. (1992). *Postmodern consumer research: The study of consumption as text.* Newbury Park, CA: Sage.

Hodges, R. (1988). *Primitive and peasant markets.* New York: Blackwell.

Holt, D. (in press). How consumers consume: A taxonomy of baseball spectators' consumption practices. *Journal of Consumer Research.*

Hudson, L., & Ozanne, J. (1988). Alternative ways of seeking knowledge in consumer research. *Journal of Consumer Research, 14*(4), 508-521.

Johnson, A. (1989). Horticulturalists: Economic behavior in tribes. In S. Plattner (Ed.), *Economic anthropology* (pp. 49-77). Stanford, CA: Stanford University Press.

Kotler, P., Haider, D., & Rein, I. (1993). *Marketing places: Attracting investment, industry, and tourism to cities, states and nations.* New York: Free Press.

Larsen, H., Mick, D., & Alsted, C. (1991). *Marketing and semiotics.* Copenhagen: Handelshøjskolens Forlag.

Lave, J. (1988). *Cognition in practice.* New York: Cambridge University Press.

Leiss, W., Kline, S., & Jhally, S. (1986). *Social communication in advertising: Persons, products and images of well-being.* New York: Methuen.

Levitt, T. (1984). *The marketing imagination.* New York: Free Press.

McCracken, G. (1988). *Culture and consumption: New approaches to the symbolic character of consumer goods and activities.* Bloomington: Indiana University Press.

Mick, D., & Buhl, C. (1992). A meaning-based model of advertising experiences. *Journal of Consumer Research, 19*(3), 317-338.

Nash, J. (1994). Global integration and subsistence insecurity. *American Anthropologist, 96*(1), 7-30.

Orlove, B., & Rutz, H. (1989). Thinking about consumption: A social economy approach. In H. Rutz & B. Orlove (Eds.), *The social economy of consumption* (pp. 1-57). Lanham, MD: University Press of America.

Plattner, S. (Ed.). (1989). *Economic anthropology.* Stanford, CA: Stanford University Press.

Roseberry, W. (1989). Peasants and the world. In S. Plattner (Ed.), *Economic anthropology* (pp. 108-126). Stanford, CA: Stanford University Press.

Sack, P. (1992). *Place, modernity, and the consumer's world.* Baltimore: Johns Hopkins University Press.

Sherry, J. F., Jr. (1987). Heresy and the useful miracle: Rethinking anthropology's contributions to marketing. In J. Sheth (Ed.), *Research in marketing* (pp. 285-306). Greenwich, CT: JAI.

Sherry, J. F., Jr. (1989). Observations on marketing and consumption: An anthropological note. In T. Srull (Ed.), *Advances in consumer research* (pp. 555-561). Provo, UT: Association of Consumer Research.

Sherry, J. F., Jr. (1991). Postmodern alternatives: The interpretive turn in consumer research. In T. Robertson & H. Kassarjian (Eds.), *Handbook of consumer behavior* (pp. 548-591). Englewood Cliffs, NJ: Prentice Hall.

Sherry, J. F., Jr. (1993). *Cultural dimensions of international marketing.* Working paper, Northwestern University, Kellogg School, Department of Marketing.

Sherry, J. F., Jr. (1994a). *Bottomless cup, plug-in drug: A telethnography of coffee.* Working paper, Northwestern University, Kellogg School, Department of Marketing.

Sherry, J. F., Jr. (1994b). *The soul of the company store: Nike Town Chicago and the emplaced brandscape.* Working paper, Northwestern University, Kellogg School, Department of Marketing.

Sherry, J. F., Jr., & Sternthal, B. (Eds.). (1991). *Advances in consumer research* (Vol. 19). Provo, UT: Association of Consumer Research.

Shopping hits home. (1994, September 5). *New Media,* pp. 26-28.

Solomon, M. (1994). *Consumer behavior.* Boston: Allyn & Bacon.

Thompson, C., Locander, W., & Pollio, H. (1989). Putting consumer experience back in consumer research: The philosophy and method of existential-phenomenology. *Journal of Consumer Research, 16*(2), 133-146.

Thompson, C., Locander, W., & Pollio, H. (1990). The lived meaning of free choice: An existential-phenomenological description of everyday consumer experiences of contemporary married women. *Journal of Consumer Research, 17*(3), 346-361.

Umiker-Sebeok, J. (Ed.). (1987). *Marketing and semiotics: New directions in the study of signs for sale.* New York: Mouton de Gruyter.

Wallendorf, M., & Anderson, P. (Eds.). (1987). *Advances in consumer research* (Vol. 14). Provo, UT: Association for Consumer Research.

Wilkie, W. (1990). *Consumer behavior.* New York: John Wiley.

Willis, S. (1991). *A primer for daily life.* New York: Routledge.

Afterword

Learning to See II

William D. Wells

The chapter "Learning to 'See': A Folk Phenomenology of the Consumption of Contemporary Canadian Art," by Carole Duhaime, Annamma Joy, and Christopher Ross (Chapter 10) shows that the exhibits in the Montreal Museum of Contemporary Art present opportunities to learn to see. It also shows that the outcomes of those opportunities depend partly on the contents of the exhibits and partly on the predispositions of the visitors.

The chapters in this sourcebook also present opportunities to learn to see. As at the Montreal Museum of Contemporary Art, the outcomes of those opportunities will depend partly on the exhibits and partly on the viewers.

Postmodern and Interpretivist Researchers

One set of viewers includes "postmodern" and "interpretivist" researchers. Like the artists at the Museum, these viewers will be scouting for good ideas. They will examine objects, materials, and forms from very close and draw inspiration from them.

Members of that segment will find quite a lot to go on. In "Monadic Giving: Anatomy of Gifts Given to the Self," by John Sherry, Mary Ann McGrath, and Sidney Levy (Chapter 11), for instance, they will find some interesting examples of how sentence completions and dream scenarios can add to understanding of consumers' motivations. They will test those two uncommon methods in their own minds and file their thoughts for future reference.

446

If they are especially interested in gifts, they will be especially interested in that chapter's comments on the "bittersweet affect" associated with gift giving. They will also be especially interested in the "labor value theory of worthiness" and in the observation that "volitional ceremonial self-care" is sometimes part of a larger contest between entrapment and empowerment. In "Monadic Giving," as in the other chapters in this volume, postmodern and interpretivist researchers will find method and substance for their own constructions.

Rita Denny's "Speaking to Customers: The Anthropology of Communications" (Chapter 9) presents additional nonstandard instances. In that exhibit, group interview respondents write "editorials" and "magazine articles" aloud. This unfamiliar task produces provocative illustrations of the "indexical properties of the language" and the persuasive effects of "marked" or "foregrounded" communications. Here, unusual data and unusual analysis combine to show how verbalizations reveal unconscious links between speakers and subjects and how mistaken syntax can send unintended messages.

"West African Marketing Channels: Environmental Duress, Relationship Management, and Implications for Western Marketing," by Eric Arnould (Chapter 4), shows how conventional constructs bring order and meaning to unconventional information. In that exhibit, key organizing ideas—"primary task environment," "low demand density," "parasitic intermediaries," "illicit rent seeking," "downstream partnering," "concessions of credit," "concessions of quality," and "channel niching," among others—emerge from (largely) American views of business relationships and channels of distribution. Integrated with kinship concepts from earlier work—and imposed upon firsthand interviews, on-site observations, and secondary data—those First World images explain Third World transactions. Like the methods and metaphors in "Monadic Giving" and "Speaking to Customers," the objects, materials, and forms in "West African Marketing Channels" have the capacity to help postmodern and interpretivist (and other) researchers master First, Second, and Third World research problems.

Those chapters—and their companions in this collection—present analogies to the future. Having examined those exhibits, visitors have new patterns to apply to new creations.

🕮 Traditional Academic Researchers

In their study of the Montreal Museum of Contemporary Art, Duhaime, Joy, and Ross show how implicit rules based on "early introduction to the process of seeing" interfere with new vision. In the same vein, it seems highly likely that implicit rules based on early introduction to traditional research methodology will interfere with learning from these chapters.

Many researchers raised on carefully contrived experiments and "falsification" of theoretical propositions will write off this collection as interesting anecdotes, perhaps, but hardly scientific knowledge. Many researchers raised on survey research methods will write it off as mere conjecture based on biased samples.

In extreme cases, reactions will resemble those of Taiwanese ritual specialists (see John McCreery's Chapter 8): "In public encounters, they would treat [others] with respect. In private, however, they freely accuse [rivals] of ignorance . . . moral turpitude . . . and outright evil" (McCreery, Chapter 8). Some visitors will not learn anything. To some ritual specialists, this collection will forever be—at best—"weird science."

But, given the turmoil in the softer disciplines (see Sherry's Chapter 1), some traditional researchers might be more open-minded. On reading Dan Rose's "Active Ingredients" (Chapter 2), for instance, some might decide that semantic differential ratings of fictional products by college students do not capture all we need to know about encounters between objects and individuals. In following that single case, they might decide that they have been performing brain surgery with blunt instruments.

Those most apt to attain that insight are researchers who have already decided, with Janeen Costa (Chapter 6) that their own work

> must involve a greater exploration of *how* . . . behaviors differ; *why* the differences . . . are manifest by some individuals and groups and not by others . . . ; *when* and *under what circumstances* [behavior varies or remains the same]; and [its] *underlying meaning.* (Costa, Chapter 6).

This conversion may resemble Caroline's appreciation of Kounellis:

> She moved very quickly toward the objects, read the titles, and then moved away from them . . . to get a better view. . . . Clearly, . . . contemporary art . . . makes her see things in a totally different perspective. She said, "The world is so drab: Reality is drab . . . and then you see this work which suddenly makes you see things. It's like being in another reality." (Duhaime et al., Chapter 10)

When traditional research has become "drab," the exhibits in this sourcebook can evoke new vision. This sudden insight can have the quality of "following a narrow winding sidewalk and . . . entering a new doorway" (Duhaime et al., Chapter 10).

Researchers who enter that new doorway will have become more effective. Having shed convenient self-deception, they will have prepared themselves to face how real things really happen.

🎐 Action Researchers

A third segment includes scholars who help policymakers intervene in real-world situations. They study humans on-site anywhere. Regardless of academic background, they are in practice applied anthropologists.

Unlike intramural purists, members of this segment are not interested in jousts between orthodox and heterodox magicians "fought with conjurations, mundras and spirits" (McCreery, Chapter 8, quoting Wolf, 1974). As far as they are concerned, the social sciences—like the *Tao-tsang*—are reference libraries containing a "a vast and motley collection of texts whose value . . . lies precisely in the fact that . . . they represent the accretion of numerous sources" (McCreery, Chapter 8).

To action researchers, the exhibits in this sourcebook represent potential answers to real questions. Unencumbered by allegiance to denominations, they take all the help they can get from anywhere they can get it.

Type I Relevance

In some cases, important help comes from sanctified reminders. For instance, action researchers and their clients all know that new brands confront traditions handed down from generation to generation. However, in the absence of Barbara Olsen's "Brand Loyalty and Consumption Patterns: The Lineage Factor" (Chapter 7), they might neglect the critical dynamics of this well-known phenomenon. One of the most serious mistakes a marketer can make is to underestimate the hazards in the environment. New brands often fail, and that is one of the main reasons.

Action researchers and their clients all know that source incredibility can veto evidence. In the absence of "Speaking to Customers" (Denny, Chapter 9), they might be tempted to assume that righteous facts will overcome entrenched suspicions.

Museum managers all know that people get confused in unfamiliar situations. In the absence of "Learning to 'See' " (Duhaime et al., Chapter 10), they might forget—as the managers of the Montreal museum forgot—that first-time visitors need guidance.

Regardless of how action research turns out, policymakers often say, "We knew that already." And so they did. But in complex real-world situations, sanctified reminders bring important propositions from background into foreground. Then, resonance with intuition turns them into action.

Type II Relevance

In other cases, "relevance" means direct transfer of method. Sentence completion, dream scenarios, on-site observation, key informants, in-depth interviews, introspection—all are applied research alternatives. Like Montreal artists, applied anthropologists have insatiable appetites for patterns.

In particular, action researchers will be impressed by the fusion of qualitative and quantitative analysis, the integration of primary and secondary data, and the employment of old concepts for new purposes in Arnould's "West African Marketing Channels" (Chapter 4) and Richard Reeves-Ellington's "Anthropology and TQM: Improving Sales Force Participation in Overseas Markets" (Chapter 5). Action researchers all know that tough problems demand triangulation. They all know that one view is inadequate and that the liabilities of one source must be offset by the assets of others.

Type III Relevance

A third kind of help is much less dependable. Because resources are never finite, applied anthropologists and their clients keep hoping that published findings will transfer intact to real-world situations. Suffering from a policy ailment, they keep hoping that some professor will have written a prescription.

Sometimes, published findings do apply to real-world problems. An action researcher who wants to sell fur coats, or who wants to persuade consumers not to buy fur coats, might decide that conclusions in "Monadic Giving" (Sherry et al., Chapter 11) transfer directly to the fur coat market. Or an action researcher caught up in a public relations firestorm might decide that "Speaking to Customers" (Denny, Chapter 9) gets at the essence of a current crisis.

But there would always be nagging reservations: What proportion of fur coat purchases are self-gifts? How adequately do Sherry, McGrath, and Levy's respondents represent all fur coat self-givers? Can I bet the company on Denny's EMF observations?

Faced with such doubts, action researchers and their clients often demand custom-tailored, problem-centered data. When that happens, they are likely to conclude—correctly, in this context—that less focused findings are "irrelevant."

Type IV Relevance

But relevance has a fourth, much more important meaning. Like all problem solvers, action researchers and their clients perseverate. Constrained by their assumptions, they reiterate the same old answers to the same old questions.

Sometimes, reiteration works: Familiar methods solve familiar problems. But sometimes, reiteration does not work. The problem may be new, or old methods may not give good answers. When reiteration does not work, action researchers need new vision. When the familiar is inadequate, they need to free themselves from preconceptions.

Then, they go outside. They talk to colleagues who have coped with cognate problems, or they hire consultants or browse through academic publications. In going outside, they do not expect to find complete solutions (although that sometimes happens). They do expect a different point of view, in the most literal meaning of that expression.

The decisive impact of a different point of view is most evident in "Malinowski, Magic, and Advertising: On Choosing Metaphors" (McCreery, Chapter 8). Here, the question was, how can I as a copywriter and creative director identify potentially effective advertising propositions? The key insight was: Effective advertising resembles effective magic. The literature did not say that. Rather, the literature provided a point of view that made the insight possible. Once the insight was attained, it led to answers to still further questions: Why is truth alone never enough? Which is the "bigger" idea? How can I know which idea is most "campaignable?"

Of the four types of relevance, Type IV is by far the most consequential. It is not limited to specific situations. It has the capacity to restructure reality. It makes the previously unknowable knowable.

⚝ Back to the Museum

Like a visit to the Montreal Museum of Contemporary Art, a visit to this sourcebook offers all four types of relevance: sanctified reminders, materials and forms for new constructions, copiable discoveries, and new perspectives.

Although anyone can take all four offers, the fourth is certainly the most important. As Caroline put it, "You see this work which suddenly makes you see things" (Duhaime et al., Chapter 10). When you suddenly see things, you are in a new reality. Your vision and your touch improve, and you are closer to good answers to your hardest questions.

Index

Aaker, D., 210, 247, 251, 257, 262
Abstract understanding, 296
Abu-Lughod, L., 406
Academic apartment syndrome, 32
Academics, visiting museums, 369
Acculturation-based consumer behaviors, 7
Achrol, R. S., 119, 125, 126, 132, 156
Ackerman, L. S., 191
Action anthropology, 106
Action researcher, 178-182, 449-451
Active universe, 62-66
Activity, shaping with materials, 63
Addiction, capitalist culture and, 73-74
Administrative arrangements, higher
        education and, 283-286
Adnography, 25
Advertising:
    aesthetic effects and, 317-318
    as religion, 312-313
    baby boomers and, 234
    brandscapes and, 17
    communication through, 305-307
    creativity and, 322-323
    magic and, 306, 309-327
    socialization and, 257
Advertising game, 322
Advocacy, 27, 33
Aesthetics:
    ads and, 317-318
    museum experience and, 355

target hardening and, 7
Affect:
    ethnic self-identification and, 225
    gifts to self and, 409
Africa, marketing channels in, 15-16,
        105-107, 109-161, 447
African American households:
    battery discards and, 88, 99, 100-101
    consumer behavior and, 225
Age:
    museum clientele and, 354, 368-370
    battery discards and, 88, 95-96, 97-98,
        102
Age-based group, 222-223
Agnew, J. C., 8, 438, 442
Agricultural cooperatives, 128, 131
Agricultural products, channel relations
        and, 120, 122, 124-132
Alderson, W., 273
Aldrich, H., 234
Alexander, J., 106
Alexander, P., 441
Alpers, S., 357
Alsted, C., 438
American Demographics, 225-226
Analytical processes, total quality
        management and, 172, 185-186
Anderson, A., 174, 183-184
Anderson, P., 11, 12, 441
Andreasen, A. R., 110, 156

About the Contributors

Eric J. Arnould is currently Associate Professor of Marketing at the University of South Florida where he teaches consumer behavior and qualitative data collection and analysis. He has taught both in anthropology and in marketing programs. After completing his doctorate in social anthropology in 1982, he pursued a Wenner-Gren Foundation postdoctoral fellowship in marketing at the University of Arizona. Before entering academia, he worked for almost a decade on economic development problems in West Africa as a consultant to the U.S. Agency for International Development, the United Nations, and CARE. He is active in a number of professional organizations and publishes in a variety of marketing and social science journals, including *Journal of Consumer Research*, where he has been among the pioneers in the application of ethnographic methods to consumer behavior, *Human Organization*, and *Journal of Marketing Research*. His current research interests include services marketing, channels relationships in West Africa, and ritual and consumer agency. Consulting interests include recreational services and improvements in channels efficiency in West African marketing systems. He speaks French and Hausa, plays guitar, is an outdoor enthusiast, and enjoys being a parent.

Janeen Arnold Costa is Assistant Professor of Marketing in the David Eccles School of Business and adjunct Assistant Professor of Anthropology at the University of Utah. She received her doctorate in cultural anthropology from Stanford University in 1983 and undertook a postdoctoral position in marketing at the University of Utah in 1988. Having taught for several years in social anthropology, Janeen joined the marketing faculty at the University of

Utah in 1989. Her research focuses on social and cultural dimensions of consumer behavior and marketing, including assessment of the role and influence of culture, gender, class, and ethnicity, and cross-cultural marketing, particularly in the context of tourism. She organized and chaired two conferences on gender and consumer behavior in Salt Lake City in 1991 and 1993. Her research has been published in *Journal of Marketing, Journal of Macromarketing, Advances in Consumer Research, Research in Consumer Behavior, Advances in Non-Profit Marketing*, and *Anthropological Quarterly* and in numerous other books and conference proceedings. She was editor of *Gender Issues and Consumer Behavior* (Sage, 1994) and coeditor of *Research in Consumer Behavior, Volume 6* and *Marketing in a Multicultural World: Ethnicity, Nationalism, and Cultural Identity* (Sage, 1995).

Rita Denny is a partner with the B/R/S Group, Inc., a San Francisco-based firm specializing in qualitative market research and consulting. For the past 10 years, she has applied an anthropological framework to the analysis of American consumer behavior, calling on linguistic, semiotic, and symbolic traditions for interpreting consumer attitudes, perceptions, and behavior. Results of these analyses are typically used for developing advertising or more general communication strategies. Clients include companies such as Apple Computers, Chrysler/Jeep, Quaker Oats Company, and Boeing Company. She received her doctorate in anthropology from the University of Chicago.

Carole Duhaime, an Associate Professor, École des Hautes Études Commerciales, Montreal, has a doctoral degree from the University of Western Ontario, Canada. She has published in various journals, including the *Journal of Macromarketing, Gestion, Possibles,* and *Journal of Consumer Satisfaction, Dissatisfaction, and Complaining Behavior,* and in various conference proceedings, including those of the American Marketing Association, the Administrative Sciences Association of Canada, and ESOMAR. Her research interests include audience studies in museums, strategic planning in museums, and consumer behavior.

Annamma Joy is an Associate Professor in the Department of Marketing at Concordia University and holds degrees in anthropology and business from universities in India and Canada. Her research interests cover topics such as culture and consumption, marketing of the arts, gender, ethnicity, and marketing and development. She has published a number of scholarly publications, is author of *Ethnicity in Canada*, and has presented papers at various marketing conferences. Recently, her articles have appeared in the *Journal* *of Macromarketing, Journal of Social Behavior and Personality, International Journal of Research in Marketing, Journal of International Consumer Marketing, Advances in Non-Profit Marketing, Research in Consumer Behavior,* and the *Canadian Journal of Administrative Sciences.* She has also published in refereed proceedings of the American Marketing Association and Association of Consumer Research. She is also the recipient of the Charles Slater Memorial Award given by the *Journal of Macromarketing* in 1991, and a recipient of the Society for Visual Anthropology for a video production on Mayan women weavers of Guatemala (guest coproducer). She is currently on the editorial board of the *Journal of Consumer Research, Journal of Macromarketing, Culture, Consumption and Markets,* and *Journal of Transnational Management.*

Sidney J. Levy is Professor of Behavioral Science in Management, J. L. Kellogg Graduate School of Management, at Northwestern University. He is a psychologist, having earned his doctorate from the Committee on Human Development, University of Chicago. He is a licensed psychologist in the State of Illinois and a member of the American Marketing Association; he received the Fellow Award from the Association for Consumer Research in 1982. He was named A. Montgomery Ward Professor of Marketing for 1983 and became the Charles H. Kellstadt Distinguished Professor in 1986. In 1988, he was named American Marketing Association/Irwin Distinguished Marketing Educator. He was elected president of the Association for Consumer Research for 1991. He was chairman of the Kellogg School marketing department from 1980 to 1992. His central interest is in studying human behavior in everyday life activities, exploring interpersonal relations, work activities, consumer behavior, public response and communication. His research examines social memberships, cultural influences, symbolic interaction, and complex motivation in personality. Discussion of these explorations with their theoretical and practical consequences have appeared in the *Harvard Business Review, California Management Review, Public Administration Review, Merrill-Palmer Quarterly, Business Horizons, Journal of Marketing, Journal of Consumer Research, Journal of Retailing, Journal of Business Research,* and *Personnel Journal.* His articles have been widely anthologized. He and Philip Kotler have received the Alpha Kappa Sigma Award for best article in the *Journal of Marketing* and received the Maynard Award for the best theoretical article in the *Journal of Marketing.* He wrote *Living With Television, Promotion: A Behavioral View, Promotional Behavior, Marketing, Society, and Conflict,* and *Marketplace Behavior—Its Meaning for Management.* As a principal in Social Research, Inc. for many years, he has directed and participated in research investigations on behalf of numerous organizations, including major corporations, media, and various public and private agencies.

John McCreery, an adman and anthropologist, is International Creative Director at Hakuhodo, Inc. He received his doctorate from Cornell University in 1973. An avid consumer of consumer research, he is frequently called on to explain Japanese consumers and creative proposals to non-Japanese clients. He notes, "In Taiwan, I studied magicians. Now in Japan, I've joined the guild."

Mary Ann McGrath is an Associate Professor of Marketing at Loyola University, Chicago. She received her MBA and doctorate in marketing from Northwestern University. Her research interests include retail interactions and retail ambience, gift exchanges, and the application of a variety of qualitative methods to elicit the consumer perspective.

Barbara Olsen received her doctorate in anthropology from the Graduate Faculty of the New School for Social Research and is Assistant Professor of Marketing at SUNY, Old Westbury. She was previously the founder and president of IMC Marketing Group, Ltd., an advertising agency with offices in New York, Los Angeles, London, Paris, and Hamburg serving diverse companies, including Chemical Bank, Pfizer, Columbia Pictures, Lorimar, and Twentieth Century Fox. She continues to consult clients in the profit and nonprofit service sector. Her ethnographic research conducted over two decades in the Caribbean focused on cultural and economic development. Currently, her research is directed toward a historical analysis of advertising and its impact on changing patterns of consumer behavior.

William L. Rathje is a Professor in the Bureau of Applied Research in Anthropology at the University of Arizona. His research interests include the archaeology of early civilizations, Mesoamerica, and modern material culture studies. He is author of numerous journal articles and coauthor of *Rubbish: The Archaeology of Garbage*. He is the founder and director of the renowned University of Arizona Garbage Project, a historical archaeological enterprise (now entering its third decade) that has greatly improved our understanding of contemporary material culture.

Richard H. Reeves-Ellington is currently a Fulbright Professor at the American University in Bulgaria, where he teaches strategic planning, international business, and international management. His home affiliation is the School of Management at SUNY, Binghamton. He is a trained anthropologist who has spent 33 years in international business, 16 of which were spent living and working in Germany, Mexico, Australia, and Indonesia. In the remaining 17 years, his business travel has kept him in Japan, East and Southeast Asia, the Near East, and parts of Africa more than 175 days a year. He is a frequently invited speaker at American Anthropological Association annual meetings and has published articles relating anthropology to business.

Dan Rose teaches anthropology at the University of Pennsylvania where he is Professor of Anthropology and of Landscape Architecture. He has contributed to literary anthropology in the recent collections *Anthropology and Literature* and *Anthropological Poetics*, and at the University of Pennsylvania Press he edits the Series in Contemporary Ethnography. His ethnographic studies include the community of ultralarge corporations in the United States and abroad and it is to the formation of capitalist culture worldwide that he brings a poetic of inquiry. Recent articles address the linked themes of the social organization of commerce, the rhetorical and pragmatic language used there, and the challenges to ethnographic theory and practice in studying market culture. Two of his artist's books have been collected by the Museum of Modern Art and he is also author of *Patterns of American Culture, Living the Ethnographic Life,* and *Black American Street Life.*

Christopher Ross is an Associate Professor, Faculty of Commerce and Administration, at Concordia University and has a doctoral degree from the University of Western Ontario, Canada. He has consulted with organizations such as Humpty Dumpty Foods Ltd., Air Jamaica, Workers' Savings Bank, Jamaica Teachers' Association, and Jamaica National Savings Committee. He has published in various journals, including the *Journal of Macromarketing, Journal of Global Marketing, Possibles,* and the *Journal of Marketing Education* and in various conference proceedings including those of the American Marketing Association, the Administrative Sciences Association of Canada, and the Marketing Education Group (UK). He is also the corecipient of the Charles Slater Memorial Award given by the *Journal of Macromarketing* in 1991. His research interests include marketing and development, marketing education in developing countries, and marketing in nonprofit organizations.

John F. Sherry, Jr., Professor of Marketing, is an anthropologist who teaches graduate and executive courses in marketing behavior, international marketing, and consumer research at Northwestern University's J. L. Kellogg School of Management. He has twice been a member of the prestigious American

Marketing Doctoral Consortium Faculty. His current research interests are in symbolic communication, macromarketing issues, and cultural risk management. He has conducted fieldwork in the urban United States, Ireland, Belgium, the French West Indies, Japan, and Thailand. He has served as a consultant to corporations in foreign and domestic operations. Among his clients are such firms as Procter & Gamble, Coca-Cola Company, Quaker Oats Company, Motorola, General Foods, Ralston Purina, Sears, Arthur Andersen and Co., Young and Rubicam, Ogilvy and Mather, Cramer and Krasselt, Hill Holliday, Upjohn Company, Rouse Company, Frank J. Corbett Inc., Quest Inc., and the St. James Strategy Group. He has conducted proprietary studies for companies in the areas of brand equity, consumer needs assessment, segmentation, advertising effectiveness, strategic planning, product design, interorganizational relations, retail design and atmospherics, cultural risk management, and employee assistance programming. He conducts corporate training seminars in qualitative research design, rapid appraisal techniques, and intercultural relations. An associate editor of the *Journal of Consumer Research,* he is also on the editorial boards of the *Journal of Business Research, Journal of Managerial Issues, Journal of International Consumer Marketing, Culture, Consumption and Markets,* and *Design Issues.* Some of his work has appeared in the *Journal of Consumer Research, Journal of Consumer Psychology, Journal of Global Marketing, Journal of Retailing, International Journal of Research in Marketing, Industrial Relations Guide, Journal of Macromarketing, Public Culture, Research in Marketing, Anthropology and Humanism Quarterly, Journal of American Culture, Florida Journal of Anthropology, Journal of the Steward Anthropological Society,* and *Environmental and Architectural Phenomenology.* He has contributed chapters to a number of books and manuals and is coeditor of *Marketing Theory* and *Advances in Consumer Research.* He has also won awards for his scholarly articles and poetry.

MasaKazu Tani is a Research Specialist in the Department of Anthropology at the University of Arizona. He received a BA in Western history from Waseda University, Tokyo and a MA and doctorate in anthropology from the University of Arizona. As an archaeologist, his main interest is in method and theory, especially in the relationship between material culture and human behavior. His investigations include not only the "old" materials archaeologists conventionally study but also modern materials, such as garbage, from contemporary households. He first joined the University of Arizona's Garbage Project in 1985 and since then has jointly conducted numerous studies of household and commercial garbage and has studied various aspects of contemporary consumer behavior through garbage.

William D. Wells joined the faculty of the School of Journalism and Mass Communication of the University of Minnesota in 1992 as the first Mithun Land Grant Professor of Advertising. There he teaches courses in communication research and in persuasion and conducts basic and applied research on substantive and methodological topics related to advertising. After receiving an AB degree from Lafayette College, and MA and doctorate degrees from Stanford University, he joined the faculty of the Psychology Department of Rutgers University in 1954. In 1966, he joined the faculty of the Graduate School of Business of the University of Chicago as Professor of Psychology and Marketing. In 1974, he joined the advertising agency Needham, Harper and Steers as Vice President and Director of Corporate Research. In 1991, he retired from DDB Needham Worldwide as Executive Vice President and Director of Marketing Services. He is coauthor, editor, or coeditor of five books, including *Advertising: Principles and Practice, Planning for R. O. I.: Effective Advertising Strategy,* and *Lifestyle and Psychographics* and more than 60 journal articles. He has served on the editorial review boards of the *Journal of Consumer Research, Journal of Consumer Psychology, Journal of Advertising Research, Journal of Marketing, Journal of Marketing Research, Psychology & Marketing, Marketing Research,* and *Current Issues and Research in Advertising.* He has been elected a Fellow of the Association for Consumer Research and a Fellow of the American Psychological Association and has served as president of the Association for Consumer Research, and president of the Consumer Psychology Division of the American Psychological Association. He has received the Distinguished Professional Contribution Award from the Society for Consumer Psychology and both the William F. O'Dell Award and the Paul D. Converse Award from the American Marketing Association.

Gerald Zaltman is the Joseph C. Wilson Professor of Business Administration at Harvard Business School. He has previously been the Albert Wesley Frey Professor of Business at the University of Pittsburgh and the A. Montgomery Ward Professor of Business at Northwestern University and has been a visiting professor at the Stockholm School of Economics and INSEAD. He holds a doctorate in sociology from Johns Hopkins University and an MBA from the University of Chicago. He has been cited in surveys conducted by the American Marketing Association as one of the five leading scholars in marketing and among the top five researchers whose works are most frequently cited in the published literature. He is recipient of the Richard D. Irwin Distinguished Educator Award, the Association for Consumer Research Fellow's Award, and the Knowledge Utilization Society's Scientific Achievement Award. He is author, coauthor, or editor of 26 books and monographs and is a frequent contributor to professional journals and conferences. His most recent book, *Hearing the Voice of the Market* (with Vincent P. Barabba), has been published in several languages. Current interests focus on the epistemology of the managerial mind and on the elicitation of consumers' mental models using visual and other sensory metaphors. He is the developer of the "Zaltman metaphor elicitation technique" (ZMET), a recently patented research tool for eliciting socially shared mental models.